The Times

HISTORY OF THE WAR

VOL. VII.

PRINTING HOUSE SQUARE.

PRINTED AND PUBLISHED BY "THE TIMES,"
PRINTING HOUSE SQUARE, LONDON.

1916.

CONTENTS OF VOL. VII

CHAPTER CVIII.

THE FIRST GERMAN AIR RAIDS ON ENGLAND.

The Zeppelin Danger—Official Scepticism and Ignorance in England—Aeroplane Raids in December, 1914—From Yarmouth to Sandringham—Raids on North East Coast and East Anglia—Zeppelins at Southend—Ramsgate and Dover—First Attack on London May 31, 1915—Government Policy of Secrecy—June Raids on East Coast—A Zeppelin Destroyed by British Aeroplane—Raids in July and August—A Picturesque Description—Second and Third Raids on London—An American Account—The Raid of October 13—German Jubilation—Raid on the Midland Counties January 31, 1916—Public Opinion and "Control of the Air."

AT the beginning of the war there was much speculation about the possibility of aerial attacks upon England. It was common knowledge that Germany had at least 13 airships of the rigid type, capable of flying from 46 to 50 miles an hour. One Zeppelin had travelled 1,800 miles in a single journey, and had remained in the air for 35 hours at a time. Since the distance from Heligoland, where airship sheds had long been reported to be under construction, to Yarmouth was only 280 miles, it was obvious that, given suitable weather conditions, a Zeppelin could not only cross to our coast and return, but could sail over large areas of England, unless we had some means to check it.

It was taken for granted that the main purpose of Zeppelins on journeys such as these would be to attempt to drop explosives on harbours, docks, ships and military positions. The tendency in England was to minimize the possibility of serious danger from such raids, and even, at one time, to question the possibility of aircraft being of any service in war. As late as 1911 the then Master-General of Ordnance, who was in charge of aeronautics at the War Office, said, "We are not yet convinced that either aeroplanes or airships will be of any utility in war." If this stage of scepticism had been passed, it was still believed by many at the opening of the war that England had little to fear from aerial attacks. One favourite theory was that, while a Zeppelin might reach this country, it would find it very difficult to escape, as it would at once be attacked by a number of aeroplanes and destroyed. This view was apparently accepted by the responsible authorities, for Mr. Winston Churchill, in a speech on March 17, 1914, said: "Any hostile aircraft, airships, or aeroplanes which reached our coast during the coming year would be promptly attacked in superior force by a swarm of very formidable hornets."

Events have shown that the British authorities at that time did not allow sufficiently for the great height at which Zeppelins can travel, nor for the fact that, while the airship could operate successfully at night time, darkness was the least suitable time for aeroplanes in the stage of development which they had reached, on account of the difficulties of starting and of landing in the dark, as well as of seeing or hearing the airship from a machine flying aloft.

The German Government and the German people had thrown their full energies into the development of aircraft for war. In England Lord Montagu of Beaulieu and Lord Northcliffe, and *The Times* and *Daily Mail* for many years did their utmost to arouse the country to the

ZEPPELIN OVER THE LONDON DISTRICT.

need of preparation, but they had to overcome the usual resistance opposed by the national slowness to take up new ideas as well as the conflicting claims of better understood demands upon the public purse. It is not too much to say that, during the first few months of the war, the responsible authorities in this country did not take the aerial menace seriously and did not regard it as within the range of possibility that England would experience any real danger from the flying machines of the enemy. It was held that the work of the German Zeppelins in the attacks on the forts at Liége and in the bombardment of Antwerp bore out this view. This idea was not confined to officialism. A supposedly authoritative writer in a prominent London newspaper in the autumn of 1914 declared that "The Zeppelin danger is a great deal exaggerated. It is, I am convinced, a German bluff rather than a reality. If the Zeppelins could do really effective mischief their deeds would have spoken for them long ago, and there would not be all this German advertisement of what they are going to do one day."

Some precautions were taken in London and throughout the country. A number of anti-aircraft guns, most of them, as was afterwards proved, of absurdly inadequate calibre, were planted at vital points. The street lights of London were subdued, sky signs were obliterated, and householders were ordered to darken the windows of their lighted rooms at night time. The rays of searchlights wheeled over the London sky each night for several hours.

The first German attacks did not come until the end of December, 1914. An aeroplane flew over the East Coast and dropped a bomb or two on the sands there. On Christmas Eve an aeroplane appeared over Dover and dropped a bomb in a garden. The bomb was probably intended for Dover Castle, but it fell harmlessly a few hundred yards away. Some British aeroplanes immediately arose in pursuit of the invading aeroplane, but before they could over-haul it it had escaped.

On Christmas Day a German airman passed Sheerness under cover of a fog, and flew far up the Thames. He was first seen over the Isle of Sheppey, slightly to the south of Sheerness, flying at a height estimated at about 9,000 feet. Anti-aircraft guns at once opened on him, but they fell short. Lost to view in a mist, he was not seen again until well up the river. Fire was once more opened on him from our guns. Rising higher to escape the shells, he made a complete half-circle. By now, several British aeroplanes were in pursuit, and the German, seeing that it was hopeless to attempt to go farther, turned back. Thousands of people had a good view of this—the first real air battle on the British coast. Shells were bursting in the air apparently all round the German. Time after time it seemed that he had been hit, yet time after time he escaped. Men could not fail to admire the skill with which he handled his machine. At one point a sudden dip of the aeroplane seemed to show that a shot had got home. Still, however, he kept on, circling, dodging, twisting, climbing and diving with almost incredible swiftness to escape his pursuers. He made straight for the sea and escaped. Weeks afterwards a rumour was received that some fishermen had found a body away out in the sea which was believed to be that of the German airman, but no satisfactory confirmation was forthcoming.

After this there came a pause of about three weeks. Then, on the evening of January 19, 1915, the people of Yarmouth were startled by the sound of loud explosions in their streets, as though big guns were firing among them. Lights were at once extinguished, the authorities turning off the electric supply at the main. For some hours little could be learned of what had happened. Word went round that two Zeppelins had arrived over the town and had dropped nine bombs. Two persons were killed—Samuel Alfred Smith, aged 53, a shoemaker, and Miss Martha Mary Taylor, aged seventy-two, an old lady living with her sister. These were the first two victims of

AT ST. PETER'S PLAIN, YARMOUTH, JANUARY 19, 1915.
Interior of a room showing damage done by a bomb. Small picture: Searching for pieces of shell.

SCENES AT KING'S LYNN, NORFOLK, JANUARY 19, 1915.

Destroyed houses in Albert Street.

Small picture : Removing furniture from their ruined homes.

enemy aircraft in this country—a man of advanced middle-age, and a woman past the allotted three score years and ten. Both Smith and Miss Taylor were blown to pieces. A few houses were more or less damaged, some holes were blown in the roadway, and a few persons were injured. No military or naval damage of any kind whatever was caused. From Yarmouth the raider went on to Sandringham and King's Lynn. The King and Queen had been spending Christmas at Sandringham House, and it was naturally suggested that the Germans were deliberately attempting to kill them. They had left, however, on the morning before the raid. A bomb apparently intended for Sandringham dropped just outside the little village of Dersingham, about a mile away, and did no damage. At King's Lynn four houses were wrecked, several more damaged, two civilians were killed, and others slightly injured. The bombs used were of two kinds, explosive and incendiary. The explosive bombs at first contained charges of from 30 to 100 lbs. of trinitrotoluene. Later on, even larger charges were employed. The incendiary bombs were charged with thermit, a mixture of a metallic oxide and powdered aluminium, which burst into flames on striking the ground, kindling instantly a burst of fierce heat, sufficient to consume anything immediately around. One of the King's Lynn victims was the widow of a soldier who had recently been killed in France. The mother of the other victim, a boy of fourteen, told the story of what had happened in language whose very simplicity made it the more effective. "We were all upstairs for bed, me and my husband, with baby and Percy, when we heard a buzzing noise. My husband put out the light. I saw a bomb fall from the sky and strike the pillow where Percy was lying. I tried to wake him, but he was dead, and then the house fell in. I knew no more."

The accounts of this raid upon a purely civilian population aroused furious indignation in England, and caused a feeling of almost stupified amazement among neutral nations. The German naval attack upon the unfortified seaside town of Scarborough in the previous month had given some evidence that Germany intended to wage war on women and children with merciless severity, and in disregard of all dictates of humanity. But even Scarborough had not led people to expect that German aircraft would seek to kill English civilians, apparently for the mere pleasure of killing, or in the hope that the nation would be terrorized.

In America, in particular, the expressions of indignation were numerous and emphatic. "Is it the madness of despair ?" asked the *New York Herald*, "or just plain everyday madness, that has prompted the Germans to select for attack peaceful and undefended resorts on the English east coast ? What can Germany hope to gain by these wanton attacks on undefended places and this slaughter of innocents ? Certainly not the good opinion of the people of neutral nations." The German official description of the raid as "attacks on some fortified places" aroused derision. The real German purpose was apparently to strike terror by means of "frightfulness," the murder of non-combatants and the destruction of private property. It soon became clear, however, that whatever effect the raids might have on the British people, they would certainly not terrify them. The attack on Yarmouth and district quickened recruiting throughout the country and intensified the national determination to wage the war to the end against a foe which could descend to such methods.

RAID OVER TYNESIDE, APRIL 14, 1915.
Bombs dropped from Zeppelins.

GERMAN BOMBS.
Found at Ipswich after the raid.

These raids, small as their immediate results were, yet demonstrated one thing. The German Press proclaimed that German genius had at last ended the legend that England was invulnerable owing to her insularity. It was certainly proved now that the seas no longer protected England from attack. Should she hope to keep her shores inviolate, and to allow her people to live in the safety that they had enjoyed for more than two centuries, she must be prepared to meet invaders from the sky as well as on the water. The coming of the German airships was the beginning of a new chapter in the history of this country.

The real German defence was summed up in a semi-official message published at the time. "The German nation has been forced by England to fight for her existence, and cannot be forced to forego legitimate self-defence, and will not do so, relying upon her good right." There were great rejoicings throughout Germany, and the Press drew glowing pictures of

[By permission of "The Aeroplane."

THE GONDOLA OF ONE OF THE GERMAN DIRIGIBLES.

The crew of the Zeppelin, together with four engines of 200 h.p. are accommodated in two of these long gondola-shaped cars—one placed forward and the other aft.

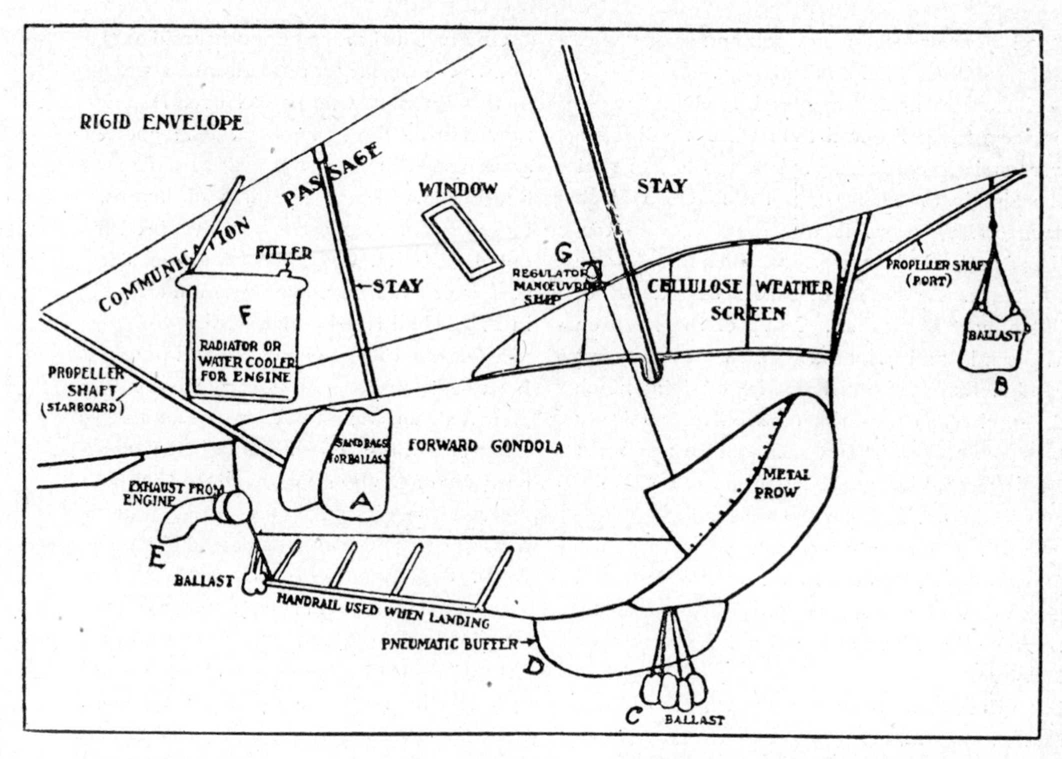

DIAGRAM NAMING THE DIFFERENT PARTS OF THE ZEPPELIN.
Illustrated on the opposite page.

the Zeppelins making further long flights over England, dropping death everywhere. "We shall not allow these wonderful weapons, which German intelligence invented, to grow rusty," said the *Cologne Gazette.*

Over a month passed before the next attempt. On Sunday evening, February 21, a Quartermaster-sergeant of the 20th Hussars was sitting in his house in Butt Road, Colchester, with his wife, just about to begin supper, when they were startled by a tremendous explosion at the back of the building. Their child, a baby a few months old, was sleeping in the bedroom upstairs, and the father rushed up to rescue it. Although the room was partly wrecked, and the house riddled with fragments of shell, the child was unharmed. Every pane of glass in the windows of the house was broken, a corrugated iron shed in the garden was torn to pieces, and many windows in adjoining houses were blown out. This, however, was all the damage done. A German aeroplane had come over the Essex coast and had dropped a bomb. The aeroplane seemed to have travelled from the direction of Braintree, due east of Colchester, to Coggleshall. It was flying at a great height, and the noise of its propellers could scarcely be heard. It dropped two bombs at Braintree and one at Coggleshall, doing, however, practically no damage in those places. Two soldiers, finding one of the bombs in a field outside Braintree, placed a stick through the handle and carried it towards the river. It burst into flames on the way, but they ran on with their burden, and threw it into the water.

The German summer air campaign against England may be said to have begun in earnest on April 14. On that day there was a futile attack on the Tyneside. A German airship was seen near Blyth soon after 8 o'clock in the evening. From there it passed Bedlington, Morpeth, and a large area of the mid-Tyne district, one of the most important shipbuilding centres of the country. As soon as news of the arrival of the raiders reached the authorities lights were at once turned out in most of the places they were likely to pass, in accordance with arrangements made in advance. The result of thus plunging a whole community into sudden darkness was in many cases extremely awkward. Trams were stopped. Newspapers were held up. Concerts and theatrical entertainments were interrupted, the audiences being informed that orders had been received to put out lights in public buildings. In nearly every case the people took the inconvenience very good-naturedly. In some concert halls they stood on their feet in the dark and sang "God Save the King" before dispersing.

Elaborate arrangements had been made between the police and the military, and these were strictly carried out. The result was that the airship found below it little save a black countryside, where it was impossible to distinguish the docks and works which it had come to attack. A number of bombs were dropped, but almost at random. Many of these fell on Wallsend and Hebburn with insignificant results. Some fell on Blyth without doing much damage. The windows of a Salvation Army barracks at Bedlington and some windows at Dudley were blown out. A house was set on fire at Carlington, but the fire was quickly extinguished. It was supposed at the time that the pilot of the Zeppelin lost his reckoning and mistook the broad estuary of the River Wandsbeck for the mouth of the Tyne. No lives were lost in this raid and the only person reported injured was a lad at Bedlington, who had a slight wound on the head.

The raid on the North-East Coast was intelligible, for here the Germans were attacking an important shipbuilding centre, but a raid upon East Anglia which followed, on April 16, was one whose only evident aim was to cause indiscriminate destruction. Special indignation was aroused by the airship attacking Henham Hall, beyond Southwold, the country house of Lady Stradbroke, which had been turned into a hospital for wounded soldiers. No fewer than twenty-three bombs were aimed at this building, but the aim of the Germans was so bad that the nearest of them did not get within 100 yards of the house. This attack upon a hospital was so senseless that it was believed that the raiders mistook the building for some other which they supposed to be of military importance. Bombs were also dropped at Lowestoft, doing some damage to property but no injury to any person. Thirteen bombs were dropped at Maldon. The side of a house was blown out, a workshop was destroyed and a fence was riddled with bullet holes, but little other damage was done.

On the same day a German aeroplane flew over Kent and dropped five bombs on Faversham and Sittingbourne without doing any damage. A British aeroplane set out in pursuit, but, owing to the great height of the invader, some 8,000 or 9,000 feet, found it impossible to reach it. In Sittingbourne a blackbird was killed and an apple tree uprooted.

On April 30 there came another raid on the East Coast. Apparently several aircraft were engaged in this attack. One passed over Harwich and moved in the direction of Ipswich; another was seen over Cromer; a third was observed at Southwold. Large numbers of bombs, both incendiary and explosive, were dropped throughout the district. Only one of the bombs dropped at Ipswich did any considerable harm. It fell in Brookshall Road and set fire to three houses, piercing the roof of one house and falling into a back bedroom where a young girl was sleeping. Here it struck a chest of drawers standing within a few feet of the bed and burst into flames. The occupier of the house rushed into the room and rescued the girl. At Bury St. Edmunds the airship dropped a number of bombs on to the town. Several fell in the Butter Market, where fires were started and some damage to property was done. Two shops were burned to the ground before the fire was got under.

Early in May the Germans turned their attention to the Thames valley and Kent. On May 3 an aeroplane passed over Dover, doing no damage. On May 10 another attacked Southend, dropping nearly a hundred bombs at random over an area of five square miles. The Germans apparently aimed at reaching London, and they actually approached Romford railway station, 12½ miles from Liverpool Street. Soon after two in the morning the people of Southend were aroused by a terrific explosion, far surpassing in magnitude the sounds of heavy firing from Shoeburyness and Sheerness to which they were accustomed. A syren had been attached to the electric light works of the town and it was arranged that, at the first sign of the arrival of a Zeppelin, the syren should be sounded to warn the inhabitants. The entire district was quickly afoot. But unfortunately the sound of the syren served another purpose. It drew the Zeppelin to the spot like steel to a magnet. Guided by the sound, it was able to locate the town, and it promptly started scattering bomb after bomb all around. Some bombs were dropped on Leigh and some on the little inland village of Rochford. A number of houses were destroyed. An incendiary bomb crashed through the roof of a double-fronted house, just escaping the bedrooms, and exploded in the hall. The people within had a miraculous escape. They jumped from the first floor bedroom windows into the front garden. A boarding-house was destroyed, and a butcher's shop had the shutters blown out. One woman was killed, the

THE PILOT IN THE FORWARD GONDOLA OF A ZEPPELIN.

wife of a labourer employed by the Southend Corporation and an active Salvation Army worker. A bomb fell full on the house, making a hole two feet square in the roof, and then penetrated into the room in which husband and wife were asleep. It burst into flames, and in a very short time the whole room was ablaze. The husband carried an invalid daughter to a place of safety and then returned for his wife, but, in spite of every effort, it was impossible for him to reach her. Before he could again get into the bedroom the flames almost overcame him. Jumping from a window, he fell heavily to the ground and was severely injured. His wife was burned to death. A timber yard was gutted, and the total damage was estimated at £20,000.

The people of Southend had rushed into the streets at the first alarm, many of them not

IN WEST ROAD, SOUTHEND.
Houses on fire.

waiting to dress and others half dressed. The town was in darkness, and the crowds, staring up, could see the body of the Zeppelin outlined against the sky. The incendiary bombs dropping from it appeared like balls of fire as they fell to earth. The streaks of light in the sky and the blazing houses around lit up the heavens like the first glories of sunrise. The troops and the local authorities tackled the fires resolutely and before long they were got under. It seemed to many that night that the whole town must surely be destroyed, and it was hard to realize next day that the real damage had been so trivial. Many of the bombs fell into fields or in gardens.

This attack upon Southend should have brought home to those responsible for the defence of London the need for more adequate preparations. Apparently, it failed to do so. The argument was still freely advanced that Zeppelin raids, however spectacular and awesome to those who beheld them, did not convey any real menace to our national security. The net result of the German aerial campaign against us during the first nine months of the war was, critics declared, half a dozen people killed, a few injured, and damage amounting to a few scores of thousands of pounds. These critics pointed triumphantly to the fact that the Germans had not succeeded in their different raids in doing any damage of military or naval importance. They had lost their way on the Tyneside, they had apparently lost their way on the East Coast, and when they aimed at buildings like Henham Hall they missed them. All they could do was to scatter bombs indiscriminately, and most of the bombs they threw fell harmlessly upon waste spaces, gardens, or countryside. It was declared that the civilian population ought to take such small risks with equanimity, and people at home should be glad to share in this trivial degree the perils of their sons and brothers on the battlefield. It was further argued that it would be highly unwise to divert our strength, in however small a degree, from the military problems of our various fronts in order to protect us against occasional and largely futile raids.

Arguments such as these were based on great misconceptions. While it was true that the Germans had so far not effected any great damage, many failed to recognize that they were working in a new field, and that the raids up to this stage had been largely experimental. The amount of damage done is not always to be reckoned up in the number of deaths, or in the value of property destroyed. A new element had been introduced into war. One disturbing fact was that we had failed to produce effective means for fighting the Zeppelin. In the attack on the Thames valley, British biplanes had quickly risen and pursued the invader. In the later flights there was little evidence of their meeting any direct opposition save from anti-aircraft guns. This apparent apathy caused considerable comment. What were the authorities doing ? Where were the " swarms " of " hornets " of which Mr. Churchill had spoken ? Why were these raiders allowed to come, time after time, and to retire unmolested ?

The Germans made no secret whatever of their delight at what had been accomplished, or of their ultimate purpose. These attacks were but the preliminaries to the great coming campaign against London. " London has not felt it yet," declared the *Hamburger Nachrichten.*

Early in the morning of May 17 a Zeppelin passed over the coast towns of Kent and dropped between twenty and thirty bombs on Ramsgate. The Zeppelin circled around the coast about midnight. It attempted to approach the Essex side, but was driven off southwards by the heavy fire of anti-aircraft guns from the forts at the mouth of the Thames. It hovered over Ramsgate until it sighted a conspicuous landmark, St. George's Church, and then, centring on it, rained fully two dozen bombs on the place in rapid succession. Most of the people were asleep in their beds. Bombs struck the Bull and George Hotel. The entire front of the building, ceiling, and floors, and everything between, was brought down. Two visitors from Thornton Heath were staying in the hotel at the time. Their room was completely shattered, as was the room below, and they were hurled among the *débris* at the bottom and badly injured. A barmaid at the hotel was also hurt. A provision shop opposite had all the glass of its windows broken, and the children of the manager awoke to find their bed covered with splinters. An explosive bomb partly wrecked a toy and china bazaar, and the proprietor had a narrow escape, the bombs bursting within a few yards of his room. From Ramsgate the airship circled around and moved southwards, passing over Broadstairs and Deal in the direction of Dover. Twenty-three bombs fell harmlessly in the fields in a village near Deal. The Zeppelin reached Dover and hovered over the port. British aeroplanes had now come up, and when it saw them it sheered off to sea.

Word had been sent to Dunkirk, where there was a station of the Royal Naval Air Service, and eight naval aeroplanes set out to meet the Zeppelin and cut it off. Three of the British aeroplanes got quite close, and attacked at close range. Flight-Commander Bigsworth flew 200

THE AIR RAID ON SOUTHEND, MAY 10, 1915.

A boarding-house struck by a bomb which demolished the roof.

Small picture: View of a house showing the hole made by a bomb, in which two people were killed.

feet above the Zeppelin and dropped four bombs upon it. According to the official statements, a large column of smoke was seen to come out from one of its compartments. The Zeppelin then rose to a great height with its tail down, apparently seriously damaged. The crew kept up a heavy fire upon the British airmen, but there were no casualties.

A second raid was made on Southend on May 26, about 11 o'clock at night. An airship, or perhaps two, approached the place from the north-east, probably in order to avoid the forts at Shoeburyness, and first attacked the centre of the town. It remained for some time stationary, the crew directing their bombs upon one building, a new laundry, which was apparently mistaken by them for a barracks or for an electric light works. Over a score of bombs were thrown immediately around this building. Not one struck it, and not even a pane of glass in the building was broken. One woman, hearing the noise of the attack, went to her door to see what was the matter. Just then a bomb burst in the road immediately in front of her, and a fragment of the shell struck her on the head and injured her so seriously that she died a few days afterwards. A lady visitor to the town was stepping off a tram when a bomb fell on her head, killing her on the spot. The audiences had just left the local theatres, and the streets were fairly full of people. One young lady had gone with her mother and her sister-in-law to meet her father, who had arrived by a late train. As they were walking along, talking together, a bomb fell directly on her, killing her instantly. A little girl, seven years old, living in Broadway Market, was terribly injured. An incendiary bomb dropped through the roof into her bedroom. She was badly burned about the head, back, and legs, the petrol from the bomb setting fire to the bedclothes before she could be rescued. Her elder sister went to her assistance with great courage. A lady was in bed when a bomb dropped into the room, setting it on fire. She was rescued, but was badly burnt about the body. Thirty bombs were dropped on Leigh, but only two houses were hit, the majority of the bombs falling on the roadways and gardens. Twelve bombs were dropped over Westcliff. The special constables and the National Guard did good service in rescuing the injured and in helping to put out the fires. During the raid a heavy fire was maintained on the Zeppelin by anti-aircraft guns. The raider remained, however, at a great height, apparently indifferent. The guns could not touch it.

The effect of these two attacks upon Southend was undoubtedly serious from a certain point of view, although wholly negative as a military operation. This town and its neighbouring districts of Westcliff and Leigh have, almost in a generation, risen from fishing villages to the status of great residential suburbs. Here is a place by the sea, within easy reach of London, where the Londoner of moderate means can afford to live and whence he can reach his business in town every day with comparative ease. Attracted by this, tens of thousands of London families had settled here. Now, after the raids, there was a great exodus. Many hundreds of families stored or sold their furniture and found homes elsewhere. "Why should we remain needlessly in a danger zone ?" they asked.

The first attack on London was made on the evening of the last day of May, 1915. Zeppelins passed over Colchester at 10 o'clock, and at twenty-three minutes past ten the people in one of the poorest and most crowded quarters of the East End were startled to find bomb after bomb, mainly of an incendiary type, dropping among them. Apparently no warning of the approach of the enemy had been received, even by the authorities, and no measures had been taken to meet it. The attack was short, sharp, and severe while it lasted. The incendiary bombs dropping in narrow lanes and crowded tenements might have been expected to kindle great fires and to cause many casualties. Actually they did not accomplish this. Six people were killed. A young couple were standing in a narrow passage-way when an incendiary bomb fell just by them, rebounded and ignited, severely injuring them. A middle-aged man and his wife were in bed when a bomb dropped on their house and set it on fire. In spite of every attempt at rescue, it was impossible to get near because of the great heat. Afterwards they were both found dead in the bedroom. Both were naked, save for a band of guernsey on the man's arm ; evidently he had had some clothes on and they were burned off by the fire. The man's arm was around the woman's waist. The two, awakened by the explosion, and finding it impossible to escape, had knelt by the bed together, spending their last moments in prayer. Another woman in the same house jumped from the window to avoid the flames,

THE AIR RAID ON SOUTHEND, MAY 10, 1915.
Watching the Zeppelin at work.

and was so injured that she subsequently died. A little girl, aged three years, was burned in her bed.

The attack produced great excitement and resentment in the East End of London. There had already, earlier in the month, been riots there against German tradesmen allowed to remain and do business among us. These riots broke out afresh. Angry mobs surrounded the premises of people in Shoreditch suspected of being of German nationality, and attacked shops. Barricades that had been erected in front of windows were pulled down, and considerable damage done. Men suspected of being Germans were chased off.

The scenes in the streets in the early hours of the morning following the raid will not soon be forgotten by those who witnessed them. The whole population was up, most of the people not having been in bed that night. The inhabitants crowded into every roadway or by-street near the scene of the outrage, exchanging experiences, telling of narrow escapes, and recalling particular instances of heroism of men in putting out fires and in rescuing threatened women and children during the attack. The police set to work to eliminate all signs of the

AT BURY ST. EDMUNDS, APRIL 30, 1915.
Demolished houses in the Butter Market.

raid, and a day or two later it was difficult, even for the most curious visitor, to find any trace of it. The damage had been amazingly slight, and the Germans must have been disappointed to find Londoners, as a whole, almost indifferent to the blow they had struck at them.

Up to this time, the authorities had permitted the publication of fairly full accounts of the raids, and in some cases had allowed even maps giving the route taken by the raiders to appear. Now they rushed to the other extreme. Almost immediately after the raid of May 31, and before the morning papers could print any description of what had happened, official directions were circulated forbidding the publication of any news about air raids or descriptions of them save those issued by the authorities. The notice was as follows:

The Press are specially reminded that no statement whatever must be published dealing with the places in the neighbourhood of London reached by aircraft, or the course proposed to be taken by them, or any statement or diagram which might indicate the ground or route covered by them.

The Admiralty *communiqué* is all the news which can properly be published.

These instructions are given in order to secure the public safety, and the present intimation may itself be published as explaining the absence of more detailed reports.

This policy of the suppression of all non official news of aerial raids was strictly enforced until the beginning of February, 1916, not only for British newspapers of every kind, but for cabled and written descriptions to neutral countries. London correspondents of Imperial and foreign newspapers were warned that the prohibition applied to descriptions sent by mail, and even purely descriptive accounts giving no names of places were relentlessly censored.

This policy of extreme secrecy proved to be a mistake. Had the authorities confined themselves to suppressing the publication of the exact localities reached by the aircraft, and of other details likely to be of use to the enemy, they would have had public opinion behind them. One effect of the absolute suppression of non-official details was to destroy the confidence of large sections of the public in the official statements, and to encourage people to believe absurdly exaggerated rumours of the damage done. Civilians who witnessed a Zeppelin raid for the first time nearly always imagined the casualties and the loss of property to be much greater than they actually were. The sight of a few injured persons carried along on stretchers gives the untrained observer the impression of great loss of life. The glare of a few simultaneous fires makes it appear for the moment as though whole neighbourhoods were burning.

In every district where an attack took place many of the residents wrote long letters to their friends describing the scenes. Many such letters, written under the stress of great emotion, were greatly, if unconsciously, exaggerated. These personal narratives were eagerly sought for in the absence of newspaper reports, and were circulated all over the kingdom and handed from friend to friend. These accounts took the place of the descriptions of trained and experienced newspaper reporters. Thus, in place of descriptions of the raids written by men whose life's work it was to get at the truth and record the real facts, the nation had the series of uncensored, over-coloured, privately written narratives. In America, London correspondents having been refused permission to send any details, the newspapers had to fall back upon the personal narratives of returned visitors, who repeated the worst of the rumours, often in still more exaggerated form. Thus the net result of the policy of silence was to produce a wholly false impression, during the autumn and winter, of what had taken place.

Suspicion of the official statements was greatly strengthened by one unfortunate incident. A raid was made on a large town in the north-east of England, a town in close and immediate business touch with almost the whole of the United Kingdom. Officially, immediately after the raid, the number of deaths was given as five. The figure was wrong, and everyone knew it was wrong. By the end of a week public rumour had placed the number of deaths at 100, 200, and in some quarters even at 300. How the wrong total came to be issued was never explained. Some days afterwards the correct figure was officially stated—24

AT MALDON, ESSEX.
A demolished workshop in Spital Road.

deaths—but it was too late to correct the harm done. The fact is that those responsible for the publication of war news showed at this stage a total misapprehension of the psychology of the British nation. In place of seeking to minimize the accounts of the damage and forbidding the publication of photographs, they ought to have told everything to the full. The mistake was to some extent recognized in February, 1916, when the Press was once more allowed to resume its legitimate function, so far as air raids were concerned.

In June the Germans once more turned to the East and the North-East Coast. On June 4 there was a raid, doing some slight damage ; and two days later there was another, by far the most serious of any that had yet happened. The raiders succeeded in reaching a town on the East Coast during the night and bombed it at their leisure. One large drapery house was struck and was completely wrecked, the entire building—a somewhat old one—collapsing. Adjoining these premises, with only a narrow roadway between, there was one of the most beautiful Norman churches in England. The church was wholly uninjured save a few of the panes in the glass windows. A rumour was spread over the country, and was generally believed, that a large number of girls and women "lived in" on the draper's premises, and were killed when the house was struck. This rumour was false. The drapery firm had ceased to house its attendants on the premises for a couple of years before the raid. Some working-class streets were very badly damaged, a number of houses destroyed, and many people injured. It was one of the peculiarities of this raid that, unlike most of the others, all the people injured were struck while indoors. The total casualties here were twenty-four killed, about sixty seriously injured, and a larger number slightly injured.

The outrage was quickly avenged by a young British naval airman, Flight Sub-Lieut. R. A. J. Warneford, in one of the most brilliant aerial exploits of the war.

Mr. Warneford, who was only 22 years of age, was the son of an Anglo-Indian railway engineer, and before the war was in the mercantile marine. He came home to "do something" for his country, enlisted in the 2nd Sportsman's Battalion on January 7, was transferred in February to the Royal Naval Air Service, passed the tests for a pilot's certificate within a few days, and was given a commission. He was noted at the flying school as one of the most brilliant pupils the instructors had ever known. A month after obtaining his commission he went to France, where his reckless daring soon made him conspicuous in a service where venturesomeness is the general rule. On the morning of June 7 at 3 a.m. he encountered a Zeppelin returning from the coast of Flanders to Ghent, and chased it, mounting above it and sailing over it at a height of 6,000 feet. Zeppelin and aeroplane exchanged shots, and when the Zeppelin was between one and two hundred feet immediately below him he dropped six bombs on it. One bomb hit the Zeppelin fairly, causing a terrific explosion, and setting the airship on fire from end to end. Warneford's aeroplane was caught by the force of the explosion and turned upside down, but he succeeded in righting it before it touched the ground. He was forced to alight within the German lines. Nevertheless he restarted his engine, though not without great difficulty, and in due course returned to his station without damage. Only the framework of the Zeppelin was left, the crew being all burned or mangled, and the body of the machine being completely destroyed. The flaming framework dropped on the Convent School of St. Amandsberg, killing one nun and burning two Sisters who had rushed into the street with children in their arms. The machine on which Mr. Warneford made this attack was a Morane "Parasol," a little monoplane with a pair of wings raised well above the pilot's head. This construction gives the aviator full view on either side below, thus enabling him to take good aim for bomb dropping. The Morane of that type was also noted as a quick-climbing machine, a very decided advantage in attacking Zeppelins.

The story of Mr. Warneford's triumph sent a thrill through England. The King promptly sent a personal telegram of congratulation to him, and conferred upon him the Victoria Cross. The telegram ran as follows :

"I most heartily congratulate you upon your splendid achievement of yesterday, in which you singlehanded destroyed an enemy Zeppelin.

"I have much pleasure in conferring upon you the Victoria Cross for this gallant act.

"George R.I."

Next day the French War Minister, on the recommendation of General Joffre, awarded Warneford the Cross of the Legion of Honour.

FLIGHT SUB-LIEUTENANT R. A. J. WARNEFORD, V.C.
Killed at Buc Aerodrome, June 17, 1915, shortly after he had been awarded the V.C. and the French Legion of Honour.

It was known that he was returning on a visit to England. A splendid public welcome was prepared for him. He went first, however, to Paris, and there in company with Mr. Henry Needham, an American journalist, he set out on a new Henry Farman biplane, which he proposed to take by air to Dunkirk. Mr. Warneford and his passenger had risen to 700 feet when the machine wobbled violently for a few seconds, and then overturned, throwing them both out. They were both killed instantly. The return to England was different from that which had been anticipated. In the late evening of June 21, a fortnight after the deed which won him fame, the train carrying Mr. Warneford's body came into Victoria Station. Thousands of people had assembled there to pay their final tributes to the hero

BOMB-DROPPING APPARATUS OF THE GERMAN "ROLAND."

The apparatus consists of three parts—the bomb tubes, the tube covers, and the pedal board. The bomb tubes are arranged in a plate let into the floor of the fuselage, a little behind observer's seat. The pedal board is operated by the foot of the observer. Round the neck of the bomb is a circumferential groove, and when the bomb has been pulled up into the tube the fork engages this groove and holds it fast. Pressure on the foot pedals, however, withdraws the fork from the groove in the neck, allowing the bomb to drop. In order to obviate mistakes the pedals and tube covers are painted in corresponding colours.

and the little procession of the coffin covered by the Union Jack, mounted on a gun carriage, and guarded by seamen of the Royal Naval Division moved out amid the bared heads of the silent crowd to the Brompton Cemetery.

Whom the gods loved they gave in youth's first flower
One infinite hour of glory. That same hour,
Before a leaf droops from the laurel, come
Winged Death and Sleep to bear Sarpedon home.
(Iliad, xvi. 676–683.)*

* By B. N. in *The Times*, June 23, 1915.

The destruction of the Zeppelin by Mr. Warneford and a successful attack by two British naval airmen on German airship sheds to the north of Brussels were followed by a slight pause in the German campaign. The next raid was made on the night of June 15, on the North-East Coast. Two Zeppelins appeared to approach from the north-east, and left flying south-east to east. They flew at a height of 5,000 feet, and, although anti-aircraft guns promptly opened on them, they were apparently not struck. The shrapnel from these guns, in falling, caused slight damage. The Zeppelins dropped about two dozen incendiary bombs in one district and were enabled to do a certain amount of damage owing to a curious oversight. The roof windows of one shop had been blackened in order that the lights from it should not show against the sky. A certain amount of the blackening had been rubbed off, so that the lights afforded a mark for the Zeppelins, which dropped a number of bombs, doing considerable damage to property, but causing no loss of life. On the other hand, some very important premises over which the Zeppelins passed that night were in total darkness and were not attacked at all, the Zeppelins failing to discover them. This was by no means the first proof of the value of darkness in foiling the raiders.

Having attacked the shops, the Zeppelins sailed across a river and came to some other buildings. Here, apparently, a number of workmen ran out into the open to see them. The workmen were caught by the bomb explosions; 14 men and youths were killed and 13 injured. The damage to property here was slight. A policeman was killed not far off, and other casualties brought the total number of deaths to 16. As the Zeppelins sailed up towards the North Sea they dropped a bomb in the Market Place of one town, but only succeeded in shattering some window panes. This raid was much better planned than the attack upon the same country a few months before. It was clear that in the interval the enemy pilots had made themselves fully informed of all the details of the topography of the district.

"Punish England" was the note of the German comment over these raids. "In spite of our U-boats, England feels the war which she has incited far less than is appropriate and necessary," said a writer in the *Hamburger Nachrichten*. "England's shamelessness is not only abominable; it drives the blood to our heads and makes us desire and demand a hard punishment for this frivolous and huckstering people. Therefore we cannot rain bombs enough on England, nor can enough of her ships be destroyed."

There was only one raid in July, on the 3rd, an unsuccessful attempt by aeroplanes and seaplanes to attack Harwich. August, however, witnessed no less than three big incursions, inflicting casualties far exceeding those of any previous month. On August 9 a squadron of airships visited the East Coast, dropping incendiary bombs over a large area and killing one man, nine women, and four children, besides wounding at least 14 others. The Zeppelins were aided by the extreme darkness of the night and by a fog which hung over some places. They were met by sustained gun-fire from our land defences. One Zeppelin was struck and damaged; as it tried to return it was attacked by aircraft from Dunkirk with such success that its back was broken, its rear compartments were damaged, and it was completely destroyed. During this raid one of our pilots, Flight Sub-Lieut. R. Lord, was killed in landing in the dark.

In the second August attack, on the 12th, two Zeppelins visited the East Coast, killing four men and two women, and injuring three men, eleven women, and nine children, all civilians. They also caused serious damage to 14 houses. The official report stated that they were engaged at some points, but succeeded in getting away from our aircraft patrols. Our men believed that one of the Zeppelins was damaged. Practically all the casualties in this raid happened in one quiet little country town. A number of people had gathered in the streets to watch the Zeppelins, never anticipating that they would be attacked. Two Zeppelins hovered over the place, coming quite low. A subaltern in charge of infantry in a village outside opened rifle fire on them. They retorted by dropping bombs on the little town. One bomb fell among a group of humble folk standing at a street corner, injuring several in a frightful fashion and wrecking many houses.

What was the impression made on the countryside by these attacks? Here is an account written at the time by a spectator of one of the most picturesque of the raids on the East Coast:

"It was a shepherd who first picked out the Zeppelin, a typical East Coast shepherd of the old type, with smock and long beard.

" 'There um be,' he called excitedly, pointing high up, eastwards. 'There um be, shutting out the stars.'

" His trained eye noted at a glance that there was darkness where some stars ought to be visible, darkness caused by the intervening body of the airship. Just then a powerful searchlight covered the spot and revealed the invader. The hackneyed description 'like a cigar' exactly expresses its appearance. It was moving swiftly, it was very far up, and consequently it looked unexpectedly small. The rays of the searchlight lent it a sudden glory, like a heavenly messenger of glistening gold hovering about the earth. 'It's ten thousand feet up,' said one onlooker. Surely that little thing could not be the German terror of the skies !

" Five searchlights now played on it. A gun spoke from seawards with a dull, heavy report. The Zeppelin dropped sharply out of the line of the lights. 'They've hit it !' one man shouted hoarsely. A long sigh, a sigh of irrepressible emotion, passed through the watching crowd.

" No such luck ! Our attention was suddenly drawn ahead. Small streaks of light were tearing through the skies earthwards. Two of them burst into furious flame as they struck the earth and burned themselves harmlessly out ; others disappeared into nothingness. These were incendiary bombs. We found later that those which had fallen into soft fields had been driven by the force of their descent into the earth, thus being rendered harmless.

" Again came the sound of gun-fire. This time it seemed directed at something out at sea. Could there be more than one Zeppelin in the attack ? Why could the heavy darkness not lift and show us what was happening ? Just then the dancing searchlights seemed to concentrate above our station. All eyes turned upwards. Directly overhead, lower, bigger, a thing no longer remote, but near us, formidable, awesome, floated the German airship.

" No one shouted. No one showed sign of fear. But there was a sudden silence, a sudden stiffening. A German bomb dropped now could scarcely fail to miss our group. No bomb came, and almost in a second the Zeppelin, moving upwards and onwards, had gone.

" The air was alive with sound coming from every quarter of the compass. Great machines were buzzing, droning, clamouring furiously. Where they were and what they were the darkness kept men from seeing. From somewhere there came the faint sound of the 'rip-p' of a machine gun. Then came an ear-splitting detonation. It started like a hiss ; it ended with a roar that bade fair to rend our ear drums. 'S-s-ss-ss-ssh-SSH BOOP—BANG.' Judging from the sound, half the countryside might have been torn away. 'It's an explosive bomb,' whispered the expert.

" Down below, I knew, the artillerymen were standing at their long grey guns waiting for the word and the moment to swing them round on their movable platforms, elevate them and fire at the invaders. In the hangars our aircraft were ready. Were they able to go out to-night and attack the enemy in the sky ? Word was passed round, no one knew from where, that our aeroplanes were making a cross move and cutting off the Zeppelins as they came back after completing their circuit.

" Then the whole thing passed. The droning ceased. There was no more dropping of bombs,

BROUGHT DOWN NEAR YPRES.

A German aeroplane. The body of the aviator, who was killed, is seen lying across the machine.

THE GIANT TWIN-PROPELLED WAR BIPLANE.

German machine fitted with two engines of 100 h.p. to 150 h.p. each. In the centre is a nacelle which contains seats for three men—two gunners and the pilot.

no more firing. The searchlights were turned off. 'You had better turn in,' said the experienced hands. 'The show is over for to-night.' Looking around, one could see the crowds that had been drawn from everywhere leaving their points of vantage, going homewards.

. . . . .

"A few hours later we heard the results of the raid. Most of the bombs had dropped harmlessly in fields, gardens, and streams. One or two had landed in a small country town near by, doing some damage. In the morning I went to view the scene.

"In daylight it seemed impossible at first to believe that the events before midnight had been a reality. The countryside was at its fairest and best. The hedges were a mass of flowers and crimson berries. Wild honeysuckle was blooming freely. The fat game rose lazily on the wing and flew into the neighbouring coverts as I approached. A piece of waste land was a blaze of deep red, covered with heather in full flower. The pear trees and the apple trees were laden with ripening fruit. What had countryside such as this to do with war and death in the air ?

"I came to a typical rural town, really little more than an over-grown village, with one long street and with side roads of quaint two-storied houses, some built in the eighteenth century, some older still.

"It was at a point where two or three side streets meet that the tragedy of the raid happened. Here, as everywhere else, the people poured into the street at the first rumour of another visit. A little crowd assembled here, the barber, the fireman and his young son, a labourer and his wife, a stable boy, and the like. They were trying to locate the Zeppelin by the noise, when it suddenly appeared right over their heads. 'It warn't a quarter of a mile up,' said one survivor. 'We could ha' brought it down with an eighteen-pounder gun,' said a veteran volunteer.

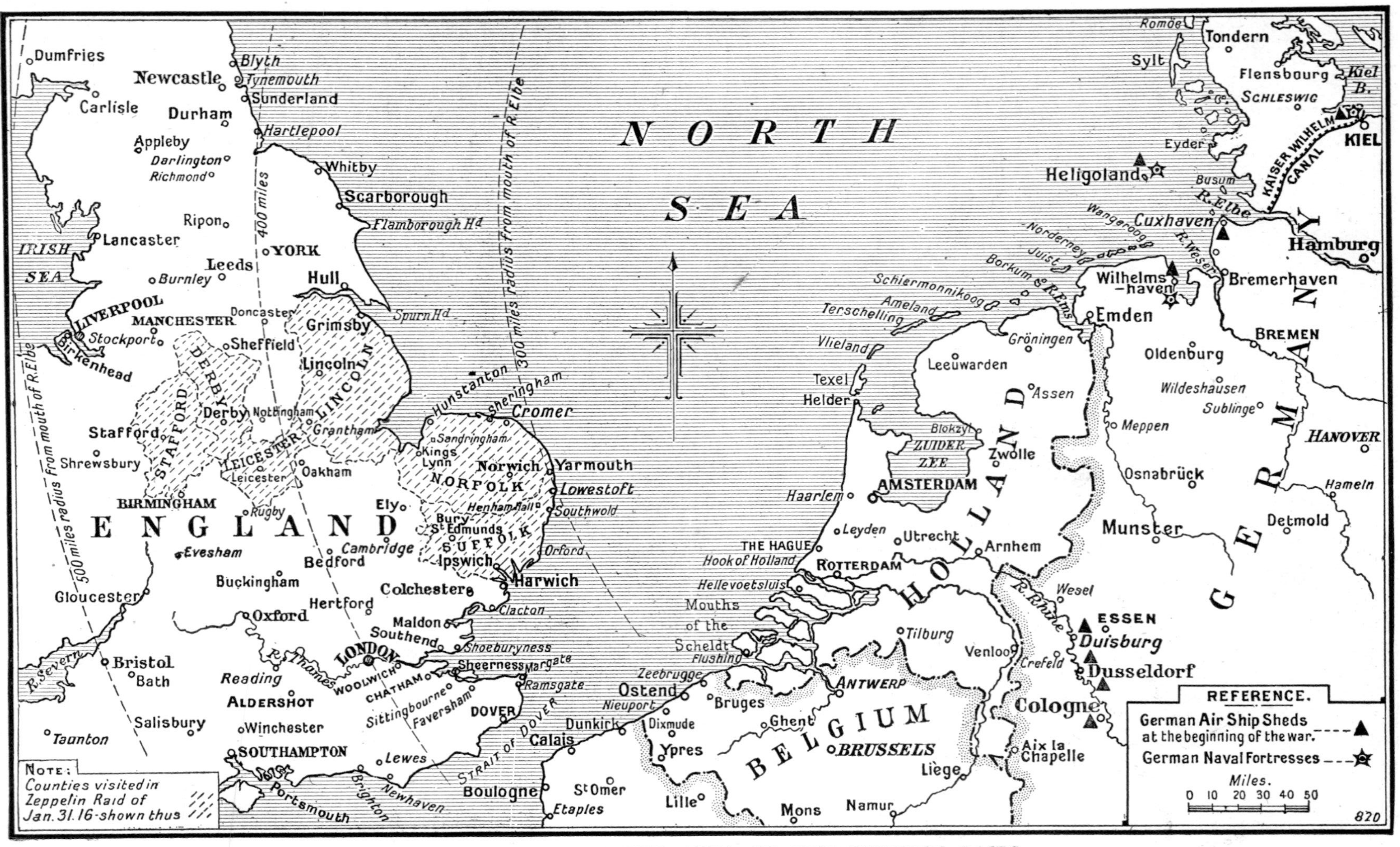

MAP TO ILLUSTRATE THE AREA OF THE ZEPPELIN RAIDS.

"Into the middle of this little crowd of old men, women and young children, the Germans dropped one of their most powerful bombs. It struck the roadway in front of one house and exploded. The little slightly built houses on either side were knocked down as a child might knock down a house of bricks. Some houses had their roofs largely taken off. Some cottages had their floors shaken out. The explosive moved mainly in one direction, making a line of death and disaster. Fragments and splinters struck into buildings hundreds of yards away.

"As for the little group of humans—how can one dwell on them, the boy with his legs torn off, the woman blown out of human resemblance, the fireman and his son killed as they stood hand in hand, the wife killed as she was stepping out to her husband ! Six killed and twenty odd wounded, all of them simple countryfolk. A great bag for a mighty raid, truly !

"The Germans dropped two more shells after the first. One struck a garden, made a big hole in the earth, tore an apple tree into splinters, and broke innumerable panes of glass in a line of greenhouses. The third fell in the stable of a little inn, killing the pony, wrecking the stable, and breaking some of the windows of the inn. Mine host is grieving over his pony and his stable, telling everyone that he is not insured. But I do not think that he will do very badly out of the incident. His little bar has become a place of pilgrimage. Three quickly enlisted assistants cannot keep pace with the demands of the armies of customers pouring in, to drink his beer and view the damage.

. . . . . .

"The thing that strikes one most about the bombardment of peaceful, quiet, rural parts is its futility. Actually, the amount of damage done by the raid was equal to what might come from a bad thunderstorm, when some parties of people were caught by the lightning under the trees.

"We are to be terrorised, say the German commentators. But if this countryside is any proof, terror is the last feeling created. People are angered, embittered, braced up for further action. Recruiting is quickened, and more people go to the munition factories. But—terror ? The parties of holiday-making children, whose laughter I can hear in the fields beyond as I write this, are the best answer to that threat."

The third August raid, on the 17th, again on the Eastern Counties, succeeded in killing ten persons and injuring fifteen men, eighteen women, and three children. The Zeppelins came once more under the fire of our anti-aircraft guns, and one was again believed to have been hit.

The brief details published about these raids and the growth of rumours of all kinds caused much dissatisfaction. People were disappointed that enemy aircraft were allowed to visit this country time after time, apparently with impunity. After each raid glowing German accounts were published of what had been accomplished, and there came an uneasy feeling in many quarters that our own authorities were possibly keeping back the real truth. *The Times* dealt with this aspect of the matter in a leading article on August 19, which attracted widespread attention. "We wonder," it said, "whether the Government quite realize the effect these announcements (of raids) in their present form are having upon the public mind and upon their own position in the public estimation." It pointed out that our extreme reticence and the lateness in the publication of our reports caused the British accounts to be discredited in neutral countries and caused widespread public irritation at home. "The Government do not seem to know how intense this feeling has become. The expressions of indignation against the Ministry on this point are for the most part extremely unfair. The authorities concerned, by suppressing information which might be useful to the Germans, are doing their best to shield the public from attack. They have no other motive, for we do not for a moment think that the full facts are improperly held back. But the fact remains that this feeling of irritation exists, and that the Government would do well to take account of it. Whether they could not disclose a little more, without telling the Germans anything that they do not know already, is a matter which they must decide for themselves. In any case we think they would be wise to issue an authoritative statement, both for neutrals and for this country, of the principles on which they are acting."

The censorship was defended by Mr. Balfour in a letter addressed to a correspondent, and officially circulated through the Press Bureau. Mr. Balfour declared that the results of the enemy air raids had been magnified out of all proportion by ill-informed rumours, and he combated the suggestion that unpleasant truths were being deliberately hid from a nervous

IN AN ENGINE GONDOLA OF A ZEPPELIN.

On the left of the car is a man with machine gun on the lookout for attacking aircraft.

public. The following is the full text of his letter:

"ADMIRALTY, S.W.,

"*August* 28.

"DEAR SIR,—You ask me why the accounts published in this country of enemy air raids are so meagre, while the German narratives of the same events are rich in lurid detail. You point out that while these narratives are widely believed in neutral countries, the reticence of the censored British Press suggests a suspicion that unpleasant truths are being deliberately hid from a nervous public.

"Compare the following accounts, which, though the historian would never guess it, relate to the same airship raid:

TRANSLATION. Headlines of *Deutsche Tageszeitung*, August 11, 1915.	August 10, 1915.
AIR ATTACK ON THE DOCKS OF LONDON.	The Secretary of the Admiralty makes the following announcement:—
On the night of the 9th–10th of August our Naval Airships carried out attacks upon fortified coast towns and harbours on the East Coast of England.	A squadron of hostile airships visited the East Coast last night and this morning between the hours of 8.30 p.m. and 12.30 a.m.
In spite of strenuous opposition, bombs were	Some fires were caused by the dropping of incendiary bombs, but these were quickly extinguished and only immaterial damage was done.

BOMB-DROPPING FROM A ZEPPELIN.

dropped on British warships in the Thames, on the docks of London, on the torpedo craft base at Harwich, and on important positions on the Humber.

Good results were observed.

The airships returned safely from their successful undertaking.

The following casualties have been reported :—1 man, 8 women, and 4 children killed ; 4 men, 6 women, and 2 children wounded.

One Zeppelin was seriously damaged by gun fire of the land defences, and was reported this morning being towed into Ostend. She has since been subjected to continual attacks by aircraft from Dunkirk under heavy fire, and it is now reported that after having had her back broken and rear compartments damaged she was completely destroyed by explosion.

"Now it is plain that if one of these stories is true the other is false. Why not then explain the discrepancy and tell the world in detail wherein the German account distorts the facts ?

"The reason is quite simple. Zeppelins attack under cover of night, and (by preference) of moonless night. In such conditions landmarks are elusive, and navigation difficult. Errors are inevitable, and sometimes of surprising magnitude. The Germans constantly assert, and may sometimes believe, that they have dropped bombs on places which in fact they never approached. Why make their future voyages easier by telling them where they have blundered

BRITISH AEROPLANES.

Testing machines at sunset.

in the past? Since their errors are our gain, why dissipate them? Let us learn what we can from the enemy; let us teach him only what we must.

"Nobody will, I think, be disposed to doubt that this reticence is judicious. But the question may still be asked whether it is used not merely to embarrass the Germans, but unduly to reassure the British. How ought we to rate the Zeppelins among weapons of attack? What have they done? What can they do?

"To this last question I do not offer a reply. I cannot prophesy about the future of a method of warfare which is still in its infancy.

"I can, however, say something of its results during the past.

"That it has caused much suffering to many innocent people is unhappily certain. But even this result, with all its tragedy, has been magnified out of all proportion by ill-informed rumour. I am assured by the Home Office that during the last 12 months 71 civilian adults and 18 children have been killed; 189 civilian adults and 31 children have been injured.

"Judged by numbers, this cumulative result of many successive crimes does not equal the single effort of the submarine which, to the unconcealed pride of Germany and the horror of all the world, sent 1,198 unoffending civilians to the bottom in the Lusitania. Yet it is bad enough, and we may well ask what military advantage has been gained at the cost of so much innocent blood.

"The answer is easily given. No soldier or sailor has been killed; seven have been wounded; and only on one occasion has damage been inflicted which could by any stretch of language be described as of the smallest military importance. Zeppelin raids have been brutal; but so far they have not been effective. They have served no hostile purpose, moral or material.

"Yours faithfully,

"ARTHUR JAMES BALFOUR."

The official report of the next air raid, of September 7, was briefer than ever. It simply announced that hostile aircraft again visited the Eastern counties and dropped bombs. "It is known that there have been some fires and some casualties, but particulars are yet unavailable."

The second and third air raids on London were made on the evenings of September 7 and 8. On the first night, outlying districts were attacked. On the following night, a serious and concerted raid was made on the very heart of London. The Zeppelins came between 10 and 11 o'clock. The theatres and music-halls were all open, the streets were full of the usual evening crowds, and life was going on with its usual animation. Suddenly the sound of explosion after explosion could be heard, first the bursting of bombs, then the rapid firing of anti-aircraft guns. Zeppelins were plainly visible aloft, as the searchlights shone on them. People came out of restaurants and stood in the streets gazing at them. From the roofs of houses, fires could be seen eastwards and northwards. One bomb fell in a square almost surrounded by hospitals. Hundreds of windows in a children's hospital near by were broken, and the sick children were aroused from their sleep by the tremendous explosion. It seemed as though the Zeppelins were taking special aim at St. Paul's Cathedral and at the British Museum, although they failed to touch either. Afterwards one of the German raiders stated that an anti-aircraft gun had been placed under cover of St. Paul's, a statement wholly false.

Perhaps the most splendid work in meeting the raid that night was done by the London Fire Brigade. "One fire, in particular, which for a time threatened to be really serious, was confined and subdued with a rapidity as splendid as anything known in the history of fire-fighting in this country. One of the heroes of that night was a fireman named Green, who penetrated a blazing building time after time, saving people there. When it was believed that all were out, word came that there were still two upstairs. Green returned, forcing his way into the upper floors of the now furiously burning and almost collapsing house. At one point he could go no farther, and the flames almost caught him. He had to jump into the roadway to escape, and injured himself so seriously that he died shortly afterwards. His name was enrolled among those of the heroes of the London Fire Brigade.

Most of the buildings damaged were in poor districts. Three or four houses in one ancient slum centre, beloved by mid-Victorian novelists, were badly wrecked. No public institution of any kind was hit, no fire station, and no arsenal. The public outside the immediate areas where the bombs fell regarded the attack as a great spectacle. It was impossible, in spite of warnings, to keep people in their houses. They crowded into the streets to get a better view. In some of the theatres the managers announced from the stage that a Zeppelin raid was on, and the performances were continued as usual. At the St. James's Theatre, for instance, Sir George Alexander begged the people to remain in their seats. But they needed no begging. They sat quietly as a matter of course.

"The Zeppelin passed right over our house and was there potted by anti-aircraft guns," said an old clergyman. "One of the fuses, weighing 1 lb. 5 oz., fell six feet from my front door, just where I had stood, and it was hot when I carried it in. It was a terrific but very splendid sight, and it had for me something exhilarating in it; for, like most old men, I

THE RAID OVER A LONDON DISTRICT, SEPTEMBER 8, 1915.
View of a Zeppelin lit up by searchlights and surrounded by shrapnel smoke.

have felt so selfish at home out of danger, and now at any rate one is allowed to feel that we may take our share of it after all." One bomb exploded near a passing motor omnibus. There were twenty people in the vehicle. Nine of them were killed and eleven injured, the driver having both his legs blown off, and dying shortly afterwards in hospital.

The Home Secretary issued subsequently a statement concerning the raid in which some of the tragedies were described. Here is a typical extract from his report :

"Somewhere in the vast area of London's suburbs there is a little block of houses standing almost by itself and divided up into small flats. On the ground floor there were sleeping a widow, her daughter, aged 18, and a young man whom they kept as a lodger. On the first floor was a family with three children, two of them girls, and on the second floor a working man and his wife with five children, four of them girls and one a boy. The bomb dropped squarely on the roof of the house. As the labourer and his wife, who were on the second floor, described it, the whole partition wall beside their bed gave way and disappeared ; the man pushed his wife out into the centre of the room, and went off to find his children. Two of them, who slept in the room under the spot where the bomb fell, had vanished with room, bed and everything, and their bodies were found two days later under the *débris* of the house. Of the others, the boy, aged eight, ran for safety to the staircase, which was blown away, and in the dark fell down into the hole where his sisters' bodies were buried in the ruins. Of the first floor inhabitants, two were missing altogether, and their bodies were subsequently recovered. Of the ground floor, where apparently the worst effect of the explosion took place, it is sufficient to say that part of the body of the man who occupied it was found 150 yards away."

One of the few impressions of the raid permitted to be printed by the Censor was written by an American journalist, Mr. William G. Shepherd. Quotations from it serve to show how the attitude of the people impressed a neutral visitor :

"Traffic is at a standstill. A million quiet cries make a subdued roar. Seven million people of the biggest city in the world stand gazing into the sky from the darkened streets.

"Here is the climax to the twentieth century !

"Among the autumn stars floats a long, gaunt Zeppelin. It is dull yellow—the colour of the harvest moon.

"The long fingers of searchlights, reaching up from the roofs of the city, are touching all sides of the death messenger with their white tips. Great booming sounds shake the city. They are Zeppelin bombs—falling—killing—burning.

"Lesser noises—of shooting—are nearer at hand, the noise of aerial guns sending shrapnel into the sky.

"'For God's sake, don't do that !' says one man to another, who has just struck a match to light a cigarette.

"Whispers, low voices, run all through the streets.

"'There's a red light in the sky over there ; our house may be burning,' exclaims a woman, clutching at a man's coat.

"'There are a million houses in London ; why ours particularly ?' he responds.

"A group of men talking French stand gazing up from the street. They are in waiters' clothes and have rushed out from the upper room of one of the most luxurious hotels in the world.

"'The devils !' exclaims one, and then—

"'We've got it ! It can't get away There's shrapnel all around it !'

"'O my neck !' says a pretty girl in evening wraps. 'I can't look up a minute more.'

"But she does.

"All about you are beautifully garbed women and men in evening dress. Ohs and ahs long drawn out—exclamations of admiration like the sounds made by American crowds, watching fireworks, greet the brilliantly white flashes of shrapnel.

"Suddenly you realize that the biggest city in the world has become the night battlefield on which 7,000,000 harmless men, women, and children live.

"Here is war at the very heart of civilization threatening all the millions of things that human hearts and human minds have created in past centuries.

"If the men up there in the sky think they are terrifying London they are wrong. They are only making England white hot mad.

"The redness of a burning building fills the sky The dome of historic St. Paul's Cathedral

AIR RAID ON LONDON, OCTOBER 13, 1915.
The effect of an explosion on wood-paving.
Small picture : Interior of a room used for business purposes.

looms up against the redness. You pass the old church in a side street.

"At the gateway stands the old verger, half dressed. It has been his duty for the last fifty years to guard the church against thieves and fires as other sextons have guarded it for centuries past. But he's got a bigger job on his hands than any of them ever had before.

"The verger's white-haired wife stands beside him. They are talking with three girls such as never come into the lives of church sextons except on nights like this. They are pointing out to the aged couple, with cheaply jewelled fingers, the slowing fading yellow form of the Zeppelin."

The German official report, which was declared officially in England to be grossly in error in most cases as to where the bombs were dropped, was as follows :

The East India Docks were attacked and a large shed full of ammunition was burned to the ground. At the London Docks a warehouse was destroyed and several ships were hit by bombs, some being destroyed. At the Victoria Docks a large cotton warehouse was burned to the ground and in the same neighbourhood blocks of houses were destroyed or damaged in St. George Street and Leman Street. The City, and particularly the newspaper quarter, was bombarded with especially good success. The Tower of London and London Bridge, which are armed with guns, were bombarded. Houses—sometimes whole blocks of them—were damaged or destroyed in Liverpool Street, Chancery Lane, Moorgate, Bishopsgate, Aldgate, and the Minories.

The London and South-Western Bank was burned to the ground and much money, valuables, and papers are believed to have been destroyed. The *Morning Post* building was seriously damaged and a branch of the London Bank reduced to ashes. The subway and railway traffic was interrupted for a time owing to bomb damage. Much damage was done to Woolwich Arsenal. In Enfield a battery with searchlights was silenced. The Hampton Power Station was hit. In Croydon extensive factories were hit and great fires were noticed.

RAID ON LONDON, OCTOBER 13, 1915.
Wrecked houses in the suburbs.
Small picture: Hole made by bomb in a London business thoroughfare.

In Kentish Town an especially strong searchlight battery was noticed and bombs were dropped on it. A whole row of searchlights went out. At West Ham and East Ham the railway was bombarded. At Ipswich a battery was bombarded, and its fire became noticeably weaker.

The German airship was the object of an unusually hot fire, but it was not damaged. Four aeroplanes attacked the airship without success.

One immediate result of the raid was to arouse a storm of protest against what was felt to be the very inadequate measures of defence provided for London. This protest was none the less severe because little could be said about it in the newspapers. Criticism centred, in particular, upon the calibre of the anti-aircraft guns, which were apparently unable to reach the enemy.

Shortly afterwards, Admiral Sir John Percy Scott was placed in charge of the gunnery arrangements for the aerial defence of London. This appointment gave great general satisfaction and did much to restore public confidence, for Admiral Scott's reputation in gunnery had been long established. Naval men knew what he could do by the fine results he had obtained when captain of the *Scylla* in the Mediterranean, and when captain of the Gunnery School at Whale Island. But to the general public he was most familiar as the officer who mounted guns on carriages that enabled them to be taken to Ladysmith for the defence of that town against the Boers. A man of great originality, accustomed to tackling fresh problems, ready to appreciate new issues—as was strikingly shown by his attitude over the submarine question immediately before the war—it was felt that under him all that could be done would be done.

There were four more raids in the United Kingdom in September, 1915. A Zeppelin flew over the East Coast on September 11, doing no damage; there was a raid over the East Coast on September 12, when the damage was trifling; there was another on the 13th on the East Coast with no damage, and a raid over Kent on the same day, when several persons were wounded.

Before Admiral Scott could complete his arrangements for the better defence of London, the Metropolis was again attacked. On October 13, about 9.30 at night, fire was opened from the skies on the centre of London. That same evening parts of the Eastern Counties were attacked. In London alone 32 were killed and 95 injured, and the total casualties for the whole area of the raid that night were 56 killed and 113 wounded. A number of houses were damaged, and several fires started. The bombs used were in many cases of a very large size. One of them, striking the roadway, penetrated into the subway containing gas and water mains, bursting them. Most of the victims were ordinary working folk, doing their ordinary work. Motor omnibus conductors died in the street, a messenger boy was killed

RAID ON LONDON, OCTOBER 13, 1915.

In the suburbs: Houses struck by bombs, where two people were killed and two severely injured. Small picture: Hole made by bomb, the explosion from which wrecked six houses.

when delivering a message, a potman died at his work, a caterer was killed while returning from a Masonic lodge, a carman's daughter was injured in the legs and lingered until next morning, a waitress was done to death while returning home from a Young Women's Guild, and so on.

The inquests on the victims revealed many tragic facts. A woman told how she and her husband, a railway guard, were standing outside a place of amusement. She was struck, but was not injured. When she found her husband, he was lying at the point of death. A man in a public house had both thighs smashed. A woman was wounded in the face and breast, and the lower part of her spine was smashed. A young woman of twenty-three, an assistant in a milk shop, was killed while on her way to a railway station. One bomb made a hole in the pavement six feet across, killing the driver and conductor of a passing motor omnibus and a special constable who was a passenger. A police inspector told how in one case a parapet was blown away, and in another an entire top storey of a building was shifted. A boy of thirteen left home to go to a place of amusement where he was employed to run errands. He received such injuries to the arms, legs and chest that he died in the hospital next day. A newsvendor, aged seventy-four, a naval pensioner and old age pensioner, was killed. He had his old age pension forms, two Five Pound War Loan vouchers, and some money on him when struck. A house decorator, forty-five years of age, was out looking for work when a bomb burst near by; he was picked up badly injured. He turned to a doctor and asked him to attend to another man first. He himself died almost immediately afterwards.

The British official report stated that some houses were damaged and several fires started, but no serious damage was caused to military material. Anti-aircraft guns and the Royal Field Artillery, attached to the Central Force, were in action. Two aeroplanes of the Royal Flying Corps went up, but, owing to the atmospheric conditions, only one aeroplane succeeded in locating an airship. This aeroplane, however, was unable to overhaul the airship before it was lost in the fog. An airship was seen to heel over on its side and to drop to a lower level.

A fuller official report, issued by the Home Office, stated that there were five positive areas in which damage had been done. The first of these was an area in which there was little or no residential property, but some large buildings devoted to various kinds of business in comparatively wide streets. Here bombs were dropped containing high explosives, which in four cases fell upon the street and in the fifth upon the back premises of one large building thronged with people. One of the bombs, which was apparently of a large size, penetrated the street into the subway containing gas and water mains, and in exploding melted the gas pipes, setting alight a fire which, though slight in extent, lasted for several hours. The explosion of this bomb damaged the buildings around considerably and destroyed almost all the glass in the neighbourhood. It was responsible for a number of casualties.

The second area contained a large block of residential flats, some employed as offices. In this area there were no casualties, although several narrow escapes. The third area contained two damaged business premises, the first of them a large modern building constructed of reinforced concrete; the fourth was a district consisting entirely of working class property with small, low buildings. One group of small houses in this area was entirely destroyed by this class of bomb. In the last area covered by the raid—this time in a suburb—the property consisted of detached or semi-detached houses surrounded by small gardens. Here the largest number of bombs was dropped, the entire number falling within 600 yards, no less than five within fifty yards, and three into a single small garden.

There were many astonishing escapes. In one instance a bomb fell on a narrow passage separating two houses, the entire fronts of which were blown out, causing the upper bedroom floors to collapse. In one of the upper bedrooms a mother and daughter were sleeping. They were hurled into the street from the place where the ground floor window should have been, both escaping with their lives. A bomb fell right on the centre of a large house, killing two children instantly, and severely injuring the father and mother. At another point, where the bomb fell into the street, a young man was saying good night to a woman at the open door of the house. He was immediately killed by a fragment of the bomb, and the woman was severely injured. Here also an old man, who was walking on the pavement, had his arm blown off, and died in the hospital shortly afterwards.

TAKING COVER ABOVE LOW-LYING CLOUDS.
A suggested method of observing from a car suspended below a Zeppelin.

The German General Staff report on this October London raid stated that—

In addition to dropping bombs on the English capital, the waterworks at Hampton, and the town of Woolwich where there is a great arsenal, were heavily bombarded. Great fires are reported to have followed the explosion of the Zeppelin bombs.

The text of the German Admiralty's statement follows:

"German airships during the night of October 13–14 attacked the City of London and nearby

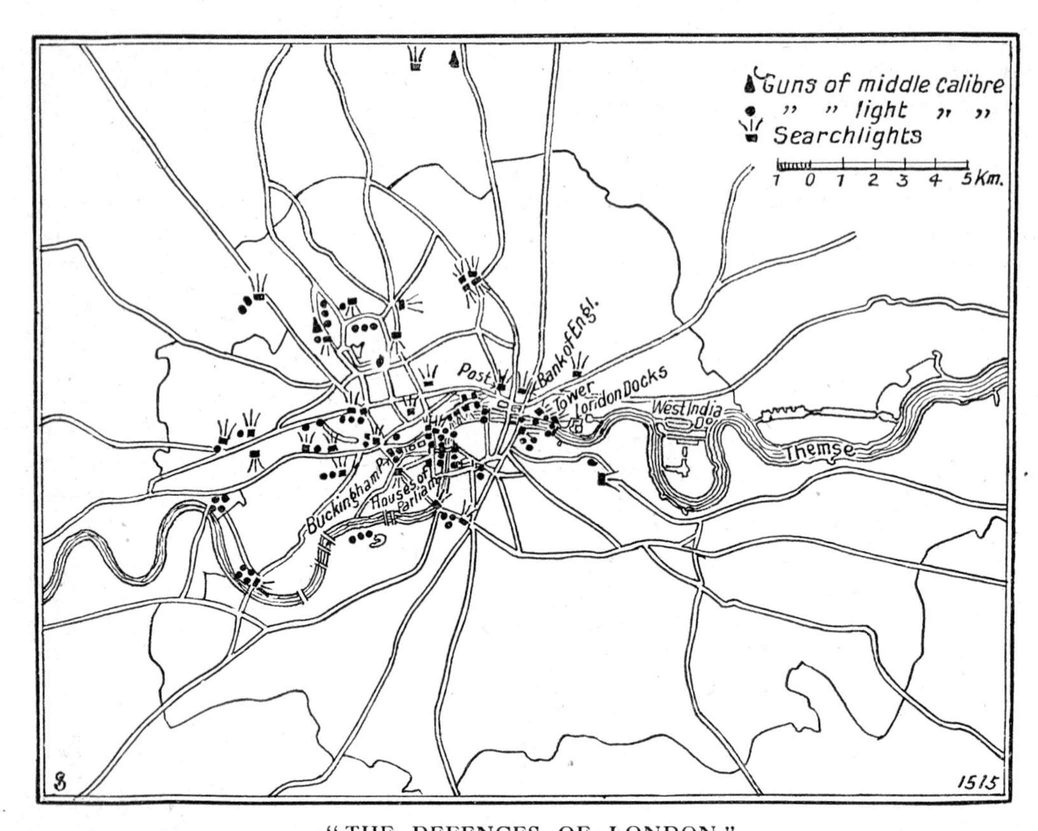

"THE DEFENCES OF LONDON."

This imaginative map was officially supplied to the German Press in December, 1915, for propaganda purposes.

important establishments as well as the batteries of Ipswich.

"Several attacks were made especially on the City of London.

'The docks of London, the waterworks at Hampton, near London, and Woolwich also were heavily bombarded with incendiary bombs.

'At all the places attacked important explosions and great fires were observed.

"All the airships returned safely, although they were vigorously attacked on passing over the English coast."

That evening one little country town in the Home Counties was unexpectedly attacked. The people and the authorities there had imagined that they were safe. There were no munition works in the district, and no war manufactures, the place was not of military importance, and it was hard to believe that its placid old streets could be the scene of war. The street lamps were kept alight as usual and the church clocks chimed the hours as they had done for centuries. In the evening, just as the clocks were striking 10, a Zeppelin appeared overhead. It was believed that it had been injured by an anti-aircraft gun on the hills beyond the town. It poured out its entire cargo of bombs, forty-four in all, as quickly as possible, on to the streets below. Had the bombs all exploded the town might well have been blown to pieces. Most of them failed to explode. A group of men stood outside a local club looking at the aircraft, when one of the bombs fell among them, killing them, and damaging the houses around. Several houses were injured, some badly, but the deaths were very few indeed. Next morning the local authorities had bills printed and pasted over the broken houses pointing out that deeds such as these showed what Germany was, and calling on the men who had not enlisted to come forward and serve their country.

The effect of the raids was twofold. On the one hand, they led to a call for reprisals and to a great deal of feeling that the Government was not sufficiently active in defence preparations. But they also led to an immense quickening of the national determination to see the war through to an end. Even in the towns that suffered most there was no panic, and nothing like panic. People did not like the raids, and did not profess to like them. They did not treat them lightly or regard them indifferently. But the suggestion put forward in German quarters that because of the raids England might be coerced into loosening her grip upon Germany was not even discussed.

A man who attempted to argue in public in England in the autumn of 1915 that his country should make peace because of the effect of the raids would have been regarded as a harmless but hopeless lunatic, and people would not have thought it worth while even to controvert his views. If the purpose of the Germans was "frightfulness," terrorism and the striking of fear into the heart of England, then they entirely failed.

After the raid on London of October 13, 1915, there came a pause of over three months. The Germans doubtless recognized the practical impossibility of conducting Zeppelin raids safely across the North Sea during the stormy and uncertain weeks of the autumn. Recalling the experiences of the previous year, the public generally anticipated a renewal of the raids towards the end of January. This anticipation proved correct. Early on the morning of Sunday, January 23, 1916, a hostile aeroplane, taking advantage of the bright moonlight, visited Dover and dropped nine bombs in rapid succession, then making off seawards. Here, as on previous attempts, the raider failed to cause any naval or military damage, but some fires were started by an incendiary bomb. One man was killed, and two men, one woman and three children slightly injured. Later in the day two hostile aeroplanes made a second attempt, but were driven off by heavy fire. On the following day a German aeroplane passed over Dover at 4 o'clock in the afternoon. Two British machines rose in pursuit and the anti-aircraft guns opened on it, but it got away These excursions were possibly reconnaissances to discover the nature and range of any new British anti-aircraft armament.

A few days later, early in the evening of Monday, January 31, the enemy struck in earnest at the East Coast and Midlands. The raiders arrived early, about 4.30 in the afternoon, and the last of them did not leave the English coast until nearly five in the morning. They entered, apparently, through Norfolk and crossed through Lincolnshire into Derbyshire

AIR RAID IN THE MIDLANDS, JANUARY 31, 1916.

Class of workmen's dwellings demolished by Zeppelin raiders. Many of the inhabitants were killed and injured.

THE RAID OVER THE EASTERN COUNTIES, JANUARY 31, 1916.

View of houses where a woman, girl, and boy were killed.

Small picture : A house in which five people were killed.

and Staffordshire, then circling around through Leicestershire, Norfolk and Suffolk. Their evident purpose was to reach Liverpool, and apparently the pilots believed that they had done so. They lost their bearings and struck instead at a town in Staffordshire. News of the arrival of the hostile aircraft quickly spread over the country. The entire train service in many parts was suspended and travellers were kept waiting in some cases half the night in by-stations. It was thought that the aircraft were aiming for London and every preparation was made there to meet them. In the case of other raids London had received no warning; now for some hours a large proportion of the population knew that at any moment attack might come. London endured its hours of suspense stoically.

The raid was undoubtedly a surprise. Staffordshire, where the Germans struck with special force, had not anticipated danger from aircraft and few precautions had been taken there against it. In some of the places there were no plans whatever for meeting hostile aircraft; in others, even arrangements for warning the authorities had not been considered. This was made a subject of great complaint afterwards. The Lord Mayor of Birmingham published an official statement on the following Saturday, in which he stated that he and the Chief Constable had on the Friday interviewed the Home Secretary and various military and other authorities, making suggestions for the better protection of the district and for the more uniform darkening of the whole Midland area, and urging the necessity of earlier warning of the approach of hostile aircraft. At a meeting of the Worcestershire County Council it was stated that in the raid the police were not informed by the local military authorities until two hours after they had received intimation that Zeppelins were coming, and therefore necessary precautions were delayed. It was mentioned that 45 bombs were dropped on the borders of that county.

The most serious damage, as already stated, occurred in one town in Staffordshire. Here no warning had been given to the people of the approach of a Zeppelin, and no provision made against any danger. There were two distinct raids in the Staffordshire area, the first between eight and nine o'clock, and the later about one o'clock. In all, 30 people were killed in this county, and at least 50 persons injured. Some families were wiped out altogether, four being killed out of one family and five of another. One man was coming out of his house when a bomb fell at his feet and killed him. His little boy, who was following him, had his arm blown off. A man left his wife and three of his four children in the house at a time while he went to a picture theatre. His wife said that she would go to visit her mother. On returning home he went to his wife's mother's house, and found mother, children, and the wife's mother, five in all, among the *débris*. A boy of twelve and a boy of nine left home to visit their grandmother. The boy of twelve was killed outright and the boy of nine died later in a doctor's surgery. At one point the bombs formed a huge crater in the road, setting the gas main on fire, and wrecking several houses. From evidence at the inquests it appeared that several of the bombs were loaded with bullets and charged with high explosives. One of the most tragic instances in this district occurred at a mission room, where the sister of a well-known minister was conducting a service attended by 200 women and girls. A bomb dropped between the mission room and church, struck the lady on the head, and killed her instantly while she was speaking, injuring two clergymen at her

IN THE EASTERN COUNTIES, JANUARY 31, 1916.

A Mission Hall wrecked by a bomb, which struck the ground a few yards in front of the building. A lady who was addressing the meeting and three members of the congregation were killed.

side. A Congregational Church was shattered. An incendiary bomb fell on the roof of a theatre full of people. The audience rose to their feet and made as though to get out, but the leading actor urged them to remain calm, and started the National Anthem. Everybody joined in the singing, and then remained in the darkened theatre until the raid was over. Close by there was a meeting in a school hall, and a number of children and some adults were present. After the first explosion the minister in charge started the hymn "Jesu, Lover of my Soul," which the whole congregation took up and sang through.

The raid on Staffordshire was the more terrible because of its utter unexpectedness. The first intimation that people had of it was when the bombs burst from the sky among them. It says much for the character of the folk there that they kept their heads through it all. Very many of the victims in Staffordshire were women and children. At one inquest on thirteen persons who had been killed, the Coroner urged the jury to return a verdict to the effect that death in each case was due to the explosion of a bomb dropped from enemy aircraft. The jury refused to accept the Coroner's suggestion and brought in a verdict against the Kaiser and the Crown Prince, as being accessories to and after the fact. The Coroner urged that there was no evidence produced that day to show that the Kaiser or the Crown Prince were accessories. But the foreman replied that the jury declined to alter their verdict.

Leicestershire was also taken completely by surprise. Ten persons were killed in one town. Warning was given before seven o'clock in the evening, and the place was thrown into darkness, but in this case the darkness did not save it. The ten persons who were killed were three men, aged 51, 49½, and 27, four married women, aged 49, 44, 42, and 29, a single woman of 25, a girl of 16, and a youth of 18.

A boy with a bandaged head told how he was with his father in a shop at eight o'clock on Monday night when he heard an explosion, and they thought at first that there was an accident at some works Then another explosion was heard and the boy going to the door called out excitedly "Bombs! Bombs!" His father followed him, was struck, and died in a quarter of an hour. The widow of the man of 51 came to the Court. She told in trembling tones how her husband, a fitter, left to go to work at 5.45 on Monday evening, That was the last time she had seen him alive. A husband related how he left his wife and child for half an hour and when he returned he found the wife lying dead with a wound in the forehead. A soldier in the R.A.M.C., stationed down south, told the Court that he last saw his wife, aged 44, his son aged 18, and his daughter aged 16 when he was at home on leave at Christmas. He was summoned back on the Tuesday morning and found they were all dead. Many people in the Court joined with the man in his tears as he told his story.

News of the approach of Zeppelins reached another Midland town about seven in the evening. The railway and tramway services were immediately stopped and soon the enemy aircraft came into view. Bombs were dropped on the countryside around; one completely demolishing a parish room, another blowing the roof off a large building, and others killing two men. In another town when the warning was received hooters and buzzers were sounded. Works were closed down, lights put out, and the tram service stopped. The town was in a very short time so darkened that when a Zeppelin passed over it less than an hour afterwards, it dropped no bombs. The sound of the firing upon other towns was plainly audible, and for some time the lights were all kept down. Then shortly before midnight lights were relit. Soon afterwards a Zeppelin returned to the place and threw some 15 bombs on it, none of which, however, did much harm.

In another town the scenes at the Coroner's Court when the inquests were held were affecting in the extreme. There had been two men victims over 50 years of age here, four women, and seven children killed. The Court was filled with relatives, and many of the witnesses were weeping so bitterly that it was scarcely possible for them to give evidence. One man who had lost his wife, a missioner, was unable to control his sobs. Another man had lost his little son, aged six, and his daughter, aged 11. A young widow had lost her daughter. So the tales of grief went on.

Little damage was done in Norfolk and Suffolk. Three persons were killed in Lincolnshire and seven injured. Zeppelins were sighted in several parts of the East Midlands and damage was done to one or two buildings. Many stories were related of amazing escapes, and there were many others of pitifully heavy losses. It made it none the better that most of the victims were people in poor circumstances,

HOW ZEPPELINS WERE GUIDED HOME.

After a Raid: A Lighthouse, in Germany, with keepers signalling to the crew of a passing airship.

labourers and workmen of different types, their wives and children.

The British official reports were very brief. The first intimation was:

"A Zeppelin raid by six or seven airships took place last night over the Eastern, North-Eastern, and Midland Counties.

"A number of bombs were dropped, but up to the present no considerable damage has been reported.

"A further statement will be issued as soon as practicable."

Later on, there was a second bulletin:

"The air raid of last night was attempted on

an extensive scale, but it appears that the raiders were hampered by the thick mist.

"After crossing the coast the Zeppelins steered various courses, and dropped bombs at several towns and in rural districts in

Derbyshire, Lincolnshire, and
Leicestershire, Staffordshire.

"Some damage to property was caused.

"No accurate reports were received until a very late hour.

"The casualties notified up to the time of issuing this statement amount to 54 persons killed and 67 injured."

This was followed by a supplementary message:

"Further reports of last night's raid show that the evening's air attacks covered a larger area than on any previous occasion.

"Bombs were dropped in

Norfolk, Leicestershire,
Suffolk, Staffordshire,
Lincolnshire, Derbyshire,

the number being estimated at 220.

"Except in one part of Staffordshire, the material damage was not considerable, and in no case was any military damage caused.

"No further casualties have been reported, and the figures remain as:

Killed	54
Injured	67"

These losses were subsequently increased to:

"Killed:	Men	33
	Women	20
	Children	6
	Total ...	59
Injured:	Men	51
	Women	48
	Children	2
	Total ...	101
	Grand total	160"

The German official statement showed how the invaders had mistaken their route:

"On the night of January 31 one of our naval airship squadrons dropped large quantities of explosive and incendiary bombs on docks, harbours, and factories in and near Liverpool and Birkenhead; on the ironfoundries and smelting furnaces at Nottingham and Sheffield, and the great industrial works on the Humber, and near Great Yarmouth.

"Everywhere marked effects were observed in the gigantic explosions and serious conflagrations. On the Humber a battery was also silenced.

"Our airships were heavily fired on from all directions, but were not hit and safely returned."

This account was described by the British Press Bureau as "utterly inaccurate," and as "affording further proof that the raiders were quite unable to ascertain their position, or to shape their course with any degree of certainty."

The raid on the Midlands finally demonstrated to the nation as a whole the need of a real and sustained attempt to obtain mastery of the air. Even the most unimaginative recognized that while it was possible for enemy aircraft to come in force and remain for twelve hours at a time over the heart of England, dealing death indiscriminately, we could not regard our position as secure.

CHAPTER CIX.

THE ITALIAN OFFENSIVE IN 1915.

SITUATION AT OUTBREAK OF WAR IN MAY, 1915—THE FOUR ITALIAN ARMIES—EFFECT OF THE POLITICAL DELAYS ON ITALIAN STRATEGY—FIRST ADVANCE ON THE ISONZO—THE TRENTINO AND TIROL—ANALYSIS OF THE OPERATIONS—MISTAKES AND DISAPPOINTMENTS—THE ADVANCE ON THE CARSO—TOLMINO—MONTE NERO—THE ITALIAN GAINS—ACHIEVEMENTS OF THE ALPINI TRENCH WARFARE—THE SUMMER CAMPAIGN—SUCCESSES IN THE TRENTINO—COL DI LANA—THE OCTOBER OFFENSIVE—BOMBARDMENT OF GORIZIA—REVIEW OF THE OPERATIONS IN 1915.

ON May 22, 1915, two days after the historic meeting of the Italian Chamber which conferred extraordinary powers upon the Government, the order for general mobilization was published. In point of fact the army had been practically ready to move for a considerable time, its cadres full and its transport prepared. Italy had announced an armed neutrality to the world, and the Salandra Government had taken care that the announcement should not be a mere piece of bluff. When the final inevitable rupture with Austria-Hungary came, the situation found strong Italian armies massed near the frontier, with everything in readiness for attack at those points where an offensive was practicable.

In Chapter LXXXI. it was explained that "Italy's strategical plan, imposed upon her by geographical conditions, must be to hold on the north and push towards the east." Only the eastern front afforded the opportunity for an offensive on the grand scale, and in order to make such an offensive possible it was necessary to secure the positions on the flank. This meant a limited offensive in the Trentino and Cadore, where it was absolutely essential to rectify the disadvantageous frontier which Italy had been forced to accept in 1866. A new line had to be won before defence was sure.

On May 25 King Victor Emanuel left Rome for General Headquarters, nominating his uncle, Prince Thomas of Savoy, Duke of Genoa, as his "Lieutenant-General" during his absence at the front. The King assumed the supreme command, but the actual control of operations was in the hands of the Chief of the General Staff, General Count Luigi Cadorna. The sub-Chief of the General Staff, General Count Porro, acted as Chief of Staff.

Four "armies" took the field, two on the eastern and two on the northern frontier, while a force independent of any of these, but not given the title of "army," was detailed to operate in the rugged and difficult Carnic Alps. The First and Fourth Armies, on the northern front, were under the command of Generals Brusati and Nava, while the Second and Third Armies, destined for the great offensive towards the east, were commanded by General Frugoni and the Duke of Aosta. The fifth independent command, whose infantry consisted mainly of Alpine troops and Bersaglieri, was entrusted to General Lequio. Of these commanders Generals Frugoni and Lequio had both seen service in Libya. General Frugoni had been second in command to General Caneva in Tripoli, and General Lequio had distinguished himself by his conduct of a short but brilliant mountain campaign in March and April, 1913, when he marched from

WITH THE ITALIAN ARMY
Mitrailleurs posted on a mountain.

Kasr Gharian to the Tunis border and crushed the obstinate resistance of the Berbers under Suleiman El Baruni.

Here it may be well to go back for a moment to the period immediately before war was declared. After the outbreak of war it was very commonly believed, especially in the Army, that the plans of the Government and the General Staff were gravely prejudiced by the political crisis which had shaken Italy during the first half of May. It is not possible to speak with certainty, but an examination of certain important dates certainly lends colour to the belief that the manœuvres of the Giolittian party turned the military situation to the disadvantage of Italy.

The denunciation of the Italian Alliance with Austria was conveyed to the Austrian Government by the Duke Avarna on May 4, and it was evident that from this moment Austria would hasten her preparations against an Italian attack. Up to May 4 it appears that Vienna had declined to believe in the failure of the formal negotiations which had been in progress since March 27. Italian mobilization was not complete on this date, but a very few days more would have furnished a sufficient number of troops for a rapid offensive. Perhaps such an offensive could have been undertaken at once, in consideration of the known fact that Austria, heavily engaged in Galicia, and still watching the Serbian frontier with some apprehension, had left little more than skeleton forces on some parts of the Italian frontier. It is in any case difficult to believe that Italy would have taken such a step as the denunciation of the Austrian alliance unless she had been prepared to follow it immediately by active warlike operations. Parliament had been summoned for May 12, and it is at least reasonable to suppose that the Salandra Government, relying upon the vote of confidence which the Premier had demanded, and received, in March, intended to present the Chamber and the Senate with a *fait accompli*. Even if this were not the intention of the Government, even if the beginning of hostilities were to be deferred until Parliament had been informed of the situation, the Italian offensive would have begun, at latest, on May 15.

What followed the denunciation of the Austrian alliance is well known. The action of the Government was paralyzed by the knowledge that Signor Giolitti and his lieutenants, who controlled the majority of both Houses, had entered into negotiations with Germany and Austria, in defiance of the vote of confidence which had been passed only seven weeks previously. When the situation became clear to those in power, the re-opening of Parliament was put off until May 20, and Signor Salandra handed his resignation to the

King, a resignation which was practically an appeal to the country. The answer of the country was not uncertain, but precious days had been lost. The Italians crossed the frontier at least nine days later than they would have done if there had been no political crisis. Perhaps the real delay extended to a fortnight. In any case, taking even the minimum period, it is easy to estimate what a difference it must have made to the military situation. General Cadorna started his campaign without an advantage which he had hoped to have and upon which he had quite justly calculated—the advantage of surprise. The Austrians were given notice of attack in time to enable the whole position on the frontier to be altered.

The first offensive movements were quickly carried out. On May 24 General Cadorna was able to announce that on that day Italian troops had occupied Caporetto (Karfreit) on the middle Isonzo, various heights between the rivers Judrio and Isonzo, and the towns, or rather villages, of Cormons, Versa, Cervignano, and Terzo. The small bodies of Austrian troops which had been left behind in the Friuli plain to keep in touch with the Italians were retiring upon the Isonzo, destroying bridges and burning villages as they went.

On the same day the troops on the Trentino frontier crossed into Austrian territory at many points and began the "push" which was to carry forward the frontier to a line more easily defended. Monte Pasubio and other important positions near the frontier were seized on May 24. Monte Altissimo, the highest peak of the Monte Baldo mass, was occupied on May 26, and on the following day the little town of Ala fell before the Italian advance. The advance continued, and the height of Coni Zugua, to the north-east of Ala, was rushed successfully. The Austrians had half completed a fort on this ridge, and the works already finished would have been difficult to take. But only a small detachment held the position, and it had perforce to retire before greatly superior numbers. Coni Zugua practically dominates Rovereto, and its occupation, together with that of the Monte Baldo

ON THE ISONZO FRONT.
Austrian troops firing on an Italian outpost.

ITALIAN ARMOURED SOLDIER.
A Captain of the Engineers Corps with breastplate, helmet, shoulder-pieces, and chainwork to protect mouth and ears.

mass, completely changed the situation in the valley of the Adige. The Austrians no longer had an open gate giving upon the plain around Verona. The Italian position on the main road leading into Italy was now V-shaped, the centre held back on the low ground, the wings running diagonally forward to the heights on either side of the valley. Within a few days the position was further strengthened by a considerable advance in the Vallarsa, to the east of Coni Zugua, while an artillery duel, of which the Italians had decidedly the better, was going on between the Italian forts in the Sette Comuni and the Austrian forts on the Lavarone plateau. All along the Trentino frontier similar movements were taking place. Italian forces were concentrated near the Stelvio and Tonale passes, and Alpine troops climbed to the frontier on the great mass of the Adamello group, while a quick move forward was made in the Val Chiese, or Val Giudicaria. Here, in a few days, the position took on an appearance very similar to that in the Adige valley. The troops in the valley advanced successively to Ponte Caffaro, Darzo, and Storo, while the steep and difficult ranges were occupied by strong detachments which pushed forward until the flanks were well in advance of the centre. By this movement the Italians came in touch with the Lardaro group of fortifications, which stood in the way of further progress until guns of heavier calibre should be available, but the main objective was practically assured. Italians and Austrians now met on level terms. An advance for either side was equally difficult, and the position was further consolidated by the occupation of the Val d'Ampola, which climbs the rugged hills to the east of the Val Giudicaria and descends to Bezzecca and the Ledro valley. To the east of the Adige valley a similar situation quickly developed. Italian troops pressed up the Val Sugana until they were within five miles of Borgo. Fiera di Primiero and the greater part of the Cortina d'Ampezzo valley were occupied without opposition, while the wedge of Austrian territory that thrusts down upon the Cordevole valley also fell into the possession of the Italians, the Austrians taking up their positions on the far side of the Livinallongo valley.

In the Trentino and Tirol, a fortnight after the outbreak of war, the Italians were well forward upon Austrian territory. Immense natural difficulties still stood in the way of a successful offensive, but they had pushed so far up the valleys and seized so many dominating positions that an Austrian offensive was now faced with difficulties nearly as great.

ITALIAN ARMOURED SOLDIER.
A Lieutenant in the Engineers Corps.

BERSAGLIERI TROOPS ON THE MARCH.

The ordinary marching rate of the Bersaglieri is four miles an hour, with a pace of thirty-four inches, and they double at a rate which works out at about nine minutes to the mile.

The primary objective of the First and Fourth Armies was already secured.

During these preliminary operations there was not much actual fighting. The Austrians were quite clearly not in a position to contest the first moves of the Italians, and their covering troops fell back at once upon the groups of forts or prepared defensive lines that lay well within their frontiers. There was no severe fighting and losses were slight.

Farther east, where General Lequio's mountain troops had made an immediate push for the main passes on the Carnia frontier, hard fighting was taking place; for the Austrians, too, had dashed for the passes. On this sector also the advantage of terrain lay with the Austrians. Although the Carnia frontier, as far east as Monte Lodin, follows the watershed along the mountains, the conditions on either side of the boundary line are sharply different. On the north the ground rises in a comparatively gradual ascent from the Upper Gailthal; on the Italian side, along a considerable front, the dividing range breaks off in a steep escarpment nearly 3,000 ft. above the approaching valleys.

The main pass is that known as Monte Croce Carnico (or Plöcken). At this gap in the range the conditions were roughly equal as far as the terrain is concerned, and though the Austrians reached the pass first, the Italians were able to hold on to its approaches in spite of repeated attacks, and finally to drive the Austrians back. But the mountain crests on either side of the pass, to east and west, were in possession of the enemy, and until they were cleared the Italian position was precarious. The Alpini fought their way up the precipitous slopes until, a fortnight after the outbreak of war, they had driven the Austrians from the summits of the peaks and ridges to the east of Monte Croce Carnico. A few days later they occupied Zellonkofel, to the west of the pass, and proceeded to consolidate their positions

ITALIAN ALPINE ARTILLERY.

An artillery mule being lowered on to a ledge in the Alps on the Italian frontier.

along the line of dominating points which they had wrested from the enemy. Before the middle of June the line was solidly established. Much remained to be done in the way of assuring adequate communications, for the Alpini and the mountain guns were stationed on cliffs and ridges where no paths led. But here, too, the door was now shut—the back-door that is supposed to have figured in the offensive planned against Italy a few years before the war by General Conrad von Hötzendorf. The Carnia front was blocked, and the valleys that run down from the frontier to the Tagliamento were no longer a danger to the flank of the armies engaged in the main operations on the eastern frontier.

It has already been said that the main operations began well. The progress reported on the evening of the first day of war seemed to show an army well on the move. It was known that the Austrians had prepared positions along the line of the Isonzo, and that the first real clash of arms would come there. But information went to show that even after the period of grace that had been given them the Austrians were scarcely ready, and great hopes were entertained that a quick move might succeed in breaking the lines of defence before they were fully manned. The best opportunity for a quick dash lay along the plain to the west of the Isonzo below Gorizia, and expectation ran high that the attacking forces would succeed at once in obtaining a footing on the Carso, thereby outflanking Gorizia. And once well on the Carso Trieste would not seem far off.

At the best the line of the Isonzo presents great difficulties to an attacking force. For two-thirds of its course from the Plezzo valley to the sea, from Saga to just above Gorizia, the river flows with extreme swiftness, pent in a narrow gorge. And on the farther bank rise ridge upon ridge of hill, line upon line of natural fortress. From Gorizia to the sea the fall is relatively slight, and the river, when it is not in flood, runs down in a broad shallow stream. In the summer it presents the appearance characteristic of many rivers of Northern Italy — a wide expanse of stones with the shrunken waters winding slowly in a narrow channel. On the eastern bank, a few miles south of Gorizia, the ground climbs quickly to the low plateau of the Carso, which dominates the plain to the west, and is in turn dominated by higher ground to the north and east. The Carso plateau from the Gorizia valley to Monfalcone is only about seven miles wide, and it is thrust forward like a bastion into the low ground, forming a blunt salient. The Isonzo flows close beneath it as far as Sagrado, where the plateau bends back to the south-east, while the river continues its south-westerly course for a few miles before turning down to the sea. A canal runs along the line of the Carso from Sagrado to Monfalcone, the water to fill it being diverted from the Isonzo by means of a large dam which is built across the river near Sagrado. It is necessary to have these details in mind in order to understand the difficulties which faced the Italians as they made their advance upon the Austrian lines.

In the summer the Isonzo would present no very great obstacle to an attacking army. In an ordinary year by the end of May the spring floods would be over, and the waters would be fairly low. But in 1915 the winter was long; the snows melted late; and when the Italians reached the line of the river they found it in heavy flood. On the upper and middle reaches, where it was running like a giant mill-race, the greatest difficulties were experienced in effecting a crossing, but here the obstacle was at least narrow, and the engineers were able after several attempts to make a way to the farther bank. But delay meant less on the upper reaches. From Gorizia to the sea it meant almost everything.

The first military delay arose out of the mistake of the general commanding the cavalry, who had been instructed to make with all speed for the bridges, railway and road, that cross the Isonzo at Pieris, to guard them, and push on towards the southern half of the Carso plateau. If possible, he was to obtain a footing on the Carso and hold there at all costs. He received news that the Pieris bridges and their approaches were mined, and while he was debating whether to risk his command on the dangerous ground, the Austrians blew up the bridges. It is generally believed that a quick dash would have caught the Austrians unawares and saved the bridges. In any case, the general was immediately dismissed. He had only hesitated, but war will not tolerate hesitation. In this way the cavalry were deprived of their one chance. From the early days of June they were mainly employed in transport duties, but many officers were drafted into the artillery.

The delay in the main advance may not have been very great, but it happened at a time when every moment mattered, and at a place

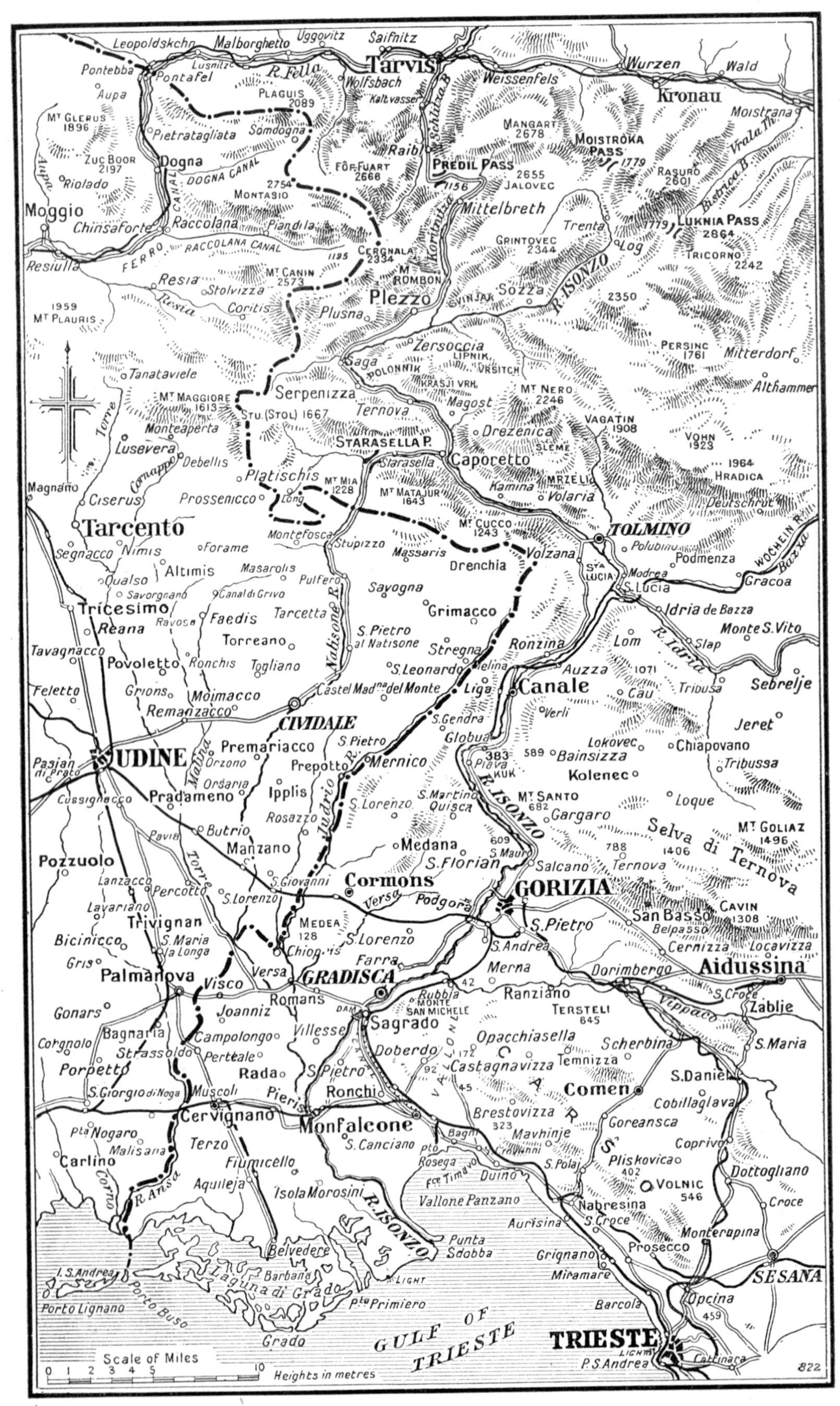

THE OPERATIONS ON THE ISONZO.

that was of particular importance for the advance of the Italian forces. The Pieris bridges cross the Isonzo at the point where the river curves farthest to the west. For this reason the passage of the Isonzo in this region was a much less arduous business than it was farther north. The Carso and the enemy's lines on the rim of the plateau were a good four miles from Pieris, a distance that gives a fair chance to troops crossing the bridges. But with the destruction of the bridges the Italian right wing was held up ; only for a few days, but this was long enough to matter gravely when every moment counted. And this delay, which affected the troops to the north as well, was in addition to the loss of the chance, perhaps only an off-chance, of the cavalry succeeding in their dash for the Carso.

Perhaps the failure of the cavalry to perform the task assigned to it would not have mattered if the Isonzo had not come down in sudden spate. On May 27 the points for crossing the river had been chosen and arrangements were well under way when the shallow stream became a roaring flood. This meant a good deal of delay, and the swollen state of the river made the crossing a difficult matter, but when the crossing had been safely accomplished the troops found a much worse barrier ahead. It has been explained that at Sagrado there was a dam across the Isonzo, built for the purpose of diverting the necessary amount of water into the Sagrado-Monfalcone canal. As soon as the Italians had passed the river at Pieris the Austrians closed the dam, destroyed the mechanism for opening it, and blew out one bank of the canal with dynamite. The flood waters of the Isonzo did the rest. The low-lying country at the foot of the Carso, from Sagrado nearly to Monfalcone, was inundated over a large area, and the advance of the Italians against the southern half of the Carso was effectually blocked. North of Sagrado the country was not flooded, but the wide bed of the Isonzo was brimming with the suddenly swollen waters, and here, it must be remembered, the river practically formed a moat to the fortress of the Carso.

The delay was of the utmost value to the Austrians. Their positions had already been well prepared, and many guns had been on the line of defence for some time, but there was almost certainly still a shortage of men in the trenches at the beginning of the war, and it was reported that the number of medium-calibre guns and machine-guns was greatly increased between the declaration of hostilities and the arrival of the Italians at the foot of the Carso.

Following on the first announcements of the Italian advance into Austrian territory, the official reports were silent for five days regarding the operations in the plain of Eastern Friuli. The bulletin of May 30 ran as follows :

> "Friuli Frontier." The positions on the left bank of the Isonzo, controlling the passage of the river, have for a long time been fortified by the Austrians and provided with medium-calibre guns. The enemy also hold strongly certain points on the right bank, covering the town of Gorizia. In addition, the heavy rains have caused the flow of the rivers to be exceptionally swollen and swift.

Reading this report at the time it was published, it was not possible to realize all that it meant. Yet it seems that these few words in fact admitted the downfall of the hope that the Italian advance might reach the Austrian positions before the very small gap between the sea and the natural ramparts of the Alps was made secure against all but the slow operations of trench warfare. The unworthy manœuvres of the Giolittians, the indecision of a commander, and the sudden hostility of Nature had combined to reduce to very meagre proportions the chance that had promised so fairly.

For six days, from May 28 till June 3, the flood waters of the Isonzo held up the Italian advance against the Carso. On June 4 the river was falling rapidly, and it was possible to throw troops across. At dawn on June 5, covered by a heavy artillery fire, a couple of battalions crossed in boats near Pieris and drove back the Austrian covering troops on the low ground between the river and Monfalcone. Pontoon bridges were quickly put together, and troops were poured across. Monfalcone was occupied two days later.

In the meantime the left wing of the Italian force in the Friuli plain was well forward on the line of the Isonzo, but co-operation with the centre and right was hampered by the inundations already described. Along the foot of the Carso, between Sagrado and Monfalcone, and stretching far into the plain, lay a wide lagoon. The crossing of the Isonzo at Pieris, which should have laid open the way for the main attack on the Carso, only gave access to a narrow strip of dry land between the flooded country and the sea. Another bridgehead had to be won, this time close under the enemy's chief line of defence, before it was possible to attack along the line of the Carso. And the attempt had to be made at an isolated spot, more or less in the air, for the floods prevented support and diversion on the right.

The first attempt to establish the new bridgehead was made on June 9. On that day fighting took place all along the course of the lower and middle Isonzo, to the north of Gorizia, near Plava, where another bridgehead was to be established, against the heights on the right bank of the Isonzo, which cover Gorizia, and on the extreme right of the Italian line, in the neighbourhood of Monfalcone. The point chosen was just above Sagrado. Here the bed of the Isonzo is between 300 and 400 yards in width, but an island of gravel and sand divides the river into two streams, and the fall of the river is less at this point, so that even in time of flood the current was comparatively slow.

It was late on the evening of the 9th that the first troops crossed in boats. Two battalions reached the far side, while the engineers worked at the bridge, or rather the first stage of it, from the right bank to the island. The advance guard occupied the village of Sagrado, which was deserted, and began to explore the slope of the Carso. They were suddenly attacked on the left flank by a force of Austrians from Sdranssina, but this attack was easily repulsed. The Austrians were driven off, and in the darkness they left a number of prisoners in the hands of the Italians. When day broke the bridge was nearly, but not quite, completed, and as soon as it was light enough to see the Austrians opened a heavy artillery fire

AN EARLY MORNING SURVEY.

The King of Italy at the front, watching the shooting by heavy artillery in the rear at the fortress of Malborghetto. The first on the left is General Brusati, A.D.C. to the King; the third from the left (X) is King Victor Emanuel; and the fifth is Colonel Ricci, Commander of the Artillery.

Top picture: The King of Italy watching an artillery duel on the mountain heights.

ITALIAN 13-INCH GUN ON THE TRENTINO FRONT.

Getting ready to fire a shell over the mountain. Bottom picture: Heavy gun aiming upwards towards the summit of a high mountain.

on the working parties and, inflicting a good deal of loss, drove them to cover on the right bank of the river. Repeated attempts were made to go on with the work, but the Austrian shells destroyed the bridge entirely, and the men on the far side of the river were completely cut off. They retired from their positions on the slopes and entrenched themselves near the river, along a line that was practically "dead ground." They had to lie close, for the margin of safety was not great, but the enemy's machine-gun fire for the most part swept harmlessly over their heads and sprayed the river beyond. A more anxious time was in store for two companies which were stranded on the island cut off from either shore. They protected themselves against machine-gun fire by burrowing in the gravel, and their appearance, stretched out on the ground, perhaps induced the Austrian gunners to turn their fire in some other direction. To those waiting on the right bank of the river the prostrate figures looked like corpses. But when night fell, and boats were sent across to bring back the isolated troops on the other side, it was found that the men on the island had lost only

AN ITALIAN MORTAR IN ACTION.

15 killed and about 50 wounded. The two battalions on the far side were also brought back safely, with the prisoners they had taken soon after landing.

It became evident that the successful passage of the river at this single spot, where the enemy were able to concentrate a very heavy fire, was exceedingly difficult to accomplish. Troops could be thrown across by night in small numbers, but the establishment of a secure bridgehead was another matter. Further bridging materials were hurried forward, and in the meantime steps were taken to deal with the floods which were blocking the way to the Carso below Sagrado. On June 11 two medium-calibre guns, which had been brought right up to within a quarter of a mile of Sagrado, broke the dam across the Isonzo in two places, so that a great quantity of water was diverted back to the natural channel, instead of flowing into the broken canal and thence over the country. But inspection showed that the breaches made in the dam were insufficient, and a detachment of engineers volunteered to blow it up. They succeeded in escaping the notice of the enemy's sentinels long enough to place and prepare their mines. The alarm was given a little before they had finished, and the las part of the work was conducted under a storm of fire. But they withdrew safely, and a few moments later the dam blew up.

No fresh inrush now fed the lagoon at the foot of the Carso, and the water slowly began to subside. But the process was very slow, and on the 15th still another attempt was made to cross the river near Sagrado. It failed, and the decision was taken to wait until the attack could be made all along the line of the Carso. It was not until the 18th that a general forward movement could be made. Three weeks had slipped past since the Isonzo came down in flood and blocked the Italian advance just as it was on the move, already later than it should have been.

The water had not altogether drained off when the advance began that was to fill the gap between Sagrado and Monfalcone, and complete the investment of the Carso. The troops toiled through liquid mud or splashed in water that was sometimes up to their knees.

By the 23rd the villages at the foot of the Carso south of Sagrado-Fogliano, Redipuglia, Vermagliano and Selz, were all in the possession of the Italians, and on that night still another attempt was made to cross the Isonzo north of Sagrado. On this occasion boats were used, and only 150 men got across before the Austrians got the range and prevented the operation being continued. The little detachment which had reached the farther side succeeded in making their way past Sagrado to their comrades at Fogliano. On the evening of the 24th the attempt was renewed. The light was dim, but the enemy had the range, and the men in the boats suffered heavily. By ten o'clock half a battalion was on the farther shore. But nearly as many had been killed or wounded. There was a lull in the furious artillery duel that had been going on all the evening. The Italians ceased firing first, and the Austrians seem to have thought that the attempt to cross had been deferred again. But all through the night the Italians were labouring at the construction of a bridge. Once again daybreak found the work incomplete, but boats were used to complete the passage across the river, and another half battalion succeeded in reaching the left bank before the bridge was smashed by direct hits from the Austrian guns. About a thousand men had reached the other side, and these immediately rushed the village of Sagrado, which was occupied by a detachment of Austrians, and entrenched themselves on the outskirts. This time there was to be no turning back. There was support on the right, and the order was given to get men across at all costs. Attention was turned to the bridge opposite the village, which had been half destroyed by the Austrians. It had been avoided before because the Austrians had the exact range; but now the engineers were instructed to brick up the broken ends and provide a crossing for infantry at least. Communication for heavy material had been assured by the advance on the right, and if only a sufficient number of men could be got across at this point, and the slopes beyond the village occupied, the position would be greatly improved. The bridge was swept by rifle and machine-gun fire from the foremost Austrian trenches on the slopes opposite, and enfiladed from the left bank of the river farther up, but field guns were pushed right forward and succeeded in keeping down the enemy's fire sufficiently to allow of the bridge being repaired. An entire regiment (three battalions) reached the farther bank, crossing by small detachments on the light structure that was hastily put in place by the engineers, and by the following morning another regiment had followed. The brigade stormed the lower slopes of the Carso and drove the Austrians from the observation posts which had served to direct the artillery fire upon the bridge. The conformation of the Carso is such that the river where it passes

AN ITALIAN MOUNTAIN CATERPILLAR.
One of the big guns in position on a mountain ridge.

INSIDE AN ITALIAN STRONGHOLD.
Italians firing on enemy's forts.

Sagrado is hidden by a spur from all but a short section of the Austrian lines. These trenches were rushed, and the enemy's artillery had to fire without eyes. A hail of shrapnel and high explosive was directed against the bridge, but the damage done was extraordinarily slight, and before long a pontoon bridge in a still more sheltered position was thrown across the river.

The conformation of the Carso explains the persistence with which the Italians drove at Sagrado instead of attempting a crossing in another place. Sagrado and Fogliano form the extreme point of the blunt salient made by the plateau, and Sagrado in particular is sheltered from the fire of the Austrian main positions. Its occupation, once the river was crossed, gave a secure footing to the attacking forces, from which it was possible to drive a wedge into the Austrian lines. This wedge was quickly made by the occupation of Castello Nuovo, a villa situated at the end of a wood that runs up the slope from Sagrado to the edge of the plateau. It was a hard fight through the wood, which was sown with mines and laced with wire entanglements, but the Italian infantry would not be denied, and the Austrians were driven out and back to their second line of trenches. Castello Nuovo was occupied on June 27, and by that date the Italians had firmly established the bridgehead they required for a general attack upon the ramparts of the Carso plateau.

The story of the crossing at Sagrado has been told in some detail, for this was the centre-point of the preliminary operations against the Carso. But it was only the central episode of a fight that raged for days, or rather weeks, along the line of the lower Isonzo, from above Gorizia down to the sea. And all along the upper valley as well from below Plezzo, battle was closely joined. The position of the Carso has been roughly described, but in order to understand the general situation it is necessary to go into some detail regarding the terrain round Gorizia. Just as the Carso makes a salient angle jutting into the plain of Friuli, so the plain runs a salient into the high ground, a wedge pushed forward just north of the Carso, so that the two salients dovetailed. The wedge of low ground is longe and narrower than the bastion of the Carso and bends slightly upwards to the north, to where the Isonzo issues from its mountain gorge and

AUSTRIAN RIFLE-GRENADE THROWER.

turns south-westwards towards the plain. Just in this bend lies Gorizia, backed by low hills, with higher hills to the north-east and north—Monte San Daniele, Monte San Gabriele, and Monte Santo on the left bank of the Isonzo, and Monte Sabotino on the right bank, and running down from the long ridge of Sabotino a furrowed mass of upland with the hog-back of Podgora thrust forward so as almost to hide the town from the west. Podgora falls steeply on to the Isonzo, and Gorizia lies just on the other side of the river, looking south-westwards to the plain. The open space between Podgora and the Carso is only three miles across, and the Isonzo bars the entrance. Looking from Monte Quarin, a low spur that juts out into the plain near Cormons, or from Monte Medea, an isolated hill farther south, from which Attila is said to have watched the burning of Aquileia, Podgora suggests itself for a moment as the key position. But in country like this there is no real key position. Podgora is swept from Sabotino and the hills on the other side of the river. Sabotino is dominated from Monte Santo and San Gabriele. And other ramparts lie behind. The whole country is a giant ridge and furrow. It is as though a drunken ploughman-god had run amok with his gargantuan plough, remembering dimly, in the back of his bemused mind, that he must drive his furrows north and south.

The Austrians had occupied and fortified with every device known to modern warfare Monte Sabotino (2,000 ft.) and Podgora (800 ft.), and linked them up by lines of trenches running through the broken country that lay between. In this way they could best defend the passage of the river, and in this way they held an admirable bridgehead for a possible offensive, if the course of the war elsewhere had allowed them to bring the necessary forces to the Italian front.

Against these positions at the end of May the Italians drove full tilt. They attacked along the whole of the enemy's defensive line, from Monte Sabotino to the Carso, but the two main efforts were directed against Monte Sabotino and Podgora. The attack was conducted with the utmost vigour, but the defences were too strong for the means of offence which the Italians then had at their disposal. The main obstacles consisted in the lines of wire entanglements, which in places were 50 metres deep. It had been hoped that the soldiers would be able to get through by the aid of wire cutters, but the Austrians had provided against this weapon by using a very strong wire, nearly as thick as a pencil. Frontal attacks on Podgora and Sabotino failed, in spite of the reckless heroism displayed by the soldiers, who renewed the offensive again and again. An attempt to outflank the Podgora position was no more successful, owing o the very strong lines constructed by the Austrians beyond the village of Lucinico, running from the foot of the hill towards the Isonzo and covering the main railway and road bridges opposite Gorizia. The village was stormed after a fierce fight from house to house, but the hedge of entanglements beyond blocked the way. A tremendous effort was made to break through. A field gun was run right forward to within 150 yards of the entanglements, and before both gun and gunners were destroyed by the enemy's fire a lane had been blown through the mass of wire. It was too narrow, and the heavy fire from other guns at longer range had not done sufficient damage to the obstacles to right and left of the gap. The assaulting troops were met by a converging fire that mowed them down. The Italians had to fall back to the village. Less than a mile separated them from the river, and Gorizia lay just beyond, but it was clear that a rush was impossible. On this front as elsewhere throughout the whole theatre of war, siege operations were necessary to success. Careful study and long preparation were the

SECTION OF AN AUSTRIAN MOUNTAIN BATTERY.
Climbing over heavy ground to take up a position in the mountains.

ITALIAN TROOPS DRAGGING A HEAVY GUN TO A NEW POSITION.

first essential. The Italians had to settle down to learn trench warfare.

Meanwhile, farther up the river, ground had been gained. A bridgehead had been won at Plava, by dint of great exertion and at heavy cost. Above Plava the Isonzo makes a curve to the westward, and below the village turns back again to flow south-east to the narrow opening between Monte Sabotino and Monte Santo. It was hoped that from Plava it might be possible to work southward and threaten Monte Santo, the position which was the chief support of the Austrian lines on the right bank of the Isonzo Monte Santo, crowned by a convent and a pilgrim church, the road to which is fringed with many shrines and way-side crucifixes, had become a huge fort, filled with guns of every calibre. It commanded the Gorizia position on the south and the Plava salient on the north ; it backed Sabotino and Podgora, and stood ready to hammer a possible occupation of those heights.

At the back of the village of Plava stands a conical hill, now known as " 383 " (its height in metres above sea-level), connected by a ridge with the mountain mass of Bainsizza. South-east of " 383," on the edge of the Bainsizza group is a peak known as Kuk, one of the innumerable Kuks to be found in mountainous Slav countries. There are at least six Kuks in the region of the middle Isonzo, varying in height from 2,000 to nearly 7,000 feet. The word means simply a " hill " or a " peak." This Kuk, known to the Italians, redundantly, as Monte Kuk, was strongly held by Austrian artillery, placed there in support of the infantry trenches nearer the river.

On June 8 the order was given to cross the river at Plava, and that evening the attacking forces moved silently down the road that leads from San Martino Quisca by the wooded slopes to the river. The pontoon was barely ready when the early dawn came. The alarm came with the light and the bridge was soon destroyed. Next night some 200 men succeeded in crossing the river in a small boat, and a platoon led by a sergeant surprised and captured, without a shot being fired, the Austrian pickets in the village. The following day passed quietly. The Austrians had apparently not discovered the capture of their pickets, and the 200 Italians spent the day in reconnoitring the

ITALIAN MOUNTAIN MACHINE-GUN BATTERY.
Taking up a position on the summit of a mountain pass.

ITALIAN SOLDIERS HAULING A HEAVY ITALIAN MORTAR ABOVE THE MOUNTAIN SLOPES

Getting over difficulties in the high Alps. The road over which the gun travelled was constructed of timbers laid crosswise, after the style of railway sleepers. On these timbers parallel planking was placed to take the mortar wheels.

enemy's positions, which they found to be well prepared. They succeeded in acquiring much useful information without being discovered. On the night of the 10th another attempt was made to construct a bridge, but morning again found the work unfinished, and the Austrian guns destroyed the labours of the night. On the night of the 11th a new method was attempted A raft was constructed and attached by a cable to the shore. The current and a steering oar did the rest, and two battalions reached the far side of the river, crossing fifty at a time. Well served by the information given by the reconnoitring party, the officer commanding decided to attack "383" at once. Dividing his forces, he attacked the hill on the northern and southern slopes, and by midday the Italians had won a way to the summit. They were speedily counter-attacked, but they held on until strong enemy columns advanced from north and south simultaneously, not directly against the hill, but towards the village of Plava, with the object of cutting off the small Italian force. The Italians were compelled to restrict their lines and withdraw to the lower slopes of "383" in order to assure their communications with the river. During the night seven more battalions were rafted across the river, and a fresh attack on the hill was prepared. The same lines of attack were followed, but this time each column consisted of a regiment instead of a battalion. The remaining three battalions held the bridgehead against a flanking movement. Midday saw the advance begin, and immediately a very heavy artillery fire opened from Kuk, which was augmented by medium-calibre guns on Monte Santo, less than five miles away. The Austrian guns were well hidden, and the Italian artillery was unable to keep down their fire, so that the right-hand column in particular suffered very severely, and the advance was slow. The left column, half protected by the hillside from the Austrian gunfire, made better progress and soon came in contact with the trenches defending the summit. They attacked fiercely, again and again, in spite of heavy machine-gun fire, and they were joined after a time by the right-hand column. But the two columns, converging upon the narrow ridge and becoming almost a compact mass, offered a fatally easy mark to the enemy. Men fell fast, and the right-hand column, which had already suffered very heavily, began to give way. The enemy counter-attacked, but were met by a firm front, and the Italians retired slowly down the wooded slopes. They dug themselves in halfway up the hill, and waited for night to fall.

Reinforcements were sent across the river that night, and the following night the engineers succeeded in constructing two bridges. An attack was planned for the 15th, but the plan of advance was altered. While the forces already on the hill were to make a direct attack, a column was to attempt an enveloping movement from the north by way of Globua, a village, or rather group of cottages, on the river bank, about a mile north of Plava. But this column, on reaching Globua, found itself flanked on the north by an unexpected line of trenches. It was evident that in view of this obstacle the enveloping movement could not be carried out to time, and the attack was broken off almost before it had begun. It was renewed the following morning. The flanking column was protected by a battalion which had orders to hold the enemy at Globua at all costs, and divert his attention from the advancing force. The battalion held: it was led out of action in the evening by a young subaltern.

The general attack succeeded, in spite of cement trenches and deep wire entanglements. Here, too, wire-cutters were useless owing to the thickness of the wire, and the first men got through by half crawling, half burrowing beneath the lower wires, while their comrades drew the fire of the machine-guns and died where they stood. When the first men had torn a portion of trench from the hands of the Austrians, others struggled through somehow. By evening the enemy's positions, which were placed below the crest of the hill, were taken. The crest emerges bare and rocky from the woods that climb nearly to the top; the enemy were in force on the far side, and the naked hilltop seemed too good a mark for Kuk and Monte Santo. It was resolved to give the troops a rest and wait till next morning for the final attack. But a group of men belonging to various battalions, who had lost their officers and pushed on by themselves, reached the crest the same night. They returned in the darkness when they found they were unsupported.

Next morning the summit of "383" was occupied. As soon as the Italians of the left-hand column moved to the attack, the Austrians came at them with the bayonet. But as they reached the attacking force they were taken in flank by the troops of the right-hand column,

A POISON CLOUD.
An Italian gas attack against the Austrians on the Isonzo.

which emerged suddenly from the trees and took them by surprise. The Austrians were thrown into complete confusion, and many were killed or captured. The remainder were easily driven back, and Hill "383" remained in the hands of the Italians. Many counter-attacks were made during the months which followed, but the Italians held fast to what they had won. On the other hand, it was long before the zone of occupation on the left bank of the river was widened to any appreciable extent. Successive generals in command at this point displayed an inexplicable lack of activity that resulted in their removal. It was hard upon Italy that the magnificent conduct of her troops during the early days of Plava did not lead to more important results.

At the beginning of the war it was part of the Italian plan of campaign to force a crossing of the Isonzo at Tolmino, and on May 25 Italian forces appeared on the hills opposite the town, above Volzana (Woltschach). They found the Austrians ready, and it was the Austrian artillery that opened the ball the following day. The Italians proceeded to feel for the enemy, and they soon discovered that they were faced by a resistance much more formidable than they had expected.

Tolmino is an important position, for it is here, or rather a little below the town, at Santa Lucia, that the Wochein railway joins the Isonzo valley. This railway deserves a few words. Two branches of recently constructed line run from Villach and Klagenfurt respectively, meet at Rosenbach, and strike south through the Karawanken range to Assling, on the Tarvis-Laibach railway. This part of the line is known as the Karawanken railway, while the continuation from Assling to Santa Lucia is the Wochein railway properly so-called. Of this new system Bædeker writes as follows: "This line, built in 1901–6 in face of great engineering difficulties, provides, in connexion with the Tauern railway, a new and more direct communication between Salzburg and south-east Germany and Trieste. The railway, itself an object of interest with its 47 tunnels and 49 large and 678 small viaducts, traverses a beautiful district, hitherto untouched by any main line of communication." As far as the Tauern and Karawanken railways are concerned, the statement as to the shortening of distance is exact. With regard to the Wochein railway, it can hardly be said to apply. The route from Assling to Trieste via Laibach is about 40 miles longer than the new route viâ the Wochein and the Isonzo valley, but the difficulty and expense of the new route would hardly seem to be compensated for by the difference in length, especially as the country through which it passes is more beautiful than productive—the capital of the Wochein, Wocheiner Feistritz or Bistritza Bohinska, is a village of 700 or 800 inhabitants. The Wocheiner railway is, of course, a strategic line, that would one day have served for the Austrian offensive so frequently talked of in Austrian military circles.

Tolmino is essentially a frontier town. It is really only a village, with less than 1,000 inhabitants, but it is a military depôt of some importance, with barracks, stores and hospital accommodation. And the bridges which cross the Isonzo at or near the town are perhaps unnecessarily large and solid for the modest purposes they would serve in time of peace.

The Isonzo valley widens out considerably just above Tolmino, which is set in a little plain, back from the river. South of the town the river, which flows south-eastwards nearly all the way from Saga, makes a right-angle turn and flows, roughly, south-west until it reaches Plava. In the angle made by this sharp bend rise two hills with a saddle between them ; Santa Maria and Santa Lucia are the names they go by now, from the villages that lie at the foot of each. The ridge of Santa Maria runs east and west, and that of Santa Lucia north and south ; Santa Lucia has two summits placed like the humps on a Bactrian camel. Both hills are thickly wooded, with intervals of grassland, but the summits are bare of trees. Santa Maria and Santa Lucia were the only positions retained by the Austrians on the right bank of the Isonzo, with the exception of Podgora and Sabotino, and, like these two hill fortresses, they held the Italians in check for many months. On the left bank of the Isonzo, isolated in the middle of the little plain of Tolmino, rises a curious cone-shaped hill, wooded to the summit, known as Hill 428. To the north rises Vodil Vrh, over 3,000 feet high, the southern spur of the great ridge that runs by Mrzli Vrh and Sleme (both over 4,000 feet) to Luznitza and Vru (Monte Nero, 7,365 feet) and thence by Vrata, Vršitch, and Lipnik to Javorček and the Plezzo valley, sending out a branch—Krasji Vrh and Polonnik —along the left bank of the Isonzo above Caporetto.

Tolmino blocked the Italian advance from the outset, and it is evident that our allies were

ITALIAN INFANTRY IN ACTION.
Operating with the 81st Regiment.

hardly ready to undertake serious operations there at the beginning of hostilities. They rightly attempted a rush, but when this was checked by the unexpected strength of the Austrians, time was necessary in order to prepare a regular investment. The communications on the Italian side of the frontier were ill-adapted for an attack on Tolmino. There was an excellent road to Caporetto from Cividale, but between the Natisone and the Judrio, among the tangled mass of hills west of Tolmino, there was only one tolerable road, which changed to little better than a track some six miles short of the frontier. It was not until August that the first real assault was made upon the Austrian positions at Tolmino, though there was daily fighting of the kind that this war had made familiar, and the Italians were gradually pushing forward their lines.

Farther up the Isonzo valley operations had been more successful. Caporetto, on the right bank of the Isonzo, was occupied the first day of the war, but across the river rises the wooded height of Volnik, which looks as though it ought to have given trouble. The difficulty was avoided by the dispatch of a flanking column through the hills north of the Caporetto road, which crossed the Isonzo higher up, scaled the Polonnik ridge, and threatened the Austrian flank from Krasji Vrh. Thus threatened, the Austrians fell back upon the Kru, or Monte Nero, chain. The name Monte Nero arose from a confusion between the two Slovene words Kru, which means a rocky peak, and is applied to various points in the Julian Alps, and Cru, which means black. Monte Nero is an unsuitable name, for the great ridge is a light grey limestone, that shows like pearl in the sunlight, but too many memories had grown up round the new name for the old one to come to its own again.

On June 2 General Cadorna was able to announce that Italian forces had gained a firm footing on the highest point of the Monte Nero chain. There had been two days of anxiety owing to the floods which caused so much trouble in the Isonzo valley. The bridge at Caporetto had been destroyed by the Austrians, and the temporary bridges thrown across by the Italians were carried away on May 28, so that the advance troops which had struck up into the mountains were isolated. Two days later communications were re-established, and on June 1 the Italians, who had beaten off a strong counter-attack the day before, were in possession of the highest peak on the ridge, the real Kru. Bersaglieri, Alpini and infantry of the line had shared the preliminary advance, but the last and hardest task naturally fell to the Alpini. The attack on the summit was made from two points, one of which looks inaccessible to any kind of military operation. The south-western approaches to the summit are steep enough, but to the north the ridge runs towards Vrata with its western edge, the side of the attack, an almost sheer wall of rock. There are two great cracks in the rock face, and it was by this climbers' route that a picked company of Alpini ascended to the attack, while a more numerous column pushed up the steep stony slope farther south. The attack took place on a dark and misty night, and it was hoped that the Austrians might be surprised.

The mountaineering party on the left bound their feet with rags so as to lessen the noise of their advance, and when they came to the last precipitous climb they roped themselves in groups. They had nearly reached the crest of the ridge when they were discovered. The Austrians hastened to repel this unlooked-for attack, and while their attention was diverted to the men who were clinging like flies to the rock faces, the main advance came up, and the summit was captured.

By this move the Italians had driven a wedge into the Austrian positions in the mountains, and they gradually extended their occupation. For a fortnight the Austrians made repeated violent attacks, on one occasion bringing up six battalions from Plezzo by the road that runs up between the Polonnik ridge and the northern part of the Monte Nero chain. While an attack was made from the east, this force endeavoured to reach the Italian positions from behind. They were blocked by detachments of Alpini and Bersaglieri, who had occupied Krasji Vrh and the saddle between this ridge and Monte Nero, but it was clear that positions on the main ridge more to the north had to be secured in order to check further attacks from this quarter. The occupation of Monte Nero was a necessary prelude to a movement upon Tolmino from the north, working down by way of Mrzli and Vodil, and in order to ensure this occupation it was essential to dominate Plezzo, which was used by the Austrians as a magazine and base of operations. Two actions were planned for May 14, one against the Vrata ridge running northward from Monte Nero,

TRENCH WORK IN THE MOUNTAINS.

Italian troops making a breastwork of boulders covered with branches, on a hillside.

and one against Kozliak, a spur to the southwest of the position held by the Italians. This spur, which was still partly occupied by the Austrians, though they had lost the lower extremity of it, known as Pleca, borders the wide dreary slope of stony *débris* that stretches across to the tawny ridge of Luznitza. The attack on Vrata was made by two columns of Alpini. One climbed along the rocky ridge from the Monte Nero summit, while another attacked from below. The Alpini were armed with hand grenades, rifles, and bayonets, but their instructions were not to fire until they were right upon the enemy. They wrapped their feet again, and some of them took off their boots to walk more noiselessly, and they reached the trenches on Vrata, after another extraordinary effort, just before dawn. Once more the Austrians were taken by surprise—they probably thought a night attack on those rocky cliffs was impossible, though they had had one warning. A whole battalion was killed or captured, and Vrata was securely occupied. The attack on Kozliak, also conducted by two columns of Alpini, was equally successful. One column attacked from the front, while another came down from Monte Nero, and taking the enemy in the flank sent him in hasty retreat to the eastward.

A few hours after the occupation of Vrata the Austrians attempted to retake the lost position. To the north and north-east they appeared to be in some force, and a persistent fire was kept up on the Italians, who were busily occupied in adapting the Austrian trenches to their own uses. Under cover of this heavy fire a Hungarian Honvéd battalion attempted a turning movement. The way was blocked by a single company of Alpini, who lay hidden among the rocks and waited till the advancing Hungarians were within 300 yards before they fired. The unexpected volley shook the Hungarians badly, and many fell. They realized that retreat was impossible, and came bravely at the Italians. But the way was rough and steep, and the Alpini are good shots. The attack wavered and stopped, and the men fell into confusion. Seizing the moment, the Alpini leapt at them with the bayonet, and in a few minutes the survivors of the battalion had surrendered. On that day the Italians took over 600 prisoners, including 30 officers, and two machine guns.

During the next week the Austrians made several further attacks, and on June 21 Alpini and Kaiserjäger met for the first time. The Kaiserjäger had come from Galicia, from the famous Fourteenth Army Corps, which had suffered very heavily in the fighting in the Carpathians. The reputation of the Kaiserjäger as mountain fighters is justly very high, but they met more than their match in the Alpini. Their attack was repulsed, the Alpini counter-attacked, and the day ended in the Italians gaining a good deal of ground. By the 23rd they were established on the green slopes of Javorček, within touch of Plezzo. The Plezzo valley was now threatened from three sides. The Italian guns could sweep it from Saga. The occupation of the Sella Prevala, at the head of the Val Raccolana in Carnia, two days after the beginning of the war, had given an observation post for heavy artillery, and the rapid progress which was being made with the road to the top of this mountain barrier promised an increase of pressure from this direction. And now an advance threatened from the east. Plezzo was no longer a suitable concentration point for the Austrians.

But the war was settling down. As the Italians advanced they found the Austrian resistance more tenacious. The enemy was undoubtedly resourceful, and learned quickly. In the mountains, to begin with, he had trusted in himself and in the natural advantages of position. Soon he learned to trust to nothing but wire. Wire entanglements sprang up at 6,000, 7,000, 8,000 feet above the sea. They girdled rocky peaks and defaced the eternal snows. In the mountains, wherever they could move, the Alpini held the whip hand, but movement became more difficult.

The Austrians had had ten months of war, and during that time, if they had lost heavily, they had learned much. They had learned that even a modern fort is all but useless against modern heavy guns, and they knew that defence could only be ensured by hidden gun positions, and, if possible, by guns that could be moved without too much difficulty. The Italians knew this, too, theoretically, and they quickly learned what it meant in practice. They battered Fort Hensel to pieces, at Malborghetto. They smashed up Fort Hermann at Predil. They silenced Luserna, Spitz Verle, and Busa Verle, on the Lavarone plateau, and sadly changed the appearance of Pozzi Alti, on the Austrian side of the Tonale Pass. But the Austrians withdrew their guns from the damaged forts, and hid them in cunningly constructed gun pits. They dug and blasted galleries, and laid down rails in them, so that the positions of the guns might be easily altered. They made a fortress out of every position that had to be defended, and yet it was generally hard to tell where their lines lay.

By the end of June it was trench warfare all along the front. In the Trentino and Tyrol, except in certain places, the war had not yet taken on the aspect it had assumed in the rest of Western Europe. Italians and Austrians faced one another at longer range, with a mile or two miles of No-Man's Land between, where patrols went out and skirmished and came back. In the valley of the Adige, for instance, in Val Giudicaria and Val Cismon, these were the conditions as late as September. There were outpost trenches and isolated redoubts in close touch with the enemy, but the main lines lay

ALPINI FIGHTING AMID ETERNAL SNOWS.

In action above the snow-line on Monte Nero: an Italian machine-gun section attacking an Austrian position.

well apart. But on the north-eastern and eastern fronts, from Monte Piana, south of Schluderbach, right down to the sea, the opposing forces, wherever the terrain allowed it, had come to close grips by the end of June. Monte Piana was occupied partly by Italians and partly by Austrians. The Italians were preparing for a push at the head of the Sexton valley. They held the frontier summits and passes in the Carnic Alps, but the Austrians clung to the farther slopes and came to the attack repeatedly. On Freikofel, Pal Piccolo and Pal Grande, east of the Plöcken Pass (Monte Croce Carnico), the trenches were separated by a distance of from 80 to 200 yards.

On the Isonzo it was the same. The first rush of the Italians had carried them right up to the main Austrian positions, and when it was found impossible to break through they dug themselves in and prepared for the offensive that the conditions demanded. This came in the early days of July. The Italians were under Sabotino and Podgora. At the Gorizia gap they were a bare mile from the bridges over the

ITALY'S ALPINE TROOPS FIGHTING IN THE CARNIC ALPS.

Isonzo. On the glacis of the Carso they were firmly established at Castello Nuovo, they were entrenched on the lower slopes of Monte San Michele and Monte Sei Busi, but Monte Kosich and the heavy guns at Duino had prevented them from making much headway against the southern rampart of the plateau. At the beginning of July pressure began all along the line of the lower Isonzo. Sabotino and Podgora were fiercely attacked, and while little impression was made upon the first, the Austrians were finally driven off the top of Podgora by the infantry rushes which followed a tremendous artillery fire. The wooded summit of the hill was swept and devastated. Breaches were made in the wire entanglements by means of tubes of gelatine carried forward by devoted parties of volunteers who practically vowed themselves to destruction. The top of Podgora was gained, but a terrible converging fire rained upon the exposed ridge from Monte Santo, San Gabriele, San Daniele, and all the Austrian artillery positions at the back of Gorizia. The Italians hung on for some time, but were finally forced to retire to the comparative shelter of the western slope of the hill, about a hundred yards below the summit. Meanwhile good progress was being made on the Carso, as progress goes in trench warfare. Bit by bit, almost yard by yard, the Italians fought their way up the steep slope and on to the edge of the plateau, wresting a trench here and a trench there from the stubborn enemy. The centre held firm at Castello Nuovo, while the wings climbed slowly, very slowly, at Monte San Michele and Monte Sei Busi. The Austrian positions on Monte San Michele supplied excellent observation posts for the artillery of all calibres that was disposed along the line of the " Vallone," the big depression in the Carso that runs from the Gorizia levels down past Doberdo to the east of Monfalcone. The Italians, on the other hand, were still fighting blindfold, struggling uphill to win positions from which they could see. Aeroplanes did good service, but a satisfactory observation post is worth many aeroplanes as far as controlling fire goes. Still they gained ground, slowly, but some of the ground they won they could not hold. They had taken and lost Monte Sei Busi more than once. It was important to hold this insignificant rise, for it gave an eye upon Doberdo, but it was terribly beaten by enemy artillery fire, and the Austrians always counter-attacked very strongly at this point, realizing its importance. Gradually, the Six Holes that gave the hill its name were multiplied manyfold by the shattering impact of large-calibre shells.

Still, on balance, the Italian line of trenches was always pushing a little farther forward. The Austrians felt the danger, and before the middle of July reinforcements had begun to concentrate. These reinforcements were very necessary, for on July 18 the steady pressure of the Italians suddenly developed into a determined attack upon the Carso. Furious fighting went on for three days. The Italians gained trench after trench and captured 3,478 prisoners. On the fourth day, July 21, the Austrians attempted a flank attack upon the Sagrado bridgehead, but they were easily driven off, and left 500 prisoners in the hands of the Italians. On the morning of July 22 came the great Austrian counter-attack. It was directed mainly against the left wing and centre of the Italian forces on the Carso, for here the rise was steepest and the river nearest. It was doubtless hoped that an attack pressed home would drive the Italians into the river, capture the bridgehead, and leave the besiegers of the Carso with all their work to do again. The attack was conducted with the greatest vigour. Long lines of Austrians poured over the edge of the plateau—from Monte San Michele, from San Michele del Carso, from Marcottini. But as they came over the skyline and down the slope, their masses stood out a clear mark for the Italian artillery, and they lost very heavily before they reached the Italian lines. The Italian first line held against the onslaught, and when the reserves came up they turned defence into attack. The Austrians were driven up the hill, leaving 1,500 prisoners, and the Italians gained a footing higher up the slopes. Hard fighting continued. On the 25th the Austrians attacked again, this time on the Italian right at Monte Sei Busi. The hill was won and lost several times, and at the end of the day the greater part of it was in Italian hands. Meanwhile there had been an advance on the left. The wood known as Bosco del Cappuccio, on the southern declivity of Monte San Michele, was stormed and held, and a further advance was made, but could not be maintained. A regiment of Bersaglieri reached the summit of San Michele, and hung on for seventeen hours, till they were ordered to retire. On the bare stony crest of the hill, where it was hard to find shelter, for the rock is only a few inches below the surface of the ground, the guns of Gorizia and the Vallone plastered their shells.

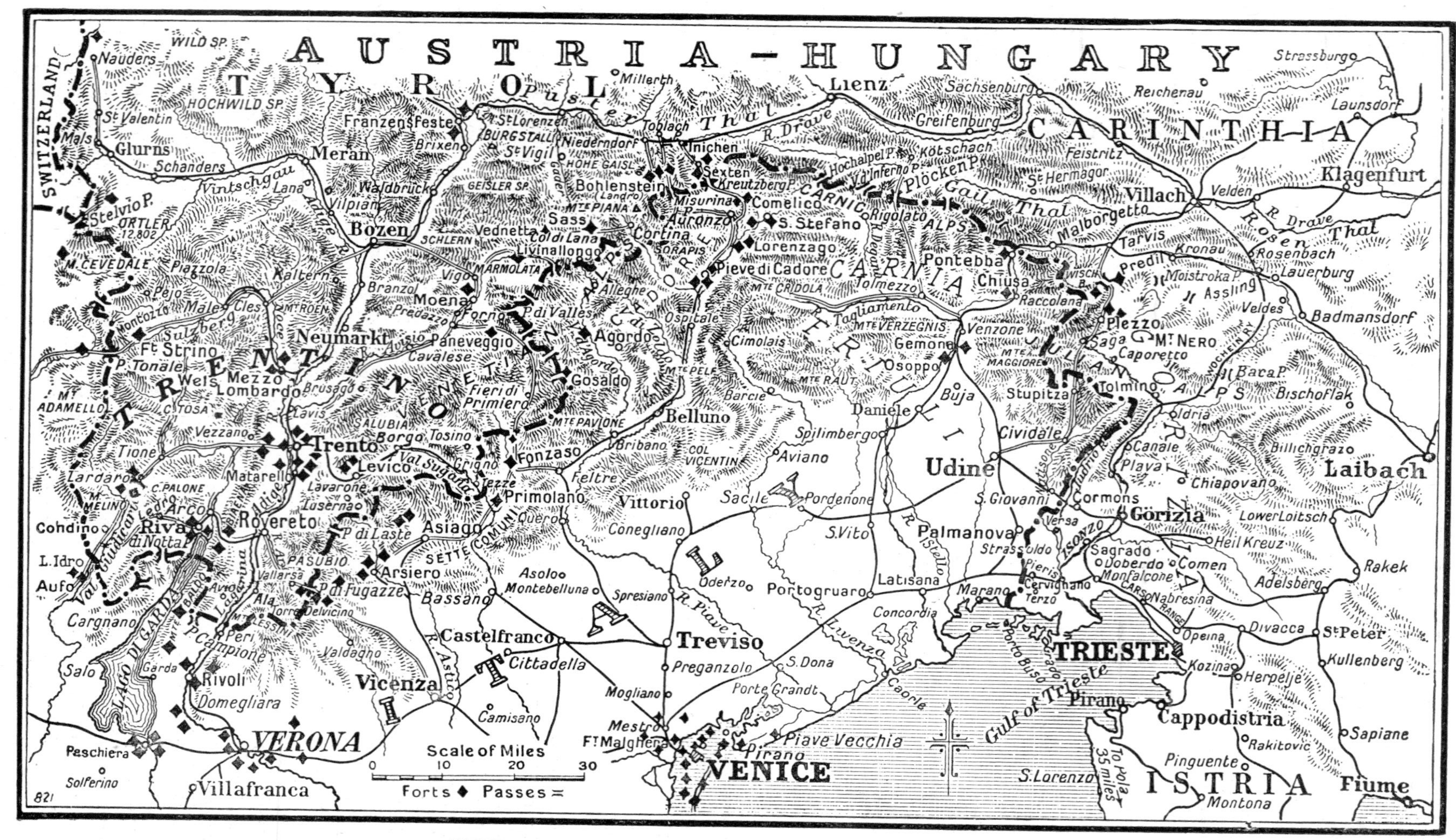

THE TRENTINO AND CADORE FRONTS.

The colonel commanding the regiment maintained that he could have stuck to the ground he had won; but he was one of very few officers left out of sixty.

The battle of the Carso raged all through the last days of July and the first week of August. It ended by the Italians being firmly established on the edge of the plateau. They were nearly at the top of Monte San Michele, they were on the saddle of San Michele del Carso, and they had at last wrested Monte Sei Busi from the enemy. They had taken nearly 20,000 prisoners, and they could see the Vallone before them. They were to settle down to two months' comparative peace, the peace that is obtainable under desultory artillery fire and continual bomb-throwing, while a new offensive was prepared.

All through the summer, including the weeks when the fighting on the lower Isonzo almost exactly resembled the periods of "quiet" on the western front, the operations in the high mountains continued without ceasing. It is impossible to go into detail regarding the work done. Space would not admit of more than a catalogue of names and dates, and even to those who spent several weeks on the mountain front and studied the operations closely, there comes a sense of bewilderment in trying to sort out the impressions and give the right proportion to the ceaseless encounters that took place on plateaus and ridges and peaks that it is difficult to associate with any kind of military operations. Perhaps, in a way, the sense of bewilderment is actually increased by a knowledge of the country where this war is being waged, and an experience of the methods which had to be adopted. For all the while, as one composes a bare narrative of the events, the little gains and the isolated combats, there comes the oppressive memory of narrow gorges, huge bare ridges and rock precipices, of mountains that were trackless and desolate but suddenly became alive with men and guns. Guns everywhere; enormous 12-inch howitzers where no road was until the engineers had dug and blasted and driven their way along the route of an old mule track that led up to some desolate pass; field-batteries and even six-inch guns dragged up incredible steeps; mountain batteries crowning Dolomite cliffs that used to be held a task for the holiday climber—the dominant feeling is wonder that war can be waged here, and progress made by any human effort. The "why" of a movement is clear enough to anyone with a map. To one who has seen the difficulties the question "how" must always be uppermost.

History tells us how the great armies of other days marched through the passes that cut the barrier of the Alps, and how the mountain valleys saw great battles. But modern war has left the valleys. There is no room there. It has spread up and over the mountains themselves—7,000, 8,000, 10,000 feet above the sea. You enter the Cortina or Misurina valleys, the Val Cordevole or the Val d'Andraz. The war is not here, though you may be 5,000 feet above the sea. It is always "up there," on the mountains to right and left, that the real work is going on. The valleys only touch the real edge of war when the Austrian gunners, in a fit of temper, bombard the villages that have been wrenched from their hands. They plaster Misurina with high-explosive and destroy a hotel belonging to a German; they lob 12-inch shells over Monte Cristallo to disturb the desolate peace of Cortina d'Ampezzo; they bombard the hospital of a village they have been forced to abandon (but which was not occupied by their adversaries), a hospital full of sick and women and children, and follow the wretched fugitives with shrapnel till they are out of range. That is the war that the high valleys know.

The Austrians had this excuse for their bombardment of villages, though not for their behaviour in the case of the hospital mentioned above—the hospital outside Pieve di Livinallongo—that they could not see exactly where they were firing. They were no doubt searching for Italian guns when they rained shells at random into a valley, for the guns that harassed them continually from unknown positions. One by one, throughout the long weeks of fighting in the mountains, the Austrians lost the observation posts they held early in the war. Even after the first line of their mountain fortifications had fallen, and the Italians had established something like an equality of conditions in regard to terrain, the Austrians still, for the most part, were able to look down upon the invaders of their fastnesses. They still held the higher peaks fronting the new Italian line, and the occupation of these was necessary to the consolidation of the positions won by the attacking forces, and to the next step in an advance. The Alpini units which naturally formed the first line in all the most arduous districts were not to be denied, and point after point was torn from the Austrians. In this way, in many places, they

AN ITALIAN SENTINEL.
Wearing the warm, white outfit, the colour of which makes him almost invisible in the snow.

were not only driven back upon their second-line positions, but the defence of these became more difficult on account of their complete inability to detect the placing of the Italian guns. Yet even with this handicap upon the defence an offensive in the mountains seemed impossible of success to anyone who looked at the great ramparts that faced the Italians. Only the knowledge that some of these barriers had already fallen compelled the belief that others too might fall.

Naturally, the pressure in the mountains, if more continuous, was not so strenuous as in the plains. The objective was different, for Austria could scarcely receive a vital wound in Tyrol, and many parts of the defensive line must be considered practically impregnable against any forces which the Italians could spare from the main operations. Yet very useful progress was made all along the mountains from west to east. A brief summary of the operations will show what was done, and how it was never possible for the defenders to feel reasonably safe, or to detach sorely-needed troops from the Trentino and Tyrol.

Looking at a map of the Trentino, the great wedge of Austrian territory thrust down upon the plains of Northern Italy, it will be seen that, in addition to the main central route by the Adige valley, there are six subsidiary highways that lead in or out of the district—three to the west of the Val d'Adige, and three to the east. This assumes the Trentino to be bounded on the north by a straight line running east and west from Monte Cevedale to the Marmolata, crossing the Adige valley south of Bozen. On the west there are the Stelvio, Tonale and Val Giudicaria routes ; on the east the Vall'Arsa, the Val Sugana, and the great road that runs by Cavalese and the Val Cismon past Fiera di Primiero to Feltre. These routes are themselves linked up and fed, in most cases, by other important highways. The road to the Tonale pass, for instance, is fed by two converging routes, from Bozen via Kaltern and the Mendel pass, and by way of Mezzo Lombardo and Cles ; and it sends a link southward to join the Trento-Val Giudicaria road at Tione. This road again is joined near the frontier by the road that runs from Riva on the Lake of Garda, by Ponale Bezzecca and the Val d'Ampola to Storo, while Riva is approached by road from Trento and by train and road from Mori. Similarly, on the eastern side of the wedge, a new military road, barely completed at the beginning of the war, runs from Fiera di Primiero to Strigno, near Borgo, in the Val Sugana, while the Lavarone plateau, south of Levico, is laced with military roads.

The Stelvio and Tonale routes do not call for much notice. Neither of these mountain routes really lend themselves to military operations on more than a very limited scale. Both are sufficiently fortified, and there was little in the way of fighting in either district, except for artillery duels, during the first seven months of the war. On the Tonale the Italian big guns smashed up Forts Pozzi Alti and Saccarana, and considerable damage was caused to the Strino fortifications, farther east. But on the whole there is little of interest to record at those two gaps in the great Alpine wall, though there were some extraordinary isolated encounters on the mountains themselves. In the Val Giudicaria, on the other hand, useful progress was made by the first push forward and the general position was consistently improved, though it was only late in the autumn that any

AT A HEIGHT OF NEARLY TEN-THOUSAND FEET.
Italian trenches in the snow of the Tonale Zone, in the western Trentino.

ITALY'S SOLDIER-MOUNTAINEERS.
On the march through a mountain pass on the Austro-Italian frontier.

important advance was made. The first move forward occupied the little wedge jutting into Italian territory. It is interesting to follow the line of the great Trentino wedge, and note how all along the frontier there are little wedges thrust forward to dominate the routes of approach—to block an Italian advance or cover an Austrian invasion. The hills between the Lago di Garda and the Lago d'Idro show one such wedge; Monte Baldo and the mountains east of Ala fill another; Monte Pasubio is another, the bastion that dominates the frontier at the Vall'Arsa; the Lavarone plateau with its forts is still another, while a fifth strengthened the Austrian frontier in the Val Sugana, and a sixth, the Colli di Santa Lucia, dominated the Cordevole valley. The frontier of 1866 is a monument to the foresight of the Austrians who succeeded in imposing it upon men to whom its details were unknown.

By the middle of June all these wedges had been occupied by the Italians, with the exception of the Lavarone plateau, whose numerous works opposed too formidable an obstacle to the forces available for what was, after all, a minor operation. A considerable time was then spent in fortifying the new line gained, bringing up big guns to dominating positions and generally securing the weak flank. It is a point that is a good deal discussed whether, in fact, a greater initiative on the part of army and corps commanders at this period would not have gained a great deal more ground. There was a strong feeling in the army that a quick offensive in the Trentino and Cadore would have carried many positions that still barred the way months afterwards. According to information that seems worthy of acceptance, the Austrians were not adequately prepared, at the beginning of the war, to defend the country south of Trento. A rapid converging attack up the Val d'Adige and the Val Sugana, might possibly have carried the Italians to the gates of Trento, isolating and putting out of action the immensely powerful defensive lines on the Lavarone and Folgaria plateaus. This criticism must be taken with all reserve. It seems well founded, but the materials are not yet fully available for forming a judgment, and it must always be remembered that the main stake was being played for farther eastward, and that the first duty of the Trentino and Cadore armies was to hold.

To the west of the Lake of Garda the advance did not progress quickly after the early days of the war, and for months practically no news came from this quarter of the front, except the reports of skirmishes on the mountain slopes or an episode in the continuous bombardments between the forts in the Tonale pass. But in the middle of October, when people were beginning to talk of winter quarters, as far at least as mountain warfare went, a sudden move came among the hills west of Garda, and this was the beginning of considerable activity along the front between the Alps and the lake.

The first step was the occupation of Pregasina,

a village perched on the cliffs overhanging Lake Garda, only about three miles below Riva. Farther west a strong attack carried the two mountains—Monte Melino and Cima Palone—which face one another across the Val Giudicaria about three miles north of Condino. Monte Melino dominates the entrance of the Val Daone into the Val Giudicaria, and Cima Palone, besides acting as a second sentinel over this point, dominates the head of the Ledro Valley. It was strongly fortified by trenches cut in the rock, and a number of prisoners were taken in the assault. This point once secured, the whole Italian line between Garda and the Val Giudicaria moved forward to occupy the Ledro Valley. Fighting went on continuously for many weeks, the Austrians contesting the ground with great bravery and counter-attacking many times. But the end of the year saw the Italians firmly established on the northern side of the Ledro valley and close up to the Lardaro group of forts. Their line ran from the Mascio ridge, north of Cima Palone, to the summit of Monte Vies, and from thence under Monte Pari to the lower slopes of the Sperone (" the spur "). They were on the Ponale road within two miles of Riva, but the road that runs under the Rocchetta, cut in the cliffs above the lake, with several tunnels through the rock, is useless for an advance. The way of approach to Riva must be found elsewhere.

On the other side of the lake, between Torbole and the Adige valley, a similar advance took place, upon the little valley that crosses from Mori to Nago, joining the Adige and Sarca valleys. The railway from Mori to Riva runs through this glen, up the Sarca valley and down to Arco. The Italians were now on the lower slopes of Biaena, the mountain that forms the main guard of Rovereto on the west. Big guns from Biaena had held back the Italians in the Adige valley for many weeks. For a considerable time Biaena dominated the valley, for the Italians were short of heavy artillery at the outset of the war. There were guns to check an Austrian offensive; there were not guns to cover an attack. But by the autumn guns were available, and the Italian grip on Rovereto gradually closed. Biaena was kept busy from the south, while attacking forces pushed slowly forwards on the east side of the Adige valley, down the slopes from Zugni Torta and down the Vall'Arsa. By the end of the year the Italians were on

ITALIAN MOTOR TRANSPORT.
Resting after a descent from a mountain height.

ITALIANS IN ACTION AGAINST THE AUSTRIANS ON THE ROAD TO PONTEBBA.

Austrian artillery firing from the sides of the mountains. In the foreground are the Italians, behind breastworks of stones, covered with leaves; to the left is a barricade of tree-trunks across the road.

the outskirts of Rovereto. They held Dante's Castle on the hillside to the south. They were pressing in from the Vall'Arsa, and up the Adige to where it is joined by the Leno. But the Austrian guns on Monte Ghello still had a say in the matter, and eastward rises Finonchio with its fortifications. Eastward again are the Folgaria forts, and beyond them, on the far side of the Val d'Astico, the great group of works on the Lavarone plateau. It is not easy for an enemy to approach Rovereto from the east. Yet Finonchio at least must fall before Rovereto could be occupied without ensuring its immediate destruction by Austrian shell fire. And there were guns on Stivo to the west.

There was no attempt at a general attack upon either of the grouped fortifications mentioned above. Long slow artillery duels went on for many weeks, but there was comparatively little infantry movement. At the end of August, however, the Italians advanced from Monte Maggio, on the frontier and took, successively, Monte Maronia and Doss del Sommo, two important points on the south-western rim of the Folgaria plateau. This move enabled Italian heavy guns to be brought within more effective range of the Folgaria forts, but no further advance was then made. The same may be said of the Lavarone-Luserna plateau. In the early days of the war the Italians silenced two of the Austrian forts, Spitz Verle and Busa Verle, and established themselves on the north-east of the plateau, near the village of Vezzena. Here for many months the positions remained practically unchanged, but halfway through December the Italians advanced from the Val Torra and secured a footing on the south-east corner of the plateau by occupying Cima Norre.

In the Val Sugana a quick move brought the Italians within touch of Borgo, but the period of consolidation which followed gave the Austrians time to throw forward a new line to protect Trento. When the offensive was resumed in August, the Italians found Panarotta, the mountain that rises north of Levico, turned into a giant fortress. Subsequent operations seemed to be directed towards turning the Panarotta position. Towards the end of August they occupied Monte Salubio, north of Borgo and from there they worked up farther, and held the slopes of Setole at the junction of the Calamento and Campelle valleys.

Farther east, where the mountains rise still higher and steeper, there was more fighting, and, where progress was aimed at, more progress. Omitting the Fiera di Primiero zone and the Val Cismon, where the first step placed the Italians in possession of the line they required, the operations in the Dolomite country were practically continuous. The occupation of Cortina d'Ampezzo furnished a base for a double advance, westward by the Falzarego Pass and northward to where the road bends towards Schluderbach. The whole Cortina valley and its mountains were quickly occupied, thanks to the amazing feats of the Alpini who established themselves upon Monte Cristallo and the three Tofana peaks, besides seizing Col Rosa and Fiammes. And where the men had climbed, mountain guns followed, even to the peaks, while field guns were placed in almost incredible positions. The advance to the north was linked up with a similar advance from Misurina, and a great deal of hard fighting took place near Schluderbach, where attack was met by counter-attack, and the formidable Landro fortifications blocked the way.

The advance by way of the Falzarego Pass combined with the forward movement in the Cordevole valley to bring about some of the hardest and most extraordinary fighting of the war. For these two lines converge upon Col di Lana, the mountain that figured so prominently in the official dispatches. Col di Lana stands out curiously among its surroundings, for it is a more or less ordinary mountain peak. With Monte Pore, which it faces across the Val d'Audraz, it forms as it were an oasis of Alp among the fantastic Dolomite crags all around.

While the Italian guns from the south and east covered the advance, a force of Alpini which had previously occupied the Cima di Falzarego and a part of the Sasso di Stria came down and established a footing on the eastern slopes of Col di Lana. This was in the middle of July, and by the end of the month an infantry force had crossed the Livinallongo valley, and seized the ridge that leads from Pieva (Buchenstein) to the Col di Lana. By the middle of August the Italian trenches had crept up close under the Austrian positions, which by this time were immensely strong. The Austrians had no guns on Col di Lana itself, but they raked the mountain side from their positions at Corte and Cherz, down the Livinallongo valley to the west, and in the trenches there was an ample supply of machine guns and bombs.

Repeated attempts were made to storm the Austrian lines. Col di Lana became invested from three sides, for the Alpini worked round by the Little Lagazuoi and partly held the cliffs of the Settsass. But the Austrians held on grimly, hurling the Italian attack down the steep sides of the mountain many times. The Italians gradually got into position for the final onslaught, and towards the end of October the Austrian resistance began to be broken down. Trench after trench was taken, till at length, on November 7, the summit of Col di Lana was occupied by the Italians. The attack was led by Colonel "Peppino" Garibaldi, grandson of the Liberator, and it was only successful after a singularly bloody encounter. On the following day the Austrians made a desperate effort to recapture the summit. Their attack was repulsed, and the Italians extended their occupation to Monte Sief, to the north-west of Col di Lana. Hard fighting followed on the ridges between Col di Lana and the Settsass, where the Austrians still had a foothold, and on November 18, and again on the 23rd, the Austrians came again to the attack. They were thrown back with heavy loss, but their artillery fire worked havoc among the Italians. The bare summit of the mountain was too exposed, and it was reluctantly abandoned for more sheltered positions a little way down. The actual summit remained unoccupied by either Italians or Austrians, but the Italians now dominated the situation.

The importance of Col di Lana lay first in the fact that it looked right down the Cordevole valley into Italy, as far as the Lago d'Alleghe, and furnished an admirable observation post for the enemy. The Italians had already shut the doors of their house, but until Col di Lana was taken there was a window still open for a prying eye. Moreover Col di Lana was the first key to the Livinallongo valley and the approaches to the Pordoi Pass and the Abtei Thal or Val Badia. The Abtei Thal seemed an unlikely route, for it was too much isolated from any other Italian line of advance. If, on the other hand, an advance should come by way of the Pordoi, the Italians were ready to support it by harassing the enemy's defence from the Fedaja and San Pellegrino passes. But this was a move that promised better on a map than from a knowledge of the country.

Going eastward along the mountain frontier from the Val Popena and Monte Piana, past the Tre Cime di Lavaredo (the Drei Zinnen), now firmly held by the Italians, the next point of interest is the pass of Monte Croce Comelico, where the Italians pushed across the frontier and occupied Burgstall and Seikofl, on either side of the valley.

Eastward again, among the wild mountains of Carnia, there is a point that deserves special attention, for it was the only point where the Austrians had gained any footing in Italian territory. Between the Val di Sesis, that runs down to the Piave valley, and the Rio di Fleons, that joins the Degano valley, two rugged masses of mountain push down into Italian soil from the main frontier chain—Monte Chiadenis and Monte Avanza. The Austrians established themselves upon these ridges in the early days of the war, and it was not until the end of August that two columns of Italian troops, attacking from the valleys east and west, drove the Austrians back on to Austrian soil. A fierce counter-attack followed, but the Italians held. The Austrians appear to have attached particular importance to the passes that lead into Italy from the Gailthal. They dashed for the passes at the beginning of the war and, when they were driven off the summits by the combined skill of the Alpini and the Italian guns, they attacked persistently. The line Pal Piccolo, Freikofel, Pal Grande, which fell into Italian hands on June 9, was the object of almost continuous attack, and the Austrians never seemed to give up hope of retaking the three peaks that figured so often in General Cadorna's reports. They attacked farther east as well, and early in October a very determined effort was made, along a fifteen-mile front, from the Plöcken eastward, to drive the Italians from their lines. The attempt failed completely, in spite of a long artillery preparation; the Austrians had particularly favourable gun positions facing the frontier line, and they expended a great deal of ammunition. After October there was relative quiet, though the Austrians always kept testing their opponents in the hope of finding a weak spot. But the Alpini were at home on these mountain-ledges. They could hold there for ever.

At the Pontebba-Pontafel gap in the main chain of the Carnic Alps the war had taken the form of a long artillery duel. The Malborghetto fortifications, and particularly Fort Hensel, were reduced to ruins by the Italian guns, but the Austrians still held their own. Farther east the Italians crossed the frontier at various points, and threatened the railway

ITALIAN CAVALRY ENTERING AN AUSTRIAN VILLAGE.

from the south, but at this point the movements of the attacking forces necessarily depended upon the results of the fighting on the main front. A successful assault on the Isonzo might mean an advance upon Tarvis, but until the main line could be broken farther south operations on a large scale were hardly to be expected in this zone. War had changed greatly since Masséna defeated the Archduke Charles at Tarvis, in 1797, and by this single battle opened the road to Vienna.

All through the summer a steady pressure was directed against the Austrian front in this sector, from the Fella Valley down by the Predil Pass to Plezzo. The Austrian fortifications at Raibl and above Plezzo were hammered to pieces, and the Austrian infantry were gradually pushed back and down, till the Italians dominated the Austrian valleys. Austrian reinforcements coming down from the Predil to Plezzo were harassed by the Italian guns, and this fact, together with the Italian occupation of Monte Rombon at the beginning of September, caused the abandonment of the Plezzo valley by the Austrians. They still held the slopes of Svinjak, the mountain that fills the angle where the Koritnica and the Isonzo join their waters, and they still occupied the approaches to the Predil and the valley of the Upper Isonzo, though the Italian forces which had come down from Monte Nero and gained a footing on Javorček were threatening

WATCHING THE ENEMY.
An instrument used by the Italians for watching the operations of the Austrians.

the latter position. There was a good deal of fighting in this district in September, the Austrians trying to recover their lost ground, without any success.

On the Monte Nero chain, operations may be said to have come to a close towards the end of July, when a detachment of Alpini, advancing along the top of the Luznitza ridge, found itself confronted by an immense belt of wire entanglement, with an Austrian trench on the far side. An advance was impossible, and Austrians and Italians now faced one another across the wire hedge, with the dreary stone slopes falling steeply away on either side.

Meanwhile, as summer came on, Tolmino was closely invested. The Italians worked down from the north and gained a footing on the upper slopes of Mrzli Vrh, though the Austrians still held the summit. Repeated attacks failed to dislodge the Italians, and they continued their progress along the slopes of Vodil. These troops linked up with others from the right bank of the river, and the town was invested from the north-west and west, the Italians holding the bridge of San Daniele. In August a strong attack was made upon the two wooded hills of Santa Maria and Santa Lucia, on the right bank of the river below the town, and the Italians won their way to the saddle of Santa Lucia between the two camel humps. But here, as so often, they were swept off the bare hill by concentrated artillery fire. They withdrew below the crest and dug themselves in. The usual routine of trench warfare followed on both hills, and here the Austrians added liquid fire to their other means of defence. The offensive was resumed in October, and the greater part of both hills was occupied. But the Austrians held desperately, and no further progress was made.

On October 18 a general bombardment began along the whole of the lower Isonzo line from Plava to the sea, and on the morning of the 21st the great offensive that had been in preparation for many weeks was begun. Prolonged fighting followed of the fiercest description. The main objectives were:

1. An enlargement of the Plava bridgehead, with the object of enabling Monte Santo to be attacked from the north.
2. The occupation of the Austrian lines on the right bank of the river, from Monte Sabotino to below Podgora.
3. The Carso Plateau.

Comparatively little progress was made in the Plava zone. The operations here had been unfortunate almost from the first. After the occupation of Hill 383 an unaccountable inaction had followed upon the heroic struggle which had resulted in the taking of the hill. Successive generals in command at this point showed a disinclination to make sufficient use of the troops at their disposal, and an extension of the bridgehead which might have been effected by energetic action in June or even July was delayed while the Austrians were given time to strengthen their lines to the north and south. Various changes were made among the junior generals, and finally, towards the end of September, the general in charge of the whole sector was relieved of his command. More energetic action followed, but by this time the task had become infinitely more difficult, and though the Italians succeeded in extending their lines for some distance both to north and south, it was found impossible to capture the dominating position of Kuk, the occupation of which was the first step towards a movement against Monte Santo. In this way the attack upon the Gorizia line had to be made without the hoped-for support from the north.

The offensive against Monte Sabotino and Podgora was conducted with the utmost determination, and between attack and counter-attack the fight went on almost unbrokenly for six weeks. After many days' hard fighting the Italians succeeded in gaining ground between the two hills and working round towards the back of Podgora. They established themselves among the broken hills round Oslavia and pressed down upon the little village that lies underneath Podgora, opposite Grafenberg, the industrial quarter of Gorizia. Farther north the attacks upon Monte Sabotino were renewed again and again. Early in November the hill was actually taken, but owing to a misunderstanding the reserves did not arrive in time, and the shattered brigade that had gained the position in spite of fearful losses was swept back by the Austrian counter-attack. Monte Sabotino is tunnelled and galleried with countless trenches. Its capture was an extraordinary feat, and but for a blunder in staff work its occupation would almost certainly have continued.

The offensive slackened at the beginning of December, but up to the end of the year fighting was almost continuous along this sector. The Italians won trenches, lost them, won and lost them again, but on the balance they were always gaining a little, and they were now close upon the bridge crossing the Isonzo into Gorizia. Towards the end of this long struggle the heavy guns were turned upon Gorizia for the first time. The town could have been blown to pieces months before, but the Italians refrained from bombarding it as long as possible. Advantage was taken of this restraint, and the Austrians placed guns in the town itself, so that it was no longer possible to spare it.

Meanwhile an equally fierce attack was being made upon the Carso, with very similar results. Some progress was made on the southern rim towards the lake of Doberdo, but the chief struggle took place on the San Michele slopes and the saddle of San Martino del Carso. In the end part of the San Michele summit was occupied, and the Church of San Martino, while a number of trenches were taken and held on the northern slope of the Carso, where it drops to the Vippacco (Wipbach). The bloody fighting here recalls the struggle on the Wipbach (then known as the Frigidus) 1,500 years before, when Theodosius met the Gauls and ten thousand of his Gothic auxiliaries were slain. It was of this battle that Claudian wrote, with what Gibbon calls "intolerable wit," how "the snow was dyed red; the cold river smoked; and the channel must

AN ITALIAN SEARCHLIGHT ON THE BATTLEFIELD.

have been choked with carcases if the current had not been swelled with blood." But the battle of the Frigidus was fought in a day. The contest on the Vippacco still continued.

The Italian offensive in October and November failed to break through the Austrian lines, though on several occasions the breaking point was almost reached. The Italian infantry displayed a bravery in attack that was beyond all praise. The southerners, who had been looked on as inferior material, showed a spirit and tenacity which the troops of the north found hard to equal. Their opponents may have fought with less *élan*, but they held like bulldogs and counter-attacked whenever the chance came. The qualities of the Hungarians were specially noticeable. They fought with a dogged courage that could hardly be surpassed, and any but the best troops would have given way before the determined onslaughts of the Italians.

Two criticisms of the Italian army may find a place here. They are Italian criticisms, and they are given here, because the fact that they were freely expressed in Italy held out the best hopes for the future. The Italian Army, like the British Army, suffered from defects in staff work, and the chief defect was the same in both cases—a failure to get the reserves on the scene in time. A second defect was a lack of technique in trench warfare. Each army had to learn for itself, and the Italians had had a shorter experience of trench work than their Allies. Where it was possible, as in the case of the Alpini and their extraordinary feats on the mountains, to use the technique learned in peace time, the results called for nothing but praise.

Much had been learned during the last offensive, and confidence in the future was unshaken. In the meantime, among all who had attempted to follow the operations on the exceptionally difficult front from the Alps to the sea, the work of the Italian Army called forth the warmest admiration. What Italy had already accomplished in the face of immense obstacles, natural and artificial, constituted a very notable military achievement.

CHAPTER CX.

AUTUMN AND WINTER OF 1915 ON THE EASTERN FRONT.

Situation after the Fall of Vilna—The German Line—Advances towards Polotsk and Minsk—The Offensive against Dvinsk—Its Failure after Fierce Fighting—Russian Victory of Platonovka—The Riga Sector—German Autumn Offensive—German Successes—Advance on Riga Abandoned—Attempt on Rovno—Battle on the Middle Styr—Fighting between the Strypa and the Sereth—November Lull on the whole Front—Concentration South of Pripet Marshes—Russian Success on the Dniester—Outlook at the New Year.

THE fall of Vilna on September 18, 1915, marks practically the close of the great Austro-German advance into Russia, which began in May, although it was not the end of the offensive. A new "balance" was reached on the Eastern front towards the end of September; the line on which it was established was not, however, that which the German commanders had intended to attain before winter. They had not stopped on the strong and convenient line of defence, offered by the Niemen and Bug, but with heavy sacrifices had advanced into the interior of Russia, through the marshes of the Pripet and the forests of Lithuania. Such ambitions as an immediate march on Petrograd, Moscow or Kieff, were frequently supposed to have been their goal. In reality their purpose appears to have been much simpler. They tried to establish themselves before winter on a line which could have been held with comparatively small forces, and on which the initiative would have been almost entirely with them. The topographical configuration of Western Russia and the consequent development of its railway net marked out clearly the Riga–Dvinsk–Rovno–Kamenets Podolski front* as the line best suited for their purpose.

The most important part of that front, its real backbone, is the Vilna-Luniniets-Rovno railway; it was in the autumn of 1915 the only railway line between Brest-Litovsk in the west and the Dnieper in the east, connecting the northern and the southern areas in the Russian theatre of war. The side which held the whole of that line would have had an obvious and most important advantage in being able to maintain direct communication between these two areas; if necessary, it could have made up by mobility for numbers. Had the Germans been able to gain, moreover, the important railway junction of Minsk, they would have established a strategic "vacuum" in front of the central part of their line, as our Allies could hardly have maintained themselves in its neighbourhood in view of the inferiority of the means of communication which they would then have had at their disposal. The German positions would have been well provided with lateral roads and railways, and the Russian front would have been thrown back beyond the Dnieper on to the Vitebsk-Kieff line.

The German position in the centre was to be protected by the establishment of similarly strong lines on the flanks. At the northern end the line of the Dvina forms for the Vilna district the natural shield against the north east. The river, and the road and railway

* See the large coloured map supplied in Volume V. (Chapter XCV.).

"The Times Photograph."

THE TSAR WITH THE TSAREVITCH ON THE BATTLEFIELD SALUTING HIS TROOPS.

which run along it, form an excellent base for a defensive position; they offer splendid communications and render possible quick concentrations. The towns of Riga and Dvinsk are the strategic keys to that position. No wonder that the Germans were prepared to make even the heaviest sacrifices, if only at that price they could have gained possession of the Dvina line.

At first sight it is less obvious which was the most favourable line of defence for the Austro-German forces at the southern end of the Eastern front. South of Rovno the marshy, winding courses of the numerous tributaries of the Pripet approach the parallel valleys of the left-hand tributaries of the Dniester, and offer a succession of strong, natural strategic positions. Yet there were good reasons for the enemy for aiming at establishing himself on the line of the River Zbrutch, with the town of Chotin, or on that of the River Smotritch, with the town of Kamenets Podolski, if he could only have taken Rovno (for without Rovno he could not possibly have attempted in the south an advance beyond the line of the Strypa or of the Sereth). The most obvious reason for the Austrians desiring to reach the Zbrutch was sentimental: it forms the eastern frontier of Galicia; not until they reached it could they have boasted of having "freed" their entire territory from the Russian "invaders." Secondly, considerable economic advantages would have been gained by an advance in that region; in the whole of Austria there is no other agricultural district as fertile as is the so-called "Podolia,"* the high plateau north of the Dniester. Thirdly, an advance or retreat in that region was likely to affect the strategic position of Roumania. Lastly, the reaching of the eastern frontier of Galicia would have implied very considerable strategic advantages. The lines of the different left-handed tributaries of the Dniester are *by nature* of more or less equal strategic value; this equality has been, however, destroyed by the different degree of development of the means of communication in Austrian and in Russian Podolia. The latter can be described even now as practically innocent of roads and railways. Only one single railway line runs through Russian Podolia, and crosses the frontier at Volotchisk, and only one single first-class road runs, parallel to the frontier, from Proskuroff to Kamenets Podolski. Some twenty years before the war conditions in Austrian Podolia were not very much better. All that had, however, changed. A railway parallel to the frontier, connected, east of the Sereth, Tarnopol with Zaleshchyki. Three railways, running east and west, reached the frontier itself, at Volotchisk, Husiatyn and Skala; three more approached it at the termini of Zbarazh, Gzhymaloff and Ivanie Puste (north of Mielnitsa). The country between the Strypa and the Zbrutch was covered by a net of high roads, which found its equal in Galicia only in the extreme west round Cracow, and was good even if judged by West-European standards. In fact, the means of communication between the River Strypa and the Russian frontier were superior to those west of the Strypa—*i.e.*, behind the line on which the advance of the Austro-German armies was arrested in September, 1915. The high development of the means of communication in Austrian Podolia explains the con-

* "Podole" means "in the hollows"; that name was probably given to the district because almost all its towns and villages lie deep in the cañons of the rivers.

siderable strategic importance which was attached to that district.

On September 7 the Austrians captured Dubno, having previously occupied Lutsk, and on September 18 the Germans entered Vilna. It seemed as if the enemy was to attain his goal. Unexpectedly the tide began to turn. On the same day on which the Austrians entered Dubno, their forces on the south suffered a severe defeat*; on September 23 our Allies re-entered Lutsk. The Russian armies round Vilna, which seemed during a few days in danger of being cut off, effected a brilliant retreat, suffering very small losses, and began to drive back towards the west the advanced bodies of German troops, which were roaming east of Vidzy and Vileika. Early in the autumn of 1915 the Germans had thus realized one part of their scheme; they held the important centre of Vilna and the Vilna-Baranovitchy railway line. Everywhere else they were standing "on the threshold"; they were facing "the promised land" without being able to enter it. Frantic efforts to complete their scheme fill the history of the next few weeks—viz., the short season during which an advance was still possible in the muddy plains and marshes of Eastern Europe.

* Cf. Chapter XCV, pp. 506–8.

During the fortnight following on the fall of Vilna the German armies under General von Eichhorn and the right wing of the group commanded by General von Below strove to complete the success which they had achieved in the neighbourhood of Vilna, by an advance to the east. In Lithuania, the country of lakes and forests, operations on a large scale are limited almost entirely, especially in autumn, to the lines of the main roads and railways. In the region of Svientsiany the Germans tried to follow up their original piercing movement by an advance towards Polotsk, along the Svientsiany-Postavy-Bereswetsh railway, and through the valley of the Disna. The movement was undertaken by five cavalry divisions with strong infantry support. By success in that quarter the Germans would have gained a flanking position with regard to Dvinsk, and might have effected at the same time a strategic envelopment of the Russian armies under General Evert, which in the centre were retiring in an easterly direction. To hamper their withdrawal, German cavalry detachments were sent out against the Molodetchna-Polotsk

["*The Times Photograph.*"]

RUSSIAN MAXIM GUNS IN ACTION.

railway, which, east of the river Narotch, approaches very close to the Svientsiany-Bereswetsh line. Meantime, two powerful German army-groups were pressing on concentric lines against Minsk, following the railways which connect it with Vilna and Baranovitchy. If either of these two groups had succeeded in hurling back the opposing Russian forces, the retreat of the troops along the other line would have been seriously endangered. On the extreme right wing, following the northern edge of the Pripet Marshes, the Germans were attempting from the south, along the road to Niesviz and Slutsk, an enveloping movement against the Minsk-Bobruisk line.

The struggle which thus developed on the fall of Vilna on the Svientsiany-Baranovitchy front—i.e., in the region which might best be described as the northern centre of the autumn front—lasted unabated for about a fortnight. At first the main fighting raged round Smorgon and Vileika. With something like astonishment, states the German report of September 25: "The Russians are still resisting our advance on the line Smorgon-Vishneff." But even more was in store for them. "In the Vilia region above Vileika," says the Russian official *communiqué* of September 26, "desperate actions continue. We captured the village of Resterka. The Germans delivered a series of attacks near Vileika, pushing them on many occasions so far that bayonet fighting ensued. All these attacks were repulsed.

"In the district north-west of Vileika our troops carried with a bayonet charge the fortified village of Ostroff and recaptured the village of Ghirty.

"On the Smorgon front and south of the town fighting continues."

During the following two days the Germans continued their onslaughts west of Vileika; in fact, their offensive developed into a pitched battle. One attack followed the other, and the fighting never slackened. At several points the Germans were pouring in their heavy artillery fire "in the approved style." On September 27, 10,000 heavy shells were dropped in a sector held by a single Russian regiment. Although pressed hard at times our Allies succeeded in holding their ground, and in inflicting heavy losses on the enemy. "One of our armies operating in this region," says the Petrograd *communiqué* of September 28, "captured from the Germans during the past week 13 guns, including five of large calibre, 33 machine-guns and 12 ammunition wagons. Over 1,000 unwounded Germans were taken."

As the result of about a week's fighting between the Disna and the Niemen our Allies extricated their advanced detachments, straightened out their front, cleared their lines of communication of enemy raiders, and even succeeded by a counter-offensive in pressing back the enemy at several points (especially in the Vidzy-Smorgon sector). The Russian right wing advanced westward down the Vilia

A SCENE IN THE PRIPET MARSHES.

"The Times photographs."

"THE TIMES" CORRESPONDENT STANDING BY A RUSSIAN HEAVY GUN.

Small picture: Armoured cars.

and up its two tributaries, the Narotch and the Servetch. The German cavalry which had cut the Polotsk railway at Krzyvitchy, on the Servetch, and had spread to the south-east as far as Dolgvinoff, near the sources of the Vilia, was driven back and the Polotsk railway was cleared of Germans. Our Allies maintained themselves round the hard-contested town of Vileika and the important railway-junction of Molodetchna and recaptured Smorgon. The German advance was stopped and depression began to spread in the ranks of the enemy. "This depression," says the Russian official report of September 30, "manifests itself in more and more frequent instances of the abandonment by the Germans on the battlefield of slightly wounded soldiers, of wagons on the line of their retreat, of the throwing away of arms and projectiles, and of disorder and nervousness in their firing."

Also farther south the German attempt met with very little success. The enveloping movement made no progess, and the fighting assumed the character of frontal attacks, with hardly any gains for the Germans to counterbalance their heavy sacrifices. All attempts to cross the Niemen east of Novogrodek or to press forward along the Baranovitchy-Minsk railway, ended in failure.

Then in the first days of October the German offensive in the northern centre began to "fizzle out." Withdrawals to the Western front and to Serbia seem to have excessively depleted their reserves; when met by the stubborn resistance of an enemy whom they described as beaten and flying, and possibly imagined to have reached that condition, the Germans found themselves unable to exert sufficient pressure against his lines so as to pierce them. Soon autumn rains and bad roads began to hamper more and more the activity of the Germans, and a long lull set in on the front between the Disna and the big Marshes. The thick red line which on the coloured map in Part 65 of this History marks the Russian front towards the end of October, 1915, still roughly defined its position at the New Year of 1916. Our Allies had maintained themselves in full possession of the highly important railway junctions of Molodetchna and Minsk.

Whilst attempting an offensive against Minsk and along the Polotsk railway, the Germans were also pressing their attack against Dvinsk. Towards the end of September the following order, issued to the German troops operating in that district, came into Russian hands: "Tens of thousands of your comrades, who with unbounded valour forced the Russian front at Svientsiany, are in danger as long as Dvinsk remains in Russian hands. It is necessary to capture it in order to avert the danger threatening your comrades ; this is your duty to these heroes." Indeed, the capture of Dvinsk would have been decisive for the entire offensive east of Vilna. With the Germans firmly established at Dvinsk, and threatening an advance against Polotsk by the road and railway which run along the right bank of the River Dvina, the position of our Allies in the northern centre opposite Svientsiany and Vilna would have become practically untenable. But the capture of Dvinsk proved by no means an easy task.

As a strategic centre Dvinsk is certainly equal in importance to Vilna, Brest-Litovsk and Rovno, and second perhaps only to Warsaw. It forms the junction of two of the most important Russian railways, the Petrograd-Vilna-Warsaw and the Moscow-Smolensk-Riga lines. Moreover, a branch line connects Dvinsk, by way of Ponevesh and Shavle, with the Baltic port of Libau ; at Shavle it is met by a narrow-gauge railway from Tauroggen, which the Germans had constructed since the summer of 1915. Dvinsk is also the centre of a network of roads.

Situated in the angle between the Dvina line and the Lithuanian front, Dvinsk served as pivot for the Russian armies operating in the lake district to the east of Vilna. The part which it played in the Russian scheme might in certain respects be compared with that of Verdun in the West. It would, however, be a mistake to think of Dvinsk as of a fortress ; in strategic discussion one ought to speak of the Dvinsk district much rather than of the town of Dvinsk. The town was the object to be defended, and not the defending factor. It lay 8 to 20 miles behind the Russian lines which enveloped and sheltered that vital centre of communications, which is also one of the principal gates to the Dvina line. From Illukst near the Dvina, the Russian front extended across the Ponevesh railway, near Garbunovka, towards Lake Sventen. From here it ran across wooded hills towards Lake Ilsen and Lake Medum, then, cutting the high road north-east of Novo Alexandrovsk and the Dvinsk-Vilna railway near Kruklishki, it reached Lake Gaten in the neighbourhood of the village of Gateny. At that point the line curved, following henceforward due south a chain of small lakes of which Lake Gaten forms approximately the centre. At the southern end of the chain lies Lake Drisviaty, the biggest in the Dvinsk region. Together with the neighbouring Lake Obolie it may be taken to form the southern end of the Dvinsk front.

A COLD DRINK.
Russian troops enjoying their cup of ice cold water.

CLEARING FOR ACTION ON THE DVINA FRONT.
Russian Gunners Extricating a Gun from the Snow.

As long as the Russian line south of Lake Drisviaty stood firm, our Allies in order to keep Dvinsk, had merely to hold the 27 miles of the Illukst-Drisviaty front, which, moreover, nature itself had provided with strong defences. Had the Germans succeeded in reaching the Dvina east of Dvinsk, the position of the Russians in that town would have become extremely precarious. Lying in a river curve, convex in the direction of the enemy, Dvinsk would have been exposed to a cross fire.

In the course of August and September several attempts had been made by the Germans against the Dvina line at different points between Dvinsk and the Baltic Sea. Towards the middle of September fighting in the neighbourhood of Dvinsk assumed the regular stationary character of trench warfare. The Germans were massing heavy artillery in the rear, whilst trying to push forward towards the Russian lines by means of saps. The operations culminated on September 24 in a fierce battle fought along the whole front between the Dvina and Lake Drisviaty. Supported by a hurricane of fire of their artillery, the Germans delivered repeated attacks against the Russian positions; certain trenches changed hands

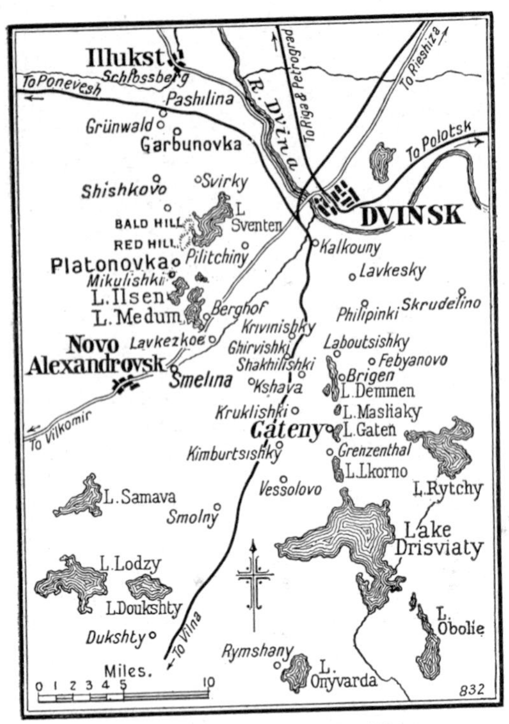

THE DVINSK FRONT.

several times, but at the end of the day the Germans had hardly any gains to record. On the next day our Allies recaptured also the village of Drisviaty, which commands the lake isthmus, and the Germans found themselves reduced to the same position which they had occupied before the commencement of their September offensive.

In the course of the following ten days fighting round Dvinsk lost somewhat in intensity and was limited to violent artillery duels and local attacks, in which particular trenches and groups of trenches were won and lost. During the fortnight October 4–18 the German offensive against Dvinsk changed its character. The operations in the sector between Lake Medum and Lake Drisviaty lost in importance, the enemy concentrated his main endeavours in the region between Illukst and Lake Sventen. The attacks south of Dvinsk had stood in close connection with the offensive from the Svientsiany district against Polotsk. This having failed completely, the enemy lost his main chance of outflanking the army defending Dvinsk by reaching the Dvina from the east; a piercing movement from the north-west was now attempted along the Illukst road and the Ponevesh railway. Had the Germans succeeded in that attack they would probably have followed it up by an attempt to force the crossing of the Dvina below Dvinsk, thus threatening the retreat of the Russians from that district.

The Russian official *communiqué* of October 5 gives the first intimation of a new battle developing in the sector between Illukst and Lake Sventen. At first the Germans attempted an advance near the village of Shishkovo; in the next few days the main attacks centred round the village of Garbunovka, about two miles south of the Ponevesh railway, and about nine miles north-west of Dvinsk. "There was an extremely desperate fight all day yesterday near the villages of Pashilina and Garbunovka,"

GERMANS REPAIRING THE DAMAGED RAILWAYS IN RUSSIA.

BRIDGES DESTROYED AND REPAIRED.

German "Saw Mills" used for cutting the required size planks for repairing bridges. Bottom picture: Ingenious Russian method of delaying German advance—Goods train blown up on a railway bridge.

says the Petrograd *communiqué* of October 10. "It diminished in intensity towards the evening. The village of Garbunovka was taken, lost, and retaken several times and was finally abandoned by us under the enemy's fire. . . . Near Pashilina the Germans were at first successful, but towards the evening the development of their offensive was checked to the east of that village." On October 10 the village of Garbunovka was retaken by our Allies. For another week the battle raged round Illukst, Garbunovka and Shishkovo, with no advantage to the Germans except some small gains near Illukst, which were balanced by losses in other sectors of the line.

The general commanding the German forces before Dvinsk had confidently expected to enter the town by the end of September; a month later he stood still in approximately the same positions, having wasted something like 40,000 men in his hopeless attacks against the Russian lines. This estimate of the German losses, which competent observers described in October, 1915, as conservative, is the more significant, as towards the end of the month the German forces massed directly under Dvinsk numbered only six divisions of infantry and two cavalry brigades, or about 80,000 bayonets. "But the lack of men," wrote *The Times* correspondent in a despatch of October 25, "is compensated by strength in artillery, including, besides a huge number of field batteries, a large number of heavy guns up to 8·2 inches, mortars and siege guns from Königsberg and Kovno." Moreover, reinforcements were coming, for the Germans were as yet far from regarding their attempt against Dvinsk as lost. General von Lauenstein, who replaced von Morgen on the Dvinsk front, continued the operations with even greater obstinacy, though in the long run with no better success.

After a short lull, fighting recommenced, and on October 23 the Germans scored their first marked success in the Dvinsk region. After long and vigorous artillery preparation, they

ARTILLERY FIGHTING ROUND THE LAKES NEAR DVINSK.

In the foreground is seen a Russian battery hidden near a burnt farm. Farther away are two lines of Russian infantry trenches, with barbed wire entanglements before them, some German shells are bursting over them. Farther still are three lines of German trenches, and on the hills beyond the burning village, shelled by the Russians, are the German batteries.

attacked the Russian trenches west of the town of Illukst; at first their attack was repulsed, but towards the close of the day, they succeeded in breaking through, and after a desperate battle in the streets, occupied the town. It seemed as if that success was to open up a new chapter of the battle before Dvinsk. "In the region to the east of Illukst," says the Russian *communiqué* of October 25, "furious fighting with the advancing Germans continues without cessation." During the next few days the enemy strove frantically to make full use of his advantage and develop his offensive. On October 27–28 he succeeded in breaking through the Russian front near the village of Garbunovka and to the south of it, and in reaching the western outskirts of the big forests which extend between the Illukst-Shishkovo road and the Dvina. Here, however, his advance was brought to a stop by our Allies promptly strengthening their defences east of Illukst, by excellent artillery work, and last but not least by the brilliant counter-offensive carried out by our Allies in the district of Platonovka.

The Dvinsk front was held by an army deemed one of the most valiant and best disciplined among the Russian hosts, which was moreover, abundantly supplied with artillery and ammunition. In the ten days of fierce fighting in the region of Lakes Sventen and Ilsen, which ended on November 11, it fully justified its high reputation. According to the Petrograd correspondent of *The Times*, who visited personally portions of the battlefield and had the privilege of hearing the accounts of the Russian commanders, that battle, best described as the Battle of Platonovka, must be regarded as one of the most important events on the northern front since the Russian Army withdrew from Poland. In the words of the distinguished veteran who has been directing the operations at Dvinsk: "After two months' patient resistance of the enemy's continuous offensive we were at last able, a fortnight ago, to assume the offensive ourselves and compel the Germans to recede from their positions and in their turn adopt defensive tactics. I think the German failure on this front will assume a permanent character"—a prophecy fully borne out by the events, or rather the absence of events during the following months.

The Russian offensive between Lakes Sventen and Ilsen had more than one aim in view. The German advance south-east of Illukst had been arrested, but considerable reinforcements were known to be under way; these had to be diverted. In the region of Lake Sventen the German lines were approaching too closely to Dvinsk; the German heavy artillery had to be prevented from getting within range of the town. The Russian positions in the sector of the two lakes presented several serious tactical disadvantages; these could be remedied only by means of a successful advance. But that advance itself was rendered enormously difficult by the bad tactical position of the Russian forces.

On October 31, the day which marks the beginning of the Russian offensive, the line of our Allies extended from the southern shore of Lake Sventen to the northern extremity of Lake Ilsen, over a distance of about three miles. The whole region presents a succession of swamps and hills, some denuded, others crested with pine trees. There is water everywhere, only the sand hills stand out—bastions for an army on the defensive. The main heights of the isthmus between Platonovka and Lake Ilsen were in the hands of the Germans who had strongly fortified them. They held also a range of hills on the western shore of Lake Sventen, from which they could sweep by their artillery fire its shores and waters. The Russian forces between Lakes Sventen and Ilsen were practically isolated, in so far as lateral connections were concerned. The flanks of the neighbouring corps to right and left were separated by almost the whole length of these respective lakes.

The Russian offensive consisted of two distinct movements: one detachment composed of two regiments was sent out to take the hills on the western bank of Lake Sventen (Red Hill and Bald Hill), and if possible to gain touch with the neighbouring corps. Another group of regiments proceeded to attack the hills round Platanovka; this movement had, however, to be preceded by the former.

The following is the description of the fighting near Lake Sventen given to the Petrograd correspondent of the *Times* by the colonel of one of the two regiments which led the way:—

"We had to secure a lodgment in the promontory nicknamed by our men the 'Dog's Tail.' My scouts crossed the lake at night, dug themselves in and annoyed the enemy holding the brickyard situated upon a slight eminence at the northern part of the promontory. A Lettish officer commanded the scouts and organized the whole landing. Being a native of the place, he was able to take advantage of every latent resource afforded by the country. Thus he managed to discover a small fleet of boats and added to them by constructing a number of rafts. During the night our men gradually reinforced the scouts. On the following day we rushed the brickyard. This gave us a larger foothold to deploy one of our regiments and storm what we called Bald Hill, while another regiment gave its attention to Red Hill, to the south-west.

" Our advance was very slow. The Germans had a large number of maxims, three times as many as we had, also automatic rifles, and freely used explosive bullets. But on our side we had our artillery massed in several lines east of Sventen and Medum, including field and heavy guns under good control, so that we could pour in direct or flanking fire at will. Three days passed chiefly in artillery preparation for our final attack. The infantry advanced slightly. Our artillery observers were in the trenches correcting the fire of our guns. On November 3, the enemy began to pour in a fierce flanking fire from their guns west of Ilsen.

" When the scouts and supports moved from the Dog's Tail promontory, our neighbouring corps began to advance also, and we finally extended our right flank and gained direct contact. But all this time we were suffering heavily from the enemy's maxims on the heights.

" Bald Hill and Red Hill were won on the third day. The enemy counter-attacked and retook the first-named heights. Our position was now a very critical one. The waters of the lake in our rear cut off all hope of immediate reinforcements or of eventual retreat. We had to retake Bald Hill at all costs, and we did it. My men were tremendously encouraged

GERMAN CAVALRYMEN AS GUNNERS.

A useful weapon used by the German cavalry. One man loads while the other fires the machine rifle.

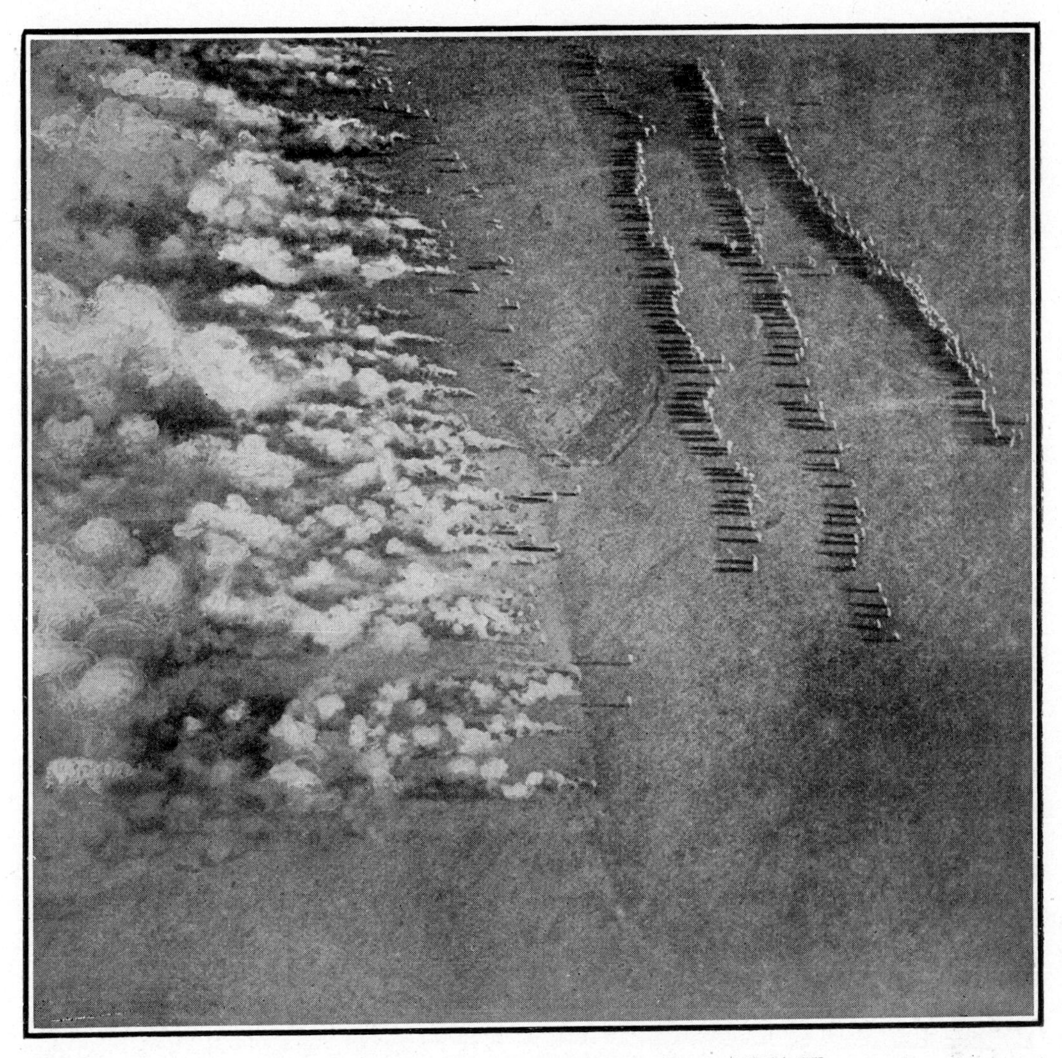

AIRMAN'S VIEW OF A GERMAN GAS ATTACK.

This picture, taken by a Russian airman, illustrates the beginning of a German gas attack, the poisoned cloud rolling before a westerly wind towards the Russian lines after being released from the gas-cylinders. On the right are lines of German troops awaiting the order to advance.

by the hurricane fire kept up by our artillery. Many of them had witnessed the terrible effects of the German hurricane fire. For the first time they saw that our own artillery was not only equal but even superior to anything that the Germans could do. Our gunners telephoned to me asking when they should stop so that our men should not suffer from their fire. It seemed to me that our shells were bursting perilously near, and I asked them to cease fire. A half company then attacking Bald Hill was immediately mown down by the German machine-guns. I at once signalled to the gunners 'keep on firing,' and only when our skirmishers were within 250 paces of the German trenches the hurricane was suspended and we went for the Germans with the bayonet, but they did not wait."

The enemy division which had been proceeding to Illukst was diverted to stem the Russian advance. But in vain; the Russian line between the lakes being freed from the galling fire from the hills, fought its way westward. Its advance led over difficult and swampy ground, which delayed its movements. One regiment remained for eight days and nights under heavy fire, receiving food only at night, yet the men never wavered and in the end forced their way forward. The heights of Platonovka, Selikishki, and Mikulishki were captured, the German line was thrown back for a distance amounting at some points to no less than three miles, the Russians gained the entire western shore of Lake Sventen and the north-western half of that of Lake Ilsen—the battle was won. It was won moreover at a loss considerably smaller than that inflicted on the enemy. The total Russian casualties

RUSSIAN ARTILLERY IN ACTION.

did not exceed 7,500, including many cases of frost-bite, whereas a conservative estimate of the enemy's losses placed them at 20,000.

When, shortly after the battle, *The Times* correspondent visited the new Russian trenches, he was struck by the good work done in them by the Russian soldiers after ten days of severe fighting. "The trenches were dry and as comfortable as they could have been made within the space of a few days. There was overhead cover for the men at the loopholes, and a strip of tarpaulin to shelter them so that within this miniature abode two men could rest and at the same time be ready to stand up instantly to the loophole in case of an attack. Here and there communication trenches led to well-dug, bomb-proof shelters where the men could warm themselves. Thanks to excellent distribution of communication trenches, hot food could be brought up to the men twice daily. The conditions were as good as they could possibly be under the circumstances, and the men were cheerful and well-nourished. . . ."

Very different were the conditions which he found in the conquered German trenches.

The contrast between the Russian and the German trenches suggested that the tales of suffering and hardship and complete moral collapse that had been told a few days ago by the 700 German prisoners taken during the battle were probably true. Their rations had been reduced to one-third of a pound of bread, while the terrific Russian bombardment rendered it impossible to light a fire in the trenches. I walked along about a mile of these abandoned works. The trenches were badly dug, evidently by prentice hands, and although the Germans had occupied them for some weeks they did not compare in point of comfort with the Russian trenches completed only a few days ago. The awful stench, due to the absence of all sanitary arrangements, the dirt and disorder in the shelters, and the almost complete absence of fire-places—all argued that the occupants were not men fitted to serve in the field, and were too depressed to care what became of them. A quantity of accoutrements still remained in the trenches. The Russian soldiers had already removed the arms and ammunition, of which a large quantity was secured. The prisoners explained that the men had refused to carry off the weapons belonging to their dead comrades.

The victory of Platonovka was followed up by a Russian advance near Illukst. "Left of the Dvina, north of Illukst," says the Russian *communiqué* of November 24, "we captured, after fighting, the farm of Yanopol." Situated on the river about 20 miles below Dvinsk, Yanopol possessed considerable strategic importance. From this point the enemy several times attempted to cross the river in the hope of effecting an envelopment of the Dvinsk army. Moreover, the loss of Yanopol changed the German position in the Illukst region into an even more pronounced salient, and one more difficult to hold, than it had been previously. Even there, in the one sector in which the Germans had gained ground during their autumn offensive, they were unable to maintain it in full, to say nothing of a farther advance. "North-west of Dvinsk, in the region of Illukst, near the village of Kazimirichki," says the Petrograd *communiqué* of November 29, "the Germans, on the night of the 28th, opened a violent artillery fire on our trenches, and at dawn took the offensive. In face of the concentrated fire of our artillery and rifles the Germans withdrew to their trenches, thereby coming under the fire of their own batteries. Taking advantage of this situation, our troops in turn delivered a counter-attack, as the result of which the enemy was driven out of the farm of Kazimirichki and the wood to the west of the farm.

"A portion of our troops at the same time forced their way into Illukst and occupied the suburb on the east side of the place. Developing our success, we occupied the two cemeteries of the village and part of the German trenches farther to the south."

In their precipitate flight from Yanopol, the Germans abandoned the official records of one battalion, in which was found some interesting correspondence of the Higher Command. It appeared from it that repeated requests for further reinforcements were sent by the German commanders on the Dvinsk front, but no sufficient help was received for a continuation of the offensive. This might have been due partly to a general shortage of reserves, partly to the conviction, which was bound to gain ground, that the attempt at forcing the Dvinsk front was hopeless. Anyhow, the fighting in that sector closed with the end of November, 1915.

Whilst the right wing of von Below's army was trying to hack its way through in the district of Dvinsk, its left wing was hammering at the other gate of the Dvina line, the Riga sector. Smaller engagements, incidental attempts to break through at particular points, and a preparatory struggle for positions had been proceeding in that region ever since the beginning of August. About the middle of October the operations round Riga assumed the character of a vigorous general offensive. Six army corps, supported by a very considerable artillery force were gathered on the 70 miles front extending along a semi-circle from Lake Shlotsen, near the Gulf of Riga, to Linden on the Dvina. In reality this concentration was even more serious than the mere numbers would indicate as, owing to the nature of the ground, operations in the neighbourhood of Riga are limited to certain definite lines.

On October 14, when the new German offensive began to develop, the enemy lines followed in the main the course of the River Aa from Shlock (near the sea) to Mitau; from there their front ran along the River Ekau, and then, following the Mitau-Kreutzburg railway, approached the Dvina opposite the bridgeheads of Friedrichstadt and Jakobstadt (in this district, half-way between Riga and Dvinsk, an attempt had been made by the Germans, towards the end of August and in the beginning of September, to force a crossing of the Dvina, but had failed *). Three main lines of attack against Riga were open to the Germans. The direct line for a frontal attack against the town followed the Mitau-Olai-Riga road and railway. An advance along these was by no means easy. Between Mitau and Olai, which lies about half-way to Riga, the road and railway cross the Rivers Ekau and Misse and several of their tributaries; the country round is a low, wooded plain and offers plenty of possibilities for defence. Beyond Olai an advance is even more difficult as it leads across the big Tirul Marsh. It is true, during their advance into Poland the Austro-Germans had been able to overcome even greater obstacles as, *e.g.*, the Tanev Marshes,†

* Cf. Chapter XCV., p. 503.
† Cf. Chapter LXXXV., p. 160 and Chapter XCI., pp. 343-4.

BIG GUNS ARRIVE IN RUSSIA FROM JAPAN.
Russian Officers inspecting the new weapons.

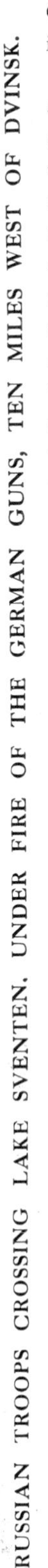

RUSSIAN TROOPS CROSSING LAKE SVENTEN, UNDER FIRE OF THE GERMAN GUNS, TEN MILES WEST OF DVINSK.

but then they had an overwhelming superiority in artillery which they possessed no longer in October, 1915, against General Ruszky's forces in front of Riga.

The other two possible lines of advance against Riga were flanking movements. The one led along the Tukkum-Shlock-Riga railway, between Lake Babit and the sea. An advance along that line presented disadvantages of such serious nature that at first it seemed unlikely to be at all attempted, and in fact it was not tried by the Germans except as their last chance, in November, after all other attempts had failed. The only possible road from Shlock to Riga runs quite close to the shore, and is exposed to fire from the sea, which was a serious matter for the Germans as, since the time of their naval reverses in August, 1915, our Allies had gained complete mastery in the Gulf of Riga.

For a flanking movement against Riga from the east, the ground was most favourable in the district of Uexkuell on the Dvina, about 12 miles upstream from the town. In the neighbourhood of Uexkuell, opposite the villages of Repe and Klange, the Dvina divides, forming the islet of Dalen, which is about five miles long and one or two miles broad. A small left-hand tributary which joins the Dvina opposite Dalen, the River Kesau, offered still further facilities for the throwing of a pontoon bridge across the river. This sector became in the second half of October the scene of bitter fighting and of perhaps the most dangerous German move against Riga.

On October 14 the Germans opened their offensive by crossing the River Ekau, near the village of Grunwald. During the next two days a desperate battle was fought with changing success for the station of Gaurosen and also near Gross Ekau and west of the farm of Misshof on the Missa. On October 16 the enemy succeeded in driving back the Russian troops near Gross Ekau towards the River Jεne , and fought with some success near the station of Neugut. During the next few days fighting extended to the neighbourhood of the Mitau-Olai line and some advance was made by the Germans near the villages of Kish and Herzogsdorf. Then followed their chief blow against the eastern flank. "In the wooded region to the north of the Mitau-Neugut railway," says the Russian official *communiqué*, of October 13, "the Germans succeeded in advancing to the north. Everywhere in this region

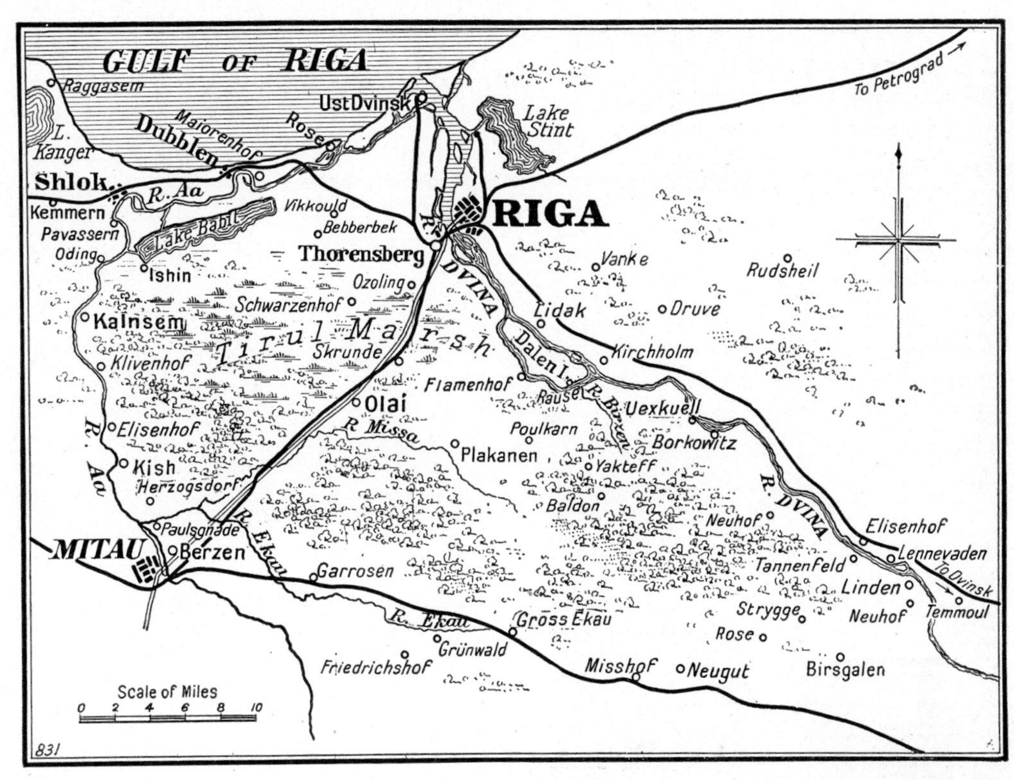

THE RIGA FRONT.

terrific fighting is going on." By October 20 the Germans reached Borkowitz on the Dvina, about 14 miles from Riga and only about two miles above the islet of Dalen, scoring their biggest success in the entire offensive round Riga. The true story of it, coming from a competent source is this: The Germans were able to break through the Russian left flank between Neugut and the Dvina, because a single regiment had been left to guard a stretch of something like 15 miles, and having been for a month almost continuously engaged, it was unable to resist the advance of a whole brigade of fresh German troops. Reinforcements reached the Russian front on the Missa in time, and enabled our Allies to drive back the enemy, but for some unaccountable reason, the hard-pressed regiment was neither reinforced nor relieved. The general commanding the —— Corps could not be found, in order to give the necessary orders, and his absence from Riga lasted two whole days. Curiously enough, that Russian general had a very German name. He had a short shrift and was promptly replaced by a well-known Slav commander.

Following on the success east of Neugut, the Germans forced a passage across the Missa near Plakanen, and reached the village Repe on the right bank of the Kesau. "In an action near the village of Repe, south-east of Riga," says the official Petrograd *communiqué* of October 24, "the Germans succeeded in capturing the village. Near the village of Klange, north of Repe, we inflicted enormous losses on the enemy by our sustained fire." Furious fighting developed on the next day in the Uexkuell district on the left bank of the Dvina. Accounts of that fighting published in the *Novoe Vremya* emphasize the appalling severity of the artillery fire on both sides. The earth shook for many miles round from the force of the exploding shells, while rockets ceaselessly shed a lurid light over the field of battle. At 8 p.m. the Germans began a first attack which was repulsed by the fire of "M." Regiment, on which devolved almost the entire weight of the defence positions. Up to 3 a.m. the regiment had repelled six furious onslaughts. Then came the critical moment of the seventh attack. From all sides dense columns of the enemy crept up and impetuously hurled themselves on the tired Russians. Artillery and maxims opened a murderous fire, and the regiment charged with the bayonet and hurled back the foe with heavy losses, which for the evening totalled at least 800 slain. On the following night the assaults were renewed with the same result.

Yet the Germans persisted in their attempts at crossing the Dvina. The results to be gained were such as to justify even heavy sacrifices. On one occasion they thought themselves near their goal; in reality they were walking into a trap. The Russians had lured them on to the island of Dalen and then promptly opened fire from two opposite sides, inflicting terrible losses on the foe. At Riga the public assembled on the bridge over the Dvina and watched thousands of German corpses floating down the stream. Other Riga residents followed the progress of the artillery battle from the high railway bridge near the station. One of the arms of the Dvina, called the Little Dvina, was clogged with German corpses. In the battles in this region the enemy lost 7,000 prisoners.*

AUSTRIANS USING AN ACID-THROWING APPARATUS.

About the same time as the German right wing reached Borkowitz on the Dvina, their centre had advanced up to Olai, half-way between Mitau and Riga, but was unable to advance any farther. The Petrograd correspondent of *The Times*, summing up on October 28 the results of a fortnight of the most desperate efforts on the part of the Germans, denied that the German offensive had achieved any marked success or threatening Riga. They now stood on a front of about 50 miles, extending from the shores of the Gulf by Schmarden, Kalnsem, Olai, Plakanen, to the Dvina opposite the island of Dalen. The sector of that line nearest to the Dvina was that between Dalen and Plakanen being distant 10 or 11 miles, most of the German front receded from Riga to a distance of from 17 to 27 miles.

On October 31 the German autumn offensive against Riga entered on its last stage. The main interest during the first half of November centred round the attempts to break through in the Shlock region, between Lakes Kanger and Babit and the sea. According to reliable estimates the enemy had concentrated two or three army corps in the maritime section, and had brought up heavy artillery, conveyed to Libau by sea, and from there by powerful tractors. The German offensive began on October 31 with attacks near Kemmern and Tchin, at the western extremity of Lake Babit. The fighting continued for several days, spreading to Raggasem at the north-eastern end of Lake Kanger. As the battle developed it began slowly to turn to the advantage of our Allies. On November 7 the Russians succeeded in advancing between Shlock and Lake Babit, and also south of the lake. On the next day they reoccupied the district east of Kemmern, capturing "a large quantity of munitions and material which the Germans had abandoned during their precipitate retreat." The fighting culminated on November 10 in a battle in which the Russian fleet co-operated effectively with the land batteries. According to a description given by M. Ksiunin, correspondent of the *Novoe Vremya*, the artillery preparation began in the morning, and the enemy's positions were drenched with a rain of shells. Thereupon the Germans attempted to assume the offensive, but were instantly beaten back by a counter move of our Allies. One of the Russian units took the enemy in the rear, subjecting him to a cross-fire from rifles and maxims.

In one of the trenches the Germans displayed the white flag and held up their hands, but the Russians, taught by bitter experience, were too wary to be caught by this transparent

* The Russian official *communiqué* of November 15 states that during the preceding month the Russian troops had taken prisoners 674 officers and 49,200 men, both Austrians and Germans, and had captured 21 guns, 118 machine-guns, 18 trench mortars and three searchlights. A large proportion of that haul was, of course, made during the fighting on the Styr and Strypa.

RUSSIANS PLACING A SEARCHLIGHT IN POSITION.

After the apparatus which is brought up by horses to the position it is to occupy, the searchlight is elevated and connected with the battery.

device, and not a man or a hostile company survived.

The Russian advance was attended by incredible difficulties, the troops going forward amid thawing snow in the swollen marshes, and with a German maxim posted on every mound and elevation. The Russians entrenched overnight before Kemmern, and early the following day the advance was resumed, the men being obliged in many places to wade waist deep in icy water.

The Fleet continued to render splendid sup-

THE FATE OF A VILLAGE BETWEEN THE OPPOSING ARMIES.

port, and its shells, bursting far into the enemy's dispositions, blew up his trenches, dismantled his batteries, and cut off his connexion with his reserves. At length the enemy, unable to stand this punishment any longer, fled in disorder, and the Russians surged into Kemmern. Pausing merely long enough to take prisoners, they pressed on farther.

The eleven days of almost uninterrupted fighting resulted in a German defeat, and all attempt at an advance against Riga along the sea was given up for the present. In fact, at a few places our Allies continued to drive back the enemy; they gained complete control of Lake Babit, and achieved considerable progress on the shores of Lake Kanger, which is about 25 miles west of Riga. The Petrograd official *communiqué* of November 24 mentions a further Russian advance in the district west of that lake.

Isolated attacks in the neighbourhood of the farm of Bersemünde, opposite the islet of Dalen, were, late in November, the last flickerings of the German offensive against the line of the Dvina. The complete failure of that offensive is in certain respects comparable with the defeat which the Germans had suffered on the Bzura-Rawka line in the last days of January, 1915. It proved once more that the Russians were as fighters more than equal to their opponents, and that the Germans had little chance of breaking through their lines when the Russian troops received sufficient support from their artillery and did not suffer from a shortage of ammunition.

THE STYR, FROM KOLKI TO RAFALOVKA.

The troops of General Ivanoff, in their dashing counter-offensive on the middle Styr, had re-entered the town of Lutsk on September 23, taking prisoners eighty officers and about 4,000 men. The capture of that bridgehead by our Allies was a bold and successful stroke, but it would hardly have been advisable for them to try to maintain the advanced position which they won in the big bend of the river. Whilst the Austro-German forces north-east of Lutsk remained in possession of the left bank of the Styr in the region of Kolki, and south-east of Lutsk held Dubno and the left of the Ikva, the intervening district would have formed for our Allies a dangerous salient. They voluntarily abandoned it, and even the enemy had no elaborate tales to tell about the extraordinary feats of his proverbial heroes. "Yesterday," says the Vienna *communiqué* of September 27, "the enemy evacuated the positions north-west of Dubno, and in the Styr sector near Lutsk fell back in an easterly direction." It was on a straight front extending from Rafalovka, Tchartorysk and Kolki to the Ikva south of Dubno, that the Russians decided to meet the new offensive by which the enemy planned to complete his advance in the southern area of the Eastern theatre of war.

The first Austro-German offensive against Rovno, in the beginning of September, took the form of a concentric attack which followed mainly the two railway lines: from the north-west it proceeded from the direction of Kovel, and from the south-west along the Brody-Dubno-Rovno railway. Its failure resulted in the adoption of a slightly different strategic plan. Having received fresh reinforcements, Linsingen in the beginning of October concentrated his main forces for an advance on Sarny, the junction of the Kovel-Kieff and the

Vilna-Rovno railways. Baranovitchy, the northern terminus of the portion of the line which crosses the Pripet Marshes, was already in the hands of the Germans. Could they have established themselves also at Sarny and obtained a lateral connexion with the armies in the northern area, the position of our Allies round Rovno would have become untenable. They would have found themselves outflanked from the north, and the strong defences of Rovno would have had to be abandoned practically without fighting. The German attempt at an outflanking movement from the north was, moreover, accompanied by a new battle in the south, fought on the now historic fields of Novo-Alexinets and on the edges of the Podolian high plateau over the Strypa.

In the neighbourhood of Sokal, some 23 miles north of Lutsk, the River Styr approaches within only a few miles of the River Stochod, another tributary of the Pripet. The space between them is filled by a marshy depression which extends from south-east to north-west, and follows the right bank of the Stochod almost down to the point at which the Kovel-Sarny railway crosses that river. Near Sokal the Styr changes its course and assumes a predominantly easterly or north-easterly direction till it is joined by the River Kormin, about three miles east of Tchartorysk. It then turns to the north-west, forming a big bend between the Komaroff-Tchartorysk-Mayunitche road and the Kovel-Sarny railway. On the line of Polonne (the point at which the Kovel-Sarny railway crosses the Styr) the distance between the Styr and the River Stochod amounts to about thirty miles. For a few more miles north of the railway line the Styr traverses fairly high ground, then it enters again a swampy depression which links up with the big marshes of the Pripet. Between Kolki and Rafalovka, on a stretch of about twenty miles, the absence of marshes along the Styr renders conditions favourable for an offensive. Moreover, the concentration within that region of roads and railways, which naturally seek higher ground and easy river crossings, marks it out for a modern battlefield. It became the main theatre of the fighting on the Styr during the autumn of 1915.

For almost two months lasted the desperate battle on the Middle Styr, in which the Austrian and German forces under General von Linsingen met the Russian troops of General Brussiloff—the same who as commander of the

AUSTRIAN PRECAUTION AGAINST CHOLERA.
Distilling drinking water.

RUSSIAN ARTILLERY GOING INTO ACTION.

Eighth Army had, in the summer of 1915, carried out the skillful retreat from the Central Carpathians by Lvoff to Volhynia. Two separate areas can be distinguished on the battlefield round Tchartorysk, which formed the central and most essential part of the Styr line. The northern part of the lines centred round the Kovel-Sarny railway. The high-road which runs through Rafalovka formed its northern limit (though minor engagements took place also beyond it); in the south it was enclosed by the marshy course of the Okonka, a small left-hand tributary of the Styr, which joins its valley south-west of the town of Tchartorysk, forming several small islands and spreading out into a wide marsh. The town of Tchartorysk lies entirely within the northern sector. The second area extended south of Tchartorysk, and north and east of Kolki, between the River Styr and its right-hand tributary Kormin. The Kolki-Garaymovka road formed its approximate southern limit. These two distinct areas were usually referred to in the official *communiqués* by the chief towns as the districts of Tchartorysk and Kolki, which names may be kept as the most convenient descriptions.

The battle of the Styr began on September 27 with a German offensive in the southern area. Having crossed the river at Kolki, the enemy spread out to the east. Three days later his advance was, however, stopped on the line Novoselki - Kulikovitche - Koshishtche - Tchernish. Then for weeks the fighting continued to oscillate east and west of that line. Attacks and counter-attacks followed on one another with that almost monotonous regularity which is characteristic of regular trench-warfare. The bare statements of small advancements and retirements, as given by the official reports, devoid as they are of all dramatic, human detail, are dry bones to the reader. Yet they contain the essential summary of big and important operations. The entries taken—*e.g.*, from the Russian *communiqués* of October 6–11, and relating to the district of Kolki, may serve as an illustration:—October 6: "South-west of Tchartorysk the enemy was thrown back towards the village of Novoselki, leaving in our hands some 150 prisoners and a quick-firing gun. In the region of the villages of Krasnovola and Koshishtche we have had several conflicts with the enemy, who was progressing towards the east."

October 8: "By an energetic attack . . . our troops, notwithstanding a violent hail from quick-firing guns and repeated counter-attacks by the enemy, occupied his positions east of Milashoff . . . and carried by assault the village of Tchernish."

October 10: "Fighting continues near Milashoff. . . ."

October 11: " . . . our troops, supported by artillery fire, occupied the eastern side of the village of Tchernish . . . with very slight losses."

RUSSIAN ARTILLERY STARTING FOR THE BATTLEFIELD.
Huge horse-teams hauling big guns through the snow.

The same names continue repeating themselves in the Kolki district to the very end of the battle of the Styr—a testimonial to the magnificent endurance of the Russian defenders. By holding out in that sector they covered, against an outflanking movement from the north, the district of Rovno, and especially its outposts round Derazno, and also enabled the adjacent forces in the district of Tchartorysk to meet by a counter-offensive the impending German attack along the Kovel-Sarny railway.

The Russian advance in the northern sector began on October 3. "Our troops," says the Petrograd *communiqué* of October 4, "crossed successfully the Styr near Polonne and drove the enemy from the village of Tsminy. We made an equally successful crossing near the village of Kozlintse, above Tchartorysk." On the same day our Allies took the village of Kostienovka, on the Rafalovka high-road, and the village of Sobieshtchitse to the north of it, capturing two quick-firing guns and over 200 men. During the next three days the Russian troops reached the Optova-Voltchek-Lisova-Budka line, about 6 miles west of the Styr. Then followed a fortnight of obstinate fighting on both sides of the River Okonka, the border line between the two areas : the Germanic forces had advanced in the Kolki district, our Allies had made good their counter-offensive west of the Rafalovka-Tchartorysk. Each side was now threatening to outflank the other ; this state of unsafe balance could not continue and a decisive action was imminent. At first the Austro-German troops succeeded in driving back our Allies. Having concentrated about three army corps in the district of Tchartorysk, they pressed back the Russian forces and captured the town of Tchartorysk ; they thereby rendered necessary a retreat towards the Styr, also farther north, west of Rafalovka.

On October 17 came the Russian counter-stroke. In the north our Allies recaptured on that day the villages of Sobieshtchitse and Podtcherevitche, taking over 1,500 prisoners. South of the Okonka they occupied the village of Novoselki and its bridgehead on the Styr, capturing two whole companies of the 41st German Infantry Regiment, with their commanders. "Our troops, who captured yesterday 50 officers and 1,900 soldiers," sums up the Petrograd *communiqué*, "also took 6 machine-guns and a large quantity of arms and munitions abandoned by the enemy, while they themselves lost only one officer and 50 men."

The success of October 17 was followed up by a new advance on the next day. The town of Tchartorysk was carried by a sudden attack. "Turning simultaneously the flanks of the Germans operating in this district," says the Russian report of October 19, "we captured over 700 soldiers of the 1st Kronprinz Grenadier Regiment, with 28 officers, including the commander of the 3rd Battalion." The German forces fell back beyond the villages of Budka and Rudka. During the next few days the Russians extended their hold on the western bank of the Styr up to Komaroff. The situation of the German forces, which were now daily losing thousands of men, was becoming precarious, and fresh reinforcements had to be hurried up to the front. About October 25 the Austro-German forces assumed a counter-offensive on the Lisova-Budka line and round Komaroff. During the following week every day each side reported heavy fighting and big captures of prisoners. Our Allies had to fall back before overwhelming numbers. Then in turn, on receiving reinforcements, they again advanced. "We broke the enemy's lines south-east of the village of Budka," says the Russian *communiqué* of November 10, "and during the pursuit of the retreating enemy our troops occupied this village, as well as the forests to the south and north. Towards midday we made prisoners 50 officers and over 2,000 men, of whom half were Germans. We took about 20 machine-guns." During the next few days, however, the Russians were again compelled to retire. The enemy reports of November 15 announced the capture of the western bank of the Styr, including the town of Tchartorysk. "Four weeks' tenacious and glorious fighting for Tchartorysk has caused the retreat of the Russians to their original positions," was the triumphant claim of the Austrians, as if they and their Allies had never intended to advance beyond the Styr. Even so, their joy was short-lived. "Left of the Styr," says the Petrograd *communiqué* of November 20, "the enemy was unable to hold the ground which he occupied, and on November 19 we reoccupied the town of Tchartorysk and the village of Kozlintse, on the left bank of the Styr below Tchartorysk."

Meantime the advanced autumn was rendering operations more difficult and, when, the enforced lull set in, the Austro-Germans forces still always stood on the western bank of the Styr, far away both from Sarny and Rovno.

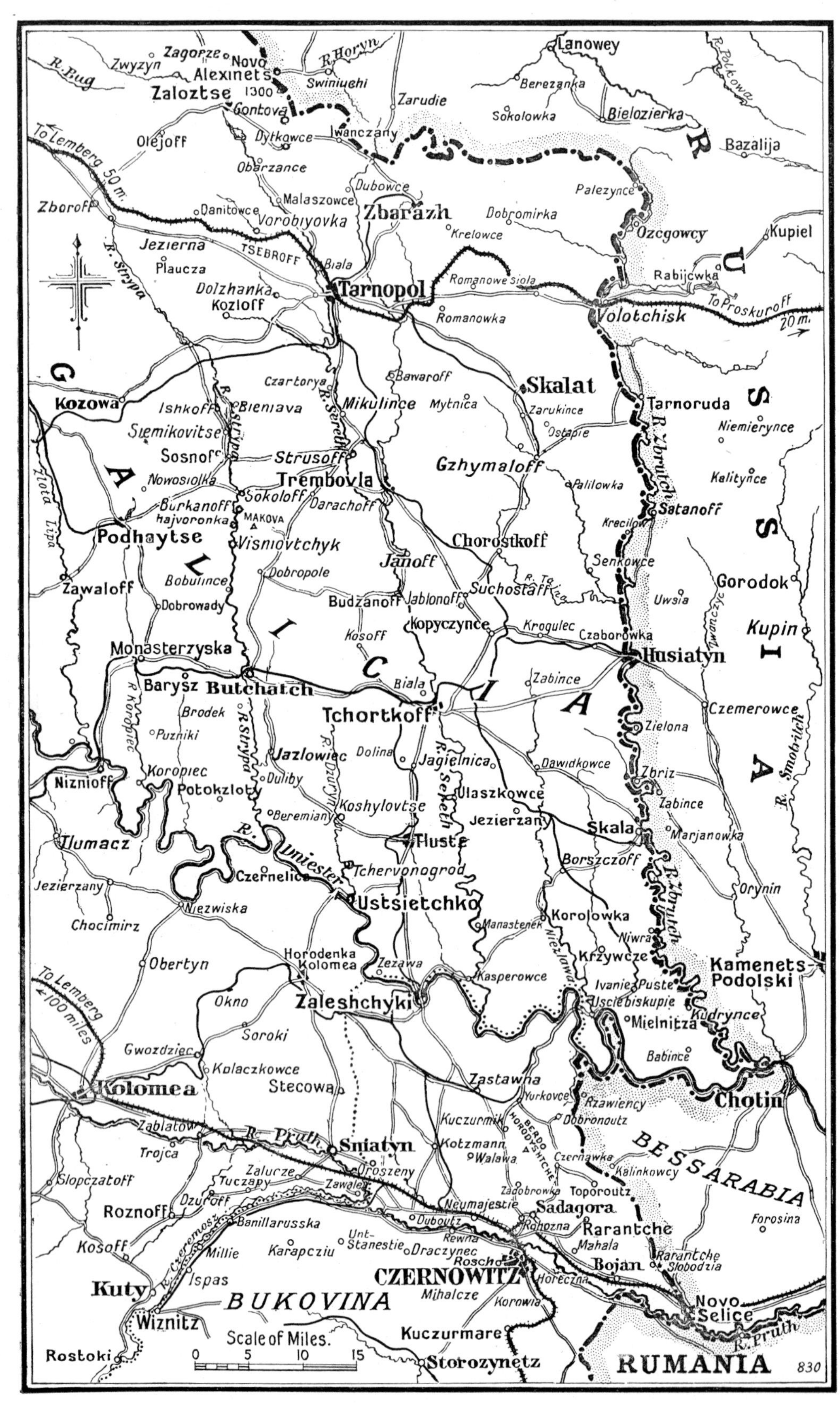

THE FIGHTING ON THE STRYPA.

The southern flank of the Russian positions in Volhynia was held by the troops under Generals Shcherbatoff and Leshitsky. Their line extended from the Ikva above Dubno, across the upper reaches of the Sereth, along the range of heights on the eastern bank of the Strypa, down to the Dniester. Up to a few miles east of Zaleshchyki the northern bank of the Dniester was in the hands of the enemy. In the country between the Dniester and the Pruth the positions extended in the autumn of 1915 close to the frontier of Bessarabia and the Bukovina.

At the northern end the district of Novo-Alexinets formed the key to the positions. It lies near the sources of the Ikva, Horyn and the Sereth. The rivers surround it from three sides and, though as yet small streams, they form serious tactical obstacles as their courses are lined with wide marshes which, at many points, deepen into ponds and small lakes. Round Novo-Alexinets, between the lake of Zaloztse on the Sereth and the upper courses of the Horyn and Ikva, rises a range of thickly wooded heights about 1,300 feet high. The marshy valley of the Sereth east of these hills is almost a mile wide. South of Zaloztse special importance attached to the sector between Vorobiyovka and Dolzhanka. It formed the gate—or, perhaps, rather the bridge, being a strip of elevated ground between two deep depressions—to Tarnopol, the chief centre of roads and railways in Northern Podolia. The hard contested heights of Tsebroff form part of that ridge; their importance lay in that they dominate the road and railway leading from Lvoff by Zlochoff and Zboroff to Tarnopol.

From the Zboroff-Tarnopol railway in the north to the Dniester in the south, between the Stryра and the Sereth, lies the part of the Podolian high plateau which, at the southern end of the Eastern front, was throughout the autumn of 1915 the scene of the most important fighting. The valleys of the parallel left-hand tributaries of the Dniester cut the Podolian plateau into a series of square segments. The tableland between the Strypa and the Sereth forms a slightly inclined plane rising towards the west and the south. Most of it is a perfectly open high plateau, with hardly any forests, not even trees, except on the hills which line the river-valleys in the northern part, and, in the south, in the neighbourhood of the cañons. The drainage of a large part of that high plateau is rather poor and its depressions—though anyhow they still exceed as a rule the 1,000 feet contour-line—tend to be marshy. The geological structure of the country is, however, such that once the river has cut down to the sub-strata of sandstone the character of its bed and banks undergoes a complete transformation. The wide, marshy valleys, with their strings of little lakes, change into narrow cañons, of which the banks descend either in terraces or in straight, steep inclines; in the local language the slope of a cañon is usually called by the expressive description of "wall." These cañons are the characteristic feature of the Dniester belt. Its bigger tributaries naturally begin to form them farther north than the smaller brooks; thus, *e.g.*, in the

IN THE TRENCHES.
Russian machine gun at work.

case of the Strypa the change sets in round Sokoloff (between Siemikovitse and Burkanoff), in the case of the Dzhuryn not until a few miles above Koshylovtse. The border-line between the two types of river-valley is usually of special tactical importance: marshes and ponds no longer impede an advance, but the cañon has not yet reached the depth, nor are its banks as yet sufficiently precipitous, to form a serious natural obstacle to military movements.

It was the peculiar configuration of the river banks which marked out the neighbourhood of Siemikovitse and Burkanoff for the battle-ground of the Middle Strypa. As a matter of fact, Siemikovitse lies still within what might be called the marshy zone. North of it the Strypa widens out into a lake about four miles long and more than half a mile wide. But

POISON-GAS FROM A HILL
Russian soldiers sheltering behind their

whereas most of the small lakes in that region are surrounded by marshes covered with rushes, the banks of the southern end of the Ishkoff Lake rise more suddenly, and the access to the water presents no difficulties. For over a mile after leaving the lake the Strypa cuts a narrow course between fairly high, though not steep, banks. At this point the Tarnopol-Podhaytse road crosses the river, and this is undoubtedly its easiest crossing within the northern area. The main disadvantage, from the point of view of military operations, lies, however, in the narrowness of the space afforded to them, for between Siemikovitse and Sokoloff the river widens out again into swamps which are practically impassable, especially in autumn. Below Sokoff begins the cañon of the Strypa and here, inside big river loops, surrounded by forest, lies the village of Burkanoff and the hamlet of Hajvoronka, after Siemikovitse the most important battlefield on the Strypa. The cañon which, 15 miles farther south, below Butchatch, attains a depth of about 400 feet, is as yet hardly 150 feet deep. The favourable character of the river crossings naturally finds its counterpart in the system of roads: on a stretch of about five miles between Sokoloff and Visniovtchyk three roads approach the Strypa from the east, whilst in the next ten miles not a single one leads across it.

During the fortnight, September 27 to October 11, smaller engagements were of almost daily occurrence in the district of the Tsebroff heights and along the Strypa front. Each side was testing the strength of the other's positions and preparing to strike a blow. The Germans were planning one from the direction of Butchatch, but our Allies got in theirs first, and after short preliminary fighting scored a decisive success in the sector Burkanoff-Hajvoronka, and carried also the Makova Height, a few miles south-east of Burkanoff; being one of the few high hills in an almost complete plain, it dominates a large part of the ground between the Strypa and the Strusoff-Darachoff-Butchatch road. "Following up the success gained the previous day," says the Petrograd *communiqué* of October 12, "our troops forced the enemy's last line of defence and occupied two rows of trenches. They also stormed a work and farm on a height east of the village of Hajvoronka.

"This position constituted a strong fort with a whole system of trenches covered in and connected by a corridor with loopholes protected by steel plates. Round the works where placed two rows of barbed wire. In the redoubt 252 men surrendered and we captured a gun and three machine-guns. In an attempt to retake the lost work the enemy launched a counter-attack with large forces, but was repulsed.

"By a fresh effort in the same region as the village of Hajvoronka we forced the enemy's line on Mount Makova, where we captured a whole Austrian battalion.

SIDE TUNNEL IN BUKOVINA.
steel shields until the gas-cloud passes.

"As a result of the fighting in the whole of this sector the enemy was completely defeated and began to retire in disorder beyond the Strypa. Our troops pursued him closely and entered the village of Hajvoronka by a bridge which was on fire. Towards the evening we crossed the Strypa.

"Our cavalry, which had been thrown forward to break up the enemy's force, sabred many and captured a convoy. Our trophies this day consisted of 60 officers and over 2,000 men taken prisoners, four guns, and 10 machine guns."

On the next day our Allies enlarged their gains on the Strypa by capturing Visniovtchyk, a village a few miles south of Burkanoff. Meantime, the fighting round Hajvoronka continued with undiminished violence. The armies in Podolia included some of the finest Russian cavalry divisions which, even under the extraordinarily difficult conditions of trench warfare, frequently managed to carry out successful charges against the enemy lines. "A detachment of our cavalry," says the Russian report of October 13, "left the village of Hajvoronka without being perceived and, deploying rapidly along the front on horseback, charged the enemy's lines. With a courage full of self-sacrifice the cavalry crossed three lines of the entrenched enemy, putting him to the sabre. The enemy after some irregular firing took to flight."

Meantime, General von Bothmer was hurrying up reinforcements, throwing some of his best German troops into the fighting. On October 13 the enemy delivered four bayonet attacks against the Russian trenches round Hajvoronka. Under the pressure of the fresh enemy forces, our Allies withdrew to the eastern bank of the Strypa, retaining, however, their gains round Burkanoff and on Mount Makova.

The next Russian stroke was delivered on October 21, in the district of Novo-Alexiniets. "By a powerful *coup de main*," says the Petrograd *communiqué* of October 22, "we carried yesterday part of the enemy's positions. Similarly we captured part of the enemy's positions in the region east of Lopushno, north of Novo-Alexiniets. During the day we captured in this fighting 148 officers and 7,500 prisoners, two howitzers, and a number of machine-guns." Even the Vienna official report of the same day acknowledged the Russian success, stating that the Austrian front had been withdrawn "before the pressure of superior forces on a length of three miles and to a depth of 1,000 paces." During the next few days a battle was fought of the kind which in trench warfare usually follows on changes in the line. At its close, about October 26, our Allies were still in possession of most of the newly-acquired ground.

On October 30 the Austrians assumed the offensive north of the Dniester. Holding the belt of forests and cañons on the left bank of

RUSSIAN MOTOR-CYCLISTS RESTING.
The soldier at the door of the Windmill is keeping guard.

the river between Butchatch and Zaleshchyki, they had a distinct tactical advantage in that region, and the initiative lay with them. Before the movement had time to develop it was stopped by a vigorous Russian counter-offensive which was opened on the following day in the sector of Siemikovitse. Seriously threatened from that quarter, the enemy had to relinquish for the time being all attempts at a flanking movement from the south. "After fierce bayonet fighting," says the Russian report of November 1, "our troops occupied the village of Siemikovitse. . . . The majority of the Germans defending the village were bayoneted and the others were captured." But the passage across the Strypa at Siemikovitse, between the lake and the marshes, was too narrow to admit a proper deployment of forces, and our Allies had, therefore, to undertake the much more hazardous attempt of crossing the lake in boats. This was successfully carried out during the night of October 31-November 1. "Landing during the night on the opposite bank," states the *communiqué* of November 2, "and breaking through several barbed wire entanglements, some of which were under water, our troops attacked the enemy, and dashing into his trenches bayoneted the majority of the Germans and Austrians defending them. We took about 400 prisoners.

"The fighting continues on the Strypa near the village of Siemikovitse, at the southern extremity of Lake Ishkoff. On November 1 our troops carried by assault the village of Bakovice, south of Siemikovitse, and the forest of Bakovice.

"It has now been established that in the fighting on October 31 and November 1 on the Strypa we captured altogether 80 officers and 3,500 German and Austrian soldiers."

This was, however, only the beginning of the fighting at Siemikovitse, one of the most peculiar battles fought in the war; forces amounting on either side to nearly an army corps, were contesting a front about one mile and a half wide, whilst batteries of all calibres were developing regular hurricanes of fire from the opposite banks of the lake and of the marshes which intervened between the two armies north and south of the causeway of Siemikovitse. South-west of the village of Siemikovitse and north of Sosnoff, between the swamps of Bicniava and the marshy valley of a small brook which joins the Strypa below Sosnoff, rises a ridge, about 1,200 feet high. Making use of its broken ground and of the cover which it affords, the enemy attempted on November 2 an attack against the village of Siemikovitse. At first he succeeded in penetrating the Russian front, but a

Russian counter-offensive cut off the advanced body which had entered the village. Five thousand men, Germans and Austrians, were taken prisoners. During the following days also the Austrian and German reports claimed considerable hauls of prisoners. "Fighting by General Bothmer's troops in and near Siemikovitse continued yesterday," reads the Berlin *communiqué* of November 4. "The number of prisoners captured in the village fighting was increased to 3,000." Considering the narrow space within which the battle was fought, and the many dangers of being cut off from all possibility of retreat by the lake and the marshes, it seems but natural that each side should have suffered heavy losses in prisoners.

During the next few days the enemy succeeded in regaining most of the ground on the western bank of the Strypa. Then a lull set in in the fighting. It was again broken towards the end of the month, when the Austrians attempted to regain a foothold also on the eastern side of the river. By a skilful counter-attack the Russians managed to drive them back and to pin their retreating columns to the river. A fearful struggle ensued; in preference to surrendering, the Austrians threw themselves into the water, where they were either drowned or perished by the fire of the Russian batteries. Russian military correspondents paid a generous tribute to that piece of stoicism, characteristic of the greatly improved *moral* of the Austrians in Galicia in comparison with the troops engaged at the beginning of the war. "Whereas a year ago flight and surrender were common phenomena in the ranks of the Austrian Army," wrote in December, 1915, *The Times* correspondent from Petrograd, summing up Russian expert opinion, "to-day the Austrians flee far less frequently and surrender with the utmost reluctance."

Toward the end of November a complete lull in the fighting set in along the entire Eastern front; the opposing forces were still facing one another practically on the same lines which they had held two months earlier, at the conclusion of the Russian retreat from Vilna. The German plan of gaining a front in the East which, owing to superiority of communications and the possession of a lateral connection across the Marshes of the Pripet, could have been held by forces very much inferior to those of the attacking side, had failed completely. On the Dvina and everywhere south of the Marshes, our Allies maintained themselves in positions in which they had the use of equal, if not superior, systems of roads and railways. The problem of initiative for the future was far from having been solved in the way in which the Germans had wished and expected to see it done. The German offensive in the summer of 1914 was to have "settled" for good the war in the West.

AN AMBUSH.
Russians skirmishing in a village in Galicia.

RUSSIANS IN THE TRENCHES. [" The Times Photograph."

Commanding Officer directing operations from observation point in the front line.

It broke down at the very gates of Paris, in the battle of the Marne. The campaign of 1915 was to have "knocked out" Russia. After a successful advance of five months, during which, with comparatively very few reverses, the Austro-German armies had been progressing on the average by about two miles a day, their offensive broke down between 10 and 15 miles in front of Riga and Dvinsk, of Rovno and Tarnopol. As it was the crust of the western area and of its system of defence remained in the hands of our Allies. Gradual in time, spread out over a front of many hundreds of miles, the final breakdown of the Austro-German offensive in the East failed to strike the imagination of the public, as had the dramatic collapse of their advance in France in the early days of the war, when every development was still followed with breathless attention. And yet the two events are comparable in intrinsic value. In either case the Germans had conquered by their previous advance a country to exploit, to oppress, and to boast about at home and abroad; but in either case they failed to reduce their opponents to a state of strategical and military impotence. Their enemies came back, determined to reclaim the lost countries and provinces and to right the wrongs inflicted upon them.

In both cases the final failure seems to have been due in part to similar causes: an exaggerated idea of the results already achieved and an under-estimate of the remaining striking power of the enemy, led to a premature withdrawal of forces from the area in which a decisive victory had been nearly gained. In either case, that withdrawal of troops was an important, though by no means the only, cause of the final failure. In September, 1914, the Russian invasion of East Prussia brought about a transfer of forces from France to the East. In September, 1915, a very considerable number of troops was withdrawn from Russia to meet the Franco-British offensive at Loos and in the Champagne, and to co-operate with the Bulgarians in the Serbian campaign. The agreement with King Ferdinand had to be carried out and the Austro-German armies on the Russian front had to pay in failure part of its price.

About the middle of September the enemy forces in Russia were estimated at about 130 divisions. The following account given by the *Russky Invalid* may be taken as representing their strength, even after the first withdrawals had been made for the Serbian front: "Under the command of von Below, in the section Riga-Dvinsk-Svientsiany, 12 divisions, of which five are cavalry; under the command of Eichhorn, in the section Svientsiany-Vilna-Orany, 15 divisions, including three cavalry; in the section Orany-Slonim-Pinsk, 47 to 50 divisions under von Hindenburg; in the section Pinsk-Dubno-Brody-Tarnopol and Novo Selice 54 divisions, including 10 cavalry. Relatively the strongest is the Austro-German group of which 80 per cent. is German, distributed on the Orany-Slonim-Pinsk line, constituting the enemy's centre. The left wing from Grodno to Riga is solely German, even the right wing being 30 per cent. German." In October, 1915, only 50 out of the total of 170 German infantry divisions stood on the Russian front, whilst 110 were concentrated in the West and 10 were engaged in Serbia. In addition to the 50 German divisions, our Allies were faced by 40 Austro-Hungarian infantry divisions and some 23 Austro-German cavalry divisions, making a total of about 113 divisions. The difference of 17 divisions, *i.e.*, about 13 per cent. of the original strength, may seem small, but then the number of divisions is not the only factor by which the strength of the army is to be judged; one needs further to know to what strength the divisions were maintained, and there were many indications of the Austro-German command allowing in the autumn of 1915 its effectives on the Eastern front to fall far below the normal level. Finally, it must be remembered that it is the marginal force which makes the offensive strength of an army; on a front of over 700 miles a very considerable number of troops must be kept all the time as a force of observation. Only that which is left over and above the number required for the defence of the static part of the front can be formed into a driving force and used as a battering ram against a chosen sector of the line.

During the lull in December, 1915, the Austro-German command strengthened again its effectives on the Russian front. The Serbian campaign had practically come to an end, and there was no immediate danger of a new Franco-British offensive in the West. The political situation in the Balkans continued uncertain, and as the Germans could not make up their mind to risk their prestige in an attack

THE GERMAN ADVANCE IN POLAND.
Distributing eatables captured from the Russians.

against Salonica, they hoped to keep up the spirits of their Allies and to intimidate neutrals by a coup in the so-called "political corner"—*i.e.*, on the Strypa, the Dniester, and in the Bukovina, where the southern end of the Eastern Front touches Rumania.

About the New Year of 1916 the best Russian military authorities estimated the hostile forces in the Eastern theatre of war at 120 infantry and 23 cavalry divisions, with corresponding artillery. The entire front, from the Gulf of Riga to the Rumanian border, was divided into four sections. The section from Tukkum to the Upper Niemen was under Hindenburg, thence to the Pripet was under Prince Leopold of Bavaria, thence to the Ikva under Linsingen, thence to Rumania was under the Archduke Frederick.

The group of armies under Hindenburg remained where it had stood at the beginning of autumn. After a brief summer campaign (it had not begun moving until after the Austrian defeat at Krasnik in the beginning of July) and after an exhibition of impotent goodwill on the Dvina, it settled down to a heroic rest, waiting for the armies in the south, composed mainly of Austro-Hungarian troops, to set the stone rolling again. In the centre, Prince Leopold of Bavaria continued with his "Sancho," General von Woyrsch, an ever more legendary existence.*

The main concentration of forces took place south of the Pripet Marshes. Some 800,000 men, including six or seven German army corps —*i.e.*, 250,000 to 300,000—were gathered between the mouth of the Stochod and the Rumanian frontier. On the extreme left flank, the German army of General von Linsingen was transferred into the marsh district, whilst the line of the Styr was handed over to the Fourth Austro-Hungarian Army under Archduke Joseph Ferdinand (this army now included all the Polish Legions, gathered for the first time into one army corps). In winter, whilst the ground was frozen, the conditions in the marshes were, of course, much more favourable than they had been in autumn, when that district had been assigned to the Austro-Hungarian and Polish troops; on the other hand, the districts of Rafalovka and Tchartorysk had proved rather "exposed," and a resumption of fighting on the Styr was soon to be expected. Next to the Army of Archduke Joseph Ferdinand stood the First Austro-Hungarian Army under General von Puhallo. The front extending from the Ikva to the Upper Strypa was held by the Second Austro-Hungarian Army under General von Boehm-Ermolli. On the Middle Strypa stood the Army of Count Bothmer, composed largely of German troops. The line of the Dniester and the Bukovina was held by the Sixth Austro-Hungarian Army under General von Pflanzer-Baltin; it had been fighting in that corner ever since the early spring of 1915.

On December 23 fighting was resumed at the southern end of the Eastern front. This time our Allies were, in appearance, the attacking side. In reality the so-called Russian offensive in Bessarabia, to the "failure" of which the enemy Press devoted endless columns, was merely a preventive move, forestalling a planned enemy advance from the Bukovina. Mr. V. Chelnokoff, Mayor of Moscow, who visited the Russian Headquarters towards the end of January, 1916, is reported to have said that the Russian Staff was completely satisfied with its results; the blow which had been prepared against the Russian positions had been successfully anticipated. Moreover, there may have been still another reason for Russia's almost demonstrative display of activity in Bessarabia. For months news had been current about the massing of troops in Southern Russia; about the middle of February, 1916, the fall of Erzerum made it clear to the world at large for which front at least considerable portions of that army had been meant. An offensive on the Bessarabian frontier, undertaken towards the end of December, was naturally of the nature to distract the attention of the enemy and to cover up the preparations for the master-blow which was to come from the Caucasus.

The most natural line for a Russian offensive, because the most threatening for the enemy, led through the "gap" between the Dniester and the Pruth, where an advance to a fairly considerable depth could be effected on a limited front, as the "belt of the Dniester" affords sufficient flank-cover from the north. It is, however, only the absence of big rivers across that region which gives it on the map

* It is interesting to mark that Prince Leopold, who at his first appearance on the Warsaw "stage" in August, 1915, was introduced to the world as chief of a group of armies, in a "birthday article," devoted to him by the *Neue Freie Presse* in February, 1916, was referred to merely as commander of the Ninth German Army. Some German political schemes concerning Poland had failed, and Prince Leopold was the loser.

BETWEEN TWO FIRES.

Russian cavalry dashing through a burning village, being fired on by German infantry.

the appearance of a "gap." In reality it is barred by a range of hills called the Berdo Horodyshtche, covered with fine oak forests. The Yurkovce-Sadagora-Mahala high road marks approximately the western and southern limit of the wooded hills, which rise from 300 to 800 feet above the level of the wide open fields on their western edge, and of the Pruth valley round Czernowitz. East of Mahala, in the valley of the River Hukeu, the hills and forests recede to the north, and for some distance their border faces to the east ; the

MOTOR TRANSPORT.
Motor wagons receiving final adjustment.
Lower picture: In a repairing shop.

villages of Rarantche and Toporoutz lie at their foot. A few miles north-east of Toporoutz the line between forest and plain runs again due east; on a large-scale map it can be distinguished by an almost continuous chain of small villages, huddled at the foot of the hills.

The following description was given of the two villages of Toporoutz and Rarantche by an eye-witness who visited them soon after the battle: "Toporoutz is a big village, and lies at the foot of a very steep hill. Its huts are burnt down. Shrapnel set fire to them. . . . Yet in the middle of the battle the peasant-folk continued to go about their work, until they had to be removed, as unnecessary casualties were becoming too frequent. . . . Next to Toporoutz lies Rarantche, covered by a height with two small forests. Their trees must be lovely in spring-time, but all that is left of them now are trunks and branches broken by gun-fire. Across the hill run the parallel lines of the opposite trenches. Since September, 1914, that hill has seen many a battle, but none as desperate as the last. . . . Here, as elsewhere, were to be found all the newest technical inventions of military art: electrified wires, mine fields, barbed wire, wolves' holes. (In what form has modern development in these years approached far-off, secluded lands !)

"Rarantche is a big village, in certain ways a town. It has three churches; of these, the Greek-Orthodox church is a big stone building, the Roman Catholic church is small. A few huts were burnt down, a few civilians were killed. In the cemetery rest soldiers of all nationalities—it has again grown much larger. . . ."

The progress of the battle on that front can hardly be described to one who does not know the country except in the vague and obscure terms of the official reports mentioning the taking of nameless trenches, or in the baro figures expressing the numbers of captured prisoners. The broken ground offered scope for skilful manœuvring. Enfilading fire from well-placed batteries, sapping, mining—all these devices were used. The much-contested ridge between the two villages was carried by our Allies. Important heights dominating the approach to Czernowitz were captured. The general position of the Russian troops can be said to have been considerably improved. Besides that one could merely tell the tale of the heroic deeds, sufferings and deaths of Tcherkiss fighters from the Caucasus, of patient Russian moujiks, of Slav peasants from Moravia and Croatia dressed in Austro-Hungarian uniforms, and of Magyars and Germans, the master races of the Hapsburg Monarchy.

Whilst the Russians were storming the hills on the Bukovina frontier a fresh struggle was raging on the old battlefields on the Styr and the Strypa. Tchartorysk and Kolki became again the centres of fierce fighting, which extended this time also farther south to Olyka, on the Rovno-Kovel railway line. Once more our Allies established themselves on the Miedviezhe Hills, and once more the enemy tried to counter their advance by an offensive in the Kolki district. In short, the alternate advances and retirements, the crossings and recrossings, the flanking movements and countering attacks, which in the autumn of 1915 received the grim and gruesome nickname of the "Polesie* Quadrille" repeated themselves in January, 1916. Similarly the *danse macabre* was resumed in the districts of Tsebroff, Burkanoff and Butchach—and about

* Polesie is the popular name given to the Pripet basin.

WOUNDED ON A RAILWAY SIDING.

On the left is a wounded Russian having his wounds dressed, while the troops who are on their way to the fighting-line look on with sympathy. On the right is a wounded German.

A SCREEN OF FIRE ALONG THE RUSSIAN FRONT.

The Enemy attempts to stop the Russian advance.

the middle of January, at the end of the so-called New Year's battle, both sides stood on the Styr and Strypa practically in the same positions as they had held at its beginning. Just one more chapter had been added to the history of stationary trench warfare. Again the Austro-German Headquarters and their Press noisily proclaimed to the world the "breakdown of the Russian offensive," although there was nothing to indicate that on the Styr and Strypa either side was more on the offensive than the other, or that either side contemplated an offensive on a considerable scale in the middle of winter. The losses on both sides were considerable, and probably more or less even. Their sum total was not far from 150,000.

The signal Russian success at Ustsietchko on the Dniester, on February 9, may be taken as the close of the winter battle in Galicia. By the capture of that important bridgehead—in fact, the most important between Nizhnioff and Zaleshchyki—our Allies opened for themselves a door into the much-contested region of Kolomea. Considering the merely preparatory character of the winter fighting, the capture of Ustsietchko can be described as an achievement of considerable strategic significance.

If a success from the strategic point of view, it was a real feat from that of tactics. The town of Ustsietchko lies in the cañon of the Dniester, at its junction with the Dzhuryn. The cañon is at that point 500 to 600 feet deep. The Dzhuryn meets the Dniester at a sharp angle. The Tluste-Horodenka road crosses the Dzhuryn in the town of Ustsietchko and then, before crossing the Dniester, runs for almost half a mile up that river—*i.e.*, along the southern arm of the angle formed by the two rivers. This circumstance proved of the greatest tactical importance: the bridgehead of Ustsietchko lies at the base of the angle formed by the Dzhuryn and the Dniester, and the Austrians held the mountain and the forest which intervene between Tchervonogrod * and the *bridgehead* of Ustsietchko. In other words, the Russians were not approaching the Dniester and the bridgehead across a plain, but had to negotiate the cañon of the Dzhuryn before they got within reach of their objective. To the fortress which the Austrians had established on the ridge intervening between the two cañons *The Times* correspondent from Petrograd, who visited the battlefield, applied the very happy description of "a miniature Gibraltar." Whoever knows the wild, ragged, rocky sides of the winding Podolian cañons, with their ravines, terraces and galleries, will easily appreciate the meaning of his comparison, and also the opportunities which Nature offered here to the technical art of the Austrian commanders, and the difficulties which our Allies had to overcome. The blow which their achievement meant to the Austrians is best shown in the flat denial of the capture of Ustsietchko which was issued from Vienna. But a few days later the news came of further fighting, this time at Michaltche, on the south-western side of the Dniester, thus clearly illustrating the value of Austrian *démentis*.

* Tchervonogrod (literally the "Red Town"), now a mere village, is one of the oldest historic townships of Eastern Europe. In the ninth century it was the seat of Ruthenian princes; it is known in mediæval chronicles as the *castrum rubrum*. From that town the whole country got the name of "Red Russia." A truly princely palace, situated deep in the cañon of the Dzhuryn, shows that also in more recent times it has had its great days.

Everybody felt at the time that these small, almost insignificant, moves, which the average student of the campaign could hardly have marked on his map, were in reality the prelude to much greater events in a no longer distant future.

On January 2 the Tsar addressed a speech to the Knights of the Order of St. George; having thanked them for their valiant and self-sacrificing services, he concluded with the following sentences of truly historic importance: ". . . be assured that, as I said at the beginning of the war, I will not conclude peace until we have chased the last enemy from our territory, nor will I conclude such a peace except in full agreement with our Allies, to whom we are bound not by paper treaties, but by true friendship and blood."

A few days later General Polivanoff, Russian Minister of War, reviewed the military situation in an interview with the special correspondent of the *Journal* at Petrograd. He described the acute munitions crisis of 1915, and the way in which it was remedied, the building up of new industries in Russia and the employment of all national resources for the services of the army. Whilst the industrial mobilisation had thus been proceeding, new armies had been raised and trained. He summed up the position in the following sentences:

PAY DAY.

A Russian Paymaster and his assistants on the battlefield.

"Thanks to the mobilization of the great mass of men ordered some months ago and the doubling of the number of our depôts, we have now a permanent reserve of a million and a half of young recruits, which will permit us to feed the various units without sending to the front men with insufficient military training. Behind the four Allies there are the natural resources of the whole universe. Behind the Army of the Central Powers are exhaustion and shakiness. There is only one way to express our final success and that is in the words—the war will continue to the end."

CHAPTER CXI.

THE NAVY'S WORK IN 1915.

THE NAVY'S TASK AND THE LESSONS OF WAR—CHANGES AT THE ADMIRALTY IN 1915—LORD FISHER AND MR. CHURCHILL—MR. BALFOUR AS FIRST LORD—CONSTRUCTION POLICY—CONTROL OF THE NORTH SEA—PATROL WORK—DESTROYERS IN ACTION—THE METEOR'S EXPLOIT—WORK ON THE BELGIAN COAST—THE GERMAN SUBMARINE "BLOCKADE"—SUBMARINE WARFARE—BRITISH COUNTER-MEASURES—THE SUBMARINE MENACE "WELL IN HAND"—BRITISH BLOCKADE POLICY—OPERATIONS IN THE BALTIC—THE NAVY AND THE DARDANELLES—WORK IN THE ADRIATIC—THE NAVY AND THE PERSIAN GULF—THE CONQUEST OF GERMAN COLONIES.

THE part played by the Royal Navy during the last nine months of 1915 was not remarkable for dramatic incidents or decisive effect. No battle was fought on the grand scale, and no large offensive movements, apart from those necessitated by cooperation with the Allied military forces, and by the operations at the Dardanelles, were undertaken. No attempt was made by the Germans to bring about an engagement of the first magnitude, nor again to inveigle the Grand Fleet into a position of their own selection. The High Sea Fleet remained behind the protection of its barrier of submarines, mines, sand-banks, and land fortifications.

It was the intervention of the British Fleet that robbed Germany of the speedy victory upon which she had so confidently relied at the outbreak of war, and during 1915 the force under Sir John Jellicoe continued to assert an unchallenged, if only a conditional, command of the seas, and in a strategic sense to dominate the war. Behind its buckler, the ocean pathways were held, the enemy's sea trade paralysed, and the maritime communications secured from material interference and molestation. At the same time it exerted a strangle-hold upon the economic condition of Germany which, although it had not yet won the war, promised inevitably when drawn tighter to hasten its end victoriously for the Allies.

So far, the sea war had followed a normal and expected course. It was not surprising that after the action of January 24, when their battle-cruisers suffered discomfiture and loss, the High Sea Fleet should remain inactive. The disparity of his navy in numbers, in gun-power, and in efficiency, which had been so strikingly demonstrated, was alone sufficient to account for the decision of the Supreme War Lord not to accept the challenge to battle offered by the British Fleet. But while it was thought unwise to send the main fleet out for the purpose of engaging a superior force, the much-vaunted process of attrition, by which equality between the opposed navies was to be attained, had also completely come to naught. It was this failure, and that of the efforts by the raiding cruisers in the outer seas to destroy British commerce, which led to the adoption of an alternative scheme for starving England.

The distinctive features of the so-called submarine blockade were the sinking of passenger ships and traders without warning, and a general war upon mercantile traffic, in which neutrals as well as Allied vessels suffered. While in the use of the under-water boats to the extent of their opportunity the record of Germany's naval officers was characterised by skill and daring, their methods were marked

DODGING AN ENEMY SUBMARINE.
The zig-zag wake of a French torpedo boat in the Mediterranean.

by so little regard either for the dictates of humanity or the laws of warfare that their acts drew down upon them and their masters the reprobation of the world.

The performances of the submarines were, indeed, so startling and spectacular that there was some inclination to attach undue importance to this class of vessel. Its successes, however, were attained mainly by stealth and surprise, and not by reason of any inherent superiority as a fighting agent. Neither against warships nor in the raid against merchantmen did the submarine find it possible to accomplish any result of great military value. While there was serious loss of life, the effect of the destruction of a certain amount of useful shipping was altogether disproportionate to the effort employed. The British seamen, put upon their mettle to meet the novel menace, were not long before they devised measures of protection, and thus a truer estimate of the submarine as an instrument of naval warfare was obtained. With further development its value might be expected to increase, but it had so far proved itself no more than a useful adjunct to the battle fleet. Such lessons as could be drawn from the naval incidents of 1915 did little to modify opinion in regard to the types of vessel which should be represented in an effective navy. Nothing yet pointed to the extinction of the battleship and battle-cruiser as the principal representatives of naval power. The advantages of superiority in speed and armament received further demonstration in the scuffles between the lighter craft on outpost duties as well as in the more important actions between larger vessels.

Apart from the measures taken to counteract the activity of the submarine, the British Navy supplied the requisite support upon which the whole of the operations on sea and land depended. With the assistance of the fleets of the Allies the lines of communication with the various centres of military activity in the Mediterranean were kept open, and the reinforcement of the armies by men, stores, and every provision for their continued effectiveness was maintained. In earlier chapters the great tragedy at the Dardanelles, which began with the naval action on February 19 and continued until the concluding act upon which the curtain was dropped when the last British and French soldiers left Helles on January 10

1916, was set forth. Whatever may be the historian's verdict upon the "gamble" at the Dardanelles, the performances of the seamen and soldiers must redound to their imperishable honour. The conditions under which the sea engagements took place, the landing was made, and the withdrawal effected, were quite unexampled in the record of the world's wars, and never before had there been displayed greater endurance, heroism, and valour. France, Britain, and the Dominions have every reason to be proud of the achievements of their sons on the Gallipoli Peninsula. Throughout the operations, as Sir Ian Hamilton said in his dispatches, "the Royal Navy has been father and mother to the army. Not one of us but realizes how much he owes to Vice-Admiral de Robeck; to the warships, French and British; to the destroyers, mine-sweepers, picket boats, and to all their dauntless crews, who took no thought of themselves, but risked everything to give their soldier comrades a fair run in at the enemy."

Connected with the Gallipoli adventure was the change in the administration of the Navy, which came about when Lord Fisher, on May 14, 1915, placed his resignation of the office of First Sea Lord in the hands of Mr. Asquith. It was not accepted until nearly a fortnight later, and the reason for Lord Fisher's action was not explained. During the interval a change of Ministry occurred, and a Coalition Cabinet was formed, when it was found that Mr. Churchill had also left the Admiralty and had been succeeded in the office of First Lord by Mr. A. J. Balfour, with Admiral Sir Henry Jackson as First Sea Lord. For about six months afterwards Mr. Churchill held the sinecure of Chancellor of the Duchy of Lancaster, which office he resigned on November 11, 1915, and in the explanation of his conduct which he made in the House of Commons four days later he complained that, in regard to the "legitimate war gamble" at Gallipoli, as Mr. Churchill himself called it, he "did not receive from the First Sea Lord either the clear guidance before the event or the firm support afterwards which I was entitled to expect." To this charge the only reply made by Lord Fisher was the following statement next day in the House of Lords:

"I ask leave of your lordships to make a statement. Certain references were made to me in a speech delivered yesterday by Mr. Churchill. I have been 61 years in the service of my country, and I leave my record in the hands of my countrymen. The Prime Minister said yesterday that Mr. Churchill had said one or two things which he had better not have

ANSWERING THE "S.O.S." MESSAGE.
British torpedo-boat destroyer going to the assistance of a steamer torpedoed by a German submarine.

THE BRITISH EVACUATION OF GALLIPOLI.
Big guns leaving Suvla Bay in broad daylight.

said, and that he had necessarily and naturally left unsaid some things which will have to be said. I am content to wait. It is unfitting to make personal explanations affecting national interests when my country is in the midst of a great war."

To what extent responsibility for the fiasco at the Dardanelles rested upon these two men, or to what degree it was shared by others, was not made clear. In the new Board of Admiralty one other change was made, the Duke of Devonshire succeeding Mr. George Lambert, M.P., as Civil Lord. Vice-Admiral H. F. Oliver remained as Chief of the War Staff, and Admiral of the Fleet Sir Arthur Wilson also continued to be associated with the Admiralty in an advisory capacity.

In one notable respect, the change at the Admiralty was followed by a complete change in policy. During the Churchill-Fisher administration, information on the subject of the whereabouts of the Fleet, its constitution and movements, had been consistently refused. Every measure necessary to maintain secrecy in regard to these matters was taken, and the actual situation of the Fleet was, as Mr. Churchill picturesquely phrased it, "lost to view amid the Northern mists." About two months after Mr. Balfour became First Lord, the Archbishop of York was permitted to visit the Fleet and to supply an account of his fortnight's stay with the seamen to *The Times*. After this exception had been made, excursions to the various naval bases became frequent, it was understood at the suggestion of the Foreign Office, and not only Allied but neutral journalists and other representatives of foreign countries were taken on board the vessels and shown the naval establishments at these places. Information thus obtained was published in the form of articles in the world's Press, and to a large extent the veil of mystery which had enveloped the principal British naval force in the war was withdrawn.

There were many indications that during 1915 the strength of the British Fleet both absolutely and relatively had undergone considerable augmentation. Not only did the journalists who visited the naval bases mention the names of vessels which had been under construction, but in official dispatches it was made evident that new classes and types of ships had been added to the Fleet. Mr. Ashmead-Bartlett, the official "Eye-Witness" at the Dardanelles, was permitted to describe several types of vessels of the monitor class and other ships which had been adapted by modifications of construction to meet the submarine menace, but Admiral Bacon, in his dispatch of the operations off the Belgian coast, mentioned several such vessels by name. Mr. Churchill, in his apologia, also spoke of his successor as First Lord finding himself, week by week, upborne upon an ever-swelling tide of deliveries of craft of all kinds, and of a kind best suited to the purposes of this war, as a consequence of Lord Fisher's return to the Admiralty in 1914. No man, he said, had ever been able to put war purpose into the design of a ship like Lord Fisher. Then in regard to the Grand Fleet, there was no doubt that during the period under review its standard of efficiency was considerably improved by constant sea training and frequent gun practice. The tangible results of the Navy's ubiquitous and all-powerful activity were felt in the inviolability of our shores and in the unaffected conditions of the daily lives of the people. Not always, however, was this sufficiently recognized, for, as Lord Crewe said in Parliament, on February 15, 1916, "we had come to take the protection of the Navy so much as a matter of course, like the shining of the sun or the falling of the rain, that we sometimes forgot to be grateful." A tribute was manifestly due, however, to the endurance, fortitude, and skill of the seamen, who were severely tried, not only by the exceptional vigilance demanded owing to the stern necessity for perpetual watch and ward, but by the strain of the constant climatic discomforts and adverse weather conditions of service by night and day in the North Sea.

In justice to our seamen also, the tremendous power of the Fleet to which they were opposed should not be under-valued. When the war began, the naval strength of Germany was only second to our own, and her capacity for ship and gun construction was nearly on an equality with that of this country. It was made manifest in many ways that the increase in the striking power of their navy during 1915 was not to be estimated by the use made of it. Germany had not relinquished the hope of smashing our naval power, but the selected moment did not arrive. So long as her navy remained undestroyed, there could be no relaxation in vigilance, for there were always risks and possibilities, and it was essential, therefore, to make every possible use of our own shipbuilding and engineering resources. Germany mocked the world when she said that she was fighting for the freedom of the seas. It was for the subjugation of those who had really made the seas free that she was fighting —and intriguing—and no other nation had enjoyed the freedom of the seas in the past more than she had herself. What kind of freedom other nations would enjoy if her greed for power were satisfied the action of her various agents fully demonstrated.

The naval aspect of the war at the end of 1915 was made clear in a letter which Mr. Balfour addressed to an American correspondent. He said:

If anyone desires to know whether the British Fleet has during the last year proved itself worthy of its

ON THE LOOK-OUT FOR ENEMY SUBMARINES.
Officers on the bridge of a French war vessel in the Mediterranean.

BRITISH DESTROYER STRANDED IN THE EASTERN MEDITERRANEAN.

The port side of the H.M.S. Louis, which ran aground during a south-westerly gale.

traditions, there is a very simple method of arriving at the truth. There are seven, and only seven, functions which a fleet can perform :

It may drive the enemy's commerce off the seas.

It may protect its own commerce.

It may render the enemy's fleet impotent.

It may make the transfer of enemy troops across the sea impossible, whether for attack or defence.

It may transport its own troops where it will.

It may secure their supplies, and (in fitting circumstances) it may assist their operations.

All these functions have so far been successfully performed by the British Fleet.

During 1915, therefore, the British and Allied Fleets fulfilled their mission, and proved that the potency of sea power was not an illusion.

After the battle of the Dogger Bank on January 24, 1915, and largely as a result of that engagement, there was a period of comparative quiet up to the end of the year. Undoubtedly the severe drubbing received by the German battle-cruisers, and the light cruisers and torpedo craft accompanying them, was one of the main causes for this. The result of the action, moreover, might have been more decisive had it not been for the unfortunate shot which wrecked one of the Lion's feed tanks and placed her out of action. It must have been obvious to the Germans that this sort of raiding was much too risky to be profitable. That this was fully recognized seems to be borne out by the removal, which was reported soon afterwards, of Admiral von Ingenohl from his command of the High Sea Fleet. A favourite of the Kaiser, this officer took charge of the Fleet in January, 1913, having previously been Commander-in-Chief in China. Earlier still he had commanded the Emperor's yacht. His successor in the High Sea Fleet was Vice-Admiral von Pohl, who, as Chief of the Admiralty Staff, had signed the declaration of the waters around the British Isles as a "war zone" as from February 18, 1915, and it may have been for the purpose of supervising the actual carrying into effect of this policy that he was placed in command of the Fleet. Although it was not so called, the British counterstroke to this attempt of Germany to "starve England into submission" by submarine warfare on merchant shipping took the shape of a blockade of the enemy's territory, with the object, as far as possible, of preventing commodities of any kind from reaching or leaving him. These two blockades formed a substantial, if not the main, part of the naval operations in the North Sea and adjacent waters during 1915.

The control which the British Fleet maintained in these waters was of a very effective character, and remarkably complete. No single enemy ship, apart from submarines, was enabled to come within reach of the coasts of Great Britain, nor, so far as was known, did any succeed in breaking through the naval guard into the Atlantic. The measures taken soon after Lord Fisher's return to office to declare the whole of the North Sea a military area, the reduction of navigation lights, the stoppage of fishing in certain localities, and the closing of East Coast ports to trawlers of foreign registry, proved their worth in enabling the Fleet under Sir John Jellicoe more efficiently to regulate traffic and to check hostile or suspicious movements. Journalists who visited a naval base in the autumn of 1915, and boarded certain warships, were informed that the Grand Fleet was assisted day and night by 2,300 auxiliary craft, mine-sweepers, patrol boats, and the like. The constitution of this vast auxiliary organization lessened the strain upon the officers and men of the main fighting Fleet at the same time that it strengthened their grip upon the enemy by the consistent watch on his outlets. As Mr. Frederick Palmer, the American author, wrote after his visit afloat in September, 1915, the "hardest part of the war for the Navy was the early days, when the Fleet was continually at sea looking for battle. Now, securely ready, it could steam out to action immediately the patrols, which are continually sweeping the North Sea, reported any signs of the enemy."

Two losses of armed merchant cruisers which occurred early in 1915 illustrated the arduous and perilous character of patrol service in bad weather. On January 25 it was officially announced that the Viknor, formerly the cruising yacht Viking, which had been taken into the Navy and commissioned on December 12 by Commander E. O. Ballantyne, R.N., had been missing for some days, and must be accepted as lost with all hands. Bodies and wreckage which were washed ashore on the north coast of Ireland indicated that the vessel had sunk in that locality, either on account of the rough weather which prevailed at the time, or probably by striking a mine after being carried out of her course. On February 24 it was officially stated that the Clan McNaughton, formerly of the Clan steamship line, which had been commissioned for patrol duties, had been missing since February 3, and no further news of her was received. Unsuccessful search was made, and wreckage, supposed to be portions of the ship, was discovered, pointing to the probability that a mine had destroyed the vessel, although this could not be definitely established. About 500 officers and men perished in these two ships. The submarine also constituted a menace to the patrol service, but whether due to the vigilance displayed, or because the efforts of the "U" boats were mainly directed to the attack on commerce, the loss from this cause was comparatively negligible. The only ship reported sunk by submarine while engaged on patrol duty was the Bayano, armed merchant cruiser, which was torpedoed at 5 a.m. on March 11 off Corsewell Point, in the Firth of Clyde. About 200 of her crew, including Commander H. C. Carr, in command, were lost, the vessel going down within four minutes of being struck.

Three months later, on the morning of June 10, the British Navy lost its first torpedo boats to be sunk in the war, the cause being a submarine attack. It was officially announced that these boats, Nos. 10 and 12, were operating off the East Coast at the time, and only one submarine was mentioned. The survivors were 41 in number, the complement of each boat being about 35. Among those

IN THE NORTH SEA.
Manning a quick-firer during patrol work.

ATTACKING COMMERCE IN BRITISH WATERS.
A German submarine shelling a British merchant vessel on her way to an English port.

lost was Lieutenant Edward W. Bulteel, R.N., the commander of No. 12. The torpedo boats belonged to a class of thirty-six, originally called "coastal destroyers," which were built between 1906 and 1909. They were of 215 tons displacement, and had a speed of 26 knots with oil fuel. Although they were constantly at sea in all weathers, the torpedo boats of the British Navy were practically immune from mishaps, and during the first eighteen months of the war Nos. 10 and 12 were the only boats reported lost by enemy action. Most of them were known to have been employed upon escort duties, and this absence of casualties in transportation testified to the skill and efficiency of the service. Two other torpedo mishaps were also officially reported in June. On the 20th the cruiser Roxburgh, Captain B. M. Chambers, was struck by a torpedo from a submarine off the Firth of Forth, but the damage was not serious, and the vessel steamed into port with no casualties. On the 30th the destroyer Lightning was similarly damaged and reached harbour, but fourteen of her crew were missing after the occurrence. The Lightning was one of the oldest class of British destroyers, built in 1894–5.

The fighting which took place in the North Sea, as will be understood from what has been already said, was confined to small affairs between outpost vessels, in which the British craft usually held their own, though not at times without loss. On May 1 there was a series of such affairs in the neighbourhood of the Galloper and North Hinder lightships. In the forenoon the destroyer Recruit, an old boat of the 30-knot type, built in 1896, was torpedoed and sunk by a submarine. Four officers and twenty-one men were saved by the trawler Daisy. About 3 p.m. two German torpedo boats attacked a division of British patrol vessels, consisting of the Barbados, Lieutenant Sir James Domville, Bart., R.N. (commanding the division), Columbia, Miura, and Chirsit, under the command of Royal Naval Reserve officers. The German boats approached the division from the westward, and began the action without hoisting their colours. After an engagement of a quarter of an hour the enemy broke off the fight. The Columbia was sunk by a torpedo, and of her crew of 17 only one man was saved. Lieutenant-Commander W. H. Hawthorn, R.N.R., who commanded her, was stated by the Admiralty to have displayed gallantry and good seamanship on many occasions. On the Germans breaking off, the direction of their retreat was communicated to a division of the Third Destroyer Flotilla, composed of the Laforey, Leonidas, Lawford, and Lark, which chased the enemy, overhauled them, and sunk both the torpedo boats after a running fight of about one hour. Two German officers and 44 men were rescued, and there were no casualties on the British side. Small though these actions were in importance, they revealed the traditional qualities of determination and devotion to duty of the British seaman. Sir James Domville, on being attacked by the German torpedo craft, commanded his division of weak fishing vessels with skill and gallantry. He remained at the wheel of his own boat after the skipper had been wounded, and personally worked the helm. The Admiralty announced that generally he handled his ship in a seamanlike manner under heavy fire, to avoid being torpedoed. On the other hand, there was afforded a further illustration of the callousness of German methods in the treatment accorded to the crew of the trawler Columbia after she was sunk. A lieutenant and two men were taken on board one of the German torpedo boats, and when the latter were afterwards sunk the Germans, on being asked what had become of these British seamen, said that they were below, and time was short. In contrast to this action of the Germans in leaving their prisoners to drown was the strenuous effort made by the British seamen to rescue their enemies; 46 men of the 59 in the German boats were saved, and Lieutenant Hartnoll, R.N., even went into the water himself to rescue a German.

Just as the German submarines during the month of June gave evidence of their activity by the torpedoing of the Roxburgh and Lightning, so in the following month the continued work of British submarines was again illustrated. The only clash of arms in the North Sea during July was the sinking of a German destroyer of the "G 196" class, on the 26th, by a British submarine under the command of Commander C. P. Talbot. The submarine was on patrol at the time off the enemy's coast, and although neither full particulars nor the number of the British submarine were published officially, the incident bore a resemblance to that nine months earlier, when Commander Max K. Horton sunk the German destroyer "S 116" off the Ems. Commander Talbot

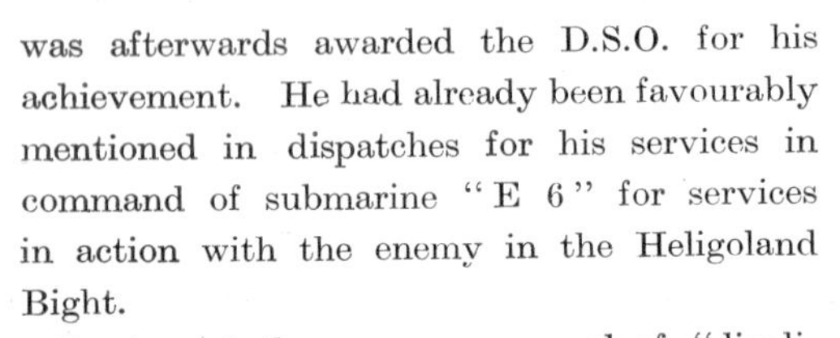

[Russell

COMMANDER C. P. TALBOT,

Commanding a British submarine which sank a German destroyer in the North Sea, July 26, 1915.

[Tale

CAPTAIN E. P. C. BACK,

Commanding the British cruiser Natal, destroyed by internal explosion on December 30, 1915.

was afterwards awarded the D.S.O. for his achievement. He had already been favourably mentioned in dispatches for his services in command of submarine "E 6" for services in action with the enemy in the Heligoland Bight.

In August there was a renewal of "liveliness" on the part of the Germans in the North Sea, which mainly centred round the doings of the auxiliary cruiser Meteor. This vessel was formerly a Hamburg-Amerika liner. During June she came into prominence as a commerce raider in the Baltic. Having been equipped with mines, and the means to lay them, she "broke through the British forces," according to the German account, on the night of August 7. Next day she met the British armed patrol vessel Ramsey, commanded by Lieutenant H. Raby, R.N.R., which was sunk with the loss of half her crew of about a hundred, including the commander. The Germans stated that they destroyed the Ramsey "after a splendid manœuvre," and according to unofficial accounts this manœuvre consisted in the Meteor disguising herself as an ordinary merchant ship, with masked guns and torpedo tubes, and flying Russian colours. The Meteor subsequently burned the Danish merchant vessel Jason, off Horn's Reef, and later transferred the crew of that ship and the survivors from the Ramsey to a Norwegian steamer. As regards her minelaying activities, a wireless message from Germany to the Sayville Station, U.S.A., stated that she succeeded in reaching the Orkneys and in laying a new field in that neighbourhood. Whether this was so or not, the British destroyer Lynx had the misfortune to strike one of her mines on August 9, and was sunk with the loss of about seventy officers and men, this total including Commander John F. H. Cole and Lieutenant Brian Thornbury, the commander and first lieutenant of the vessel. Four other officers and twenty-two men were saved. The Lynx was a comparatively new destroyer, of the "K" class, launched in 1913, and up to the time war began she had been serving in the Fourth Flotilla, attached to the Home Fleet. At length, on August 9, a stop was put to the brief but exciting career of the Meteor. A squadron of British auxiliary cruisers got on her track, but the German commander, cunning to the last, was not going to risk a fight with superior force. Before the cruisers could overtake his vessel, he blew her up by detonating her remaining mines, having first ordered the crew to take to the boats. They were only some fifteen miles from the German coast, and succeeded in making good their escape. Thus ended a romantic adventure of the kind which had been rather scarce up to that time. It was thought at first that the Meteor started out on a similar mission to that of the Königin Luise — also a Hamburg-Amerika liner — which attempted on the first day of the war to get into the Thames estuary and strew a number of mines, but was caught and sunk off the Suffolk coast. Another and equally plausible theory

British Naval men boarding an Arab dhow in order to search for contraband.

The captured dhow on fire and sinking after a British war vessel had confiscated its contraband.
Centre picture: Prisoners and rifles on board a British war vessel.

ARAB SMUGGLERS IN THE PERSIAN GULF.

GERMAN COAST DEFENCE IN FLANDERS.

Bottom picture: A big gun in position on the coast.

was that she hoped to break through the North Sea guard and reach the trade routes to begin commerce raiding, as the Berlin had tried to do some months earlier, but without avail, being driven to take refuge at Trondhjem. Whatever her object, however, the measure of success the Meteor attained under a dashing and enterprising captain highly pleased the Germans, and when the crew returned to Kiel they received a great ovation, in which Prince Henry of Prussia took part.

The British Fleet suffered another misfortune in the same week as the Meteor's exploits occurred. This was the torpedoing of the auxiliary cruiser India off the island of Hellevoer, near Bodö, at the entrance to the West Fiord, Norway. Commander W. G. A. Kennedy, with 21 other officers and 120 men of the ship were saved, but 10 officers and 150 men lost their lives. In attacking the India at the spot at which she was torpedoed, about two and a quarter miles from land, the German submarine violated international law, and the Norwegian Government sent a protest to Berlin on account of this disregard of neutral rights in connexion with what had always been maintained to be Norwegian territorial waters.

In the last four months of 1915 there were fewer events of martial significance to record in connexion with affairs in the North Sea. The stranding and loss of the cruiser Argyll, on October 28, emphasized afresh the perils to which the seamen are constantly liable apart from those connected with the action of the enemy. The Argyll, under the command of Captain J. C. Tancred, grounded off the east coast of Scotland, and became a total wreck, but fortunately her crew were saved. More deplorable, on account of the sacrifice of life involved, was the blowing up of the cruiser Natal on December 30, by an internal explosion. The vessel was in harbour at the time, and Captain E. P. C. Back, Commander John Hutchings, 23 other officers, and 380 men were killed or drowned.

We may now turn to a very important and highly interesting phase of the Navy's work in Home waters during 1915, the support given to the Army operating in the region of the Belgian coast. The early work of the naval flotilla under Rear-Admiral the Hon. H. L. A. Hood has already been described (Vol. III., p. 154). After the bombardment of Zeebrugge on November 23, 1915, other bombardments followed at frequent intervals. On December 1 airmen cooperated in an attack on Zeebrugge. On the 10th the Germans admitted that British warships had opposed an advance attempted in the region of Nieuport. On the 16th the monitor squadron, repaired and refitted after its arduous and hazardous work during October and November, was back off the coast bombarding Westende. The opening of the new year saw no slackening of the naval efforts, and the airmen from the Dunkirk station especially distinguished themselves. Their cooperation took the shape of spotting the fall of the shells from the warships, and also of bomb attacks on objects of military importance. On February 12 and 16 an unprecedented stroke was delivered on submarine bases, railway stations, gun positions, and military objects in the Bruges-Ostend-Zeebrugge district, when 34 and 48 aeroplanes respectively made attacks under the direction of Wing-Commander C. R. Samson, assisted by Wing-Commander A. M. Longmore and Squadron-Commanders J. C. Porte, I. T. Courtney, and C. E. Rathborne. Never before had so many machines been employed together for an attack of the kind, and as a spectacle this arrival of clouds of aircraft over the enemy's positions was a brilliant and dramatic one. There were several air attacks on a smaller scale against the Mole at Zeebrugge, submarine works at Hoboken, near Antwerp, and the like. Operations by the warships were also continued as occasion demanded. On April 3 some German minelayers, whilst endeavouring to extend the minefields off Zeebrugge, were reported to have been fired upon and driven into port. A month later, on May 7, the first loss of a naval vessel off the Belgian coast occurred when the destroyer Maori, Commander B. W. Barrow, was struck by a mine and foundered. The crew took to their boats as the destroyer was sinking. Her sister-ship, the Crusader, Lieutenant-Commander T. K. Maxwell, was in company, and lowered her boats to assist in picking up the Maori's crew, but before this could be done the Germans opened fire from shore batteries, and the Crusader, after being under fire for one hour and a half, had to leave her boats and retire. In all, seven officers and 88 men were taken prisoners into Zeebrugge.

In April, 1915, Rear-Admiral Hood was succeeded as Admiral Commanding the Dover Patrol by Vice-Admiral R. H. S. Bacon. Under the new commander, the vessels in this force were destined to play a prominent part in the Allied advance on land which developed in

GERMAN COAST DEFENCE IN FLANDERS.
German marines sniping on sand dunes.

BRITISH WARSHIPS SHELLING THE BELGIAN COAST BETWEEN NIEUPORT AND WESTENDE.

OFF THE BELGIAN COAST.
The gun turret in a British monitor.

September and October. On the evening of August 22 Vice-Admiral Bacon left England with a force of no less than 80 vessels. In this total were included several new monitors, the existence of which in use in home waters was officially revealed for the first time. One group was named the Lord Clive, Sir John Moore, Prince Rupert, General Craufurd, Marshal Ney, and Prince Eugene, and besides this class with soldier names there were others with numbers like the M 25. There were also trawlers and drifters, for mine-sweeping and other duties, and a new class of "fleet messengers," understood to be fast motor-boats. With this strangely-assorted force, organized and equipped since war broke out, attacks with important results were made on six occasions, and on eight other days bombardments, on a smaller scale, of fortified positions took place. The damage inflicted on the enemy was known to have included the sinking of one torpedo-boat, two submarines, and one large dredger, the total destruction of three military factories and damage to a fourth, extensive damage to the locks at Zeebrugge and the destruction of 13 guns of large calibre, in addition to the destruction of two ammunition depôts and several military storehouses, observation stations and signalling posts, damage to wharves, moles, and other secondary places. The personnel of Vice-Admiral Bacon's command was made up largely of officers of the Royal Naval Reserve, whose fleet training had necessarily been scant, and by men whose work in life had previously been that of deep sea fishermen, but the manner in which all overcame the difficulties attendant on the cruising in company by day and night under war conditions of such a large fleet was highly commended by the Admiral, and the results, he said, showed how deeply sea adaptability is ingrained in the seafaring race of these islands. Three vessels, the armed yacht Sanda, drifter Great Heart, and mine-sweeper Brighton Queen were lost in the operations, and the casualties were 34 killed and 24 wounded, which were proportionately small considering how the ships were constantly exposed to gunfire, aircraft, mines, and submarines off an enemy's coast.

The nature of the work performed by the Navy in the North Sea in 1915 was valuable and effective. Except on the Belgian coast, it did not include any offensive operations, and it was rather of a useful and laborious character. Reference has already been made to the expansion of the Fleet to meet the heavy calls upon it. Not only drifters and trawlers for mine-sweeping, armed yachts and other vessels for patrol duties, motor-boats for dispatch carrying and the like, but many entirely new vessels of novel design were introduced. Indeed, throughout the year the Fleet was being increased considerably in numbers and, even to a larger extent, in material strength. In addition to the vessels under construction when war broke out, which were completed and passed into service under Sir John Jellicoe, there was a vast fleet of new ships laid down

THE LAST MOMENTS OF A TORPEDOED TRANSPORT.
Sinking of the French liner Carthage by a German submarine off Cape Helles.

since the war. Not all these additional ships, of course, joined the naval force in the North Sea, but it must have been due to the general augmentation of the Fleet there that the large demand upon what Mr. Churchill called the "surplus ships" for the undertaking at the Dardanelles could be met without the strain which would otherwise have been caused being felt.

The work accomplished by the destroyers in the North Sea was beyond all praise. Under conditions of exceptional severity and extreme discomfort, they performed their allotted tasks with success. To them fell the protection of the trawlers and drifters sweeping constantly for mines, or employed upon outpost duty, and the immunity from mishap of the big ships of the Grand Fleet during their periodical cruises and sweeps through the North Sea was also a tribute to the vigilance of the torpedo craft in attendance. The work of all those craft, too, which come under the generic term of "auxiliaries" has received commendation which was well deserved. In "The Fringes of the Fleet," Mr. Rudyard Kipling wrote :

> Words of command may have changed a little, the tools are certainly more complex, but the spirit of the new crews who come to the old job is utterly unchanged. It is the same fierce, hard-living, heavy-handed, very cunning service out of which the Navy as we know it to-day was born. It is called indifferently the Trawler and Auxiliary Fleet. It is chiefly composed of fishermen, but it takes in everyone who may have maritime tastes—from retired admirals to the son of the sea-cook. It exists for the benefit of the traffic and the annoyance of the enemy. Its doings are recorded by flags stuck into charts ; its casualties are buried in obscure corners of the newspapers. The Grand Fleet knows it slightly ; the restless light cruisers who chaperon it from the background are more intimate ; the destroyers working off unlighted coasts over unmarked shoals come, as you might say, in direct contact with it ; the submarine alternately praises and—since one periscope is very like another—curses its activities ; but the steady procession of traffic in home waters, liner and tramp, six every sixty minutes, blesses it altogether.

As to the spirit of the men, in spite of the hardships they endured and the grey dulness of their lives in waiting and watching for an enemy who remained sheltered behind the protection of his fortified bases, the Archbishop of York bore striking testimony in describing in *The Times* on July 28, 1915, his ten days' visit to the Fleet. Said Dr. Lang: "Their one longing is to meet the German ships and sink them ; and yet month after month the German ships decline the challenge. . . . Officers and men have all the responsibilities of war without the thrill and excitement of battle. Day by day they have to be ready for action. Leave is almost impossible. . . . Yet in spite of all they are full of *cheerfulness.* Every captain had the same word—nothing could be better than the spirit of the whole crew."

In December, 1914, Admiral von Tirpitz proclaimed, in an interview with an American journalist, the intention of Germany to employ submarines as a weapon against British merchant vessels. What would America say, he asked, if Germany were to declare a submarine war against all hostile merchant vessels ? Asked by the interviewer if he was considering such measures, the Admiral replied : "Why not ? England wishes to starve us : we might play the same game and encircle England, torpedoing every British ship, every ship belonging to the Allies that approached any British or Scottish port, and thereby cut off the greater part of England's food supply." The threat thus revealed was accepted with enthusiasm in Germany, and it was eventually formulated in the shape of a "warning to peaceful shipping," published in the Imperial Gazette on February 2, 1915, and of a declaration of the waters around Great Britain and Ireland as a "war zone," published in the same journal on February 4. In the one case, merchant ships were urgently warned against approaching British ports, since the German Navy was to act with all the military means at its disposal against the transports which were about to convey to France large numbers of troops and great quantities of war material, and the traders "may be confused with ships serving warlike purposes." In the other case, Vice-Admiral von Pohl issued a long statement charging the Allies, and especially Great Britain, with illegal acts and violations of international law, which it was asserted had been the real cause of the German proclamation.*

The motives which led the Germans to adopt a policy of submarine war on merchant shipping were probably many-sided. Leaving out of account here its political aspects, and the moral effect which may have been hoped for from the extension of "frightfulness" from land to sea warfare, the situation from the naval point of view was clearly defined. Each successive effort by which the Germans had sought to nullify the effect of the supremacy possessed by the British Fleet had failed. They had first tried mine-laying on an extensive scale, using mercantile ships under neutral colours and similar wiles for the purpose. This was counteracted by the expansion of the mine-sweeping flotillas, and the battle in the Heligoland Bight was a salutary blow to the torpedo craft which had made a few dashes into the North Sea and attacked the fishing fleets. Then the submarine assaults upon the Grand Fleet and its attendant vessels had attained but a small result, a few old cruisers being the principal victims of this form of the war of attrition which had for its object the whittling down of our sea strength. There followed the cruiser raids upon the East Coast, but after two safe expeditions of this kind to Yarmouth and Scarborough a third ended disastrously for the raiders when they were brought to action by Sir David Beatty off the Dogger Bank on January 24,

* The text of this proclamation will be found in Vol. V., p. 270.

OFF THE ENEMY'S COAST.
A torpedo-boat destroyer's crew resting.

VIEW OF THE GERMAN SUBMARINE U36 SHOWING THE LARGE SUPERSTRUCTURE, WIRELESS MASTS, QUICK-FIRING GUN, AND OTHER FITTINGS.

1915. Finally, there was the attack on the trade routes in the outer oceans, which, by careful preparation in peace, combined with the skill of enterprising captains like von Müller, of the Emden, had taken its comparatively small toll of merchant shipping. The battle off the Falklands, however, destroyed the backbone of this undertaking, and it was only a few weeks before the scattered remnants of Germany's cruiser force abroad were rounded up or sought refuge in neutral ports.

The German Navy had thus to cast about for a fresh weapon to strike at England, and its choice fell upon, or maybe there was chosen for it by outside authorities, a submarine war on commerce. In peace time, opinion had been divided as to whether the submarine would come to be used in this fashion, but in the main it agreed with the view expressed by Lord Sydenham, in a letter to *The Times* on July 14, 1914—only three weeks before war broke out—as follows:

Capture of vessels at sea is an old right of war. The right to kill unresisting non-combatants, engaged in peaceful avocations, has never been recognized. The submarine cannot capture and must destroy. I do not believe that the sentiment of the world in the twentieth century would tolerate for a moment proceedings which have hitherto been associated only with piracy in its blackest form.

In the interval between the declaration of war and the introduction of the so-called submarine blockade on February 18, 1915, there had been tentative attacks on a few merchant ships by German submarines in the North Sea and English Channel. On October 20, 1914, the steamer Glitra was stopped by U17, her crew ordered into the boats, and then destroyed, and a month later the steamers Malachite and Primo were stopped off Havre by U21 and similarly treated, although in their case the gun of the submarine was used to destroy them. The Primo did not sink at once, as the Admiralty reported her still afloat next day, but on fire, the submarine having apparently to make off before completing its task, possibly because the sound of firing brought help to the vessel. This case may have convinced the German authorities that gun attack was not sufficiently decisive. On October 26, 1914, one of their submarines had, without warning, fired a torpedo into the passenger steamer Amiral Ganteaume, on passage from Ostend to Havre with 2,000 unarmed Belgian refugees on board, including women and children. Had it not been for the timely aid of another steamer, whose master promptly placed her alongside the stricken vessel, this outrage would have been as great, so far as the sacrifice of innocent life was concerned, as the Lusitania case. As it was, it called forth expressions of horror throughout the civilized world, and the Germans could not, therefore, have been ignorant of the general feeling in regard to such attacks on merchant ships. On January 21 the steamer Durward was stopped off the Dutch coast by U19 and her crew ordered to the boats, after which the vessel was blown up by bombs placed in the engine-room, with time-fuses—a more effective method of destruction than gunfire.

These early instances of submarine attack upon merchant ships served to illustrate the possibilities of such warfare to the Germans, and the attempt against the Amiral Ganteaume, the worst form of attack, elicited the opinions of neutrals on the subject. Before the blockade came into force, too, there was afforded an example of the spirit in which it was to be met by the merchant seamen upon whom it was directed. The British steamer Laertes, Captain W. H. Propert, a vessel of 4,541 tons, belonging to the Ocean Steamship Company, was sighted by a German submarine on February 10 off the Dutch coast and ordered to stop. The captain ignored the signal, rang for full speed, and steered a zigzag course. The submarine chased his vessel on the surface and, failing to get into a position for discharging a torpedo, opened fire from a gun. The Laertes was worked up to 16 knots by the efforts of her engine-room complement, and for an hour the submarine tried vainly to overtake her, shelling the vessel all the time. She also managed to get off a torpedo, which passed a few yards astern. At length, when she was only about 500 yards away, the submarine dived and made off. As a mark of appreciation "for his gallant and spirited conduct in command of his unarmed ship when exposed to attack by the gunfire and torpedo of a German submarine," Captain Propert was given a commission as temporary lieutenant in the Royal Naval Reserve, and on March 5, 1915, was received by the King, when his Majesty handed him the Distinguished Service Cross. The Admiralty also presented a gold watch to each officer, and a grant of £3 to every member of the crew of the Laertes.

When at length the submarine "blockade" opened it was not carried into effect with any sort of uniformity. According apparently to the character of the submarine commander there were various degrees of severity, though all were more or less callous of human life. No attempt was made to carry out the procedure laid down by international law of detaining, visiting, and searching merchant ships before capture, and of taking them into port for trial in the prize courts. On the contrary, the primary aim and object was destruction, even though this involved the death of or risk to many hundreds of innocent non-combatants.

SUBMARINE E13.

The vessel ran aground on the Danish Island of Saltholm, and was shelled by a German destroyer. Fifteen of her crew of thirty were killed.

A few cases will illustrate the various methods adopted by the "U" boats.

Some of the very worst crimes of the submarine raiders were those in which attacks were made by torpedo without warning of any kind or with insufficient notice to enable those on board to take to the boats. The Lusitania case, already dealt with in an earlier chapter, was the one which, from the huge loss of life, most shocked the world. It will remain for all ages an indelible stain on the German Navy. Equally callous, though the casualty list was not so high, were the circumstances attending the sinking of the Elder Dempster liner Falaba on March 28, 1915, to the south of St. George's Channel. The German submarine U28 gave her people five minutes to take to their boats, but before this period had elapsed a torpedo was fired at point-blank range—not more than a hundred yards or so—and as a result 101 lives were lost of the 237 persons on board. The submarine's crew jeered at the helpless situation of the people in the water, including women and children, and it was declared in evidence at the official inquiry by Lord Mersey afterwards that many victims might have been saved by the Germans merely by the latter stooping down and reaching out their hands to them in the water. As showing the utter disregard of the laws of humanity by the "U" boats in their campaign, the sinking of a Belgian relief ship may be mentioned, in spite of her being given a "safe conduct" permit by the German Minister at The Hague. On April 10, 1915, the Harpalyce, a four-masted steamer of 5,940 tons, was on her way from Rotterdam to Norfolk, U.S.A., in ballast. She flew a large white flag bearing the words, "Commission for Belgian Relief" in very large letters, visible for eight miles, and the inscription was also painted in large characters on the sides of the vessel. When off the North Hinder lightship she was torpedoed without any warning, and sank before the boats could be lowered, 17 of her crew of 44 losing their lives.

As some of the larger submarine boats were completed, the Germans resorted more to the use of the gun in enforcing their so-called blockade. They probably found this course more economical, as the number of torpedoes carried in each boat is limited, and except under favourable conditions these weapons are, perhaps, not so accurate as guns. Torpedoes, moreover, are costly missiles, some of those of the smallest calibre absorbing about £500 each. It was characteristic of the Germans that they endeavoured to get the most out of

BRITISH SUBMARINE AND CREW IN THE BALTIC.

Top picture: The vessel cutting its way through the broken ice.

BRITISH SUBMARINE AND CREW IN THE BALTIC.

them, however, for on April 13, 1915, the French Ministry of Marine asserted that, contrary to Article 1 of the Hague Convention, which forbids the use of torpedoes which do not become harmless after they have missed their mark, examination of torpedoes from German submarines which were found in the English Channel proved that their immersion apparatus had been systematically jammed, so as to turn the torpedo into a floating mine. Many thrilling stories filled the newspapers, during the time the "blockade" was at its height, of submarines attacking ships with their guns, and of the stubborn and heroic resistance and general coolness under fire displayed by the merchant seamen. A typical occurrence of this kind was the experience of the steamship Vosges, Captain J. R. Green, of the Moss Line. While on passage from Bordeaux to Liverpool, this vessel was sighted on March 27, 1915, by a German submarine off the western entrance to the English Channel, about 60 miles west of Trevose Head. "I had always made up my mind," said Captain Green afterwards, "to make a fight of it in such an emergency, and I ordered all steam up in order to get away. I turned my stern to the enemy, and then ensued a duel of skill. Foiled of using his torpedo, the submarine manœuvred to bring his gun into action, and his superior speed, despite the fact that we were making over 14 knots, enabled him to do so." For an hour and a half, with the submarine ever getting nearer, this unequal combat was maintained. The bridge of the steamer and her funnel were both riddled with shell, and the engine-room was also pierced, the chief engineer being killed whilst exhorting his men to further efforts. The submarine, baffled by the determination of the British seamen not to give in, then gave up the chase and sheered off, but the Vosges was so severely damaged that she sank about two hours later, a patrol yacht fortunately arriving in time to take off the survivors. "I wish," said Captain Green, "I had had a gun. If I had, there would now be one enemy submarine less. We have one satisfaction, and that is that the German did not see us sink." King George, it was announced on April 10, had awarded him the Distinguished Service Cross, and the Admiralty granted him a temporary commission as lieutenant in the Royal Naval Reserve. As in the case of the Laertes, gold watches were presented to the officers and £3 to each of the crew.

A third form of attack was that by aircraft. This had very unsatisfactory results from the

A German sailor, barefooted and holding on to a rope, watching his comrades swimming towards the submarine.

British sailor hauling a German up the side of the submarine while another leans over to lift him on deck.

GERMAN SAILORS RESCUED FROM DROWNING BY THE CREW OF A BRITISH SUBMARINE.

German point of view, as no vessel was reported to have been destroyed by aeroplanes, although several attempts by these machines were made. Many vessels of neutral countries, of course, suffered during the blockade, and among those damaged from the air was an American steamer, the Cushing, which was assaulted on April 28, about midway between Flushing and the North Foreland. The fact that the ship had her name painted on both sides in letters 6 feet high, and that she was flying the American flag, did not safeguard her from the attentions of the aeroplane, and two bombs were dropped, but only slight damage was caused. A much more successful and general mode of attack was that described in the case of the Durward, of placing bombs in the engine-rooms of steamers. Besides being more economical from the German standpoint, this procedure was more humane, since the time taken for the "U" boats' crews to reach the vessels and fix the explosives also allowed the merchant seamen opportunity to escape in their boats. Yet another method, adopted very largely in the case of cargoes of wood-pulp from Scandinavia and the like, was for the Germans to set fire to ships and leave them burning hulks, dangerous to the navigation of friend and foe alike.

This review would be incomplete without reference to the one bright feature of the "blockade" on the German side—the combination of adherence to duty with humanity towards those whom they were ordered to attack which marked the conduct of certain of the German submarine commanders. The name of Otto Weddigen at once springs to mind in this connexion. In command of U29, this officer figured in various episodes of the blockade in March, 1915. On the 11th he attacked and sank the steamer Aden-wen, off the Casquets, and so considerate were his methods that in this and other exploits he earned for himself the nickname of "the polite pirate." He gave the crew of the steamer ten minutes to launch their boats, observing, "We wish no lives to be lost." He noticed that one seaman fell into the water, and thereupon sent a suit of dry clothes for him At the same time he informed the master of the vessel how sorry he was to have to destroy his ship. Later on, he stopped and destroyed the French steamer Auguste Conseil, off the Start, and in taking leave of the vessel's crew, he asked them to "give his compliments to Lord Churchill." Two or three months later, when the "U" boats sought to create a fresh impression by attacks on the fishing fleets, and when many fishermen were brutally done to death without being given a chance for their lives, a welcome exception to the general practice occurred when the commander of one submarine allowed the crew of a trawler he attacked to get away in their boat. "We are not Prussians," he declared to the skipper; "it is only the Prussians who would let you drown."

Among the odd events which marked the "blockade," one of the most dramatic was the

"THE POLITE PIRATE."

Otto Weddigen, who commanded the U29, which figured in various episodes of the blockade in March, 1915.

bombardment of the towns of Parton, Harrington, and Whitehaven on August 16. This was rather a clever exploit on the part of the submarine commander who carried it out, and on this account was conspicuous in comparison with other incidents, for in spite of the gloating joy which characterized the German newspapers in referring to the submarines' work, there was no great amount of skill demanded to destroy harmless merchant ships, or lay in wait to hit a huge liner with a torpedo at short range. The shelling of these Cumberland towns, however, had an historic interest as well, for it was here that Paul Jones, the American seaman, carried out his raid during the War of Independence in April, 1778. He sailed from Brest in command of the sloop Ranger, and appearing off Whitehaven, surprised the garrison and landed. Reaching the half-ruined battery supposed to be able to defend the harbour, he spiked its old guns and captured the pensioners who manned them. He ordered the 300 ships in harbour to be set on fire, but before this could be done, the alarm was raised and he beat a hurried retreat. Thus the German commander who turned up off the same coast showed his acquaintance with British naval history. He

BRITISH SUBMARINE COMMANDERS.
Commander Max Horton (marked with a cross).

shelled the three towns mentioned for about an hour, but no material damage was done beyond that caused by a few shells which hit the railway embankment north of Parton and delayed traffic for a short time. Some fires were also caused, but there were no casualties.

It will have been gathered that the Germans were not allowed to have things entirely their own way, so far as the merchant seamen were concerned. The manner in which the British crews met the new menace was magnificent, and shed lustre on the already high traditions of their service. Speaking at a meeting of the Navy League on March 24, 1915, Lord Sydenham said that "Sea-power did not begin and end with ships of war. One of the most startling features of this war was the employment of the general maritime resources of the country, and the seafaring population drawn upon for dangerous duties had shown great heroism. Merchant captains showed no dread of German pirates, and were learning how to deal with them." From King George downwards there was natural appreciation expressed of the work of the merchant service in this connexion. His Majesty graciously accepted in August, 1915, a copy of the annual report of the Merchant Service Guild, and in so doing said he realized what magnificent work had been done by the brave officers and crews of his merchant service during the months of war. On February 28 the first case of a merchant vessel turning the tables on a submarine occurred in the English Channel. The Thordis, a small coasting steamer of 501 tons, was on her way from Blyth to Plymouth with coal when she sighted a submarine's periscope off Beachy Head. The master, John W. Bell, ordered his little crew of twelve on deck in case of an emergency, and the submarine was observed to cross the bow of the collier to the port side, where a position was taken up thirty to forty yards off. Then the wake of a torpedo was noticed, but in the swell which prevailed at the time it missed. Captain Bell then determined to go for his assailant. He put his helm hard over to starboard, and ran over the periscope, which was torn away against the side of the collier, a crash and crunch being felt at the same time under the keel of the ship. No trace of the submarine was seen afterwards, but oil was observed floating on the water. On being dry-docked at Plymouth, the Admiralty announced that the injuries to the keel and propeller of the Thordis confirmed the evidence that the vessel rammed and in all probability sank a German submarine after the latter had fired a torpedo at her. For this feat Captain Bell and his crew earned the prizes of £500 offered by the *Syren and Shipping* newspaper and other private donors to the first British merchant steamer to sink an enemy submarine, and the captain's share was publicly presented to him by the Lord Mayor of London at the Mansion House on April 12, 1915.

It was not, however, left to the merchant service to fight the submarine raiders, but the Royal Navy put into execution counter-measures which met with great success. Naturally, the character and scope of these were not divulged, but that they accomplished their

A German submarine shelling and chasing a Danish steamer while on a voyage to Iceland.

The steamer managed to escape, and afterwards the crew rescued several Russian sailors whose vessel had been sunk by the same submarine, which had abandoned the survivors to the mercy of the sea.

THE GERMAN SUBMARINE CAMPAIGN AGAINST MERCHANTMEN.

purpose was clear not only by the failure of the Germans to "blockade" Great Britain, but by the manner in which they found it expedient, after six months' trial, to accede to American requests to abate the virulence of their warfare against non-combatants. About this time, journalists who were permitted to visit the Grand Fleet were shown a map marking points where German submarines had been sighted, and the results of the attacks on them classified under "Captured," "Supposed Sunk," and "Sunk." When asked how these boats were caught, the officers replied, "Sometimes by ramming, sometimes by gunfire, sometimes by explosives, and in many other ways which we do not tell." During the first ten days of March two submarines, U8 and U12, were sunk by British destroyers off Dover and the Firth of Forth respectively, and U29 (Commander Weddigen's boat) by another warship, but after this the Admiralty decided not to issue particulars of such losses inflicted on the enemy. On August 26, 1915, when Squadron-Commander A. W. Bigsworth was successful in destroying, single-handed, a submarine by bombs from his aeroplane off Ostend, this incident was revealed, with the following explanation:

It is not the practice of the Admiralty to publish statements regarding the losses of German submarines, important though they have been, in cases where the enemy have no other sources of information as to the time and place at which these losses have occurred. In the case referred to above, however, the brilliant feat of Squadron-Commander Bigsworth was performed in the immediate neighbourhood of the coast in occupation of the enemy, and the position of the sunken submarine has been located by a German destroyer.

LIEUTENANT-COMMANDER CROMIE.

LIEUTENANT-COMMANDER GOODHART.

The mystery attaching to the number of German submarines accounted for inspired a good deal of speculation at this time. Thus an American journal stated on September 23 that it was positively known that 67 had been sunk since May, 5, 28 of these being of the newest and latest construction. In answer to a question on this matter, Mr. Balfour stated in Parliament on September 30 that an inevitable margin of doubt attached to any attempt to estimate the numbers of enemy submarines destroyed, because a submarine was not like an ordinary vessel, and there was every gradation from absolute certainty through practical assurance down to faint possibility. Facts like these were not fitted for statistical statement. Although, therefore, the British people could not have their very natural curiosity satisfied on this interesting point, the effect of this and other authoritative pronouncements was to show that, as Lord Selborne said, the Navy had the submarine menace well in hand.

In addition to the attitude adopted towards the German campaign by the Royal Navy and the Mercantile Marine, a third stand was made in the region of diplomacy. As a measure of reprisal for the wanton and illegal attacks on

SQUADRON-COMMANDER BIGSWORTH,
In the uniform of a Lieutenant, R.N.

shipping, Mr. Asquith on March 1 outlined in the House of Commons certain measures which were to be adopted in reply to what he described as the "organized campaign of piracy and pillage" undertaken by the enemy. Henceforth, he declared, the British and French Governments held themselves free to detain and take into port all ships carrying goods of presumed enemy destination, ownership, or origin, the object being to prevent commodities of any kind from reaching or leaving the German Empire. No mention was made in the speech of "blockade," "contraband," or other technical terms, the reason being, said the Premier, that "the Government were not going to allow their efforts to be strangled in a network of juridical niceties," but their policy, he added, would be enforced without risk to neutral ships or to neutral and non-combatant lives, and in strict observance of the dictates of humanity. The text of the official Proclamation giving effect to these views was published in the *London Gazette* on March 15.

In carrying out the policy the Admiralty established a "cruiser cordon" for the detention of the ships carrying goods of presumed enemy origin or destination. The nature or composition of this force was not revealed, nor was it stated who the officer in command was; but on August 7 a number of awards were announced by the Admiralty to officers and men "in recognition of their services in the patrol cruisers since the outbreak of war," and some of those honoured were shown by the "Navy List" to have been serving under Rear-Admiral D. R. S. De Chair, whose flagship was the Alsatian, armed merchant cruiser. In a note to these awards it was stated that the Commander-in-Chief of the Grand Fleet spoke in the highest terms of the manner in which the patrol cruisers had performed their arduous task, especially during the winter months, under exceptionally bad weather conditions. They had suffered severe losses, said the Admiralty, both in officers and men, and had been exposed continually to dangers from mines and submarines. An idea of the working of the patrol cruisers and their satellites may be gained from an article published in *The Times* on October 6, 1915, in which Mr. Gilbert Hirsch, an American journalist, described how the sea passage north of Scotland was kept by the Navy. Relating how he visited the harbour-master's office, he said :

Through the window to the commander's left a dozen of the Government's small harbour boats were to be

CAPTAIN JOHN W. BELL,
Master of the Thordis, who, together with his crew, earned the prizes of £500 for the first British steamer to sink an enemy submarine.

seen moored to the quay, and beyond them, dotting the harbour, more than a score of neutral merchant vessels. Some of these, like the Oscar II., on which I had just crossed, were detained only temporarily, for examination of passengers or cargo. Others were prizes, to be held till the end of the war.

These were the flies caught in the great web spun by the British across the northern trade route. Beyond the harbour's mouth, in the waters about these Orkney Isles, about the bleak Shetland Islands to the north, and the Hebrides to the south-west, along the eastern coasts of Scotland, and out across the North Sea towards the Norwegian shore, converted cruisers on patrol duty are for ever weaving their criss-cross courses, with Dreadnoughts waiting within easy call. . . . I pictured a similar web centring at Dover, in which all the Channel shipping becomes enmeshed; a third at Gibraltar,

COMMANDER E. C. BOYLE.

Awarded the Victoria Cross for most conspicuous bravery, in command of Submarine E 14, when he dived his vessel under enemy minefields and entered the Sea of Marmora, April 27, 1915.

which controls, even more effectively, traffic between America and the Mediterranean ports. And I got a vivid idea of the completeness with which England dominates transatlantic intercourse; I understood for the first time what Englishmen mean when they declare that "Britannia rules the waves."

The manner in which the British and French Governments established this cordon was the subject of Notes from the United States, which would have preferred the procedure to be modelled strictly on precedent and a regular blockade declared. It is beyond the scope of this chapter to enter into the legal and diplomatic questions thus raised, but it may be noted that in some measure the force of the American contentions was recognized when, on October 26, an Order in Council was published modifying the British prize law by the abrogation of Article 57 of the Declaration of London. By this article the flag which a ship was entitled to fly was sufficient evidence and guarantee of her character. Experience had shown, however, that it was necessary to go beyond the nationality of the flag to the nationality of the owner, and therefore it was decided to revert to the old prize law formerly in force, under which, even if an enemy had only a part interest in a ship, that part could be condemned and its value realized by various methods known to the Courts.

At what date British submarines first penetrated into the Baltic was not officially disclosed, but very early in 1915 they made their presence known there. When the light cruiser Gazelle was torpedoed off the island of Rügen on January 25, Swedish newspapers referred to the attacking submarine as British. So long as the greater part of the opportunities for submarine work was denied to the boats on account of the ice their activity did not attract so much attention as at a later period. An admirable summary of the Russian Fleet's work from the outbreak of war to the end of March, 1915, was contained in a report of Admiral von Essen, the Commander-in-Chief, to the Tsar. This statement showed that during the first period of the war the German Fleet confined its activities purely to observing the naval measures adopted by Russia for the protection of her coasts.. This allowed time for the Russian defences to be placed in order and extended farther out to sea. The area reserved for the movements of the defending fleet was carefully mined, and entirely closed to merchant shipping. Later on there were several skirmishes between cruisers and outpost vessels, and although most of these were of an indecisive character the Russian seamen proved their worth. The Germans also used submarines to a considerable extent to try and reduce the strength of the Russians. Within two months, said Admiral von Essen, twenty submarine attacks were delivered, only one of which, that on the cruiser Pallada on October 11, 1914, was successful. In ten cases the torpedoes missed their mark, and in the nine others the Germans were unable to use the torpedo at all. Generally

The Anglia as she appeared shortly after striking the mine.

The stern of the Anglia rising out of the water. Some of the wounded were transferred to the boats, while others, unable to retain their precarious footing, slipped into the sea, and were saved by sailors.

The last of the Anglia.

THE SINKING OF A BRITISH HOSPITAL SHIP IN THE ENGLISH CHANNEL.

AN ENCOUNTER OFF THE BELGIAN COAST.
Two French torpedo-boats attacking a German destroyer off Ostend.

speaking, the report concluded, the Russian Fleet during these first eight months of war gained much experience in dealing with the modern weapons at the disposal of the Germans. Its numbers were not diminished, but, on the contrary, had been increased by new ships, and the morale and confidence in the future of the Russian sailors was stronger than ever.

With the melting of the ice, there was a natural development in hostilities, but the command of the Baltic remained in dispute, in spite of the superiority of force possessed by the Germans. Early illustration of this was afforded when the Russian Fleet supported the successful raid into East Prussia from March 18 to 22, 1915, during which the town of Memel was captured. The fact that there was no German naval force at hand to deal with the Russian warships, without the cooperation of which the enterprise could not have been carried out, indicated that the Germans were caught napping. They apparently poured forth their wrath in sending a division of seven battleships, with a score or more torpedo craft, to cruise along the Courland coast and fire on the coast villages at Polangen and elsewhere during the next few days. About two months later the great German campaign against Russia began, and on both sides the naval forces cooperated with and conformed their movements to the undertakings of the troops on shore. Libau, at one time a Russian naval base, but since 1910 an open maritime town, fell to the German Army, supported by gun-fire from the ships, on May 9, and gradually the Germans began to extend their activity higher up the coast to Windau and other places, until the time came for them to make an effort in force against the Gulf of Riga. It was a matter of deep regret that before these operations developed, however, Admiral von Essen, a brave and resourceful officer and a capable Commander-in-Chief, died in hospital at Reval from pneumonia. Sir John Jellicoe and Sir David Beatty were among those who expressed their condolence. Vice-Admiral Kanin was appointed to be the new Commander-in-Chief, a choice which was fully justified by the successful handling of the Russian sea forces during the next few months.

In the week beginning on August 16, 1915, a large German fleet endeavoured to seize control of the waters of the Gulf of Riga. The success of this operation would have had an important bearing upon the military situation in this region, as it might have made possible the transport by sea of reinforcements to the invading army of General von Below, and perhaps turned the Russian flank. But the enterprise failed, and the Germans eventually retired with loss. After mine-sweepers, protected by the heavier ships, had cleared the waters at the entrance, the enemy succeeded on August 18 in penetrating into the Gulf, favoured by the thick fogs and misty weather prevailing. For the next two days reconnaissances were made, but on the 21st the Germans, influenced by the losses they had sustained and the barrenness of their efforts, evacuated the Gulf. This abandonment of the enterprise, coming at a time of great depression owing to the German military advance in the eastern theatre of war, had an enormously reassuring effect in Russia and throughout the Allied countries. It is not surprising that some exaggerated stories became current in regard to it. One of these, told to the Duma itself, was that four barges full of troops had attempted to land at Pernau, but had been annihilated, but the fact was that the vessels were empty steamers sunk by the Germans to block navigation. However, the Russian official *communiqués* showed that two cruisers and not less than eight torpedo craft of the Germans were either sunk or put out of action during the week's fighting, whereas the Russians lost only the gunboat Sivoutch, which was sunk in Moon Sound, after a brave defence, by a German cruiser.

Apart from the Riga fighting, the year in the Baltic was chiefly distinguished for submarine operations. A number of British boats were placed under the Russian Admiral, and their successes were very striking. On July 2 a battleship of the "Pommern" type was torpedoed, and on August 19 the battle-cruiser Moltke was likewise hit and damaged. On October 23 the cruiser Prinz Adalbert was sunk off Libau, on November 7 the light cruiser Undine suffered a similar fate off the south coast of Sweden, and on December 17 the light cruiser Bremen and a torpedo boat were sunk. On July 30 a large transport was sunk, and on October 16 the Russian *communiqué* reported that five German transports had been destroyed by British submarines and a sixth forced to run ashore. At the end of September the Russo-British submarines directed their efforts towards a fresh field when they began to attack German merchant ships. During October these vessels were sunk or driven ashore at the rate of something like one or two a day, and although this rate was not maintained, the reason was due to the decrease in traffic, which remained in port rather than risk being intercepted. This turning of the tables upon the Germans had a great moral as well as a material effect—it showed that two could play the game of setting submarines to attack the floating trade, while at the same time it stopped the supply of iron ore and other minerals into Germany from Scandinavia. The impotence of the Germans to deal with the submarine menace was also a marked feature. They resorted to extensive minelaying, but were unable to keep the British boats out of the Baltic, or to frustrate their activity and that of the Russian submarines in its waters. The British submarine commanders who specially distinguished themselves in this work were Commander Max K. Horton, Commander Noel F. Laurence, and Commander F. A. N. Cromie.

In previous chapters the great battles to obtain control of the Gallipoli Peninsula have

THE CAMEROON CAMPAIGN.
British gunboat on the Wuri River.

BRITISH SUBMARINE IN ACTION IN CONSTANTINOPLE HARBOUR.

Turkish transport, "Stamboul," sunk by Submarine "E 11," commanded by Lieutenant-Commander M. E. Nasmith, V.C.

been fully described. The big engagements, however, cover but a comparatively small part of the work which was performed by the Royal Navy during the eleven months in which the adventure lasted. That work revealed qualities which shed lustre on the high traditions of the Service, and as the facts became known to the world the cause for marvel was, not that the enterprise did not achieve its object, but that it accomplished so much. Mr. Churchill gave the first official hint of a coming adventure when he said, in the House of Commons, on February 15, 1915, that the victory at the Falkland Islands swept away difficulties in the employment of our naval strength. "It set free," he said, "a large force of cruisers and battleships for all purposes; it opened the way to other operations of great interest." He showed that while there was a powerful German cruiser squadron still at large in the Pacific or the Atlantic it had to be watched for and waited for in superior force in six or seven different parts of the world at once. He also said that the strain upon the Navy in the early months of the war had been greatly diminished by the abatement of distant convoy work and by the clearance of the enemy's flag from the oceans. The way was thus clear for the employment of our naval resources in a new offensive undertaking, and the choice fell upon an attempt to force the Straits of the Dardanelles with the aid of the "surplus fleet," as Mr. Churchill called it, of the Majestic, Canopus, and similar classes.

There was some mystery at first as to whether the plan for a purely naval attack on the outer forts had a naval origin or not, but in his valedictory speech on November 15, 1915, Mr. Churchill showed clearly that it had not. After dealing with the evidence in favour of action at the Dardanelles, he said that Lord Fisher favoured a joint operation of the Fleet and the Army in this quarter, and that his schemes involved the cooperation of Powers which were neutral and of an army which was not available. The futility, in fact, of ships attacking without a military force to follow up and make good their work was obvious. As was said in a previous chapter,* "Even if the initial attacks were to be delivered by ships alone, it must have been manifest from the very beginning that at some stage of the enterprise military assistance would be required. Ships might have forced the Straits, but they could not occupy Constantinople." All the conditions, therefore, pointed to a joint operation being necessary, but a mistake was made when the naval part of the undertaking was put into execution before its military counterpart was available or ready. Action opened on February 19 with the bombardment of the forts at Cape Helles and Kum Kale with deliberate long-range fire, and in the afternoon six battleships, the Vengeance, Cornwallis, Triumph, Suffren, Gaulois and Bouvet, closed and engaged the forts with their secondary armaments, the Inflexible and Agamemnon supporting at long range. All the forts except one on the European side were apparently silenced, and no Allied ship was hit.

Of the first phase of the campaign, Mr. Churchill said it "was successful beyond our hopes." "The outer forts," he said, "were destroyed; the Fleet was able to enter the Straits and attack the forts in the Narrows." Mr. Ashmead-Bartlett, however, in a long letter to *The Times*, on November 24, 1915, said in reference to this statement:

> This is the first time I have ever heard this view expressed, because almost all naval men who took part in the early bombardments with whom I have spoken express the opinion that it was the difficulty in smashing the outer forts which first opened their eyes to the true nature of what their task would be when the time came to attack the Narrows. The first bombardment was on February 19, and was confined to the outer forts at Helles, Seddul Bahr and Kum Kale. These works were fully exposed, and can be partly enfiladed. They mounted old-fashioned Krupp guns, mostly 9.5's, and some larger, but the extreme range was only some 10,000 yards. They were erected, in fact, to sweep the entrance to the Straits, and not to oppose a long-range attack from the sea.

Proceeding, Mr. Churchill said that "across the prospect of the operations a shadow began to pass at the end of the first week in March. The difficulties of sweeping up the mine-fields increased, and although great success was obtained by the ships in silencing the forts, they were not able at that stage to inflict decisive and permanent damage. The mobile armament of the enemy began to develop and become increasingly annoying." Mr. Ashmead-Bartlett interprets the "shadow" as being the parting of the ways between Mr. Churchill and Lord Fisher. "It would seem," he wrote in his letter to *The Times*, "as if Lord Fisher became sceptical of the whole enterprise directly he realized the inability of the Fleet to clear the enemy's minefield, or to locate any other underwater defences, the difficulties of silencing the forts of the Narrows by long-range direct fire, and the inability of the Fleet to knock out the mobile batteries on both sides of the Straits.

* Vol. V., page 365.

IN GERMAN EAST AFRICA.

Destruction of the Königsberg: Hauling a wrecked seaplane aboard a British warship.

He evidently realized that none of the conditions precedent for a successful attempt to force the Narrows had been fulfilled, and under the circumstances the Fleet might be faced with a grave disaster." On Mr. Churchill the difficulties appeared to have the effect of increasing his determination to rush the matter through. It was decided, so he told the House of Commons, that the gradual advance must be replaced by more vigorous measures. Vice-Admiral Sackville H. Carden, then commanding the Allied Fleet, "was invited to press hard for a decision, and not to be deterred by the inevitable loss." The Admiral was, however, stricken down with illness on the 16th, and invalided by medical authority, when Rear-Admiral John M. de Robeck, second-in-command, took his place, with the acting rank of Vice-Admiral. The attack in force took place on March 18, and failed with the loss of the British battleships Irresistible (Captain Douglas L. Dent) and Ocean (Captain A. Hayes-Sadler), and the French battleship Bouvet, the last-named sinking with the greater part of her crew. Mr. Churchill evidently thought, and led the public to believe also, that this action on March 18 was a deliberate attempt to force a passage through the Narrows and reach Constantinople, but careful study of the facts concerning it proves that it was nothing of the kind, and was never intended to be so by the officers commanding. It was only an attempt to clear the triple minefield below the Narrows. Mr. Ashmead-Bartlett stated in his letter to *The Times* that, in addition to the three capital ships sunk outright, the French battleship Gaulois was run ashore on Rabbit Island to prevent her sinking, and the battle-cruiser Inflexible was so badly damaged by a mine that it was thought at one time she must sink. He added :

The Fleet was prepared, of course, to take advantage of any favourable condition that might possibly arise for a dash through, but it was hardly within the scheme of operation that this dash should take place on the same day. The plan of campaign was for the Fleet to silence the forts at the Narrows, those at Kephez Point and Fort Dardanus, to enable destroyers and trawlers to sweep the minefield, which they had hitherto been unable to do. . . . But the facts underlying the naval attack are simple, and the merest tyro can understand them. We attempted a most difficult operation, as usual underestimating our opponents and without any adequate information on the essential points. We persisted in our effort, even when none of the conditions precedent to forcing the Narrows—on which the experts based their consent—were fulfilled. In consequence we got a fair and square beating, at which we cannot complain. We went all out on March 18. There were no half-measures. How many Englishmen would have slept soundly in their beds that night had they known that our latest and greatest Dreadnought, the Queen Elizabeth, was a long way up the Straits throughout the whole of the 18th amongst drifting mines, one of which actually knocked out the Inflexible, of the same division and on the same alignment, off Aren Koi ?

After March 18 it was decided to substitute

for the purely naval operation a joint naval and military attack, and on the 19th the Admiralty in their official *communiqué* stated that "The operations are continuing, ample naval and military forces being available on the spot." Unfortunately, as already narrated in Chapter XCII., though the troops were on the spot, they had been wrongly loaded in the transports, and Sir Ian Hamilton, having reluctantly decided that the cooperation of the whole of his force would be required to enable the Fleet effectively to force the Dardanelles, had first of all to redistribute the troops in the transports to suit the order of their disembarkation. It was impossible to do this at Mudros, and therefore all the ships had to return to Egypt. A whole month elapsed before the military force was able to attack the peninsula on April 25, with the result known. This delay probably sealed the fate of the expedition. The invaluable element of surprise was lost. Had the Army been on the spot and ready to land when the Fleet began to bombard on February 19 it is difficult to see how, in view of the facts revealed later, it could have failed in its purpose.

We have already told the tale of the landings in Gallipoli. Further information concerning the Navy's part in that stupendous undertaking serves to emphasize the warm-hearted eulogy passed by Sir Ian Hamilton. To the difficulties, already of a considerable and unprecedented magnitude, in which the seamen had to labour to support the Army on shore, to keep it supplied with food and munitions, to protect its reinforcements and transport its wounded, there were added others when the arrival of enemy submarines took place. The first of these boats to arrive was believed to be a vessel commanded by Lieutenant-Commander Otto Hersing, the successful assailant of the Pathfinder in the second month of the war. He was said to have left Wilhelmshaven on the day the British landed in the peninsula, and he reached the Straits exactly a month later, when he torpedoed the battleships Triumph and Majestic. A description of their sinking, as well as of the destruction of the Goliath by a Turkish destroyer has already been given. Henceforth the right wing of the Army had to be left to take care of itself during the night, it being too dangerous for ships to be stationed at this point. The news of the Goliath's destruction seems to have determined Lord Fisher's attitude towards the Dardanelles under-

IN GERMAN EAST AFRICA.

A British seaplane about to start on a scouting expedition.

taking, for he resigned next day. The increasing drain upon ships and men caused by the expedition, for no apparent result, evidently convinced the First Sea Lord that stronger action was necessary than an expression of his "doubts and hesitations" which the Prime Minister said in Parliament on November 2 had been in the mind of the Government's chief naval adviser before the naval attack was begun.

The advent of submarines off the Straits changed the aspect of the naval force there. The big ships had to retire to sheltered harbours, protected by booms and nets, and for a short time the Fleet was represented by destroyers and small craft, whose work was beyond all praise. These frail, unprotected vessels rendered noble service under extremely dangerous conditions, being frequently under fire to which they could not reply. At length the deficiency was made good by the utilization of a fleet of monitors which had been ordered in the previous year for another purpose by Lord Fisher. These vessels, so constructed that they can carry the guns of a cruiser or battleship, according to their size, without having the vulnerability to submarine attack of those types, began to arrive in July. Three classes of monitors were mentioned, one with two 6-in. guns, another with one 9·2-in. forward and a 6-in. aft, and a third with two 14-in. guns. Old cruisers of the Edgar class also appeared, having been structurally adapted to render them practically immune from torpedo attack. Owing to the bulges on their sides, they were known as "blister ships." They played an important rôle on the occasion of the new landing at Suvla Bay on August 6 and the subsequent operations, when they commanded every vantage-point and kept the Turks from showing themselves near the cliffs and from counter-attacking.

Towards the end of 1915 the enemy submarines were reinforced, whether by boats sent out from German ports or by craft transported in sections to Austria and re-launched into the Adriatic was uncertain ; probably in both ways. Baulked of opportunities for attacking the Fleet on the spot at the Dardanelles, their activity was diverted to the long line of communications through the Mediterranean, and in the last three months of the year their chances in this connexion improved owing to the dispatch of a new expedition to Salonika. At first, owing mainly to the surprise which they effected, the "U" boats achieved a certain amount of success. On August 14 the transport Royal Edward was sunk in the Ægean with the

IN GERMAN EAST AFRICA.

A raft constructed of seaplane floats used for getting supplies ashore.

ON THE RIVER TIGRIS.

British troops re-embarking on board a vessel after a fight with the Turks in Mesopotamia.

loss of about 1,000 lives, and subsequently the Southland, Ramazan, Marquette, Woodfield and Mercian were also sunk or damaged by submarine attack. A new group of boats got through the Straits of Gibraltar in the first week of November, as stated by the French Ministry of Marine, and off the North African coast they destroyed several merchantmen. On November 7 the Italian liner Ancona was torpedoed without warning, and also shelled, being sunk with the loss of about 300 lives. On December 30 the P. and O. Company's steamer Persia was torpedoed and sunk off Crete, with the loss of 200 lives. Here again no warning was given. Whether the attacking boats in this new campaign were Austrian or German was uncertain, and it was also reported that Turkish submarines were being utilized. Another locality where they attained a measure of success was on the western frontier of Egypt, the armed boarding steamer Tara and the Egyptian gunboats Prince Abbas and Abdul Moneim being destroyed in the Bay of Sollum. By the end of the year, however, the preventive measures taken by the Allies in concert had appreciably lessened the submarines' activity. Many suspected places were examined for possible stores for the raiders, and some were occupied by Allied forces, including the Kaiser's villa at Corfu.

A brilliant chapter in the history of the Dardanelles undertaking is that concerned with

THE FRENCH CRUISER LEON GAMBETTA.
Torpedoed in the Adriatic by an Austrian submarine.

the doings of French and British submarines which penetrated into the Sea of Marmora. After negotiating all obstacles in the tricky and hazardous passage through the Dardanelles, and passing under the minefields, these vessels up to October 26 had succeeded in sinking or damaging two battleships, five gunboats, one torpedo boat, eight transports, and 197 supply ships of all kinds. This activity had a marked effect on the reinforcement and supply of the Turkish Army in the peninsula. The great exploits of Commanders Boyle and Nasmith have been described (Vol. VI., p. 96). More than one submarine entered the harbour at Constantinople itself and attacked shipping at the wharves, and the Turkish powder mills at Zeitunlik and railway cutting near Kara Burnu were also shelled. The measure of risk attaching to this work was shown by the heavy losses sustained by the Franco-British flotilla, the submarines Saphir, Mariotte, Joule and Turquoise, E.15, AE.2, E.7, and E.20 being sunk or captured during the year.

The naval situation in the Adriatic throughout 1915 resembled that in the North Sea in that no important fleet actions took place. The Austro-Hungarian Fleet was contained at Pola by the Franco-British forces from August, 1914, to May, 1915, when the Italian Navy joined in the task, and although "liveliness" increased after this it was confined to coast raids and affairs between outposts. When the entry of Italy into the war relieved his force of its duty as immediate guard over the Adriatic, Admiral Boué de Lapeyrère, who had commanded the Franco-British Fleet since the return to England in August, 1914, of Admiral Sir Berkeley Milne, issued an Order of the Day in which he referred to the remarkable endurance with which the work had been done. He thanked his subordinates for the tireless zeal, energy, and abnegation which every one of them had displayed in supporting him in the most arduous and thankless tasks which naval forces ever had to accomplish. On October 10 the retirement of the Admiral, owing to ill-health, was announced, and Vice-Admiral d'Artige du Fournet was appointed Commander-in-Chief in his place.

In the war of attrition by submarine, mine, and other methods, both sides suffered a few losses. The Austrian light cruiser Zenta was sunk on August 16, 1914, in a sweep up to Cattaro by the Allied Fleets. On December 28 the French submarine Curie tried to enter Pola harbour, but became entangled in the defence obstructions and was captured, when the Austrians renamed her the Zenta in memory of their lost cruiser. French submarines operating in the Adriatic were rather unlucky, no success being reported by them up to the end of 1915, while in addition to the Curie the Fresnel and Monge were lost. The former was destroyed on December 5, 1915, off San Giovanni di

Medua, being attacked while aground; and the latter on December 28 off Cattaro. Austrian submarines were more successful, and in 1914 attacked the Waldeck Rousseau and Courbet, neither of which, however, was sunk. On April 27, 1915, they torpedoed and destroyed the cruiser Leon Gambetta, in which nearly 600 men were lost, at the entrance to the Otranto Straits, and on July 7 and 18 respectively the Italian cruisers Amalfi and Giuseppe Garibaldi were sunk. On June 11 a British cruiser of the "Liverpool" class was torpedoed, but only damaged. The Austrian flotilla had several losses during this warfare. The first boat reported sunk was the submarine which attacked the Waldeck Rousseau on October 17, 1914. On July 1, 1915, U.11 was seriously damaged in an air attack by a French aviator, Sub-Lieutenant Rouillet, who hit the boat with two bombs. A fortnight earlier another novel combat had taken place—a duel between submarines. The Italian boat Medusa was torpedoed by an Austrian submarine and sunk, and divers who went down to examine the wreck found the hull of an Austrian boat as well, showing that both combatants in this action went to the bottom. Oddly enough, a second duel of the kind occurred in the Adriatic on August 11, when the Austrian submarine U.12, which had torpedoed the Courbet in the previous December, was torpedoed by an Italian submarine and sunk with all on board. Two days later U.3 was also sunk, and about one-half of the Austrian flotilla was reported to have been accounted for at this time.

Towards the end of 1915 the naval control of the Adriatic by the Allies became of increased utility because of the need for transporting an Italian Army to Albania and for bringing away Serbian troops and refugees. The dispatch of an expeditionary force to Valona was accomplished with complete success, and reflected great credit upon the Italian Navy. It was officially stated at Roma that 260,000 men were moved between the western and eastern shores of the lower Adriatic, under the escort of the Allied Fleet, and a large quantity of animals were also carried, 250 steamers being needed for the work. During the same undertaking 300,000 cwt. of materials were transported in 100 steamers, mostly of small tonnage so that they might be able to put in on the opposite shore. The Austrians threatened this enterprise by 19 submarine attacks, and by

THE SURVIVORS OF THE CREW OF THE LEON GAMBETTA.

activity in the air, by mining certain areas, and raids by torpedo craft and cruisers, but such was the efficiency displayed by the Allied seamen that only three small steamers were lost, two by striking mines and a third by being torpedoed after she had discharged her cargo. Not a single Serbian soldier was lost at sea. Considering that these operations were carried on in a restricted area of water, and along routes well known to the enemy and without alternatives, it was a magnificent achievement of which the Italian Commander-in-Chief, Admiral the Duke of the Abruzzi, and the Allied admirals associated with him, may well have been proud.

The naval position in the Black Sea attracted increased attention when Bulgaria entered the war on October 14, 1915, and on the 27th the Russian Fleet bombarded the port and harbour of Varna. One or two of the new "Dreadnoughts" were engaged, with other battleships, and the railway station, custom house, wireless station, and other military objects were destroyed. Rear-Admiral R. F. Phillimore, formerly Principal Naval Transport Officer at the Dardanelles, was present in the Russian flagship as Chief of the British Naval Mission, and it was afterwards reported that he inspected the naval bases in the Black Sea. The Russian forces made good use of their control of its waters, and destroyed hundreds of Turkish craft carrying supplies to Constantinople. In such skirmishes as took place with the Ottoman Navy, moreover, they asserted their superiority, even the battle cruiser Goeben being worsted, proving that her efficiency as a fighting unit had been greatly lowered. The Turks' losses included the cruiser Medjidieh, sunk by a mine near Odessa on April 3, 1915. She was refloated two months after by the Russians. Once or twice hostile submarines were reported to have appeared, whether German, Turkish, or Bulgarian was not known definitely, but they achieved no success, and on July 15, 1915, one boat was reported to have been sunk. Six submarines sent in sections to Varna for the protection of the port were unable to prevent its bombardment, during which they also suffered loss and damage.

There remains to be noted the assistance and support given by the Royal Navy to the military expeditions on the rivers at the head of the Persian Gulf and in the various German Colonies. These enterprises were not only rendered possible by the protecting shield of the Grand Fleet, but owed no small measure of their success to the help given on the spot by the seamen. In Mesopotamia a naval brigade accompanied the expeditionary force, and a gunboat flotilla also cooperated. In September, 1915, Sir Mark Sykes, describing the operations in Mesopotamia, mentioned in terms of high praise the conduct of the seamen of the Royal Navy and Royal Indian Marine serving there. The flotilla working with the expedition, he said, included paddle steamers which once carried passengers, armoured and armed tugs, a launch carrying 4·7-in. guns, "a steamer with a Christmas-tree growing amidships, in the branches of which its officers fondly imagine they are invisible to friend or foe," and a ship which started life as an aeroplane in Singapore, shed its wings but kept its aerial propeller, took to the water and became a hospital. This fleet, he added, was the cavalry screen, advance guard, rear guard, railway, headquarters, heavy artillery, line of communication, supply depôt, police force, field ambulance, aerial hangar, and base of supply of the Mesopotamian Expedition.

Lastly, the indispensable character of the Fleet's help to the conquest of the German Colonies was fittingly acknowledged by General Botha, who, after the final surrender of German South-West Africa in July, 1915, said at Capetown that "the success of this expedition would have been impossible but for the help of the British Navy, for whose protection South Africa ought ever to be grateful." The same was true of the operations against the Cameroons, which were crowned with success in February, 1916, and in which naval officers and men afforded assistance and support in many ways, notably by the transport of heavy naval guns several hundreds of miles to the siege of Garua and other places. In East Africa a blockade of the entire German coast was declared on February 28, 1915, and a blow at the enemy's power was struck when the monitors Severn and Mersey, under Captain E. J. A. Fullerton, ascended the Rufigi River and knocked out the German cruiser Königsberg, which had been hiding there since October, 1914. This daring and difficult task was completely successful on July 11, 1915, the two shallow-draught monitors, aided by aeroplanes spotting, bringing their heavy guns to bear with telling effect. The episode afforded another illustration of the working of that long arm of sea power which had throughout the war been the mainstay of the Allies.

CHAPTER CXII.

THE DARDANELLES CAMPAIGN (IV.): SARI BAIR AND SUVLA BAY.

SITUATION AT END OF JUNE, 1915—SIR IAN HAMILTON'S PLANS AND THE BRITISH GOVERNMENT—THE NEED OF REINFORCEMENTS—DELAYS IN LONDON—SUVLA BAY LANDING MISUNDERSTOOD—THE JULY PREPARATIONS—THE GREAT ATTACK ON AUGUST 6—ANALYSIS OF THE OPERATIONS—SARI BAIR—DETAILS OF THE ASSAULT—CAUSES OF FAILURE—THE SUVLA BAY LANDING—THE OPERATIONS DESCRIBED—SIR IAN HAMILTON'S CRITICISMS—GENERAL STOPFORD'S RECALL—SITUATION ON AUGUST 15.

THE present chapter almost concludes the story of the great and tragic failure of the British and French forces to dislodge the Turks from the Gallipoli Peninsula, to open the passage of the Dardanelles, and to reach Constantinople. The inception of the Gallipoli campaign and the phase of exclusively naval attacks were dealt with in Chapter XCII. The great Battle of the Landing was described in full detail in Chapter XCIV. The first two months of land fighting were recounted in Chapter XCVIII., and the wonderful work of the Australian and New Zealand Army Corps was discussed separately in Chapter XCIX., entitled "The Spirit of Anzac." The present chapter takes up the general narrative of the land fighting from the end of June, 1915. It explains briefly what happened at Gallipoli during the month of July, and then describes concisely the brilliant attempt made at the beginning of August by mixed forces from the Anzac area to capture the ultimate heights of the Sari Bair mountain, together with the principal episodes of the ill-starred landing at Suvla Bay on August 6–7, 1915, and the following days. The records, official and unofficial, of the Dardanelles Expedition are in most respects so voluminous, especially with regard to the later phases, that any narrative is bound to be merely selective. Kinglake, who took thirty-two years to complete his classic history of the Crimean War, would have required a century and treble his eight volumes to have written the story of the Dardanelles campaign on the same scale. As the area of the whole war expanded, and the numbers engaged grew ever more huge, so it became impossible to record all the facts with the minuteness practised in previous wars. Never before had warfare been seen on so huge a scale, for never since the great though far smaller incursions of barbaric Asiatic hordes into Europe had the conception of "a nation in arms" been put fully into actual practice. The fall of cities almost ceased to excite emotion; battles which in older eras would have convulsed the world only aroused transient interest; and minor engagements in every theatre of war, which would once have been meticulously noted in every detail, passed into oblivion in a few days and were never recorded at all. No section of the war was

TAKING SHELLS TO THE FRENCH BATTERIES.

more constantly marked by these small but often fierce minor conflicts than the Gallipoli campaign. They were so numerous that even the Commander-in-Chief, Sir Ian Hamilton, was unable to mention most of them in his dispatches. He was soon obliged to content himself with picking illustrative episodes from a form of warfare which was constant and severe.

At the end of June, 1915, the Franco-British line across the end of the peninsula had just previously been slightly advanced. The French, on the right of the line, had seized on June 21 the heights above the small stream known as the Kereves Dere, and the British had captured the cleft called the Gully Ravine, on the left of the line near the sea. The positions in the Cape Helles area were never afterwards materially altered. To the end the village of Krithia was not reached, and the heights of Achi Baba remained unscaled. The position at Anzac was also, when June ended, very much what it had been some weeks earlier, though various small advances had been made during the interval.

During July Sir Ian Hamilton's plans were largely governed by the inadequacy of his supply of high explosives. He kept the enemy on the alert by a constant routine of "bombing, sniping, and mining," but he was only able to make one important attack, which was delivered on July 12 and 13. Meanwhile the Turks at Krithia had received reinforcements which were reputed to number 10,000 men, and they made a half-hearted general attack about dawn on July 5. The enemy left their trenches and advanced across the open ground. They were allowed to come within point-blank range, and then were mown down by a murderous fire from rifles and machine-guns. No Turk succeeded in reaching the British or French trenches; very few were able to get back to the shelter of their own defences.

The Allied attack on July 12 was meant to form a sequel to the Battle of the Gully Ravine, described in Chapter XCVIII. The capture of the gully had driven back the Turkish right, but before Krithia the Turks had succeeded in retaining possession of their advanced trenches. Sir Ian Hamilton sought to storm the forward system of trenches along a front of 2,000 yards, from the mouth of the Kereves Dere to the main road from Krithia to Sedd-el-Bahr. The French Corps attacked on the right and the 52nd (Lowland) Division on the right centre. The French were to attack in full force at once. The right of the 52nd Division was to attack simultaneously, but the left of the Division was to attack in the afternoon. The 29th Division was to make a diversion on the British extreme left, and the Anzacs were to hold the attention of the troops confronting them far away beyond Gaba Tepe.

In pursuance of this plan, the French and half the 52nd Division dashed forward at

7.35 a.m., after the enemy's positions had been "prepared" by bombardment. They captured the first two lines of Turkish trenches with the greatest ease. The 1st Division of the French Corps, on the extreme right, made their way onward until they had established themselves in trenches on the very banks of the Kereves Dere. The 2nd French Division got no farther than the first two trenches, and the right (155th) Brigade of the 52nd Division were in a similar position.

On the left of the 155th Brigade a single splendid battalion, the 4th Battalion of the King's Own Scottish Borderers, charged impetuously deep into the enemy's lines, and all but a remnant of the battalion was destroyed. Sir Ian Hamilton said they "pressed on too eagerly," captured the third line of trenches, stormed the slope beyond, and were still carrying all before them when they came under a disastrous cross-fire from the artillery of the French and of the enemy. They were therefore, added Sir Ian, "forced to fall back with heavy losses to the second line of enemy trenches." Lieutenant Mellon, who did not witness the charge, but collected details from the survivors, gave a somewhat different version, which was published by Colonel C. W. E. Duncombe more than six months afterwards. The story told to Lieutenant Mellon was that the battalion was ordered to take two intervening trenches said to be weakly held, and then to advance another 150 yards in order to seize a new Turkish trench which had been "spotted" from an aeroplane. The battalion was given a plan showing the three trenches. A couple of companies advanced, took the two intervening trenches, but found that the supposed new one was a dummy. A terrific Turkish rifle and machine-gun fire burst upon the doomed companies, who were caught in the open without shelter, and very few escaped. The officer commanding the two supporting companies rushed his men forward when he saw a few stragglers returning. The supporting companies actually reached the dummy trench, found it strewn with the dead bodies of their comrades, and were themselves half-destroyed. The remnant fell back to the second intervening trench, which they held. The dummy trench remained an impassable zone. Every man who tried to reach it to

FIRING A FRENCH HEAVY GUN.

MAJOR-GEN. W. DOUGLAS,
Who succeeded Lieut.-Gen. Hunter-Weston as Commander of the Eighth Corps.

bring back the wounded was killed. Neither Turk nor Scot ever set foot in the area again, and those who did not return were reported missing.

A great deal of indiscriminate fighting followed all along the line, for the Turks continued to resist. In the afternoon the 157th Brigade forming the left of the Lowland Division, charged on their allotted sector in accordance with the plan of battle, and took all three lines of trenches before them. They had advanced about 400 yards, while the 155th Brigade and the French Corps had made progress to the extent of from 200 to 300 yards. Towards evening the whole line was ordered to stand fast, but all night long it had to face resolute counter-attacks, and at 7.30 next morning signs of exhaustion were visible among the tired troops. The right of the 157th Brigade gave way for a time under a bomb attack. On the afternoon of July 13 a fresh general attack was made at 4.30 p.m. by the Allies all along the line, the British having been reinforced by a brigade of the Royal Naval Division. The final result can be summed up in a sentence. In the centre of the Allied line of attack the Turks more or less held their own, and their third trench was not taken; but the French right and the British left made good the Turkish advanced positions confronting them, and thus gained new and valuable entrenchments. The Nelson battalion of the Royal Naval Division fought with conspicuous determination on this day; but the Portsmouth Battalion, equally indomitable, suffered the same experience as the 4th King's Own Scottish Borderers on the first day of the battle. At the same spot, and in just the same way, they charged too far, and were severely reduced in numbers in consequence. Sir Ian Hamilton afterwards specially mentioned the 5th Royal Scots Fusiliers (Lieutenant-Colonel J. B. Pollok-McCall), the 5th King's Own Scottish Borderers (Lieutenant-Colonel W. J. Millar), and the 6th Highland Light Infantry (Major J. Millar) for having fought with distinction in this action. The Turks were badly shaken by the two days' fighting, and over 500 Turkish prisoners were taken. The total Turkish casualties were estimated at 5,000, while the British lost 3,000 killed and wounded. The French escaped more lightly, but General Masnou, commanding the 1st Division of the French Corps, received a wound which proved mortal.

On July 17 Lieutenant-General Hunter-Weston, commanding the VIIIth Corps, left the peninsula, and directly afterwards was invalided home, where he received the K.C.B. for his energetic share in the operations. He was eventually succeeded in the command of the VIIIth Corps by Major-General W. Douglas. In a farewell order to the troops under his immediate command, Sir Aylmer Hunter-Weston specially expressed his gratitude to "the magnificent French artillery for their inestimable support repeatedly given." It may be noted at this point, though not in the strict chronological order of events, that on August 8 a Turkish battleship, the Hairredin Barbarossa, was torpedoed by a British submarine at the entrance to the Sea of Marmora. The Barbarossa had previously been moored in the Straits between Maidos and Chanak, and her long-range indirect fire had occasionally troubled the Anzacs a great deal. She had a displacement of 10,600 tons, and a principal armament of six 11-inch guns. The Barbarossa had originally been a German battleship, and in 1910 she was sold by the thrifty Germans to their Turkish dupes at an extortionate price. About the same time a useful Turkish torpedoboat, the Berk-i-Satvet, was also torpedoed by the British.

Before describing the last great combined attempt to dislodge the Turks from the peninsula, the plans of Sir Ian Hamilton, and his communications to the British Government, must be explained. The Second Battle of Krithia was fought on May 6, 7, and 8. Its broad result was failure, and it ought, therefore, to have led to a reconsideration of the whole position at the Dardanelles. Neither on the spot nor in London was there any such broad reconsideration. Sir Ian Hamilton's only thought was to "press on," and as he saw that his forces were too weak he cabled on May 10 asking for two fresh divisions. He got one, the 52nd Division. In London the Dardanelles position appears to have received no serious consideration at all during May. The Lusitania had been torpedoed on May 7, and the public mind was still preoccupied with the great disaster. The General Staff at the War Office had practically ceased to exist. Lord Kitchener was to all intents and purposes performing the duties of Chief of the General Staff, and he had other distractions nearer home. The British advance in the Festubert area had begun on Sunday, May 9. That week the Military Correspondent of *The Times* published his famous dispatches revealing the grave shortage of shells, and the Government were instantly in jeopardy. On May 15 Lord Fisher resigned, and the political crisis was thereby accentuated. At such a moment the voice of Sir Ian Hamilton was to Ministers in London as of one calling vainly in a distant wilderness. There were none who would heed him.

By Monday, May 17, Sir Ian Hamilton seems to have finally realised that the expected landing of Russian troops on the Black Sea coast of European Turkey had been finally abandoned, and that thenceforth the Allies in Gallipoli could look for no military aid from Russia in the neighbourhood of Constantinople. The reason was obvious. On May Day von Mackensen and his phalanx had begun their great attack against the Russians on the Dunajec in Galicia. It took Europe a fortnight or more fully to realize what was happening, but by May 16 the Russian armies had withdrawn from the Carpathian passes. On May 17, a Monday, Sir Ian Hamilton cabled pointing out that, if all hope of Russian help had gone, he would require not two more divisions, but two additional Army Corps. He was addressing deaf ears. By May 18 the whole country knew that a Coalition Government was in process of formation, and the next fortnight was passed in the task of making a new Ministry. Few looked towards Gallipoli. Sir Ian Hamilton fought the Third Battle of Krithia on June 4 with weak forces, but its chief result was to reveal the growing strength of the enemy.

During the month of June Lord Kitchener, in the words of Sir Ian Hamilton, "became persuaded of the bearing of these facts" about the Dardanelles. He promised to send three divisions of the New Armies and the infantry of two Territorial Divisions. These troops were to begin to arrive at Mudros on July 10, and their concentration was to be complete by August 10. The promise was kept, but a month of infinite value had been lost. For

Lafayette.

LIEUT.-COL. W. J. MILLAR,
Who commanded the 5th King's Own Scottish Borderers.

ARTILLERY AT SUVLA BAY: A GUN-POSITION.

the new operation Sir Ian Hamilton contemplated he required dark and moonless nights. He lost all July owing to the inattention of the Ministry and the War Office. When the second week of August came he had to choose between striking at once with troops mostly disembarked straight out of the transports, or waiting another month for the next dark nights. He struck at once and lost; but in estimating the causes of his failure it should not be forgotten that it was Lord Kitchener, and not Sir Ian Hamilton, who gave the Turks another month's grace in July. Had the Imperial General Staff been then in working order, the appeals from the Dardanelles would have received instant consideration. Possibly the desirability of fresh operations might also have been considered from a different angle.

Sir Ian Hamilton had thus at last got his two additional Army Corps on their way, and something over, and his next problem was to consider how best to utilize the new forces at his disposal. He considered that he had the choice of four courses, as follows:

1. He might land all his reinforcements at Cape Helles or elsewhere in the southern sector, and continue to try to force his way up the peninsula from its tip. He rejected this course (*a*) because the space available was narrow, and there was no room for such masses of troops to deploy; (*b*) because, even if he took the village of Krithia, the Achi Baba height was now too well fortified to be assailed; (*c*) because there was no good new landing-place between Cape Helles and Anzac which would not be exposed to converging artillery fire.

2. He might land at the Asiatic side of the Straits, and march on Chanak. He rejected this course, because, in his opinion, both the old and the new operation would be weak. He would have to continue his old attacks in the peninsula, and they would be in no greater strength. He would not have enough new forces to make the new operation a reasonably certain success.

3. He might land at Enos or Ebrije, in the Gulf of Xeros, and march round to seize the neck of the peninsula at the Bulair lines, thus cutting the land communications of the Turkish Army at Gallipoli. He rejected this course (*a*) because Ebrije had "a bad beach"; (*b*) because the distance by sea to Enos would impose too great a strain on the fleet-sweepers and trawlers and other vessels constantly engaged in carrying supplies; (*c*) because the powerful Turkish Army in Thrace would then have to be reckoned with; and (*d*) because, even if he could seize the isthmus at Bulair, the Turks would still be able to obtain supplies by ferrying them across the Straits from Chanak. The question was often asked: Why go to Enos or Ebrije? Why not land a little above the isthmus of Bulair? The answer was that the first few miles of coast above the Bulair

lines were exposed to the guns on the isthmus, and that beyond lay the marshes at the mouth of the Kavak Dere river, where a landing was impossible. If the bad beach at Ebrije was excluded, it was believed, though the evidence as to the coast between the Kavak Dere and Enos does not seem quite conclusive, that there was no good landing-place nearer than Enos.

4. He might reinforce the Anzacs, and direct them to make a strong push to capture the Sari Bair mountain. He might simultaneously make a fresh landing in Suvla Bay, well to the north of the Anzac position, and so surprise the Turks that it would be possible for the reinforced Anzac forces, after capturing Sari Bair, to get across the waist of the peninsula and seize the town of Maidos, on the Narrows. The Turkish Army at Krithia and on Achi Baba would thus be isolated. This was the plan which Sir Ian Hamilton decided very early to adopt.

For a long time after the plan had been tried, and had failed disastrously, the British public remained under a misconception about its character. It was believed in England that the landing in Suvla Bay was the main feature of the new operation. This was not the case, nor was there ever any such suggestion on the spot. Even Ministers seemed to have only a hazy idea of what was intended. Speeches were made in Parliament in terms which appeared to imply that the Suvla Bay attack was the essence of the business. It was not until the extremely belated publication of Sir Ian Hamilton's final dispatch on January 6, 1916, that the truth became clear. He explained in this dispatch that Anzac was meant to deliver "the knock-down blow," while the Suvla Bay landing, and a big containing attack on Krithia and Achi Baba, were both "complementary operations." The Sari Bair mountain was, he said, the key to his whole tactical conception; and dispassionate study of his scheme and published orders shows that this must have been so.

Yet another misconception long lingered in the public mind. It was widely thought that the whole combined operation failed because the Suvla Bay landing came to grief. The gradual revelation of the facts showed far otherwise. It is true that the advance of the Suvla Bay forces through the depression between Sari Bair

BRITISH CAVALRY AND ARTILLERY HORSES JUST AFTER THE LANDING AT SUVLA BAY.

THE HILLSIDE AT SUVLA BAY: BRITISH TROOPS PREPARING A BIVOUAC.

and the Anafarta Hills was expected to "smash the mainspring of the Turkish opposition to Anzac," but the Anzac attack eventually failed of itself, because, although brilliantly and heroically delivered, it just fell short of full achievement in the end for reasons which will be presently related. There will always be great differences of opinion about the causes of final failure. It may well be argued that if the Suvla Bay forces had not dallied, but had gained a great success, the Anzacs and their reinforcements might have held on to the new positions they won so arduously; yet the balance of probability is against the assumption that the attack was primarily lost at Suvla. The tactical scheme was a good one, and was probably the best of the four courses which Sir Ian Hamilton formulated. The assault on Sari Bair had a strong chance of success, and it very nearly succeeded. The real and ultimate cause of failure was probably not the generals, nor the untried troops at Suvla, nor the lack of water, nor defective staff work in some sectors, though all these were important contributory factors. The dominating factor, the ultimate cause of failure, was probably the difficult and diversified character of the terrain and the very great advantages which the area in dispute gave to the Turks. In other words, the last great battles fought at Gallipoli were lost by the Allies not only by their own mistakes, but still more because they were attempting an exploit which in that intricate and tangled wilderness of heights and hollows, of woods and scrub and patches of open plain, left much to chance; and it happened that on that occasion the luck was with the enemy. Earlier in the year the British expedition might have tried and succeeded, but they never overcame the consequences of the months that were lost, for from first to last it was their misfortune to be too late. The fault lay principally in London.

The details of the great attack from Anzac were left largely in the hands of Lieutenant-General Sir William Birdwood, who commanded the Anzac position. It was believed that the landing at Suvla Bay was also very largely his idea, and it was never any secret that to the last this tenacious and extremely able soldier always believed that the Gallipoli peninsula might be won, and that he withdrew from it with the utmost reluctance. Nor, indeed, was the resolution of Sir Ian Hamilton any less firm, for he maintained throughout, and after his return to England, that the enterprise should not be abandoned. These views of the principal commanders were long shared by the British Government, but they were not endorsed by the preponderating weight of competent military opinion in other areas of the war. Yet the attack on Sari Bair in August showed that Sir Ian Hamilton and Sir William Birdwood had at least substantial grounds for their contention.

Throughout July the secret preparations for the great thrust went unceasingly forward. The scheme was dominated by the almanac, and the actual date was fixed long beforehand. The final reinforcements were due to arrive in the first days of August. The crescent moon would rise on the night of August 6–7 at 2 a.m. It was, therefore,

BRIG.-GEN. A. H. BALDWIN.
Commanded 38th Infantry Brigade.

decided that the operations were to begin on August 6, and that the landing at Suvla Bay was to be made after dark on that day. Sir Ian Hamilton recapitulated his principal objects in these words:

(1) To break out with a rush from Anzac and cut off the bulk of the Turkish Army from land communication with Constantinople.

(2) To gain such a command for my artillery as to cut off the bulk of the Turkish Army from sea traffic, whether with Constantinople or with Asia.

(3) Incidentally to secure Suvla Bay as a winter base for Anzac and all the troops operating in the northern theatre.

Suvla Bay had originally been quite wrongly believed to be exposed to bad weather. It also received little consideration when the first land operations were planned in March and April, because the early attacks were governed too exclusively by consideration of the domi-

RECAPTURING A TRENCH AT GALLIPOLI.

nating heights and the practicable depressions in the interior of the peninsula. As a matter of fact the bay was submarine-proof, and was fairly well protected against all gales except those from the south-west; and old dwellers in Constantinople, who professed some knowledge of Gallipoli, had always contended that Suvla Bay was the place which should have been selected for the original landing. Many devices were practised during the weeks of waiting in order to mislead the enemy. Troops were concentrated at the island of Mitylene, off the coast of Asia Minor, and the island was solemnly inspected by Sir Ian Hamilton and Admiral de Robeck. Fresh maps of Asia Minor were made in Cairo, and the enemy's spies were allowed to learn of their existence. The warships visited various places on the Asian coast, and the monitors ostentatiously took soundings and sought fresh ranges for their guns between Gaba Tepe and Kum Tepe. These and other ingenious ruses were simple enough to practise, and they threw the enemy off their guard; but the real problems were harder to solve. No one of the available bases could contain the reinforcements, and on August 5 the new forces were still scattered at various places in the Ægean. Some had been landed at Anzac, others were on transports at Imbros, Tenedos, and even at Mitylene, 120 miles away. The water question, about which much was afterwards heard, caused the most intense anxiety. A storage reservoir holding 30,000 gallons was secretly built at Anzac, and distributing pipes were laid from it; but the scheme went wrong at first owing to the breakdown of the stationary engine on which it depended. Vast quantities of petroleum tins were sent for in order to carry water in other areas, but a collision between two steamers delayed their arrival. A pack mule corps was organized, chiefly for the transport of water. A steamer was specially filled with water-pumps, hose, tanks, troughs, and other appliances intended for the rapid utilization of the wells and springs which were known to exist in the open country near Suvla Bay. Water-lighters and a tank-steamer to tow them were provided, and there was a "parent water-ship" at Imbros. The mules furnished for carrying water numbered 4,650, and there were 1,750 water-carts. If the water supply went wrong at Suvla Bay, it was not through lack of preparation, but rather because the arrangements for distribution were inadequate, owing to the inexperience of those charged with this important task.

Sir Ian Hamilton decided to control the triple attack he had planned from his headquarters in the island of Imbros, which was "the centre of the cable system." He explained afterwards that, in his view, if he had committed himself at the outset to any one of the three theatres he would have lost his "sense of proportion." At Imbros he was 45 minutes from Helles, 40 minutes from Anzac, and 50 minutes from Suvla. He could also, he said, best control from Imbros the two divisions he held in reserve, and throw them in where they were most required. His decision was afterwards questioned in many quarters. It was urged that at Helles only a containing attack was planned, and it was to be delivered by troops and commanders who were thoroughly familiar with the ground. Sir Ian Hamilton himself acknowledged that, although the Anzac attack was vital, "there was nothing in its course or conduct to call for my personal intervention." He had left all the Anzac arrangements to Sir William Birdwood, and rightly had the fullest confidence in his judgment. The troops designated for the landing at Suvla Bay were raw, the generals were unfamiliar with the character of the warfare at Gallipoli, and, if the Suvla operation was complementary, it was nevertheless of the utmost importance to the tactical scheme. Sir Ian Hamilton did not visit Suvla until 5 p.m. on the evening of August 8, although it was only 50 minutes' steaming distance from his headquarters. This must be held a serious error of judgment. Either the Commander-in-Chief or his Chief of Staff should have been there much earlier. Another criticism afterwards made, that the Suvla Bay attack should have been entrusted to veteran troops who might have been replaced at Helles and Anzac by portions of the new arrivals, was probably more questionable. Time was short, and the exchange of units would have been a difficult operation for the Navy, upon whom a tremendous and complex burden had already been imposed ; yet the Suvla Bay Army Corps might have been stiffened by a few veteran units.

The last great combined assault upon the Turkish positions in Gallipoli began in the afternoon of Friday, August 6, with the attack at the southern end of the peninsula, which was meant to hold the enemy forces gathered before Krithia and Achi Baba. The 88th Brigade

INDIAN TROOPS AT THE DARDANELLES. [*"Times" Photograph.*

Gurkhas resting before returning to the trenches.

ROYAL NAVAL DIVISION'S ARMOURED CARS IN ACTION.

Armoured cars which advanced over bridges constructed across the British trenches right up to the enemy's firing-line at Achi Baba.

of the 29th Division sought to capture 1,200 yards of the Turkish front opposite the British right and right centre. The 42nd (East Lancashire) Division simultaneously endeavoured to take two small trenches which enfiladed the main advance. The whole British attack had failed by sunset, although on the left wing of the advance long sections of the enemy's trenches were seized and held for a time. The repulse was entirely unexpected. The Turkish trenches were found to be packed with troops, and it was discovered from prisoners that the Turks had actually been preparing to attack the British line within the next hour or two. Two fresh Turkish divisions had arrived for this especial purpose. The Turks fought, moreover, as they had never fought in June and July. They had recovered their spirit, and had been greatly heartened by the news of the sweeping German advance on the Russian front. They attacked in turn on the morning of August 7, but were driven back.

Sir Ian Hamilton felt on August 7 that it was imperative for him to continue his attack on the Krithia front, as otherwise Turkish reinforcements might be directed to Anzac and Suvla. He chose a double line of Turkish trenches, about 800 yards long, which lay to the east of Krithia, and launched the 125th and 129th Brigades at this section of the front at 9.40 a.m. The Turks resisted with as much ardour as on the previous day. The 125th Brigade took the first line of the trenches allotted to them, and small parties reached the second line; but the 129th Brigade were not so fortunate, and in an hour had made no substantial progress. There was a vineyard, about 200 yards long by 100 yards broad, lying west of the Krithia road, where there was much desperate fighting on August 7 and 8, as well as on succeeding days. The 6th and 7th Lancashire Fusiliers held the vineyard against desperate counter-attacks all through the Saturday and Sunday, although both battalions lost heavily. Other units took a hand in the struggle for the vineyard, including the 4th East Lancashire Regiment and the 1/9th Manchester Regiment. A subaltern of the latter Territorial battalion, Lieutenant W. T. Forshaw, received the Victoria Cross for his personal bravery at the northern corner of the vineyard. "He treated bomb-throwing," said eye-witnesses, "as if it were snowballing"; and Sir Ian Hamilton testified in his final dispatch that Lieutenant Forshaw was "largely instrumental in the repulse of three very determined onslaughts." In one attack he shot three Turks with his revolver at close quarters, and he threw innumerable bombs. Lieutenant Forshaw stuck to his corner continuously for 41 hours, refusing to budge when his detachment was relieved. The Turkish attacks on the vineyard died away on August 9. Three nights later they made a desperate assault and took it, but they were cleared out by bombs, and the coveted spot was made part of the British lines. The net result of the Helles portion of the operations was that useful minor advances were made and consolidated, while the real purpose of the fighting, which was to keep the Turks in this area busy, was more than

FRENCH COLONIAL TROOPS
In the first-line trenches.

accomplished. The enemy were so thoroughly alarmed that they even reinforced the Krithia line although hard pressed elsewhere.

The operations from Anzac must next be recounted. Reinforcements had been stealthily poured into the Anzac sector for two or three nights preceding the great attack, and had been concealed in prepared hiding-places. The water supply had also been greatly developed. On the morning of August 6 Sir William Birdwood had at his disposal 37,000 rifles and 72 guns, while two cruisers, four monitors, and two destroyers lay opposite the Anzac heights to give him further assistance. The land forces were divided into two portions.

One portion was to deliver the grand assault on the rugged heights of Sari Bair, and the other was to hold the existing Anzac position and to make special attacks on Turkish positions immediately confronting it. The attack on Sari Bair was to be made by the New Zealand and Australian Division (less the 1st and 3rd Light Horse Brigades), the 13th Division (less five battalions), and the 29th Indian Infantry Brigade and the Indian Mountain Artillery Brigade. It was a composite force in more senses than one. Australians, New Zealanders, Maoris, Englishmen, Sikhs, and Gurkhas fought side by side in the supreme attempt to win the heights which had so long dominated Anzac. Many of the Australians and New Zealanders were veterans twice over; the Sikhs and Gurkhas had been in several fierce actions around Helles; the 13th Division (commanded by Major-General Shaw) belonged to the New Armies, and was fresh from England, but had relieved the 29th Division for a short time at Helles in order to gain experience in the field. The portion of the forces retained at Anzac consisted of the Australian Division (plus the 1st and 3rd Light Horse Brigades and two batteries of the 40th Brigade). Two brigades were kept in reserve, the 29th Brigade of the 10th Division (New Armies) and the 38th Brigade.

For three days, August 4, 5, and 6, the Turkish left and centre were slowly bombarded. At 5.30 p.m. on August 6, little more than an hour after the resolute infantry assault had been begun miles away near Krithia, the 1st Australian Brigade started its fierce attack upon Lone Pine, which must always remain one of the most famous episodes of the warfare at Gallipoli. Lone Pine was the name given to a formidable system of Turkish entrenchments on a plateau which was one of the lower southern spurs of the great mass of Sari Bair heights. It was near the southern end of the Anzac position, and was strongly held by the Turks, because it commanded one of their principal sources of water supply. The 1st Australian Brigade was chiefly composed of men from New South Wales, and was commanded by Brigadier-General N. M. Smyth. It was considerably below strength, and the supporting battalions were also weak.

BRITISH ANTI-AIRCRAFT GUN.
Fired by Electricity.

A GREAT BOMB
Used by the Allies' Airmen at Gallipoli.

When the whistles blew at the appointed minute, three successive lines of Australians swarmed out of their trenches and dashed through the scrub towards the Turkish position. Almost the first to fall mortally wounded was Lieutenant Digges La Touche, an Irish clergyman belonging to the Church of England. He had enlisted at Sydney as a private, was promoted, had arrived at Anzac from Alexandria in charge of reinforcements that very day, and though he joined in the attack at his own option, he would not be denied. The surging lines swept onward, but came to a sudden and

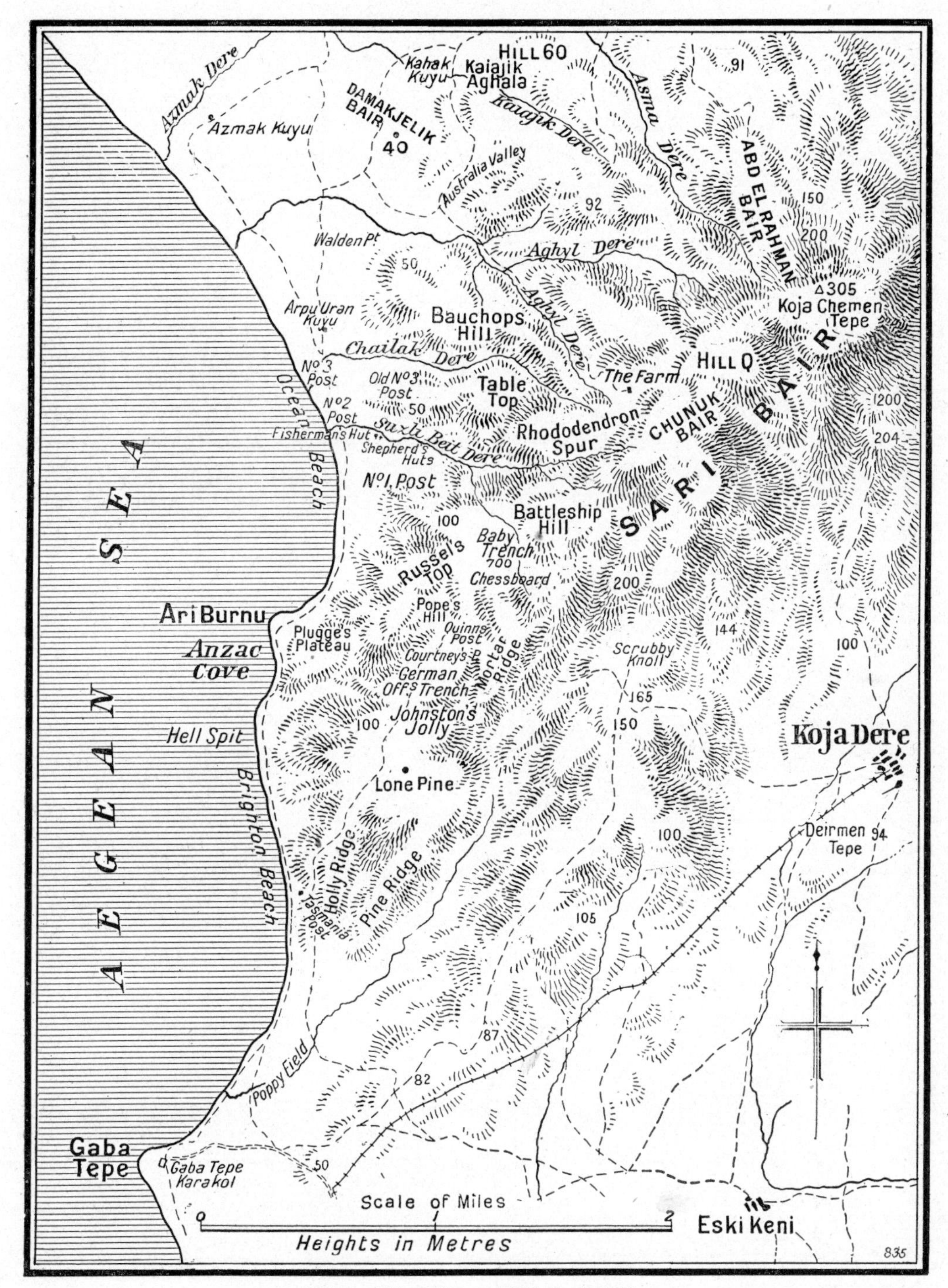

MAP OF THE ANZAC AREA.

perplexed halt on the verge of the Turkish trench; for no trench was visible, only a roof of great beams covered with earth, and impossible to move. The Turks were deep below ground, and were firing through small loopholes. It was a daunting moment, but the Anzacs were equal to the occasion, although they were being swept by a converging fire of shot and shell. They rushed over the roof, found the manholes, and dropped feet foremost into a plexus of dim passages. The fight was waged, and the trenches were won, in these narrow underground galleries. Within half-an-hour the whole system of entrenchments had passed into the hands of the men from New South Wales, whose reserves had meanwhile crossed the intervening ground under a fierce fire; but later on a thousand Turkish and Australian dead were dragged from the labyrinth of burrows. The enemy made

MULES CONVEYING AMMUNITION BOXES TO THE FIGHTING-LINE.

numerous desperate counter-attacks during the succeeding three days, but they were always repulsed, largely owing, on several occasions, to the accurate fire of the 2nd New Zealand Battery under Major Sykes. The taking of Lone Pine inflicted disproportionately heavy losses on the Turks; it was a conspicuously gallant exploit, because the Anzacs were considerably outnumbered; and it served a far more than local purpose, because it attracted the Turkish reserves, and was afterwards held to be the principal reason why so few of the enemy opposed the landing at Suvla Bay that night. The fight for Lone Pine was always regarded as the most desperate hand-to-hand conflict which occurred during the whole of the Gallipoli operations. Seven Victoria Crosses were awarded for it to Captain Alfred John Short, Lieutenant W. J. Symons, Lieutenant F. H. Tubb, Corporal A. S. Burton, Corporal William Dunstan, Private John Hamilton, and Private Leonard Keyser. Sir Ian Hamilton in his dispatch said that "one weak Australian brigade, numbering at the outset but 2,000 rifles, and supported only by two weak battalions, carried the work under the eyes of a whole enemy division, and maintained their grip upon it like a vice during six days' successive counter-attacks."

There were other brilliant attacks from the old Anzac positions on the night of August 6, including assaults on German Officer's Trench and Baby 700. The story of the dramatic charge of the First and Third Light Horse Brigades has already been told in Chapter XCIX. They won no ground, but their glory is imperishable, and they held on Battleship Hill all day on the 7th masses of Turkish reserves who ought to have been at Suvla Bay.

The Lone Pine and the other attacks did not, however, represent the main operation from Anzac. The principal business was the night attack on the summits of Sari Bair, which was under the immediate direction of Major-General Sir A. J. Godley. The mass of Sari Bair was crowned by two topmost heights, with a considerable ravine intervening. The southern height, known as Chunuk Bair, was about 850 feet high. Beyond the ravine lay a spur called Hill Q, from which the ground sloped upward to the ultimate crest of Sari Bair called Koja Chemen Tepe, just under a thousand feet high. Four columns were assigned to the operations against Sari Bair, as follows:

Right Covering Column, under Brigadier-General A. H. Russell: New Zealand Mounted Rifles Brigade, the Otago Mounted Rifles Regiment, the Maori Contingent and New Zealand Field Troop.

Right Assaulting Column, under Brigadier-General F. E. Johnston: New Zealand Infantry Brigade, Indian Mountain Battery (less one section), one Company New Zealand Engineers.

Left Covering Column, under Brigadier-General J. H. Travers: Headquarters 40th Brigade, half the 72nd Field Company, 4th Battalion South Wales Borderers, and 5th Battalion Wiltshire Regiment.

Left Assaulting Column, under Brigadier-General (afterwards Major-General) H. V. Cox: 29th Indian Infantry Brigade, 4th Australian Infantry Brigade, Indian Mountain Battery (less one section), one company New Zealand Engineers.

Divisional Reserve.—6th Battalion South Lancashire Regiment, and 8th Battalion Welsh Regiment (Pioneers) at Chailak Dere, and the 39th Infantry Brigade and half 72nd Field Company at Aghyl Dere.

All the troops had to be moved along the coast in secrecy to an outpost beyond Fisherman's Hut (known as No. 2 Post), where great quantities of gun and rifle ammunition had been stealthily accumulated. The right assaulting column was to storm the summit of Chunuk Bair. It was to advance up the Chailak Dere and Sazli Beit Dere ravines. The left assaulting column was given orders which were not made entirely clear in the documents subsequently

FORTY-ONE HOURS' CONTINUOUS BOMB-THROWING: A GALLIPOLI V.C.

When holding the north-west corner of the "Vineyard" Lieutenant William Thomas Forshaw, 1/9th Battn. Manchester Regiment (T.F.), was attacked and heavily bombed by Turks, who advanced time after time by three trenches, which converged at this point. But he held on, directing his men and encouraging them by exposing himself with the utmost disregard of danger, and throwing bombs continuously for forty-one hours. He refused to budge when his detachment was relieved.

published. Sir Ian Hamilton in his dispatch said that General Cox was to work up the Aghyl Dere and storm Koja Chemen Tepe, the final summit of Sari Bair, which will hereafter be called in this narrative Hill 305. But as it approached the Sari Bair heights, the main

Aghyl Dere ravine bifurcated, the northern fork approaching Hill 305, while the southern fork led towards Hill Q, between Hill 305 and Chunuk Bair. What happened was that when the left assaulting column reached the fork it split up, one-half going up the northern ravine against Hill 305, while the other half went up the southern ravine against Hill Q. There was thus a division of strength, which may have been intended, but the official papers give no clue.

The object of the two covering columns was to save the strength and numbers of the two assaulting columns for the main assault. They were to clear the ravines and foothills, and let the assaulting columns through. West of Chunuk Bair was a steep knoll known as Table Top, 400 feet high, with precipitous sides, and a small plateau at the summit teeming with enemy trenches. A communication trench led from Table Top to Rhododendron Spur, below the summit of Chunuk Bair. The right covering column was instructed to capture Table Top, and generally to clear the way for the assault on Chunuk Bair. The left covering column was meant to help General Cox's forces in their assault on Hill 305. It was to move far up along the beach and then strike inland and seize a low hill called Damakjelik Bair, about 130 feet high. It would thus cover the Hill 305 column against any attack from the direction of Suvla Bay, while it might also be able to help that portion of the Suvla Bay attacking forces which was landing south of Nibrunesi Point.

Before proceeding to details, the broad results of all these operations from Anzac may first be briefly summarized. They failed in their principal object, but they greatly extended the positions held by the Anzacs. The results, compendiously stated, were as follows :

First Day (August 7) : The right covering column cleared the Chailak Dere and took Table Top. The left covering column took Damakjelik Bair precisely as arranged. The right assaulting column reached the top of Rhododendron Spur and entrenched. One-half the left assaulting column worked round to the ravine of the Asma Dere, but was checked on the lower northern slopes of Hill 305. The other half of the left assaulting column reached the lower slopes of Hill Q and was there checked. That evening the bulk of the forces were re-arranged in three columns, called the right, centre, and left.

Second Day (August 8) : The right column reached and held the summit of Chunuk Bair. The centre column was driven back from the dip between Chunuk Bair and Hill Q. The left column unsuccessfully attacked the slopes of Abd el Rahman Bair, a northern spur of Sari Bair. That night the forces were again re-arranged in three columns, numbered 1, 2, and 3.

Third Day (August 9) : The captured summit of Chunuk Bair was used as a pivot. No. 1 column held Chunuk Bair and Rhododendron Spur. No. 2 column stormed the dip between Chunuk Bair and Hill Q, and saw the waters of the Narrows far below, but was driven back. No. 3 column lost its way and failed to take Hill Q, which was its objective.

Fourth Day (August 10) : The Turks retook the summit of Chunuk Bair, the dip, and the slopes of Hill Q. The attack on the Sari Bair position definitely failed on this day, after fierce hand-to-hand fighting.

Turning now to details, it must be explained that the first task of the right covering column, which was entirely composed of New Zealanders, was undertaken early on the night of August 6. General Russell had to clear the Chailak Dere and Sazli Beit Dere ravines, but he had previously to take a formidable redoubt known as Old No. 3 Post, on the slopes opposite No. 2 Post. The redoubt was captured by stratagem. For many nights previously the destroyer Colne (Commander Claude Seymour, R.N.) had been turning her searchlight on it at 9 p.m., and bombarding it for ten minutes. Then followed ten minutes' darkness and silence, succeeded by another illuminated bombardment, which always ceased precisely at 9.30. The Turks had grown so accustomed to this nightly visitation that they always evacuated the redoubt at the appointed time. On the night of August 6, when the searchlight switched off at 9.30, the New Zealanders were waiting in the adjacent scrub, and they swarmed into the empty redoubt. The Auckland Mounted Rifles disposed of such Turks as were found in the neighbourhood. Having made sure of their success, they quickly pushed on, and by 1 a.m. had cleared all Bauchop's Hill (named after the Colonel of the Otago Mounted Rifles), which was described as " a maze of ridge and ravine, everywhere entrenched." The Otago Rifles and the Maoris, while making their way into the Chailak Dere ravine, were stopped by a tremendous barbed wire entanglement flanked by en-

CAPTAIN R. R. WILLIS. SERGT. RICHARDS. CORPORAL W. COSGRAVE.

Captain Willis and Sergeant Richards were two of the three men selected by vote of the 1st Lancashire Fusiliers to receive the V.C. for gallantry during the Battle of the Landing, April 25, 1915. Corporal Cosgrave, 1st Battalion Munster Fusiliers, awarded the V.C. for most conspicuous bravery during the attack from the beach east of Cape Helles, April 26, 1915. He pulled down the posts of the enemy's wire entanglements single-handed, thereby greatly contributing to successful clearing of the heights.

CAPT. PERCY H. HANSEN. LIEUT. FORSHAW. PRIVATE ALFRED POTTS.

At Green Knoll, in Suvla Bay, when his regiment—the Lincolnshires—had been forced to retire, leaving some wounded behind, Captain Hansen led volunteers under heavy fire into the shrub, which was burning fiercely, and succeeded in saving the lives of several men who would otherwise have been burned to death ; Lieutenant William Thomas Forshaw, whose gallant deed is illustrated on page 177 ; Private Alfred Potts, 1st Berkshire Yeomanry, who, at Suvla Bay, under heavy fire, rescued a comrade by dragging him several hundred yards on a shovel to a place of safety.

AWARDED THE VICTORIA CROSS FOR BRAVERY IN THE FIELD.

GENERAL SIR IAN HAMILTON (X) AND MEMBERS

trenchments. They suffered considerably, but progress was forced with the help of engineers, backed by the Maoris. Sir Ian Hamilton said that Captain Shera and the New Zealand Engineers acted at this moment with "most conspicuous and cool courage." The principal exploit of the New Zealanders that night was, however, the storming of Table Top, whose sides were so steep that they almost seemed to bulge out like a mushroom. It was bombarded by the Colne, its precipitous heights were scaled by the undaunted New Zealanders, and by midnight they held the plateau and had taken 150 prisoners. The work of the right covering column was completely successful.

As soon as Old No. 3 Post had been taken, and while the attack on Bauchop's Hill was proceeding, the left covering column came into action. It marched by the entrance to the Aghyl Dere ravine, and took Damakjelik Bair with a rush. A battalion of the New Army, the 4th South Wales Borderers, under Lieutenant-Colonel Gillespie, led the way, and Sir Ian Hamilton afterwards bestowed the highest possible praise on the men of the battalion and their commander. They bore themselves well in the most trying of operations—a long night march with an uphill fight at the end—although at times they were enfiladed.

By midnight Brigadier-General Johnston and the right assaulting column, consisting of the New Zealand Infantry Brigade, were on their way through the Chailak Dere and Sazli Beit Dere ravines to the assault of Chunuk Bair. An hour and a half later the Canterbury Infantry had traversed the Sazli Beit Dere and were attacking the lower trenches on Rhododendron Spur. The Otago Infantry headed the force marching through the Chailak Dere, but the country was so difficult, and the opposition so fierce, that they did not debouch on the spur until 5.30 a.m. The whole column, once reunited, swept up the spur, cleared it, and entrenched there. They were a quarter of a mile from the summit of Chunuk Bair,

OF HIS STAFF AT THE DARDANELLES.

so had just been compelled to stop short of full achievement. On this day Corporal Cyril Royston Guyton Bassett, of the New Zealand Divisional Signal Company, won the V.C for his "most conspicuous bravery and devotion" in laying a field telephone wire to the new position "in full daylight and under a continuous and heavy fire."

The left assaulting column, which had farther to go, fared less favourably. It crossed the lower portion of the Chailak Dere, swerved round, and entered the Aghyl Dere. On reaching the fork in the ravine, the column divided, as already explained. The 4th Australian Brigade went up the northern fork of the ravine, while the 29th Indian Infantry Brigade moved up the southern fork. The scrub was thick, the enemy's fire was persistent, and the march proved exhausting. The Australians, whose spirit was unbreakable, got across from the Aghyl Dere into the northern end of the Asma Dere ravine. Soon after 7 a.m. they were ordered to join with the 14th Sikhs, with whom they had got into touch, and to assault the summit of Hill 305. But the Turks had been reinforced, our troops were exhausted by their long night march, the heat was growing intense, the New Zealanders were not on the top of Chunuk Bair, and eventually the assault was suspended. The Indian Brigade was likewise checked. The 10th Gurkhas, on the right of the brigade, had come into contact with the New Zealanders on Rhododendron Spur; the 5th and 6th Gurkhas were practically on the slopes of Hill Q; but the troops were all tired out, and the two main summits were still uncarried. It was decided to hold on for the rest of the day, and to resume the attack next morning. During the afternoon the forces were rearranged as follows:

Right Column, Brigadier-General F. E. Johnston: 26th Indian Mountain Battery (less one section), Auckland Mounted Rifles, New Zealand Infantry Brigade, two battalions 13th Division, and the Maori Contingent.

Centre and Left Columns, Major-General H. V. Cox: 21st Indian Mountain Battery (less one section), 4th Australian Brigade, 39th Infantry Brigade (less one

TABLE TOP, 400 FEET HIGH, WITH PRECIPITOUS SIDES, WHICH WAS CAPTURED BY THE NEW ZEALANDERS.

This position was taken by the New Zealanders on the night of August 6, 1915. Orders were given to the men not to fire their rifles, but to use bayonets. One hundred and fifty prisoners, many rifles, and much ammunition were captured.

battalion), with 6th Battalion South Lancashire Regiment attached, and the 29th Indian Infantry Brigade.

The revised plan of attack was that the right column was to take the summit of Chunuk Bair, while the left column was to make a flank assault on Hill 305 by way of Abd el Rahman Bair, the northern spur which jutted out below the topmost peak. General Johnston moved out against Chunuk Bair at 4.15 a.m. on August 8. The Wellington Battalion of the New Zealand Infantry Brigade, a battalion whose name will live for ever in the annals of the Dominion, headed the advance. There followed the Auckland Mounted Rifles, the Maori Contingent, and two battalions of the New Army, the 7th Battalion Gloucester Regiment and the 8th Welsh Pioneers. Lieutenant-Colonel Malone, of the Gloucesters, led the way, and the whole force raced with irresistible determination up the ultimate steeps. They suffered terribly, but they won the peak, and saw the Dardanelles and the coast of Asia Minor spread out before them. The summit was a second Spion Kop, and there was room there for less than a thousand men, who were exposed to a galling fire. Colonel Malone was mortally wounded while marking out the line to be held. The 7th Gloucesters lost in killed or wounded every officer and every senior non-commissioned officer. They fought on undaunted under their sergeants and corporals, enduring continuous casualties, but honourably maintaining the splendid name of the fine old marching regiment to which they were affiliated. The Wellington Battalion had gone into action 700 strong on the night of the 6th, but by the evening of the 8th it only numbered 53 effectives. Yet though the enemy's fire was so hot that there was little chance to entrench deeply, the New Zealanders and the men of Gloucester and South Wales, none of whom had dreamed of war a year before, held the peak throughout the night.

The centre column was operating from the direction of the farm above the southern fork of the Aghyl Dere, but it met with so much opposition that it made little progress that day. The 4th Australian Brigade, which constituted the left column, fared even worse. It was still on the Asma Dere, and tried to advance up the Abd el Rahman spur. The enemy were plentifully supplied with machine guns, were in great strength, and were quickly helped by powerful reinforcements. The Australians were "virtually surrounded," and before they withdrew under superior pressure

EMBARKATION OF BRITISH TROOPS.

the brigade had suffered a total loss of over 1,000 casualties since they first marched out from the beach. They clung to the Asma Dere ravine, however. "Here," wrote Sir Ian Hamilton, "they stood at bay, and, though the men were by now half dead with thirst and with fatigue, they bloodily repulsed attack after attack delivered by heavy columns of Turks." They looked anxiously for the expected support from the Suvla Bay area, but in vain, for August 8 was the fatal day when "inertia prevailed" at the new landing-place. No sound of firing floated upward from the Suvla foothills to the Australians struggling on the ridge below Sari Bair.

In the afternoon the conflict grew more desultory, and much necessary time was spent in getting up water and food to the tired troops. The one definite result of the day's operations was that the crest of Chunuk Bair had been seized. It was decided to make a supreme effort next morning, and the columns were once more rearranged as follows:

No. 1 Column, Brigadier-General F. E. Johnston: 26th Indian Mountain Battery (less one section), the

Auckland and Wellington Mounted Rifles Regiments, the New Zealand Infantry Brigade, and two battalions of the 13th Division.

No. 2 Column, Major-General H. V. Cox: 21st Indian Mountain Battery (less one section), 4th Australian Brigade, 39th Brigade (less the 7th Gloucesters, relieved), with the 6th Battalion South Lancashire Regiment attached, and the Indian Infantry Brigade.

No. 3 Column, Brigadier-General A. H. Baldwin, Commanding 38th Infantry Brigade: Two battalions each from the 38th and 29th Brigades and one from the 40th Brigade.

The instructions to the columns were concise. No. 1 column was to hold and consolidate the positions already gained on the right, and to complete the conquest of Chunuk Bair (only the south-western slopes and the small crest of the knoll were actually held). No. 2 column was to make for the dip between Chunuk Bair and Hill Q, and eventually to assist in an attack on Hill Q by this route. No. 3 column was to march up the Chailak Dere, mass behind the trenches on Chunuk Bair, sweep across the summit, along the dip, and deliver the main attack on Hill Q after the dip had been cleared by Column No. 2.

There was a tremendous bombardment of Chunuk Bair and Hill Q from land and sea at dawn on August 9; but the day was destined to end in failure. The New Zealanders and the untried men of the New Army clung with desperate valour to the summit of Chunuk Bair throughout the long day of tropical heat. They were constantly assailed, for the Turks knew that Chunuk Bair commanded the Narrows; but they never budged an inch, although greatly exhausted. No. 2 column performed the first part of its allotted task. The 6th Gurkhas, under Major C. G. L. Allanson, and a portion of the 6th South Lancashire Regiment won their way to the ridge of the dip, saw below them the road leading to Maidos and the Straits, and even rushed down the farther slopes after the discomfited enemy. But at that moment the attack was seen to have gone wrong. No. 3 column, under Brigadier-General Baldwin, should by then have been behind the trenches on Chunuk Bair ready to sweep along the dip against Hill Q. It had lost its way in the darkness amid the scrub and the rugged hollows of the Chailak Dere, and was only debouching at the Farm when it ought to have been crowning Chunuk Bair. Major Allanson was listening eagerly for the expected sound of Baldwin's advance through his forces, when Turkish shells began to fall among his Gurkhas on the ridge of the dip. There was no chance for him to lead his men unsupported up the slopes of Hill Q. Almost before he realized that Baldwin was late, the Turkish commander on the other side of the ridge had taken advantage of the confusion caused by the support of the guns. He rallied his flying troops, they rushed up their side of the dip, and drove the Gurkhas and Lancashires back towards their starting point.

That movement, comparatively small at first, settled the fate of the day, and, as many have since thought, the whole fate of the great attack from Anzac upon Sari Bair. So true it is that one little rally, one little rush, one last turn by the commander of a handful of retreating troops, may give just the change which develops into a decision. Had the Turks not rallied and cleared the dip just at that critical moment, things might have gone differently. For when Baldwin reached the Farm, and perceived that he had not time to reach the upper heights of Chunuk Bair, he promptly and quite rightly deployed his men where they stood, and shortened his line of attack. The 10th Hampshires and two companies of the 6th East Lancashires charged with the bayonet straight across to the point where the dip rose into the final summit of Chunuk Bair. They reached their goal, but were too late. The Gurkhas and the South Lancashires had fallen back, the enemy were pouring up their side of the dip in overwhelming numbers, and the day was lost. General Baldwin withdrew at length to the Farm, and the rest of the fighting that day in this area consisted chiefly of fierce but unavailing attacks on the exhausted troops who clung doggedly to the summit of Chunuk Bair.

During the night the gallant New Zealanders and the New Army troops on the summit were withdrawn, as they were naturally worn out. They were replaced by two New Army battalions, the 6th Loyal North Lancashires and the 5th Wiltshires, while the 10th Hampshires were instructed to hold the line from the summit to the Farm. The Lancashires arrived first, and their commanding officer, Lieutenant-Colonel Levinge, hastily tried to improve the trenches, which he considered dangerous. The 5th Wiltshires were delayed, and on reaching the top were disposed by an error in an exposed position, which in the darkness was thought to be well covered. The Turks were well aware that if the British could hold the top of Chunuk Bair the Narrows would be endangered. They shelled the summit vigorously at dawn on

French soldiers digging themselves in.

A busy scene at Suvla Bay: Road making. Centre picture: Naval airmen preparing the ground for pitching their tent.

SPADE WORK AT THE DARDANELLES.

A HOUSE OF SAND-BAGS: THE ARMY POST OFFICE AT SUVLA BAY.

August 10, and then hurled against it a whole division and three extra battalions. The Wiltshires were caught in the open, and "literally almost annihilated." The 6th Loyal North Lancashires were "simply overwhelmed in their trenches by sheer weight of numbers." Chunuk Bair was almost instantly lost, and the Turks swept over the crest, drove back the 10th Hampshires, drove back the rest of Baldwin's column from the Farm, and for a time carried all before them.

The struggle which followed was more fierce and desperate than any other phase of the assault on the *massif* of Sari Bair and the adjacent heights. Staff-Captain Street rallied the driven troops below the Farm, and carried them forward again. There was a long and deadly hand-to-hand conflict. Sir Ian Hamilton wrote:

> Generals fought in the ranks and men dropped their scientific weapons and caught one another by the throat. So desperate a battle cannot be described. The Turks came on again and again, fighting magnificently, calling upon the name of God. Our men stood to it, and maintained, by many a deed of daring, the old traditions of their race. There was no flinching. They died in the ranks where they stood.
>
> Here Generals Cayley, Baldwin, and Cooper, and all their gallant men achieved great glory. On this bloody field fell Brigadier-General Baldwin, who earned his first laurels on Cæsar's Camp at Ladysmith. There, too, fell Brigadier-General Cooper, badly wounded; and there, too, fell Lieutenant-Colonel M. H. Nunn, commanding the 9th Worcestershire Regiment; Lieutenant-Colonel H. G. Levinge, commanding the 6th Loyal North Lancashire Regiment; and Lieutenant-Colonel J. Carden, commanding the 5th Wiltshire Regiment.

The Turks paid dearly for the recovery of Chunuk Bair. As they swarmed in dense masses down the western side of the summit, they were assailed by a terrific fire from the British land batteries and the warships. The New Zealand and Australian Artillery, the Indian Mountain Artillery Brigade, and the 69th Brigade Royal Field Artillery, poured a concentrated hail of shell upon them. The ten machine-guns of the New Zealand Infantry Brigade tore gaps in the Turkish ranks at close range until their barrels were red-hot. But the fighting round the Farm was too close and deadly to give the guns much chance. There hand weapons and cold steel decided the issue. Sir William Birdwood sent up the very last two battalions from his General Reserve, and at 10 a.m., after a five-hours' battle, the Turkish attack was spent. By nightfall there was no Turk on the British side of the heights; but the enemy held the top of Chunuk Bair, and the great operation was finally declared to have failed. How near it was to success, what a touch-and-go business the whole attack had been, this narrative has sufficiently shown. That day, it may be noted, the enemy also attacked the 4th Australian Brigade in the Asma Dere, and the 4th South Wales Borderers far away on Damakjelik Bair. The attacks were repulsed, but both forces suffered further heavy losses, and the Borderers lost their gallant commander, Lieutenant-Colonel Gillespie.

The close of the story of the attack from Anzac on Sari Bair may be given in Sir Ian Hamilton's own words :

By evening the total casualties of General Birdwood's force had reached 12,000, and included a very large proportion of officers. The 13th Division of the New Army, under Major-General Shaw, had alone lost 6,000 out of a grand total of 10,500. Baldwin was gone, and all his staff. Ten commanding officers out of thirteen had disappeared from the fighting effectives. The Warwicks and the Worcesters had lost literally every single officer. The old German notion that no unit would stand a loss of more than 25 per cent. had been completely falsified. The 13th Division and the 29th Brigade of the 10th (Irish) Division had lost more than twice that proportion, and, in spirit, were game for as much more fighting as might be required. But physically, though Birdwood's forces were prepared to hold all they had got, they were now too exhausted to attack —at least until they had rested and reorganized. So far they *had* held on to all they had gained, excepting only the footholds on the ridge between Chunuk Bair and Hill Q, momentarily carried by the Gurkhas, and the salient of Chunuk Bair itself, which they had retained for forty-eight hours. Unfortunately, these two pieces of ground, small and worthless as they seemed, were worth, according to the ethics of war, 10,000 lives, for by their loss or retention they just marked the difference between an important success and a signal victory.

At times I had thought of throwing my reserves into this stubborn central battle, where probably they would have turned the scale. But each time the water troubles made me give up the idea, all ranks at Anzac being reduced to one pint a day. True thirst is a sensation unknown to the dwellers in cool, well-watered England. But at Anzac, when mules with water "pakhals" arrived at the front, the men would rush up to them in swarms, just to lick the moisture that had exuded through the canvas bags. It will be understood, then, that until wells had been discovered under the freshly-won hills, the reinforcing of Anzac by even so much as a brigade was unthinkable.

The grand coup had not come off. The Narrows were still out of sight and beyond field gun range. But this was not the fault of Lieutenant-General Birdwood or any of the officers and men under his command. No mortal can command success; Lieutenant-General Birdwood had done all that mortal man can do to deserve it. The way in which he worked out his instructions into practical arrangements and dispositions upon the terrain reflect high credit upon his military capacity. I also wish to bring to your Lordship's notice the valuable services of Major-General Godley, commanding the New Zealand and Australian Division. He had under him at one time a force amounting to two divisions, which he handled with conspicuous ability. Major-General F. C. Shaw, commanding 13th Division, also rose superior to all the trials and tests of these trying days. His calm and sound judgment proved to be of the greatest value throughout the arduous fighting I have recorded.

As for the troops, the joyous alacrity with which they faced danger, wounds and death, as if they were some new form of exciting recreation, has astonished me—old campaigner as I am. I will say no more, leaving Major-General Godley to speak for what happened under his eyes : "I cannot close my report," he says, "without placing on record my unbounded admiration of the work performed, and the gallantry displayed, by the troops and their leaders during the severe fighting involved in these operations. Though the Australian, New Zealand, and Indian units had been confined to trench duty in a cramped space for some four months, and though the troops of the New Armies had only just landed from a sea voyage, and many of them had not been previously under fire, I do not believe that any troops in the world could have accomplished more. All

A CORNER OF ANZAC: BRITISH DUG-OUTS.

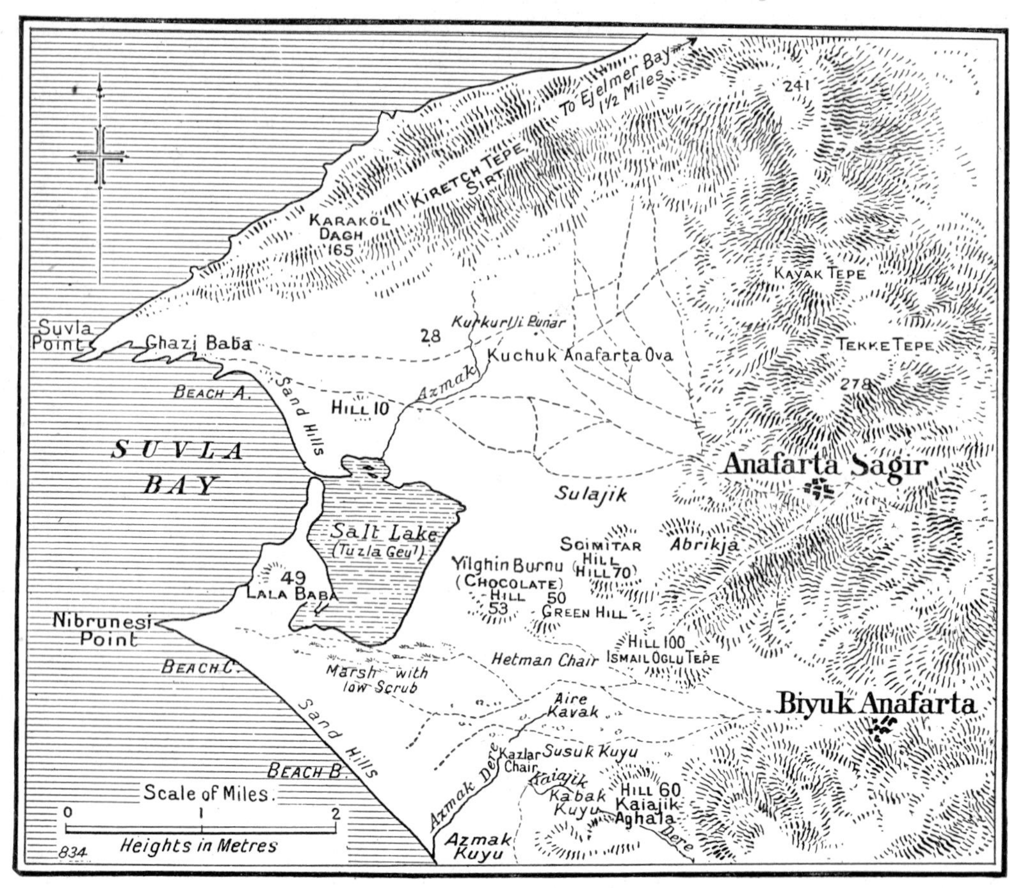

MAP OF THE SUVLA BAY AREA.

ranks vied with one another in the performance of gallant deeds, and more than worthily upheld the best traditions of the British Army."

Let the verdict be written at once. The conception of the attack on Sari Bair ridge, coupled with a fresh landing at Suvla Bay, was strategically and tactically sound, except in one or two details. The attack on Sari Bair came within an ace of success, within a hair's-breadth of such a victory as might have transformed the whole position on the Gallipoli Peninsula. Only a very close and careful study fully reveals the reasons which led Sir Ian Hamilton and Sir William Birdwood to maintain to the end of the whole campaign that persistence, together with sufficient reinforcements, would have given them the triumph they sought, and perhaps have changed the face of the war on the eastern front. But these considerations should be always examined with due reference to the current situation in the other theatres of the war in the middle of August, 1915.

While the great attack on Sari Bair was being made and lost, the new landing at Suvla Bay was begun, and soon failed to achieve its immediate purpose. The operations at Suvla Bay were in charge of Lieutenant-General the Hon. Sir Frederick Stopford, K.C.M.G. General Stopford was sixty-one years of age, and was a Guardsman. He entered the Army in 1871, fought in the Egyptian and Sudan campaigns in the eighties, and in the Ashanti campaign in 1895. He was Military Secretary to Sir Redvers Buller in the South African War, commanded the London District during 1906-09, and had since been Lieutenant of the Tower of London. It was understood that Sir Ian Hamilton was himself instrumental in securing General Stopford's appointment to a command at the Dardanelles. General Stopford arrived in the Aegean in July, and was given command of the 8th Corps on the Krithia front for eight days, in order that he might gain a little local experience. On July 24 he assumed command of the 9th Army Corps, then assembling at Mudros. This was the Corps designated for the landing at Suvla Bay, less the 13th Division (sent to Anzac) and the 29th Brigade of the 10th Division.

Suvla Bay was a wide semi-circular indentation of the coast, bounded on the north by

Suvla Point and on the south by Nibrunesi Point. The extremity of the latter cape was exactly five miles from Anzac Cove, following the line of the beach. Nibrunesi Point was a low spit, but from Suvla Point the coast rose beyond the bay into the ridge of hills called the Kiretch Tepe Sirt, which at their highest point were perhaps 700 feet high. The ridge extended north-eastward towards Ejelmer Bay, but the heights also curved inland and formed the Anafarta group of hills, which at their highest point, Tekke Tepe, were 882 feet high. The Anafarta hills were divided from the Sari Bair *massif* by a valley, on the north side of which stood the village of Anafarta Sagir, otherwise known as Kuchuk (Little) Anafarta, while on the opposite side, beneath the northern spurs of Sari Bair, was the village of Biyuk (Big) Anafarta. The Anafarta Valley gave easy access to two other valleys which led through cultivated land to the Narrows. The Anafarta hills rose four miles back from the bay, and the intervening gently sloping plain was partly cultivated and partly covered with low scrub, together with a fair number of isolated trees. From the plain rose three or four low eminences, the most conspicuous of which were soon known to the troops as Chocolate Hill, the Green Hill, and Scimitar Hill. The shores of the bay were shallow and muddy, and in the foreground was a sandy causeway, behind which lay the Salt Lake, more than a mile long and nearly a mile wide in its broadest part. The Salt Lake was really a morass, which was dry enough to walk over in summer, except after heavy rain. Between the Salt Lake and the sea, in the direction of Nibrunesi Point, was a knoll called Lala Baba, well over 100 feet high.

The Turks were known to have a ring of trenches round Lala Baba, a few more trenches on Hill 10 (at the northern end of the Salt Lake) and some primitive defences on the ridge beyond Suvla Point. They had a little redoubt and a few guns on Chocolate Hill, and more guns on Ismail Oglu Tepe (Hill 100), a mile farther inland. These guns included a 4·7 and a 9·2, but they were trained on Anzac. It was believed, and the assumption proved to be approximately accurate, that the enemy only had about 4,000 troops in the Suvla Bay area, where they did not expect a landing. There were three battalions in the Anafarta villages, a battalion at Ismail Oglu Tepe, another at Chocolate Hill, outposts at Lala Baba and Ghazi Baba, and gendarmerie on the Kiretch ridge.

The plan of attack at Suvla Bay provided that the first landing should be made by the three brigades of the 11th (Northern) Division, then concentrated at the island of Imbros. They were to leave in destroyers and motor-lighters after dark on August 6, and to begin disembarkation at 10.30 p.m., an hour after the Anzacs were timed to rush "Old No. 3 Post." Three landing beaches were chosen, two outside the bay south of Nibrunesi Point, and one inside the bay, north of the Salt Lake and opposite

LIEUT.-GEN. THE HON. SIR F. STOPFORD, K.C.M.G., K.C.V.O.
Commanded the Ninth Army Corps at Suvla Bay.

Hill 10. The last-named was called Beach A. Beach C was a little south of Nibrunesi Point, and about a mile from Lala Baba. Beach B was a mile and a half lower down the coast, and little more than a couple of miles from Old No. 3 Post. The allotment of brigades was as follows: Beach A, 34th Brigade; Beach B, 32nd Brigade; Beach C, 33rd Brigade. Sir Ian Hamilton had wanted to land all the brigades outside the bay, but yielded to the desire of General Stopford to send the 34th Brigade to Beach A, "unfortunately, as it turned out," he said, because the beach proved to have a bad landing-place. The broad scheme

THE CAUSEWAY AT SUVLA BAY.

was that the 11th Division was to seize and hold the principal heights in the plain, but especially Chocolate Hill and Ismail Oglu, and also the ridge of the Kiretch Tepe Sirt (Sirt means summit, Tepe means hill), between the plain and the coast to the north of the bay. The remainder of the Army Corps would, it was hoped, make good the Anafarta Hills, and work across the Anafarta Valley against the northern slopes of Sari Bair. If the Anzacs and the Suvla Bay forces combined to drive the Turks off Sari Bair on to the Kilid Bahr plateau, Sir Ian Hamilton hoped to seize a new line across the peninsula from Gaba Tepe to Maidos, with a protected line of supply from Suvla Bay.

The 11th Division, commanded by Major-General Hammersley, sailed from Imbros at the appointed time, and the landing at Beaches C and B was effected without opposition. But there was trouble at Beach A. The Turks were on the alert on the shores of the bay, and it was afterwards said that searchlights were used from the Anafarta Hills. The lighters grounded far from the beach, and some of the men had to struggle ashore through nearly five feet of water. The Turkish outposts on Lala Baba and Ghazi Baba (a hill near Suvla Point) set up a flanking rifle fire. Some of the enemy even got among the troops on the beach. One battalion of the Northumberland Fusiliers seems to have been landed opposite the Salt Lake, quite close to Lala Baba. The original Beach A was eventually shifted nearer Ghazi Baba. The various difficulties were gradually overcome, and on the whole the landing of the 11th Division was successfully accomplished.

Although farthest away, the 32nd Brigade was first in action. Marching through the darkness along the coast from Beach B, the 9th West Yorkshires and the 6th Yorkshires found their way unswervingly to Lala Baba, and without firing a shot dashed up the height with fixed bayonets. They carried it swiftly, but Lieutenant-Colonel E. H. Chapman, who was in the van shouting "Come on, the Yorkshires," fell dead on the summit, shot through the neck. The 32nd Brigade than pushed on along the sandy causeway to support the 34th Brigade, part of which was in difficulties before Hill 10. A single battalion, the 11th Manchesters, had meanwhile sturdily made its way up the Karakol Dagh (Police Mountain or Hill) towards the ridge of the Kiretch Tepe Sirt, where they were driving back the few hundred gendarmerie posted on the summit. By this time dawn was breaking, and the two brigades had got into some confusion, which was heightened by the arrival of Turkish shells in their midst. Sir Ian Hamilton wrote: "No one seems to have been present who could take hold of the two brigades, the 32nd and 34th, and launch them in a concerted and cohesive attack. Consequently there was confusion and hesitation, increased by gorse fires lit by hostile shell, but redeemed, I am proud to report, by the conspicuously fine, soldierly conduct of several individual battalions." The position near Hill 10 was eventually retrieved by two battalions of the 34th Brigade, the 9th Lancashire Fusiliers and the 11th Manchesters, which drove the enemy at the point of the bayonet off Hill 10, where the scrub was burning furiously.

With the dawn came two Highland mountain batteries and one battery of the 59th Brigade, Royal Field Artillery, which were landed at Beach B. Some of the guns were quickly placed on Lala Baba. Dawn brought also six battalions of the 10th (Irish) Division, under Brigadier-General Hill, from the island of Mitylene, 120 miles away; disembarked strictly to time by the marvellous organization of the Royal Navy. But five of the battalions were landed at Beach C, instead of Beach A, as was intended, and they had to march between three or four miles under fire before they came into action near Hill 10. They were thus fatigued at the outset, for the day soon grew hot, and local plans again went awry. The remaining three battalions of the 10th Division, with an odd battalion left afloat from the first six, were landed beyond Beach A near Ghazi Baba. With them came the commander of the Irish Division, Lieutenant-General Sir Bryan Mahon, a dashing cavalry officer who had seen much service in the Sudan and in South Africa. It was Mahon who led the cavalry, camel corps, and maxims in that last swift pursuit of the Khalifa in the wilds of Kordofan which ended in the grey dawn near the wells of Gedid. Mahon rode a dead heat with Plumer in the race from north and south to relieve Mafeking. He had been commanding the Lucknow Division

[Elliott & Fry.

MAJ.-GEN. SIR BRYAN T. MAHON, K.C.V.O., C.B., D.S.O.
Commanded the Irish Division.

[Lafayette.

MAJ.-GEN. FREDERICK HAMMERSLEY.
Commanded the 11th Division.

in India on the eve of the war, and had been promptly given one of the first commands in the New Armies after hostilities began.

General Mahon on landing instantly turned his attention to the ridge of the Kiretch Tepe Sirt, along which his Division was ordered to operate. The 11th Manchesters had already won a foothold there, but the Irishmen pushed on until they were firmly astride the western end of the ridge. The 6th Royal Munster Fusiliers specially distinguished themselves in this advance. Although only about 700 gendarmerie were on the ridge, they proved to be better entrenched than was expected. The troops began to suffer much from want of water, and Sir Ian Hamilton afterwards reported that no sufficient attempt was made to develop the local water supplies, both in this and in other areas of the Suvla operations. While General Mahon was occupied with the ridge, the enemy in the level lands below had been retreating from Hill 10 towards Sulajik and Kuchuk Anafarta Ova (plain). They were pursued by the 34th and 32nd Brigades of the 11th Division, and by the 31st Brigade of the 10th Division. The 31st Brigade had been meant to advance on the left of the 11th Division, but in the confusion of the day found

STORMING THE RIDGE OF BURNT HILL, SUVLA BAY—THE HILL-TOP VICTORIOUSLY SURMOUNTED.

itself far out in the plain, where it bore the brunt of such desultory fighting as occurred. The 31st Brigade consisted of the 6th Royal Inniskilling Fusiliers, the 6th Royal Irish Fusiliers, and the 6th Royal Dublin Fusiliers, the last-named being an attached battalion. No mention has yet been made of the doings of the 33rd Brigade. It had remained south of the Salt Lake, had experienced less opposition than the others, and after a smart little fight had captured Chocolate Hill with few casualties early in the afternoon. In this assault the 6th Lincolns and the 6th Border Regiment did admirable work ; but the Turks were increasing in strength, and the brigade was unable to reach Ismail Oglu Tepe, as had been hoped.

The Suvla Bay scheme of operations had, in short, already gone terribly wrong. How much it was amiss can be gauged by Sir Ian Hamilton's original instructions to General Stopford. He was told to land the 11th Division at 10.30 p.m. on the night of August 6. He was to seize Lala Baba, Ghazi Baba, Chocolate Hill, Ismail Oglu Tepe, and the Kiretch ridge, before daylight. The 11th Division was considered sufficient to attain these objectives, and it was hoped, with certain qualifications, that the fresh troops arriving after daylight would be able to advance on Biyuk Anafarta and lend a helping hand to the Anzacs on the northern slopes of Sari Bair. The programme was left unfulfilled to an extent almost ludicrous. The only eminence taken during the hours of darkness was Lala Baba. Chocolate Hill was carried the next afternoon. Instead of landing at Beach B, whence it might have made for Biyuk Anafarta, as Sir Ian Hamilton apparently intended, the Irish Division was put ashore near Suvla Point. But it has also to be said that the task imposed upon the 11th Division, a body of raw troops never in action before, was excessive. They were expected to land, fresh from home, in an unknown country in dense darkness, without guides, and under opposition, and to take half a dozen widely separated points before daylight. Even the Guards Division would probably have come to grief in such an enterprise. Among the many causes of the failure at Suvla Bay, the too extensive scheme prepared for the first night's operations cannot be disregarded. Entrusted to newly formed troops, a large proportion of whose officers were equally without experience, the scheme of the night surprise was probably foredoomed.

When night fell on August 7, the British forces in the Suvla area were extended from Hetman Chair (meadow), through Chocolate Hill, the hamlet of Sulajik, to the western outskirts of Kuchuk Anafarta Ova. General Mahon's force was astride the Kiretch ridge. The night passed quietly, for the Turks were terribly alarmed at the appearance of the 9th Corps at Suvla Bay. They made no attempt to counter-attack, and they even hurried off their few guns after sunset. They were numerically weak and badly needed reinforcements. During the night, too, the New Zealanders and the Welsh and the men of Gloucester had captured the summit of Chunuk Bair, so the enemy had their hands full elsewhere.

If ever a Corps had a great chance, it was the 9th Army Corps at daybreak on August 8 at Suvla Bay. They had passed a quiet night, the enemy were few, were obviously dispirited, and had removed their guns. The incredible happened, however, and throughout that critical and vitally important day of August 8 the 9th Army Corps never bestirred itself to make any attempt to advance. The story is so extraordinary that it had better be told in Sir Ian Hamilton's own dramatic and pointed words :—

> And now (on August 8) General Stopford, recollecting the vast issues which hung upon his success in forestalling the enemy, urged his Divisional Commanders to push on. Otherwise, as he saw, all the advantages of the surprise landing must be nullified. But the Divisional Commanders believed themselves, it seems, to be unable to move. Their men, they said, were exhausted by their efforts of the night of the 6th–7th and by the action of the 7th. The want of water had told on the new troops. The distribution from the beaches had not worked smoothly.
>
> In some cases the hose had been pierced by individuals wishing to fill their own bottles; in others lighters had grounded so far from the beach that men swam out to fill batches of water-bottles. All this had added to the disorganization inevitable after a night landing, followed by fights here and there with an enemy scattered over a country to us unknown. These pleas for delay were perfectly well founded. But it seems to have been overlooked that the half-defeated Turks in front of us were equally exhausted and disorganized, and that an advance was the simplest and swiftest method of solving the water trouble and every other sort of trouble. Be this as it may, the objections overbore the Corps Commander's resolution. He had now got ashore three batteries (two of them mountain batteries), and the great guns of the ships were ready to speak at his request. But it was lack of artillery support which finally decided him to acquiesce in a policy of going slow which, by the time it reached the troops, became translated into a period of inaction. The Divisional Generals were, in fact, informed that, "in view of the inadequate artillery support," General Stopford did not wish them to make frontal attacks on entrenched positions, but desired them, so far as was possible, to try and turn any trenches which were met with. Within the terms of this instruction lies the root of our failure to make use of the priceless daylight hours of August 8.

TURK AND BRITON.

A British soldier giving a wounded Turk a drink from his water-bottle.

Normally, it may be correct to say that in modern warfare infantry cannot be expected to advance without artillery preparation. But in a landing on a hostile shore the order has to be inverted. The infantry must advance and seize a suitable position to cover the landing and to provide artillery positions for the main thrust. The very existence of the force, its water supply, its facilities for munitions and supplies, its power to reinforce must absolutely depend on the infantry being able instantly to make good sufficient ground without the aid of the artillery other than can be supplied for the purpose by *floating* batteries.

This is not a condition that should take the commander of a covering force by surprise. It is one already foreseen. Driving power was required, and even a certain ruthlessness, to brush aside pleas for a respite for tired troops. *The one fatal error was inertia. And inertia prevailed.*

Late in the evening of the 7th the enemy had withdrawn the few guns which had been in action during the day. Beyond half a dozen shells dropped from very long range into the bay in the early morning of the 8th no enemy artillery fired that day in the Suvla area. The guns had evidently been moved back, lest they should be captured when we pushed forward. As for the entrenched positions, these, in the ordinary acceptance of the term, were non-existent. The General Staff Officer whom I had sent on to Suvla early in the morning of the 8th reported by telegraph the absence of hostile gun-fire, the small amount of rifle fire, and the enemy's apparent weakness. He also drew attention to the inaction of our own troops, and to the fact that golden opportunities were being missed. Before this message arrived at general headquarters I had made up my mind from the Corps Commander's own reports that all was not well at Suvla. There was risk in cutting myself adrift, even temporarily, from touch with the operations at Anzac and Helles ; but I did my best to provide against any sudden call by leaving Major-General W. P. Braithwaite, my Chief of the General Staff, in charge, with instructions to keep me closely informed of events at the other two fronts ; and, having done this, I took ship and set out for Suvla.

On arrival at about 5 p.m. I boarded H.M.S. Jonquil, where I found corps headquarters, and where General Stopford informed me that the General Officer commanding 11th Division was confident of success in an attack he was to make at dawn next morning (the 9th). I felt no such confidence. Beyond a small advance by a part of the 11th Division between the Chocolate Hills and Ismail Oglu Tepe, and some further progress along the Kiretch Tepe Sirt ridge by the 10th Division, the day of the 8th had been lost. The commander of the 11th Division had, it seems, ordered strong patrols to be pushed forward so as to make good all the strong positions in advance which could be occupied without serious fighting; but, as he afterwards reported, "little was done in this respect." Thus a priceless twelve hours had already gone to help the chances of the Turkish reinforcements which were, I knew, both from naval and aerial sources, actually on the march for Suvla. But when I urged that even now, at the eleventh hour, the 11th Division should make a concerted attack upon the hills, I was met by a *non possumus*. The objections of the morning were no longer valid ; the men were now well rested, watered, and fed. But the divisional commanders disliked the idea of an advance by night, and General Stopford did not care, it seemed, to force their hands.

So it came about that I was driven to see whether I could not, myself, put concentration of effort and purpose into the direction of the large number of men ashore. The Corps Commander made no objection. He declared himself to be as eager as I could be to advance. The representations made by the Divisional Commanders had seemed to him insuperable. If I could see my way to get over them no one would be more pleased than himself.

Accompanied by Commodore Roger Keyes and

AFTER A BATTLE.

Carrying British wounded through the trenches.

AT A BURIAL SERVICE.
Three Army Chaplains (Church of England, Roman Catholic, and Presbyterian) attend the burial of fallen heroes.

Lieutenant-Colonel Aspinall, of the Headquarters General Staff, I landed on the beach, where all seemed quiet and peaceful, and saw the Commander of the 11th Division, Major-General Hammersley. I warned him the sands were running out fast, and that by dawn the high ground to his front might very likely be occupied in force by the enemy. He saw the danger, but declared that it was a physical impossibility, at so late an hour (6 p.m.), to get out orders for a night attack, the troops being very much scattered. There was no other difficulty now, but this was insuperable ; he could not recast his orders or get them round to his troops in time. But one brigade, the 32nd, was, so General Hammersley admitted, more or less concentrated and ready to move. The General Staff Officer of the division, Colonel Neil Malcolm, a soldier of experience, on whose opinion I set much value, was consulted. He agreed that the 32nd Brigade was now in a position to act. I, therefore, issued a direct order that, even if it were only with this 32nd Brigade, the advance should begin at the earliest possible moment, so that a portion at least of the 11th Division should anticipate the Turkish reinforcements on the heights and dig themselves in there upon some good tactical point.

In taking upon myself the serious responsibility of thus dealing with a detail of divisional tactics I was careful to limit the scope of the interference. Beyond directing that the one brigade which was reported ready to move at once should try and make good the heights before the enemy got on to them I did nothing, and said not a word calculated to modify or in any way affect the attack already planned for the morning. Out of the thirteen battalions which were to have advanced against the heights at dawn four were now to anticipate that movement by trying to make good the key of the enemy's position at once and under cover of darkness.

Though these strictures sound severe, they were more gentle and restrained than the occasion warranted. The paralysis in the Suvla Bay area on August 8 was extraordinary, and it was not to be entirely accounted for either by the rawness of the troops or the scarcity of water. But it was also pointed out afterwards in England that whereas Sir Ian Hamilton's criticisms appeared to relate to August 8 alone, the offensive at Suvla Bay really began to go wrong on August 7. The slowness and confusion of the operations on August 7 must have been known at General Headquarters at Imbros on that day ; and it was urged that Sir Ian Hamilton would have been better advised if he had left the other fronts alone, and hurried to Suvla Bay, his weakest point, at least 24 or 30 hours earlier.

The four battalions of the 32nd Brigade did

FILLING A WATER CART FROM A NEWLY-SUNK WELL.

not start on the evening of August 8, as Sir Ian Hamilton desired. They moved out at 4 a.m. on August 9, their objective being the line of the Anafarta heights. The reason assigned for the further delay was that the units of the brigade were scattered, which did not accord with the information given to Sir Ian Hamilton (who stayed at Suvla on the night of the 8th). When it did advance, the opposition encountered by the brigade was at first not great. A company of the 6th East Yorks Pioneer Battalion actually succeeded in climbing to the shoulder of Tekke Tepe (Shrine Hill) north of Anafarta Sagir, the principal summit of the heights, and a point which commanded the whole battlefield. But the opposing Turks attacked the rest of the battalion, and fell on the flanks of the whole brigade, which drew back to a line abreast of Sulajik. Of the single adventurous company which crowned the heights, together with the party of Royal Engineers which marched with it, very few escaped. General Stopford reported that by nightfall on August 9 the strength of the 6th East Yorks Pioneers had declined to nine officers and 380 men.

The 32nd Brigade having fallen back into line, the whole division advanced against the Anafarta heights an hour or two later. The 33rd Brigade, which had somehow found its way back to the beach, had started forward again at 2 a.m., and was in line again by 5 a.m., soon after which hour the whole division delivered an attack along an extensive front. But the Turks had recovered from their scare. They had come back to the heights, and had brought their guns back with them. They were able to enfilade the division with shrapnel, and the attack wavered and failed. Sir Ian Hamilton wrote :—

Just as the 32nd Brigade in their advance met with markedly less opposition than the troops who attacked an hour and a half later, so, had they themselves started earlier, they would probably have experienced less opposition. Further, it seems reasonable to suppose that had the complete division started at 4 a.m. on the 9th, or, better still, at 10 p.m. on the 8th, they would have made good the whole of the heights in front of them.

The 33rd Brigade, on the right flank, got as far as Ismail Oglu Tepe, and a portion of the troops even gained the summit of that hill after a hard encounter at close quarters with groups of Turks, who were mostly slain. The men who took this important hill could not stay on it, for meanwhile the 32nd Brigade, in the centre of the line—which had done so well in the earlier operations, but was now sorely fatigued—gave way. One theory is that it was demoralised by the shrapnel fire, and another allegation, mentioned by Sir Ian Hamilton, is that "an order to retire came up from the rear." Be that as it may, the 32nd Brigade fell back on Sulajik again, and the 33rd Brigade thereupon abandoned Ismail Oglu Tepe and retired to the Chocolate Hill. Two battalions of the 34th Brigade came up on the left of the 32nd Brigade, and assisted their withdrawal. During the night of August 8 the 53rd (Territorial) Division, under General Lindley, had arrived at Suvla Bay. The division represented Sir Ian Hamilton's general reserve, and he had ordered it up because he felt that all the troops he could throw in were needed in this area. The whole division was ashore early on August 9, and two battalions of the 159th Brigade were advanced on the left front in time to render useful help.

The available records, official and unofficial, of these conflicts on August 9 are, like so much of the Suvla Bay records, scanty, confused, and contradictory. Even Sir Ian Hamilton was not able to gather many of the details he sought, and the absence of definite information was afterwards advanced as one of the reasons why his dispatch was not finished and made public until the following January. It is clear that the men still suffered terribly from thirst, and hundreds are said to have dropped out of the ranks for this reason. Another very serious hindrance was the prevalence of bush fires. The Turkish shells set the gorse and scrub alight. Scimitar Hill became suddenly ablaze, and a wall of fire 30 feet high swept over it, so transforming its appearance that it was ever afterwards called Burnt Hill. Captain Percy Hansen,* of the 6th Lincolnshires, won the Victoria Cross for "most conspicuous bravery" in one of these fires, for he led a handful of volunteers into the flames on Green Hill under a heavy hail of shrapnel and rifle bullets, and succeeded in rescuing several wounded men, who would otherwise have been burnt to death.

* Captain Hansen was also awarded the Military Cross for another deed of conspicuous gallantry at Suvla Bay on September 9, 1915. He made a reconnaissance of the coast, stripping himself and carrying only a revolver and a blanket for disguise. He swam and scrambled over rocks, which severely cut and bruised him, obtained valuable information, and located a gun that was causing much damage. Once he met a patrol of 12 Turks, who did not see him, and later a single Turk, whom he killed. He returned to the British lines in a state of great exhaustion.

The 6th Lincolnshires, on the right flank, and the 6th Battalion Border Regiment, did much to redeem the fortunes of the day, and were specially commended by the Commander-in-Chief for their "steady, gallant behaviour." The Lincolnshires lost heavily, for they went into action 700 strong, and next day had only 120 effectives. Another battalion which won much praise was the 1/1st Herefordshire Territorials. Only landed that morning, they "attacked with impetuosity and courage between Hetman Chair and Kaslar Chair, in the neighbourhood of the Azmak Dere, on the extreme right of the line."

Next day, August 10, General Stopford decided to attack the Anafarta heights again. He placed the 53rd Division in the forefront of the advance, and the 11th Division was chiefly held in reserve. By this time he had the whole of the 59th Brigade of the Royal Field Artillery ashore, as well as the two Highland mountain batteries, and a powerful backing from the guns of warships. The British bombardment had a perceptible effect upon the Turks, but the infantry attack failed once more. General Stopford said, and Sir Ian Hamilton concurred, that seasoned troops would have taken the heights; but both generals agreed that the task was too severe for units never in action before, unsupported by veteran regulars. The Turks had increased their strength threefold. It was believed that part of the well-trained Yemen Division, on its way to Krithia, had been

R.A.M.C. AT WORK: BRINGING WOUNDED DOWN A CLIFF SIDE.

[*Lafayette.*

BRIG.-GEN. P. A. KENNA, V.C., D.S.O., A.D.C.
Died of Wounds.

diverted to the Anafarta ridges; and the Turkish guns were also more numerous. Some of the Territorial battalions nevertheless showed much bravery and determination, and were well led. Two battalions of the 11th Division, the 6th (Service) Battalion York and Lancaster Regiment and the 8th (Service) Battalion West Riding Regiment, entered the action on the left of the 53rd Division at a very ugly moment and gave valuable help. At the end of the day the centre of the British line still ran through Sulajik and Green Hill. That night Sir Ian Hamilton ordered General Stopford to entrench along his whole front, which ran from the Asmak Dere through Green Hill and a little west of Kuchuk Anafarta Ova to the position held by the 10th Division astride of the ridge of Kiretch Tepe Sirt. The whole of August 11 was devoted to this work, and certain divisions were reorganised. On August 11 the 54th Division (infantry only) was disembarked and placed in reserve.

On August 12 Sir Ian Hamilton directed that the 54th Division should make a night march that night and attack at dawn on August 13 the twin heights of Kavak Tepe and Tekke Tepe, the chief summits of the Anafarta Hills. General Stopford agreed, but considered it necessary to clear first the cultivated area of Kuchuk Anafarta Ova, in order that the night march might be unobstructed. The 163rd Brigade marched out in the afternoon of August 12, moved into Kuchuk Anafarta Ova, and succeeded in its purpose, though there was some hot fighting. The enemy were in considerable strength, but fell back, and in the pursuit there happened what Sir Ian Hamilton described as "a mysterious thing." The 1/5th Norfolks were on the right of the brigade. They were led by Colonel Sir Horace Beauchamp, an officer who had seen much campaigning in Egypt, the Sudan, and South Africa. He had commanded the 20th Hussars, and was an ardent cavalry soldier, but he delighted in the sea, and was widely known in the Army as "The Bo's'un." Probably he was the only cavalry colonel who had ever devoted his leave to standing watch on the bridge of an ocean liner, in order to qualify for a master mariner's certificate. He had emerged from his retirement to take command of a battalion of the Norfolks, and on this eventful afternoon at Kuchuk Anafarta Ova he found himself less opposed than the rest of the brigade. Ever a thruster, he pressed forward, followed by most of his battalion. He was seen amid the scattered houses in the meadow-land, carrying a cane and urging on his men. The trees, at first few and isolated, grew thicker as the pursuit progressed. The day was hot, the men were suffering much from thirst, casualties were numerous, and the battalion seems to have lost formation when rising ground covered with thick low woods was reached. Many stragglers found their way back to the camp after darkness fell, according to Sir Ian Hamilton.

> But the Colonel, with 16 officers and 250 men, still kept pushing on, driving the enemy before him. Amongst these ardent souls was part of a fine company enlisted from the King's Sandringham estates. Nothing more was ever seen or heard of any of them. They charged into the forest, and were lost to sight or sound. Not one of them ever came back.

The experience of the 163rd Brigade around Kuchuk Anafarta Ova caused the projected night march against the heights to be incontinently abandoned. General Stopford urged that, even if the attack succeeded, he would find it difficult to send food and water into the hills, and his representations were accepted. It must be remembered that General Birdwood had lost the crest of Chunuk Bair two days before, and the whole original scheme had

THE RIDGE NEAR SUVLA BAY.

This was scaled by the Manchesters and the Irish Division.

therefore fallen through. General Birdwood, however, hoped to renew his attack on Sari Bair, and on August 13 it was proposed that General Stopford should co-operate by sending the 11th and 54th Divisions against Ismail Oglu Tepe, where there were guns which had the range of the Sari Bair slopes. This proposal was quickly dropped because, on further investigation, General Birdwood was unable to renew his assault. Therefore, August 13 and 14 were passed in comparative quietude at Suvla Bay.

On August 15 an attack was delivered on the left flank, with the object of gaining possession of the whole of the Kiretch Tepe Sirt ridge. The ridge was cleared, but the cost was heavy. The 30th and 31st Brigades of the 10th (Irish) Division attacked along the ridge, and the 162nd Brigade of the 54th Division supported on the right. The artillery engaged included a machine-gun detachment of the Royal Naval Air Service, the Argyll Mountain Battery, the 15th Heavy Battery, and the 58th Field Battery. The guns of the destroyers Grampus and Foxhound gave valuable aid. The conflict was severe, and for several hours was inconclusive, but eventually the 6th Royal Dublin Fusiliers made a brilliant charge and captured the whole ridge. Then came misfortune. The forward positions were difficult to hold, and as promised reinforcements failed to appear, the front trenches were evacuated. A high price was paid for this partial success. The 5th Royal Irish Fusiliers lost every officer save one, and the 5th Inniskilling Fusiliers also had serious losses in officers. The net result of the action was that the line, which had hitherto swerved back on the left, was straightened, though not so much as was expected.

The command of the IXth Corps was changed on the evening of August 15, and the reasons for the change are best given in Sir Ian Hamilton's own words :—

On the evening of August 15 General Stopford handed over command of the 9th Corps.

The units of the 10th and 11th Divisions had shown their mettle when they leaped into the water to get more quickly to close quarters, or when they stormed Lala Baba in the darkness. They had shown their resolution later when they tackled the Chocolate Hills and drove the enemy from Hill 10 right back out of rifle range from the beaches.

Then had come hesitation. The advantage had not been pressed. The senior Commanders at Suvla had had no personal experience of the new trench warfare ; of the Turkish methods ; of the paramount importance of time. Strong, clear leadership had not been promptly enough applied. These were the reasons which induced me, with your Lordship's (Lord Kitchener's) approval, to appoint Major-General H. de B. De Lisle to take over temporary command.

By the time General De Lisle took the IXth Army Corps in hand, the offensive in the Suvla Bay area was already lapsing into trench warfare of the normal and immobile kind. There was one more great and disastrous attempt to take Ismail Oglu Tepe and the adjacent positions on August 21, in which the English Yeomanry and the 29th Division suffered terrible losses. Thenceforward the story of Gallipoli, which will be brought to a close in the succeeding chapter, was one of ravages through devastating sickness, followed by tragic privations produced by the swift advent of winter. Sir Ian Hamilton was recalled on October 16, and the whole peninsula was evacuated during December and January. But from the moment further reinforcements from England were refused during the third week in August the fate of the Dardanelles enterprise was finally sealed.

CHAPTER CXIII.

DARDANELLES CAMPAIGN (V.): EVACUATION OF GALLIPOLI.

THE POSITION ON AUGUST 16, 1915—NO MORE BRITISH REINFORCEMENTS—ATTACK ON ISMAIL OGLU TEPE—REPULSE OF THE 29TH DIVISION—GALLANT ADVANCE BY THE YEOMANRY—CAPTURE OF HILL 60—ANXIETY IN ENGLAND—SIR IAN HAMILTON RECALLED—SIR CHARLES MONRO AND LORD KITCHENER AT GALLIPOLI—THE GREAT BLIZZARD IN NOVEMBER—EVACUATION OF SUVLA AND ANZAC—THE LAST MOMENTS AT CAPE HELLES—TOTAL LOSSES OF THE CAMPAIGN.

IN the preceding chapter the great attack against Sari Bair from Anzac in August, 1915, was described at length, and the operations in the Suvla Bay area of the Gallipoli Peninsula were dealt with as far as August 15. In the present chapter the story of the ill-fated Dardanelles Expedition will be brought to a close. General Stopford relinquished the command of the 9th Corps at Suvla Bay on the evening of August 15, and Major-General H. De B. De Lisle was temporarily appointed in his stead. General De Lisle served for twenty years with the 2nd Durham Light Infantry. A celebrated polo player, he captained the famous team of the Durhams for ten years in India. He fought in the early days in Egypt, led an independent column far and wide over the veldt in South Africa, and was always supposed to be the very active and able unnamed general who figured so prominently in that vivid book, *On the Heels of De Wet.* Afterwards he commanded the 1st Royal Dragoons, and he went to France on the outbreak of war at the head of the 2nd Cavalry Brigade. He ordered the charge in which the 9th Lancers, supported by the 4th Dragoon Guards and the 18th Hussars, rode at the masses of German infantry at Audregnies, near Mons, and were stopped by wire and the enemy's guns. His brigade afterwards fought with distinction at the Battle of the Marne.

The position of the Allied forces in the Gallipoli Peninsula on August 16 may be briefly recapitulated. On the Krithia line, near Cape Helles, the containing attack on August 6–8 had served its purpose by holding down the southern Turkish forces, but had effected no great advance. The attack from Anzac upon Sari Bair had failed to capture the heights, but had greatly extended the Anzac line northward, and had also brought it considerably nearer the summits of Sari Bair. The line in the Suvla Bay area ran on August 16 northward from the Azmak Dere through Hetman Chair, Green Hill, Sulajik, and Kuchuk Anafarta Ova, and across the ridge of Kiretch Tepe Sirt to the sea. The 9th Corps was, however, very much disorganized and General De Lisle was urged to get it into fighting trim again as quickly as possible.

The respective forces in the area of conflict in the Gallipoli Peninsula were estimated on August 16 to be as follows:

At Suvla Bay, under Major-General De Lisle, the 10th Division (less one brigade), 11th, 53rd and 54th Divisions, the whole force reduced owing to casualties to a total of 30,000 rifles.

At Anzac, under Lieutenant-General Birdwood, 25,000 rifles.

At Cape Helles, under Lieutenant-General Davies, 23,000 rifles.

French Corps at Cape Helles, 17,000 rifles.

Turks on Krithia and Achi Baba line, 35,000 rifles.

Turks on Sari Bair, Anafarta Hills, and in reserve in adjacent valleys and beyond Bulair, 75,000 rifles.

[It was believed that there were also another 45,000

MILITARY CROSS FOR FRENCH OFFICERS.

General Sir Ian Hamilton decorating Commandant Berthier de Sauvigny, Lieutenant de la Bord, and Lieutenant Pelliot, with the Military Cross.

Turkish rifles in reserve around Keshan, 20 miles north of the Gulf of Xeros (Saros); but these were not counted in Sir Ian Hamilton's estimate.]

Sir Ian Hamilton's view of the situation on August 16 was defined thus:—

The Turks then, I reckoned, had 110,000 rifles to our 95,000, and held all the vantages of ground; they had plenty of ammunition, also drafts wherewith to refill ranks depleted in action within two or three days. My hopes that these drafts would be of poor quality had been every time disappointed. After weighing all these points, I sent your Lordship [Lord Kitchener] a long cable. In it I urged that if the campaign was to be brought to a quick, victorious decision, large reinforcements must at once be sent out. Autumn, I pointed out, was already upon us, and there was not a moment to be lost. At that time (August 16) my British divisions alone were 45,000 under establishment, and some of my fine battalions had dwindled down so far that I had to withdraw them from the fighting line. Our most vital need was the replenishment of these sadly depleted ranks. When that was done I wanted 50,000 fresh rifles. From what I knew of the Turkish situation, both in its local and general aspects, it seemed humanly speaking a certainty that if this help could be sent to me *at once* we could still clear a passage for our fleet to Constantinople.

It may be judged, then, how deep was my disappointment when I learnt that the essential drafts, reinforcements, and munitions could not be sent to me, the reason given being one which prevented me from any further insistence.

Sir Ian Hamilton, it will be observed, really asked for the instant embarcation of another 100,000 men. The probability was that so great an additional force could neither be sent nor munitioned in mid-August, 1915. Whatever the reason given may have been, it was manifest that the British Government were not disposed to send more troops to Gallipoli at that particular period. Recruiting in England had slackened. Warsaw had fallen eleven days earlier. There were secret apprehensions about the attitude of Bulgaria. The bulk of the Ministry were on that date still in favour of holding on at Gallipoli, but they wished to run no more risks there. They feared to press forward, and they feared to leave the peninsula. They dreaded the effect evacuation might have upon public opinion at home and in India, and they were further quite unnecessarily anxious about the views of Australia and New Zealand. Above all, they were daunted by the belief, which eventually proved entirely erroneous, that Gallipoli could only be evacuated at the cost of a terrible slaughter of rear-guards. The consequence was that irresolution prevailed in the Cabinet. Yet the Coalition attempted to make the public understand that the position at Gallipoli was grave and precarious. Ministers were dismayed to find a large section of the British Press actually professing to believe that the attack on Sari Bair and Suvla Bay had been a great success and laying stress on the fresh ground gained by the Anzacs, regardless of the definite failure of the great offensive. On August 25, after the further attacks about to be recounted here, the Government issued a statement explaining to the public that the true objective had not been gained; but it was worded so guardedly that it was some weeks before the bulk of the nation understood how unfavourable the situation at Gallipoli really was.

When Sir Ian Hamilton found that he could expect no more help from England, he resolved to attack again with such troops as were at his disposal. He brought the "Old Guard of Gallipoli," the incomparable 29th Division, secretly and by night in trawlers from Cape Helles to Suvla Bay. The 29th Division had been chiefly under the command of General De Lisle since the departure of Sir Aylmer Hunter-Weston, but at this period it was in the temporary charge of Brigadier-General Marshall. Mr. Ashmead Bartlett wrote that the arrival of the 29th Division at Suvla Bay "stimulated the whole Army." Sir Ian Hamilton also brought from Egypt the 2nd Mounted Division, consisting of 5,000 Yeomanry who had been dismounted and were to serve as infantry. The 2nd Mounted Division was commanded by Major-General Paton.

The new attack was delivered on August 21,

FAREWELL GROUPS AT SEDD-UL-BAHR.

General Brula (X) the Commander-in-Chief of the French Army at the Dardanelles, and his staff.

BEFORE THE EVACUATION: AN INCIDENT OF INDIVIDUAL BRAVERY IN GALLIPOLI.

Two men of the 1st Royal Munster Fusiliers bringing two uninjured horses back to the British lines during a Turkish bombardment.

and was chiefly directed against Ismail Oglu Tepe, an artillery position which commanded both Anzac Cove and the Suvla beaches. Ismail Oglu Tepe was a hill which " rises 350 feet from the plain, with steep spurs jutting out to the west and south-west, the whole of it covered with dense holly oak scrub, so nearly impenetrable that it breaks up an attack and forces troops to move in single file along goat tracks between the bushes." The capture of this hill was considered an essential preliminary to the seizure of the Anafarta heights. It had, indeed, been included in the scheme laid down for the operations on the night of the first landing. It was a difficult position to attack at the end of the third week in August, for the Turks were by that time in great strength. There was no cover for the assailing columns except Lala Baba, on the verge of the sea, and Chocolate Hill. The rest of the way was open plain, with a slight rise, swept by artillery fire. " For a mile and a half," said Sir Ian Hamilton, " there was nothing to conceal a mouse."

The 53rd and 54th Divisions were ranged from the Kiretch ridge to Sulajik, their duty being to hold the enemy on their part of the front. The 29th Division, from the direction of Chocolate Hill, was to storm Scimitar Hill and afterwards to assault Ismail Oglu Tepe. The 11th Division, farther to the right, was to clear the Turkish trenches around Hetman Chair and Aire Kavak, and afterwards to co-operate by moving on Ismail Oglu Tepe from the south-west. Two brigades of the 10th Division were in reserve at a point unnamed, and the 2nd Mounted Division was held in reserve behind Lala Baba. General Birdwood was to co-operate from the left of the Anzac line in the direction of Kabak Kuyu and Susuk Kuyu. The 29th Division and the 11th Division went into the front trenches on the night of August 20.

The attack was timed for the afternoon, because it was hoped that the sun would then be in the eyes of the Turkish gunners, while showing clearly the line of their trenches. Ill-luck once more attended the British plans. Suvla Bay was enveloped in " a strange mist," which almost concealed the enemy's lines, while it threw the British positions into strong relief against the sun's rays. General De Lisle had at his disposal two Field Artillery Brigades (very short of horses), two heavy batteries, the two Highland mountain batteries, and two batteries of 5-inch howitzers. There were also 24 machine-guns on Chocolate Hill and Green Hill, and several warships were in attendance. The preparatory bombardment, which lasted from 2.30 to 3 p.m., was, however, greatly handicapped by the bad light. The guns were chiefly concentrated on Ismail Oglu Tepe and Scimitar (Burnt) Hill, while the enemy's fire was principally directed against Chocolate Hill. The bush and scrub soon became alight, and fierce fires were quickly raging in various areas.

At 3 p.m. the infantry advance began on the right of the line, and almost at once the scheme began to go wrong. The 34th Brigade of the 11th Division charged and carried the Turkish trenches between Hetman Chair and Aire Kavak with great ease. The 32nd Brigade, on the left of the 34th, was less successful. It advanced against Hetman Chair, from which point a communication trench ran to the south-west corner of Ismail Oglu Tepe. The trench was a formidable loopholed line with an overhead cover. The Brigade took the wrong direction, moving north-east instead of due east, and on correcting its line of advance in open country met with a severe repulse. The 33rd Brigade, hurried up to redeem the error, lost its bearings and was divided. Part of the Brigade marched north-east, exactly as the 32nd Brigade had done, and the rest of the Brigade swerved south to Susuk Kuyu, a spot which had been left to General Birdwood to deal with. The failure of these two Brigades practically decided the fortunes of the day, for the 29th Division was therefore eventually enfiladed.

The 29th Division advanced from the direction of Chocolate Hill at 3.30, half an hour after the infantry attack on the right. Its first objective was Scimitar Hill, which was meanwhile furiously bombarded by the warships and the land batteries. The 87th Brigade was entrusted with the task of attacking this height. The 86th Brigade was to advance up the valley between Scimitar Hill and the Ismail Oglu Tepe spur, in order to assail the latter position. The 88th Brigade, which had been greatly diminished in numbers on the Krithia line on August 6, was held in reserve. When the 87th Brigade emerged from its trenches it was greeted by a terrific rifle fire from the Turks, who stood up on the crest of Scimitar Hill and blazed away regardless of the shells falling around them. The 1st Inniskilling Fusiliers reached the foot of the hill on the western side, and the 1st Border Regiment pushed undaunted to a point on the

BRITISH TROOPS ADVANCING ACROSS SALT LAKE TO ATTACK ANAFARTA.

southern side. Twenty minutes after they had left the trenches both battalions charged impetuously up the hill with fixed bayonets. The Inniskillings almost reached the top, but were swept by shrapnel fire and machine-guns. The Border Regiment actually surmounted the crest, but the Turks held their ground, and there was a violent hand-to-hand struggle in which both sides lost heavily. The two battalions were by this time under a deadly cross-fire, and though the Border Regiment managed to clear some trenches, both battalions had to fall back. Some inadequate cover on the slopes of the hill was clung to for a time, but at last the Brigade withdrew to its trenches, greatly reduced in numbers. The withdrawal was in any case inevitable, for the 86th Brigade had failed to make good its advance up the adjacent valley towards Ismail Oglu Tepe. It had encountered a fierce bush fire, and had also been badly hammered by the terrible rifle fire from Ismail Oglu Tepe and the trench leading to Hetman Chair. It was at this moment that the failure of the 32nd and 33rd Brigades was keenly felt. The indomitable 29th Division for once found the odds against them too heavy, and though the troops advanced again and again, they were always in the end beaten back.

The 5,000 Yeomen forming the 2nd Mounted Division had meanwhile been waiting in reserve behind Lala Baba, close to the beach. When it was seen that the attack was going wrong, the Division was ordered to advance to a fresh position behind Chocolate Hill. "Led," as Mr. Ashmead-Bartlett afterwards wrote, "by men bearing some of the best-known names in England," it advanced across the dry bed of the Salt Lake in open order. The Division was assailed instantly by a well-directed and destructive shrapnel fire. Sir Ian Hamilton said :—

> The advance of these English Yeomen was a sight calculated to send a thrill of pride through anyone with a drop of English blood running in their veins. Such superb martial spectacles are rare in modern war. Ordinarily it should always be possible to bring up reserves under some sort of cover from shrapnel fire. Here, for a mile and a half, there was nothing to conceal a mouse, much less some of the most stalwart soldiers England has ever sent from her shores. Despite the critical events in other parts of the field, I could hardly take my glasses from the Yeomen; they moved like men marching on parade. Here and there a shell would take toll of a cluster; there they lay; there was no straggling; the others moved steadily on; not a man was there who hung back or hurried.

By the time the Yeomanry, already somewhat thinned, had reached their new position behind Chocolate Hill, and in rear of the 88th Brigade, it was 6 o'clock and the light was failing. Yet the whole landscape was lit by the flames from the bush fires, and the roar of the bombardment and the roll of musketry increased until the din was deafening. The 2nd South Midland (Mounted) Brigade, commanded by Brigadier-General the Earl of Longford, was thrown forward in the hope that the Yeomen might retrieve the fortunes of the day. The 2nd South Wales Borderers had previously advanced to the southern side of Scimitar Hill, where the battalion had dug itself in. The 2nd South Midland Brigade consisted of the Bucks Yeomanry, the Berks Yeomanry, and the Dorset Yeomanry. Heavy toll was taken from the Brigade as it advanced in the twilight over the open plain, and at first, said the official account, "the advance had in places to be almost by inches." Many conflicting versions of the subsequent episodes that evening were afterwards published, but though written in all good faith, some of them were evidently at variance with the actual facts. Plain and hills alike were wreathed in smoke and mist. The onlookers at a distance could only see dimly through the gathering gloom. The Yeomen themselves, plunged in a literal fog of battle, could hardly gain a definite idea of what was happening. Sir Ian Hamilton presumably had the best opportunities for ascertaining afterwards the course of the fighting, though even his accounts of the Suvla Bay actions were often necessarily incomplete. His version was that the left of the 2nd South Midland Brigade "reached the foremost line of the 29th Division, and on the right also they got as far as the leading battalions" (presumably the South Wales Borderers near the southern face of Scimitar Hill). He went on to say :—

As soon as it was dark, one regiment pushed up the valley between Scimitar Hill and Ismail Oglu Tepe, and carried the trenches on a small knoll near the centre of this horseshoe. The regiment imagined it had captured Ismail Oglu Tepe, which would have been a very notable success, enabling as it would the whole of our line to hang on and dig in. But when the report came in some doubt was felt as to its accuracy, and a reconnaissance by staff officers showed that the knoll was a good way from Ismail Oglu Tepe, and that a strongly-held semicircle of Turkish trenches (the enemy having been heavily reinforced) still denied us access to the top of the hill. As the men were too done, and had lost too heavily to admit of a second immediate assault, and as the knoll actually held would have been swept by fire at daybreak, there was nothing for it but to fall back under cover of darkness to our original line.

The regiment that took the knoll was not officially named. One Berkshire Yeoman, Private Alfred Potts, remained for forty-eight hours under the Turkish trenches with a wounded comrade, although he was himself wounded in the thigh. Eventually he dragged his companion on a shovel nearly three-quarters of a mile to the British trenches. For this act of devotion and gallantry he received the Victoria Cross. The Royal Bucks Hussars suffered very heavy losses, particularly among their officers. Lord Longford, who commanded the South Midland Brigade, was killed during the action, as was also Brigadier-General P. A. Kenna, V.C. Lord Longford was at one time in the 2nd Life Guards, General Kenna had been in the 21st Lancers, had seen much campaigning, and had won his V.C. on the Nile in 1898. A well-known cavalry officer, the gallant Sir John Milbanke, V.C., commander of the Sherwood Foresters, and previously in the 10th

A CHARGE BEFORE EVACUATION.
Australian troops charging near a Turkish trench.

THE EVACUATION OF GALLIPOLI.
Lord Kitchener and General Birdwood passing through Mudros.

Hussars, also fell during the battle. But the heaviest aggregate losses were those of the 29th Division, which once more suffered partial destruction. It had 5,000 casualties during the day. The operations at Suvla Bay on August 21 failed so completely at every point that it may well be doubted whether, in view of the discouraging conditions, such a desperate frontal attack should ever have been undertaken at all. The expediency of the decision which flung forward the 2nd South Midland Brigade at sunset was specially open to question.

On the same day an important independent action was fought under the direction of Sir William Birdwood south of Suvla Bay, which had the excellent result of firmly linking up the Suvla Bay and the Anzac forces, previously only connected by outposts. A column was constituted in the Anzac area, consisting of two battalions of the New Zealand Mounted Rifles, two battalions of the 29th Irish Brigade, the 4th South Wales Borderers, and the 29th Infantry Brigade. The force was placed under the command of Major-General H. V. Cox, an officer of the Indian Army, who had fought in six previous campaigns, and had been in command of a brigade on the North-West Frontier when the Great War began. His column was divided into three sections. The left section was to complete the link from Damakjelik Bair to the troops on the right of the 11th Division; the centre was to seize an important well at Kabak Kuyu; the right section was to capture the eminence known as the Kaiajik Aghala, on the north-east side of which the Turks had made trenches. The Kaiajik Aghala was a little south-west of an important height styled Hill 60, which commanded the Biyuk Anafarta valley from the south. It was really a spur of Hill 60. The whole of this subsidiary operation went with a swing from the outset, and was the redeeming feature of an unfortunate day. The attack was made in the afternoon. The left section secured the ground desired, the Indian Brigade in the centre got the well, and the right section, under Brigadier-General Russell, fought its way to the Kaiajik Aghala and dug itself in below the summit. Russell's troops were severely bombed during the night, but held their own. They were reinforced early next morning by the 18th Australian Infantry, a newly arrived battalion, and at 6.30 a.m. on August 22 an attack was made on the summit of the Kaiajik Aghala. The Australians, who suffered many casualties, carried 150 yards of the Turkish trenches, but were enfiladed and forced to fall back. The New Zealand Mounted Rifles, in face of strenuous opposition, took 80 yards of trenches. The Turks made several counter-attacks, but the ultimate result of the whole action was that the Suvla and Anzac forces satisfactorily though gradually linked up their lines. It should be noted that throughout this conflict the 4th Australian Brigade, which held the ground south of the Kaiajik Dere (a Dere is a valley with a stream), rendered constant assistance, and their rifle fire accounted for hundreds of Turks on the hill. The Brigade also sent an assaulting party of 300 men across the gully under a fire so heavy that only a third of the party got through ; but they stayed there, and were not dislodged.

The attack on the Kaiajik Aghala was followed on August 27 by the brilliant capture of Hill 60 by troops from Anzac. General Cox was again in charge. He had at his disposal detachments from the 4th and 5th Australian Brigades, the New Zealand Mounted Rifles Brigade, and the 5th Connaught Rangers. The Turks, who well knew what was coming, had scored Hill 60 with trenches. The attack was made at five in the afternoon after a preparatory bombardment, but the British guns had not silenced the enemy, who poured in a fierce fire from rifles, machine-guns, and field-guns, as well as from a heavy battery. The centre of the attack consisted of three lines of troops, the Auckland and Canterbury Mounted Rifles being in the first line, the Otago and Wellington Mounted Rifles in the second line, and the 18th Australian Infantry in the third line. The 5th Connaught Rangers, commanded by Colonel Jourdain, were on the left, and the detachments from the 4th and 5th Australian Brigades on the right. The attack of the New Zealanders was magnificent. They charged to the top of the hill, and engaged in a desperate hand-to-hand combat, which lasted intermittently until 9.30 p.m., by which time nine-tenths of the trenches on the actual summit were in their hands. The 18th Australians gave them a vigorous backing. On the right the detachments from the 4th and 5th Australian Brigades were held

DECIDING ON THE EVACUATION OF GALLIPOLI.

Lord Kitchener and General Birdwood in the trenches. Smaller picture : General Birdwood and Colonel Sir Henry McMahon, High Commissioner of Egypt, thirty yards from the enemy trenches.

FOR GALLANT DEEDS IN GALLIPOLI.

Lieutenant-General Sir Bryan Mahon (X) decorating officers and men of the French army.

up by a battery of machine-guns. They advanced in three lines of a hundred men each, and nearly the whole of the force, both officers and men, was either killed or wounded. A few who were unscathed managed to join the New Zealanders in the trenches on the summit. On the left 250 men of the Connaught Rangers had swept round and seized the northern Turkish communication trenches, and Sir Ian Hamilton said that they "excited the admiration of all beholders by the vigour and cohesion of their charge." The Irishmen stood their ground with desperate gallantry until long after dark, when they were bombed into withdrawal. The 9th Australian Light Horse tried to recapture the lost trenches, but failed. All night the situation was critical, and it was only saved by the stubborn grit of the New Zealanders. They clung to the summit like bulldogs. "Nothing would shift them," wrote Sir Ian Hamilton. "All that night and all next day, through bombing, bayonet charges, musketry, shrapnel, and heavy shell, they held on." Their indomitable tenacity won Hill 60. At 1 a.m. on August 29 the 10th Light Horse made another attack on the northern communication trenches, captured them, and held them with the aid of the 9th Light Horse, which had advanced from another direction. Hill 60 passed into the possession of the Allies, and it was the last important position won by the Mediterranean Expeditionary Force at the Dardanelles. Sir Ian Hamilton's concluding comments on the action were as follows:

This gave us . . . an outlook over the Biyuk Anafarta valley, and safer lateral communications between Anzac and Suvla Bay. Our casualties in this hotly contested affair amounted to 1,000. The Turks lost out of all proportion more. Their line of retreat was commanded from our Kaiajik Dere trenches, whence our observers were able to direct artillery fire equally upon their fugitives and their reinforcements. The same observers estimated the Turkish casualties as no less than 5,000. Three Turkish machine-guns and forty-six prisoners were taken, as well as three trench mortars, 300 Turkish rifles, 60,000 rounds of ammunition, and 500 bombs. Four hundred acres were added to the territories of Anzac. Major-General Cox showed his usual forethought and wisdom. Brigadier-General Russell fought his men splendidly.

The story of the next few weeks was thus summed up by Sir Ian Hamilton, who had meanwhile organized "a minor offensive routine of sniping and bombing":

From this date onwards . . . the flow of munitions and drafts fell away. Sickness, the legacy of a desperately trying summer, took heavy toll of the survivors of so many arduous conflicts. No longer was there any question of operations on the grand scale, but with such troops it was difficult to be downhearted. All ranks were cheerful; all remained confident that, so long as they stuck to their guns, their country would stick to them, and see them victoriously through the last and greatest of the crusades.

Lieutenant-General the Hon. J. H. G. Byng, K.C.M.G., took over command of the 9th Army Corps at Suvla Bay on August 24. There was considerable submarine, seaplane, and airplane activity at the Dardanelles and in the Sea of Marmora in August and September. Flight-Lieutenant Edmonds, flying in a seaplane, dropped a heavy bomb on a Turkish transport packed with troops. The vessel sank and most of the men on board perished. On September 3 the Kaiser bestowed the Order Pour le Mérite on Enver Pasha. On September 7 it was announced that a British submarine had sunk in the Sea of Marmora a transport carrying 11-inch guns to Gallipoli. On October 8 Sir Ian Hamilton reported that during the month of September, as a result of "patrol actions, bomb attacks, and rushing of houses" every night, there had been an average gain of 300 yards along the whole four miles of the Suvla front. The real difficulty of the Expeditionary Force during this period was the growing prevalence of sickness. Several hundred men were sometimes added to the sick-list in a single day. A great many of the cases were comparatively slight. One complaint which grew epidemic was called "the three days' fever." It did not produce any eruption, was seldom serious, and was hardly ever fatal. The infection was believed to be borne by mosquitoes.

The British public had become slowly aware of the gravity of the position at the Dardanelles, and it was freely stated in private at the beginning of October that the Government were finding great difficulty in coming to a decision. The landing of Franco-British forces at Salonika began on October 6. The next day Austro-German armies crossed the Danube, the Drina, and the Save, and Belgrade was captured on October 9. By October 14 Bulgaria and Serbia were formally at war. On the same day Lord Milner, in the House of Lords, made the first really important public criticism of the Dardanelles Expedition by saying: "When I hear statements that it would be a terrible thing to abandon our Dardanelles adventure because this would have so bad an effect in Egypt, in India, upon our prestige in the

ADMIRAL DE ROBECK AND STAFF.

Left to right: Commander Somerville, Wireless Officer; Commander Hood, Naval Secretary; Lieutenant Bowlby, Flag-Lieutenant; Flag-Commander Ramsay, Major Godfrey, R.M.A., Captain Lambert Commodore Keyes, Vice-Admiral de Robeck, Captain McClintock, Commander Millot, French Naval attaché.

THE EVACUATION: LAST BRITISH VESSELS LEAVING THE DARDANELLES.

East, I cannot help asking myself whether it will not have a worse effect if we persist in that enterprise and it ends in complete disaster." Lord Lansdowne replied by deprecating so public a suggestion, but he acknowledged that the development in the Balkans had created a new military situation, which was "being examined in all its bearings." Lord Ribblesdale supported Lord Milner, and urged the Government to "get out of the unfortunate adventure at the Dardanelles." There could be no doubt that the view expressed by Lords Milner and Ribblesdale represented the growing trend of public opinion in Great Britain, which had been shocked by the increasing disclosures regarding the tragic failure in August. A number of Liberal members had already tabled a motion in identical terms calling upon the Government to appoint a Select Committee to inquire into the initiation, conduct, and position of the Dardanelles campaign, though this motion was afterwards dropped.

But the Government had, in fact, already taken certain steps. On October 11, two days after Belgrade fell, Lord Kitchener had telegraphed to Sir Ian Hamilton asking for an estimate of the losses which would be involved in an evacuation of the peninsula. Sir Ian Hamilton replied on October 12 "in terms," he said, "showing that such a step was to me unthinkable." On October 16 he was recalled by telegraph, and only on his arrival in London on October 22 was he informed that the Government "desired a fresh, unbiassed opinion, from a responsible Commander, upon the question of early evacuation." The new Commander-in-Chief of the Mediterranean Expeditionary Force was General Sir Charles Carmichael Monro, K.C.B., who had fought in Indian frontier campaigns and in the South African War, had been Commandant of the School of Musketry, and was commanding the Second London Division on the outbreak of war. He was holding a high command in France when he was sent to the Dardanelles, and he left London for the East on October 22. In the meantime, Sir William Birdwood was placed in temporary command of the Dardanelles operations. Sir Ian Hamilton left the Gallipoli Peninsula on October 17.

The Government, although effecting these changes in the command, had by no means made up their mind to evacuate the Gallipoli Peninsula. Many Ministers were believed still to dread the consequences of withdrawal, and others, with Mr. Winston Churchill at their head, favoured a continuance of the operations. Sir Edward Carson, the Attorney-General, held that Gallipoli should be evacuated, and that more strenuous efforts should be made, if possible, to rescue Serbia. Because he considered that the Government were not pursuing "a clearly-defined, well-thought-out, and decisive policy" in the Eastern Mediterranean, he resigned from the Ministry on October 18. By the beginning of November General Monro had reported in favour of evacuation, though his views were kept secret, and the Government remained indisposed to accept his advice without further consideration. On November 2 Mr. Asquith made a long statement in the House of Commons upon the naval and military situation, in the course of which he referred to the Dardanelles. He said the inception of the operation was most carefully considered, in conjunction with the best naval and military experts; that the Cabinet fully approved; and that it was formally decided, in the first place, to make a purely naval attack. He defended the objects of the expedition, and claimed that it was at that moment holding up 200,000 Turks and preventing them from doing incalculable mischief in other parts of the Eastern theatre. "If anybody," he said, "is responsible for the initiation of this enterprise in the Dardanelles, nobody is more responsible than I." Sir Edward Carson, who spoke next, taunted the Cabinet because, he said, "you have never been able to make up your mind, and you have not now made up your mind, as to whether you ought or are able either to proceed with these operations, or whether you ought boldly to withdraw your men and save the suffering and the loss that goes on from day to day with absolutely no hope of any satisfactory result." Other members made severe speeches, and Lord Charles Beresford declared that the Government "know perfectly well that we shall never get through the Dardanelles."

Ministers made no reply to these criticisms, but within a day or two it became known that Lord Kitchener had gone to the Dardanelles to look at the position for himself. It was believed that he shared the views of those Ministers who disliked the idea of withdrawal, but by the time he left Gallipoli he had decided to confirm General Monro's recommendation. He reached Mudros on an early day in November, and discussed the position with General Monro and the corps and divisional commanders. Afterwards he inspected the Cape Helles area, as

WEST BEACH, SUVLA.
Getting ready to leave.

well as Anzac and Suvla Bay. He climbed to Russell's Top at Anzac, and to the Corps observation post at Suvla. He also went through the front firing trench at Anzac where the Light Horse had charged, and he was then within 20 yards of the Turkish trenches. At the time of Lord Kitchener's visit the front at Anzac and Suvla alone formed a line twelve miles long. On the completion of his investigations, and in view of the situation elsewhere, he favoured evacuation. The Cabinet were notified of his conclusions by telegraph, and even then there was some further Ministerial hesitation. It was understood that Mr. Bonar Law headed the Ministers who eventually carried the decision to withdraw, but the Cabinet as a whole were largely influenced by the revised opinions of the military and naval experts, who had come to the conclusion that evacuation need not involve heavy losses. In this conclusion the experts were thoroughly justified in the event.

The secret decision to evacuate Gallipoli was believed to have influenced Mr. Winston Churchill's decision to resign the somewhat ornamental post he then held in the Cabinet as Chancellor of the Duchy of Lancaster. He made a personal statement in the House of Commons on November 15, in which he announced his intention of joining the Army in France. In the course of this statement he made an elaborate defence of his share of responsibility for the Dardanelles Expedition. "If," he added, "there were any operations in the history of the world which, having been begun, it was worth while to carry through with the utmost vigour and fury, with a consistent flow of reinforcements, and an utter disregard of life, it was the operations so daringly and brilliantly begun by Sir Ian Hamilton in the immortal landing of April 25." Three days later Lord Ribblesdale startled the country by saying in the House of Lords that it was common knowledge that Sir Charles Monro had "reported in favour of withdrawal from the Dardanelles, and adversely to the continuance of winter operations there." The statement of Sir Charles Monro's recommendation was quite correct, but it was certainly not common knowledge, and right up to the moment of evacuation a large proportion of the public never realized that withdrawal was intended.

The operations at Gallipoli during the month of October had fully partaken of the deadly monotony of trench warfare. On the night of October 28 H.M.S. Hythe, an auxiliary mine-sweeper, commanded by Lieutenant-Commander Bird, R.N.R., was sunk in collision with another vessel off the coast of the peninsula. The loss of life included two military officers, one naval warrant officer, nine seamen, and 143 military rank and file. The Turks attacked the extreme right of the Anzac position four times within an hour on the evening of November 4, but were quickly repulsed. On November 14 the Admiralty announced that submarine E 20, Lieutenant-Commander Clyfford, R.N., had been sunk in the Sea of Marmora. The commander and three other officers, and six men were rescued by the Turks and made prisoners. On November 15 the Turkish trenches in the neighbourhood of Krithia ravine were successfully attacked. Portions of the 4th and 7th Royal Scots, 7th and 8th Scottish Rifles, and Ayrshire Yeomanry, all of the 156th Brigade, were employed. Three mines were exploded under the enemy's trenches, and the infantry carried 280 yards of trench east and west of the ravine, the total British losses being under 50 killed and wounded. The Turks counter-attacked without success two nights afterwards, and further counter-attacks on November 21 were equally futile. The French Corps was very busy with under-ground warfare towards the end of November. Towards the end of November, too, the Turkish artillery fire increased in "quality and quantity," as a result of the opening of the Danube route to Germany, and the consequent arrival of fresh supplies of munitions.

A terrible gale of rain and snow, accompanied by a swift fall of temperature, struck the Gallipoli Peninsula on November 27, and lasted three days. The bad weather had arrived a month earlier than was expected, although fortunately the hurricane was followed by a fortnight's calm. The gale caused much suffering to the forces both ashore and afloat. The Australians were particularly affected. being unused to rigorous winter weather.

WEST BEACH.

A busy scene two days before the evacuation.

ANOTHER SCENE ON THE WEST BEACH AT SUVLA.

Many of them saw snow for the first time on that occasion. The storm began with twelve hours' rain, which flooded the trenches and dug-outs, and soaked the men to the skin. The Turks fared even worse, and some were drowned; their bodies were washed down the gullies into the British lines. Others climbed out of their trenches and were promptly shot down by the Anzacs. The rain was followed by a piercing north wind and a black, biting frost, which froze the water round the feet of the men as they stood. With the north wind came the snow, and the tempest grew into a veritable blizzard. In some of the trenches the men were only kept alive by being forced to work hard all night with pick and shovel.

One Corps alone lost 204 men dead from frost and exposure in two nights. Before the blizzard from the north began, a rain-cloud burst over the 9th Corps at Suvla Bay with such intensity that it resembled the action of a waterspout. The trenches became rushing torrents, in which, as in the case of the Turks, some of the men were drowned. The three days' hurricane cost the Gallipoli Expedition 6,000 men, who had to be removed sick; and it was therefore more deadly in its results than some of the battles. Since the days of the Crimea no British Army had been exposed to more suffering from the elements, but the troops bore their trials without complaint. They welcomed the spell of "mild Riviera weather" which followed the gale.

Lord Kitchener arrived again in London on November 30, after having paid visits to Greece and Italy. On December 21 Mr. Asquith made to the House of Commons the astonishing announcement that all the troops at Suvla and Anzac had been successfully removed, with the bulk of their stores. Only a few men were wounded, not more than half a dozen in both areas. The guns, numbering 200, were got away with the exception of seven, which were blown up at the last. The dominating feeling in Great Britain was one of intense relief. So great was the rejoicing that there was even some tendency to speak of the withdrawal as though it amounted to a great victory. Australia and New Zealand expressed approval of the decision. Mr. Hughes, the Prime Minister of the Commonwealth, said: "The news of the evacuation with insignificant loss has been received in a spirit of devout gladness, chastened by keen regret that the withdrawal was found to be imperative."

The Government decided that the methods adopted in the evacuation should be kept secret until after the conclusion of the war. Very few details were therefore published. Broadly speaking, the plan was to withdraw the forces gradually in the darkness of night during several nights, while keeping the front trenches manned almost until the end. The whole undertaking was actually spread over ten nights, and was divided into three periods. During the first period the winter stores and miscellaneous articles were removed; in the second period everything but a minimum of food and ammunition was shipped, and the first drafts of men were embarked; the final stage, which at Suvla only took two nights, was the embarcation of guns, transport animals, and the main body of troops. The Turks had no suspicion of these deliberate preparations, which were conducted with extraordinary skill and stealth. There were over 80,000 Turks entrenched before the Suvla and Anzac lines, at distances varying from 20 yards to half a mile, or in reserve close behind; and only the most extreme caution prevented them from discovering what was afoot. Mr. Ward Price, who witnessed the evacuation, wrote:

> With quiet efficiency, with regularity, even without noise, it was done. It may be said that the only "fighting" that took place in connexion with the embarcation was that which occurred in the Australian brigades to decide who should have the privilege of staying to the last. Many men paraded before their commanding officers to protest vigorously against being ordered to go on board the transports while men who had arrived on the Peninsula after themselves were allowed to stay an hour or two longer with the rearguard.
>
> At Suvla the 200 men who formed the ultimate rearguard had been the first to land there in August and, suffering heavy loss, had set foot ashore almost on the very same spot where, on the night of December 20, they held the final barrier until the work of embarking the last details was completed.

The enemy were completely deceived. On the afternoon of December 20 a vigorous attack was begun in the Cape Helles area against some trenches at the head of the Krithia ravine. With the help of fire from warships, the trenches were taken with small loss, and held against counter-attacks delivered that night. This operation helped to divert the enemy's attention. At 3.30 a.m. on the morning of December 21 a huge mine was exploded by the Anzacs near Russell's Top. It was fired by electric contact from a distance, just as the last troops were leaving the beach; and as it had been driven under the Turkish trenches it was considered that the enemy must have suffered a hundred casualties. The Turks thought the Anzacs were about to attack, and for forty minutes they blazed away furiously with their rifles at the empty trenches. Some stragglers who had lost their way in the maze of trenches were not fetched off from the Anzac beach until 8 a.m. The Australians left many letters of farewell to the Turks, assuring them that they

GALLIPOLI.
Troops embarking.

were clean fighters and that the Australians hoped to meet them again. A gramophone was left in a conspicuous place in the trench on Walker's Ridge, with its disc on and the needle ready to play "The Turkish Patrol." Bonfires of bully beef, biscuits, and rice—only a small proportion of the stores—were lit before the last troops left. By daybreak every transport had vanished from the coast and only one or two warships remained. When the sun was well up, the Turks on the Anafarta ridges began bombarding Chocolate Hill, Lala Baba, and Hill 10 with more than

AFTER THE EVACUATION.
Captain Davidson, of H.M.S. "Cornwallis," and General Byng.

their usual violence, and it was apparently hours before they discovered what had occurred. Few among the departing troops knew how well the luck which had so often deserted them served them at the end. As a matter of fact, the Royal Navy, to whose splendid organization the success of the withdrawal was chiefly due, found that sufficient small craft could be concentrated for the final embarcation 24 hours earlier than was originally planned. The last movements were therefore made a night earlier, and it was fortunate that the departure was accelerated. On the night of December 21 a tremendous southerly gale sprang out of a clear sky. Had the original date remained unaltered, it would assuredly have found some thousands of men ashore and unable to embark. Thus good fortune, which had so often been denied them, was with the Anzacs and the 9th Corps in the closing episode.

Sir Charles Monro issued a Special Order of the Day on December 21, in which he congratulated all ranks on "an achievement without parallel in the annals of war." Next day he was appointed to the command of the First Army in France and Flanders, and Sir William Birdwood remained in supreme charge at the Dardanelles. General Birdwood had been wounded on the top of the head in the preceding May, but the wound was thought to be slight, and he never went on the sick list. After the evacuation of Anzac he had the wound examined, and it was found that he had been carrying a large piece of bullet in his head for seven months without knowing it. On December 22, on the Krithia front, Second Lieutenant Alfred Victor Smith, of the 1/5th Battalion, East Lancashire Regiment, met with his death under circumstances so remarkable that his splendid self-sacrifice sheds a glow over the last melancholy days at Cape Helles. The Victoria Cross was posthumously conferred upon him, and in making the announcement the *London Gazette* said:

> He was in the act of throwing a grenade when it slipped from his hand and fell to the bottom of the trench, close to several of our officers and men. He immediately shouted out a warning, and himself jumped clear and into safety; but, seeing that the officers and men were unable to get into cover, and knowing well that the grenade was due to explode, he returned without any hesitation and flung himself down on it. He was instantly killed by the explosion. His magnificent act of self-sacrifice undoubtedly saved many lives.*

When Suvla and Anzac were evacuated, it was announced, probably as a blind, that the Krithia line would be retained. Some neutral

* Second Lieutenant Smith was the only son of Mr. W. H. Smith, Chief Constable of Burnley, and he had been at Gallipoli since May. He was 24 years of age. Writing to his father, Brigadier-General Tufnell said:

"Possibly he thought he could extinguish it; more likely he deliberately forfeited his life to save others from death and injury. Whatever his thoughts may have been, his act was one of bravery such as I personally have never heard surpassed. There was only one result possible. The grenade exploded, and he lost his life. I am afraid no decoration can compensate for the loss of your only son, but the explanation must make you the proudest man in England, when every one reads the story and couples the memory of his name with that old and honoured phrase 'A soldier and a gentleman.' The admiration expressed in these lines is not mine alone, but that of every officer and man in the brigade I have the honour to command."

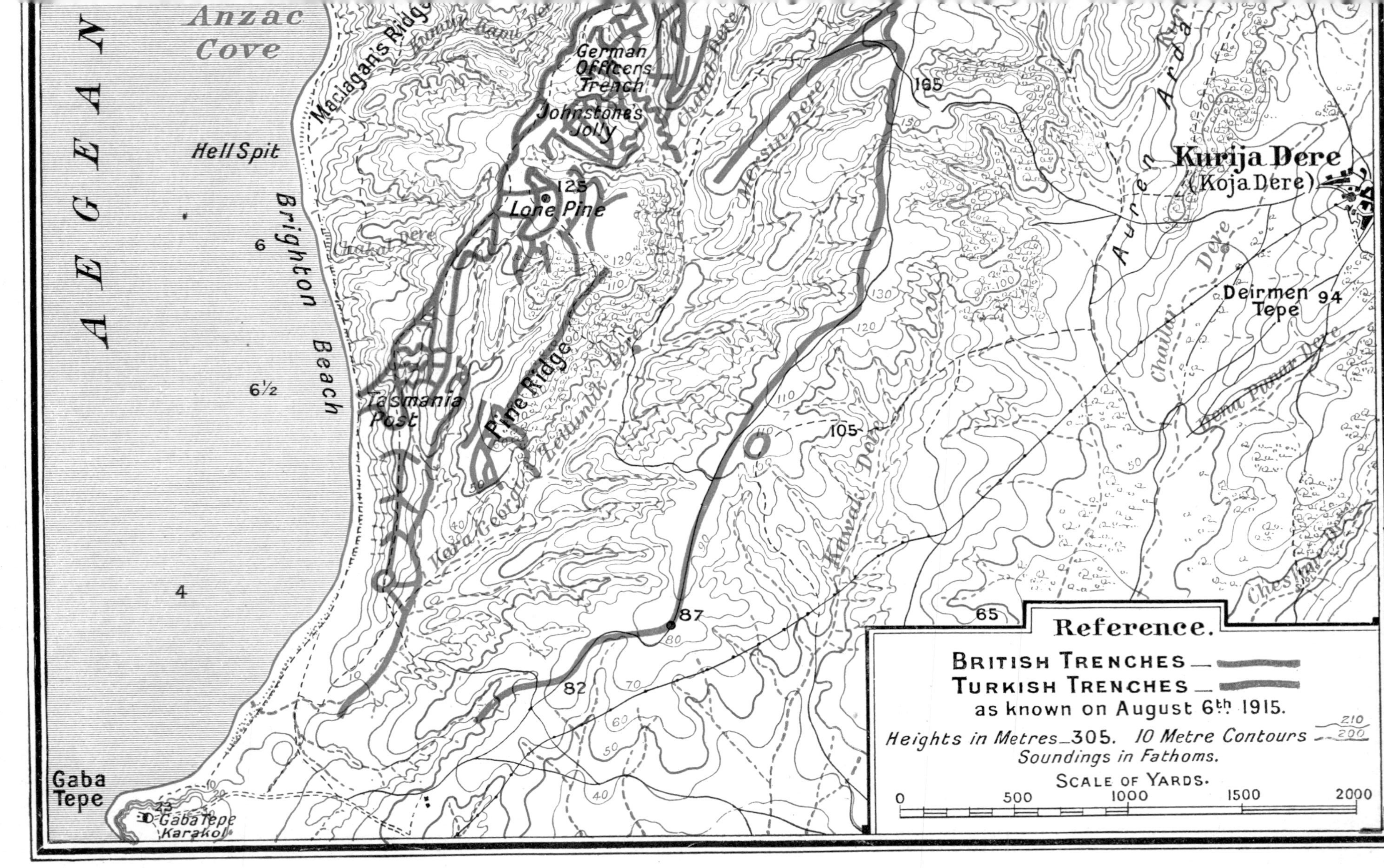

Based upon a War Office Map, 1916.
By permission of Controller of H.M. Stationery Office.

THE TRENCHES AT ANZAC.

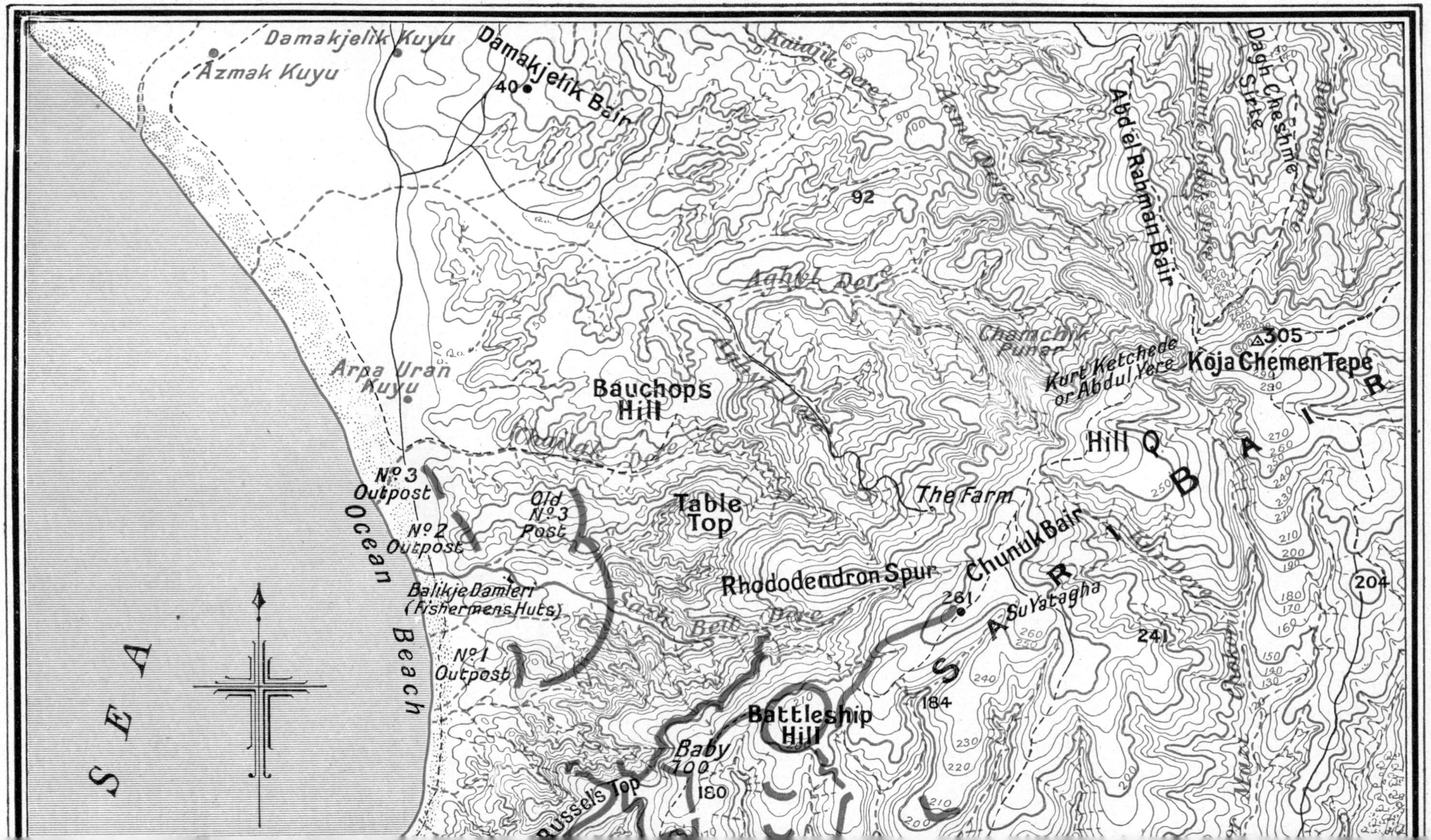
SEA
Damakjelik Kuyu
Azmak Kuyu
Damakjelik Bair
40
Kaiajik Dere
Asmak Dere
Abd'el Rahman Bair
Dagh Cheshme Sirte
92
Aghyl Dere
Chamchik Punar
Kurt Ketchede or Abdul Yere
Koja Chemen Tepe
305
Arpa Uran Kuyu
Bauchops Hill
Chailak Dere
No 3 Outpost
Ocean Beach
No 2 Outpost
Old No 3 Post
Table Top
The Farm
Hill Q
Chunuk Bair
Rhododendron Spur
Balikje Damleri (Fishermens Huts)
Sazli Beit Dere
261
Su Yatagha
241
204
No 1 Outpost
SARI BAIR
184
Battleship Hill
Baby 700
180
Russel's Top

correspondents, notably Mr. Granville Fortescue, who had seen the conflict from the Turkish side, had urged that the Krithia line should be held at all costs, because it was the "key position" of the Dardanelles, and likely to be 'more important than Gibraltar." Whether there was any further hesitation in London was not publicly explained, but the French Corps began to prepare to go as soon as Anzac was emptied, and on December 29 formal orders to evacuate the whole Cape Helles area were made known. The Turkish artillery fire had greatly increased in intensity, but the Turkish infantry had deteriorated in quality, and there was not much apprehension about an infantry attack. The methods adopted at Anzac and Suvla were altered for the Cape Helles withdrawal. The shipments of troops were spread over a longer period. The French Corps, a British Division, and the remaining Yeomanry got away under cover of darkness at the very beginning of January, 1916. By January 4 nearly all the French and 10,000 British had gone. The French used Beach V, and the bulk of the British embarcation was undertaken at Beach W, better known as Lancashire Landing (see Vol. V., pp. 453–4). On the nights of January 5 and 6 the evacuation continued in a steady and unhurried fashion. On the afternoon of January 7 the Turks began a heavy bombardment accompanied by musketry fire, and they sprang two mines near Fusilier Bluff, on the extreme left of the British line. At 4.15 p.m. it was seen that the Turks had fixed bayonets all along their front, and their officers were perceived endeavouring to persuade them to advance. But the Turkish first-line army had mostly been destroyed, and the new formations were unwilling to move. The only advance actually made by the enemy was near Fusilier Bluff, where there was a brisk fight, in which the British repulsed the Turks, losing themselves five officers and 130 men killed and wounded. The Staffordshires had the honour of bearing the brunt of the very last action fought on the Gallipoli Peninsula.

Several thousand men were got away on the

SCENES DURING THE EVACUATION OF GALLIPOLI.

A shell from the Turkish guns bursting near the River Clyde.

night of January 7, and by the morning of January 8 most of the guns had gone also. In the afternoon the sea became very rough, and the embarcation on the last night was greatly impeded. Gully Beach and Beach Y were used to some extent, until the sea became too high. The final embarcations were made at Beach W and Beach V, and at the latter spot the troops passed through the holes in the River Clyde, exactly as had been done at the original landing. Most of the last batches of troops were afloat by 2.30 a.m. on January 9, and the last man left the River Clyde at 3.35 a.m. He was the principal military landing officer. There may have been slightly later embarcations at Beach W. The very last act of the beach parties was to fire great mounds of stores and ammunition, and as the ships moved off, a tremendous explosion of ten tons of explosive material marked the end of the attack on the Dardanelles. Seventeen guns were left behind and destroyed, but of these six were French naval guns, and all were worn out.

The British losses on land at the Dardanelles, including the Royal Naval Division and al Anzac units, were as follows up to January 9, 1916:

	Killed.	Wounded.	Missing.	Total.
Officers ...	1,745	3,143	353	5,241
Other ranks	26,455	74,952	10,901	112,308

Grand Total—117,549, of which number 28,200 officers and men were recorded as killed or died of wounds.

The French losses are not included in these numbers; and it should also be noted that in addition to the losses in action, 96,683 sick cases were admitted to hospital at or from the Dardanelles between April 25 and December 11, 1915.

Mr. Asquith in the House of Commons on January 10, 1916, said that the retirement from Gallipoli was one of the finest operations in naval or military history, and it would take an imperishable place in our national history. The mistakes of the British Government at Gallipoli, as well as of those responsible for the unsupported naval attack and for the various cardinal blunders of strategy and organization, will probably find an almost equally imperishable place in the annals of war.

EVACUATION OF GALLIPOLI.
The last Turkish prisoners from Suvla.

CHAPTER CXIV.

THE DARDANELLES AND THE BALKANS: INTERVENTION OF BULGARIA.

POLICY OF THE ALLIES IN THE BALKANS—RESULTS OF THE BALKAN WARS—ATTITUDE OF BALKAN STATES IN 1914—POSITION AT BEGINNING OF DARDANELLES CAMPAIGN—M. VENIZELOS ON GREEK INTERVENTION—HIS DEFEAT AND RESIGNATION—BULGARIA'S CLAIMS—NEGOTIATIONS WITH THE ALLIES—TURCO-BULGARIAN AGREEMENT—FAILURE OF THE MACEDONIAN NEGOTIATIONS—GERMANY'S DIPLOMATIC TRIUMPH—THE RUSSIAN ULTIMATUM—BULGARIA AT WAR—M. VENIZELOS RETURNS TO POWER—HIS SECOND RESIGNATION—THE ALLIES AT SALONIKA.

AS we have seen, the initiation and the gradual development of the Dardanelles campaign were very greatly influenced by political rather than military considerations. As in so many other critical phases of a war that was not of their making, the Governments of the Allies lacked clearness of vision and definite community of purpose in their attitude towards Turkey, towards the Balkan States, and towards the solution of the whole problem of South-Eastern Europe. In the years before the war they had been engaged in a desperate attempt to keep all the Great Powers of Europe united precisely in regard to that problem, and to solve it by agreement. When, in 1914, the Germanic Powers abandoned pacific and "European" pretences, and set out to destroy Serbia and to complete the German domination of Turkey, the Allies sought rather to counteract and defeat this policy than to promote a positive counter-policy of their own. Certain undertakings were, indeed, entered into with Russia against the event of the conquest of the Dardanelles and Constantinople, but, in the main, the Dardanelles campaign was inspired less by clear political conceptions than by a general hope that it would cut knots which diplomacy had failed to unravel, and, while administering a severe check to Germany's eastern ambitions, would restore the conditions necessary for further diplomatic labours.

It was, indeed, obvious that the opening of the Dardanelles would have immense political consequences. It might restore the Balkan League of Serbia, Greece and Bulgaria—this time with the adhesion of Rumania. It must in any case determine the policy and relations of all the Balkan States. Unfortunately failure was no less certain than success to determine the course of events in the Balkans. It soon appeared that, having failed to negotiate a Balkan agreement before embarking upon the Dardanelles enterprise, the Allies would fail to obtain an agreement during the progress of uncertain and, indeed, unsuccessful military operations. The spring and summer of 1915 were occupied in feverish diplomatic effort. But diplomacy secured the help neither of Greece nor of Rumania, and in the autumn, before the Allies had resolved to abandon the costly Dardanelles campaign, hopeless though its prospects had become, Bulgaria had thrown in her lot definitely with the Central Powers, and Serbia, who had twice driven the Austrians off her soil, was exposed to invasion of a kind

THE KING OF GREECE.

which she was powerless to resist. The diplomacy of the Allies had suffered a severe defeat.

We shall not attempt here to analyse the whole causes of this political failure. Our narrative will in the main tell its own tale. But let us note at once the official account of the policy of the Allies which was given to the House of Commons on October 14, 1915, by Sir Edward Grey. It was, he said, at the outset of the war the desire of the Allies that "the war should not spread in the Near East." When, however, Germany forced Turkey to intervene, the Allies "concentrated on working for Balkan agreement." They considered that agreement among the Balkan States could be secured only by "mutual concessions," which required "mutual consent." But the "acute divisions" in the Balkans were such that the policy of embitterment, promoted by the Central Powers, overcame the policy of reconciliation. Sir Edward Grey added—and this was the gist of his case:

In my opinion it is clear that nothing outside a preponderating advantage to the Allies in the course of military events in Europe would have enabled us to make the policy of Balkan union prevail over the opposite policy of bringing about Balkan war.

In other words the Balkan policy of the Allies was, for better or worse, based upon the expectation of military successes sufficient to turn the scale. It is said that in the spring of 1915 the King of Bulgaria declared that he would intervene on behalf of the Allies when they began to hammer at the gates of Constantinople. When the obvious failure of the Dardanelles campaign was added to the Germanic conquest of Galicia—freeing him from the fear of any immediate intervention by Rumania—Ferdinand intervened on behalf of Germany and Austria-Hungary.

The first Balkan War (1912) was, in its origin at any rate, a real war of Liberation, fought for the freedom of the Christian population of the Balkan Peninsula from the misrule of Turkey. It was rendered possible by the conclusion, after years of unsuccessful diplomacy, of an alliance between Serbia and Bulgaria, followed by the conclusion of a Treaty between Bulgaria and Greece and other arrangements which completed the Balkan League. The central feature of the Serbo-Bulgarian Treaty of 1912 was a provisional settlement of the vexed question of the partition of Macedonia—that immensely complicated problem of mixed races and mixed creeds. The settlement was provisional, especially inasmuch as the north-western area of Macedonia remained a "contested zone," and much was to depend upon ultimate arbitration by Russia. No sooner had the arms of the Balkan States triumphed over Turkey than—largely by reason of the dissensions of the Great Powers—Balkan unity was again broken. Serbia, refused the outlet to the Adriatic that was her due, required "compensation" in Macedonia. Germany and Austria-Hungary fomented the consequent feud, and encouraged Bulgaria to attack her allies. The second Balkan War ended in the defeat of Bulgaria. This defeat was sealed by the intervention of Rumania. The Treaty of Bukarest (August, 1913) deprived Bulgaria of the bulk of her expected gains. It gave her, indeed, some additional territory to the south-east, with a strip of coast on the Ægean and a port at Dedeagatch. But on the one hand the Turco-Bulgarian frontier, joining the Ægean and the Black Sea, ran to the west and not to the east of Adrianople; on the other hand Bulgaria was not only excluded from the "contested zone" of Macedonia, but was cut off from most of the territory allotted to her by the Treaty of 1912

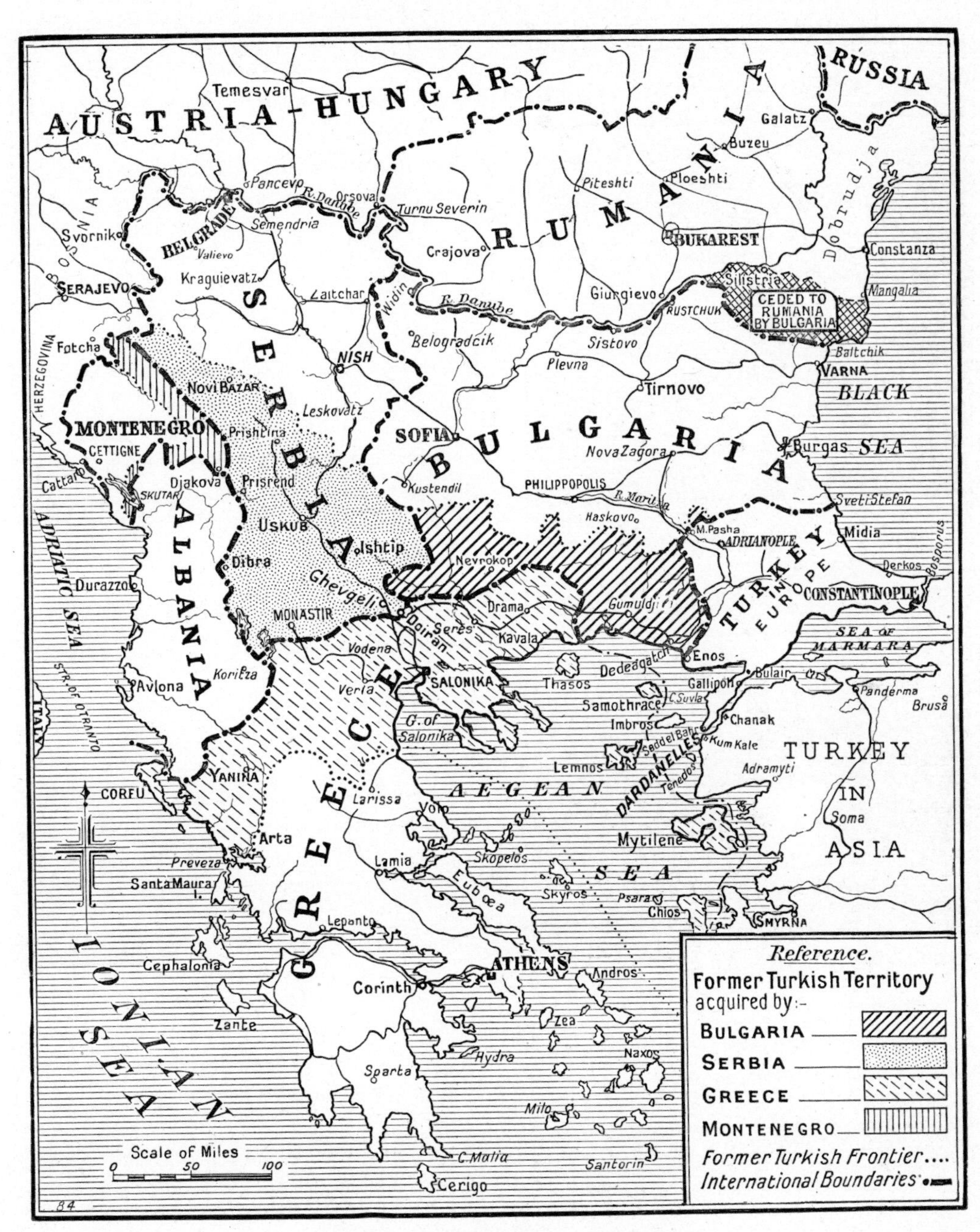

BALKAN FRONTIERS, 1913-1915
(Showing terms of Treaty of Bukarest).

with Serbia, and by the agreements with Greece. Bulgaria owed her humiliation to the criminal act of her King and to the intrigues of the Central Powers. But Europe had no reason to be proud of the Treaty of Bukarest, which could not be justified by any principles of nationality The most that could be said for it was that its temporary acceptance was perhaps preferable to attempts at revision which had no prospect of success. The real hope was that, having defeated the Central Powers and removed their malevolent influence, the Allies would restore justice in South-Eastern Europe, and solve the Macedonian problem with the rest of the problems which had been poisoned by German policy.

Meanwhile the actual situation in the Balkans during the first year of war was this. Serbia was guarded against Bulgaria by her alliance with Greece—the scope of which, as will be seen, was a matter of some dispute. Bulgaria was checked also by the fear of Rumanian intervention. On the other hand, Bulgaria was quite certain not to remain content with

M. HADJI MICHEFF.

The Bulgarian Minister, leaving the Legation in London, October, 1915.

mere neutrality. Both in Turkey and in Macedonia she would endeavour to repair the losses of the Balkan Wars. Into which scale would King Ferdinand hold it the more profitable to throw his weight ? He could be trusted to decide ruthlessly and selfishly, without regard for Bulgaria's historic debts to Russia on the one hand, and England on the other. And it was well known that he thought more of his vanity, often wounded by the contempt in which, he fancied, his person was held in Petrograd and London, than of the loss and humiliation to which he had exposed his adopted country by the German-made Second Balkan War. Unfortunately the failure of the Dardanelles expedition and the set-back to Russia's arms in the summer of 1915 were to give him the excuse that his craven heart desired, and enable him to emerge as the ally of William II. and the "Saviour of Macedonia."

From the outbreak of the Great War in August, 1915, Bulgaria was prolific in declarations of tranquillity and good intention. Greece being pledged to join Serbia in the event of Bulgarian aggression, Bulgaria promoted—already, it would seem, under German and Austrian auspices—much talk of an entente between Turkey, Bulgaria, and Rumania, as the result of which Bulgaria should acquire Kavalla, the much coveted port on the Ægean, at the expense of Greece, and satisfy all her claims in Macedonia. Meanwhile the Bulgarian Government repeatedly declared its determination to maintain neutrality. Sofia seems to have expected Rumania to take early action against Hungary, and hoped then to destroy the Treaty of Bukarest and to obtain what was called "a complete rearrangement of frontiers in the Balkans." To these ends there was a considerable display of Anglophil sentiment, with revived reminiscences of Bulgaria's debt to English Liberalism under Gladstone. In October Balkan prospects and possibilities were affected by the death of King Charles of Rumania, a Hohenzollern Prince whose powerful personality and experienced statesmanship had been for half a century a considerable factor in all the problems of South-Eastern Europe. His death undoubtedly made Ferdinand of Bulgaria seem a bigger figure among the little Balkan statesman of the time, and when Turkey's intervention increased the probability of Rumanian action, Sofia began to blackmail Bukarest. Bulgaria required a "mandate" for the occupation of Macedonia, and immediate "restitution" of everything accorded her by the Serbo-Bulgarian Treaty of 1912.

Germany now developed great diplomatic activity. In December the veteran Marshal von der Goltz, on his way to Turkey, paid a demonstrative visit to Sofia, bearing an autograph letter from the Emperor William to King Ferdinand. In January, 1915, the German banks made Bulgaria an advance of £3,000,000—belated fulfilment of an agreement for a loan of £20,000,000 concluded in the summer of 1914, by which Germany secured valuable economic concessions. Further advances to the total amount of £3,000,000 were promised in the course of two or three months. Needless to say, Bulgarian diplomacy insisted that these financial operations were devoid of political significance, and "Anglophil" Bulgarians were permitted to renew their assurances of sympathy with the Entente. All that was true was that Bulgaria was not yet irrevocably committed to the Central Powers.

When, then, in January, 1915, the Allies decided upon the great venture at the Dardanelles, they were in almost complete uncertainty as to the future course of events in the Balkans, and in particular as to the policy of Bulgaria. But they believed that the hour had come for Greece to strike, in the spirit of her treaty obligations to Serbia and on behalf of the just aspirations of Hellenism. There is no doubt that the military councils in London were influenced by confidence in Greek intervention—a confidence supported by the diplomatic reports and also by the less trustworthy assurances of all too international finance. We must now record briefly the disappointment of these hopes.

While King Constantine seemed to be bent upon maintaining in perfect equilibrium his affection for England and France and his admiration for the German army, the great Greek statesman and Prime Minister, M. Venizelos, held from the beginning of the Great War that the welfare of the Balkans and the future of Greece were bound up with the victory of the Allies. In December, 1915, long after the events here narrated, the King defended his policy in a conversation with a special correspondent of *The Times*. "The pitiable condition of Belgium," he said, "was always before my eyes." His desire was "at all costs to keep his country from sharing the perils and disasters of the great European conflagration." M. Venizelos thought otherwise. He held that the operations of the Allies against Turkey were Greece's crowning opportunity. He recommended armed intervention, and he was ready to make to Bulgaria the concessions necessary for Balkan solidarity, finding compensation for Greece in Asia Minor. His policy and his courage were worthy of the man who had five years before, by his solution of the Cretan crisis, saved both Greece and the dynasty.

Acting upon these views, M. Venizelos entered into detailed negotiations with the Allies, and in January received definite proposals for intervention from the British Minister at Athens, Sir Francis Elliot, on behalf of the British Government. On January 24 he sent a close analysis of Greek policy and interests to King Constantine. M. Venizelos observed that the British communication "again confronts

BULGARIAN INFANTRY IN ACTION.
Smaller picture: type of Bulgarian infantryman.

M. VENIZELOS.

Greece with one of the most critical periods in her history." He proceeded :

> Until to-day our policy simply consisted in the preservation of neutrality, in so far, at least, as our treaty obligation to Serbia did not oblige us to depart therefrom. But we are called to participate in the war, no longer in order to fulfil simply moral obligations, which, if realized, will create a great and powerful Greece, such as not even the boldest optimist could have imagined only a few years back.
>
> In order to obtain these great compensations great dangers will certainly have to be faced. But after long and careful study of the question I end with the opinion that we ought to face these dangers.
>
> We ought to face them chiefly because, even though we were to take no part in the war now, and to endeavour to preserve our neutrality until the end, we should still be exposed to dangers.

M. Venizelos then pointed out that, if Serbia were crushed by another Austro-German invasion, there was no reason why the invasion should stop short at Greece's Macedonian frontier, or why it should not advance to Salonika. Alternatively, Bulgaria, at the invitation of Austria, might be expected to occupy Serbian Macedonia. M. Venizelos continued :

> What would be our position ? We should then be obliged to hasten to the aid of Serbia unless we wished to incur the dishonour of disregarding our treaty obligations. Even if we were to remain indifferent to our moral debasement and impassive, we should have to submit to the disturbance of the Balkan equilibrium in favour of Bulgaria, who, thus strengthened, would either now or some time hence be in a position to attack us, when we should be entirely without either a friend or an ally. If, on the other hand, we had then to help Serbia in order to fulfil the duty incumbent upon us, we should do so in far more unfavourable circumstances than if we went to her assistance now, because Serbia would already be crushed, and in consequence our aid would be of no, or at best of little, avail. Moreover, by rejecting now the overtures of the Triple Entente, we should, even in the event of victory, secure no tangible compensation for the support we should have lent.

As these passages show, M. Venizelos took a very definite view of the treaty obligations of Greece in the event of any attack by Bulgaria upon Serbia. This matter was at the root of the differences which arose between M. Venizelos and King Constantine. In the subsequent statement to the correspondent of *The Times*, which we have already quoted, the King said : "The Greco-Serbian Treaty deals with a Balkan war, and a Balkan war alone. It was only to come into force in case either Greece or Serbia was attacked by Bulgaria alone. Clearly it did not refer, and was never intended to refer, to the case of Serbia being attacked by two of the great military Powers of Europe as well as by Bulgaria."

Having laid down the principles, M. Venizelos proceeded to define his policy. Greece must seek the cooperation not only of Rumania, but also of Bulgaria. To this end she must no longer refuse all discussion of concessions, and no longer, as hitherto, oppose any important concessions by Serbia. She must "make adequate concessions to Bulgaria." Now that Greece could look to the realization of her national aims in Asia Minor, she could afford to make concessions. Greece should withdraw her objections to concessions by Serbia to Bulgaria, "even if these concessions extend to the right bank of the Vardar." She should even "sacrifice Kavalla, in order to save Hellenism in Turkey, and to ensure the creation of a real Magna Græcia." In return Bulgaria should promise active cooperation in the war, and, before the actual cession of Kavalla, should agree, under the guarantee of the Entente

SIR FRANCIS ELLIOT,
British Minister at Athens.

ELECTION SCENES IN ATHENS.

Gendarmes charging a crowd in the streets.
Inset picture:
Cheering a Venizelos voter.

Powers, to the frontier arrangement essential to "a definite ethnological settlement in the Balkans." If Bulgaria extended beyond the Vardar, Serbia should cede the Doiran-Ghevgeli district to Greece. If, on the other hand, "Bulgaria's greed" made cooperation impossible, Greece should at least obtain Rumania's cooperation, without which Greek intervention in the war would be too dangerous.

In a second letter, two days later, M. Venizelos explained that, painful though the cession of Kavalla would be, it would be compensated by the acquisition of much larger Greek territory in Asia Minor. When, however, the German loan to Bulgaria was concluded, he himself no longer favoured territorial concessions to that country.

The arguments of M. Venizelos prevailed, however, neither with the King nor with the Greek General Staff, and the whole history of Greece from the opening of the Dardanelles campaign in January, 1915, down to the intervention of Bulgaria in October, the subsequent crushing of Serbia, and the evacuation of Gallipoli, was that of a dramatic political struggle, which, however, left Greece still "neutral," but with her territory occupied by allied forces based upon Salonika.

During February M. Venizelos continued to press unsuccessfully for intervention. At the beginning of March, on the eve of the great naval attack at the Dardanelles, he resigned office, and appealed to public opinion on behalf of the policy for which he could not obtain the approval of the King. The King responded by restoring to office the Germanophil Chief of the General Staff, who had been dismissed for an attack on M. Venizelos. A Cabinet was formed by M. Gounaris, with an avowed policy of neutrality. After a brief absence from Athens M. Venizelos returned in April, and, as a preface to the General Election which was inevitable owing to the strength of M. Venizelos's majority in the Chamber, there was an unseemly wrangle between the late Premier and the Crown, M. Venizelos being forced to publish his letters to the King which we have already summarized, while the King and the Government insisted upon M. Venizelos's readiness to sacrifice Kavalla and other gains of the second Balkan War, and disputed M. Venizelos's declaration that the King had originally approved his policy and authorized negotiations with Bulgaria. The Government found means to postpone the elections, and M. Venizelos left Greece. Meanwhile excitement in Greece was kept at fever heat by events at the Dardanelles. In May the King became dangerously ill, and there was plenty of evidence that, while the country warmly favoured the policy of M. Venizelos, King Constantine was still a national hero, assured not only of the devotion of the army but of the affectionate loyalty of the people. In the middle of June, however, when the belated elections were at last held, M. Venizelos, who had himself returned to Greece, won two-thirds of the seats in the Chamber.

PRINCES BORIS AND CYRIL OF BULGARIA.

The illness of the King still served to keep M. Venizelos, even under these conditions, out of office. The Premier, M. Gounaris, declared that "unfortunately the King's condition does not permit of the taking of any other decision than that of awaiting the meeting of the Chamber; the doctors are of opinion that it is impossible for the King to discuss the political situation without endangering his life." Similarly, the proposal of a Regency was defeated by the argument that, according to the Greek Constitution, the initiative in this matter also rested with the King, and "the present state of the King's health excludes all possibility of proposing such a measure to him." In the middle of July, in spite of all protests, M. Gounaris obtained from the King a decree postponing the opening of Parliament for a month. When the Chamber at last met on August 16, the Venizelist candidate for the presidency of the Chamber was elected by a large majority. The Gounaris Government resigned, and M. Venizelos returned to office.

We must now revert to Bulgaria before describing M. Venizelos's second, but again unsuccessful, effort to secure the intervention of Greece on the side of the Allies.

We have seen that Bulgaria's financial transactions with Germany in January, 1915, already acted as a check upon M. Venizelos's conciliatory policy. The Allies, however, regarded the matter as only one move in the German game, put the best appearance they could on the situation, and entered into negotiations with Sofia. The British Government by the middle of February, or sooner, had given Bulgaria to understand that her national aspirations were regarded with sympathy, and that there was every prospect of satisfactory negotiations, provided that, if concessions were made at the expense of Serbia, it was certain that Bulgaria would enter the war against Turkey. In their subsequent explanations British Ministers laid great stress upon this point—that concessions must depend upon Bulgaria's definite promise of armed co-operation. In his speech on October 14 Sir Edward Grey said that this was "an essential preliminary," and that, "if Bulgaria was to realize her hopes and aspirations, she must cooperate in the common cause in which the hopes and aspirations of other neighbouring States who were to make concessions to her were engaged." The Allies were, indeed, bound in honour to Serbia, and also unable to propose terms unjust to Greece. The reply of German diplomacy was prompt. Affecting to desire only Bulgaria's neutrality, Germany and Austria-Hungary offered freely, at the expense of Serbia and Greece, more gains in Macedonia than the Allies could "in common fairness," as Sir Edward Grey said, offer for Bulgaria's cooperation. On the other hand, they began to prepare the way for Turkish concessions to Bulgaria in Thrace. On March 13, at the very moment that a British Military Mission were visiting Sofia, *The Times* correspondent in the Balkan Peninsula reported "efforts recently made by Germany to induce Turkey to restore to Bulgaria the territory in Thrace accorded to her by the Treaty of London." As *The Times* correspondent said, this proposal "aimed at embroiling Bulgaria with the Entente Powers, and would compromise the future of Macedonia."* It proved to be the key to Germany's diplomatic success.

When the Bulgarian Sobranye closed at the end of March—not to meet again until King Ferdinand and the Radoslavoff Government, which had no majority in the Sobranye, had imposed a Germanophil policy on the country—the Premier, M. Radoslavoff, made an emphatic declaration of the resolve of the Government to maintain neutrality. Its effect was somewhat marred by the news that, in insolent repetition of an almost identical operation in November, 1914, there had been a considerable raid of Bulgarian irregulars into Serbian territory in the neighbourhood of Strumnitza. The affair seems to have been organized by the Austrian Military Attaché at Sofia, Colonel Laxa, who was spending large sums in bribery, not only of Turkish and Bulgarian refugees from Serbian Macedonia, but of Bulgarian officials. M. Radoslavoff loudly disclaimed responsibility for the incident, and began to issue "interviews" and Press *communiqués* to the effect that the Entente could have Bulgarian cooperation in return for only a part of the zone of Macedonia which was

* Yet Sir E. Grey said in the House of Commons on November 9 that "reports of Bulgarian negotiations with Turkey came from various Balkan sources *as early as April.*"

KING FERDINAND OF BULGARIA AND ONE OF HIS GENERALS.

"uncontested" according to the Serbo-Bulgarian Treaty of 1912, together with the cession of Seres, Kavalla, and Drama by Greece. During April there was, indeed, considerable optimism as to the prospect of a settlement among those who could best gauge the currents at Sofia, and it was, perhaps, unfortunate that those who were responsible for the military operations at the Dardanelles showed a peculiar lack of understanding of the political situation and of the value of obtaining in advance the Balkan assistance of which they were soon to stand sorely in need. Shaken by the intervention of Italy at the end of May, disturbed by the belief that Rumania was pledged to Italy, and not yet satisfied about Bulgaria, Germany at this time turned on Rumania. The German Press now threatened, now coaxed, Bukarest, some writers using language such as that "those who do not or will not know that our military situation is brilliant should learn the fact from the language and attitude of our diplomacy," while other writers advocated "fair and just" concessions to Rumania.

But, in any case, Bulgaria made extravagant demands. Early in May, M. Radoslavoff made

GENERAL MOSKOPOULOS
(On left) the Greek Commander at Salonika.

proposals which involved the cession at the expense of Serbia not only of the "uncontested zone" but of Uskub, and the cession by Greece of Seres, Kavalla, and Drama. On May 29 the Entente Powers gave their reply, and on June 15 Bulgaria made new proposals. They were officially stated to have made "a favourble impression," and to be a possible "basis for negotiations." But the Allies were not ready with their decision. They embarked upon long and difficult, however friendly, negotiations with Serbia. Six weeks elapsed before they delivered their reply to the Bulgarian proposals of June 15. Meanwhile Bulgaria had come to terms with Turkey. Then six more weeks elapsed before definite offers were made to Bulgaria. In this time Germany had completed her diplomatic victory.

The presentation of the Bulgarian Note of June 15 to the Entente Powers coincided with a great accentuation of German efforts. The immediate consequences were dramatic enough. On June 24 it was announced at Sofia that the German Minister, Dr. Michahelles, was absent in Berlin and would not return to his post, his place being taken provisionally by the German Military Attaché in Constantinople. This officer was a certain Colonel von Leipzig. He had been employed for years as a German agent in Turkey. He had been Military Attaché at Constantinople in the days of Abdul Hamid. He had afterwards retired, but was sent back again to Constantinople at the beginning of 1915. The object of his "provisional" mission to Bulgaria was the conclusion of a Turco-Bulgarian agreement at Turkey's expense. He reached Sofia, and seems to have prepared an agreement upon the basis of the acceptance of all Bulgaria's demands—the cession of Adrianople and everything up to the line drawn from Enos to Midia. Bulgaria, in fact, was to recover all that she had lost in Thrace in 1913. Colonel von Leipzig then returned to Turkey. In a few days he was dead. The German Press was supplied with an ingenious story of how he had paid a visit to the Dardanelles, and, while waiting at the railway station of Usunköprü for a train to take him back to Constantinople, had opened his suit case and been killed by the accidental explosion of a revolver which was lying among his clothes. In reality he had been murdered by the opponents of Turkish concessions to Bulgaria.

Germany, however, was not to be deterred by such trifles, and, although there was a momentary lull in the Turco-Bulgarian negotiations, they were continued upon a more moderate basis than that of the concessions negotiated by Colonel von Leipzig. As regards Bulgaria, Germany had a powerful tool in the notorious M. Rizoff, who had been appointed Bulgarian Minister in Berlin, and pressure upon Turkey was facilitated by the increasing scarcity of munitions at the Dardanelles. Rumania steadily resisted German demands for the passage of war material through her territory, and the German Press clamoured for a right of way through Bulgaria. The idea was noisily propagated that the most pressing military task of the Central Powers was to open a road "from Hamburg to Baghdad," by means, first, of Turco-Bulgarian cooperation, and, secondly, of a great new offensive against Serbia, which would finally break the resistance of the brave little State which had twice inflicted crushing defeats upon Austria-Hungary, and would put Bulgaria in immediate possession of Macedonia.

On July 26, while Entente diplomatists were still placing trust in Bulgarian good faith, and putting the last touches on their reply to the Bulgarian Note about Macedonia, *The Times* correspondent in the Balkan Peninsula announced the practical completion of an agreement ceding to Bulgaria the Turkish portion of the Dedeagatch Railway. He said :—" Under the new arrangement Bulgaria obtains the whole extent of the line traversing Turkish territory, together with the stations Karagach, Demotika, and Kuleli Burgas. The Bulgarian frontier will coincide with the course of the river Maritza, all territory to the west becoming Bulgarian." Noting the Bulgarian assurances that the cession of the railway " implied no engagement of a political character," *The Times* observed that it was " improbable that Turkey would have made concessions so large without some certainty of a political *quid pro quo*."

The truth seems to have been that Bulgaria still retained a nominal, or highly conditional, freedom of action, and Germany may even have countenanced the continuation of the Bulgarian negotiations with the Entente Powers about Macedonia, especially as they were well calculated to cause serious friction among the Allies. But to all intents and purposes the die was now cast. It may be that the Bulgarian Government—which, it must be remembered, had no reason to believe that the country approved of the new Germanophil policy—was not entirely insincere, even after the events of July. But the Bulgarian General Staff freely expressed belief in the victory of the Central Powers, and Ferdinand was only awaiting the moment to throw in his lot with Germany.

On August 4 the Entente Powers delivered their reply to the Bulgarian Note of June 15. On the same day they made " collective representations " in Athens, where M. Gounaris was still clinging to office. But the centre of diplomatic interest was now Nish, the temporary capital of Serbia, where it was officially announced that Russia, Great Britain, Italy, and France had made " representations of an

GREEK INFANTRY ON THE MARCH.

BULGARIAN ARTILLERY

entirely friendly nature, with the hope of removing the causes of friction between the Balkan States and of establishing an entente between them in order to bring the war nearer to final success." The German Press again became violently excited. "It is no longer possible," wrote the *Vossische Zeitung*, "to disturb the agreement between Bulgaria and Turkey. The active fabrication of Notes which has now suddenly begun again on the part of the Quadruple Entente is merely intended to throw sand in the eyes of the world. Of course, the diplomatists of the Quadruple Entente know only too well how matters really stand with Bulgaria." But if they knew, they made no sign.

The strain upon Serbia was very severe. After all her sufferings and all her victories, she was called upon to restore hard-won territory to her treacherous and insatiable neighbour. And the prospect was not improved by what was known of the arrangements between the Entente Powers and Italy. Great secrecy was observed about the Treaty concluded at the end of April which secured the intervention of Italy in the war at the end of May, but it was known to contain provisions regarding especially Dalmatia—both the Dalmatian mainland and the Dalmatian islands—which caused dismay in Serbia and among all the Southern Slavs. Thanks, however, especially to the wisdom and patience of M. Pashitch, Serbia bowed to necessity, and did her best to serve the common interests of the Allies as well as the cause of Balkan unity The whole future of Serbia was at stake. In spite of the inevitable opposition of military opinion, M. Pashitch held fast. Serbia, he said, would go on striving for an agreement with Bulgaria "on condition that the vital interests of both countries be respected." For the rest, Serbia would "fight in accordance with the plans of the Allies." Parliament supported him. On August 24, the Serbian Skupshtina, after three secret sittings, passed the following resolution :

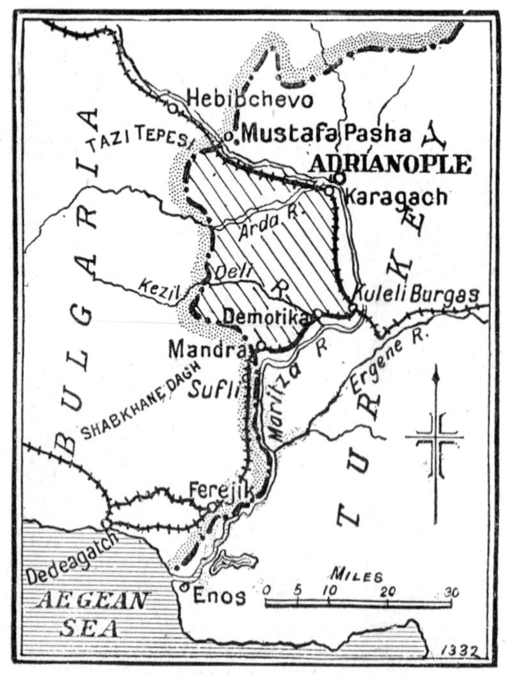

THE TURKISH CONCESSIONS TO BULGARIA.

> The Chamber, rendering homage to the fallen heroes and renewing its decision to continue side by side with Serbia's Allies the struggle for the liberation of the Serbo-Croatian-Slovene people at the price of the sacrifices indispensable for the protection of the vital interests of our people, approves the policy of the Government.

Although, however, the principle of concessions had thus been accepted, the concessions themselves had by no means been determined, and Germany and Austria-Hungary redoubled their efforts at Sofia. Reports were carefully circulated to the effect that a strong Austro-German attack on the north-east frontier of Serbia had been fixed for the middle of September, and that the Kaiser had irrevocably resolved "to wipe Serbia off the map" on his way to Constantinople. Unfortunately, just because the German announcements were so deliberate, they found little credence in responsible quarters. It was still solemnly maintained that Germany "had not the men" for a new offensive. Such views were particularly prevalent in official quarters in England, and it was the demonstration by the German offensive of the unsatisfactory character of the military advice upon which the British Government relied that led, in the autumn and winter of 1915, to important reforms—especially the formation of a real General Staff with a Chief who, although Lord Kitchener remained Secretary of State for War, was placed in direct communication with the Cabinet.

Meanwhile the diplomatic negotiations dragged on, in spite of all warnings. The attitude of the Bulgarian Government was one of the utmost suspicion, and the nearer the diplomatists seemed to come to a settlement, the more insistent Sofia became that Bulgaria must have not only promises but actual and immediate occupation of the ceded Macedonian territory. At the end of August the Kaiser sent the Grand Duke Johann Albrecht of Mecklenburg, formerly Regent of Brunswick, upon an urgent mission to the Bulgarian Court, accompanied by diplomatic officials. The Grand Duke spent nearly a fortnight with King Ferdinand, and was afterwards received with great honours at Constantinople. On September 10, M. Radoslavoff admitted that the Turco-Bulgarian convention, already described, was an established fact, although he still maintained the pretence that it "involved no political engagements." At the same time Bulgaria called to the colours the Macedonian Bulgarian bands, and all Bulgarians of Macedonian or Thracian origin. A strict Press censorship was imposed, and journals which criticized the Germanophil policy of the Government were confiscated.

On September 14 the Entente Powers made at last definite proposals to Bulgaria, proposals of an extremely liberal kind. They would have given Bulgaria the whole of the "non-contested" zone of Macedonia, including Monastir, and also Doiran and Ghevgheli. They held out also the promise of a friendly Serbo-Bulgarian agreement regarding the "contested zone" of Macedonia, and diplomatic support of the Bulgarian demand for the cession by Greece of Kavalla and by Rumania of the portion of the Dobrudja between Silistria and Varna. In order to allay any just suspicion about the fulfilment of the contract, the Allies were, it seems, willing themselves to occupy the valley of the Vardar. Such terms were all, or more than all, that Bulgaria had any right to expect. They ended all her

ARRIVAL OF BRITISH TROOPS AT SALONIKA.
Patrol marching through the streets.

ALLIED TROOPS IN GREECE: BRITISH TROOPS RESTING BY THE ROADSIDE WATCH FRENCH TROOPS ON THE MARCH.

grievances, and left her free to satisfy also her full ambitions in Thrace.

But if Bulgaria had at any recent period of the negotiations been sincere, it was now too late. It soon appeared that she was practically committed to participation in an Austro-German campaign against Serbia, and, on the other hand, as the price of the Dedeagatch railway concession and whatever other secret spoils Germany had promised, had pledged herself to cooperation with Turkey.*

On September 17, all the leaders of the Opposition in the Sobranye made a desperate effort to check the policy of the King. In an audience which lasted for more than two hours they remonstrated with him in even violent terms, and declared emphatically that the policy of compliance with the demands of Germany was contrary to the traditions, wishes, and interests of the people. But it was all of no avail.

On September 20 M. Radoslavoff announced to his followers the signature of a convention with Turkey for the maintenance of "armed neutrality" on the part of Bulgaria. On September 23 the decree of mobilization was issued. Even now Bulgaria professed to desire peace and a willingness to continue negotiations about Macedonia. On September 24 M. Radoslavoff officially assured the British and Russian Ministers that the Bulgarian mobilization was not directed against Serbia. To the Greek Minister he described the mobilization as merely a preventive measure. On September 28 Sir Edward Grey said in the House of Commons:—"My official information from the Bulgarian Government is that they have taken up a position of armed neutrality to defend their rights and independence, and that they have no aggressive intentions whatever against Bulgaria's neighbours." Sir Edward Grey referred to the "warm feeling of sympathy for the Bulgarian people" that was traditional in England, and added:

> As long as Bulgaria does not side with the enemies of Great Britain and her Allies, there can be no question of British influence or forces being used in a sense hostile to Bulgarian interests, and as long as the Bulgarian attitude is unaggressive, there should be no disturbance of friendly relations. If, on the other hand, the Bulgarian mobilization were to result in Bulgaria assuming an aggressive attitude on the side of our enemies, we are prepared to give to our friends in the Balkans all the support in our power, in the manner that would be most welcome to them, in concert with our Allies, without reserve and without qualification.

But the situation was hopeless. On October 2 the state of affairs was officially described in London as one of "the utmost gravity." On October 3 Russia addressed to Bulgaria the following Note:

"Events which are taking place in Bulgaria at this moment give evidence of the definite decision of King Ferdinand's Government to place the fate of its country in the hands of Germany. The presence of German and Austrian officers at the Ministry of War and on the staffs of the army, the concentration of troops in the zone bordering on Serbia, and the extensive financial support accepted from our enemies by the Sofia Cabinet no longer leave any doubt as to the object of the present military preparations of Bulgaria.

M. RADOSLAVOFF.

"The Powers of the Entente, who have at heart the realization of the aspirations of the Bulgarian people, have on many occasions warned M. Radoslavoff that any hostile act against Serbia would be considered as directed against themselves. The assurances given by the head of the Bulgarian Cabinet in reply to these warnings are contradicted by facts.

"The representative of Russia, bound to Bulgaria by the imperishable memory of her liberation from the Turkish yoke, cannot sanction by his presence preparations for

* It should, however, be observed that some competent critics have held that it was only after the Russian ultimatum that Bulgaria definitely pledged herself to military action. According to this view there was, indeed, no longer any hope of Bulgarian intervention on the side of the Allies, but it was conceivable that, without military pledges from Bulgaria, the Germanic Powers would be unable to attack Serbia.

fratricidal aggression against a Slav and allied people.

"The Russian Minister has, therefore, received orders to leave Bulgaria with all the staffs of the Legation and the Consulates, if the Bulgarian Government does not within twenty-four hours openly break with the enemies of the Slav cause and of Russia, and does not at once proceed to send away the officers belonging to the armies of States which are at war with the Powers of the Entente."

France and Great Britain associated themselves with the Russian representations. No satisfactory reply was received from Bulgaria. On October 5 the Russian, French, and British Ministers at Sofia asked for their passports. Bulgaria was at war. On October 7 it was announced from Berlin that the Austro-German offensive had begun, and it was claimed that the Drina, the Save, and the Danube had been crossed "in many places."

We must now return to Greece. M. Venizelos had, after many delays not altogether relevant to the welfare of his country, returned to power, as we saw, in the middle of August. He maintained close contact with the Entente Powers, and took part in the negotiations about Macedonia which culminated in the proposed concessions to Bulgaria. By the middle of September the situation became extremely menacing, and before M. Radoslavoff had declared his arrangements with Turkey, Greece had definite diplomatic information that Bulgaria was pledged to Germany. On September 18 M. Venizelos had a long audience of King Constantine, and discussed with him the threatened Austro-German invasion of Serbia and the whole Macedonian question. It was announced that the King and M. Venizelos were in complete agreement about the policy to be pursued. As already stated, the Entente Powers had, in connexion with their offers about Macedonia, mentioned to Bulgaria the possibility that their troops should occupy the valley of the Vardar. On September 21 * M. Venizelos, seeing that Bulgaria had proclaimed a policy of "armed neutrality," invited France and Great Britain to send 150,000 men to Salonika, and gave the express undertaking that Greece would mobilize. On September 23, immediately after the Bulgarian general mobilization, King Constantine received M. Venizelos, and signed the mobilization decree. It was generally believed that Greece had definitely decided to fulfil her treaty obligations to Serbia, and that the intervention of Bulgaria would immediately be followed by the intervention of Greece. On September 29 M. Venizelos said in the Greek Chamber:—"Notwithstanding an universal desire for peace, the Greek nation is ready to defend the integrity and vital interests of the country, and to resist every attempt on the part of any Balkan State to establish a predominance which would mean the end of the political independence of the other States." But great difficulties had arisen, and M. Venizelos was sharply opposed, by the Greek military authorities as regarded the Salonika landing and the coming campaign, and by a Germanophil group of politicians, led by the veteran M. Theotokis, who were still in favour with the King. On October 2, in spite of all opposition, M. Venizelos, under a merely formal protest, informed the French and British Governments of Greece's approval of the landing. On October 4 he again addressed the Chamber. He said that Greece would not "take material measures to prevent the passage of the Anglo-French armies which were hastening to the aid of the Serbians, the Allies of Greece, who were threatened by the Bulgarians." But on the following day King Constantine repudiated M. Venizelos's declaration, and he once more resigned office, being succeeded by a Ministry formed under the nominal leadership of M. Zaimis.

The new Government reaffirmed the neutrality of Greece. "The result," as Mr. Asquith said afterwards in the House of Commons, "was that Serbia, without Greek support, was left to bear the brunt of a frontal invasion by Germany and Austria and a side attack from the King of Bulgaria." The Allies remained at Salonika, and consolidated their position there, but, as will be seen later on, they were unable to render effective aid to Serbia in her hour of greatest tribulation. Belgrade was occupied on October 9, and Serbia was soon overrun by the invaders.

* Mr. Asquith in the House of Commons, November 2, 1915.

CHAPTER CXV.

BRITISH WAR FINANCE 1914-1915.

Great Britain's Immense Financial Problem—Government Policy in 1914—The Bank of England—Guarantee of British Bill Acceptances—The Stock Exchange Moratorium—Minimum Prices—The Foreign Exchanges—Votes of Credit—Mr. Lloyd George's First War Budget—First War Loan—Imports and Exports—Stock Exchange Reopened—Second War Budget—Mr. McKenna Chancellor of the Exchequer—Second War Loan—Thrift and Retrenchment Campaign—Government Delays—American Exchange—Anglo-French Commission at New York—Mobilization of American Securities—Third War Budget—New Taxation—Issue of Exchequer Bonds—National Income—Wheat Prices—Board of Trade Returns—Outlook at End of 1915.

THE financial history of the first year and a half of the war made it clear that the economic endurance and power of adaptation possessed by the great industrial States and the power of organized credit had been, in almost all quarters, very greatly underestimated. It had not been realized to what an extent production could be increased and to what an extent consumption could be reduced.

The mobility and power of recuperation displayed by the British credit system showed its intrinsic strength under an almost unimaginable strain. That we should have been able in the first nineteen months of a conflict involving two-thirds of the peoples of the world to raise and equip an army of a size never previously contemplated by us, to carry on our foreign trade at a comparatively high level, and at the same time to provide funds to the amount of over £1,700,000,000 for the purpose of carrying on the war—a sum equivalent to considerably more than one-half of the national income during that period—may be justly regarded as great achievements, which before the war would have been looked upon as utterly impossible of accomplishment. But a still greater proof of our economic strength was afforded by the fact that, notwithstanding the tremendous financial disturbance caused by the war, we found it possible practically to double our revenue from taxation.

The various emergency measures which were adopted immediately after the outbreak of war in order to preserve British credit were fully described in Vol. I. (Chapters XI. and XII.). On November 27, 1914, Mr. Lloyd George, then Chancellor of the Exchequer, made an important statement in the House of Commons with regard to the action which the Government had taken to meet the abnormal economic conditions which had been created by the war and the reasons which had guided the Government in taking such steps

Mr. Lloyd George said the Government had

RIGHT HON. R. McKENNA,
Chancellor of the Exchequer.

undertaken responsibilities that no Government had ever been called upon to undertake in the past. Their defence was that the circumstances were of an unusual character. That was the first great war that had ever been fought under modern conditions. In the great Napoleonic wars practically all the countries of the world were self-contained. Great Britain had one-third of its present population. It raised its own food. The total imports and exports of the country together came to about £86,000,000 in those days. In 1913 the imports and exports together came to about £1,500,000,000. The Government had not merely their own business to run, they were an essential part of the machinery that ran the whole international trade of the world. They provided the capital to raise the produce; they carried half the produce, not merely of their own country, but of the whole world. They provided the capital that moved that produce from one part of the world to another. They were transacting half the business of the world by means of the bill on London. A great war affecting nearly two-thirds of the whole population of the world crashed into this fine delicate paper machinery: confusion was inevitable and undoubtedly there was great confusion. The deadlock that ensued was not due to any lack of credit in this country. It was entirely due to the fact that there was a failure of remittances from abroad. When the war broke out there were between £350,000,000 and £500,000,000 of bills of exchange in circulation which bore British signatures. At that time most of them had been discounted; the cash had been found from British sources and the failure was not due to the fact that Great Britain had not paid her creditors abroad; it was entirely due to the fact that those abroad could not pay Great Britain. When the moratorium came there appeared to be something like a failure of British credit, but it was not a British failure at all—it was because remittances could not be obtained from foreign countries. It was vital to the credit and good name of Great Britain that those bits of paper which were circulating throughout the globe with British names upon them should not be dishonoured.

The Government considered that it was a very great national emergency and that the consequences of a false step might be very serious for the trade of the country. They eventually set up a permanent Committee to assist the Government. It consisted of Mr. Austen Chamberlain, Lord St. Aldwyn, Lord Revelstoke, the Governor of the Bank of England, the Lord Chief Justice of England, and Sir John Bradbury. They first of all declared a moratorium, to give everyone time to look round. Then they decided that some step should be taken to restore the national exchange, and the Government agreed to advance Treasury notes to bankers at Bank rate to the extent of 20 per cent. of their deposits. At first the bankers availed themselves of this currency facility to the amount of nearly £13,000,000, but by the end of November, 1914, the amount had fallen to only £244,000.

The official correspondence with regard to the issue of notes by the Bank of England in excess of the limit allowed by law at the time of the outbreak of war is of great historical interest. It was issued (rather tardily) as a White Paper at the end of October, 1915:

I.—LETTER FROM THE BANK OF ENGLAND TO THE CHANCELLOR OF THE EXCHEQUER, DATED AUGUST 1, 1914.

August 1, 1914.

SIR,—We consider it to be our duty to lay before the Government the facts relating to the extraordinary demands for assistance which have been made upon the Bank of England in consequence of the threatened outbreak of hostilities between two or more of the Great Powers of Europe.

We have advanced to the Bankers, Bill Brokers and Merchants in London during the last five days upwards of 27 millions sterling, upon the security of Government Stock, Bills of Exchange, etc., an unprecedented sum to lend, and which, therefore, we suppose, would be sufficient to meet all their requirements; although the proportion of this sum which may have been sent to the country must materially affect the question.

We commenced this morning with a reserve of £17,420,000, which has been drawn upon so largely that we cannot calculate upon having so much as £11,000,000 this evening, making a fair allowance for what may be remaining at the branches.

We have not up to the present refused any legitimate application for assistance, but having regard to the depletion of the reserve, we fear that unless we obtain authority to issue Notes against Securities in excess of the amount permitted by law it will shortly become necessary to curtail the facilities which under present conditions we regard it as essential to offer to the trade and commerce of the country.—We have the honour to be, Sir, your obedient servants,

WALTER CUNLIFFE.
R. L. NEWMAN.

II.—LETTER FROM THE PRIME MINISTER AND CHANCELLOR OF THE EXCHEQUER TO THE BANK OF ENGLAND, DATED AUGUST 1, 1914.

Treasury Chambers, Whitehall, S.W.
August 1, 1914.

GENTLEMEN,—We have the honour to acknowledge the receipt of your letter of this day to the Chancellor of the Exchequer in regard to the extraordinary demands which are being made upon the Bank of England in consequence of the threatened outbreak of hostilities between two or more of the Great Powers of Europe.

In the circumstances represented, His Majesty's Government recommend that, if the Bank of England shall find that, in order to meet the wants of legitimate commerce, it is requisite to extend its discounts and advances upon approved securities so as to require issues of Notes beyond the limit fixed by law, this necessity should be met immediately upon its occurrence, and in that event they will not fail to make application to Parliament for its sanction.

No such discount or advance should be granted at a rate of interest less than 10 per cent., and His Majesty's Government reserve it to themselves to recommend, if they should see fit, the imposition of a higher rate.

After deduction, by the Bank, of whatever it may consider to be a fair charge for its risk, expense, and trouble, the profits of these advances will accrue to the public.—We have the honour to be, Gentlemen, your obedient Servants,

H. H. ASQUITH.
D. LLOYD GEORGE.

On November 9, 1915, Mr. Asquith, in reply to a question in the House of Commons whether the authority given to the Bank to suspend the Bank Act had been cancelled, said that the authority of August 1 was never acted upon, and was superseded by the provisions of the Currency and Bank Notes Act, 1914, which received the Royal Assent on August 6. On August 7 and 8, as adequate supplies of currency notes were not for the moment available, certain notes of the Bank of England were used at the request of the Treasury for the purpose of advances to bankers under the Currency and Bank Notes Act, the maximum excess involved being £3,043,000. By August 10 the position as regards the bank notes had become normal in all respects.

The next step the Government took was to

M. RIBOT,
The French Minister of Finance.

guarantee the due payment of all bills accepted by British houses, and to offer the accepting houses reasonable time in which to collect the debts due to them and meet the bills. Great Britain's national wealth included £4,000,000,000 of good foreign securities—the greater part representing investments in countries unaffected by the war—and in addition there were assets in this country in the shape of land, collieries, factories, railways, and harbours, worth another £13,000,000,000. The Government felt that with assets such as these it would be a criminal act of negligence to allow the credit of the country to be even in doubt for 24 hours in respect of £350,000,000, most of it owing to their own people. They decided, therefore, that the time had come to hypothecate the credit of the State in order to maintain the financial equilibrium.

These, then, were the three steps the Government took:—(1) the preparation of a moratorium, (2) the issue of currency facilities, and (3) the guarantee of the due payment of the bills. By these means the unimpeachable character of the British bill of exchange was maintained and anything resembling a financial catastrophe entirely averted. Bills amounting to £120,000,000 were discounted in this country; £350,000,000 to £500,000,000 of bills which were out at the outbreak of war had most of them been disposed of by the end of November in the ordinary course. There were at the end

WAR SAVINGS CAMPAIGN.
Mr. McKenna addressing a meeting at the Guildhall.

of November, 1914, £12,500,000 of bills that had not arrived at maturity. It was estimated that by the end of the war there would be about £50,000,000 of bills of all classes in "cold storage"—*i.e.*, bills which could not be dealt with because they related to belligerent countries and were impossible to collect.

Before the Government brought the moratorium to an end there were three things to consider:—(1) The position of many people who still could not carry out their contracts owing to the war, (2) the restoration of the foreign exchanges, and (3) the reopening of the Stock Exchange.

With regard to the first point the Government thought the best way to deal with it was by the passing of the Courts (Emergency Powers) Act, which provides that no man can put any legal process in operation without first of all obtaining the sanction of the Courts, and if the debtor is able to establish the fact that his inability to meet his debts is due to circumstances arising out of the war then relief must be given to him during the period of the war and for such time as the Courts think fit.

The second matter was the restoration of the exchanges. In spite of the Government having undertaken the discounting of bills there was still trouble in the foreign exchanges. As long as the drawers and endorsers of the bills were still held responsible they did not care to undertake any fresh liability. Foreign banks, foreign drawers, foreign endorsers and endorsers and drawers in England were very chary of incurring fresh liabilities unless other liabilities could be liquidated. This interfered with the action of the exchanges, and they were not being restored as rapidly as was desired. After full consideration the Government found that the best way of restoring the old machinery was to release the endorsers of the pre-war bills and simply retain the liability of the acceptors.

The difficulty with regard to the Stock Exchange was the fact that about £90,000,000 had been borrowed against Stock Exchange securities before the war began. If the banks had pressed for the repayment of these loans, a mass of securities would have been placed upon the market and the value of all securities might have been reduced to a deplorable level. The Government, who would in all probability be the only borrowers in the market for a considerable time to come, would have had to pay incredible rates of interest. The Government was asked whether, if there was a guarantee that those securities would not be placed upon the market until six months after the war, they would be prepared to advance money for the purpose of enabling those who had lent money on the securities to get some of their cash to carry on until the war was over. It was found that out of the total advances of about

£90,000,000 between £40,000,000 and £50,000,000 had been advanced by the banks and about £40,000,000 by other firms, institutions, and corporations. The Government told the banks they would not advance them a single penny. They had assisted them on their bills of exchange and given them currency facilities and therefore they would have to make their own arrangements with the Stock Exchanges. But the Government agreed to advance to lenders other than banks 60 per cent. of the value of their securities on July 29, 1914, on the express condition that the banks undertook not to put their securities on the market until six months after the war. That was one of the things that helped to restore confidence. Settlement day (November 18) had been regarded with considerable apprehension by everybody on the Stock Exchange; but it passed so quietly that it did not interfere with the huge Government war loan that was put on the market at the same time, and, in addition, there was not a single application for Government credit. It was important that the Government should have some control over the Stock Exchanges, so they stipulated that the Stock Exchanges were not to be re-opened until they had the sanction of the Treasury, and only on conditions that the Treasury thought right to impose in the national interests.

The Liverpool Cotton Exchange was re-opened under a guarantee of a similar nature. Assistance was also given to many small traders in provincial towns who had been sending goods to the Continent without having bills of exchange.

On December 22, 1915, the Chancellor of the Exchequer, in reply to a question as to what amount was advanced by the Treasury to firms in London to enable them to meet their obligations in the early days of the war, said it was undesirable to give figures in detail, and he was unable to give separate figures for London. The total amount advanced under the Treasury schemes formulated with a view to the protection of credit at the outbreak of war was about £200,000,000, and the amount outstanding at November 31, 1915, was £35,500,000; so that over 82 per cent. of the original advances had been repaid.

The various measures taken by the Government for the purpose of re-establishing credit were favourably received, and the economic system rapidly adapted itself to the new conditions. The Moratorium came to an end on November 4, but early in September—although it was not publicly declared—the Banks really came from under it and carried on their business as if no Moratorium existed. Some amount of irritation was felt with regard to the action of certain banks which showed a disposition to withhold credit facilities, but a warning from the Chancellor of the Exchequer appeared to have had satisfactory results.

The mid-August Stock Exchange settlement, which had been postponed under the Moratorium, was practically completed on November 19, and it was carried through with astonishing ease.

[*Elliott & Fry*

VISCOUNT ST. ALDWYN.

The affairs of a small number of members were wound up under the new liquidation rule, but the amount of stock which was carried over under the Emergency Rules was much smaller than had been anticipated. The House remained closed until the end of the year. "Street" dealings were carried on under stringent conditions, the principal condition being that all bargains were for cash and no members were allowed to do business in certain securities—principally trustee securities—below the minimum prices which had been fixed by the Committee. These prices were in almost every case the mean prices of July 29.

The recovery of the internal credit system

from the first shock of war was very rapid, and it was no doubt accelerated by the failure of the German Army to march on Paris, and by the dramatic success of Admiral Sturdee's ships in the Falkland Islands battle. At the end of July, 1914, the total deposits of the London Clearing Banks amounted to £597,000,000 ; on December 31, 1914, they were £657,000,000. The calling in of our credits abroad which automatically followed the outbreak of war resulted in a very large addition to our gold reserve. At the end of July, 1914, the Bank of England held £38,100,000 in gold ; by the end of the year the Bank held about £69,000,000 in gold.

Notwithstanding the special measures taken by the Government to restore the foreign exchanges they remained in a disorganized condition. At first the principal difficulty was with regard to the American exchange. When war broke out the United States owed Great Britain about £90,000,000, payable within a short time. Exports and imports were stopped and those who had already exported goods to America and wished to bring their money back were unable to do so, except at a loss, because there was little exchange on London, and no gold available ; any exchange that could occasionally be bought was between 5 and 6 dollars, as against a parity of 4.8665, which meant a loss of about 20 per cent. Immediate measures were taken in the United States to facilitate the export of cotton, and in order to cause the exchanges to operate the American Bankers raised a fund of £20,000,000 in gold and arranged to transmit this gold to Ottawa for the account of the Bank of England. By these and other means the American Bankers succeeded in bringing the Exchange in New York down to a normal level by the end of 1914.

Towards the end of November the advance in the rouble created considerable difficulty, and on December 4 it was announced that the British Government, in consideration of the shipment of £8,000,000 in gold from Russia to London had arranged with the Bank of England to discount Russian Treasury Bills to the further amount of £12,000,000. By this means the Russian Government obtained funds in England to the total amount of £20,000,000.

A conference between the Chancellor of the Exchequer and M. Ribot and M. Bark, the Finance Ministers of Russia and France respectively, was held at Paris at the beginning of February, 1915, on questions affecting the financial relations of the Allies. At the close of the conference the following statement was published :

> The Finance Ministers of France, Great Britain and Russia have met together at Paris to examine into the financial questions arising out of the war.
>
> They are agreed in declaring that the three Powers are resolved to unite their financial resources, equally with their military resources, for the purpose of carrying the war to a successful conclusion.
>
> With this aim in view, they have decided to recommend to their respective Governments to take over in equal shares the advances made, or to be made, to the countries which are now fighting with them, or which may find themselves in the near future in a position to take up arms for the common cause.
>
> The amount of these advances will be covered by the individual resources of the three Powers as well as by the issue at a suitable opportunity of a loan in the name of the three Powers.
>
> The question of the relations to be established between the Banks of Issue of the three Powers was the subject of a special understanding.
>
> The Ministers have decided to proceed jointly with all purchases which their Governments have occasion to make from neutral countries.
>
> They have adopted the financial measures necessary to facilitate Russian exports and to re-establish, so far as possible, the parity of Exchange between Russia and the other Allies.
>
> They have determined to meet again according as circumstances may require. The next conference will be held in London.

Italy declared war on Austria-Hungary on May 31, 1915, and in the early part of June it was announced that the Minister to the Italian Treasury had conferred with the Chancellor of the Exchequer at Nice, when proposals for the financial co-operation of the two Powers were discussed and arrangements concluded on behalf of their respective Governments.

On November 16, 1914, the House of Commons granted the Government a second Vote of Credit amounting to £225,000,000, and an addition of 1,000,000 men to the regular army. The Prime Minister explained how the first vote of £100,000,000 had been expended and gave a detailed account of the purposes to which the new Vote of Credit would be applied. The bulk of it was for the army and navy, but loans to our Allies and to the Overseas Dominions accounted for nearly £75,000,000. Mr. Asquith stated that the war expenditure was between £900,000 and £1,000,000 per day. In asking the House to pass the vote for 1,000,000 more men Mr. Asquith announced that the regular army then under arms amounted to 1,100,000 men, but that was not enough. He stated that the Government would not charge interest on the loans of £10,000,000 to the Belgian Government and £800,000 to the Serbian Government while the war lasted.

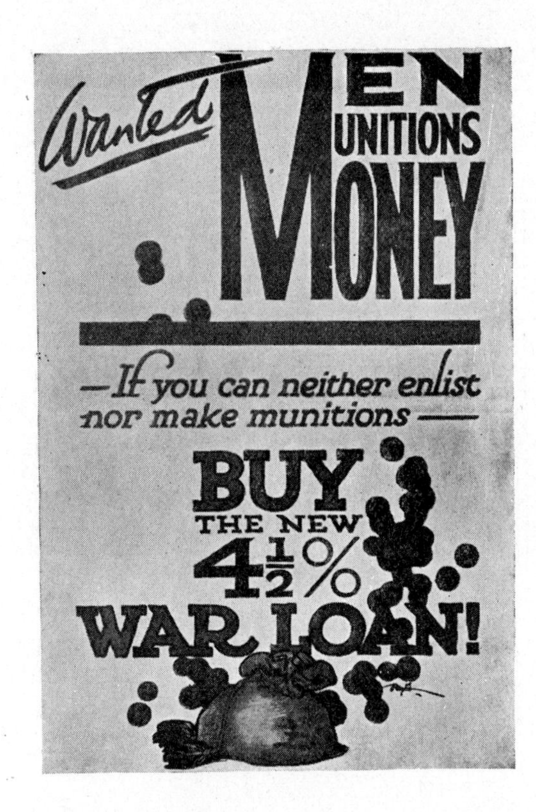

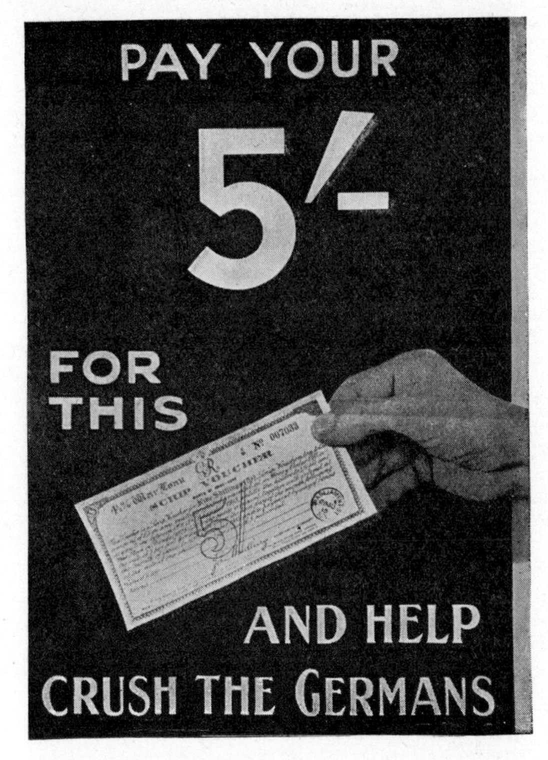

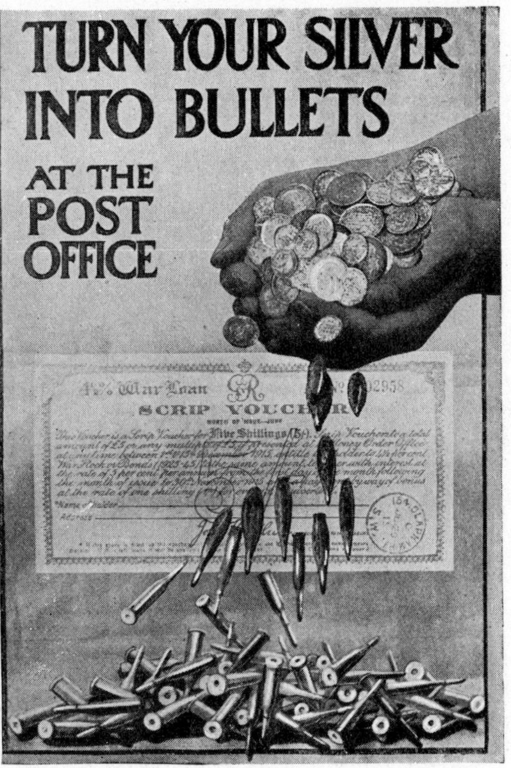

POPULARIZING THE WAR LOAN.

Posters explaining its object.

On November 17 Mr. Lloyd George introduced his first War Budget. He said the Budget estimate for the financial year to March 31, 1915, was £207,000,000. By reason of the war the Treasury would be short of that amount by £11,000,000. He estimated the actual war expenditure for the eight months to March 31st, 1915, at £328,000,000. That meant that he had to find a total sum of £535,000,000, leaving a deficiency not yet provided for of £339,000,000. He announced the following increases in taxation :—

(1) The Income Tax and Super Tax to be doubled—*i.e.* raised from 1s. 3d. to 2s. 6d.—but for the year to March 31, 1915, the increase was to be collected only in respect of one-third of the income. The rate for earned income to be increased from 9d. to 1s. 6d., but for the year to March 31, 1915, the rate to be only 1s.

(2) The duty on beer to be increased by 17s. 3d. per barrel.

(3) The duty on tea to be increased by 3d. per lb.

The new taxation was estimated to produce £15,500,000 in the year to March 31, 1915, and £65,000,000 per annum thereafter. Mr. Lloyd George proposed to obtain a further £2,750,000 from the suspension of the Sinking Fund. This left a deficiency of £321,000,000. As £91,000,000 had already been borrowed, mainly by the issue of Treasury Bills, it was necessary to borrow £230,000,000 to carry the Treasury on to the end of the financial year.

AT THE BANK OF ENGLAND.
Testing Sovereigns.

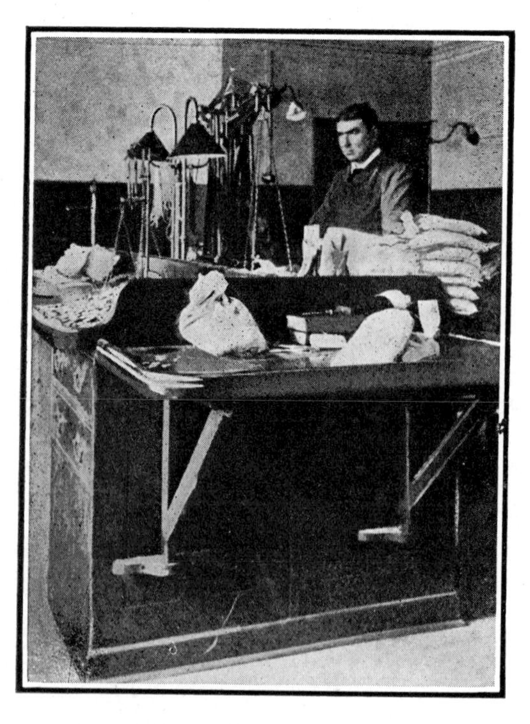

AT THE BANK OF ENGLAND.
The Weighing Counter.

The Chancellor of the Exchequer then announced the terms upon which the first War Loan would be issued.

The first War Loan, which was limited in amount to £350,000,000, took the form of a 3½ per cent. security, to be redeemed by the Government at par on March 1, 1928, or, subject to three months' notice at any time between March 1, 1925, and March 1, 1928. The issue price was fixed at 95 per cent. Mr. Lloyd George stated that the Government had already had £100,000,000 offered firm. Not less than £100 could be applied for. Mr. Lloyd George stated that the Bank of England had agreed to give important credit facilities in connexion with the loan. For a period of rather more than three years—that was from the date of the issue of the loan until March 1, 1918—the Bank would be prepared to make advances against the deposit of war stock or bonds, without collateral security, of amounts equal to the issue price of the stock or bonds deposited without margin at a rate of interest 1 per cent. below the current bank rate. Allowing for redemption the yield worked out at about 4 per cent. The loan was fully subscribed within a week. The banks took about £100,000,000, and the remainder of the loan was subscribed by nearly 100,000 investors.

The returns of the Bankers Clearing House for 1914 showed the effect which the war exercised upon the London Money Market during the first five months of the war. Up to the end of July, 1914, the total amount passed through the Clearing House amounted to £10,241,299,000, an increase of £490,932,000. On the outbreak of war the figures fell rapidly, and at the end of August the increase had disappeared. The grand total for the year 1914 was £14,665,048,000, a decrease of £1,771,356,000 as compared with 1913.

As the war directly involved five of our principal customers, it was inevitable that it should exercise a profound influence upon the course of our foreign trade, but as a matter of fact the actual disturbance was very much less than might have been anticipated.

The Board of Trade returns for the five months, August–December, 1914, were as follows:—

IMPORTS (000's omitted).

		Decrease compared with corresponding period 1913.	
		Amount.	Per
1914.	£	£	Cent.
August	42,362	13,613	24·3
September	45,425	16,303	26·5
October	51,559	20,172	28·1
November	55,987	12,480	18·2
December	67,555	3,560	5·1

EXPORTS (000's omitted).

		Decrease compared with corresponding period 1913.	
		Amount.	Per
1914.	£	£	Cent.
August	24,211	19,899	45·1
September	26,674	15,750	37·1
October	28,602	18,020	38·6
November	24,601	20,154	45·0
December	26,278	17,043	39·3

RE-EXPORTS.

		Decrease compared with corresponding period 1913.	
		Amount.	Per
1914.	£	£	Cent.
August	4,420	3,730	45·7
September	5,274	1,578	23·1
October	7,179	2,376	24·8
November	5,643	2,357	29·5
December	5,870	3,858	39·6

Immediately after the outbreak of war the imports fell heavily. The figures for August were 24·3 per cent. less than in August, 1913. The decline continued until October, when it amounted to 28·1 per cent. In November there was a marked recovery, and for December the decrease amounted to only 5·1 per cent. The effect of the war on the export trade was much more serious. The falling off in August amounted to 45·1 per cent. and this was only reduced to a decrease of 39·3 per cent. in December. The re-export trade was almost as badly affected as the export. The principal cause of the recovery of the imports trade was the rapid expansion of the imports of foodstuffs. There was a heavy falling off in the imports of

THE "SILVER BULLET" CONFERENCE IN PARIS.

M. Bark, M. Ribot, and Mr. Lloyd George—the Russian, French, and British Ministers—in Session at the Ministry of Finance, Paris.

ARRIVAL OF £10,000,000 WORTH OF ENGLISH GOLD IN NEW YORK.
Twenty-three automobiles, containing the gold, on the way to the Sub-Treasury.

raw materials. The principal falling off in exports was in manufactured goods—mainly cotton manufactures—and coal. The general result for the year was that the imports were valued at £697,433,000, as compared with £769,034,000, in 1913. The exports, including re-exports, were valued at £430,231,000 as compared with £525,461,000 in 1913. The excess of imports over exports was £171,713,000 as compared with an excess of £133,917,000 for 1913.

The London Stock Exchange was reopened on January 4, 1915, after having been closed for five months, an occurrence for which there was no precedent in the history of that institution. The restrictions imposed by the Treasury were severe and had for their object the prevention of all speculative transactions and any kind of trading with the enemy. The House was permitted to remain open between the hours of 10.45 a.m. and 3 p.m. The minimum prices of trustee and a number of other securities, which were fixed while the Stock Exchange was closed, were revised, and no business was permissible in these securities below the prices fixed. It was provided that all bargains must be for cash, and transactions in options and arbitrage business were prohibited. No dealings were allowed in any new issues made after January 4, 1915, unless specially allowed by the Committee and approved by the Treasury. Every bargain had to be officially "marked" and recorded. No securities were a good delivery unless supported by a declaration by a broker or banker that they had remained in physical possession in the United Kingdom since September 30, 1914, and had not since the outbreak of war been in enemy ownership. No securities to bearer or endorsed in blank were good delivery, unless impressed with the Government stamp dated previous to October 1, 1914. During the period the Stock Exchange was closed, prices seemed to have reached their level pretty well in the "street" dealings, and there was no wholesale marking down of prices on the re-opening. It will be recalled, however, that between July 20 and July 30, 1914, there was a depreciation in the aggregate valuation of the securities included in the table published in the "Banker's Magazine," of £190,000,000. The outstanding feature of the re-opening was that business was much better than most people had anticipated, and the public appeared to welcome the provision that all prices must be recorded.

On February 11 the Prime Minister made an

interesting statement in the House of Commons upon the subject of food supplies and prices. Wheat, he said, was 72 per cent. dearer than it was in February, 1914, flour 75 per cent., British meat 6 per cent., foreign meat 12 per cent., sugar 72 per cent., and coal 15 per cent. higher. The general level of retail food prices on February 1, 1915, as compared with those of the preceding July, had increased by 24 per cent. in London, by 23 per cent. in other large towns, and by 20 per cent. in small towns and villages. So far as the Government could make out there was very little evidence of a diminution on any important scale in the country's consumption; and Mr. Asquith came to the conclusion that, if account were taken of the men in the new army, the working class was probably consuming more food per head than in any former year.

The principal cause of the increase in the price of foodstuffs was the great rise which took place in ocean freights. Immediately after the outbreak of war there was a reaction in freight rates, but from the middle of September, 1914, onwards there was an upward movement, which continued throughout the remainder of the year, and at the end of December the berth rates from New York to England were for some classes of goods three times greater than those ruling in July, 1914. The

ARRIVAL OF £10,000,000 WORTH OF ENGLISH GOLD IN NEW YORK.
Unloading and checking the gold at the Sub-Treasury.

OVERSEA COMMERCE.

A British cruiser convoying merchant vessels.

principal causes of this movement in freights were :—

(1) The requisitioning by the British and French Governments of cargo-carrying boats of the great Trans-Atlantic lines. At the beginning of January, 1915, it was estimated that 600 ocean-going steamships had been withdrawn for transport and other war services.

(2) The huge movement of grain from the United States and Canada to European ports.

(3) The tying up of the German and Austrian mercantile marine, which represented about 10 per cent. of the merchant shipping of the world.

(4) The increased cost of coal, insurance, wages and stores.

At the beginning of February, 1915, a special report was issued by the Select Committee of the House of Commons appointed to consider a scheme of pensions for officers and men of the fighting services disabled by wounds or disease and for widows and dependents of those killed. The report recommended various increases on the pensions proposed in the White Paper issued in November, 1914. Mr. G. N. Barnes, M.P., who was a member of the Select Committee, said that the actuarial estimates submitted to the Committee provided for a total outlay extending over the whole period of £346,000,000. That sum corresponded to a figure in the White Paper of the preceding November standing at £202,000,000, so that the agitation in favour of the increase of allowances and pensions had been a very costly one for the country. Comparing the maximum yearly expenditure—the first year after the war—the figures were £8,240,000 in the November White Paper as against £13,310,000 under the new scheme.

On October 12 the Financial Secretary to the War Office stated in the House of Commons that the total amount of the payments to dependents of soldiers then exceeded £1,000,000 per week. (The number of married men's separation allowances was stated to be 857,000 on September 1, 1915.)

At the same time the Financial Secretary to the Admiralty said that the total of the weekly payments to the dependents of sailors was £200,000.

On March 1 the Prime Minister said that the two Votes of Credit already passed by the House—namely, £100,000,000 on August 6, 1914, and £225,000,000 on November 15, 1914—had been found insufficient to meet the expenditure which would be incurred up to March 31, and he therefore asked for a further grant of £37,000,000, making a total of £362,000,000. Mr. Asquith said that by the end of the financial year on March 31 the war would have lasted 240 days, and the average expenditure during that period from the votes of credit worked out at about £1,500,000 per day. He added that the war expenditure had risen rapidly, and from April 1 they would be spending over £1,700,000 a day above the normal. In order to start the new financial year Mr. Asquith then moved the fourth Vote of Credit amounting to £250,000,000, which he estimated would provide for all the expenditure up to the middle of July, *i.e.* for 100 days. He pointed out that this Vote differed from its predecessors, inasmuch as it provided not only for war expenditure but for the whole of the normal peace expenditure on the Army and Navy, which might be estimated at £220,000 per day. He said that the War Office calculated that from the beginning of April, 1915, the total expenditure on Army services would be at the rate of £1,500,000 per day, with a tendency to increase, and that the expenditure on the Navy would amount to about £400,000 per day.

Mr. Lloyd George presented his second war budget on May 4, 1915. He said the principal features of the past financial year were, (1) the cost of the war, which he estimated at £360,000,000 up to March 31, 1915, and (2) the buoyancy of the Income Tax. The yield of the Income Tax attributable to the first Budget of 1914–15 was put by Mr. Lloyd George at £46,000,000. The forecast made in November of the yield as increased by the rate levied in that Budget was £53,000,000; the actual yield was £59,279,000. The yield of the Super Tax attributable to the first Budget was £8,135,000; and, though the rates were increased in November, Mr. Lloyd George did not expect to receive more than £8,460,000. The actual yield proved to be £10,120,000.

[*Swaine.*

MR. G. N. BARNES, M.P.

The total excess of the yield of Income Tax and Super Tax over the estimate of November, 1914, was nearly £8,000,000. With regard to Customs and Excise, the November estimate was £73,900,000, and the revenue actually received came to £80,975,000, an increase of £7,075,000 on the estimate. Of that increase £3,000,000 came from forestalments, notably on spirits, tea and tobacco, and £2,182,000 was due to an increase in the consumption of spirits.

The total revenue for the year amounted to £226,694,000, an increase of £28,451,000, and the expenditure of £560,474,000, leaving a deficiency of £333,780,000.

The following is a summary of the war

M. BARK,
The Russian Minister of Finance.

charges up to March 31, 1915, and the sources from which the charges were met :

War Charges to March 31, 1915.

	£
Debt charges...	2,786,000
Army and Navy Expenditure	280,545,000
Advances by way of Loans to Dominions, Allied Powers, etc.	51,825,000
Advances for purchases of foodstuffs, etc....	14,640,000
Payments to Railway Companies	6,852,000
Miscellaneous services	3,138,000
Total estimated War Charges	359,786,000

Statement Showing How the Above Charges were Met.

	£
Suspension of part of the New Sinking Fund	3,003,000
New Taxation	23,003,000
Issue of 3½ per cent. War Loan 1925–28 ...	296,000,000
3 per cent. Exchequer Bonds, 1920 ...	47,700,000
Treasury Bills	64,150,000
Total	433,856,000
	£
Difference added to Exchequer balance brought forward	74,070,000

The new year, therefore, began with a balance in hand of £83,000,000.

It will be observed that out of a total war expenditure of £359,780,000 incurred up to March 31, 1915, no less than £76,455,000 was required for advances to the Dominions and to our Allies and for miscellaneous expenditure.

Mr. Lloyd George frankly intimated his belief that it was not a suitable moment to attempt a forecast of the probable expenditure upon the war up to March 31, 1916, or to submit proposals for that purpose. Nevertheless he submitted two estimates. The first, which showed an outlay of £638,000,000, was based upon the assumption that the war would last up to September 30, 1915, and the second estimate, which showed an outlay of £978,000,000, was based upon the assumption that the war would last until March 31, 1916. The following table contains the details of the two estimates :—

	Estimate for 6 months	Estimate for 12 months
	£	£
Army	400,000,000	600,000,000
Navy	120,000,000	140,000 000
Railways, Compensation for Bombardments, Raids, etc.	11,000,000	22,000,000
Advances to Allies and Dominions	100,000,000	200,000,000
Compensation provision of canteens...	7,000,000	10,000,000
Total	638,000,000	978,000,000

As a matter of fact the second estimate was hopelessly inadequate, the principal increase being in the Advances to Allies and Dominions, and the final estimate of the war expenditure up to March 31 was given by Mr. McKenna as £1,465,000,000.

The completion of the new Coalition Ministry was announced on June 11. Mr. Lloyd George became the Minister of Munitions and Mr. McKenna took his place as Chancellor of the Exchequer. Mr. Montagu became Financial Secretary to the Treasury in the place of Mr Acland.

The fifth Vote of Credit was moved by Mr. Asquith on June 15, the amount being £250,000,000. He said the average expenditure out of the Votes of Credit passed on March 1, during the 73 days up to June 12, was approximately £2,600,000 per day, and the Treasury had in hand an unexpended balance of £56,000,000. He estimated that the total expenditure from the new Vote of Credit would not be much less than £3,000,000 a day during the ensuing months, and it would take them on until well into September. The principal new feature in the fifth Vote of Credit was the provision for repayment to the Bank of England of advances made by them at the request of His Majesty's Government for the general purposes of the war.

The terms and conditions of the second War Loan were explained by Mr. McKenna to the House of Commons on June 21. The principal features were as follows :—

The Loan was for an unspecified amount, in order to allow for the uncertain extent to which its provisions for converting older Government securities might be utilized.

The Loan was issued at par, and carried interest at the rate of 4½ per cent. per annum.

The State had the right to repay at par in 1925, or at any subsequent date, and the stockholder could in any event demand repayment in 1945.

Holders of the first War Loan issued in November, of Consols and of 2½ and 2¾ per cent. Annuities could on certain conditions convert their holdings into new War Loan Stock.

For every £100 an investor subscribed to the new Loan he was entitled to have an equal amount of his holdings in the first Loan taken up at the price of issue, 95, (so that he had to add £5 in cash), and converted into new War Stock.

Holders of £75 of Consols could convert that sum into £50 in the new Loan by first applying for £100 of the new Loan. This arrangement made Consols exchangeable at 66⅔.

Annuities similarly were exchangeable in the proportion of £78 in 2½ per cent. and £67 in 2¾ per cent. to £50 of the new Loan.

The minimum subscription through the Bank of England was £100.

For the small investor Bonds of the new Loan in denominations of £5 and £25 were on sale at the Post Offices, while Scrip Vouchers for £1, 10s. and 5s., carrying a slightly higher interest, were also on sale at the Post Offices, until December 1, and, when they reached £5 or any multiple of £5, could be exchanged for Bonds.

An important privilege was added for holders of the new Loan in the proviso that, in the event of the issue of any later Loan (other than a short dated one) at a higher rate of interest, they would be entitled to subscribe their stock as cash into such new Loan at par.

The list of applications closed on July 10, and on July 13 the Chancellor of the Exchequer announced that £570,000,000 had been subscribed through the Bank of England, while some £15,000,000 more could be added from the Post Office Receipts.* The individual applications through the Bank of England numbered 555,000. About £200,000,000 was subscribed by the Joint Stock Banks themselves, the largest among their contributions being those of the London City and Midland Bank £21,000,000, Lloyd's Bank £21,000,000, London County and Westminster Bank,

* The receipts through the Post Office at the end of 1915 amounted to £30,642,000.

IN THE COURTYARD OF THE BANK OF ENGLAND.
Applying for prospectuses of the War Loan.

Counting pence saved by children in London schools.

£20,000,000, Union of London and Smiths Bank, £8,500,000.

A large number of holders of the first war loan and of Consols and Annuities availed themselves of the privilege of converting their holdings into the new 4½ per cent. loan, and the following table shows the amounts converted and the balances unconverted of the different issues of Government securities:

Stock.	Amount Previously Outstanding.	Amount Converted.	Balance Un-converted.
	£	£	£
Consols	536,101,000	204,000,000	332,101,000
Annuities, 2½ p.c. ..	29,812,000	7,500,000	22,312,000
Annuities, 2¾ p.c. ..	3,813,000	1,000,000	2,813,000
War Loan 3½ p.c. ..	350,000,000	135,000,000	215,000,000
TOTALS ..	919,726,000	347,500,000	572,226,000

Led by an important letter from "A Banker," printed in *The Times* of June 9, 1915, public misgivings had meanwhile been increasing as to the growth of war expenditure and the apparent failure of the Government to grapple with the question of economy and retrenchment in both public and private expenditure. To some extent, but without much actual effect, the urgency of the matter was admitted by the Government, for on June 29

TEACHING ECONOMY IN SCHOOLS.
The significance of the War Loan explained to the pupils.
Small picture: Children subscribing to the War Loan.

THE FRENCH WAR LOAN.
Exchanging gold for paper at the Bank of France.

Mr. Asquith and Mr. Bonar Law both spoke strongly at a Guildhall meeting on the need of economy. On July 6 an important debate took place in the House of Lords on the motion of Lord Midleton:

"That in view of the necessary expenditure on the war it is in the opinion of this House incumbent on His Majesty's Government to take immediate steps to reduce the civil expenditure of the country."

On July 21 Mr. Asquith announced the appointment of a Retrenchment Committee, consisting of the Chancellor of the Exchequer, Lord Midleton, Mr. H. T. Baker, M.P., Sir Leo Chiozza Money, M.P., Mr. J. Mason, M.P., Mr. Evelyn Cecil, M.P., Mr. J. H. Thomas, M.P., Sir G. Claughton, Mr. G. Farrer, and Mr. Harold Cox. The terms of reference were as follows:

"To inquire and report what savings of public expenditure can, in view of the necessities created by the war, be effected in the Civil Departments without detriment to the interests of the State."

On July 22 an important deputation of City men waited upon the Prime Minister to urge the importance of greater thrift in the public departments of the State, and in regard to private expenditure and the urgent necessity that new taxation should be imposed forthwith on all classes. Well-known Free Traders, who formed part of the deputation, urged the Prime Minister to impose new taxation upon imports not only for the purpose of raising revenue but designed to reduce the consumption of imported goods. They also pressed upon the Premier the desirability of widening the scope of the income tax and the institution of a "war profits" tax. The efforts of the Retrenchment Committee in the direction of economy were not as productive as had been hoped. On January 18, 1916, Lord Midleton, speaking at Sheffield, said that six months before, in deference to strong pressure in Parliament, the Committee had started to consider possible reductions in the Civil Service Estimates, which in twenty years had risen from £32,000,000 to £90,000,000. But the Committee had been strangely hampered by circumstances. About £35,000,000 of this increase was ruled out of consideration as being due to new policy determined upon by Parliament. For sixteen weeks — from September 9 to December 29—the Committee was kept adjourned owing to prior claims of the Budget; while of the £10,000,000 of economies which were proposed for immediate adoption, two-thirds were abandoned by the Cabinet before the House of Commons had considered them. In Ireland the Nationalist Leaders declined to associate their party with a review of expenditure at the present time. Yet in that country Civil expenditure was notoriously high. Even the Government themselves did not know what the war was costing us. In May, 1915, the deficit for the year was put at £865,000,000. In July they were told £960,000,000. In December, despite immense increases of taxation, it had risen to £1,200,000,000. For 1916–17 it would be far larger. Yet six months elapsed between the time that the Retrenchment Committee pressed the Government to place some outside check on Army and Navy expenditure and the appointment of Committees to examine it, while the Munitions Department, which had by far the largest liabilities, had not yet been examined.

The Prime Minister asked for a further Vote of Credit for £150,000,000 on July 20. He said that if the future expenditure were taken at roughly £3,000,000 per day the balance of £199,000,000 remaining from previous votes of credit would last until September 21. But the daily rate of expenditure was necessarily uncertain and it might be substantially more than £3,000,000 a day. It was expedient, he said, that the Government should accelerate and make ample provision for the obligations to the Bank of England, and be in a position to meet the financial requirements of our Allies. The latter item might grow with the adherence to our cause of States which did not take part in the war in its earlier stages. In the last vote of credit the advances by way of loan were limited to the Dominions and Protectorates and the Allied Powers. Those limiting words had been omitted on that occasion.

AT THE ROYAL MINT: MELTING THE GOLD.

Towards the end of July the tendency of the American exchange to become increasingly unfavourable created anxiety. Immediately after the outbreak of war it had been as high in our favour as $6, and as the normal "gold parity" is 4·8665 this represented a premium of 20 per cent. At the beginning of 1915 it had fallen back to 4·86, but by April a slow but steady decline set in, and the fall became more rapid towards August, while finally on September 1 the New York cable rate on London went as low as 4·50. Among the reasons

The Counting Machine.

The Rolling Room: electrical rollers for making the fillets.

AT THE ROYAL MINT.

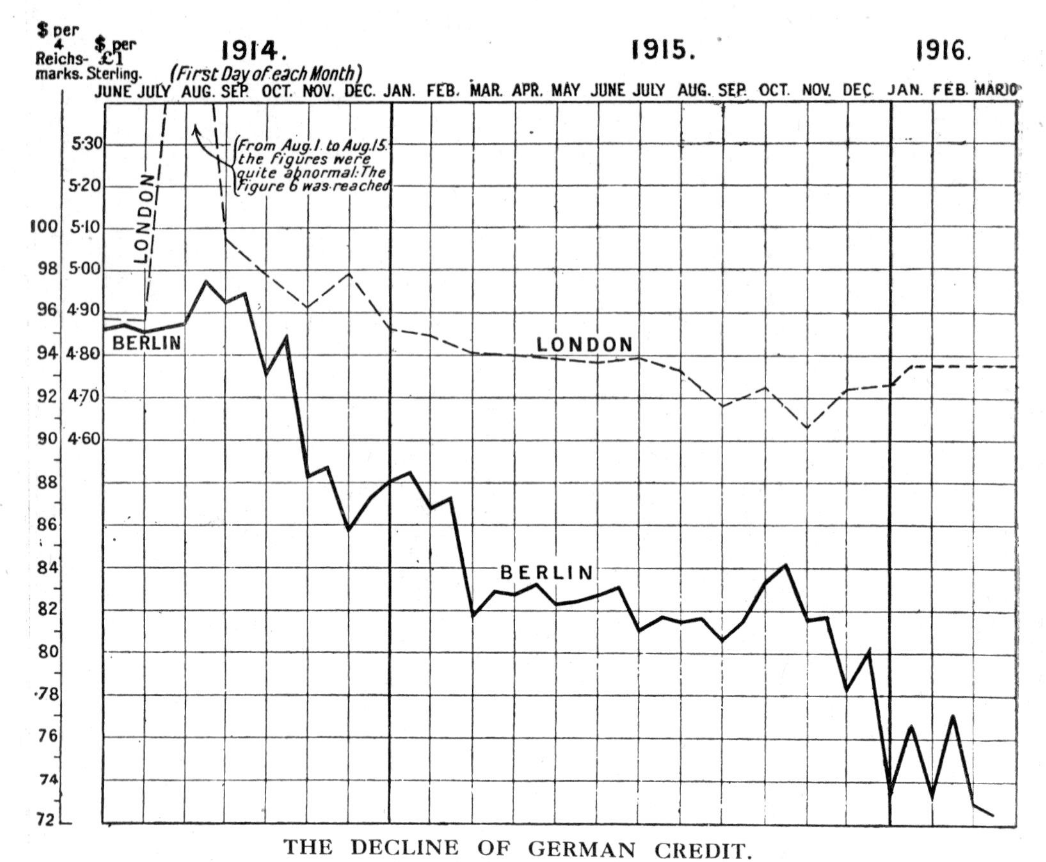

THE DECLINE OF GERMAN CREDIT.

Fluctuations of the New York Exchange on London and on Berlin: June, 1914—March, 1916.

On January 28 the German Government started a scheme for "fixing" the value of the mark for the purpose of the exchange in neutral markets. It will be noticed that in New York, after some fluctuations, the result was only that the depreciation in the mark went still further. In March, 1916, it stood at a discount of 24 per cent. In Switzerland the depreciation was 25 per cent., in Holland 29 per cent., and in the Scandinavian countries 30 per cent.

which contributed to this result were the following: (1) The finance bills which usually matured in August were practically non-existent; (2) the American cotton crop and the record wheat crop were beginning to move forward; (3) and, above all, exceedingly heavy payments had to be made in New York for the increasing purchases by the British Government for supplies on behalf of the Allies. At last serious representations were made by the leading bankers in the City to the Government, and a definite policy for restoring the exchange was concerted with France. An Anglo-French Commission was sent to New York at the beginning of September, Lord Reading, Sir Edward Holden, and Sir H. Babington Smith being the principal British envoys, and they discussed the whole position with the leading American bankers. As the outcome of these negotiations it was announced at the end of the month that the issue of an Anglo-French loan for $500,000,000 had been arranged, England and France each taking half the proceeds, and the debt constituting a joint and several obligation of the British and French Exchequers. The loan was to be issued in five-year 5 per cent. Bonds, redeemable at par, but convertible into 4½ per cent. Bonds of a fifteen to twenty-five years' currency.

The whole amount was taken by an underwriting syndicate of American bankers at 96, in order that they might make a public issue at 98. Allowing for redemption the true interest worked out at about £5 19s. 1d. per cent. There was some disappointment and a good deal of criticism as to the costliness of this loan, but the experts who knew the difficulties felt that the Commission had made a fair bargain, particularly in view of the fact that the yield on other securities available to the American public was at a very high rate, and that there was an organized movement by German-Americans to prevent American banks from participating in loans to the Allies. Subsequently the English Joint Stock Banks made arrangements whereby an additional credit of £10,000,000 should be forthcoming to prevent further fluctuations, and this sum was, if necessary, to be supported by an additional £10,000,000 or £20,000,000 from other sources.

The diagram on page 256 shows the course of the rates of exchange in New York on London and Berlin respectively from June, 1914, to March 1916. It illustrates the almost uninterrupted fall in German credit, and the effect of the steps taken to restore sterling exchange is clearly indicated.

A considerable amount of irritation was manifested in business circles that the Government had not taken the American exchange in hand earlier in the year, and had allowed it to drift until the fluctuations had become so acute as seriously to hamper trade, but the special measures taken in September were successful, and resulted in a rapid improvement. By the end of December the exchange rose to 4·74—a figure all the more satisfactory because, owing to the increased cost of freight and insurance, the working "gold parity" was now about 4·76½. The Bank, however, continued to lose gold, and in order to avoid a repetition of the difficulties experienced in July and August the Government were strongly urged to adopt a policy of preparation in connexion with the further loans which it would be necessary to arrange in the United States.

It was pointed out that although many British holders of American securities had taken advantage of the high prices ruling in New York, and the additional profit resulting from the exchange, there was still an enormous amount of such securities held in the United Kingdom. Various estimates were made from time to time by authorities on both sides of the Atlantic as to the total amount of American securities held in Great Britain before the war and the amount which had been disposed of up to the end of September. These authorities appeared to think that of original holdings of between £600,000,000 and £800,000,000 it was probable that between £150,000,000 and £200,000,000 had been sold back to America. It was suggested that large blocks of these securities should be purchased or borrowed from private lenders by the British Government, and used either for paying in dollars in New York or as collateral for future loans there.

The Treasury adopted the suggestion, and at the end of December it was announced that, with a view to facilitating the maintenance of the exchanges between the United Kingdom and the United States the Treasury were prepared to purchase certain American and Canadian dollar securities owned in Great Britain, or to receive such securities on deposit. In the case of purchase the Treasury offered the current market price to be paid either in cash or in 5 per cent. Exchequer Bonds falling due December 1, 1920, at par. In the case of securities deposited on loan the lender was to receive from the Treasury all interest and dividends paid in respect of the securities, and also by way of consideration for the loan a payment at the rate of one-half of 1 per cent. per annum, calculated on the face value of the securities. It was stipulated, however, in the case of securities deposited on loan, that

THE THRIFT CAMPAIGN.
Poster published by the War Savings Committee.

the Treasury reserved an option, if necessary, to sell them in the United States, in which case it would pay the British owners the current market price with a bonus of 2 per cent.

An interesting statement with regard to the mobilization of American securities was made by the Chairman of the Prudential Assurance Company (Mr. Thomas C. Dewey) at the annual meeting on March 2, 1916. Mr. Dewey said that the company had placed at the disposal of the Government all their holding of American securities. It was their practice to detach the sheets of coupons from the Bonds in order to facilitate the cashing of them as they fell due. These coupons had again to be attached to the Bonds, and within

JOINT WAR COUNCIL IN PARIS.

The Ministers of France and Great Britain conferring in Paris—scene in the Council Chamber at the Quai d'Orsay, November 17, 1915. On the left-hand side of the table are the British Ministers—Sir Edward Grey, Mr. Asquith, Mr. Balfour, and Mr. Lloyd George. Facing them are M. Briand, General Gallieni, General Joffre, and Admiral Lacaze.

a period of forty-eight hours over 44,000 bonds of a nominal value of over £8,750,000 were checked, removed from their own strong rooms, had their sheets of coupons attached, and were dispatched to the Bank of England. The actual Bonds themselves made up six motor-omnibus loads. The adhesive paper used to affix the sheets of coupons measured well over eight miles. A staff of about 100 was engaged until nearly midnight. The work was carried out under the personal supervision of the Directors, and when all was finished the Bank of England informed them that everything had been found correct, except that a single coupon of the value of only a few shillings had in some unexplained manner vanished.

On September 15 the Prime Minister asked the House of Commons to grant the seventh vote of credit, amounting to £250,000,000. He said the average daily rate of expenditure for the 108 days from April 1 to July 17 was £2,900,000, and for the fifty-six days from July 18 to September 11 the average was £4,200,000. Mr. Asquith said that the main reason for this vast growth of expenditure was the extent of our advances to our Allies. The next was the expenditure upon the Army, of which the principal factor of increase was the expenditure on munitions. In the case of the Navy the expenditure rose steadily until June. Since then it had shown a decline and the daily rate for the expenditure on the Navy in September was £600,000. With regard to the future gross expenditure he suggested that £5,000,000 per day would be a safe estimate. The great increase in the daily expenditure made a profound impression, and the necessity for national economy was now impressed more than ever on all competent financial critics.

Mr. McKenna presented the third War Budget on September 21. The principal items of expenditure for the year to March 31, 1916, were as follows :

		£
Navy		190,000,000
Army		715,000,000
Advances to Overseas Dominions and Allied Powers		423,000,000
Pre-and-Post Moratorium Bills		36,000,000
Purchases of food supplies, etc.		56,000,000
Interest on new War Debt		45,324,000
Total war expenditure		1,465,324,000
Consolidated Fund Services :—		
Interest, etc., on old debt	£22,055,000	
Payments to Local Taxation Account	11,925,000	
		33,980,000
Civil Service, Customs and Excise :— Inland Revenue Departments and Post Office		90,696,000
Total expenditure		£1,590,000,000

The new estimate of expenditure was £457,000,000 more than the amount estimated for a whole year by Mr. Lloyd George in May.

The estimated revenue from the taxation in force at the date of the Budget in May, 1915, was £272,000,000 and Mr. McKenna made the following proposals for new taxation :—

Income Tax.—40 per cent. added to the existing rates ; only half of the increase (20 per cent.) to be imposed for the year to March 31, 1916. The exemption limit to be reduced from £160 to £130 ; and the abatement limit to be £120 where it was £160, and where it was £150 or £120 it would become £100. Provision was made to enable the payment of the tax by instalments in certain cases. The alterations in the income tax were expected to produce an additional £11,274,000 in 1915–16, and £44,400,000 in a full effective year. Certain additions were also made to the Super Tax.

Excess Profits Tax.—This tax really constituted an additional Income Tax. The trades or professions liable to the tax included any carried on in the United Kingdom or owned or carried on in any other place by persons ordinarily resident in the United Kingdom. Farmers, officials, and professional men were exempt. Any business or trade to which the tax applied was liable to pay to the Exchequer a sum equal to 50 per cent. of the amount by which the profits for the "accounting period" exceeded by more than £200 the defined pre-war standard of profits. The tax only applied to periods of account terminating after August 4, 1914, and before July 1, 1915. Profits earned in periods ending later were to be dealt with by subsequent legislation on the same lines. The new tax was estimated to produce £6,000,000 in 1915–16 and £37,000,000 in a full effective year.

Customs and Excise.—Duty on sugar increased from 1s. 10d. per cwt. to 9s. 4d. per cwt. Tea, tobacco, cocoa, coffee, chicory and dried fruits an all-round increase of 50 per cent. in the existing duties. Motor spirits, an increase of duty of 3d. per gallon.

Imported Luxuries.—An ad valorem duty of 33⅓ per cent. or its equivalent in the form of a specific tax—that is to say on weight, instead of on price—on motor cars, motor cycles, cinema films, clocks, watches, musical instruments, plate glass.

Post Office, etc.—Some important changes in postal, telegraph and telephone rates were proposed, but the most important of all, namely the proposed abolition of halfpenny postage, was abandoned as a result of pressure brought to bear upon the Government.

The following table shows the changes effected by the new war taxation :

	Revenue received in 1913–14.	Estimate for 1915–16.	Estimate for 1916–17.
	£	£	£
Customs	35,450,000	48,000,000	62,190,000
Excise	39,590,000	54,850,000	55,130,000
Estate Duties ..	27,359,000	30,000,000	30,000,000
Stamps	9,966,000	6,500,000	6,500,000
Land Tax	700,000	660,000	660,000
House Duty ..	2,000,000	1,990,000	1,990,000
Income Tax, incl. Super Tax ..	47,249,000	116,424,000	151,002,000
Excess Profits Tax	—	6,000,000	37,000,000
Land Value Duties	715,000	350,000	300,000
Total Revenue from Taxes	163,029,000	265,674,000	344,722,000
Non-Tax Revenue ..	35,214,000	39,340,000	39,340,000
TOTAL REVENUE	198,243,000	305,014,000	384,112,000

In three years, 1914–1917, notwithstanding the enormous disturbance of the economic system occasioned by the war, the revenue from taxation was, thus, to show an increase from £163,000,000 to well over £350,000,000, an advance of £187,000,000, or 114 per cent.

Mr. McKenna said the new taxation was estimated to produce £33,000,000 in the year to March 31, 1916, and adding the estimated revenue under the previous basis of taxation the total revenue would amount to £305,000,000. The deficit for the year would, therefore, be £1,285,000,000 and the total amount of the deadweight debt at the close of the financial year would amount to £2,200,000,000, and the revenue for the new year might be estimated at £387,000,000.

AMERICA'S WAR LOAN TO ALLIES.
Mr. J. P. Morgan and Lord Reading in New York.

As a matter of fact the yield of the new taxes both direct and indirect was considerably underestimated by Mr. McKenna in September. The Chancellor anticipated that the revenue from Income Tax and Super Tax would amount to £116,424,000; up to March 18 the amount received was £118,323,000. The receipts from Customs were put down at £48,900,000, the amount received up to March 18 was £56,045,000. Excise was expected to provide £54,850,000; the amount received up to March 18 was £60,120,000. Thus with two weeks' revenue still to come in the receipts of the Exchequer were £14,000,000 in excess of the estimate.

The Budget was on the whole favourably received. The most widely discussed features were the excess profits tax, the yield from which, it was widely held, had been greatly underestimated by the Chancellor of the Exchequer, and the import duties on luxuries. A certain amount of criticism was directed to the disproportion between the growth of direct and indirect taxation, and it was pointed out that, whereas in 1888 when the national revenue was £87,424,000, direct taxes only provided 45·3 per cent. of the total tax revenue and indirect taxes 54·7 per cent., the preliminary figures for 1916–17 indicated that 66·6 per cent. of the tax revenue for that year would be derived from direct taxation and only 33·3 per cent. from indirect taxation.

Mr. Montagu, speaking in the House on October 13, warned the country emphatically about the real meaning of the cost of the war. He said that for the current year the estimated expenditure was £1,590,000,000 and the estimated revenue £305,000,000, leaving a deficit of £1,285,000,000. For next year, if the present rate of expenditure were maintained, the expenditure would be £1,825,000,000, and the revenue on the present basis was expected to realize £387,000,000, leaving a deficit of £1,438,000,000. It would be seen, therefore, he added, that our burden involved a total expenditure by the Government amounting to not less than two-thirds of the entire estimated national income. The expenditure would have to be borne by the nation almost entirely either in the form of tax or loan. Allowing for any loans which could be raised abroad, every citizen ought to be prepared to put at least one-half of his current income at the disposal of the State either in the form of tax or loan. There seemed to be an opinion that these huge deficits could be found out of the accumulated wealth of the country. But they could not tax capital which could not be realized, and much accumulated wealth was in forms which could not be converted except in so far as the property represented by it could be sold to foreign purchasers.

This striking declaration did much to attract renewed public attention to the gravity of the financial problem, and the need of drastic public

1 2 3

1. Sir Henry Babington Smith, former President of National Bank of Turkey; 2. Mr. George W. Perkins, American banker; 3. Sir Edward H. Holden, managing director of the London City and Midland Bank.

4 5 6 7

4. Mr. A. Barton Hepburn, American banker; 5. Mr. Basil Blackett, British Treasury expert; 6. M. Octave Homberg, of the French Foreign Office; 7. M. Ernest Mallet, of Bank of France.

ARRANGING AMERICA'S $500,000,000 WAR LOAN TO THE ALLIES.

Members of the Anglo-French Commission and prominent American bankers in New York.

WOMEN AT WORK INSIDE A MUNITION FACTORY ASSEMBLING FUSES.

and private economy. An important manifesto upon the subject of national thrift, signed by some of the foremost men in the world of business, was published on December 23. The manifesto declared :

In a long war success depends mainly upon the respective financial resources of the combatants, and the consequent power of one of them to maintain, or to add to its fighting strength when the other's is declining, or is not capable of expansion. It is not in doubt that the financial resources of the Allies, when fully mobilized and wisely controlled, will be vastly greater than the enemies'. . . . The Allies have assembled new armies of overwhelming strength in France, in Russia, in Italy and in Great Britain, and everything needed to equip them and to supply them with munitions has been secured, or is in process of manufacture. The only thing remaining to be done is to provide all the money needed to support these vast armies of new men and to pay for the vast quantities of arms and munitions now being manufactured in all parts of the world.

The task of finding the greater part of the immense sums of money needed by the Allies is the special duty of the British people, for they in particular possess the necessary financial resources. Their manufacturing power has not been reduced by invasion, their cities have not been destroyed, their ports have not been shut off from the rest of the world and their income has not been diminished by the absence of tourists and by other circumstances. Indeed the income of the British people has been maintained at a very high level. Their exports, though not so great as before the war, are greater than they were as recently as 1909, their income, from interest on capital invested abroad, has been reduced but little, the earnings of their ships are greater than ever, and their factories are working full time. Moreover, the effect upon the production of the nation of the mobilization of a great army has been largely neutralized by the more vigorous and effective work of the civilian population in general and of the women in particular. In the current calendar year (1915) the British people will spend about £1,300,000,000 upon war and government, and next year (1916) will need to spend about £1,800,000,000 in place of a sum of about £200,000,000 a year before the war. . . . No one can realize the vastness of the task before the nation without becoming keenly conscious that it demands the strenuous co-operation of every man and woman, youth and maiden in the country ; that the nation's energies must be completely concentrated upon the production of really essential things ; and that the production of all non-essentials must be wholly stopped. Moreover, not only must the nation avoid the consumption of all non-essentials, but must even restrict the consumption of essentials to the limits of efficiency. . . . Only by all classes, employers and employed alike, adding to and most carefully husbanding income, by selling foreign securities and by creating foreign credits, will it be possible to provide the vast sum needed by the nation and the nation's Allies.

On November 11 the Prime Minister moved the eighth vote of credit amounting to £400,000,000, and he gave the following particulars of the war expenditure from April 1 to November 6 :

	£
Army, Navy and Munitions	517,300,000
Repayments to Bank of England ...	104,000,000
Loans to Dominions and Allies	98,300,000
Food Supplies, etc.	32,500,000
Total	743,100,000

This total gave an average of £3,377,000 per day (or, including the ordinary expenditure and the interest on the war debt, £3,847,000). Mr. Asquith added, " We see no reason to suppose that during the next two-and-a-half months the total issues from the Vote of Credit we are now asking for will exceed the figure on which my last estimate was based, namely £5,000,000 a day—a safe, I will not call it a liberal, figure."

From the figures furnished by Mr. Asquith on November 11 it is possible to frame the following estimate of the gross and the net war expenditure of the British Government from the outbreak of war up to March 31, 1916 :

Period.	Gross Outlay.	Loans to Dominions and Allies and Purchases of Foodstuffs, Repayments to Bank of England, &c.	Net Expenditure.
	£	£	£
Aug. 4, 1914, to Mar. 31, 1915 ..	359,786,000	80,786,000	279,000,000
April 1, 1915, to Nov. 6, 1915 ..	743,100,000	225,800,000	517,300,000
Nov. 7, 1915, to Mar. 31, 1916 ..	677,700,000	290,000,000	387,700,000
TOTALS ..	1,780,586,000	596,586,000	1,184,000,000

Our net expenditure, without taking into consideration the capital value of pensions and allowances up to March 31, 1916, may be estimated at £1,184,000,000. A considerable proportion of the sum lent to our Allies and Dominions, £596,586,000, should be ultimately recoverable.

The eight Votes of Credit from the outbreak of war up to December 31, 1915, were as follows :

PERIOD ENDING MARCH 31, 1915.	£	£
August 6, 1914	100,000,000	
November 15, 1914 ...	225,000,000	
March 1, 1915	37,000,000	
		362,000,000
PERIOD APRIL 1, 1915, TO DECEMBER 31, 1915.		
March 1, 1915	250,000,000	
June 15, 1915	250,000,000	
July 20, 1915	150,000,000	
September 15, 1915 ...	250,000,000	
November 11, 1915 ...	400,000,000	
		1,300,000,000

A large proportion of the war expenditure during 1915 was raised by means of the issue of Treasury Bills. The rates varied as follows :

—	From April 1 to Aug. 8.	From Aug. 9 to Oct. 26.	From Oct. 27 to Nov. 11.	From Nov. 12 to Dec. 31.
	Per Cent.	Per Cent.	Per Cent.	Per Cent.
Three months' bills ..	2¾	4½	4¾	5
Six months' bills ..	3⅞	4½	4⅞	5
Nine and twelve months'bills	3¾	4½	5	5

On December 16 an issue of 5 per cent. Exchequer Bonds was announced, bearing interest at 5 per cent. per annum payable half yearly. They were issued at par and repayable at par on December 1, 1920. They were largely applied in payment for the American dollar securities purchased by the Government under the scheme described earlier. As in the case of the 4½ per cent. loan, it was provided that in the event of any future loans (other than issues made abroad or issues of Exchequer Bonds, Treasury Bills, or similar short-dated securities) being raised for the purpose of carrying on the war the Exchequer Bonds of that issue would be accepted as the equivalent of cash to the amount of their face value for the purpose of subscription to any such loan.

The total sums raised by taxation and loans from April 1 to March 4, 1916, were as follows :—

	£
4½ per cent. War Loan	586,639,000
Treasury Bills	384,376,000
3½ per cent. War Loan (balance)... ...	35,798,000
5 per cent. Exchequer Bonds	127,754,000
American Loan	50,596,000
Temporary Advances	19,952,000
Revenue	289,316,000
Total	1,494,431,000

The gold movements at the Bank of England in 1915 were particularly interesting. The stock of gold held by the Bank at the beginning of 1915 was £70,000,000. By the end of June the total had fallen to £52,000,000, and by the end of the year it had further declined to £51,500,000. The gold received by the Bank amounted to £73,625,000, and the aggregate amount taken out was £94,426,000, most of which went to the United States. The net amount of gold exported was £20,801,000.

The continued expansion of the currency notes was an important feature of the financial history of the year. It will be recalled that immediately after the outbreak of war the dearth of small currency became so great that the provision of an additional circulating medium became absolutely necessary. On August 5, 1914, Mr. Lloyd George stated that with a view to effecting an economy of gold without causing any inconvenience to the public, whilst at the same time maintaining the gold standard in its integrity, it had been decided to issue £1 and 10s. notes convertible into gold at the Bank of England. The note would be a Government note and issued on the security of the Government. The first return issued in 1915, namely that dated January 13, showed that the total notes outstanding amounted to £37,205,079, and the amount of gold held to £20,500,000, showing a ratio of gold to notes of 55·1. On August 6, 1915, the following notice was issued by the Treasury :—

In view of the importance of strengthening the gold reserves of the country for exchange purposes the Treasury have instructed the Post Office and all public departments charged with the duty of making cash payments to use notes instead of gold coins wherever possible.

The public generally are earnestly requested in the national interest, to co-operate with the Treasury in this policy by (1) Paying in gold to the Post Office and to the Banks ; (2) Asking for payment of cheques in notes rather than gold ; (3) Using notes rather than gold for payment of wages and cash disbursements generally.

Full effect was quickly given to the desire of the Treasury, and within a few months gold had almost disappeared from ordinary internal circulation.

The Treasury notice was issued at a moment when the American exchange problem was becoming one of great urgency. After that date there was a rapid increase in the amount of notes issued, and by the date of the last return issued in 1915, December 29, the amount outstanding was £103,125,099, against which £28,500,000 of gold was held, a ratio of 27·6.

Of course, in addition to the gold held by the Bank of England, there is a large amount held by the joint stock banks and in the hands of the general public. On December 7 Mr. McKenna stated in the House of Commons that the amount of gold coin held by the banks including the Bank of England was £110,200,000 on June 30, 1915, as compared with £82,800,000, on June 30, 1914. No precise statistics were available, he said, as to the amount in the hands of the general public, but the best estimate was £75,000,000 on June 30, 1915, as compared with £78,000,000 on June 30, 1914.

The Stock Exchange recovered slowly but steadily from the tremendous disturbance caused by the war, and it was computed at the end of 1915 that the outstanding loans had been reduced from £90,000,000 to less than £30,000,000.

Early in January, 1915, the Treasury announced that no fresh issues of capital would be permitted without its sanction. There had been an accumulation of money available for investment while the Stock Exchange remained closed, and in January there was quite a substantial business. Towards the end of the month nearly 3,000 bargains were marked each day. In February there was some falling off. The minimum prices were revised on March 19, and business con-

"THE LOAN OF VICTORY"

An old French couple prepared to devote their savings to their country's cause.

tinued fairly active throughout that month and during April. In May the sinking of the Lusitania, the Italian crisis, and the political crisis at home exercised a restraining influence and business reached a low ebb. In June the appearance of the war loan caused a general marking down of all investment securities which were not protected by minimum prices. July and August were idle months. In September there was a steady improvement, due in a measure to the favourable war news, and in October there was quite a substantial business passing. The great advance in American and Canadian securities had a strengthening effect on all the sections of the market. At the end of November the official minima on Consols and Corporation and on foreign Government stocks were removed and Consols became marketable at about 59. Business continued fairly active throughout December, the principal

MR. E. S. MONTAGU,
Financial Secretary of the Treasury.

feature being a substantial rise in rubber shares. The general trend of Stock Exchange prices was indicated in the table of valuations contained in the *Bankers' Magazine*, which showed a total shrinkage in the value of 387 securities between January 20, 1915, and December 17, 1915, of £207,000,000. This shrinkage would have been much greater if the minimum prices on home railway debentures and preference stocks had been removed.

The war naturally exercised a profound influence upon the national income. It was estimated that at the date of the Census of 1911 the number of occupied persons of both sexes aged 10 years and upwards was about 20,000,000 of whom 14,000,000 were males and 6,000,000 females. At the end of 1915 there were upwards of 3,000,000 men in the Army and 320,000 in the Navy. In addition there were 1,750,000 male and 250,000 female workers in the 3,000 odd factories controlled by the Ministry of Munitions, and there were nearly 1,000,000 men employed on ship construction and repairing and contributing to the general maintenance and fighting efficiency of the fleet. This transference of 6,000,000 workers from commercial production to war service and the production of munitions of war caused a tremendous disturbance of the economic system. The loss of production was, however, largely neutralized by the vigorous and more effective work of the civilian population and by the introduction of female and juvenile labour. The result of the speeding up of production and the rise in the cost of production and in the cost of living was believed to have had the effect of actually increasing the national income for the time being.

After the outbreak of war employment became very good, and before the end of the year a considerable amount of overtime was being worked, and in several trades complaint was being made of a shortage of labour. This was especially the case in the engineering, shipbuilding, woollen and leather and kindred trades. Concurrently the prices of food and many other necessaries rose. In these circumstances a movement began at the commencement of 1915 to raise wages. This movement, which in most cases took the form of bonuses, or of an increase in rates of wages limited to the duration of the war, first became evident in the trades more directly concerned with the output of munitions and the transport of troops and supplies. From March onwards, however, it spread to nearly all the principal industries, and its effects were far greater than those of any other upward movement in wages previously recorded. It was estimated that, during the whole period under review, about 4,500,000 workpeople had their rates of wages increased by over £750,000 per week—say at the rate of £39,000,000 per annum. On December 1 Mr. Asquith stated that, generally speaking, the rise in the cost of living since the outbreak of war had been, in food 40 per cent., in rent 2 per cent., fuel and light 25 per cent., clothing 30 per cent., and in other miscellaneous items 15 per cent., the general result being to show an average increase in the cost of living of about 30 per cent.

The war naturally and inevitably affected the shipping industry profoundly. At the end of 1915 Great Britain owned 19,540,368 tons of merchant shipping, but it should be borne in mind that although there were about 20,000 British ships afloat, there were only 3,600 large ocean-going steamships. The submarine losses up to the end of 1915 amounted to about 740,000 tons. In addition 234,000 tons were captured and sunk by the enemy; while 103,000 tons were sunk by mines or explosion. Including the British tonnage detained in German and Turkish ports and the miscellaneous losses due to the war, the total amount of British shipping locked up was about 1,500,000 tons, or about 8 per cent. of the total tonnage. On the other hand the new tonnage built during 1915 amounted to only 600,000 tons.

Then, about 1,700 steamships, representing nearly one-third of the tonnage of the British mercantile fleet, were employed by the Government for naval and transport services, hospital ships, etc., at the end of 1915. When account is taken of these facts, and of the locking up of 5,000,000 tons of German and Austrian merchant shipping, together with the heavy losses incurred through the war by neutral shipping, it is easier to understand the main causes of the huge rise which took place in ocean freights during 1915. Cotton and wheat are the two principal commodities shipped from the United States and Argentina to Liverpool, and the subjoined table shows the great increase in freights for those cargoes :—

WHEAT (Per Ton).

—	Before the War.	End Dec., 1915.	Increase.
	s. d.	s. d.	Per Cent.
New York	6 0	70 0	1,060
Argentina	12 0	120 0	860

COTTON (Per 100 lb.).

—	Before the War.	End Dec., 1915.	Increase.
	Cents.	Cents.	Per Cent.
New York	20	200	900
Mobile	35	200	506

Before the war Great Britain derived an income of about £100,000,000 per annum from her services to the world as carrier; the earnings from this source for 1915 were estimated to amount to not less than £300,000,000. In considering the Board of Trade returns it is important to bear this fact in mind, because the values given for our exports are "f.o.b.", that is Free on Board, and the value of the imports given are "c.i.f.", that is to say Cost Insurance and Freight.

Another great industry—agriculture—was very seriously affected by the war. At first it appeared that farmers were likely to suffer rather than gain by the war, but at the end of 1914 food prices began to rise rapidly.

The average price of wheat per imperial quarter for the year 1915 was 52s. 10d., being the highest average since 1877, in which year it

PAY DAY ON THE EASTERN FRONT.

German soldiers drawing their pay in paper money.

[*Reproduced by courtesy of "The World's Work."*

THE RUSSIAN GOLD RESERVE IN THE STATE BANK, PETROGRAD.

was 56s. 9d. The average price in 1915 was 17s. 11d. in excess of that for the previous year. The highest average price was reached during the week ended May 22, when 62s. per quarter was the average price obtained; the lowest average, 42s. 9d. per quarter, was obtained for the week ended September 18. From the beginning of August there was a steady decline in the price of wheat, due to a large extent to the prevalent belief at that time that the forcing of the Dardanelles was imminent. But after the failure of operations in that region prices showed an upward tendency, and at the end of the year the average price recorded was 54s. 9d.

The average price of barley during the year was 37s. 4d., this figure being an advance of 10s. 2d. on the average price of the preceding year and the highest since 1878. Prices fluctuated from 27s. 9d. in the week ended January 9 to 48s. 11d. in the week ended December 4. These being the lowest and highest average weekly prices respectively.

The average weekly price of oats in 1915 was 30s. 2d. per quarter. This is 9s. 2d. more than the average price for the previous year and the highest price obtained for nearly a century, the year in which that price was exceeded being 1818, when the average price was 32s. 5d. per quarter. The lowest average for the year was for the week ended September 25, the price then being 26s. 1d.; the highest average obtained was for the week ended May 22, when the price was 32s. 8d.

The accompanying diagram, which appeared in *The Times* of January 6, 1916, shows the various fluctuations in the price of wheat during the year 1915.

The agricultural index number at the end of July, 1915, touched 140—*i.e.*, 40 per cent. above the average of the years 1906–8. Agricultural labourers were among the first to respond to the call for the new armies, and in all about 250,000 agricultural workers had enlisted at the end of 1915. Wages naturally rose, the advance varying from 1s. 6d. to 3s. per week. Among our other principal industries, the coal, iron, and steel trades enjoyed a great measure of prosperity notwithstanding the growing difficulties in connexion with the shortage of labour. At the end of 1915 the woollen and leather industries were in a flourishing condition. On the other hand, several important industries, including cotton and the building and printing trades, were in a depressed condition. On the whole economists estimated that Great Britain had increased her savings from an average of about £350,000,000 per annum to well over £600,000,000, a remarkable achievement considering the disturbance caused by the war and the increased cost of living.

The Board of Trade Returns for 1915 were particularly interesting. The exports continued to show heavy decreases until July, but at a rapidly diminishing ratio. The decrease for that month was only £9,638,000, or 21·8 per cent., as compared with a decrease of £19,899,000, or 45·1 per cent. in the first month of the war. From August onwards the comparisons were made with the figures for the first five months of the war, and the increases were very substantial, amounting to as much as £11,037,000, or 44·8 per cent. in November. The monthly figures are given in the subjoined table.

EXPORTS OF BRITISH MANUFACTURES.

Month.	Amount. £	+Increase or —Decrease Compared with Corresponding Period in 1914. Amount. £	Per Cent.
January	28,247,000	19,558,000	—40·9
February	26,176,000	15,085,000	—36·5
March	30,176,000	14,342,000	—32·2
April	32,169,000	7,777,000	—19·4
May	33,619,000	8,432,000	—20·0
June	33,233,000	6,639,000	—16·6
July	34,721,000	9,638,000	—21·8
August	32,438,000	8,227,000	+34·0
September ..	32,308,000	5,634,000	+21·2
October	31,968,000	3,367,000	+10·6
November.. ..	35,639,000	11,037,000	+44·8
December.. ..	33,947,000	7,668,000	+29·1

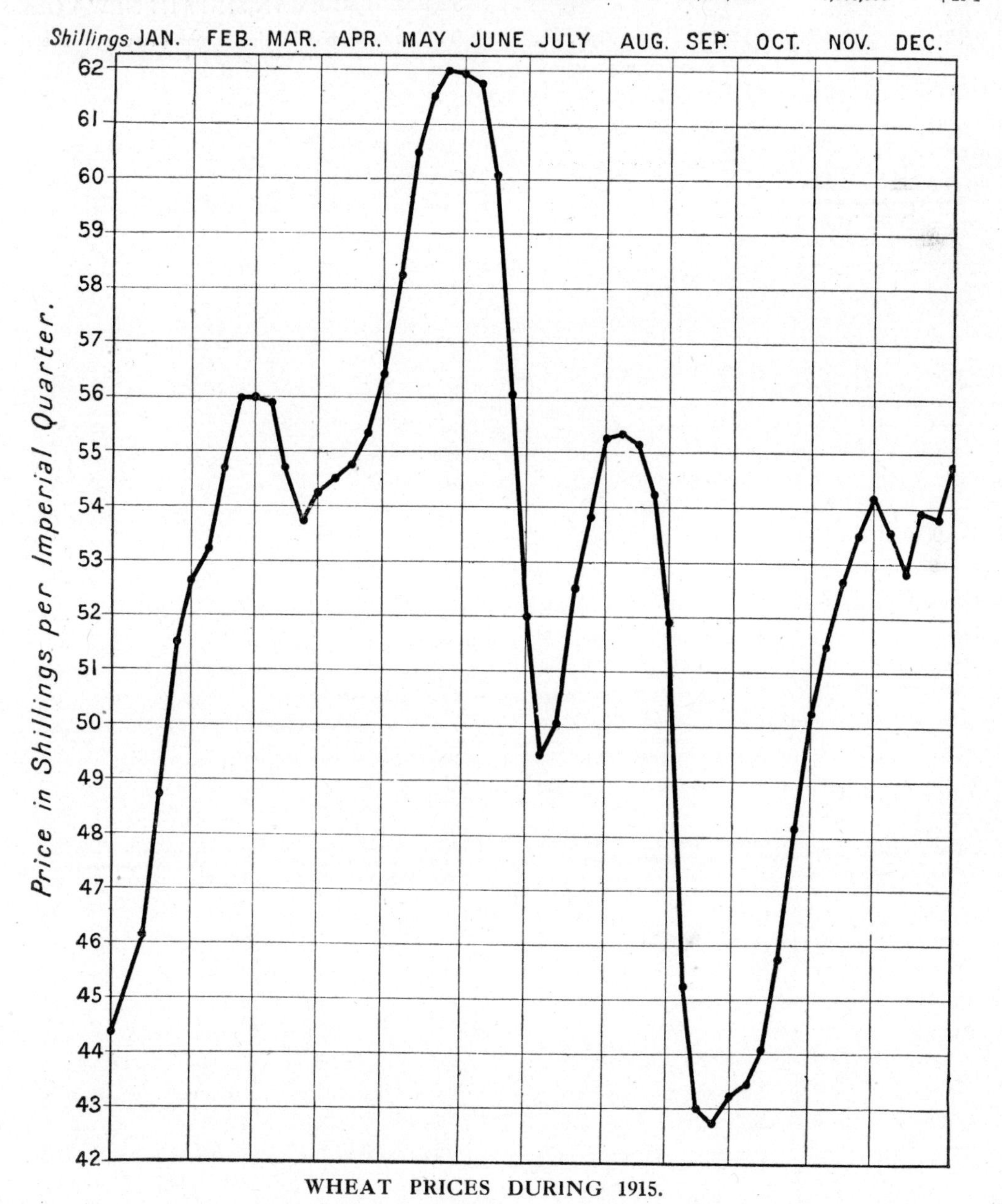

WHEAT PRICES DURING 1915.

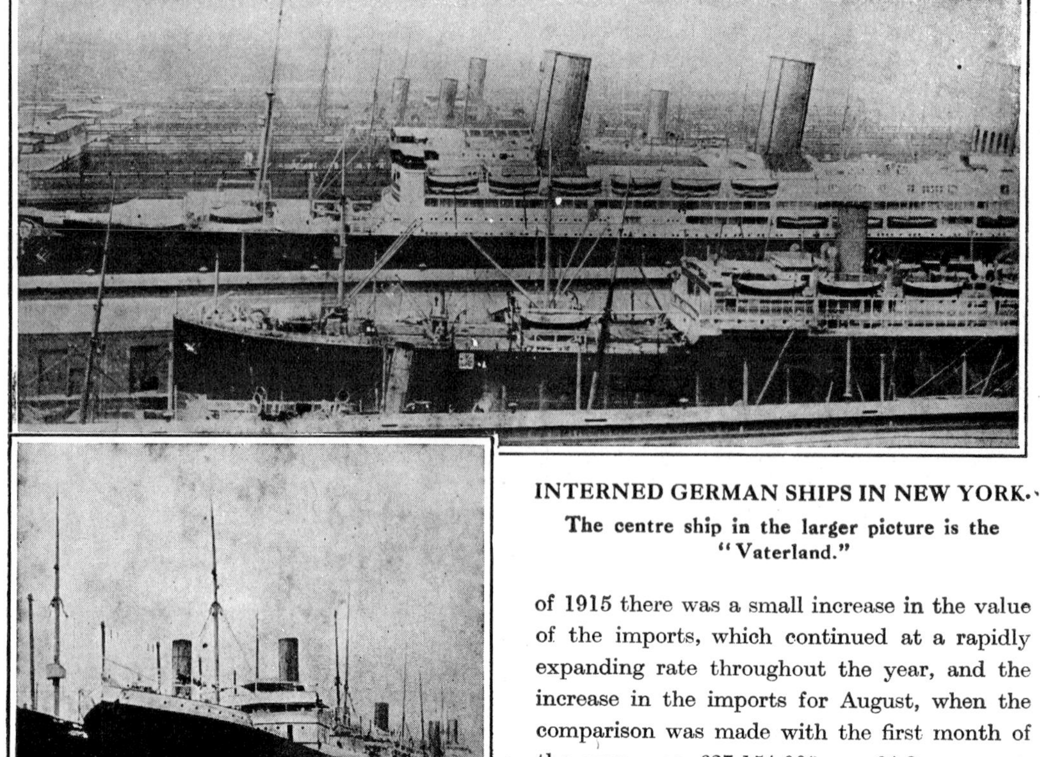

INTERNED GERMAN SHIPS IN NEW YORK.
The centre ship in the larger picture is the "Vaterland."

The total value of the British exports recorded in 1915 was £384,600,000, as compared with £430,700,000 in 1914, a decrease of £46,100,000. The bulk of the decrease was in manufactures, which were valued at £292,800,000, as against £338,600,000 in 1914. It was calculated that the volume of the exports diminished by £77,000,000, but the advance in average prices reduced it to the figures given above.

It is important to bear in mind the fact that while the Trade Returns include goods bought in the United Kingdom by or on behalf of the Allies, they do not include goods taken from British Government stores and depôts, or goods bought by His Majesty's Government and shipped on Government vessels.

The import trade made a much more rapid recovery than the export trade. In August, 1914, the decrease was £13,613,000, or 24·3 per cent. For the last month of that year it amounted to only £3,560,000, or 5·1 per cent. Our economic strength was then beginning to manifest its power and we were calling in our credits all over the world. By the beginning of 1915 there was a small increase in the value of the imports, which continued at a rapidly expanding rate throughout the year, and the increase in the imports for August, when the comparison was made with the first month of the war, was £27,154,000, or 64·2 per cent. The monthly totals are given in the following table:

IMPORTS.

Month.	Amount. £	+Increase or —Decrease Compared with Corresponding Period in 1914. Amount. £	Per Cent.
January	67,401,000	604,000	— 0·8
February	65,209,000	3,215,000	+ 5·1
March	75,591,000	8,643,000	+12·9
April	73,678,000	12,051,000	+19·5
May	71,645,000	12,545,000	+21·2
June	76,118,000	17,836,000	+30·6
July	75,548,000	16,171,000	+27·2
August	69,496,000	27,154,000	+64·2
September	70,293,000	25,286,000	+56·1
October	67,792,000	16,413,000	+31·8
November	71,647,000	16,129,000	+29·0
December	70,398,000	3,621,000	+ 5·3

The total imports of commodities in 1915 were valued at £853,756,000, or £151,721,000 more than in 1914. In the first place it is necessary to recall that a very large proportion of this increase represents the higher freights charged during 1915, the bulk of which came to the shipowners of this country. Then it must be remembered that the returns do not include the value of the Government imports of munitions, etc., which have been unofficially estimated at £120,000,000 to £150,000,000. The principal increase was in food and drink, the value of which amounted to £381,000,000, as compared with £297,000,000 in 1914. About 85 per cent. of this increase was due to the advance in prices, and only 15 per cent. to the increased volume. The imports of raw materials advanced from

£236,000,000 in 1914 to £287,300,000 in 1915. Manufactures to the value of £181,500,000 were imported in 1915 as against £160,500,000 in the preceding year.

The following table gives the monthly values of the re-exports:

RE-EXPORTS.

Month.	Amount.	+Increase or —Decrease Compared with Corresponding Period in 1914.	
		Amount.	Per Cent.
	£	£	
January	6,895,000	2,701,000	—28·1
February	6,809,000	3,419,000	—33·4
March	8,067,000	1,469,000	—15·4
April	9,957,000	832,000	— 7·7
May	10,243,319	128,200	+ 1·2
June	9,350,339	596,905	— 6·8
July	9,408,790	1,582,874	—21·7
August	7,323,749	2,903,916	+66·0
September ..	7,564,327	2,290,286	+43·5
October	7,162,000	17,224	— 0.2
November.. ..	8,313,000	2.669,000	+47·3
December ..	7,702,000	1,831,000	+31·2

The most unsatisfactory feature of the foreign Trade Returns was the enormous growth of the excess of imports over exports. In the five years 1909–13 the excess of imports over exports averaged £140,000,000 per annum. For the year 1915 the excess of imports was £370,300,000. The widening of our adverse trade balance was the principal cause of the difficulties experienced in maintaining the foreign exchanges in 1915. In normal years the excess of imports over exports is met by (1) our earnings from shipping; (2) the interest on our investments abroad, and (3) the earnings of our banking and insurance houses. The credits from these sources were not only sufficient for this purpose but they provided a fund of about £200,000,000 per annum for new investments abroad. In 1915 the ordinary investment of capital abroad was suspended, but in its place we were called upon to make special investments in the shape of loans to the Dominions and our Allies to the extent of £423,000,000.

It was estimated that after making all the necessary adjustments in connexion with the so-called "invisible imports and exports" our net deficit for the year amounted to about £400,000,000. This was mainly provided by the sale of a portion of our American and other investments, by the raising of the Anglo-French loan in the United States, and by the export of gold. Towards the end of 1915 it was realized that the adjustment of our trade balance in 1916 would be a matter of even greater difficulty than it was in 1915 unless adequate steps were taken in time to restrict the import of unnecessary commodities, and it was widely believed that it would be necessary

INTERNED GERMAN SHIPS.
Hoisting the Portuguese flag in the Tagus.

RUSSIAN STAMP MONEY.

to carry out to much greater lengths the tentative steps in the direction of the imposition of import duties on luxuries which were contained in Mr. McKenna's Budget of September.

By the end of 1915 the British people began to attain a clearer perception of the magnitude of the financial task which the war had imposed upon them.

It was pointed out by some economists that the resources of the Overseas Dominions had not yet been mobilized, and considerable significance was attached to the fact that Canada had found it possible to provide with the greatest ease credits amounting to £21,000,000 for the payment of Munitions for the War Office produced in Canadian factories. It was stated in the House of Commons that the wealth of the whole British Empire had been estimated at £26,000,000,000 and the national income at £4,000,000,000.

Another great source of economic strength was indicated in our investments abroad, which were estimated to be worth £4,000,000,000, and the bulk of these investments were in countries which are remote from the war areas.

The steady improvement in the foreign trade, notwithstanding the withdrawal of so many men from production, the intrinsic strength of the credit system, its power of recuperation and its mobility contributed to a feeling of confidence, and although it was recognized that great and far-reaching changes in our mode of living and in our fiscal system must result from the war, the new year was not looked forward to with undue anxiety so far as finance was concerned.

Back of the Russian Stamp Money; "having circulation on a par with silver subsidiary coins."

CHAPTER CXVI.

SECOND WINTER ON THE WESTERN FRONT.

Situation in October, 1915—Changes in the French and British Higher Command—Promotion of General de Castelnau—Sir Douglas Haig Replaces Sir John French—Conditions of the Allied and German Forces during the Winter—Visit of and Accident to King George—Gains and Losses in the Champagne Pouilleuse—Struggle on the Vimy Heights—Combats in Alsace and near Belfort—The Belgian Coast Fighting; Belgians re-inundate the Yser District—Operations on the British Front—German Gas Attack of December 19 in the Ypres Salient—Canadian Exploit near Messines—Fighting in the Air.

THE great offensive of the Allies in the Autumn of 1915, which was described in Chapters CIV., CV., and CVI., had obtained no great measure of success against the German lines between La Bassée and Arras and between Reims and the Argonne. For, although the losses inflicted on the enemy were severe, it had not been possible to pierce the entrenchments which stretched from the North Sea to the Swiss frontier; only here and there, and in a slight degree, had they been pushed back. In the eyes of neutrals the results of the battles of the Champagne Pouilleuse and Loos-Vimy did not counterbalance the successes which the Germans and Austro-Hungarians had won over the Russians in the summer and autumn.

In the first days of October Bulgaria joined our enemies and, as a consequence, no inconsiderable portion of the French and British effectives were transported to Salonica—too late even to help the Serbians and still less able to take the field against the German, Austrian and Bulgarian forces. The command of the Allied force here was given to General Sarrail, the saviour of Verdun in the days of the Battle of the Marne.

The inability of the Allies to act with vigour in the Near East rendered them unable to prevent the enemy occupying Serbia and Montenegro. This, together with the failure to make any real progress in Gallipoli, and the insuccess of the Indian Expeditionary Force in Mesopotamia, reacted on the strategy of the allied commanders in the west. We had wasted our troops on minor objects instead of concentrating our whole force against the principal adversary. The Gallipoli expedition was "a gamble," and proved a disastrous one. Moreover, we could not provide sufficient troops for the advance up the Tigris. These two diversions of strength from the main theatre of war seriously hampered our movements there.

All this produced a state of comparative inactivity on the western front. There were many small fights. Day after day the toll of losses mounted. But no great advantage was gained by either side. The situation here was indeed almost entirely novel in war and only faintly foreshadowed in the Russo-Japanese conflict. There for the first time we saw two armies facing one another, both entrenched. But in that case the length of the fighting lines was only a fifth of what it was from Nieuport to Belfort; the fortifications were nothing like as elaborate; and, above all, the extremities of the Russian fighting front were open—especially the right—so that the Japanese were able to attack them.

In the present instance the western flanks of the two contending powers were quite unturnable, resting as they did on the sea, while the

AFTER A BATTLE IN CHAMPAGNE.
German soldiers running into the French lines to surrender.

eastern extremities were by the nature of the country and their proximity to neutral territory equally secure. The winter time also is not favourable to great military efforts. Troops cannot move with facility, guns cannot be manœuvred over heavy roads, ammunition and food cannot be easily brought up.

The consequence of all these considerations was relative stagnation, broken only at the end of February, 1916, by the German offensive known as the Battle of Verdun.

Victory was for many reasons very necessary to the Germans; the longer they waited the stronger became their adversaries and the greater the danger of a converging attack from them.

The time of pause was therefore used by them to bring up slowly but surely large numbers of guns, piles of ammunition, and, above all, to give the troops destined for the assault of the chosen point of entry into France a period of rest and recuperation, to prepare for the desperate enterprise they were destined to undertake.

These preparations were perfectly well known to the Allies; but the oftener the Germans knocked their heads against the hard wall of their trenches the better they were pleased. Offensives conducted on the German plan involve enormous losses. The more their forces were depleted the sooner they must come to the end of their resources.

During the winter months considerable changes were made in the Higher Command of the French and British forces. On October 13 the French Minister of Foreign Affairs, M. Delcassé, resigned, and his resignation was speedily followed by that of the Viviani Ministry. At the end of October M. Viviani was replaced by M. Briand, and the civilian Minister of War, M. Millerand, by General Galliéni. The latter had had a brilliant career in the French Colonies. He had pacified Tonking, commanded the French troops who had conquered Madagascar, and organized the administration of that island. Later he had been a member of the Conseil Supérieur de Guerre, and, just before the Battle of the Marne, had been nominated Governor of Paris.

On December 2 (the anniversary of Austerlitz) Joffre was appointed Commander-in-Chief of the French armies in all theatres of war. At the same time the immediate direction of the French troops in France was entrusted to General de Castelnau.

Castelnau was born in 1851. In 1870, during the war with Germany, he joined the army from St. Cyr, the Sandhurst of France. He was appointed to the 36th Regiment as a Second Lieutenant, but obtained such rapid promotion that he was made a Captain after a few weeks. This rapid rise was due to the number of officers required to replace those who were prisoners in Germany and to lead the multiplied army raised by Gambetta. His war service included fighting with the 1st and 2nd Armies of the Loire, and he also took part in the struggle with the Commune.

Some time after the war he entered the Staff College (Ecole Supérieure de Guerre), where he greatly distinguished himself. In 1885 he was promoted to the rank of Lieut.-Colonel and posted to the 17th Army Corps. In 1896 he was appointed to the Headquarter Staff and employed in work connected with the mobilization and organization of the army. In 1899 he was placed in command of the 37th Regiment, which formed part of the 6th Army Corps which acted as a counter-check to the German forces round Metz. The knowledge of this part of the country thus gained proved invaluable when in 1914 he was posted to the command of the Army of Lorraine. In 1906 he was made a Major-General, and in 1909 was given the leadership of the 13th Division. In this position he soon showed his capacity for command, and in 1913 he joined the Conseil Supérieur de Guerre, and thus worked directly with General Joffre.

The opening phase of the war in Alsace-Lorraine was not a success, but when Castelnau assumed the direction he was able to hold the Germans at bay. After the Battle of the Marne he was called up with his army to strengthen the northern front, and he now received the appointment which placed him at the head of the French forces combating in France. Popular with his troops and believed by them and by all who come in contact with him to be a man of vigour and a general of ability, he seemed to be well suited to command the advance against the Germans.

On December 15 it was announced that Sir John French had been relieved of the command of the British Army in France. His farewell order to the Army he had commanded ran as follows :

"In relinquishing the Command of the British Army in France, I wish to express to the officers, non-commissioned officers, and men, with whom I have been so closely associated during the last sixteen months, my heartfelt sorrow in parting with them before the campaign, in which we have been so long engaged

BRITISH CYCLISTS CORPS.
On a snow-covered road in France.

CONVOYS OF THE TRANSPORT DE MATÉRIEL AND TRANSPORT DE PERSONNEL.
French troops, munitions and provisions on the way to the fighting front.

together, has been brought to a victorious conclusion.

"I have, however, the firmest conviction that such a glorious ending to their splendid and heroic efforts is not far distant, and I shall watch their progress towards this final goal with intense interest, but in the most confident hope.

"The success so far attained has been due to the indomitable spirit, dogged tenacity which knows no defeat, and the heroic courage so abundantly displayed by the rank and file of the splendid Army which it will ever remain the pride and glory of my life to have commanded during over sixteen months of incessant fighting.

"Regulars and Territorials, Old Army and New Army, have ever shown these magnificent qualities in equal degree.

"From my heart I thank them all.

"At this sad moment of parting, my heart goes out to those who have received lifelong injury from wounds, and I think with sorrow of that great and glorious host of my beloved comrades who have made the greatest sacrifice of all by laying down their lives for their country.

"In saying good-bye to the British Army in France, I ask them once again to accept this expression of my deepest gratitude and heartfelt devotion towards them, and my earnest good wishes for the glorious future which I feel to be assured.

"(Signed) J. D. P. FRENCH,
Field-Marshal Commanding-in-Chief,
British Army in France.

"18th December, 1915."

It is too early to appraise Sir John's services to his country. The circumstances under which he had to carry out his operations are not yet fully known. It cannot, however, be gainsaid that the Asquith Cabinet had set him one of the most difficult tasks ever presented to a British soldier. At Mons and during the retreat from Mons, on the Aisne and at Ypres he had had insufficient numbers, artillery and munitions. Before he was in a position to take the offensive, the Germans had had time to construct the most formidable defences which any army has been called upon to assault. When Sir John French attacked at Neuve Chapelle, the Aubers Ridge, Festubert and Loos, a considerable part of his troops were half trained, and, except at the Battle of Loos, his artillery and munitions were inadequate. No overwhelming victories were gained during his term of command by any general in the western theatre of war. But one thing is certain—viz., that Sir John kept his head, and, ably supported by his subordinate leaders, especially Smith-Dorrien, he checked the first rush of the German hordes and thus helped Joffre to turn on them and eventually drive them back.

GENERAL DE CASTELNAU.

Sir John, on his return to England, took over the command of the Home Army, and in France he was succeeded by Sir Douglas Haig, who had done so much to win the Battle of Ypres.

Directly afterwards the Chief of the Staff in France, Lieut.-General Sir William Robertson, was made Chief of the Imperial General Staff in succession to Lieut.-General Sir Archibald Murray. Sir William had had a remarkable career, having risen from the ranks. Born in 1859, he had in 1888 obtained a commission in the 3rd Dragoon Guards. For some years he was in the Intelligence Department of the Indian

Army, and subsequently passed with credit through the Staff College. As Field Intelligence Officer he had served with the Chitral Relief Force in 1895. On the Staff during the South African War, he was present at most of the principal engagements. In 1910 he was made Commandant of the Staff College, and in 1913 Director of Military Training. When the Great War broke out, he was given the command of a division, and in January, 1915, was appointed Chief of the Staff to Sir John French. According to *The Times* Military Correspondent, he had "an iron constitution, and certainly a remarkably strong will."

The responsibilities of Lord Kitchener, already reduced by the creation of the Ministry of Munitions, were further diminished on January 27, 1916, by an Order in Council declaring that Sir William Robertson "should be responsible for issuing the orders of the Government in regard to Military Operations."

Not only was there a redistribution of the Allied commands on the western front, but, to ensure proper co-ordination between their widely scattered forces, a council for the direction of the strategy of the Allied armies in all the theatres of war was instituted.

Before describing the fighting which occurred on the western front from the beginning of October, 1915, to the opening of the Battle of Verdun in February, 1916, we shall endeavour to picture to the reader the conditions under which the Allied and German Armies lived through the winter months. The opposing armies represented in numbers the population of one of those gigantic capitals which had sprung into existence since the invention of the steam engine. Few details of the units engaged and still fewer of the deeds of the troops composing them have been published. It is only possible, therefore, to give in broad outline a description of the various engagements.

The first point to be noted is that, thanks to the locomotive in its various shapes—steamer, railway engine, motor-lorry, and the many forms comprised in the word automobile—it was now possible to move troops with far greater facility and to keep them more regularly supplied with munitions and food. The hard-

ON THE WAY TO THE TRENCHES.

French troops, with supplies, travelling on a light railway to the firing-line.

WELL-SCREENED FROM THE ENEMY.
A French Sniper at work.

ships suffered therefore were very much less than had been experienced in any previous campaign, and these were also diminished by the greater care of the wounded and the great advances made in medical treatment. Typhoid fever had almost disappeared from the Army, thanks to the prophylactic treatment by inoculation ; and the scientific and rapid methods of healing and handling the wounded had enormously diminished the death rate among them.

When war broke out few preparations had been made, even by the prescient Germans, for the siege-like warfare which speedily replaced the manœuvring battles of August and September, 1914. The consequence was that, despite the fact that most of the fighting had taken place in thickly populated districts where houses, cottages and other buildings afforded some shelter, the crowding together of the large numbers of soldiers necessary to hold the lines of trenches exposed a large proportion of them to the inclemency of the winter weather. Many of the reserve men used to complete the units were unaccustomed to open-air existence, while some of them, like the Indians and the French Colonial troops, had been brought from tropical climates to France and Flanders. It might have been expected, therefore, that the hardships in the trenches and dug-outs of the winter of 1914–15 would have caused an appalling death-rate. Fortunately, the medical administration and the ease with which good food and warm clothing could be supplied to the troops in the fighting line greatly diminished the losses.

Nevertheless, the first winter had been a terrible experience to the front-line troops, and the Staffs of the French, British and Belgian Armies had during the summer and autumn of 1915 been doing their utmost to provide against the contingencies of another winter campaign.

On the British section of the front many of the trenches by October, 1915, had bricked floors and drains to carry away the water. Whole woods had been cut into logs to line the dug-outs. A young subaltern of the Royal Irish Rifles, writing on October 23, 1915, describes how the officers of the Territorial company to whom he was attached spent the evening. "They had a gramophone in the mess dug-out, on which we reeled out rag-time, while we drank whisky and soda for the first time in France, and smoked cigars ! " Behind the lines recreation huts awaited the soldier when he was relieved. Prebendary Carlile shows us the interior of a Church Army hut :

On entering the first hut we came to we were welcomed by the sound of the piano, which is the chief favourite in all huts and is strummed upon from morn to night except when the gramophone strikes up on the bar counter at the other end. The hut measures 90 feet by 21 feet, with protruding bottom sides to avoid unnecessary reflection in the sun. It was made, like all the others, in portable sections. All huts and superintendents are under military orders and the guidance of the chaplains. Ping-pong was being played in the middle and competes greatly with the boxing-gloves, which are often in keen demand. Two stoves were centres of attraction ; and tables were occupied by men writing home ; little groups of chums were comparing notes ; others trying to scrape off dried mud. At the far end, behind the temperance bar, facing an eager crowd with tin cups in hand, were the helpers, supported by two stalwart 6-feet "padres" (chaplains) issuing cocoa, kept warm in wooden boxes packed with sawdust. A magic lantern was on the shelf for use at night, dominoes, draughts, footballs, hymn-books, etc., were just beside the tins of biscuits, jams and cigarettes. The "kitchen" had been driven out under pressure to take refuge under a makeshift outhouse, composed partly of cases broken up and knocked together. Coal and coke are often difficult to obtain, and so the trees of the wood have to do their best.

In the background a vast Aldershot had sprung up in which the new armies were being trained. When not learning to bomb, bayonet or shoot, work a machine-gun, fly an aeroplane or drive a motor-car, the men played at football, listened to concerts or witnessed cinematograph shows and theatrical performances. A pantomime, *The Babes in the Wood,* specially composed by a soldier, an ex-actor on the music-hall stage, was performed on December 26. A sergeant took the part of Maid Marian and instructed Ferdinand, "A Bad Lad" (one of a pair, the other being "Kizer Bill"), in the use of the "glad eye." To wile away the time, "trench newspapers" were produced. Below is an extract from the *Leadswinger*, the bivouac journal of a field ambulance :

To celebrate November 1, our divisional band paid us a visit. The casualties, taking into account the surprise nature of the attack, are very few. Lieutenant S—— had to have his voice in a sling as the result of a too vigorous rendering of "Here we are again." He was game to the last, and was carried out on a stretcher after an attempt to outclass the trombone in the "Have a banana" passage of "Let's all go down the Strand," in which as a fact he got hopelessly stranded.

IN TRENCH TOWN.

On the "terrace" of a dug-out in the war area.

COMMUNICATION TRENCHES.

Entrance to a French trench which is in direct communication with the front line. Smaller picture: a trench connected with a building in a French village.

To the Germans, singing the "Song of Hate" or the "Watch on the Rhine," the lightheartedness of our troops was incomprehensible.

An Italian who visited the British front at the beginning of 1916 has recorded his impressions. "The way in which your Army," he said, "is fed, clothed and protected from the enmity both of man and Nature is worthy of an empire which is the greatest financial power in the world and which is ready to sacrifice in this war its wealth for the peace and freedom of Europe. . . . It is a source of wonder to the foreigner that all this should have been created under a voluntary system." He related how the British fraternized with the French, and he remarked that the British soldier "was no longer a foreigner in France." He also noted the "democratic character of the British Army," personified in the Prince of Wales mixing with a crowd of privates. "I thought," he added, "for a moment of the difference between this British Prince and the German Crown Prince. They symbolize two races, two epochs, two political systems, which could well be named Progress and Reaction."

The life of the soldiers watching the German lines was diversified during the winter months

A COMMUNICATION BREASTWORK ON THE WESTERN FRONT: RUNNING THE GAUNTLET PAST A GAP.

This form was used where trenches, owing to the nature of the soil, could not be made. It ran in serpentine fashion for miles through fields, roads, villages, and houses; these latter, of course, mostly in ruins.

by the visits of King George and of certain politicians, notably Mr. John Redmond, whose brother William had joined the Army and was serving in the field, and also by parties of bluejackets. On October 21 the King landed in France. The next day he was at Havre, where he inspected the British camps. After spending some days at the base he moved up to the Allied lines south of Arras. There on Monday, October 26, he was met by President Poincaré, who bestowed the *Croix de Guerre* on the Prince of Wales. The following day General Joffre arrived, and the King was present at a review of the French Second Colonial Corps, held in the neighbourhood of Amiens. His Majesty's Order of the Day, addressed to the French Armies, expressed admirably the feelings which animated himself and his subjects towards our splendid Allies :

"Soldiers of France,

"I am very happy to have been able to realize a desire which I have had at heart for a long time, and to express to you my profound admiration for your heroic exploits, for your dash as well as your tenacity, and those magnificent military virtues which are the proud heritage of the French Army.

"Under the brilliant leadership of your eminent General-in-Chief and his distinguished collaborators you, officers, non-commissioned officers, and soldiers, have deserved well of your dear country, which will for ever be grateful to you for your brave efforts in safeguarding and defending it.

"My armies are very proud to fight by your side and to have you as comrades. May the bonds which unite us hold firm and the two countries remain thus intimately united for ever.

"Soldiers,—Accept my most cordial and sincere greetings. I have no doubt that you will bring this gigantic struggle to a victorious conclusion, and, in the name of my soldiers and my country, I beg to address to you my warmest congratulations and best wishes."

The remainder of the day was spent in visiting the British Third Army. King George, who as a Naval officer took an interest in gunnery, paid special attention to the artillery, and watched from an observation post the enemy's positions. On the 27th he proceeded to the area of the Second Army, where he saw, among other things, an Australian artillery park and motor-ambulance convoy. Newly arrived contingents of the Canadian Corps, and a mixed brigade composed of detachments from other divisions of the Second Army, were reviewed by him, but a few hours later, when he was inspecting troops representing corps of the First Army, his horse, frightened by the cheers of the men, reared and in falling rolled on to the King's leg. The reviews of an Indian Brigade and the Guards had to be cancelled, and, as the injury was serious, His Majesty was laid up for several days. He was, however, well enough by the beginning of November to return to England, where he gradually recovered from the effects of his accident.

In the second fortnight of November Mr. Redmond crossed the Channel, and paid a visit to various Irish regiments and to King Albert. He was received everywhere with great cordiality.

At some date in November Major Winston Churchill, M.P., who, on the 11th of that month, had resigned his position as Chancellor of the Duchy of Lancaster, appears to have joined the Army in France.

At Christmas the men in the trenches were cheered by the appearance of parties of bluejackets, who had been sent by Sir John Jellicoe to see what their comrades of the sister service were doing. The sailors lent a hand in the fighting.

"Do you think I hit a Hun, sir ?" a petty officer who had been sniping asked a company officer.

"No doubt of that," was the reply.

The sailor produced his note-book, made out a document, certifying the score in legal language, and requested the officer's signature, which was given.

The arrival of the men from the Navy coincided with the departure of the Indian Corps for Mesopotamia. It had amply justified the hopes entertained of it and the measures of Lord Kitchener, whose aim when Commander-in-Chief in India had been to prepare the Indian Army for warfare against Europeans. Before the departure of the Indian Army Corps the Prince of Wales at a parade delivered a message to them from King George. :

"Officers, non-commissioned officers, and men of the Indian Army Corps—

"More than a year ago I summoned you from India to fight for the safety of My Empire and the honour of My pledged word on the battlefields of Belgium and France. The confidence which I then expressed in your

TRENCH RAT-CATCHING.
A French soldier showing his "catch" to his comrade.

sense of duty, your courage, and your chivalry you have since then nobly justified.

"I now require your services in another field of action; but before you leave France I send My dear and gallant son, the Prince of Wales, who has shared with My Armies the dangers and hardships of the campaign, to thank you in My name for your services and to express to you My satisfaction.

"British and Indian comrades-in-arms, yours has been a fellowship in toils and hardships, in courage and endurance often against great odds, in deeds nobly done in days of ever-memorable conflict. In a warfare waged under new conditions, and in peculiarly trying circumstances, you have worthily upheld the honour of the Empire and the great traditions of My Army in India.

"You leave France with a just pride in honourable deeds already achieved and with My assured confidence that your proved valour and experience will contribute to further victories in the new fields of action to which you go.

"I pray God to bless and guard you and to bring you back safely, when the final victory is won, each to his own home—there to be welcomed with honour among his own people."

The French authorities had strained every effort to ameliorate the conditions of their men. Most of the trenches had been paved, and the water in them had been drained into pits from which it was emptied by powerful pumps. The walls of the trenches where necessary were strengthened with hurdle work or revetted with planks to prevent landslides, while bombproof shelters had been provided with earthern roofs kept dry by sheets of zinc. The floors of these had been levelled and covered with planks or straw. In the second line, wooden huts had been run up with double walls, slate roofs and raised floors. In the shelters and huts were often to be found camp beds and plenty of blankets. The huts contained stoves; the trenches and shelters, coal braziers. At night the men's refuges were lit up by acetylene gas lamps or electricity. Furnaces had been constructed to burn refuse, and there was seldom any lack of excellent drinking water. When the weather became cold, hot drinks—coffee and a moderate quantity of alcohol—were served out. The proverbial ingenuity of the French soldier showed itself in a thousand different ways in providing shelter and overcoming the difficulties of the situation. The food was of good quality and, owing to the *cuisines roulantes* (horse-drawn or motor-driven camp kitchens) attached to the corps at the front, usually reached the men in a palatable form. Plenty of warm clothing had been served out; the conspicuous uniforms of the early days of the war had been in nearly all cases replaced by the new horizon-blue tunics and breeches. To keep the feet of the men in the trenches dry, waders and wooden *sabots* had been liberally supplied, and the steel trench helmet protected the head, not only from shrapnel and shell splinters, but also from rain and snow.

Like their British Allies, too, they did their best to provide amusements. Bands were improvised, very often the instruments themselves were of trench construction. Never had the *gaité de coeur* of the French soldier been more in evidence. An indirect result of the war had been to increase the quantity of game in the regions where the fighting was taking place. There was plenty of sport for the men of the Allied armies which relieved the monotony of trench life.

One great drawback was the enormous numbers of rats which made their appearance, and the letters of the combatants are full of complaints at their presence. "You literally walk on top of them," observes a French soldier, writing in November. "They breed and breed and deliver assaults, like the Germans on the Yser, by massed battalions. Like the Boches, too, they are beginning to be tormented by hunger." The rats ate everything which came in their way—motor tyres, surgical packets, clothes, as well as food. Much inventive talent was diverted to discovering new methods for killing rats, and to assist in the war against the vermin whole regiments of dogs were dispatched to the front. On December 12 a correspondent in Paris saw the singular sight of a train with 2,700 dogs leaving for the fighting line.

The French had a large portion of their territory overrun by the hated Germans, they appreciated the hideous crimes committed by them on old men, women and children, but nevertheless they, too, contrived to find means of

TRENCH RATS.

The Rat-catcher, his dog, and their "bag."

"SOMEWHERE IN FRANCE."
A peaceful winter scene.

amusement. Mr. H. Warner Allen, the representative of the British Press with the French armies, introduces us to the interior of a French café in January, 1916 :

The Frenchman takes his gaiety and love of simple enjoyment with him to the trenches, and wherever behind the lines there is a café left something of the animation of the boulevards makes its appearance there, even though it may be brought to an abrupt termination by a German bombardment. I was a day or two ago at the principal café of a certain French military town close behind the lines.

The soldier from the trenches is as fond of games as he is in civil life. Backgammon and bridge occupied a number of tables, while elsewhere two officers were engaged in a desperate game of piquet that was somewhat interfered with by the advice and exhortations of half a dozen other officers. Every now and then one man would shout across the café in tones of astonishment and pleasure at perceiving a friend whom, perhaps, he had not seen since the war began. For this café is a famous meeting-place, and during the present war civilians suddenly converted into soldiers have for a long time lost sight of friends whom they used to meet regularly in their favourite café.

That night there was a great celebration in honour of a young officer who had just received the *Croix de Guerre*. The hotel behind the café had prepared a sumptuous dinner. Songs were sung, and the merriment was kept up till the last moment allowed by the strict military laws concerning closing time. There was a certain simplicity and directness about their rejoicings. Affectations have disappeared before the reality of the war and its primitive conditions. The same amusements are shared by all classes of society alike. I was sitting at a table with two private soldiers, chauffeurs for the time being. One of them drove his own 60-horse motor-car, while the other owns a magnificent private house in the Avenue du Bois de Boulogne. At the next table there was a lieutenant wearing the *Médaille Militaire*, a proof that he had been promoted from the ranks. Of course, they saluted him with the respect due to an officer. In civil life he had been their fencing master.

For the Belgians the situation was a hard one. Nearly the whole of the country was under the heel of the invader, and it was in Belgium that the worst atrocities had been committed. Perhaps nothing brings home to one the poignant plight of the unfortunate people which first flung itself in the path of the German colossus than the story of the creation of the school of Boitshoek on the Yser front. Among the crowds of refugees who had escaped from the German clutches, were three hundred little children, who did not know whether their parents were alive or dead. The villagers of Boitshoek received and fed them, and the soldiers of the Belgian 5th Army Division, out of their scanty pay, provided a fund to build a school for and educate the little waifs. Men who had been school teachers were in the Division, and they devoted their leisure to training the children. This incident speaks

ON THE WAY TO THE FIRING-LINE.
French troops passing through a snow-covered village near their lines.

for itself. The Belgian Army had no large civilian population of its own race to minister to its comforts. Encamped in the flooded Yser district, on the edge of the sea, it was exposed to great discomfort, but the spirit of the troops was not subdued and they awaited the time when they could help to drive their hated foe headlong across the Rhine.

Turning from the Allies to the Germans: the evidence points to the fact that the enemy was at last beginning to feel the pinch of hunger, although the British Government had not enforced the blockade of Germany with sufficient rigour. Vast quantities of food (cocoa, etc.), clothing, and even war materials continued to reach the enemy through neutral countries, and the adhesion of Bulgaria to the Teutonic Powers and the consequent opening up of communications with Turkey slightly relieved the economic pressure. A prisoner captured in February, 1916, on the Flanders front, remarked: "We are nearly always hungry . . . coffee night and morning, a mince at night, no meal in the middle of the day; a piece of bread nine inches long, four inches wide, four inches thick, for three men a day; a piece of sausage perhaps once a week; no other meat; tea occasionally."

Like the Allies, the Germans had greatly improved their trenches and dug-outs, and the special correspondent of the *Vossische Zeitung*, Herr Max Osborn, describes the difference between the German lines in the winter of 1914 and those in the winter of the next year:

What impressed me most forcibly in the position I saw, which is typical of so many others, was the development of trench construction. The few rude planks used at the beginning of the war had entirely disappeared. I remember seeing trenches on the East Prussian frontier in December, 1914, and it is, indeed, amusing to think of what people called trenches then. They were merely primitive attempts, scarcely embryos, and, at the utmost, preliminary experiments. Then came the trenches that were not unlike little culverts, with a protective barrier of wicker-work. Then followed the barbed-wire entanglements. Our engineers have now invented a system of defence works which includes a combination of all the earlier devices. These latest trenches are composed of earth, stakes and netting, which at once make them rigid and ensure the necessary elasticity. These trenches have even become green with newly-grown grass since they were made. You may walk through them and yet remain quite clean—indeed, you may even begin to fancy that the stakes and wire are arranged in such a way as to produce a decorative effect. A roof protects the men from the rain, and if an unusually heavy shower happens to penetrate into the interior the water would be carried away from the gutter by an arrangement of pipes. Innumerable lamps,

A FLOODED SECTION OF THE BELGIAN LINE,
Showing the sandbag breastwork.

taken from motor-cars, provide the necessary light, and there are fans and ventilators and switchboards. All this, remember, is underground. The saps leading to the hearing posts are all provided with the same modern conveniences. As for barbed-wire protection, there is row upon row of barbed wire on the surface, through which one imagines no enemy could conceivably find his way. All these trenches give one the impression that they could hardly be reached either by bombardment or by bombs.

Yet it should be observed that Major Moraht, analysing letters from the front about the same time, told a different tale in the *Berliner Tageblatt :*

In all of them I read determination and see that our brave men have reconciled themselves to the fate of spending a second Christmas in the enemy's country, that their discipline is in no way crumbling, and that the grief at the thought of wife and child at home cannot injure their discipline. But one request I find constantly repeated—that the privations at the front should not be underestimated at home. Superhuman work is still being achieved in the fight against wind, weather and winter. The privations are particularly great in the case of those hundreds of thousands of brain workers whom the German people has sent little by little to the war.

I will not describe in detail what their bodies have to suffer although their hearts remain firm. But in order that we at home may not underestimate their privations and what they have to bear I must agree with the wish that is often expressed that people would not let themselves be deceived by the pretty pictures which now and then find their way into German newspapers as coming from the front. After the bad change in the weather in December our dug-outs really do not look like pleasant Alpine huts, and our trenches do not look like cushioned resting-places. The war against the elements must be carried on by day and night in order merely to maintain the existence of cave-dwellers. There are, no doubt, places at the front where the conditions are more favourable, but they are few. On the Western and Eastern fronts, and on the frontiers of our Allies in the Alps and on the Isonzo the strain upon endurance is greater than it ever was in all the winter campaigns of history.

If Major Moraht's correspondents wrote in the manner of the German prisoner taken in January, 1916, whose letter, published in the *Daily Chronicle*, is quoted below, he had good grounds for the above statements.

My Dear Friend.—

I have been at the front again since Sunday, and am squatting in a deep hole in the ground. I can hardly believe I ever was on leave ; it seems just as if I had had a beautiful dream. But yet it is the hard reality. When I got home they told me you had gone back again only a few days before. I should like to have had a talk with you at home. But Fritz was there from Russia. A little while before he was to have gone back Fritz got a telegram ordering him to report himself at the Ersatz battalion H.Q. I shouldn't mind having his luck.

I suppose the so-called interpellation came up for

discussion in the Reichstag yesterday—the peace interpellation? But I suppose the Imperial Chancellor will again have nothing to say in answer except that the enemy is not yet ready to make peace. And then no doubt he will give them the clap-trap about enemy countries regarding every German offer of peace as a sign of weakness. We should be glad if he would do something else. When will the thirst for blood of individual despots be quenched?

What I see now makes me sick, and I expect you feel the same. A—— and C—— and a whole lot of other Landsturm men have been called up already. So the last line are being stuck into the strait-waistcoat. It looks very desolate and sad at home, the poor devil's cheeks pale and hollow, the children naked. What is this going to lead to? They are sad pictures which horrify one. But there is still no prospect of peace.

How are you? Are you still well? In the meantime, hearty greeting from your friend, D—— E——.

Our brief sketch of the conditions of the armies in the winter of 1915–1916, must not lead the reader to conceive that either side led even a comparatively easy existence. The terrific power of modern explosives and guns, and the use by the enemy of poisonous gas and jets of fire more than counterbalanced the advantage in food, clothes and shelter, which our men possessed. The horrors of the war are graphically depicted by an officer in a cavalry regiment writing in December, 1915:

Recently I was one of a draft of 45 sent up to a place a short way behind the firing line, where I was in closer contact for some days than I had been previously with the sort of conditions these fellows have to put up with. In spite of all they have to face out in this awful war one finds the same cheery, casual spirit dominating them all. Only a few nights ago, long after we were turned in, a lot of them were passing down the road on their way down from the trenches. It was a wretched wet night, and as each platoon floundered knee deep through a sheet of water that flooded the road the humorous side came uppermost in the general uproar and confusion, and in a few moments one heard rising above the splashings a chorus of "Quack, quack, quack," and all the while the poor beggars knew well enough how long it would be before they could get dry again.

But I was telling you of our going up near the line. We were sent up to take over some German prisoners. But not many prisoners were coming in, so we turned over while waiting to police work, and especially to directing drafts and stragglers passing in and out of the trenches to their several units, and wounded on their way to the dressing stations. Heavy attacks were going on at that time.

We were quartered in a small protected "keep" on the outskirts of a village, or what remained of it. The Germans were shelling the place a good deal, and some of our fellows had pretty near shaves from shells falling close to them. Sometimes they would send over a perfectly timed "chain" of shells in quick succession, which sounded like a flight of birds streaming overhead. But beyond general wreckage and some minor casualties they did little serious mischief while we were there. The big shells sound something like a train coming along. I saw one hit the church, carrying away a large part of what remained of the tower. We slept in dug-outs and protected galleries and had a fairly dry berth, but our quarters were cold and draughty, and as for the first two nights we were without blankets or overcoats it was a poor time trying to sleep on the bare ground. We did not know we should be there overnight, so rations were short, too, to start with, which wasn't at all pleasant.

On our last night there a heavy attack broke out. I think the Germans were trying to recover some of their lost ground. I can't imagine anything more absolutely devilish than the effect produced by that sudden outburst of rifle and machine-gun fire and bombing on a still, clear night, and as I stood watching the German shells breaking over our trenches by the light of the star shells, and trying to picture what was going on, perhaps three-quarters of a mile away, I felt keenly it was there I ought to be too, throwing in my small share with those fellows holding our line through that terrible ordeal. After about three-quarters of an hour it died down again, and soon one heard just the occasional rifle shot (almost always going on), here and there interspersed with the smashing reports of our heavy guns firing just behind us.

Then I crawled back again into my hole, feeling my way through the dark, into my blanket, and wondering what some of our people at home would think if they could be dumped down for one hour in that scene of ruin.

It will be seen from the foregoing pages that a great deal had been done to ameliorate the

[*Elliott & Fry.*

LIEUT.-GEN. SIR WILLIAM ROBERTSON,
Chief of the Imperial General Staff.

condition of the men in the trenches, yet it must be remembered that this was more true of those in the supporting trenches than of those in the front line immediately in contact with the Germans. The distance between the hostile lines varied greatly. In some cases the interval between them was sufficiently great to render the passage over the No Man's Land in between so difficult that warning of an attack was certain. In others they were

PERTHES.
Remains of German Positions.

quite close, twenty to fifty yards, and local attacks whether by bombing parties or small assaults were of constant occurrence. The sniper was always on the look out to shoot a man who incautiously showed his head. There were periodical artillery attacks and trench mortars threw their heavy shells. Trenches had to be repaired without ceasing, parapets fell back into them owing to the weather or the explosion of shells. Or the parapet and trench might be successfully mined by the opponent and the whole blown into the air. Then ensued a hand-to-hand fight for the crater, one side or the other made good its footing, and the defeated side had to dig a fresh trench behind it or make a great effort to recover the lost position. In many places the water was so close to the surface or the soil so liquid that no parapet would stand. Then a breastwork of sandbags had to be constructed. This formed a conspicuous target and was constantly demolished by the opponent's artillery and had again to be made good. The weather was bad for a long period, and all the precautions to keep the trenches dry failed; they ran with water in unfavourably situated parts—*i.e.*, in depressed ground—and it was a task of great difficulty to free them. In the firing line, therefore, although distinctly improved from the winter before, the situation can only be described as very trying. In the supporting trenches it was better, and farther back, where the troops assembled after their tour of duty in front, the men were extremely comfortable. They had dry and warm lodgings, warm baths and fresh clean clothes. Compared with the state of affairs in an army of the Napoleonic period, when men did not get proper clothes, adequate food, or proper medical attention, their existence was one of comfort. Then typhus devastated armies, now it was almost unknown.

One last observation before we proceed to deal in detail with the fighting in the air and on and under the earth. The mass of the Germans were far from considering their cause hopeless. Their successes in the East had made them forget the bloody repulses they had suffered in the West. On the other hand, the British, French, and Belgians were confident of victory. The spirit of the British was that of the Buffs as described by Second Lieutenant J. Presnail of the 3rd Royal West Kent Regiment, who visited them at Christmas:

The Buffs are marvellous. Straight from the trenches, their spirits undamped by water, and defiant of gas and shell; feet swollen and sore from immersion in icy water; but thank God, though they may have "trench feet" sometimes, they always have trench hearts. I saw them and expected to find them weary and "down." Not a blessed bit of it. There they sat, on Boxing Day, munching mince-pies, and rubbing white oil into great swollen red things that faintly resembled feet. Some poor boys, whom I called to see, were—alas!—not there. They had not come back. They had done their bit—a man's ending to a man's job.

As for the French: their sentiments were voiced by the heroic General Marchand—the erstwhile African explorer, who had been wounded in the Battle of the Champagne Pouilleuse. "I expect," he wrote to a friend, "to return to the front to take up my command again in six weeks, for, in these days, one has a right to be dead, but not ill." The Belgians led by their noble King, were of a like opinion, and the only fear felt in France was the fear felt by some of the British that a premature and inconclusive peace might be concluded. "What I say is," wrote a British officer to his father on December 7, 1915, "that this war must *not* be finished until it has been carried right into the heart of Germany, so that the German people may know and understand what France, Belgium, Serbia, and Russia have gone through the last fifteen months. . . . Just think of all these poor souls resting happily . . . behind our firing line, thinking that they have done their bit to crush Germany for all time, finding that we are only seeing the show half-through. It's too awful to think of."

In Chapter CIV. the tremendous battle which began on September 25, 1915, in the Champagne Pouilleuse between Auberive on the Suippes and Ville-sur-Tourbe was described. A glance at the map is necessary for the understanding of the position at the beginning of October.* The immediate objective of de Castelnau was the Bazancourt-Challerange-Apremont railway, the most southerly of the railroads connecting the army of von Einem with that of the German Crown Prince which was operating in the northern sector of the Argonne and the region north of Verdun. That railway could be reached by a road through Auberive, by another from St. Hilaire-le-Grand which touched the line at St. Souplet, by a third from Souain to Somme Py, also on the line, by a fourth from Perthes-lez-Hurlus to Somme Py, and by the high road from Ville-sur-Tourbe through Cernay to Vouziers. The Germans had not been dislodged from Auberive nor

* A more detailed map of the German position will be found in Vol. VI, pp. 340-1.

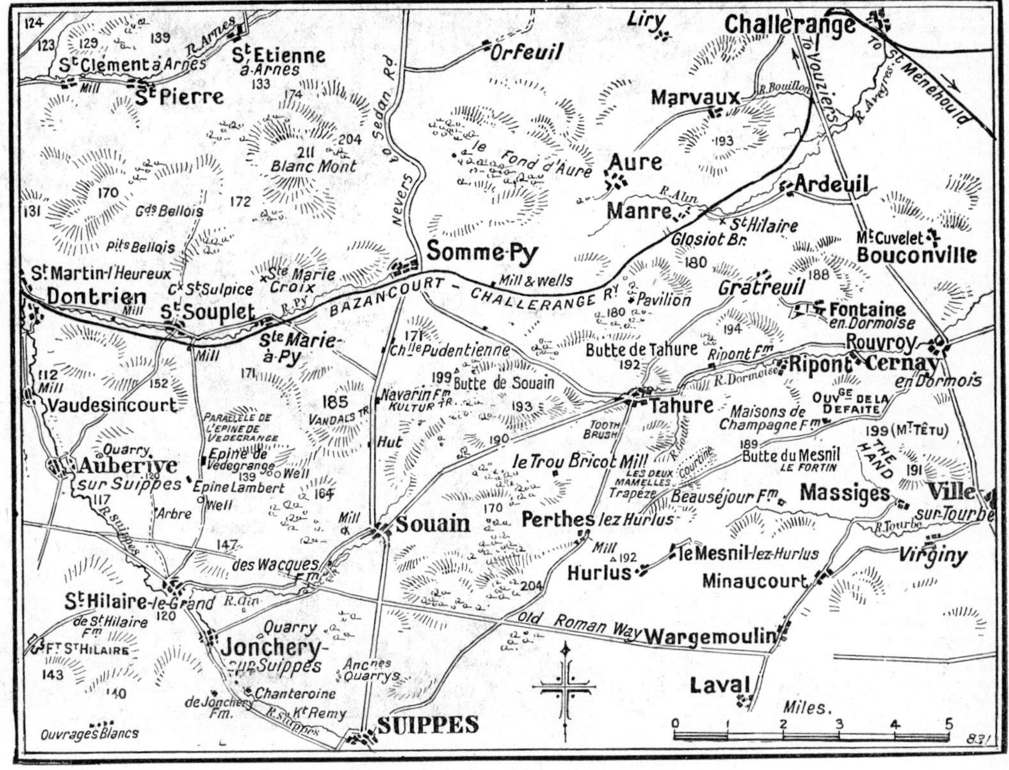

THE CHAMPAGNE FRONT.

Cl
Roundin

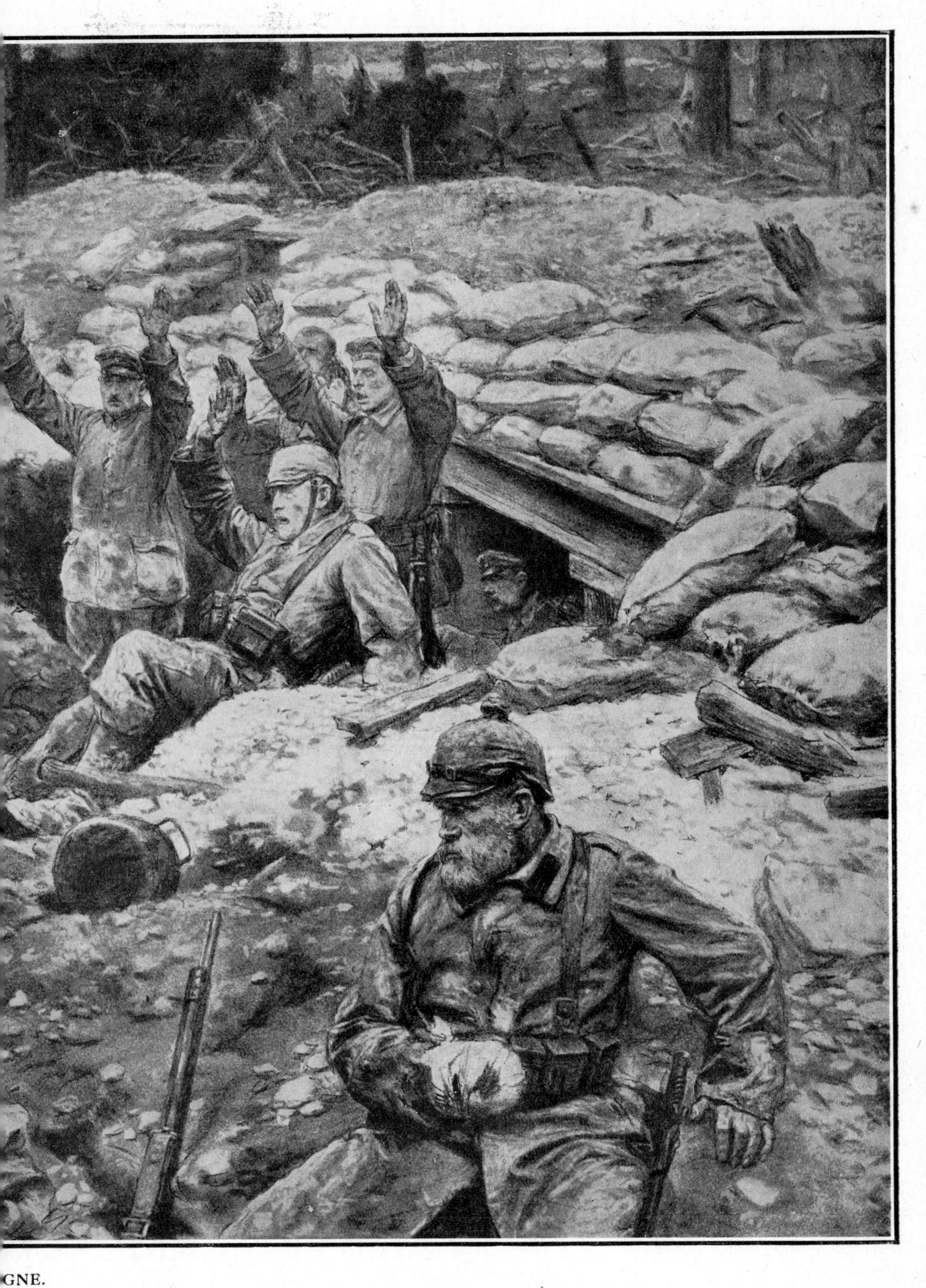

GNE.

rman prisoners.

IN NORTHERN FRANCE.
French Troops being inspected to see whether their respirators are in order.

Cernay, but the French had forced their way up the St. Hilaire-le-Grand-St. Souplet road as far as the Parallèle de l'Épine de Vedegrange, up the Souain-Somme Py road as far as the Navarin Farm on the crest of the downs, and up the Perthes-lez-Hurlus-Somme Py road to the outskirts of Tahure and the foot of the Butte de Tahure. Nearly all the German fortified posts and trenches from the Parallèle de l'Épine de Vedegrange to the environs of Tahure were now in their hands, but the Germans retained the Butte de Tahure, the village of Tahure and a salient southwards terminating in the Trapeze and the Courtine redoubts. East of this salient the French had established themselves at Maisons de Champagne, in the Ouvrage de la Défaite, and on Hill 199 (Mt. Tetu), and they had cleared the enemy from the extraordinarily strong labyrinth-like fortress called "The Hand of Massiges." During October and November the aim of de Castelnau was to straighten his line by driving the enemy out of the salient, at the base of which were the village and knoll of Tahure. The Bazancourt-Challerange railway ran within a mile of the knoll, and its interruption would have been a serious blow to the Germans. To hinder the German reinforcements coming up to strengthen von Einem's army in the Champagne Pouilleuse Castelnau employed his aircraft.

On October 1 the airship *Alsace* crossed the Aisne and bombarded the point where the railway, which from St. Ménéhould skirts the western Ardennes, crosses the Mézières-Reims railroad. The *Alsace* also dropped bombs at the railway station of Attigny on the former line. In spite of being heavily cannonaded, it returned in safety. The next day a squadron of sixty-five aeroplanes bombed the railway station at Vouziers, the aerodromes there, and the station of Challerange, where the Bazancourt-Apremont railway crosses the St. Ménéhould-Vouziers-Attigny-Rethel railway. Considerable damage was done. West of Rethel, near the railway station of Laon, a German train was cut in two by a bomb dropped by a French aeronaut. On the 3rd a French squadron went farther afield, bombing the station, railway bridge, and some military buildings in Luxembourg, while another squadron on the 4th flew over Metz and dropped forty large bombs on the Sablons station. On the 5th a railway station near Péronne was attacked, and on the 10th French aviators released a hundred large bombs on the Bazancourt-Apremont railway itself. Movements of the enemy having been signalled at Bazancourt, on the 13th nineteen French aeroplanes dropped 140 bombs on the railway station there, while others damaged the Bazancourt-Apremont railway at Warmériville, east of Bazancourt.

While the French airmen were operating against the German communications a series of fierce engagements, which in former times would have been dignified with the title of battles, went on in the area between Reims and the Argonne. On September 30 the French had gained ground on the southern side of the Tahure salient and between Mont Tetu and the Ville sur Tourbe-Cernay-Vouziers road. The

Germans had replied by two counter-attacks, which aimed at recovering the Ouvrage de la Défaite, the work north of Mont Tetu. These were defeated with heavy losses. The next day, October 1, the French made some further headway in the vicinity of the St. Hilaire-le-Grand-Saint Souplet road between Épine de Vedegrange and Auberive, capturing some machine-guns and 30 prisoners. The answer of the Germans was a violent cannonade, lachrymatory bombs being employed; but their infantry made no advance. That day in the Tahure salient the northern of the two works known as the Deux Mamelles was seized by our Allies. But the southern fort, called the Trapèze, and the Courtine to the east of the latter, still held out. Counter-attacks of the enemy were beaten off. During these and the succeeding days the artillery on both sides was exceedingly active.

On October 7 the French resumed the offensive, widening their front on both sides of the Souain-Somme-Py road in the neighbourhood of Navarin Farm, and in the eastern section of the battlefield they captured the village of Tahure and the Butte de Tahure behind it.

Round the Navarin Farm the Moroccan troops greatly distinguished themselves. Elements of the German 10th Corps, which had been brought back from Russia, garrisoned the trenches called by the French "The Trench of the Vandals" and "The Trench of Kultur." Isolated by the fire of the French artillery, they had had nothing to drink for four days and their reserve rations had just given out. They had been unable to evacuate their wounded, and the district in which they were fighting was imperfectly known to them and their officers. It is not, then, to be wondered that what remained of the garrison—10 officers and 482 privates—surrendered. The Moroccans pressed forward and surprised a German camp, but machine-guns hidden in the woods brought the advance to a standstill. Counter-attacked, the Africans retired to the "Trench of the Vandals."

Greater success attended the assault on the Butte de Tahure, where since September 28 a Normandy regiment had been digging trenches along the southern slopes. From these trenches a Picardy Division was launched against the summit of the Butte after it had been deluged with high-explosive shells. The artillery preparation is graphically described by Mr. H. Warner Allen:

We came upon the heavy guns that were bombarding the trenches near Tahure behind a precipitous hill, over which their projectiles were flying with a portentous din. The bombardment was not yet at its height and some of the pieces were resting, covered over with tarpaulins, which straggled over the ground as if they were covering gigantic spiders. Others were at work; a battery or two of long Rimailhos 105's (4·1 in.) and 155's (6·1 in.) looking very tall and smart and deadly as they made the ground quiver with their salvoes. The Rimailho is in appearance a gentleman in comparison with the 220 (8·6 in.) howitzers, evil black machines as uncanny and inhuman as Mr. Wells's Martians, which seemed to be hurling their projectiles vertically upwards. The 220's were hard at work, and one after the other in steady succession they vomited out fire and smoke like dwarfed misshapen dragons.

But of all these hideous engines the most hideous and most unnatural was the enormous howitzer. It stood apart from all the lesser monsters in a lair of its own,

A BRITISH TRENCH.

Running from the cellar of a mined house to the firing-line.

and it seemed to move of its own volition. One scarcely noticed the men around it, so insignificant did they seem. When we first saw it it was lying flat like some prehistoric monster waiting for its prey. With the aid of pulleys and a trolley the huge projectile was hauled towards its breach. Then when the breach was closed it seemed to wake up, and without any visible human agency it raised its nose over the edge of the pit in which it lived. It moved slowly upwards until one could have sworn that it was gazing intently into the clouds above the steep hillside before it. The men who had been ministering to it hastily ran aside and left a respectful distance between themselves and the monster. The non-commissioned officer who was to fire the great howitzer, as he stood back on the hillside, seemed no more important than its humblest slave.

There was a silence. Instinctively one stopped one's ears. There was a great roar, a sheet of flame, and a thin mist of fiercely driven smoke. Everything in the valley shook and trembled, while a hut covered with a tarpaulin collapsed entirely as, with a wild bellowing,

MEETING OF THE COUNCIL OF WAR AT THE FRENCH HEADQUARTERS.

Reading from left to right, the front row officers are: General de Castelnau, in charge of the French Armies on the Western Front; Sir Douglas Haig, the British Commander-in-Chief; General Wielemans, the Belgian Army representative; General Gilinsky, the Russian Army representative; General Joffre, the Generalissimo of all the French armies engaged in the war; General Porro, the Italian Army representative; Colonel Pechitch, the Serbian Army representative.

the huge shell tore through the air on its way towards the enemy. Then quietly the gun lowered its nose again and sank back into its pit with a dignified swagger that seemed to say that there was no reason to make any fuss about the matter.

Later on we went up to the hills above, and from there we could get some idea of the havoc that the monsters in the valley below were working. Every now and then the Germans would reply angrily, trying to locate the French trenches in the hillside facing us. Meantime the French were hammering away with a terrible methodical steadiness, tearing the enemy's trenches to pieces and opening a way for their infantry through Tahure to the Butte de Tahure, one of the greatest buttresses of the German second line.

As a result of the combat the summit was occupied by the French and a wedge driven into the second line of the German defences. What was more important, the village of Tahure which lies in a basin south of the Butte was exposed to fire from the north, just as Souchez had been when the summit of the Plateau of Notre Dame-de-Lorette had been taken.

While this fight was going on troops from Brittany and La Vendée had attacked the Toothbrush Wood, in which there were no less than seven German trenches one behind the other up to the crest below which lies Tahure. In the preceding days the French guns had so destroyed the trees that it was now a wood only in name. When the Bretons and Vendéans advanced they found the German trenches choked with corpses among which were numbers of famished and thirsty soldiers who promptly surrendered. From the Butte and the Toothbrush Wood, the French troops poured down into Tahure. The Germans in the village put up a poor resistance and our Allies traversing it dug themselves in 600 yards or so to the east. At 5 p.m. the Germans violently bombarded the lost positions, throwing on them great numbers of asphyxiating bombs, and counter-attacks were vainly directed against the men of Picardy on the summit of the Butte.

The next day the French, from Tahure, pushed south-eastwards up the German communication trenches towards the Butte du Mesnil and captured the Trapèze.

The latter, now exposed to fire from three sides, was connected with the enemy's second line by only a few communication trenches. A mine charged with twenty-two tons of explosives had been sprung which obliterated ninety yards of German trench, and the heaviest projectiles had been rained on the redoubts. For days and nights, the communication trenches also had been bombarded by artillery and enfiladed by machine-guns from the north. When the French penetrated into the earthworks they found that most of the garrison had fled. A couple of hundred prisoners and several machine-guns were taken. During the night of the 9th–10th the enemy attacked the French trenches east of Navarin Farm, and the next day the Butte de Tahure. Both attacks were repulsed with loss. On the 10th, 11th and 12th, the French progressed north-east and south-east of Tahure, on the edge of the Ravine de la Goutte and east of the Trapèze.

The continued successes won by the French caused the Germans to make two vigorous counter-attacks. The first directed against the French line between La Pompelle (one of the old forts protecting Reims) and Prosnes to the west of Auberive, was probably designed to divert the reserves of de Castelnau from the battlefield between Auberive and Ville-sur-Tourbe. If successful, it would have thrown the French back across the Reims-Châlons railway and the Vesle river and canal.

Several divisions drawn from the armies of von Einem and von Heeringen—the army of von Heeringen was to the west of von Einem—were concentrated along the six-and-a-half mile front. On October 18, for three hours, a torrent of shells was poured on the French first line and a curtain of asphyxiating shells was formed between the first and second line. At dawn on Tuesday October 19, when the bombardment was at its height, an immense volume of poisonous gas was discharged from the German cylinders. Behind the gas in four successive lines, separated from each other by about 300 yards, the enemy advanced. The first two lines were mown down by the machine-guns and by the soixante-quinzes. The third line entered the front trench but was bombed out by the defenders. Reinforced by the fourth line, it returned to the attack and gained a foothold in the French position. Before noon, however, fresh troops had arrived to strengthen the defence and by nightfall the Germans were everywhere driven back leaving behind them thousands of dead and wounded.

Undeterred by their losses, at 9 a.m., a similar attack was, on Wednesday the 20th, launched on a front of about five miles round Prunay on the Reims-Châlons railway. As before, vast quantities of shells and poisonous gas were employed by the enemy, but the French were ready for all emergencies. A battalion of the 137th Regiment of Prussian infantry, which managed to cross the railway, was wiped out. At other points, the enemy

THE BUTTE DE SOUAIN.
French Infantry entering a communication trench.

was held up by wire entanglements and mown down. On a stretch of less than a mile more than 1,600 corpses of men belonging to the same regiment were counted.

Between this bloody repulse and the second of the German main counter-attacks there was severe fighting along the Auberive-Ville-sur-Tourbe front. On October 22 a vain effort was made by the Germans to recover the Butte de Tahure. Two days later the French made another inroad into the Tahure salient by taking the Courtine south of Tahure and east of the Trapèze. The Courtine was 1,300 yards long, and on an average 270 yards deep. The four lines of trenches were connected by communication trenches and subterranean tunnels. By nightfall the Courtine was in the possession of the French, who had captured 200 prisoners. The next day, however, the Germans counter-attacked and recovered the centre but not the extremities of the lost work. Up to the 30th desperate fighting continued at this point, while, on October 27, another attack, accompanied by the use of poisonous gas, was made in the Prosnes region, west of Auberive.

On October 30 a desperate effort was made by von Einem to expel the French from the Butte de Tahure, from Tahure, the Courtine and other points between the Souain-Somme Py road and the Ville-sur-Tourbe-Cernay-Vouziers causeway. A copy of the Order issued by Count Schwerin commanding the 7th Division, marked "Secret. Not to be taken to the advanced lines," was captured on a German officer who had disobeyed this admonition. According to Count Schwerin not only was the Butte de Tahure to be carried but also the village of Tahure, Toothbrush Wood, the northern of the Deux Mamelles, and the Trapèze. The storming of a point in Toothbrush Wood, it was stated, would be decisive.

The orders given to the German gunners were "to engage the enemy's guns and destroy completely the positions to be attacked by an intense bombardment of several hours. . . . Our artillery in great force and a quite exceptional number of Meinenwerfer," added Count Schwerin, "will play on the enemy's lines from 11 a.m. to 4 p.m." If the weather were favourable, asphyxiating gas was to be used. The German infantry was to advance in five waves one behind the other. The Butte de Tahure was to be attacked from the north and the west. When it was carried the village

CAPTURED FROM THE GERMANS.

Transporting an Armoured Turret for a light gun to the French Lines.

was to be assaulted. A brigade was told off to retake Toothbrush Wood. The Order was illustrated by a map on which the points where the Germans were to dig themselves in were carefully marked. But Count Schwerin's programme could not be carried out in anything like its entirety, and proved, indeed, a failure.

On October 30 the Germans, attacking from a point on Hill 193 round the Butte de Tahure to the Courtine, were only successful at one spot—viz., the Butte de Tahure, where they claimed to have captured 21 officers and 1,215 men. Elsewhere they were driven back and suffered enormously from the fire of the French field-guns and mitrailleuses. On a German prisoner was found the following letter, which deserves to be quoted because of its psychological interest:

Condé, 26th October, 1915.

Dear Parents, Dear Brothers and Sisters.

I am still well, and hope it is the same with you. But in the next few days terrible events will happen, and who knows if we will come out of them safe and sound ? Things will not go here as simply as in Russia. We can see that already. These lines, therefore, will carry you my last farewell if fate should decide against me.

May you for many years continue in good health and peace. I do not die for the ideas that heroes in slippers call love of the Fatherland. I shall be one more victim of this lamentable madness that has seized upon all the peoples.

I have often dreamed of a new kingdom in which all the nations would be fraternally united, and there would be no more racial differences ; in which there would be one kingdom and one people such as that for which in times of peace the Social Democrats had prepared the way, but which in this war is shown, alas ! to be unrealizable.

I hoped to become a party leader, the editor of a great journal, to contribute towards the gathering of the different peoples in an ideal community. That was my aspiration ; I was still young, and I had educated myself in that direction.

Now this terrible war has been unchained, fomented by a few men, who are sending their subjects, their slaves rather, to the battlefield to slay each other like animals. For this war has horribly degenerated—hand-grenades, mines, and, what is worst of all, asphyxiating shells, gases, and chlorine, are now the chief weapons in close fighting.

I should like to go toward to those they call our enemies and say to them : " Brothers, let us fight together ; the enemy is behind us." Yes, since I have been wearing this uniform I do not feel any hatred toward those who are in front ; but my hatred has grown against those who have power in their hands.

We Germans wish to be at the head of the nations ; are we more advanced than a thousand years ago ? We have invented the most murderous weapons ; even the terrible attacks by means of chlorine were first made by us. It is very possible I shall not return from the coming engagement ; but for all those who do return it should be a sacred aim to avenge themselves on the small number of those who have on their conscience hundreds of thousands of human lives.*

The next day, October 31, preceded by volleys of suffocating bombs, four more attacks were delivered. At 6 a.m. one was directed against the eastern extremity of the Courtine, the second at noon against Tahure, the third two hours later on the Toothbrush Wood, and the fourth at 4 p.m. against the

*Published by the *Daily Chronicle*.

A BRITISH BATTERY AT THE FRONT.

An order arrives by telephone ; a soldier repeats it loudly ; the Officer unfolds his map hurriedly and gives the order "Tell the observer we will fire on X,"

southern crests of the Butte de Tahure. All were defeated by artillery, machine-gun, and rifle fire. Great numbers of the enemy were killed or wounded and 356 unwounded prisoners, including three officers, were captured. The next day, the Germans could not be brought to face the French fire in this part of the field. They then turned their attention to the French position north of "The Hand of Massiges," assaulting Mont Tetu, the highest point of the Plateau of Massiges. During November 3, 4, and 5 the fighting continued round Mont Tetu, but the Germans were unable to storm the hill in spite of their use of liquid fire. On the last date bodies of Germans with grenades and "Flammenwerfer" tried unavailingly to wrest the Courtine from the French, and on November 10 the enemy, after a furious bombardment, failed again to eject the French from their trenches on the southern slopes of the Butte de Tahure.

If we except the German success in regaining the summit of the Butte de Tahure, the costly operations of the enemy during October and November had been ineffective. From November 11 there was a lull in the fighting, broken by an indecisive combat on December 7 east of Auberive and another on Hill 193. At the beginning of December General Gouraud, "the lion of the Argonne," who had been wounded in Gallipoli, was given the command of an army in the Champagne district. On December 27 the Germans, who were beginning to feel the continual pressure of the French on their salient between Tahure and Maisons de Champagne, began a series of attacks west of Tahure towards Hill 193. These attacks were the preliminary to a serious offensive in which at least three German Divisions were employed from the region of the Courtine at the southern end of the salient to Mont Tetu. Asphyxiating gas shells were lavishly used, and the enemy descended from the Butte de Tahure and advanced from Ripont and from his trenches in the neighbourhood of Maisons de Champagne and Mont Tetu. Except in a small rectangle west of Maisons de Champagne, he gained no foothold in the French line.

Between this date and the opening of the Battle of Verdun on February 21 the events in the Champagne Pouilleuse call for little comment. It may be mentioned, however, that on February 5 the French guns, while cannonading the Navarin Plateau, blew up several ammunition depôts, and demolished reservoirs of asphyxiating gas, quantities of which were driven by the wind on to the German lines—a good example of poetic justice. There was also some severe grenade fighting round the Butte du Mesnil and Tahure from February 10 to 15.

The aftermath of the Battle of Vimy was almost as full of incident as that of the Battle of the Champagne Pouilleuse. As the loss of the Vimy heights would have entailed that of Lens and thus enable the British 1st and the French 10th Army to descend into the plain of the Scheldt, it is not a matter of wonder that the Crown Prince of Bavaria clung desperately

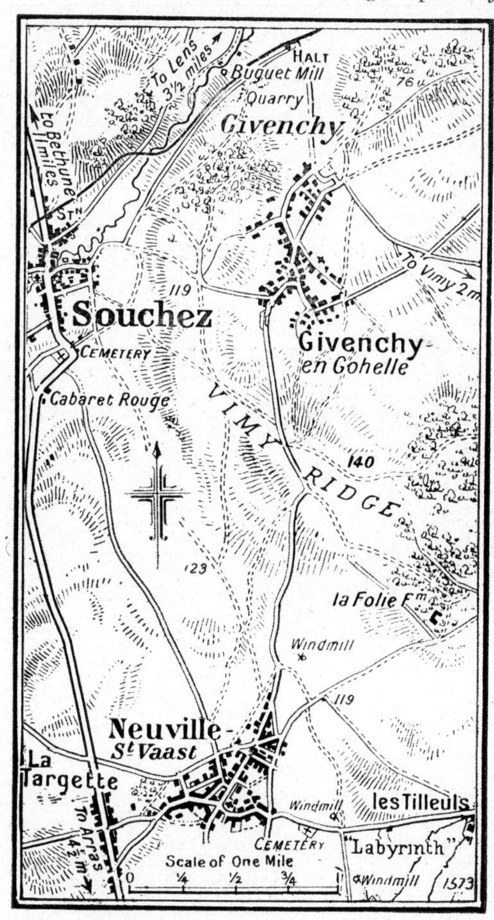

to the trenches and redoubts east of Souchez and Neuville St. Vaast. On October 16 the Germans attempted to recover the Bois-en-Hache, north-east of Souchez. The struggle continued for several days, but the French maintained their position, and on October 21 they repulsed an attack in the Givenchy Wood. On October 23 the French redoubt and advanced posts in the neighbourhood of Hill 140 were assaulted. The Germans lost heavily, and achieved no success. On October 27, by means of mines, the French wrecked the trenches and barbed wire entanglements near

ON THE WESTERN FRONT.

Inspection of French Colonial troops. A scene during the first snap of winter, November, 1915.

the Lille-Arras road, south-east of Neuville St. Vaast, and occupied the craters created by the mines. On October 30 there were several combats in the Bois-en-Hache, near Hill 140, and east of the Labyrinth. If the Germans are to be believed, the Bavarians took 200 prisoners and captured four machine-guns and three trench mortars. At the beginning of November the Germans admit that they evacuated a small salient north-east of Souchez. More fighting occurred on November 10 in the Givenchy Wood, and on November 14 round the Labyrinth. Throughout the remainder of November and also in December the struggle in this region was continued almost daily. In the last week of January, 1916, the enemy commenced a determined offensive, probably with the aim of attracting the attention of Joffre and Castelnau away from Verdun. On January 23, after a violent bombardment and the explosion of mines, the Germans stormed several hundred yards of the first-line French trench in the region of Neuville St. Vaast and got as far as the supporting trench. Counter-attacks, however, broke the efforts of the enemy, and dislodged him from most of the ground which he had carried. Two more attacks by the Germans on January 24 were unsuccessful. On January 25, preceded by mine explosions and heavy shelling, the Germans attacked the French front in the angle formed by the Arras-Lens road and the Neuville St. Vaast-Thélus road. Their gains were trifling, and the next day they were expelled from the craters caused by the explosion of the mines. Other German mines were exploded that day in the vicinity of the La Folie road. On January 28, west of Hill 140, more mines were fired by the enemy, who gained a footing in some parts of the French advance trenches. Simultaneously the French positions near the Neuville St. Vaast-La Folie road, those to the north of Roclincourt and on the road from St. Laurent to St. Nicholas, north-east of Arras, were attacked, while Arras itself, and the trenches south of the town, were fiercely bombarded. The fighting went on into February, the Germans, as was to be expected, claiming to have been successful. On February 13, at four different points, the Bavarians advanced between Hill 140 and the Neuville St. Vaast-La Folie road, but were beaten off by artillery and infantry fire and counter-attacks. The net result of the winter engagements on the Vimy heights must have been disappointing to the Crown Prince of Bavaria, who had made very little if any progress.

In Alsace there was no cessation of the struggle. On October 15 the enemy hailed shells of all calibres and heavy bombs on a front of four miles between the Rehfelsen, the Hartmannsweilerkopf and Sidelkopf, and the French position at this point was violently assaulted by the German infantry. The attack was repulsed at almost all points, but the enemy succeeded in reoccupying the summit of the Hartmannsweilerkopf. Shortly after there was a fierce struggle for the heights of the Linge and Barrenkopf, and the Germans were again expelled from the summit of the Hartmannsweilerkopf. North of the Col du

Bonhomme, at La Chapelotte and Le Violu, there were lively engagements on November 6, 7 and 8. On December 3 Thann was bombarded by the Germans. Towards the end of the month the French pushed down the eastern slope of the Hartmannsweilerkopf, taking 1,200 prisoners. The Germans promptly counter-attacked and recovered a portion of the lost ground. The Germans claim to have taken twenty-three officers and 1,530 men. This statement was probably false. For in the action of December 21 the German Higher Command alleged that their total losses had not exceeded 1,100, but Mr. H. Warner Allen himself saw 21 officers and 1,360 non-commissioned officers and rank and file who had been captured in the engagement pass before the General commanding the Army of the Vosges. Although figures furnished by the Germans are hopelessly unreliable, still that the engagement was of a desperate nature may be gathered from the notes of a *Times* correspondent at Delémont, who observed that the artillery fire in the Alsace region had been far heavier and more continuous than at any time since the war began. "It was heard," he added, "at places in Switzerland 30 miles from the frontier, and considerably farther from the scene of action."

The German troops in Alsace had been heavily reinforced, especially with heavy artillery, and it was rumoured (untruly) that Marshal Mackensen had arrived and that an effort was to be made to capture Belfort. An army corps, it was believed, had been transported to the north of the Sundgau from the Russian frontier. But as events subsequently showed, the Kaiser had decided to make his real offensive against Verdun. A feint in the direction of Belfort would be a means of drawing the French reserves away from the fortified area before which the Germans were accumulating their reserves of men, guns and munitions. To guard against the contingency the French constructed a series of formidable entrenchments along the frontier from Ffetterhausen to Delle and from Delle to the river Doubs. Whether any reserves were shifted to the Belfort region is not at present known.

On December 28 and 29 the French, notwithstanding violent counter-attacks by the enemy, made further progress in the region of the Hartmannsweilerkopf, capturing German works between the Rehfelsen and the Hirzstein. On January 2, however, they were driven back on a front of about 220 yards to trenches on the western edge of the ravine to the south of the Rehfelsen, and on January 9 the Germans, after several fruitless attacks, succeeded in taking possession of a little hill to the north of the summit of the Hirzstein. The Germans claim to have taken 20 officers, 1,083 Chasseurs, and 15 machine-guns. On January 24 some bombs were thrown by the Germans east of

THE MAIN ROAD FROM BÉTHUNE TO ARRAS.

JOURNALISTS AT THE FRENCH FRONT LISTENING TO EXPLANATIONS OF A FRENCH STAFF OFFICER.

Belfort. The French about this date suffered a heavy loss, General Serret dying of wounds received in the fighting on the Hartmannsweilerkopf. He had been Military Attaché in Berlin before the war. He had fought on the Somme and in Belgium, and was known to his soldiers as "the man of the Hartmannsweilerkopf." Mr. Rudyard Kipling, in his articles on "France at War," called him the "Governor of Alsace." According to Mr. Kipling, "except for his medals, there was nothing about General Serret to show that he was not English. He might have come straight from an Indian frontier command." In the afternoon of February 8 a German long-range gun, probably a 15-inch naval gun, fired three shells into Belfort and its suburbs. Some time before a gun of the same calibre had bombarded Nancy. Seven more shells were thrown into Belfort the next day, and this quite useless bombardment was continued on February 10 and 11. As in the case of the shelling of Dunkirk, recorded in a previous chapter, no military object was obtained by the waste of ammunition.

The moment when the German Crown Prince was to launch his great offensive against Verdun was now approaching, and on February 13 the Germans began a demonstration in the direction of Belfort, apparently under the direction of the Crown Prince, whose journey to Alsace was probably made to throw dust in the eyes of the French. Their trenches east of Sept, south-west of Altkirch, were threatened, and on February 18, after an intense artillery preparation, the French position north-east of Sept was vainly assaulted.

Of the fighting on the coast and on the banks of the Yser there is little to record. The Allied warships appear to have bombarded Zeebrugge on October 17. The night before, the Germans had attacked the French in the region of Dixmude and captured some trenches from which they were driven out at dawn. From the *communiqués* we learn that there was a great deal of reciprocal cannonading during October and November round Lombartzyde. On or about November 20 our monitors were firing at the coast batteries in the dunes near Westende. At the beginning of December the enemy surprised a French outpost between Lombartzyde and Nieuport, but the post was retaken on December 3. About this date the Belgians reinundated the Yser district and forced the Germans to abandon a considerable number of their advanced works. On the 10th British warships destroyed the wire entanglements which had been erected along the coast to prevent the Allies landing. A week later there was grenade fighting in the dunes, and on December 19 the Germans state that our monitors were again shelling Westende. The monitors repeated the operation on December 27 or 28. At the end of January, 1916, the Germans made an effort to take Nieuport. On that town and the Allied trenches no less than 20,000 shells were discharged on the 24th, but the German infantry were stopped by curtain fire of our artillery. On the 27th our monitors again bombarded the Westende region.

Between Dixmude and Ypres there were in the same period a considerable number of small engagements, which, however, led to no appreciable change in the positions of the contending armies.

It will be recollected that at the Second Battle of Ypres the Germans, assisted by poisonous gas, had forced their way across the Yperlee Canal in the neighbourhood of Boesinghe. They had been driven back to the right bank by General Putz. Boesinghe was now the point where the French army in Belgium, commanded by General Hely d'Oissel, joined on to the British Second Army. The German Higher Command appears to have considered that

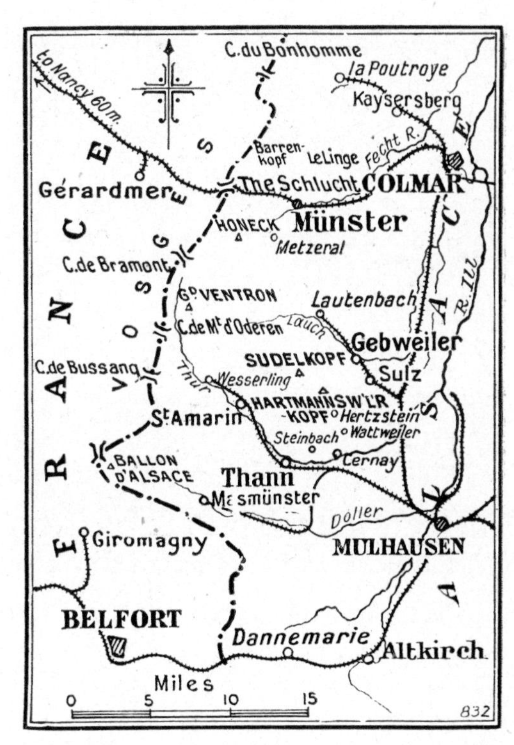

offensives against the point where the wings of armies of different nationalities met were likely to succeed, and the activities of the enemy therefore, for a time, centred round Boesinghe. Thus on November 7 we learn from a *communiqué* there was "a particularly active fight

IN THE SABOT WOODS, CHAMPAGNE.

A depôt used by the French for filling sandbags.

SECOND LIEUT. B. J. MACKLIN.
Awarded the Military Cross.

CAPTAIN M. McBEAN BELL IRVING.
Awarded the Distinguished Service Order.

with trench engines in the region of Het Sast and Boesinghe." Again, on February 12, several attempts were made by the enemy to cross the canal near Het Sast and Steenstraate. The attempts failed under the combined fire of the Allied artillery and machine-guns. On February 20 another effort, equally unsuccessful, was made at Steenstraate, and the enemy seized an unimportant point in the British line south-east of Boesinghe. Throughout the winter months the Allied guns were constantly employed in destroying the redoubts and trenches of the enemy in this neighbourhood.

With regard to the British Second and First armies which filled the gap from Boesinghe to Loos no offensive on a large scale followed the Battle of Loos and the holding battles which had accompanied it. There were, however, plenty of artillery duels, mining operations and small infantry actions which afforded opportunities to the various arms of the New Army to complete their training for the battles intended to be delivered in the spring or summer of 1916.

The artillery had now an abundance of shells. Previously a heavy bombardment by the British guns had almost always been the preliminary of an infantry attack. "We always know," said a German prisoner, "that when you begin a bombardment you're going to attack." That was no longer the case, and the enemy were kept on tenterhooks by heavy cannonading which might or might not indicate an infantry offensive. An eye-witness writing in November relates how an artillery brigade "removed some hundred yards of the enemy's trench from the map and the barbed wire in front of it," and how the Germans who had prepared to meet the rush of our oncoming men with machine-gun fire were deceived. "They will have," he said, "to re-dig their trench, to replace innumerable sandbags and thousands of yards of barbed wire under the unsleeping British eye and the surveillance of the guns that did them all the mischief." It is obvious that, apart from the damage inflicted on the Germans and the wear and tear to the brains of the German Staff officers, the bombardments were of inestimable value to the civilians who had been suddenly turned into artillerymen. One of the weak points in the New Army was its artillery. Gunners cannot be trained in a few days, but able here frequently to handle their pieces in actual warfare the improvised artillerymen rapidly became proficient. Two examples of the conditions under which they performed their duties may help the reader to realize how different was the training which they received from that which they would have received in time of peace. At Ypres on October 29, 1915, a temporary shell and cartridge magazine was struck by a German missile which ignited a box of cordite, causing a severe outbreak of fire. Acting Bombardier W. Rooney, of the 6th Brigade Ammunition Column, Royal Garrison Artillery, entered the burning magazine and brought out the remaining boxes of cordite, which were already catching fire, and the only 6-inch lyddite shell which was in the magazine at the time. On November 13, 1915,

LIEUT. G. S. M. INSALL.
Awarded the Victoria Cross.

LIEUT. J. R. McILLREE.
Awarded the Distinguished Service Order.

at Hooge, Corporal W. A. Flack, of the 27th Trench Mortar Battery, Royal Garrison Artillery, unscrewed a burning fuse from a 50-pound bomb which had fallen back into the bore of the gun owing to a misfire. The unscrewed fuse exploded as he threw it from him.

The engineers of the New Army had, like other arms, a good deal to learn, though many recruits had in civil life performed work analogous to that which they were now called upon to do. This was specially the case with the tunnelling companies largely composed of coal miners. The dangerous character of their tasks may be gathered from the following examples. On October 20 Private G. Walsh, of the 2nd Battalion Lancashire Fusiliers, attached to the 178th Tunnelling Company Royal Engineers, after the enemy had exploded a mine, went with two other men to rescue three comrades from a gallery filled with foul gas. He then made two explorations in workings which were in a very dangerous condition, and, when one of his companions was badly burned and gassed in a gallery, brought him safely to the surface. On November 10, 1915, one of our galleries, south-east of Ypres, struck an enemy gallery. Two officers, Second Lieutenant Brisco and Second Lieutenant Arthur Hibbert, entered the German gallery to investigate, Lieutenant Brisco going to the left and Lieutenant Hibbert to the right. After advancing some eighty yards, Lieutenant Brisco saw Germans at work and shot one of them with his revolver. The rest fired at him and he was forced to retire. He rejoined Lieutenant Hibbert and kept the enemy off while the latter fetched sandbags and explosives. Together they placed and exploded a charge and thus forestalled the enemy. Near Armentières, on the night of December 15–16, Lieutenant James Duncan Shepherd led a demolition party into a German trench in order to destroy mine-shafts. He could not find them, but he laid a charge and destroyed a machine-gun ensconced in a steel cupola. On December 23, 1915, near Frelinghein, a charge placed by our miners in a German gallery in order to destroy it had only partially exploded. The explosion warned the enemy, but Second Lieutenant George Fraser Fitzgerald Eagar guarded the entrance to the German gallery and shot a German while the second charge was being prepared. Another officer describes a mining operation in which he took part:

It was very interesting blowing up the mine. We waited in the early dawn during those few minutes before it went up. Here and there a sniper's rifle spoke, but elsewhere all was still. A whispered order and the men filed silently away from the part that was opposite the mine. At last everybody was at his post and nothing remained to be done except to wait and watch. Far under the ground an officer was attaching the fuse. Above him the Germans were moving in their trenches. There was no time to lose.

In the trenches the men still stood to their posts. Every few minutes we consulted our watches. Two minutes more—one minute—thirty seconds—ten, five, four, three, two—crum-boom-boom! A mass of earth and flame shot 60 feet up. Immediately all was movement. The bombers hurried to their saps; working parties started digging away earth which the shock had caused to fall in our own trenches, and officers gave orders.

We expected to get a shelling for it, but the extraordinary thing was that nothing happened at all for about an hour, and then they went to fortify the crater

THROUGH THE COMMUNICATION TRENCHES IN THE SABOT WOODS.

French troops on their way to relieve their comrades in the firing line.

(we weren't meant to occupy the thing, as it was right in their lines). Our machine-guns got a good many of them as they ran to it, and from one of our saps, which went to within ten yards of it, a sniper got several of them.

Our sappers were awfully pleased about it, because they had started mining after the Germans, so they bored this gallery out and blew it up, thus neutralizing all the German mines in the vicinity. It was a very close thing—the sapper officer told me.

In the Ypres salient the most important event was the German attack with gas on December 19. For the novel and abominable device of poisonous gas the Allied troops in the front trenches had always to be prepared. This was especially the case in salients—a wind blowing against either face was equally effective; and even if the Germans had not sufficient gas cylinders to line the whole of their front, they could be shifted to act against one side or the other as the wind changed. On this occasion news had reached the staff of the British Second Army that the Germans were about to repeat their gas experiments. An order was, therefore, circulated among the troops that smoke helmets were to be carried day and night, and that the goggles protecting the eyes against the fumes from lachrymatory shells were to be ready.

During Saturday (December 18) the wind blew steadily from the east-north-east. At sunset it dropped to a light breeze. Anticipating an attack the next day, our artillery directed a heavy fire on the points where it might be expected that the enemy's troops were massed. The German guns replied, but many of their shells, plunging into ground softened by the rain of the previous days, did not burst. The dawn of December 19 was cold and misty, which held the heavy gas down to earth and kept it from diffusing. Suddenly our men sniffed an odour like lilac. The Germans were firing lachrymatory shells. Hastily goggles were adjusted. When the cannonading was at its height a hissing was heard in the direction of the Ypres-Poelcappelle road. The gas cylinders on the north-east of the salient were being turned on. A wall of grey-green vapour some seven feet high, the smell of which could be eventually detected miles behind our lines, began slowly but steadily to move towards the British trenches. Instantly the smoke helmets were donned, and shrapnel and high-explosive shells were pumped by our artillery into the foul-smelling fog. Shrieks of wounded and dying men proclaimed that in, or behind it, masses of the enemy were making for our lines. The British, to some of whom a gas attack was a novelty, leant forward on the parapets, peeping through the eye-pieces of their helmets. A few moments later lines of gas-masked Germans, some with bombs in their hands, others with fixed bayonets, were dimly visible. They advanced, as usual, at a lumbering trot, and, in the picturesque phrase of an eye-witness, looked like "giant toads from some batrachian inferno." This spectacle was almost instantly replaced by another even more gruesome. Our machine guns and rifles had spoken and the ground was covered with corpses and with dying or wounded men. "All that was left of the vaunted attack," the same eye-witness relates, "was represented by what looked like . . . bundles of rags littering the plain." As the poisonous fog cleared our men perceived here and there a German in his uncanny headgear crawling back on his hands and knees. The sight aroused no pity. Since the Germans had taken to the use of poisonous gas and liquid fire, the temper of the British had risen. "Kill every Boche you can!" was now the slogan of the trenches.

The gas attack had failed. It was followed by a combat between opposing airmen in the clear, blue, frosty atmosphere and by incessant cannonading which lasted well into the day. To quote the British Report, "there were forty-four combats in the air. Two of the enemy's airplanes were brought down behind their lines, and others were driven down, apparently in a damaged condition." Captain Malcolm McBean Bell-Irving, R.F.A., between Lille and Ypres engaged three hostile machines. The first he drove off, the second he sent to the ground in flames, and the third nose-dived and disappeared. Upon him three other machines, possibly Fokkers, descended. He escaped them and flew off to Ypres, chasing a hostile aeroplane; but, when within a hundred yards of it, was wounded by a shell and had to return. For these fine performances he received the D.S.O.

After their discomfiture on December 19 there was a lull in the struggle for the Ypres salient but on February 11, perhaps as a feint to draw off attention from the Verdun district, the enemy resumed the offensive. At 3 a.m. on that day he bombarded the trenches east of Boesinghe, and there was some indecisive trench-fighting. The bombardment was renewed on a more extensive scale the next day but no serious infantry attack followed. On the 13th the Hooge end of the salient received

A LONELY SENTRY.
Guarding a road in Northern France.

5,000 shells and at night the Germans destroyed by mines the famous "International Trench," which ran south of Hill 60 between the Ypres-Comines canal and railway. On Monday they took possession of the site of this trench and were shelled and bombed in it until March 2, when, as will be described in a later chapter, it was retaken from them.

South of Ypres to Loos there were in the winter months a succession of incidents in which individual British officers and men won well-merited honour. For example, on the night of November 16–17 a detachment of the 7th Canadian Infantry Battalion south of Messines executed a surprise attack, designed by Lieutenant-Colonel Victor Wentworth Odlum, which was so skilfully conducted that General Joffre is reported to have circulated an account of it among the French armies in order that it might be treated as a model for similar operations. Though the moon was shining brightly, Private J. Berry, Corporals Babcock, H. Odlum and K. Weir, and Sergeants W. C. Meyerstein and H. Ashby, under the superintendence of Lieutenant William Dumbledon Holmes, worked for four hours cutting lanes through wire entanglements. They then placed a bridge over the little river Douve, about 16 yards from the parapet of a heavily manned German trench. Guided by these brave men, bombing parties slipped past the German sentries into the trench where they bombed or bayonetted a considerable number of the enemy. With the loss of only one man, who was killed accidentally, they returned, driving a dozen prisoners before them. Lieutenant John Raymond McIllree had thrown down the first German he met and felled the second with his rifle and Captain Charles Telford Costigan, of the 10th Canadian Infantry Battalion, who accompanied the party, had shot with his revolver three Germans. The last man to leave the trench was Lieutenant Archibald Wrightson, who displayed great coolness and judgment, as had done Corporal A. K. Curry. Just as the party was coming back Germans were heard approaching on the left. An officer promptly ran back to the nearest traverse and threw over it four bombs, one after the other, as fast as he could pull out the safety pins. Four deafening explosions followed, and the Canadians returned unmolested across the Douve and through the lanes in the barbed-wire entanglements to their own trenches.

The Canadians were not the only British troops to indulge in these exploits. An artillery officer in a letter to his wife, published by the *Morning Post*, writes:

It will comfort you a little for the rather doleful news from the Balkans if you'd been "Somewhere in France" this morning to see a company of a new regiment from the hearty, wholesome West of England come back after a jolly little raid on the Huns' trenches.

A company of the —— regiment was entrusted with the task of harassing the Hun. Without preliminary advertisement of an artillery bombardment, but with warning to the artillery who were to have a share in the good work at its second stage, our men, one hundred and twenty strong, slipped silently over our parapet and made for the German trench. They had means (which I had better not specify) to deal with the German wire, and these means proved quite efficacious. No German patrols were encountered. The first news the Germans had of our arrival was when an officer appeared over their parapet and shot down a German non-commissioned officer with his revolver. Then like a huge Rugby rush on the ball, the English soldiers were over the German parapet, their colonel (who, by the way, had been begged not to go with them, but insisted) at their head, shouting gaily, cheering, shooting. The Huns would not make a fight of it. Most of them scurried away like frightened rabbits to the communication trenches. Others threw up their hands, calling out "*Kamerad.*" A German officer, who showed fight, was struck down by a loaded bomb stick—his skull crushed in. Whilst the prisoners were being secured the English company divided up. Some bombed the communication trenches, others "made hay" of the German firing trench, cutting the wires, destroying the dug-outs, looting the war *matériel.*

After twenty minutes, the allotted time, the company started back for their own trench. They had twelve prisoners, a German Maxim-gun, two bags of German bombs, and some other booty. They had not sustained a single casualty and had left dead in the trench a number of Germans, variously estimated at from 20 to 48. As soon as our infantry had left the German firing trench our artillery opened fire on the German communication trenches where the fugitives had taken refuge. It was at this time, probably, that the chief slaughter of the enemy took place. They were "rattled" and in flight. Presumably the German reserves were being rushed up, and we hope that both parties met around about the points where we were raining high explosives and shrapnel from a score of batteries at the rate of one hundred shells a minute.

The Germans at this stage, 25 minutes after our men had crossed the parapet, woke up, and their artillery began a heavy bombardment of our firing trench and communication trenches. From this fire we had three killed, mainly because one of the German prisoners became obstreperous and delayed the passing of our men at a certain point. That was practically the whole cost of the enterprise. The German prisoners, when they learned that they were not to be shot—the German officers tell their men that the British always shoot prisoners—were unfeignedly glad to be captured. Probably they will be usefully communicative when they come to be examined. One prisoner was a youth of seventeen. He had been two days at the front when he was thus taken prisoner.

Now, I don't suggest that this was a great victory and that London or even a certain West Country town should be flagged. But it was a happy little incident. And it is cheering to find that when all this deadly mechanical trickery of war can be swept aside, and the Englishman meets the German as man to man, the German scurries away, and does not make any pretence of equality.

The exploit of an officer in the Wiltshire Regiment performed in or near Ploegsteert Wood south of Messines, also gives an idea of the courage and initiative displayed by men from the West Country. Second Lieutenant Bernard James Macklin on the night of December 6–7, 1915, previous to a surprise attack took three men out to cut wire. Finding six yards of water in front of the wire, he crawled through it—the month was December—and cut a lane through four rows of wire. A German listening post approached to within a few yards of him. Half frozen, he remained watching the listeners for nearly an hour. He then crawled back and made his report. The Military Cross was his reward. Lack of space precludes doing justice to hundreds of other performances no less deserving of mention.

South of Arras the British 3rd Army held the line to a point close to the Somme. Little has transpired of the fighting in this section. From the notices in which the actions of individual soldiers have been recorded by the War Office we catch, however, some glimpses of the work performed by our men. For example, at Gommercourt, between Arras and Hébuterne, on the night of November 25–26, during a bomb attack against the German trenches, Lance-Corporal H. W. Moore, of the 1/6th Battalion Gloucestershire Regiment, T.F., showed great bravery in entering shelters full of the enemy and clearing them with his grenades. When he had no more missiles left he fought his way with his fists through a group of Germans. On the same occasion Lieutenant Jasper M. C. Badgley, of the same regiment, cut through two lines of wire entanglements, and Second Lieutenant T. T. Pryce, with an assaulting column, succeeded in entering the German trenches unobserved, cleared the enemy from them, and bombed numbers crowded in deep dug-outs. Again, on December 1, the Germans near Mametz exploded a mine which partly destroyed one of our galleries, whereupon Sergeant J. Dunbabin, of the 1st Battalion Norfolk Regiment, led up his grenadiers to repel an attack, and had himself lowered down the shaft. In spite of foul gas and falling galleries he brought two unconscious men to the surface. Similar actions were performed by Lieutenant G. P. Burlton and Private R. G. Doughty, both of the same regiment. On December 6–7 a detachment of the 1st Battalion Cheshire Regiment attacked the Germans near Carnoy; Acting Corporal J. Moore, who was in charge of a "West" machine, greatly assisted the attack by keeping up rapid

IN A FRENCH TRENCH.
Watching enemy movements.

fire. A lighted bomb dropped off the cap of the machine and would have caused many casualties, but Corporal Moore groped for it in the mud, and had just time to throw it over the parapet when it exploded.

Just beyond the right wing of the British 3rd Army there was a small engagement in January. On the left bank of the Somme, west of Péronne, lies the village of Frise in marshy ground. At this point, owing to the difficulty of digging trenches in the marshes, there was a break in the French advance line. The Germans on the 28th drove the French from Frise, but their attempts to advance south on Dompierre met with no success.

The fighting in the air during the winter months was favourable to the Allies. The German anti-aircraft gunners had, however, improved, and, for defensive purposes, the enemy had secured a formidable aeroplane, the Fokker, invented by a Dutchman. The Fokker was to a large extent a copy of the Morane monoplane, and furnished with a very powerful engine for rapidly climbing to great heights. This type was most useful. The Allies possessed equally good machines, but, as the German airmen rarely ventured over their lines, had far fewer opportunities of employing them. An analysis of the evidence, especially that of the German reports (which are not likely to have minimized the successes of German aircraft), establishes that, while individual German airmen—notably Lieutenants Boelke and Immelmann—showed remarkable skill and gallantry, the Germans were very far from obtaining a mastery of the air. Nor was it in any way probable that they would so long as we had airmen of the calibre of Second Lieutenant Gilbert Stuart Martin Insall, who, on November 7, 1915, gained the V.C. under circumstances described below.

Insall was patrolling in a Vickers fighting machine, with First-Class Air-Mechanic T. H. Donald as gunner, when a German machine was sighted, pursued, and attacked near Achiet. The German pilot led the Vickers machine over a rocket battery, but with great skill Lieutenant Insall dived and got to close range, when Donald fired a drum of cartridges into the German machine, stopping its engine. The German pilot dived through a cloud, followed by Lieutenant Insall. Fire was again opened, and the German machine was brought down heavily in a ploughed field four miles south-east of Arras. On seeing the Germans scramble out of their machine and prepare to fire, Lieutenant Insall dived to 500 ft., thus enabling Donald to open on them. The Germans fled, one helping the other, who was apparently wounded. Others Germans commenced heavy fire, but Lieutenant Insall turned again, and an incendiary bomb was dropped on the German machine, which was last seen wreathed in smoke. He next headed west in order to get back over the German trenches, but as he was at only 2,000 ft. altitude he dived across them for greater speed, Donald turning his machine-gun into the trenches as he passed over. The German fire damaged the petrol tank. With great coolness Lieutenant Insall landed under cover of a wood 500 yards inside our lines. Thereupon the Germans fired some 150 shells at the machine lying on the ground, but without causing material damage. During the night it was repaired behind screened lights, and at dawn Lieutenant Insall flew his machine home with First-Class Air-Mechanic T. H. Donald as a passenger. Donald was awarded a Distinguished Conduct Medal.

Thus it will be seen that in every way the Allies held their own, and even made some slight progress. Winter was not the time for a big offensive, and they could afford to wait.

CHAPTER CXVII.

THE MENTAL FACTOR IN MODERN WAR: SHELL SHOCK AND NERVOUS INJURIES.

New Problems of Mental Strain—First Appearance of "Shell Shock"—Effect of the High Explosive Shell—"Resistance" Dependent on Training and Health—Strange Phenomena of Mental Breakdown—Loss of Memory—Temporary Dumbness and Blindness—Scientific Opinions—Precautions and Treatment of "Shell Shock"—The Mental Treatment Bill—Special Hospital Work in England—Rest Camps—Baths at the Front—"Trench-Foot"—The Disease and its Cure—"Soldier's Heart"—Research Work—Gas Poisoning and its Cure—After-Treatment of Face Injuries and Prevention of Deformity—The Work of the Doctors.

THE effect of war upon the fighting man has always been difficult to estimate, and it is probably true that the whole effect, moral and mental as well as physical, never has been estimated. Yet in all the wars of the past certain broad results have been noted and commented upon.

These results were chiefly physical and were recorded much as the discharges from a great hospital are recorded. The mental factor in war was, generally, not a very important one, or it was very badly understood. A certain proportion of soldiers broke down mentally, but this proportion was so small when compared with the proportion of wounded, and still more of sick, that it was regarded as being negligible. Thus the medical records which tell the whole story of outbreaks of plague and pestilence devote but scant attention to the mind of the fighting man.

It is not possible to feel surprised at this when one remembers that in the wars of the past the great problem which the doctors had to face was the problem of infectious disease. They had, literally, no time for any other matters. Epidemics always sprang up, and what with the sick and wounded the medical staff had its hands very full indeed.

The Great War was in a category by itself so far as medical matters were concerned. In the first place the advance of surgery had rendered the treatment of wounds a much easier matter, in the second the help of science ensured that treatment would be undertaken with good prospect of success. Again, science had met and defeated the principal epidemic, typhoid fever, and had thus rid the armies of their worst enemy. The strain upon the medical service was greatly reduced.

But the medical service itself was a very different body from the medical services of the old days. It had become, quite early in the war, a vast organization of the best medical and scientific ability in the country, an organization even in its humblest ranks of picked men.

This organization included specialists in almost every department of medicine. These men were enabled to deal with the fallen and wounded soldier not as a mere unit but rather as a patient. They had opportunity afforded them for that careful scientific work which is so essential to correct treatment. They were able to study their patients, so that from study better lines of treatment might be arrived at.

The war had scarcely begun before it was seen that the specialist would be called upon to play

FRENCH RED CROSS STATION IN A CAVE.

Rendering first aid to the wounded as they are brought from the trenches.

a great part in the solution of its medical problems. This was very apparent in regard to the poisoned wounds which began to show themselves in such terrible abundance ; it was no less apparent in regard to the nervous affections which resulted from the explosion of heavy shells.

These nervous affections indeed constituted a huge problem from the very outset. They were exceedingly frequent, exceedingly varied, and exceedingly severe. They represented a phenomenon which, if it was not new, was, at any rate, very unfamiliar to the majority of the doctors who encountered it. In the wars of the past a certain amount of trouble had arisen as the result of the explosions of shells, but this trouble had never been of a really serious character Here, on the contrary, was a force which killed without injuring, which seemed to unseat the mind itself, and to deprive a man of all his faculties while yet not a scratch could be detected upon his skin.

The first warning of a really impressive kind which the world received regarding this new and terrible factor in warfare came in the form of a strange rumour which was in circulation at the time of the Battle of the Marne. The rumour had several forms, but in its essence it told the same story. Dead men, it said, had been found standing in the trenches, apparently in possession of their faculties. Every normal attitude of life was imitated by these dead men ; their bodies were found posed in all manner of positions, and the illusion was so complete that often the living would speak to the dead before they realized the true state of affairs.

When this rumour first became current, the explanation was offered that these men had been "asphyxiated" by a new type of shell. The explanation revealed the fact that at that period a purely physical reason was regarded as necessary ; doctors and the public at large had not then taken into consideration the possibility that the cause of death might be mental rather than physical.

The asphyxia explanation did not survive long, for soon a great deal of new evidence regarding the effects of high explosive shells accumulated. Thus men were brought down to the base in the state known as the state of shock. These men presented very much the appearance of severely wounded men, only in this case no wound could be discovered. Every medical man who had given anæsthetics and watched his patients after their recovery from operation knew this state and knew something about it.

But, in addition to the cases of shock, there were found cases in which disease pictures were represented, but in which no actual disease could be detected, and it was observed that, almost without exception, the men so affected had been exposed to the effects, either immediate or more remote, of high explosive shells.

From this time onwards interest in the nervous affection of battle became profound. Neurologists were attached to the military hospitals, and nerve cases were studied as closely and as carefully as were surgical and medical cases. It was realized that the coming of the high explosive shell to the front place among the weapons of war had wrought a revolution in the types of war injuries, and so in war medicine. It became quite clear that vast numbers of men would be smitten down by the "invisible force," and that the future of these men must depend almost wholly upon the degree of knowledge of the conditions possessed by their doctors and upon the degree of enlightenment of the authorities controlling their destinies.

It was recognized from the first that the condition of shell shock was no simple one, but that very many complex factors were involved. The growth of knowledge of the subject very soon set all doubt about this at rest. One of the first observations made was that liability to shell shock or to nervous injury was by no means the same in every individual, indeed that it differed in the same individual at different times and in different conditions. Wellington's famous remark about "four o'clock in the morning courage" seemed thus to find a new application. Amongst the determining factors were the force of the explosion, the length of time during which the soldier had been exposed to shell fire, the length of time during which he had been under fire at all—*i.e.*, the

AFTER A BATTLE IN CHAMPAGNE.
German wounded waiting for an ambulance to take them off the battle-ground.

REMOVING THE WOUNDED UNDER FIRE.

degree of his experience of war, the state of the weather, the state of the campaign, the man's own health, his physical well-being, his food, his sleep, and finally his history, both personal and family.

These observations opened up a very wide vista indeed, and called for immediate and careful investigation. The first point, clearly, which had to be determined was the type of soldier who was most subject to the effects of the shock and the type of conditions in which he was most subject. The investigation was carried out by many workers, and their results were found to agree in the main particulars.

First it became clear that the experienced soldier was less liable than his inexperienced fellow, so long as the conditions surrounding him came within his experience. This was not perhaps surprising in view of the well-known effects of discipline and the equally well-known value of old and seasoned troops as against raw levies, though it remained a matter of great interest that discipline and seasoning were able to confer immunity of a kind against so violent an assault as that of a bursting shell.

The next difference which was observed was that existing between men of sound history and men in whose history there were flaws of one kind or another. Investigation along this line soon brought to light the fact that a very considerable number of the cases of shell shock occurred in individuals of a neuropathic or psychopathic predisposition or of a nervous or timorous disposition.

It became clear that the term "resistance" as applied to man has a much wider significance than had hitherto been supposed—that, in fact, resistance is a quality of the whole organism, always active and determining the course of every reaction.

Further, a curious relationship between the events of war and the incidence of shell shock was established, and it was found that a happy, or a hopeful, army is, as a unit, less subject to this condition than an overwrought, unsuccessful or disappointed one. Thus Major Mott stated in a lecture before the Royal Society of Medicine that it had appeared to him that the cases of shell shock in 1916 were less severe than those met with in the spring of 1915. He added: "I attribute this to the fact that life in the trenches has not been associated with such continuous and severe nervous strain and fearful apprehension. Our men have felt that in numbers and in effectiveness of our artillery the balance of power is no longer with the enemy. The joy of hope has replaced the depression of fear."

A speaker who followed him pointed out, further, that it was a curious fact that very few cases of mental breakdown seemed to have occurred among the troops at Gallipoli at the time of the first landing, in spite of the awful slaughter. During the first two or three weeks after this landing he saw only about half a dozen cases of nervous breakdown in the seventeenth General Hospital at Alexandria. No doubt this was due to the protective influence of the sthenic emotions which actuated almost all the men at the time.

Shell shock, then, was seen to be the end rather than the beginning of a process. In some instances it was the culminating stage in a nervous life-history ; in other cases it was the expression of physical bankruptcy. In all cases its occurrence was favoured by those circumstances which, generally, favour the onset of ill-health.

The fact that the war was being waged largely by means of high explosive shells made these observations exceedingly important, as will presently be shown.

The condition itself was so remarkable and so interesting as to merit a careful description. Its onset was determined as a rule by heavy gunfire or by the bursting of a shell in the neighbourhood of the affected man, though such a history could not always be obtained. Occasionally the victim had been buried by the shell. In these cases of burying, where presumably some actual concussion took place,

THE RETURN OF STRENGTH.
One crutch has been taken away.

the state known as "retrograde amnesia," or loss of memory extending back beyond the shock, perhaps far beyond it, was observed. Retrograde amnesia was not seen in cases in which no physical damage had occurred, in these memory-loss dated from the event. The immediate effect was almost always loss of consciousness. This loss of consciousness lasted for a long time or a short time. It affected the intellect rather than the functions of the brain which have regard to the preser-

MECHANO-THERAPEUTICS AT RENNES.
A repair-shop for wounded men.

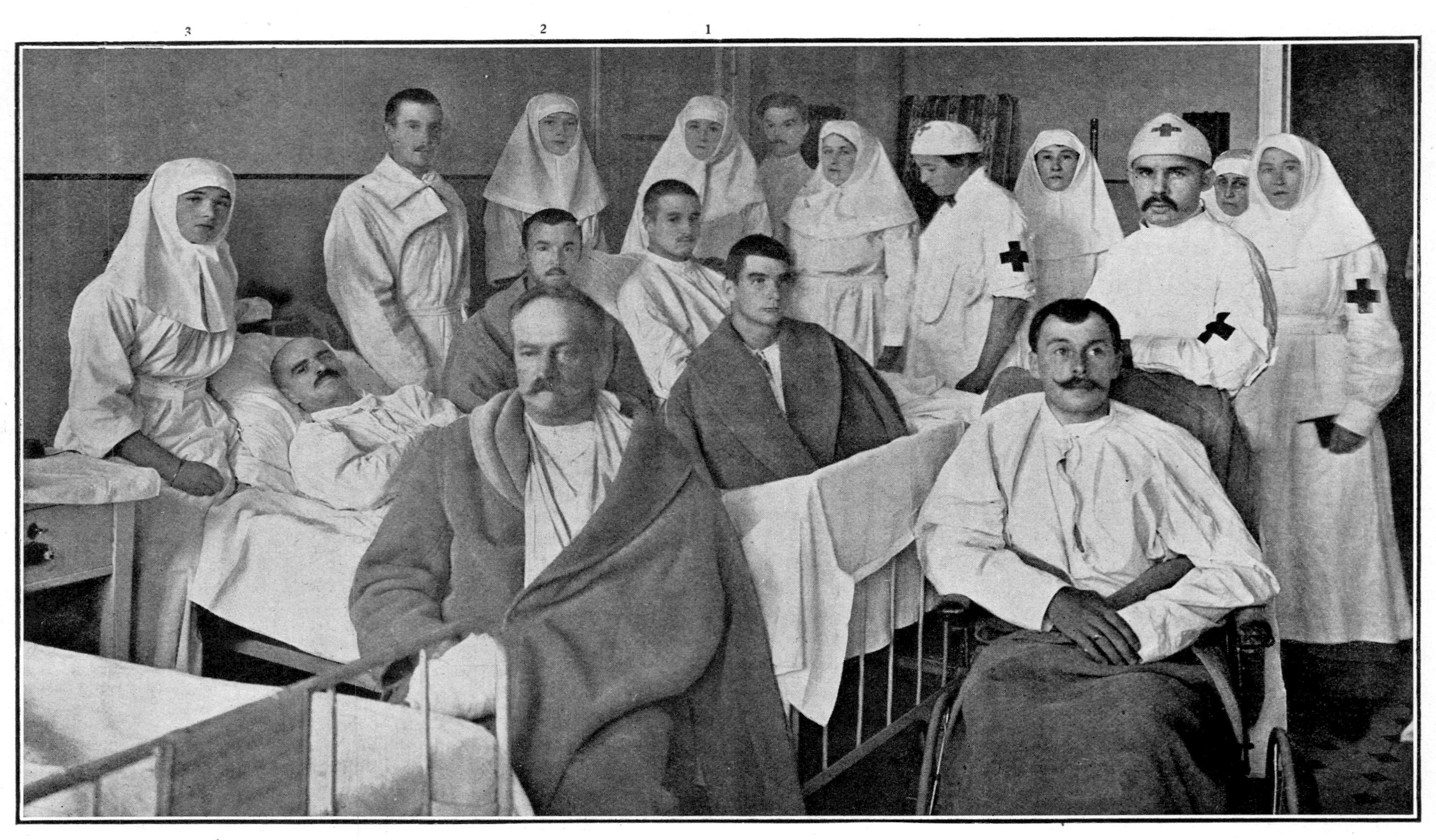

A RUSSIAN RED CROSS HOSPITAL.

(1) The Czarina and the Grand Duchesses Olga (2) and Tatiana (3) with the wounded.

vation of the individual and the species. Dr. Mott described the case of an officer whose company had dug themselves in, in a wood; he went out into the road to see if a convoy was coming. A large shell burst near him. It was about two o'clock in the morning, and quite dark. About 4.30 a.m. it was light, and the officer found himself being helped off his horse by two women who came out of a farm house. He had no recollection of anything that happened between the bursting of the shell and this incident.

In this state memory might be completely lost, so that the soldier's face was a blank. He might not remember his name; he might have no idea who he was, or how he came to be in the position in which he found himself. Near relations who visited him often found that he had no idea regarding their identity, and viewed their coming with the same stony indifference with which he regarded the whole world around him. No matter what his aptitudes and tastes might have been before the shock occurred, he lost them. One soldier, for example, was found to be unable to give any account of himself. When his name was written he did not recognize it; he did not know the season of the year. He did not recollect anything that was told him, so that his memory for recent events, as well as for the past, was lost.

Another man had been a good musician. He was asked by the doctor to sing. He failed to do this, and the doctor then began to whistle "God Save the King." The patient looked up and finished the tune. He was then invited to whistle "Tipperary," and did so on being started. From this time his expression changed—his mind had found itself. He could now whistle any of the tunes he had previously been started on. Later he began to play the piano.

It was found that the musical memory tended to return sooner than did the memory of events and persons, probably because the emotional effect of music fixed impressions upon the mind very firmly, and these impressions were therefore more easily brought again into consciousness.

In another class of case the soldier retained a very clear recollection of the event, or events, which took place at the moment when he received his shock. Thus he might be haunted by terrible visions of carnage, visions in which "flying legs and arms" figured prominently. In these cases terrifying dreams played a prominent part in the mental picture.

Men became dumb within an hour, yet many of these dumb men recovered speech almost as instantaneously as they had lost it. Written speech and silent thought, the visualisation of words, were always intact. In one case a man's companions belaboured him with a slipper until he cried out—he was cured. In another instance a man remained dumb until he saw a child about to be run over in the street, when he shouted out to warn her. He also was able to speak from that moment. In yet another case a severe shock—the unexpected news of the death of a relative—restored speech.

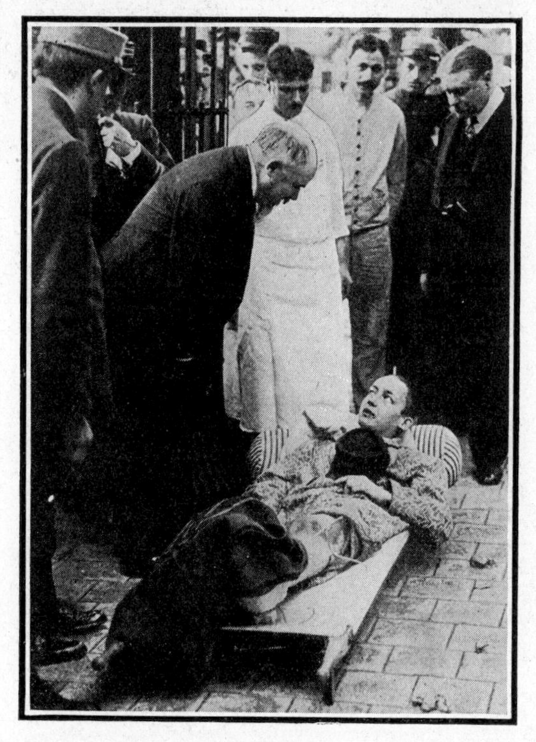

THE STIMULUS OF PRAISE.
The face of the wounded man lights up at sight of M. Poincaré.

Even more remarkable were the cases of blindness. Men were met with who possessed good eyes and active brains, who could hear and speak well, but who could not see. Blindness was relative. Yet these men recovered sight in many cases instantly. In one instance a nurse went to the bedside of one of these people at 2 a.m., and said, "You can see now." The patient, who had been absolutely blind for a considerable period of time, replied, "I can, as well as ever I did in my life." He recovered his sight. Another man saw nothing until his

IN CHAMPAGNE.
On the way to hospital.

mother came to visit him in hospital. The sound of her voice "opened his eyes" as he himself expressed it.

The deaf, too, presented another astonishing aspect of the condition. They also recovered their lost sense often with extreme suddenness, and as the result of trifling events.

This failure of sense was not in any way connected with the sense organs. The dumb man, even when unable to produce any audible sound such as a cough or a laugh, had no lesion of his vocal cords or of his larynx, the blind man possessed normal eyes, the deaf man normal ears. Nor was the brain rendered insensible to sense impressions, for in some cases the blind man could see in the sense that he was aware of an outside world but could not interpret it. In the same way the deaf man was often aware that words were being spoken, though he could extract from these words no meaning.

Again, in all cases in which a man had lost the power of speech he could write down quite easily what he desired to say. One of these men wrote, "I hear and understand all you are talking about, and I know what I wish to reply, but I am unable to utter the words."

It was known that the special senses receive stimuli from the outside world which are read off by the brain, and either stored as memory images or else translated into action or both. It was known that certain areas of the surface of the brain (cortex) dominated certain functions, while other areas received and perhaps stored impressions from the senses. For example, cases were known in which a tumour or injury of the brain had deprived its victim of his knowledge of one language, but left him in possession of his knowledge of another—an Englishman was unable to speak French, but could still speak English. This strict localization of function and sense perception was well recognized, and from the recognition of it arose the idea that any particular activity, whether of sensation or of motion, calls into play a particular set of cortical brain cells.

The adult human brain is thus an instrument of great delicacy and complexity attuned to its work, able to show with speed certain responses, and to repeat these responses over and over again. Practice has made it perfect in certain clearly defined directions. Each man has built up his own brain aptitudes, has fashioned, that is to say, his own characteristics.

Now it was recognized that this delicate brain is an object of great solicitude on the part of Nature. The brain is the only organ in the body which is completely surrounded by bone. It has a rich blood supply, and it is covered by a layer of fluid which serves to protect it from shock. But in addition to this it possesses means of its own which are capable of affording it protection against shock—internal means as against external means.

All the sense nerves of the body lead to the brain, which thus is affected at once by any stress or shock. A wound is reflected at once upon the brain by way of the sensory nerves leading from the wounded area to that organ. But the severity of the shock received varies greatly in different persons. Some men are able to "stand" a much more severe shock than are others. In the case of certain members of the community the mere sight of blood may be enough to produce a state of profound shock.

This knowledge was applied to the case of the victims of shell shock, and various deductions were drawn. The importance of a clear understanding of the condition was obvious, since only upon clear understanding can a rational treatment be built up. A great deal of attention was therefore given to what may be described as the theories of causation.

One theory tended to give prominence to molecular or chemical changes occurring in the brain itself. The tremendous force of the explosion, it was argued, was sufficient to disturb the normal chemical constitution of the blood, to liberate air from the blood, and so perhaps to set up so-called "air emboli." Again, it was noted that a shell which had exploded badly liberated carbon monoxide gas (CO.)—the gas so feared in pits. This gas exercises a profound toxic effect and may lead to instant death. It may, again, modify powerfully the vitality of the brain as a whole or in part, and so give rise to the typical symptoms of shell shock.

Another set of observers saw in the state of shell shock a state of suspended mental action. They pointed out that under the conscious mind lies the unconscious, and that the unconscious, or sub-conscious, mind is the repository of race instinct. The history of a man's ancestry is written upon his sub-conscious mind, and chief among the primitive or elemental emotions is fear. Thus when the conscious

UNDOING HIS WORK.
German helps to remove French wounded.

mind was in abeyance as the result of long continued illness or anxiety followed by shock fear tended to assert itself and to gain dominion over the whole being. It was fear which determined the blindness and deafness met with. As cure took place, the natural resistance of the individual was re-established.

Another view was that the shock of the shell released traits in the mind which had been buried and hidden during long periods, but which now again asserted themselves. Thus a case was cited in which a young man who had suffered from some religious trouble became much vexed by dreams after suffering from shell shock. The dreams indeed became a dominant in his life, and his health was seriously affected by them. Removal of the mental difficulty caused complete disappearance of the symptoms.

The types of the condition may thus conveniently be grouped under three headings:

(1) Those cases in which, as a result of shock, there was some molecular or chemical change in the brain itself.

(2) Those cases in which the condition was the end of a long process of weak health or weak nerves—"the last straw."

(3) Those cases in which some worry already present to the patient's mind had rendered him a suitable subject. After the condition had become developed, this worry would appear most probably in his dreams.

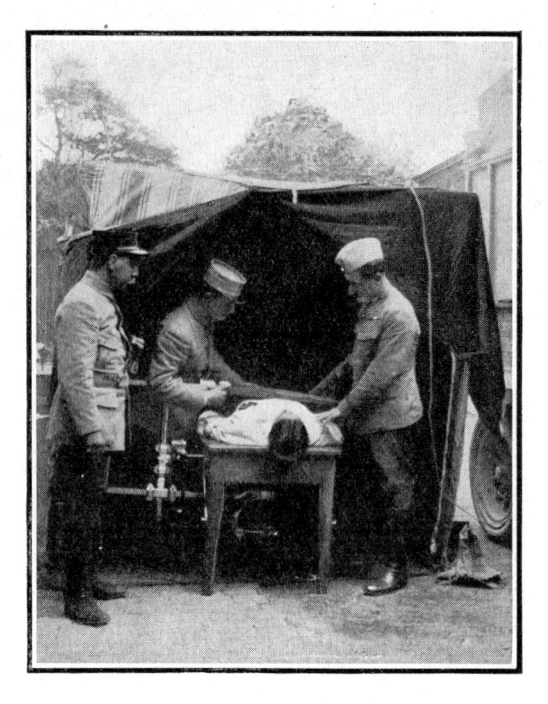

X-RAYS ON THE FIELD.

WEIGHING A CONVALESCENT.
Weights are taken daily.

This classification is necessary. In an article on a recent discussion on shell shock *The Lancet* called attention to some observations made by Dr. Henry Head, who has accomplished so much on behalf of the nerve-stricken soldier, and said that he "was not even content to allow the separate existence of the subject under discussion, holding it to be a heterogeneous collection of different nervous affections which have merely this much in common, that nervous control has at last given way. To him it would be just as reasonable to sweep up the various fruits which fall from the trees in a strong wind and then to discuss them without first stating that some fell from an apple and some from a pear tree."

The mechanism of production of the condition was also studied with great care both from the point of view of pathology and of psychology. In his Lettsonian Lectures Major Mott showed how sometimes small hæmorrhages in the brain were found; he also dealt with the aspect of causation by means of gas (CO.), and also as a result of intense atmospheric disturbance.

From the purely psychological point of view the power of dissociation shown by the brain seemed to be of great importance. Dissociation is a normal function, and is seen every day in ordinary life. Thus a blow received during a fight is frequently not felt or not noticed. Again, in sudden shock the patient frequently is cut off from his surroundings, so that he seems to hear and see nothing, and later will confess that he felt himself become "almost blind and deaf."

The healthy soldier at the moment of acute tension should be to some extent "dissociated from his brain," if that term be allowed. His brain, in order to protect itself, should partially close the avenues of feeling, and should retire within itself, so that when the terrible effects of the shell fire are carried up the nerves to the brain they will find the way partially blocked, and will be less able to reach their destination in the cells of the brain surface.

The process of dissociation lasts but a short time, though its duration is determined to some extent by the circumstances of the case. It is essentially a protective process, but the word protective must be given a liberal interpretation, and must be made to include efforts at self-preservation.

Now fear is clearly the expression of a protective mechanism, just as anger is. Fear is the emotion which impels to safety by flight, anger that which impels to safety by attack. Both these emotions have at their command many functions of the body, and chief among the functions they control is dissociation. The power of the brain to dissociate is thus exercised when the man is angry or when he is afraid. Each man, however, possesses a control over his emotions—that is to say, he can prevent the automatic action of dissociation or, better, can limit and restrain it, thus remaining in touch with his surroundings and master of events. It is this controlling power which seems to be attacked by the shock of shells and warfare, just as it is this controlling power which is attacked in civil life by illness, exhaustion, exposure, and so on. The nervous man dissociates too rapidly and too completely; he is too continually in the protective state. And he may show this in the trenches either by some splendid deed of anger which wins him honour or by some deed of fear which brings shame. The exponents of this view emphasized, therefore, the fact already re-

BEHIND THE BATTLE-LINE IN FRANCE.

French soldiers having their wounds dressed before being taken to hospital.

ON THE WESTERN FRONT.

The driver of the ambulance was struck by a stray bullet; the horses bolted, but luckily towards the British trenches, where they were stopped.

ferred to—that the worst sufferers from shell shock were men with a previous history of nervous ill-health, or men who had been subjected to great stress and hardship, or, again, men who had not been disciplined and seasoned against the shocks of war. These men had either already exhausted their powers of control from over-use or they had not developed them. They were therefore less well equipped to withstand shocks than were their more healthy or better-trained comrades.

This view, it will be seen, offered a comprehensive explanation of many of the obscure phenomena of the condition of shell shock. It shed a new light upon the supreme importance of discipline and of seasoning of troops, and also of all the measures taken to ensure the well-being of the soldiers in the field. It gave new significance to Napoleon's famous dictum: That an army fights on its stomach.

But it did much more than this. It showed also that a normal process which gets out of hand may lead to a picture of disease, or, in other words, that disease may in some cases, at any rate, be an exaggeration of or an adding to the normal. Thus fear and anger are both normal processes, so also is the shutting off of the brain—" dissociation." The normal man is able to see without seeing and hear without hearing, and this ability is essential to his well-being for it enables attention to be directed in one way and cut off from other ways. But exaggeration of the protective power gives a violent reaction to small stimuli, which reaction may be so violent that seeing without seeing becomes " functional blindness," hearing without hearing becomes " functional deafness," and so on. In this way it comes about that shell-shock victims may suffer from paralysis which is merely functional, for in certain emotional states paralysis takes place and the animal falls—and may thus save its life by becoming inconspicuous—*e.g.*, deadly fear. This is an " idea paralysis " ; it is protection carried out of the normal into the region of the abnormal. Conversely it displays weakened or exhausted control. In exactly the same way the cases of mutism are to be explained. Loss of voice is a well-known accompaniment of some emotional states and may well be protective when a single sound would mean detection. In the victim of shell shock we see the condition carried to the last extreme. Shell shock, then, does not differ materially from the so-called " functional " nervous diseases of civil life.

The victim of shell shock was thus separated at once from the so-called malingerer on the one hand and the insane person on the other. Shell shock was revealed as a disease and, which is much more important—as in some respects a preventable disease. The army doctor found himself suddenly face to face with a new world—a world in which his duty was magnified sevenfold and in which his usefulness was given an almost unlimited scope. He had forced upon him the assurance that by every jot or tittle that the health or comfort or happiness of the men under his care was weakened, by so much was the chance of these men falling victims to the high explosive danger increased —and not to the high explosive danger alone, but to all those dangers incidental to warfare which are summed up in the words " nervous breakdown."

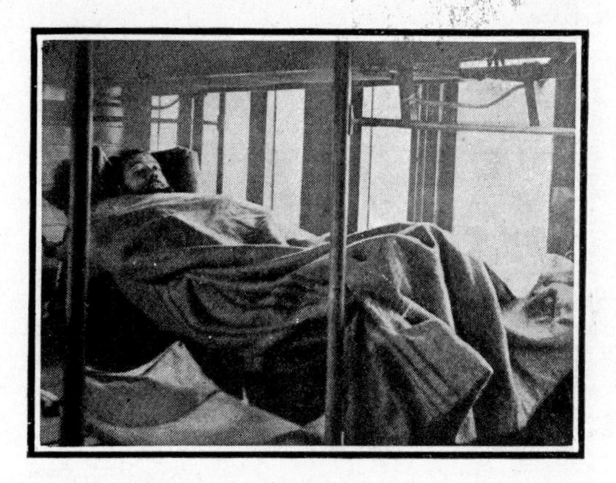

IN A HOSPITAL TRAIN.
The expression of relief on the patient's face is very evident.

The vast general importance of the conception need scarcely be insisted upon. A few of its applications must, however, be indicated. In the first place it was made quite evident that unseasoned troops must suffer greater injury from modern warfare than seasoned troops (because of undeveloped control), that they must be less effective in an important degree, and that they must be a greater burden upon the organization controlling and directing them.

In the second place it was made evident that the passage of unfit men into the ranks was not only a mistake from the social point of view, but also a danger from the point of view of the Army. The man of unfit type did not possess the power of control possessed by the fit man.

CURING SHELL SHOCK.

It is claimed that soldiers suffering from shell shock and nervous disorders can be cured by the use of this revolving wheel, which brings before the eye a constant succession of different colours. The patient can control its speed.

The danger that he would lose what little control he possessed could not be overlooked. And the infectious character of loss of control was a menace not to be disregarded.

Further, apparently insignificant details affecting the comfort and health of the troops assumed new importance. It became certain that even the smallest detail was so important as to merit careful attention. The Royal Army Medical Corps displayed a fine understanding of the situation, and set to work very early in the campaign to remove every cause of discomfort and to afford every legitimate manner of relief.

To begin with, the actual victims of shell shock were provided for. It had been established that these cases differed widely from cases of mental unsoundness, and it became abundantly clear that they must be treated upon special lines and not on any account allowed to fall under the stigma attaching to confinement in an asylum. The question was exceedingly urgent and called for settlement upon generous lines. It was taken up in a most public-spirited manner by Lord Knutsford.

Lord Knutsford's wide knowledge of hospital administration qualified him to speak with authority. He chose *The Times* as his medium, and on November 4, 1914, wrote as follows: "There are a number of our gallant soldiers for whom no proper provision is at present obtainable, but is sorely needed. They are men suffering from very severe mental and nervous shock due to exposure, excessive strain and tension. They can be cured if only they can receive proper attention. If not cured they will drift back to the world as miserable wrecks for the rest of their lives. A number of physicians have offered their services free to attend all these patients if a quiet home in London can be provided, and one in the country. The scheme has received the sanction and support of the War Office."

The appeal met with an immediate response, and Lord Knutsford soon had the £10,000 he asked for to start a hospital. He was fortunate in having a suitable house in Palace Green offered to him by the trustees of Lord Rendel's will, and he lost no time in putting his ideas into practice. Meantime the War Office made arrangements to open a hospital for men, and special facilities for the treatment of nerve shock cases were provided at the military hospitals throughout the country.

The Home Office, too, took the matter in

hand, and on April 23, 1915, Mr. Cecil Harmsworth, Assistant Home Secretary, introduced a Bill into the House of Commons in which it was provided that a man who in the service of his country suffered a nervous breakdown should receive treatment without being certified. The Act was to be cited as the Mental Treatment Act (1915).

The movement thus inaugurated was crowned with immediate success. In May, 1915, Lord Knutsford again wrote to *The Times*, stating that 100 officers had passed through the home at Palace Green and that, with but few exceptions, all had recovered from the effects of the shock of battle. The good work had been extended, thanks to the generosity of Mr. R. Leicester Harmsworth, M.P., who lent his house, Moray Lodge, Campden Hill, to provide a second home. The War Office, too, had broadened the basis of its work for the cases of shell shock and several neurological departments in London and the provinces had been organized.

Treatment was based upon the conception of the condition which has already been afforded. In the first place it was clear that the wounded mind must be rested, and must be secured against all manner of irritations. The idea was to allow the brain to regain its controlling power.

THE STAR & GARTER HOTEL, RICHMOND, WHICH WAS DEMOLISHED.

A hospital for soldiers disabled in the war is being erected on the site.

The sick men were first of all placed in quiet rooms, darkened if necessary and excluded from noise and distraction. In this peaceful atmosphere the brain in many cases gradually sank into a condition of complete repose and the terrifying dreams and visions which haunted these men became to a great extent obliterated. Sleep returned. A certain relationship with the world was established, very feebly at first, later in a more secure fashion.

Meanwhile efforts of various kinds were

HIGH FREQUENCY CURRENT AT RENNES.

One of the ways in which "after treatment" is applied.

A STIFF WRIST.

initiated to assist this process of healing. In some instances hypnotism was employed to increase the state of repose and to suggest a more collected state of mind. In the hypnotic state many of the patients were able to express the ideas which troubled them and so in some cases to obtain relief from these ideas—though in the conscious state they had been unaware that these ideas were lodged in their minds.

In other cases, however—and this illustrates the extreme difficulty of the subject—hypnosis produced rather ill effects ; it caused the patients to live over again their terrible experiences, and this was often an ordeal from which they shrank. One man found himself, while under hypnosis, back in France under shell fire, and on being awakened implored that the treatment be stopped. He had just seen his " pal's " head blown from his body by a shell.

Analysis of the wounded mind and so-called re-education was another method employed in respect of these cases. The object of this treatment was to reveal to the patient the process of mental action whereby events in his life had been woven into the fabric of the delusions and ideas which were tormenting him. For example, a man haunted by voices confessed that before the war he was bitterly jealous of, and unjust to, a friend and later suffered remorse on account of this. The voices were the externalization of his feelings of remorse. On this being explained to him he recovered. These and other lines of treatment accomplished a great deal, though cases were encountered which resisted treatment, and other cases occurred in which recovery took place suddenly as the result of some happy accident.

The second stage of treatment, as carried out by the majority of observers, was largely a stage of reintroduction to the affairs of life. The convalescent man was gradually brought back to the world, and by slow stages came to his place in the scheme of things. . . . The joy of these men when first it dawned upon them that they were on the way to recovery was often very touching, and in the sitting-room of the home in Palace Green many a moving scene was witnessed.

The after-history of the cases was on the whole good. Many returned to the front, many others were found to be able to undertake light duty at home. Only in a few cases was the breakdown permanent. These results more than recompensed the far-seeing men who had started the hospitals and justified to the full their view of the conditions.

Meanwhile the effects of the work on shell-shock were becoming apparent at the front. New ideas regarding the capacity of soldiers to stand fatigue and stress were gaining ground and the science of economy in human material was being studied.

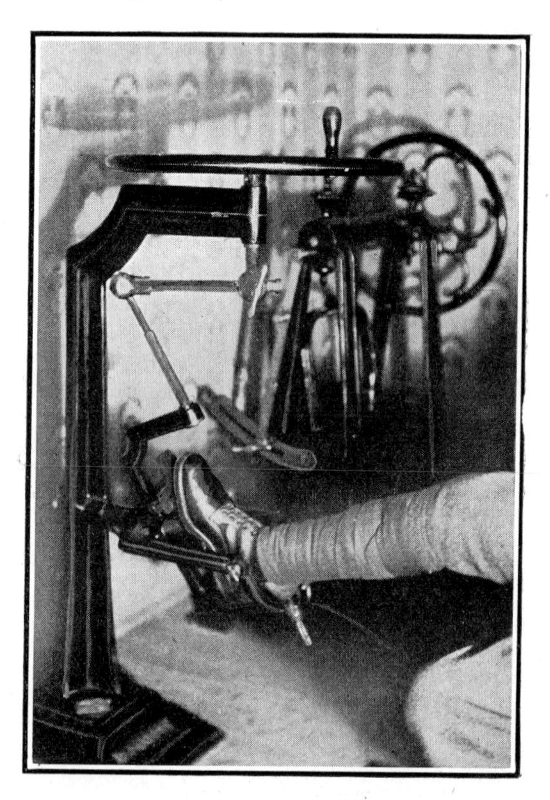

APPARATUS FOR LOOSING AN ANKLE JOINT.

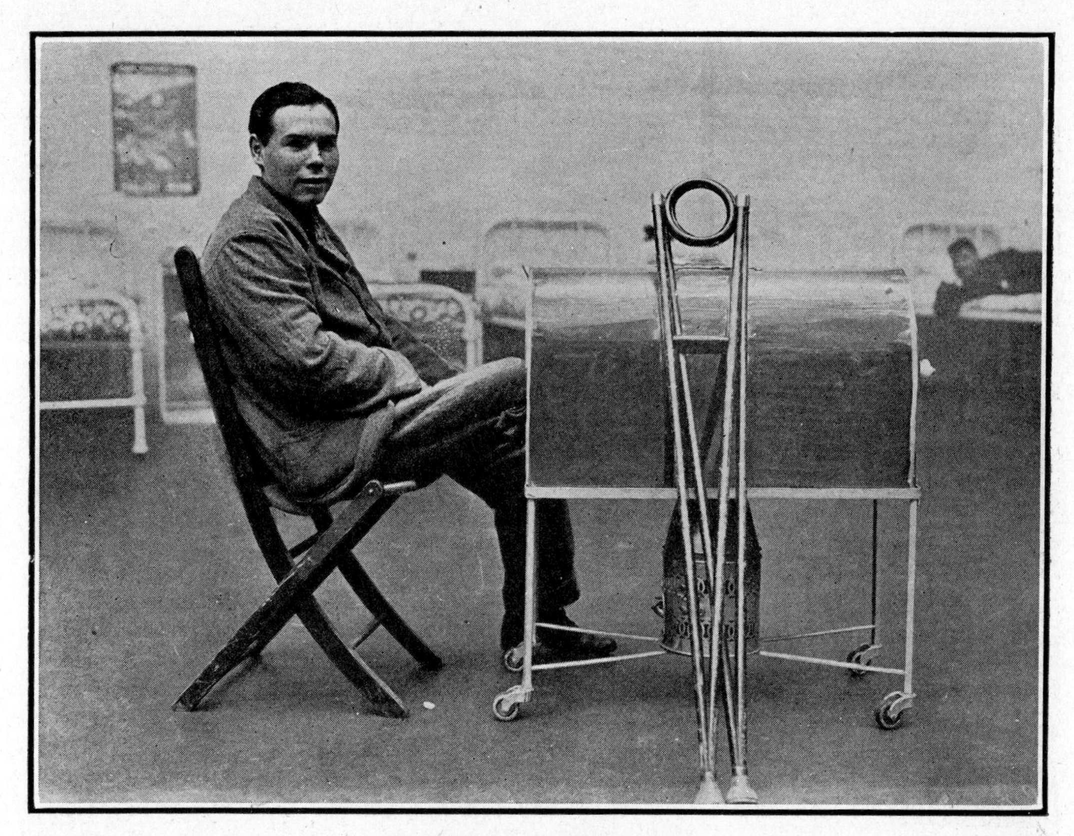

ELECTRIC HEAT BATH.

It was becoming recognized, for example, that certain broad principles must be laid down with regard to the work of the fighting man inside of the zone of fire. A man, it was perceived, labours under limitations in respect of his power of standing the great strain of the trenches. At first his power was very limited indeed; later, as the result of habitude, his power was developed to a high pitch; later still it began to wane until, if relief were not forthcoming, a breakdown might be expected.

The coming of this knowledge—and knowledge came quickly in the days when the British line in France remained unsupported and unrelieved during long periods of intense fighting—wrought a revolution in military ideas. It was no longer possible or at least expedient to work with one army. A nation required relays of armies—day and night shifts, so to speak, after the fashion of industrial life. Moreover armies had to be "salted" carefully before they could be relied upon. Certain terrible experiences in the early days had taught commanders that to rush raw troops into the firing line was equivalent to sending them to destruction. These experiences had been brought about, it is true, by dire necessity, but repetition of them was to be avoided at all costs.

The military authorities soon learned that the actual numerical strength of an army in modern conditions is no criterion of its fighting strength at any given moment, and that in fact its fighting strength depends as much upon the factors of adequate preparation and adequate rest as upon the factor of numbers. This discovery was one of the circumstances which led to the demand for more men, and reinforced the other arguments for compulsory service.

This demand, if it be viewed dispassionately, was essentially a doctor's order. The medical men in charge of the troops demanded that the soldier should not be kept in the trenches more than a certain fixed period of time, and that he should be afforded an adequate period of rest immediately after he left the firing line. They based this demand on the knowledge that if it was not granted the whole nervous tone of the fighting force would be lowered and the force made more liable to nervous injury and also to the effects of shock and alarm.

As a result of these demands very strict measures were enforced. Young troops were seasoned gradually, and no troops were allowed to grow "trench stale." After a spell in the trenches the men were returned to rest camps,

TENDING FRENCH AND GERMAN WOUNDED IN A CHURCH.

which were started upon a great scale and which very soon proved their utility.

The rest camps were really great nerve recruiting establishments. Here every kind of effort was made to relieve nerve strain and to increase nerve strength. Every sort of irritation was removed. When the men arrived at the rest camp after a period in the trenches they were usually very weary. Trench life had robbed many of them of sleep, and in any case sleep was difficult in the conditions prevailing. The constant strain on attention had produced exhaustion both of brain and body ; the wet and the mud had likewise exercised their effects. And the " minor horrors of war," the lice and other vermin which abounded in all the trenches, had added to the general discomfort.

Arrived at the rest camp, men gave themselves up at once to sleep. Some of them slept solidly for 12, 15, and 24 hours on end, in order " to make up for lost time." The relief experienced was remarkable and constituted one of the most striking vindications of the system of economy in human material which the war afforded.

When he woke up finally from his " sleep cure," the soldier went to the baths. These baths were among the show places of the front and deserved all the praise and credit bestowed upon them. An officer of the R.A.M.C. was in charge of each establishment, and the following letter from one of these baths officers reveals the nature of the work accomplished :

" Yesterday," he wrote, " I was given a new job ; have been put, with my 36 bearers, in a brewery, and our job is this : when a brigade comes out of the trenches the men are very muddy and dirty. We have to see to the washing of the men ; they are to come in to me by fifties. They go up to a big room on the second storey and undress, then they all go down to the basement where there are 50 tubs filled with hot water. They wash there and then go upstairs and dry themselves. Meanwhile their clothes have been taken and sorted out and the used up and torn destroyed and sent 200 yards down the road to another brewery, where are 24 washerwomen who wash and iron all the clothes. The men are supplied with all clean things—in the first case with new, but later on those sent to the washerwomen are ready for use, and so it goes on. We start work at 8 to-morrow morning and will go on until 5 o'clock without a break ; 1,000 men a day we have got to do. As you can imagine, we are very busy. We have had to scrub the brewery out from top to bottom, wash out 50 tubs, and we are having 2,000 towels, 500 lb. of soap, 12 acetylene lamps, 500 pairs of pants, shirts, socks, etc., so you can see it is a big business." That letter was written in January, 1915. Within a month three breweries had been taken over and their barrels sawn to make tubs, and the movement spread rapidly.

The comfort of these baths was referred to again and again in letters from the front. After the cold and wet and mud of the trenches, the warm water, the soap, and the clean, dry clothes gave a man a new outlook on life. Literally he was transformed : the hopeless weariness which had given to his face the dull, expressionless look so characteristic of the overwrought soldier, passed away. He became " twice the man " in the space of a few hours.

DRESSING THE WOUNDED IN A FRENCH CHURCH.

The clean clothes, too, meant relief from the horrible vermin which tormented the men in the trenches. It was noticed that long exposure to the attack of these vermin made a man nervous and irritable. This again lowered his resistance and rendered him more likely to break down. Fumigation of clothing and frequent changes of clothing were therefore medical as well as social measures. They were

THE COMPLETE ELECTRO CARDIOGRAPH OUTFIT.

By means of this instrument the electric waves set up by the heart beats are photographed.

a part of the great campaign of prevention which in various ways was waged continuously by the Royal Army Medical Corps on behalf of the fighting men. And, indeed, in this campaign may also be included the recreations which were provided at the rest stations—the cinematograph entertainments, the concert parties, and the various other forms of distraction.

There remained, however, a number of purely medical problems which called urgently for solution. Among these was the trouble known as "trench-feet." As a result of this trouble a great number of men suffered, during the early days, a vast amount of pain and inconvenience; good men, otherwise perfectly fit, were lost to the fighting forces, and men of all types were pulled down in health and rendered more liable to general breakdown.

Trench-foot made its first appearance during the winter of 1914–1915 when the sodden fields of Flanders became a quagmire and trenches filled with water. Men during this period had often to stand during days and nights knee-deep in water. There was no proper protection against the water which was, of course, cold.

The condition varied in different individuals but was generally characterized by a redness or blueness of the feet, by a state of the skin which resembled chilblains and, in its more severe forms, by gangrene and death of the tissues. It was thus a very severe condition—from the point of view of the administration it was as bad as any epidemic, for it laid useful men low and burdened the medical service with a huge number of incapables who had to be transported to England and then nursed back to health. Recovery was notoriously a slow business.

The first step was clearly to determine the nature of the affliction. Several investigators took the matter in hand and began to experiment, and notable among these was Professor Delepine. Professor Delepine carried out a number of investigations with a view to determining the effects of water upon the skin, (1) at ordinary temperatures, and (2) at low temperatures. It was found that neither wet of itself nor yet cold of itself was capable of producing the condition of trench-foot, but that the condition supervened rapidly when the two factors came into play at the same time, for example by evaporation. It became clear, therefore, that if steps were taken to protect the men from wet the effects of cold could to a great extent be discounted. Professor Delepine suggested the use of a light material like oiled-skin worn in the form of extensions of the boots and coming well up the thighs so that no wet should be allowed to reach the skin.

Other investigators arrived at conclusions which corresponded more or less closely with those reached by Professor Delepine. Recommendations that the feet should be covered with fat or oil were made by some and were carried out with good results in various quarters. The use of fat was, of course, only another method of excluding moisture from the skin and so eliminating one of the essential factors in the production of the condition, or it was another method of applying a non-conductor of heat and so preventing heat loss and evaporation.

Finally, a definite system of foot care was established. The men going into the trenches had their feet examined to ensure that the skin was healthy and free from cracks and abrasions. They were then provided with good thick socks to be put on after the feet had been greased. Over the socks carefully dried gum boots, or waders, coming well up the leg, were pulled on. The use of constricting leg-wear, *e.g.* tight puttees, was abandoned. Puttees were especially bad because of the very large surface afforded by them for evaporation.

It speedily became apparent that these precautions were sufficient to banish trench-foot altogether. The condition, indeed, began to disappear as soon as the precautions were instituted and medical men were told off to inspect the boots of the men coming from the trenches and to report on their condition, and the utmost care was taken to ensure that no leaky boot should pass to a soldier about to begin his trench work.

Trench-foot, as the result of these efforts, became a " crime." That is to say, that if there was an outbreak of the condition some one was held responsible for it. The outbreak could, in almost every case, be traced to some negligence. Either a man had put on his boots while they were wet inside, or he had failed to take the necessary precautions to prevent water entering his boots, or the officials in charge had allowed boots with a leak in them to pass muster.

The conquest of trench-foot was a very important matter and reflected great credit upon the men who carried it through. A considerable portion of the scientific work was carried out at the instance of the Medical Research Committee of the National Insurance Act, which thus added another item to the long list of benefits conferred by it upon the Army during the war.

Careful attention to the feet in the rest camps was of course an important feature of this aspect of the work for the soldiers' well-being. Regular inspections were carried out, and great care was taken to detect cracks in the skin and to treat them at once when detected. The result was a raising of the general comfort level both in and outside of the trenches and so a general raising of the spirit of the men—an achievement the importance of which cannot be exaggerated.

The period of rest, then, was no mere time of

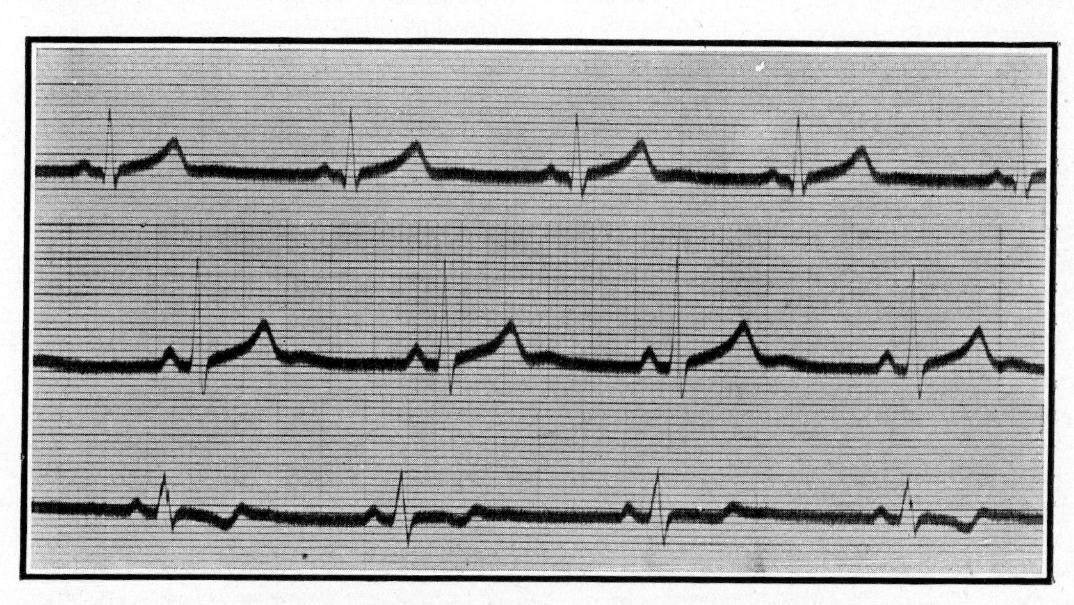

ELECTRO CARDIOGRAM OF A NORMAL HEART.

GERMAN RED CROSS TRAIN: WOUNDED WAITING THEIR TURNS.
The dull apathetic expressions of the men should be noted.

idleness. It was a vital necessity to the well-being of the forces, a true recuperation period, yielding as its fruits increased efficiency, augmented fighting value and a greater power of resistance both to disease and to the effects of modern warfare—shell-shock, neurasthenia and depression. It owed its origin in no small measure to the intelligence of the administrators of the Army Medical Service, who were quick to profit by experience and to translate the mistakes and ignorance of the past into the triumphs of the future.

While these works, dictated by a clear understanding of the mental effect of war, were in progress, another condition to which the soldier seemed very liable was forcing itself upon attention. This condition was known as the "soldier's heart," or the "irritable heart of soldiers," because it had been met with in many other wars and seemed in some way to be connected with warfare.

There were many points of similarity between the soldier's heart and the state of nerve weariness produced by high explosive shells. On the other hand, various differences were soon recognized. For one thing, the soldier's heart was not a new problem in the sense in which shell shock was a new problem. High explosive shells had produced an "epidemic" of the latter condition, they had not exercised a like effect upon the former. Whereas shell shock was relatively infrequent in other campaigns, soldier's heart was relatively frequent, and it was not clear that the introduction of massed artillery had produced any very great effect upon the incidence of the disease.

"Soldier's heart" therefore fell into a category by itself, and the study of it was entrusted to heart as opposed to nerve specialists. These heart specialists very soon discovered that a very obscure type of disease awaited their unravelling. And a knowledge of the history of the condition served to confirm that first impression.

The history of "soldier's heart" is the history of an unsolved riddle. The story begins in the days of the Crimean War, when a number of soldiers were sent back to England because they had developed a form of palpitation of the heart which proved persistent. Few of these men recovered. The second chapter of the story concerns the American Civil War, in the medical history of which "soldier's heart" seems to have played an important part. So frequent was the trouble, indeed, in this war that special investigations were instituted and a special hospital opened in Philadelphia. This hospital was presided over by Da Costa, and that eminent doctor made a prolonged and very careful study of the disease and gave to it the name which it now bears.

Da Costa's monograph on the subject presented a picture which was as true in respect of our soldiers as it was in respect of the American soldiers of his time.

"A man," he wrote, "three months or so on active service was seized with diarrhœa, annoying yet not severe. Soon rejoined, and then noticed that he could not bear exertion as well as formerly. Out of breath and unable to keep up with his comrades; dizziness and palpitation. Accoutrements oppressed him, yet otherwise he seemed well and healthy. Sought advice; was sent to hospital, where his persistent quick pulse confirmed his story. Digestive disturbances if present passed away, but the irritable condition of the heart remained, and only very slowly did this get normal or it failed to do so."

The British Government of the time gave some consideration to the question and appointed a Commission in 1864 to investigate the whole problem of heart disease in the Army. This Commission sat during four years and issued many reports. In one of their reports the Commissioners referred specifically to the "soldier's heart" and described it as "an extreme excitability of the heart, combined with some, but not great, enlargement. During rest a heart of this sort beats easily, but on the least exertion its action becomes irregular and the man becomes breathless."

The Committee ascribed this trouble to the wearing of tight accoutrements, and on their recommendation the tight accoutrements were abandoned. This, however, by no means ended the difficulty, and the cases of soldier's heart continued to arise whenever any military operations took place. Further study was, therefore, given to the matter, and in 1876 it was suggested that the condition arose as the result of what was known as "setting-up drill" —i.e., the drill given to recruits with a view to making smart men of them.

This suggestion was supported by much evidence and resulted in the abolition of setting-up drill. But no change took place so far as the soldier's heart was concerned.

The matter received little further attention until the present war, when it immediately assumed great importance, and it was realized that steps must be taken to investigate it over again. It was clear that whatever might be the cause the result was a heavy loss both to the Army and to the Public purse, for the victims of the disease became useless so far as fighting was concerned, and they remained a burden on the State in the military hospitals. The men were not actually very ill: indeed, in a broad sense they enjoyed fairly good health, but they were unable to perform any work. The mild character of their complaint encouraged the hope that they would be restored, and this tended to keep them in the Army. But this hope was seldom realized.

Acting under instructions from the War Office, the Medical Research Committee took up the question and appointed Sir James Mackenzie to open an investigation into it. This investigation was planned upon the most comprehensive lines and embraced observations made at

HEAT BATHS.
Contrast the expressions with those in the picture opposite.

A FIRST-AID DRESSING STATION UNDER FIRE.

the front, in course of transit from the front, and in the hospitals at the base and at home.

Before long it was determined that whatever else the "soldier's heart" might be, it was not heart disease as that term is usually understood.

The scientific work accomplished within recent years on the subject of the heart in health and disease forms one of the most brilliant chapters in contemporary medicine. From a state of obscurity comparable to mediæval darkness heart medicine had passed almost at a bound to a state of great enlightenment. Thanks especially to the pioneer work of Sir James Mackenzie heart diseases had been classified and rendered easily identifiable and appropriate treatments in many instances secured. This work had been carried on latterly at the London Hospital, where a special department had been instituted and special instruments installed, and already it was attracting world-wide attention and interest.

The outcome of this work was, as has been stated, a greatly extended knowledge. In the light of that knowledge it was possible to draw a distinction between "soldier's heart" and other heart conditions and to relegate the affection to a class by itself.

But the puzzle was not the less a puzzle because its limits had been defined, and it soon became evident that if it was to be solved special lines of investigation would be required. It was at this point that Sir Alfred Keogh, Director-General of Army Medical Services,

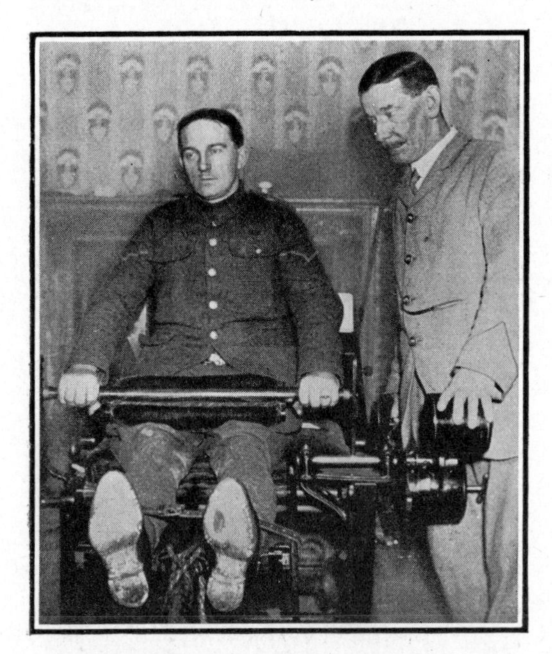

MANIPULATING THE THIGH AND KNEES.

MANIPULATING THE LEG.

displayed his administrative ability and scientific acumen by deciding, on the advice of Sir James Mackenzie, that a special hospital was necessary for the investigation and treatment of cases of soldier's heart.

The idea was a good one, for it brought into close cooperation the work of the scientific laboratory and the no less scientific work of the physician. The physician was to study the malady in mass and he was to have at his disposal the very best and most recent methods which science had produced. Nothing was to be denied him which might make for the easy solution of the many difficulties besetting his way.

This idea necessitated for its proper translation into action the cooperation of the most mature clinical and scientific minds, and the Medical Department of the War Office appointed as consulting physicians men of such great reputation as Sir Clifford Allbutt, Sir James Mackenzie and Sir William Osler. The staff of the hospital included also Dr. Lewis, consulting cardiologist to University College Hospital; Major Meakins, of Montreal; and Captain Parkinson, of the Cardiological Department of the London Hospital.

The selection of a suitable place for the work was somewhat difficult, but finally the hospital at Mount Vernon, Hampstead, known as the Hampstead Military Hospital, was chosen. It was soon evident that the choice was a good one, for the situation on the hill-top proved ideal and exercised a beneficial effect upon the spirits

1

2

3

THE HAVOC

A Study in expressions: (1) After Verdun (2, 5) Wounded

of the patients. Colonel More Reid, who had been officer in command of the hospital before its conversion, was appointed to command the new hospital.

The work had not been in progress for long before much new light had been obtained. The idea, for example, that a cheerful atmosphere and congenial surroundings would exercise a very beneficial effect upon these soldiers was justified by experience, and it was found that, as already anticipated, these were not instances of organic heart disease in the usual sense of the term. Treatment by a system of modified exercises and games such as skittles, badminton and bowls (kindly presented by the British Red Cross Society) was instituted, and laboratories were fitted up for the investigation of the cases by means of the electro-cardiograph—a very delicate instrument which enables a photographic record of the nervous impulses set up by the heart's action to be made—the ortho-diegraph —which gives an exact record of the size of the heart—the X-rays and the ordinary methods of bacteriology.

This great work began therefore under the best possible auspices and little doubt was felt that it would be productive of important results both for the army and, at a later period, for the public in general. If any proof were required that in Sir Alfred Keogh the people of England possessed an administrator of imagination and ability this heart hospital furnished that proof. It was an answer to many an ill-informed criticism and it showed that in spite of all the many matters pressing upon his attention the Director-General had time to consider the well-being of those unfortunate men who had in a very literal sense "fallen by the way."

Soldier's heart, then, was an effect of war upon the man himself; it was a mental effect as well as a physical one, for while the heart was involved in the condition, the "spirits" also were involved and that, perhaps, to a greater degree. The soldier afflicted by this malady was, so to speak, less of a man than his healthy comrades; he lived upon the edge of nervous breakdown and he felt, in his own expressive mood, "rotten." Whatever the cause of his disability might be, one thing was clear—the stress and strain of war, the cold and damp of the trenches, and the shock of the high explosives, played a part; they were contributory causes. And the stronger the man was and the better conditioned the less likely was he to suffer from this trouble.

In the course of a paper delivered before the Royal Society of Medicine in February, 1916, Sir James Mackenzie said, regarding these cases: "We must understand the life in the trenches. The story of some of these soldiers is illuminating. One in December, 1914, suffered from appendicitis and was operated on. He returned to duty three months after, and in June went to the Front. Immediately on arrival he went into the trenches and was there a fortnight. Every night was spent in repairing the damaged parapets. They were constantly being shelled. He never slept at night and occasionally got a few hours' sleep in the day—often being 24 hours without sleep. One day a shell exploded in the trench, knocking him over

4

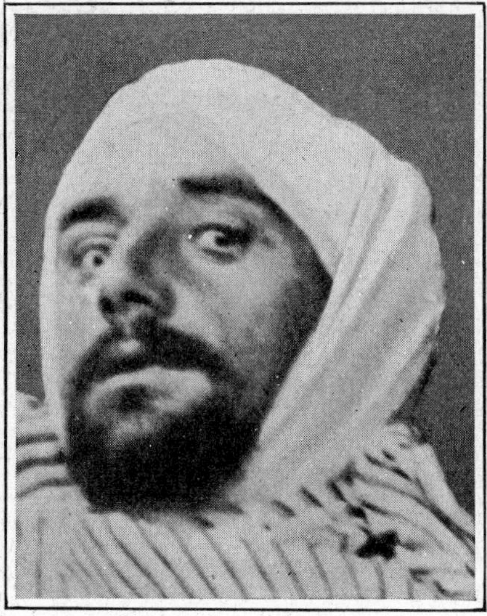

5

6

OF WAR.

(3) Gassed (4, 6) Effect of high explosive shell fire.

and rendering him partly unconscious. On regaining consciousness he stuck to his work for 24 hours, but had to give in, feeling weak and ill with pain over the region of the heart. . . . So great is the mental strain and bodily exertion with sleepless days and nights, while the trenches are frequently bombarded, that one might be disposed to consider that these two factors would be sufficient to account for all the symptoms. But we find identical symptoms present in many who have never been to the front, and who have had no excessive bodily or mental strain, but who have suffered from some febrile infection. . . . The principles of treatment should be devoted to increasing the health of the body and to bracing up the whole man, bodily and mentally. . . . The men often feel miserable, so that there is a mental side to the case which is aggravated by the supposition that there is something wrong with the heart."

But there was another type of injury inflicted by the enemy against which natural resistance availed less than against high explosive shells—though, as will be seen, natural resistance was a factor of great importance. This was not in the strict sense a nerve injury, yet its effects upon the mind of the soldier were great indeed and fully entitle it to be included in a survey of the general impress of modern warfare upon the human material of war.

This injury was what has been generally termed "gas poisoning" and was the result of inhalation of the poison gas liberated from the German trenches, and also of the gas liberated by specially constructed shells.

In a previous chapter of this history * the matter was dealt with from the point of view of the doctor. It was indicated that the gas in use in the earlier days of the war contained a large quantity of chlorine, and that steps had been taken to combat its effects by means of the use of respirators containing substances which combine with chlorine and render it inert.

After the comparative failure which attended the use of their horrible weapon the Germans began to employ a variety of different kinds of gas, and especially gases of an acutely irritating kind (lachrymatory shells) which cause a flow of lymph in the air passages and so literally drown the victim. The constitution of these gases was probably similar to the constitution of the earlier forms, but the effects produced seemed to differ at different times and in different areas.

Now, in order to appreciate the value of gas as a weapon, and also in order to appreciate the effect of it upon the soldier, it is necessary to adopt the soldier's point of view. One must attempt to see the gas cloud not as it is seen in the laboratory, but as it is seen in the trench when the wind is favourable and the enemy active and threatening.

In the first place it is necessary to realize that the soldier has probably already seen the effect of the gas cloud, and therefore there is present to his mind the picture of the sufferings which gas is capable of producing. Upon these

* Vol. VI., p. 78.

FROM BATTLEFIELD TO BASE HOSPITAL.

sufferings it is unnecessary to dilate ; they have been fully described in previous chapters. But the mental effect must be realized. It was an effect of great importance and only steady nerves were capable of withstanding it. The tension experienced while awaiting the gas cloud was extreme, and this even when the men were provided with efficient respirators and were thus, relatively, immune. Here, as in the case of the high-explosive shells, the men with steady nerves were in the best position and were more likely to escape than those whose nerves had been weakened, or whose discipline was lax.

As the cloud approached the presence of the gas became appreciable in the air. Professor Hill in a lecture before the Medical Society of London pointed out that "the effect of 1 in 10,000 chlorine is such that no man would endure breathing it who could escape from its influence. The eyes and the mucous membrane of the respiratory tract are intensely irritated and a watery exudation takes place—the inevitable effort which the living tissues make to dilute so irritant a poison." It was at this point that men unaccustomed to the gas, or men very much oppressed by it, were apt to act in a manner calculated to fulfil the hopes of the enemy. Thus in one or two instances it was observed that men, feeling the difficulty of breathing, tore off their respirators in spite of warnings, and so became asphyxiated. Other men unable to stand the strain threw themselves down and thus plunged more deeply into the heavy fumes. In other cases regiments maintained their coolness even in face of the horror, held their ground, and, thanks to their respirators and the fact that the gas is more dilute the higher up one goes, were able to endure the passage of the cloud and to meet the enemy when he charged behind it.

It is clear, then, that the mental and moral factor can be no more eliminated from consideration of this weapon than it can from consideration of the effects of high explosives, or from the causation of soldier's heart. This was obvious at once to those in charge of the troops, and the splendid stand of the Canadians at Ypres during the first great poison gas attack of April 22, 1915, will remain as a testimony to the nervous equipoise and stern discipline of that gallant contingent.

What was equally obvious was that the use of efficient respirators—*i.e.*, respirators which the men had proved to be efficient—must have a big moral value in addition to a protective value. The search for good respirators meant really the search for suitable substances to put in the respirators, for if the gas could be combined at once with some chemical which would render it inert the danger would be at an end.

The medical authorities displayed great energy in grappling with the problem and they called very eminent men to their help. The result of the work of Haldane and Barcroft and other eminent physiologists was a great and immediate improvement in the situation and a restoration of confidence which was gratifying. The men felt that they could rely upon their respirators and this knowledge steadied them. They were thus less liable to injury from the gas, for their natural power of resistance, or control, was more fully developed and was not so apt to be "stampeded."

Moreover, the soldier soon learned that his

IN THE VOSGES

A mountain dressing station.

BREATHING OXYGEN.
A method of treating the gassed.

doctors were grappling with the problem of how to relieve those who, in spite of all precautions, had been "gassed," and this again gave him confidence. (One of the most remarkable features of war is the good effect upon the *morale* of troops of an efficient medical service. The knowledge that he has good doctors behind him cheers a man almost as much as the knowledge that his guns are efficient or that there are plenty of men in reserve behind him.) The treatment of gassed patients was an exceedingly difficult problem, and at first puzzled sorely those entrusted with the solution of it. Gradually, however, methods were evolved and existing methods improved upon. In the first place the necessity of getting rid of the outpouring of fluid from the tubes was recognized so that the patient might be saved from choking—or rather from drowning.

One of the means adopted to this end was artificial respiration—*i.e.*, the means employed in cases of drowning. Forms of apparatus were constructed to facilitate this work and to keep up the artificial respiration during periods of time. Oxygen was also given in continuous stream, and methods were devised of combining oxygen inhalation and artificial respiration. Experiments on animals had shown that compressed air relieved the breathlessness just as oxygen did. As the result of these experiments it was suggested that so-called medical air-locks might be constructed after the fashion of those used in compressed air tunnel work, and patients placed in them and compressed to two atmospheres. At the end of the period slow decompression would be carried out. The difficulty here, however, was the

BEFORE A GAS ATTACK.
The men carry their respirators in tin cases to keep them moist.

BRITISH OFFICERS TESTING RESPIRATORS.
Small Picture: A type of respirator.

weight of the apparatus. Nevertheless the principle was applied in other ways with satisfactory results.

While, therefore, it could not be said that poison gas had been robbed of its terrors, much had been done to lessen these terrors and to minimize the moral effect of the gas upon the minds of the troops. The outcome of this work was a conviction, which hardened with time, that in modern warfare the fit man and the disciplined man are at a great initial advantage, and secondly that this advantage may be improved or depreciated in value by the medical staff. With the medical staff, indeed, were all the issues, for the minds of the fighting men, as well as the bodies of the fighting men, were in their care, and the minds, as was shown again and again, were more important, in the last issue, than the bodies. The medical staff could not fight battles, but they could assure victory beforehand by keeping the fighting men in fighting trim. They could minimize the effects of high explosives by insisting upon proper rest periods being afforded, and by demanding a high standard of comfort in the rest camps, adequate bathing arrangements, recreations, foot care, vermin destruction; they could lessen the chances of soldier's heart making its appearance by the same means, by close attention to the personal hygiene of the men, more especially as regards the care of the teeth, and by strict measures to prevent the outbreak of infection; finally they could "draw the sting" of the poison gas by adequate protective measures in the field, adequate recreative measures behind it, and adequate hospital measures at the base.

It is necessary to insist upon this view of the subject, because by the adoption of this view

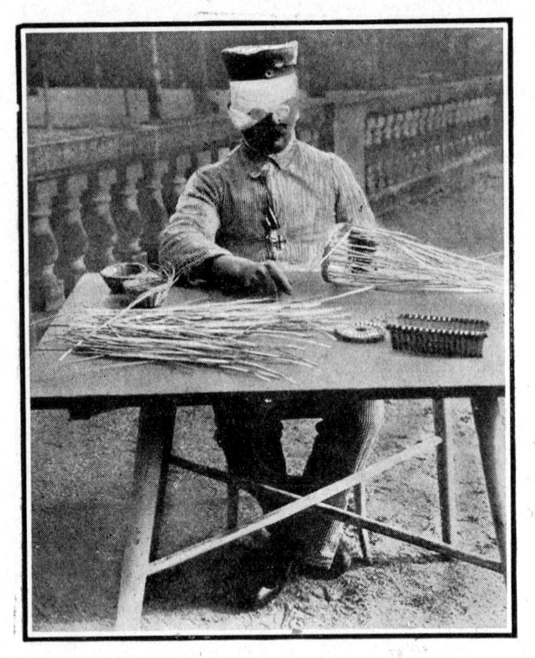

A BLINDED GERMAN SOLDIER BASKET-MAKING.

a revolution was wrought in the whole science of war. Like most revolutions this one had been anticipated to some extent by the great leaders of old time and notably by Napoleon. Napoleon was perhaps the greatest mind doctor ever given to an army. His knowledge of the value of the mental factor was astonishing and was scarcely ever at fault. In every bulletin which he issued to his troops this knowledge was revealed. His prescription for defeat was victory, the prospect of victory or the memory of it. By this alchemy drooping spirits were revived, sick men literally made whole, the effects of enemy attacks and surprises negatived and annulled. The confidence of the soldier was precious to him as the assurance of success.

It is not perhaps possible to estimate at this time how much or how little use our generals made of the great force of the mind. But one thing is certain: Had not our Medical Corps been directed by a very able man and a man of vivid imagination the essential revolution would have been postponed, perhaps until too late. Sir Alfred Keogh brought much more to his work than ripe knowledge and experience; an Irishman, he brought the imagination and the inspiration of his race. He saw his task clear, and he saw it whole; he knew the vast importance of it, and realized that in this war at any rate the doctor held in his two hands the issues of defeat or victory. It was the doctor who should make the man.

A medical service was evolved which won the confidence of the common soldier and which secured the best use of the material available. Ignorant critics poured ridicule upon the "waste of doctors" occasioned by the use of doctors to examine the boots of men coming out of the trenches. The doctors themselves, who had seen cases of trench foot, knew better; other critics sneered at the attachment of medical men "to bathing establishments"; their lack of imagination made no difference to those in authority. The great plan was adhered to. The well-being of the soldier was the unceasing care of his doctor. And the doctor's reward was to be found in the issue of almost every combat.

It would not be possible to bring this chapter to a close without a reference, however brief, to a special aspect of the work of helping the soldier back to that normal state of mind and body which is called health—the after-treatment of injuries about the face and of stiff joints. This work, indeed, though it belongs in a sense to the surgery of the war, possesses a psychological importance which is perhaps its chief claim to consideration. A man disfigured by a wound of the face can live and can work; his working capacity is not diminished. On the other hand, life for him is robbed of the greater part of its joy. He may be an object of pity, he is also, and he knows it, an object of fear. Men honour him, but they shun his company because his sorrow is too terrible to be viewed without pain. Thus he is driven in upon himself and cut off from his fellows. His world becomes a place of gloom and his mind a harbour for bitter and sorrowful thoughts. And in a lesser degree the same is true of the man crippled and deformed by wounds and by the effects of wounds and of sickness in body or limbs.

The problem of the treatment of these cases presented itself very early in the war, and in regard to the injuries of the face and jaws the credit for the earliest solution of it belongs to the American surgeons and dentists who so generously gave their services in Paris during the period of the Marne and the Aisne, and to Claude Martin, of Lyons, who was the first man to devise a scientific method of dealing with the cases.

The method of treatment adopted aimed first at preventing deformity by early and efficient measures, and secondly at curing those deformities which had already occurred. As most of the face wounds involved jaw injuries, dentistry was essential to success—not the ordinary dentistry of civil life, but that highly specialized kind which has raised the schools of France and America to a pinnacle of fame. The principles were these: complete reduction of displacement and maintenance of the remaining fragments of the broken jaw during the healing of the part; stretching of any contractions and remoulding of facial contours; fitting of permanent appliances to replace lost parts, and so to preserve the facial outlines. The first end was achieved much more easily, of course, when the case was a recent one. In other cases metal "cappings" were applied to the teeth on each side of the break and adjusted in correct relationship by means of an expanding screw. Later a solid bar of metal replaces the screw and is soldered between the cappings. The splint is firmly cemented to the teeth and mastication is thus rendered possible.

This method was described in the journal of the Royal Army Medical Corps by several dentists who visited the French schools at the Val de Grâce, École Dentaire, No. 39 Auxiliary Hospital of the Croix Rouge and the American Ambulance at Neuilly.

The stretching of scars was possible because new "scar-tissue" is easily stretched and does not tend to contract again. Stretching was carried out by an ingenious arrangement of what were practically wedges of vulcanite driven in by degrees against the hard scar until the latter gave way before them. Artificial jaws made of vulcanite could then, if necessary, be made and placed in position. These artificial jaws naturally made all the difference in the patient's appearance, rendering his deformity negligible and ensuring for him that comfort of mind which must, in other circumstances, have been lost irretrievably.

Even more remarkable was the work accomplished in respect of other regions of the face. Indeed, this work had a dramatic quality. As the result of it, that which was unbearable to the eyes became once again normal in appearance and men were rescued literally from the very deeps of despair.

The method adopted in these cases was first to secure a good healing of the original wound and then to take a plaster mould. The skin is first oiled and then the plaster applied, and a few minutes later the cast is taken. Thereafter the procedure is as follows:

"The mould having been obtained, it is dried, french chalked, and a clay or plasticine squeeze is obtained from the mould giving a positive model of the patient's dressed wound and the

EVACUATION OF WOUNDED BULGARIANS BY THE GERMAN RED CROSS.

surrounding healthy tissues; this is fixed to a board on a modelling stand and a sitting from the patient with undressed wound is obtained. Modelling now commences and such art as the sculptor may possess is brought to the test. . . . The sculptor having completed his model, he proceeds to cast it and procures the plaster positive of the wound and its surrounding structures. Another sitting is obtained and the portions which are to be hidden eventually by the metal plate are modelled in clay or wax, the edges being blended to the uninjured portions of face, thus effectively masking any trace of wounds. This is once more moulded in plaster, and the edge of proposed plate being marked on the negative a cast is obtained, edges are trimmed to marking, and the model is ready to have the artificial eye fitted to the lids; this is done from the back of the model. The plaster eyeball is dug out, the requisite thickness of lids is carefully worked down, the glass eyes placed in position, and the edges of the lids made good with the plaster.

"The model is now taken to the electrotyper, where an exact reproduction by galvanoplastic deposit is made in virgin copper $\frac{1}{32}$-inch in thickness. This is finally well coated with silver. Thin bands are soldered in on the back to clamp the eye in place. . . . The final sittings are devoted to pigmentation of the plate. . . . The results of this work were good beyond the most sanguine expectations and proved how much can be accomplished given the will to achieve, infinite patience and a high sense of duty."*

EXERCISING THE ELBOW AND SHOULDER JOINTS.

Finally the French led the way in regard to the deformities caused by stiffness after wounds had healed. Early in 1915 the Grand Palais at Paris was converted into a hospital for the physical treatment of sick and wounded soldiers, among whom a very large proportion suffered from disabled limbs. The hospital included many separate departments, all under skilled medical direction, for baths, electricity, massage, movements (by hand and apparatus), and radiology.

It was soon found that the apparatus which gave the best results was the so-called *eau courante* bath or "Whirlpool Bath." The object of this bath was to subject the injured limb to high temperature and moisture and continuous movement in a circular current of water. The motion might be that of a gentle stream or of a miniature whirlpool. The degree of heat varied from 104° to 122° F. —usually as much heat was administered as could conveniently be borne. The immersion was from 15–20 minutes daily.

The results of the use of this bath passed all expectations, and it was calculated that a huge sum, put as high as £80,000 per month, was saved the French Government in pensions. Men who appeared to be hopelessly crippled were relieved and often so far regenerated as to be fit for active service again. Milder cases recovered after short periods of treatment.

This work soon attracted attention, and a Committee of the Royal Society of Medicine, Balneological Section, went to Paris to investigate it. They reported in favourable terms, and efforts were made to have the treatment installed and begun in England.

His doctor, therefore, followed the soldier back into ordinary life, and indeed did not relinquish care of him until, so far as human power could achieve, he had been returned to the full citizenship of his world. The horrors of war were thus mitigated in yet another direction and a guarantee given to the soldiers of the new armies that their well-being was the aim and object of a vast corps of highly skilled devoted men and women. The value of that assurance cannot be overestimated; it inspired

* (*Journal of Royal Army Medical Corps*, March 1916). Paper by Captains Richard Cruise and Somerville Hastings and Sergeant Derwent Wood, A.R.A.

A FRENCH FIELD HOSPITAL IN AN ANCIENT CHURCH.

In the aisle of a church, near the Aisne River.

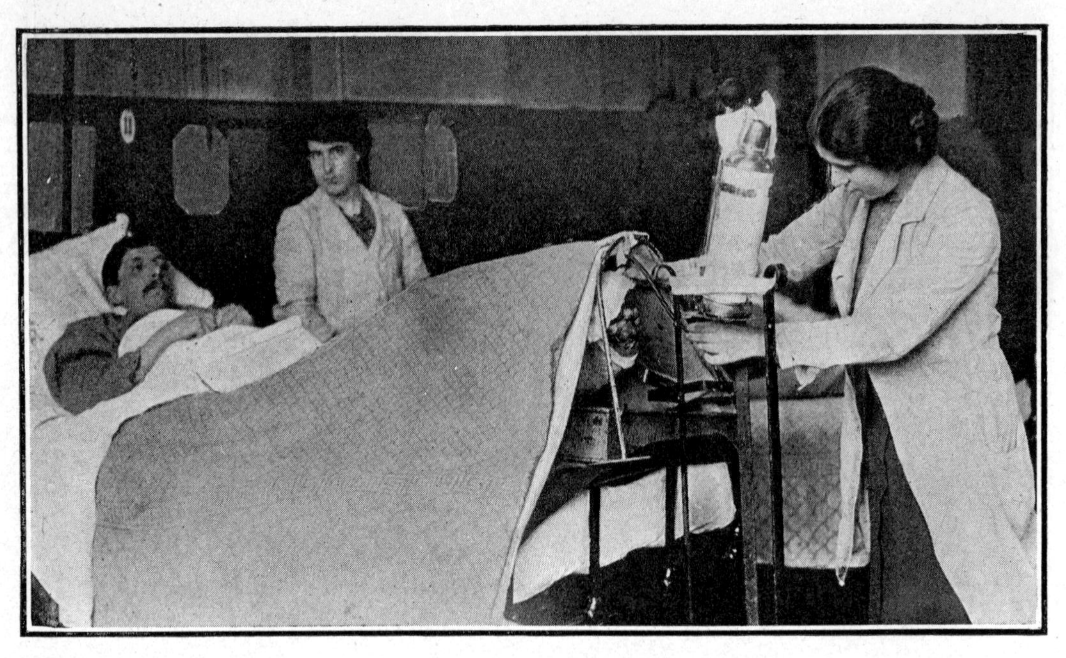

TREATMENT OF TRENCH-FOOT.

a strong feeling of confidence, and it did much to lighten the sorrow and anxiety of those to whom the soldier's welfare was the chief consideration in life. When from time to time statements regarding these great advances were published, the utmost satisfaction was awakened in the public mind, which responded by an increased generosity towards auxiliary agencies of relief like the British Red Cross and the Society of St. John.

Thus the doctor influenced opinion at home as profoundly as he influenced it in the trenches. His days were full days and his work spread before him without limitation. His it was to choose the material of war in the light of war experience, to see that the material was brought to full maturity of preparation for the ordeal about to be encountered, to guard jealously the health, happiness, and comfort of the men who had given themselves into his hands, to inspire them with confidence in their hour of trial, to shield them from the small as well as the great troubles of campaigning, to build up between them and the unseen enemy, disease, a strong buttress, to heal them when fallen, and finally to win for them relief from the effects of their injuries. It will stand to the everlasting honour of these army doctors that they were worthy of this high calling. Through the long days of doubt and danger the mind of the soldier, ever bright and hopeful, was, indeed, the mirror of their labours and the measure of their achievement.

CHAPTER CXVIII.

THE TRAGEDY OF SERBIA.

SITUATION AT END OF 1914—THE TYPHUS EPIDEMIC AND RELIEF WORK—A TERRIBLE WINTER—AUSTRIAN PREPARATIONS FOR NEW INVASION—BRITISH CONTINGENT AT BELGRADE—THE "TERROR OF THE DANUBE"—STRENGTH OF SERBIAN ARMY—THE NEGOTIATIONS WITH BULGARIA—SERBIAN PREPARATIONS AND DISPOSITIONS—BOMBARDMENT OF BELGRADE—CROSSING OF THE DANUBE—BULGARIAN INVASION OF SERBIA—ANALYSIS OF OPERATIONS—SERBIA'S HOPELESS PLIGHT ON OCTOBER 21, 1915—THE GREAT RETREAT—A NATION IN FLIGHT—SERBIAN HEROISM—ARRIVAL AT THE COAST—SERBIAN ARMIES EMBARKED AT DURAZZO—THE FAILURE OF THE ANGLO-FRENCH RELIEF EXPEDITION—WITHDRAWAL TO SALONIKA.

IT is now necessary to tell the tragic story of Serbia in the year 1915.

It will be remembered how triumphantly the Serbian army, under Marshal Putnik, had, in the last days of 1914, driven the invading Austrians out of the country. The Austrians had invaded with five army corps, advancing simultaneously from the north and north-west. For a month the Serbians, utterly lacking ammunition for their guns and almost destitute of cartridges for their rifles, had fallen back, fighting gallantly, whenever opportunity offered, with the bayonet. Late in November supplies of French ammunition, sent at the urgent insistence of the British Government, reached them. Thus strengthened, they turned upon their enemy, and the early days of December saw one of the most extraordinary campaigns in the whole history of war.

The Austrians had grown over-confident, believing that the resistance of Serbia was already broken. They had suffered their front to become unduly extended, their communications and movements were hampered by the mud. At first they offered stubborn resistance to the impetuous assaults of the rejuvenated enemy; but they were beaten at every point. Forced to fall back all along the line, they became disorganized. The difficulties of transport among the hills, with every valley a sea of mud and rivers overflowing their banks, were enormous. The Serbians gave them no rest. The retreat rapidly degenerated into an inglorious flight, and in the last days the Austrians seem to have had no thought except to escape, disembarrassing themselves of everything that impeded their flight and leaving enormous booty in the hands of the victors. Belgrade itself, which had been occupied on December 1 (N.S.), was evacuated again on December 1 (O.S.). The end of the year saw not an enemy left on Serbian soil, and among the booty which the Austrians left behind them were approximately 60,000 prisoners.

It should be stated at once, inasmuch as all manner of rumours to the contrary obtained publicity in the German and Austrian Press, that, though the Austrians, in their occupation of Shabatz and other towns and villages of north-western Serbia, had behaved with all the "frightfulness" which the Germans practised in Belgium,* the Serbians treated their prisoners with the utmost humanity. The Austrian officers at Nish were admirably accommodated and given the greatest possible freedom. They were permitted to wander

* See Vol. III., pp. 394 foll.

THE GREAT TREK SOUTHWARD.
Serbian artillerymen bringing their gun up a steep incline.

about the town—for purposes of sketching and the like—almost unguarded, and were encouraged to organize various kinds of entertainments and sports for their amusement. By the middle of summer it was a common—and obvious—joke among them that they were all growing too fat for their uniforms And this was at a time when the whole population of Serbia was, as will be seen, suffering great privations.

As for the private soldiers, they were treated with conspicuous leniency, and were employed in the most friendly way in a great number of capacities. Throughout the year the steward of the Diplomatic Club at Nish was an Austrian prisoner, who had formerly been a waiter at the Carlton Hotel, in London. They were employed as coachmen, as cab drivers, and as private servants; they were used for road-mending and taking care of parks and public gardens, and, especially, they were used as hospital orderlies. Their life was always easier, and their food no worse, than that of the soldiers of the Serbian army. They had to suffer the hardships common to all the Serbian people, but never beyond their share. That they increased those hardships for the whole population, on the other hand, is certain.

The great majority of the prisoners were captured in the fighting of what is known as the Battle of the Kolubara; that is, in the extreme north-west of the country, and there they were at first concentrated in camps about Valievo. It was in these camps that the terrible typhus scourge originated, which probably cost more Serbian lives than all the fighting of the previous winter.

Typhus is communicated chiefly, and probably only, by lice. The temporary crowding of the prisoners in masses in restricted quarters was unavoidable. In the bitter winter weather they probably herded together even more closely than was necessary. The multiplication of the lice and communication of the disease, when once it started, were inevitable. From the prisoners it spread to the Serbian army; and the Serbian soldiers, after the hardships which they had gone through and the scanty diet on which, even after their victory, they had to subsist, were emaciated and in no condition to resist disease. The mortality was dreadful. From the army, as soldiers began to return to their homes on leave, the typhus spread throughout the country. Nobody knows what the actual loss of life from this cause was during the first half of 1915; but it has been estimated that there were probably not less than 200,000 deaths.

Serbia then was almost destitute of doctors. At the outbreak of war there had only been some 350 doctors in the country, and of these over 100 had died on service. What remained were not enough for the needs of the army alone, so the civil population of the country as a whole was absolutely without medical advice or assistance. In her distress, Serbia appealed to her Allies. Her first request, addressed to France, Russia, and Great Britain, was for 100 doctors from each and for medical supplies. Each country, when appealed to, responded promptly according to its ability, as did also the United States. An International Sanitary Commission was organized with headquarters at Nish, under Sir Ralph Paget as Chairman. The 100 doctors whom France sent were scattered through the towns and villages of the northern part of the country. The United States Commission, with Dr. Richard P. Strong at its head, took over the southern part, working from centres at Skoplie (Uskub), Veles and Monastir. Nish itself was in charge of the Russians, who also had a mission at Kraguievatz. Great Britain poured in hospital units and supplies; and, in addition, sent Col. Hunter with Lieut.-Col. Stammers and 30 doctors of the R.A.M.C., to whom the Serbian Government entrusted the immediate work of fighting the advance of typhus over the country.

Colonel Hunter acted vigorously. For 15 days all railway communication was stopped, and when it was resumed, until the end of the year, on the main line north from Nish and on the branch lines to Uzitsha, Kraguievatz and Valievo, no carriages were permitted to be used but wooden-seated third-class vehicles, from which every shred of fabric or upholstery was stripped away. These bare wooden interiors were scrubbed and disinfected with formalin every day. A cordon of sanitary and disinfecting stations was drawn across the country from west to east. All soldiers' leave was stopped. In the northern part of the country, above this line, Colonel Hunter's staff set to work and practically disinfected and inoculated (against typhoid and cholera) the whole Serbian army. In all the towns and villages, every restaurant, hotel, or place of

THE ENEMY'S ADVANCE ON USKUB.

Serbian artillery on the way to a position in the endeavour to stop the enemy's advance.

public entertainment was compelled to close its doors for certain hours in the forenoon and afternoon, and in those hours the floors, walls, tables, and chairs of every room to which the public had access were scrubbed and disinfected. By these drastic measures the epidemic was successfully checked and was practically confined to the northern half of the country. By the beginning of April, 1915, it was apparent that the scourge was declining. By the beginning of June, typhus was to all intents and purposes extinct.

All authorities are agreed that no one who witnessed the horrors of the winter 1914–1915 in Serbia could ever forget them, nor, probably, can anyone who did not witness them imagine how terrible they were. Serbia was already exhausted by war. Practically the whole manhood of the country was in the army, and agriculture had been left to the very old men, the women, and young children. The supply of home products, then, was inevitably reduced. Almost all its imported articles Serbia had for many years been accustomed to draw from the north. There was a time when Austria furnished the great bulk of goods to the Serbian market, but of late years, in their characteristic way, the Germans had gradually shouldered their Austrian friends out and had obtained control of a great part of the trade, even though they had habitually sold their goods under British names—cards of German imitation jewellery labelled in English "real gems," cheap German cutlery stamped "Best Sheffield," writing paper made in Berlin with the watermark "Royal Parchment," or "Crown Stationery," matchboxes (but these were Austrian) bearing the portraits of King George and Queen Mary, of the Prince of Wales, and Lord Roberts. This confession of the superior reputation of British goods in the Balkan markets must have had its humiliation for German manufacturers, but they did not seem to mind, so long as they did the trade. But with the outbreak of war that trade stopped.

From that moment Serbia could no longer draw any supplies from the north. She had to rely for her imports on the one single-track line of railway from Salonika; and, before she could receive goods by that line, she had to make new trade connections with Great Britain or other countries—not in itself an easy thing in time of war. The capacity of that railway line was further taxed always to its utmost capacity

ON THE NISH-SALONIKA RAILWAY.

German engineers repairing the line which was torn up by the Serbians to hinder the enemy's advance.

IN THE SERBIAN MOUNTAINS.

German supply column travelling through a pass, with a file of Serbian prisoners.

in the carriage of war materials and hospital supplies, and great quantities of goods also came that way to Bulgaria and for destinations beyond. The difficulty of getting into Serbia, therefore, the ordinary necessities of life, let alone any comforts, was prodigious. The country was almost stripped of luxuries; and for the masses of the people it was a question only of supporting life by the simplest possible means and on the slenderest possible diet.

It was on a land thus destitute and a people thus enfeebled that fell, first, the winter fighting which gave some 40,000 wounded to be cared for in hospitals where no hospitals were, and, second, the still worse scourge of typhus. With the typhus also were other diseases, enteric and scarlet fever and dysentery and, later in alarming proportions, scurvy as a direct result of the poverty of the diet. In the first months, and until the early spring, there was no hospital accommodation for treating separately the various kinds of patients. The wounded in battle, the typhus patients, those suffering from small-pox, scarlet fever, enteric, or any other disease—all had to be treated together. Nor were there any hospital staffs or any medical supplies. Devoted nurses, single-handed, without a doctor or surgeon to help, strove to care for, perhaps, a couple of hundred patients of all kinds, who were laid, each touching the next, on the floor of, it might be, a warehouse or school. It was not in some cases even possible to carry the dead out daily. The dead might lie for hours beside the living; and as soon as a place was vacant some one of the dozens waiting had to be brought in to fill it. The sanitary conditions in some of these so-called hospitals were appalling; and it is not to be wondered at that every country—England, France, Russia, and the United States alike—gave many precious lives of doctors and nurses and hospital assistants before the fight was won.

To give here any detailed account of what was then done in Serbia would be impossible. It must suffice to say that of the British hospital units which did fine work must be mentioned Lady Paget's hospital at Skoplie; Lady Wimborne's hospital at the same place (though that withdrew from Serbia in the beginning of July);

ON THE NISH-SALONIKA RAILWAY.

Serbian outpost guarding the single track of the Nish-Salonika Railway which connected the main Serbian Army in the north with the allied troops to the south.

Dr. James Berry's hospital at Vrnjatska Banja, and the two Red Cross units at the same place under Major Banks; the Scottish Women, under Doctor Inglis, at Kraguievatz, with the branch under Dr. Hutcheson at Valievo; Mrs. St. Clair Stobart's field hospital, also at Kraguievatz, and, after its reorganization under Dr. Aspland, the Wounded Allies at the same place, and the two Farmers' units at Belgrade and Pozarevatz. There were other British units in Serbia; and by midsummer the staffs of all combined numbered not less than 500 persons. All were under the direction of Sir Ralph Paget at Nish. Nor should mention be omitted of Sir Thomas Lipton, who, going out with his yacht (now the Hospital Ship) *Erin*, took parties of nurses and great quantities of medical stores, on successive trips, earning great gratitude from the Serbian people of all classes, while, in addition, by his writings after his first trip in January-February, 1915, he did much to arouse public sentiment in England to an understanding of the extreme needs of the situation.

The earnestness of the efforts which England made in this respect to help Serbia in her distress may serve as some mitigation of whatever blame there may be for the failure to help her also in due season in the new trials which were preparing for her.

That Austria would accept her humiliation and defeat as final was hardly to be expected. She had been shamed in the eyes of all the world; and, above all, German irritation and contempt for her incapacity were outspoken. Very early in the year 1915, therefore, there began to be talk of a renewed invasion. Austrian official *communiqués*, issued at the end of the year, explaining away the disaster which had occurred, said that the Army "awaits new combats," and—

With respect to Serbia, a fault has been committed, which, however, will be set right. It is said that General Potiorek promised to conquer before Christmas, but war has not to be finished in a fixed time like business; it has to be continued until the victory is final.

Apparently, preparations were actually set on foot for a second invasion that winter. Some 200,000 men were massed at Serajevo, and there was talk of a combined Austro-German force being formed of 400,000. Rumours on the subject were plentiful during the first three months of 1915; and it must be assumed that the plans were abandoned only in deference to the much greater offensive which was preparing against the Russians in Galicia.

LADY PAGET.

[*Russell.*

MRS. ST. CLAIR STOBART.

Meanwhile the Serbian army was resting. It was still, in spite of all its sufferings, flushed with victory and very confident of itself; and, as it became apparent that no immediate attack from Austria was to be apprehended, projects for a Serbian offensive on the north began to take form. In this offensive it was expected that the small International Force which had been sent to assist in the defence of Belgrade and the Danube front, under Rear-Admiral Troubridge, would be able to render effective help.

The British contingent in this International Force consisted of less than 90 men, with four 2-gun batteries of naval 4·7 guns, under Lieut.-Commander C. L. Kerr, R.N., who also had a diminutive boat, hardly more than a tug, which was fitted with a torpedo tube and carried a machine gun and became famous as *The Terror of the Danube.* The guns were manned chiefly by Serbian artillerymen. A body of 30 marines, under Major B. N. Elliot, R.M.L.I., and Lieut. George Bullock, R.M., had charge of the mine-work for preventing the enemy from making free use of the river. In addition to the British members, the force included a battery of Russian guns, two French guns, and a party of French aviators. The French airmen did admirable work, both in reconnaissance and in fighting. They established a complete ascendancy over the Austrian airmen who occasionally made incursions into Serbia from across the river, the famous aviator Paulhan, in particular, who had been one of the most brilliant aerial performers in the days before the war, being decorated for a peculiarly dashing piece of work. He was alone at the Belgrade aerodrome when four hostile machines came from across the Danube. Rising to meet them, he cut one out from its companions and, chasing it over the river, shot it down so that it fell a little way on the Austrian side. Paulhan followed, descending to some 300 metres, and dropped a bomb on the wreckage of the enemy machine, to make quite sure of his work; and then, lest there should be any doubt of his feat, descended still lower and photographed the débris. All this was done while he was under fire from Austrian guns and while the other enemy machines, though they had retreated, were still in the air.

Distinction was also won for the British force by Lieut.-Commander Kerr, who, with his little *Terror of the Danube*, succeeded in torpedoing one of the big Austrian monitors which made their base (and never dared to come away from it) just beyond Semlin in the Save, an achievement for which he received the D.S.O., while all the members of the boat's crew were given Distinguished Conduct Medals. On another occasion he succeeded in tempting one of the enemy's picket boats (a craft considerably larger than the *Terror*, looking like a miniature Dreadnought and mounting two machine guns) on to a prepared mine-field where it was destroyed. The wreck stranded on a corner of Kojara Island, in mid-stream opposite to Belgrade, where, after Major Elliot and his men had plundered it of all that was worth taking away, it remained a conspicuous landmark throughout the summer.

It is known to have been the intention to furnish Admiral Troubridge with a considerably larger force if events in the Dardanelles had taken a more fortunate course. Preparations were made in Belgrade for a much larger con-

BRITISH NURSING UNIT AT VRANJA BANJA.
On the right is *The Times* correspondent (×).

MEMBERS OF THE BRITISH FIELD HOSPITAL.

Smaller picture: Sister in charge of the British Field Hospital.

tingent, but, as has been said, the number of British there never actually reached 90. The object of the International Force was to assist in the river defence of Belgrade. Belgrade itself could, as a matter of fact, never be defended. Apart from the facility with which hostile aeroplanes could reach it to drop bombs, it was always at the mercy of the Austrian guns across the river, just as the Serbians could at any time have destroyed the town of Semlin. At first there was, indeed, a good deal of shelling of both towns, but in February, 1915, after a particularly spiteful bombardment of Belgrade, the British guns turned their attention on Semlin with such determination that the Austrians sent a *parlementaire* under a white flag across the river in a rowboat to propose a friendly agreement under which each side should refrain from shelling the other's city, both confining their attention to the enemy batteries, or other legitimate military objectives, on the opposite shores. Though the proposal came from the Austrians, it was cordially welcomed by the Serbians, who, as will be seen later, were very proud of their capital city and very willing that it should escape rough usage. The agreement, then, was made, but, like most things in the war which depended only on Austrian or German good faith, was imperfectly kept on the Austrian side. Several times during the summer the enemy dropped shells into Belgrade with an accuracy which was not accidental.

A much more important task for Admiral Troubridge's force, then, than the actual defending of Belgrade was the holding of that section of the river so that the enemy craft could not use it. The Austrians had originally seven, and, after Lieut.-Commander Kerr's exploit, six monitors here, besides sundry

THE IMPRISONED SCOTTISH NURSES AND THEIR GUARD.

picket boats. It was a force sufficient to have given Austria an enormous advantage, whether for offence or defence, along the whole of the northern front, if it had been free to move about. It never was free. During the whole of the summer none of the Austrian boats, except the one whose wreckage lay on Kojara Island, dared to come down into the Danube below the junction with the Save. They were kept penned up behind Semlin, where they could be seen at any time in fine weather through a telescope from the heights about Belgrade and where they were protected by booms against the impertinent attentions of the *Terror*. In case of Serbian invasion of Austria, it was particularly desirable that the enemy monitors should be prevented from interfering with the crossing of the river.

That the plans for a Serbian offensive began to take form soon after the talk of a new Austrian invasion died out has already been mentioned. Serbia doubtless did not expect such an offensive to be an isolated movement on her part alone. She may well have dreamed of a united "push" in which Italy, on coming into the war, would cooperate on Serbia's left and Rumania might intervene on her right. Some time the correspondence may be published which will show how far a concerted plan had been worked out.

The Serbians, and especially the Serbian rank and file, were impatient for an advance, and during the month of May and until well into June it seemed likely that Serbia would make the great adventure on her own account. Various dates, from the middle of May till the end of the second week in June, were more or less authoritatively fixed for the beginning of the crossing of the Danube. The International Force at Belgrade was almost hourly expecting the intimation where the crossing was to be attempted, so that it could make the necessary preparations, for which a period of three days were to be allowed it; and all Serbia was in a state of tension and restrained excitement.

With the continuance of the Russian retirement and the concentration of Italian effort on the Isonzo front, any hope of a combined offensive had disappeared by about the middle of June. For some time afterwards there were those who continued to urge on Serbia the desirability of an offensive so as to entertain as many enemy troops on this front as possible. The Serbian Government and higher command, however, believed that they could best serve the common cause by declining to take the chances of an advance which must necessarily be attended by some risk, and by keeping its army intact, for use in some future cooperative movement, and to be a permanent menace to any German advance in the direction of Constantinople.

The Serbian Army numbered at this time

about 240,000 men of all arms, with 210,000 bayonets. The country has in all some 700 miles of frontiers, and it was exposed to attack both from the east and the west. In any event, a large part of the army would have to be held back for the protection of these frontiers. The scantiness of lines of communication and the difficulties of the Danube crossing reduced the actual force which could be effectively used in an offensive to the north, in the opinion of the Serbian higher command, to less than 100,000 men. Probably the invading army could not have exceeded 80,000. It did not appear that such a force could be of material service in diverting Austro-German attention from the Russian operations. If any serious calamity befell the expedition, however, it would be a grave matter for Serbia, ringed around with enemies as she was, and having already all her available force under arms. She had literally no reserves with which to make up for any losses. Under these circumstances the more cautious policy seemed to be the wiser one ; and in this opinion Serbia had the support of Great Britain.

Serbia, it has been said, was exposed to attack both from the west and the east. That she was exposed on the side of the Austrian territory on the west was obvious. Though less obvious to the world at large, Serbia herself always held that the danger from Bulgaria on the east was even greater. The Serbians never had any doubt of Bulgarian malevolence. In the events of the preceding winter the Bulgarians had done all that they could by raiding the railway line to prevent the ammunition, to which Serbia owed her triumph over Austria, from ever reaching her. Later, in January, 1915, similar raids had taken place on a larger scale, and these again were followed by others still more serious in the beginning of April. The usual efforts were made on the part of Bulgaria to obscure the facts, to represent that the trouble arose entirely from a revolt of Turkish inhabitants of Serbian territory, and to deny, not only that Bulgarian soldiers were concerned in the raid, but even that it began on the Bulgarian side of the frontier at all. At the worst, it was claimed, certain *komitadji* bands might have been implicated.

On the Serbian side, the evidence went overwhelmingly to show that the raiders were mostly dressed in regular Bulgarian uniforms, that they fought with regulation rifles and machine guns, and that they were disciplined and acted under officers as no *komitadji* bands ever did. In proof of their contentions the Serbians had in their possession the uniforms

GERMAN TROOPS IN A SERBIAN VILLAGE.

and equipment of the dead whom the raiders had left upon the field. The Bulgarian authorities, in reply, asserted that if there were any Bulgarian soldiers concerned they were men who had left the army and retired to civil life, and that if any rifles or ammunition were used they must have been some which were accidentally left in peasants' hands after the war of 1913.

The writer was at Strumitza shortly afterwards, and he has beside him as he writes some of the cartridges taken from the dead Bulgarians. They are regulation cartridges bearing the date 1914. He saw, moreover, the army books found on the bodies of the dead, giving their record with the colours ; and these in several cases showed that the soldiers were of recent enlistment. There is, in fact, no doubt of the falseness of the Bulgarian statements.

LIEUT.-COMMANDER C. L. KERR.

The Serbians were never under any misapprehension on this subject. They never regarded Bulgaria's neutrality as anything other than a veiled hostility which bided its time. It may be, as has been explained in a preceding chapter, that early in the year—perhaps as late as March or April—Bulgarian support might have been won, by a sufficient bribe, to the side of the Allies, to which in theory the sympathy of the Bulgarian population, from traditional regard for Russia and gratitude to England, was believed to lean. But, apart from King Ferdinand's well-known inclination to the Central Powers, it was notorious in the Balkans that the Bulgarian General Staff firmly believed in the ultimate victory of Germany. Serbians, then, never had any patience with the sanguineness of those diplomats who clung throughout the summer to the belief in the possibility of getting Bulgaria's cooperation. On the contrary, Serbia never kept less than 30,000 men, or one-eighth of her available army, within easy distance of the frontier at Strumitza, the troops being based on Veles. Towards her friendly neighbour on this side Serbia was compelled to stand perpetually on guard no less vigilantly than against her open enemies on the north and west.

Throughout the summer Serbia stood thus on guard. Soon after it was definitely recognised that the Serbian proposal to invade Austria had been abandoned, the threat of an Austrian attack on Serbia began to grow again. By the end of June the threat appeared to be formidable. There were rumours of large concentrations on the north at Temesvar, and of considerable troop movements along the valley of the Maros. It was also said that two Austrian divisions had been moved down into Bosnia. Thanks to the French airmen, however, the Serbian General Staff was kept well informed of all movements within striking distance of the frontier, and the summer passed without any such great concentration in close proximity to Serbian territory as to threaten immediate danger. Meanwhile the Serbian Army, now thoroughly rested, was increasing in efficiency, and the lines of defence on the north and west were continually being improved and strengthened.

Under the Serbian regulations all the male population fit for service was incorporated in the army. There were three bans, the first including men from 21 to 30, the second all men from 30 to 38, and the third men from 38 to 45. In addition, men from 18 to 20 and from 45 to 50 were included in the Landsturm. The War Establishment contemplated :—

A.—Ten Infantry Divisions of 1st ban troops, each consisting of 4 regiments of 4 battalions, the regiment containing about 4,500 men of all ranks. With the division were 3 squadrons of cavalry and an artillery regiment of 3 divisions of three 4-gun batteries, or 36 guns. With the miscellaneous divisional units, the full strength of an infantry division was something over 19,000 men. Total, 10 divisions, 190,000.

B.—Ten Infantry Divisions of 2nd ban troops, each division similar to those of the 1st ban,

A FRENCH ARMOURED MACHINE-GUN CAR SURROUNDED AND CAPTURED BY BULGARIANS NEAR STRUMITZA.

except that the regiments contained only 3 battalions instead of 4. The total strength of the division, therefore, was about 14,500 men. Total, 10 divisions, 145,000.

C.—Fifteen 4-battalion regiments of infantry (not made into divisions) of the 3rd ban. In addition, this ban produced a few squadrons of cavalry and some batteries of artillery, which were equipped with a slow-firing De Bange gun. Total, about 80,000.

D.—Two Cavalry Divisions, 1st ban troops, each of 2 brigades of 2 four-squadron regiments, with 2 four-gun horse batteries; or a total divisional strength of about 4,000 men. Total cavalry, 2 divisions, 8,000.

E.—The Army Troops, also 1st ban, consisting of one howitzer regiment of 5 batteries, one mountain artillery regiment of 9 batteries, and one fortress artillery regiment of 16 siege guns.

F.—The Landsturm should on paper have provided about 50 battalions, to be used for garrison duty, on lines of communication, etc.

The total combatant force included in the

BRITISH TROOPS IN SERBIA.
Heavy gun being drawn along a difficult road. Smaller picture: British and Serbian troops in the trenches.

first five of the above categories should have amounted, it will be seen, to about 425,000 men; but, after all its fighting, the Serbian Army in 1915 did not amount to more than 240,000. The infantry in physique and *moral* were of a very high quality and, in the opinion of competent foreign observers, the field artillery, armed in the main with 75 mm. Creusot quick-firing guns, was extremely good. In addition, there were the De Bange, siege and mountain guns mentioned above. Also 120 7.5 Krupp quick-firing guns, of the nearly 500 captured from the Austrians, had been used to equip 40 additional 3-gun batteries, for which there was abundance of captured ammunition. In all there were about 500 quick-firing guns. Each battalion of infantry had two machine-guns, the regulation infantry rifle being the 7 mm. Mauser. Serbia and the Balkans generally are not a country favourable to the extensive use of cavalry, which was the weakest part of the Serbian organization.*

The army, then, was small and there was no possibility of increasing it from any reserves. On the other hand, the material was very fine. The British Army doctors, from their experience in inoculating a large proportion of the Serbian soldiery, declared them to be physically the finest lot of men that they had ever seen. Their courage was undoubted. Their discipline was less rigid and more informal than that of the great European armies; but the events of the preceding autumn had shown that they could preserve their *moral* through all the disheartenment of a month of retirement and defeat and remain well enough in hand to be able to assume the offensive with extraordinary dash and vigour. They had the one conspicuous quality of having been inured to hard living and scanty fare from childhood, and were therefore able to fight almost without commissariat. The feats of endurance on the part of some regiments, of the First and Third Armies especially, in the winter fighting were almost incredible. The transport was practically all by ox-wagons, which, though slow and cumbersome, are better adapted to the bad

* These explanations supplement the discussion of the Serbian strength given in Vol. II., pp. 285-7.

roads and hilly country than some more modern vehicles would be. A fleet of heavy motor lorries had, indeed, been imported from England during the summer, but the use of these was almost entirely confined to serving the defensive positions on the line from Valievo to Ub, where excellent military roads had been made for them.

These positions, however, were never brought up to the standard of modern warfare. The Serbians, lacking experience of the effects of heavy artillery fire as it is now understood, cherished a certain contempt for trench warfare; and while, in the triple lines of defence on the north and north-west, the natural features of the broken country were utilised with great skill, the positions themselves were better suited to the kind of fighting to which Serbia had been accustomed in former wars than to the conditions which have been developed in the present conflict. The way in which they had been able to treat the Austrians in the preceding winter had perhaps made them overconfident.

It must always be borne in mind that the Serbian plans of defence were formed entirely with a view to repelling an invasion from the north or west. That they profoundly distrusted Bulgaria it is needless to repeat, and we have seen that a sufficient force was always kept along the eastern frontier to repel anything except an invasion in strength. Against such a real invasion by Bulgaria, Serbia looked to her Allies to protect her. Her alliance with Greece was explicit and seemed to ensure the cooperation of the Greek army the moment that a regular Bulgarian force crossed the Serbian frontier. Beyond Greece, however, Serbia also looked to the Powers of the Entente The little International Force at Belgrade was an earnest of the intention of those Powers to protect her. She never believed that they would suffer her to be crushed, if only because of the value of her existence as a barrier on the

REAR-ADMIRAL TROUBRIDGE (2), COMMANDER OF THE BRITISH CONTINGENT WITH THE CROWN PRINCE ALEXANDER (1), WATCHING RANGE-FINDING OPERATIONS AT BELGRADE FORT.

road to Constantinople. For her own part, assuming that she would be free to devote her whole attention to the task, it was the belief of the Serbian higher command that the Serbian Army would be able to hold indefinitely and to repel any invading force from the north or west not exceeding 400,000 men. A larger force than that, up to, perhaps, 700,000, they believed that they would be able to hold for at least a month, so as to give their friends time to come to their assistance. Their preparations never contemplated having to meet single-handed the full weight of an invasion from the north as well as the assault of Bulgaria with all her strength from the east.

During the summer and early autumn of 1915 the actual military operations in Serbia were few. There was always a certain interchange of artillery fire and constant sniping going on across the Save and Danube. Now and again there were minor incidents of some importance, as in the matter of Mishiska Ada, an island in mid-stream near Shabatz, where, in July, the Austrians succeeded in surprising the small Serbian post on the island, only themselves to be attacked by a larger force on the following day, when the island remained in Serbian hands and the Austrians lost 120 prisoners. There were frequent collisions of small forces on the Bosnian frontier, where the Serbians held throughout the year a certain tract of Austrian territory. There was a certain amount of aerial activity, a squadron of Austrian aeroplanes on one occasion penetrating as far as Kraguievatz and dropping bombs which caused a dozen casualties in the civilian population. But the most important operation of the season was the Serbian invasion of Albania.

The Serbian column, with machine and light mountain guns, left the south end of Lake

WAITING FOR THE ENEMY.

Setting up a quick-firing gun. Circle picture: On the look-out for snipers.

BRITISH NAVAL GUNS IN SERBIA.

British sailors and soldiers, assisted by Serbians, assembling a naval gun.

Ochrida on the last day of May. The country was extremely difficult, but the Serbians advanced with great dash, fighting a successful engagement at Kakrew and reaching Elbasan on June 3. They drove the enemy out of formidable positions in the Grabe Mountains and, pushing on, occupied Tirana and Kavaia and also advanced as far north as Ishmi. The Albanians were commanded by Austrian officers. The total Serbian losses were about 200, and they captured seven Austrian machine and mountain guns. Finding the enemy occupying very strongly entrenched positions in a semicircle round Durazzo, which it would have been very costly to attempt to storm, the invaders contented themselves with investing the position, and sat down to starve out Durazzo, where Essad Pasha was held a prisoner. Simultaneously with the Serbian advance, a Montenegrin force made a demonstration on the north, and Greek troops also cooperated in the south, not joining in the fighting but occupying towns after the Serbians had taken and evacuated them.

At the beginning of August it became generally known in Serbia that the Entente Powers had made proposals (which have been discussed in Chapter CXIV.) with a view to obtaining cessions of territory to Bulgaria, in order to win the latter's adherence to the Allied cause. The ideas of what would satisfy Bulgaria seem to have been shaped for her by the Allies, and they took the form of the cession by Serbia of what is known as the "non-contested zone" (*i.e.* the zone which was regarded as unquestionably Bulgarian) in the Serbo-Bulgarian Treaty of February 29, 1912. This gave to Bulgaria all that portion of Old Serbia and Serbian Macedonia south of a line drawn from Mount Golem, on the frontier a little south-west of Sofia, to the northern end of Lake Ochrida. The cession would have included the important towns of Veles, Prilep, and Monastir.

The news that it was proposed to ask the surrender of so much territory, which had so recently been acquired at the cost of so much blood, had a bad reception in Serbia. In military circles especially the feeling for a while ran very high. It was freely declared that the attempt to make the surrender would bring about the downfall not only of the

LINES OF COMMUNICATION.

Bulgarian troops repairing telegraph wires in Serbia.

Government but of the dynasty. The proposal that the territory should not be conceded immediately to Bulgaria, but that it should be held in trust by the Entente Powers, being meanwhile garrisoned by, presumably, British troops, until the end of the war, found no approval. There were those who did not hesitate to say that the terms offered by the Central Powers were vastly preferable to such a national humiliation, and that it would be better to accept the overtures which Austria was known to be making. This extreme view, however, had not much support.

To M. Pashitch, more than to anyone else, belongs the credit of withstanding and cooling down the wrath of this patriotic outburst. At the hurried conferences which took place at Nish, in those first ten days of August, it is known to have been his wise and moderate counsel which led to the temperate and conciliatory course which Serbia thenceforward followed. It has to be remembered that no Serbian at that time had any belief that Bulgaria would in any circumstances throw in her lot with the Entente. Her path, it was believed, was already chosen. The most that could possibly be hoped for from her was a promise of neutrality; and that this neutrality would be anything more friendly than the thinly veiled hostility which she had shown up to that time was not believed. In Greece M. Venizelos held precisely the same view. Both in Serbia and in Greece it is probable that the ultimate sacrifice would have been made if there had been any certainty that the sacrifice would achieve its end. In both countries, however, there was the same reluctance to make promises and consent to sacrifices which would probably only be rejected, but which might at some future time be quoted against them. If all the non-contested zone was ethnographically Serbian, it would surely be argued that under no circumstances would Serbia consent to surrender it. If an offer to surrender it could be extorted from Serbia, it would, though rejected, be equivalent to a confession on her part that she had no right to it. Such a confession might be extremely useful in some future crisis in the tangled diplomacies of the Balkan States. As M. Venizelos said at the time to a correspondent of *The Times*: "The price which might not be at all too high to be worth paying for Bulgaria's active cooperation may be much too high to be even worth discussing until we know what it is going to buy."

Meanwhile it became daily more and more evident that the time for negotiations was getting very short. Certain members of the Bulgarian Ministry at the time who were notoriously Germanophile were accustomed to be used as a channel through which German official news and views were communicated to the Bulgarian public. The accuracy of the information which came through that channel had more than once been recently demonstrated. Some weeks before it took place, these Ministers had been able to announce with exactness the date of the beginning of the German offensive in Galicia. A little later, also well in advance of the event, they had foretold the precise date of the fall of Warsaw and what Germany would do when the city came into her hands. It was unfortunate that, in contrast with the accuracy of these prophecies, distinguished Englishmen had visited Sofia with explicit predictions, which were tantamount to promises, of the date of the fall of Constantinople—a date which, at the beginning of August, 1915, had long gone by.

When, about this time, then, these authorities in Sofia began to let it be known that Germany was really about to begin the great offensive against Serbia, their announcement had considerable weight. At the middle of August they began to circulate the statement that the offensive would begin in the third week of September, and that this time the attack would be made in such overwhelming force as, in a phrase which was said to be that of the Kaiser himself, "to wipe Serbia off the map for ever." Very soon afterwards rumours grew of large movements of troops on the north of the Danube, and especially of a great concentration going on at Temesvar.

Even before this date, however, those in command of the International Force at Belgrade had grown uneasy at certain evidences of increased activity on the opposite shores of the Danube and Save. The Austrians had been permitted to occupy Semendrevo (or Semendria) Island as well as Kojara. Furthermore, they were very busy at Panchevo, where there seemed to be a not inconsiderable number of small craft. It has been said above that the Serbians were very confident of their ability to hold an invasion from the north; also that they attached great importance to the preservation from destruction of the beautiful town of Belgrade. These two motives seem to have combined to make them indifferent to whatever the enemy might be doing on the northern bank of the river. The Serbian Higher Command does not appear to have believed that any serious danger was to be apprehended either from Semendria Island or from Panchevo, and, under pressure of the civil authorities, it was undoubtedly reluctant to do anything which was likely to provoke the enemy into active retaliatory measures against the capital. Semendria Island was about four miles long, and wooded. Panchevo, some ten miles by water below Belgrade, was well sheltered, by islands and trees. At either place it was difficult, except from the reports of airmen, to know exactly what was going on. In July the representatives of the Allies at Belgrade had called the attention of the Commander of the Army of Belgrade, General Jivkovitch, to the apparent activity of the enemy at these points, but it was decided not to interfere with him.

The Serbians do not seem to have contemplated the probability of a direct frontal attack on Belgrade itself. The city, most unfortunately placed for a capital, occupied what was practically a salient, though protected by the rivers all along the front, into the enemy's territory. It was thought more likely that, as in former cases, the Austrian attack, when it came, would be directed against points to the east and west of the town, so compelling its strategical evacuation, rather than against the salient itself. If they erred in this, however, the Serbians were much more keenly alive than were the Governments of the Entente

SERBIAN INFANTRYMAN FRATERNISING WITH THE AUSTRIAN PRISONERS.

THE GREAT RETREAT.

A scene on a road outside Kralievo: war-worn troops tramping along a road to take up fresh positions.

Powers to the reality of the danger which threatened from Bulgaria. At the end of September, when the Allies still clung to a hope of winning Bulgaria's cooperation, even after her mobilization, the Serbians proposed to anticipate the enemy's action and strike first by a thrust at Sofia. The proposal, however, was discouraged, and Serbia remained in an attitude of defence.

Partly from misconception of the enemy's plans of attack on the north, partly from confidence, bred from the events of the preceding winter, that even if the Austrians (or Austro-Germans) succeeded in crossing the rivers they could be held, as they had been held before, at the lines farther back, and partly through a just appreciation of the disaster that would follow if the Bulgarians were permitted to attack unopposed on the flank, so turning the whole Serbian positions by getting round to the rear—from all these motives combined the defences of the Belgrade salient were, at the critical moment, weakened instead of being increased. All the troops were withdrawn from the immediate vicinity of the city, except two infantry regiments, the 7th and 10th, though one Division was held in reserve some forty miles to the south. The Serbian heavy artillery was all removed to the Bulgarian frontier, except two 12 cm. howitzers on Topchider Hill, as also were the French aviators, as well as all the searchlights, but one. With the exception of the howitzers at Topchider, the only guns left in Belgrade were two old Russian 14 cm. and one quick-firing 165 mm. in the fortress, two French 14 cm. at Topchider, and one two-gun battery of British 4·7 in a position at Velike Varchar. The other British guns (three two-gun batteries) had been sent to Ostrujnitza Tcholin Grob, ten miles down the Danube, and to Grotska, the western and eastern bases of the salient respectively, in accordance with the belief of the Serbian

Command that this was where crossings of the river were most likely to be attempted.

After three days of fairly heavy but desultory bombardment, at daybreak on October 6 the direct attack opened on Belgrade with immense violence. It was undoubtedly a complete surprise. The number of guns used was very large, including 9-inch and 12-inch howitzers. It was estimated that in the course of 24 hours no less than 48,000 shells of all sorts were thrown into the area of the Belgrade defences. In addition, the enemy's aeroplanes kept flying low over the city and dropping bombs wherever they pleased. To this terrific assault the city was practically unable to reply. The Allied artillery, as has already been said, was disposed not to repel an attack upon Belgrade itself, but to prevent free movement in the river of the enemy boats. The only Allied guns which were in a position to offer any active resistance to the enemy's attack were the Russian guns in the fortress. Both of the heavy guns were put out of action on the first day by direct hits, and had to be stripped and abandoned, while the quick-firer ran out of ammunition and was destroyed by the Russians themselves. The British battery at Velike Varchar did not come into action on the first day, as it could do nothing to help to repel the enemy's landing, and it was better to keep its posit on concealed until it could be used effectively.

The destruction wrought by the enemy's bombardment was almost complete. Such anti-aircraft guns as there were on the Serbian side were immediately located, and all were destroyed on the first day. The electric light, telephone and telegraph communications were all cut. The city was on fire at many points, and the whole river front was pulverized and torn to bits. During the night of the 6th the enemy commenced his landing operations, using flotillas of flat-bottomed boats which had been prepared at Jakovo, on the Save, and behind Semlin. The landing was made in two places: on the west end of Tziganlia Island, which was connected with the Serbian shore by a bridge, and at the Danube quays on the front of the city itself. It was estimated that by daybreak of October 7 between 4,000 and 5,000 men had made good their footing at these two points. The eastern portion of Tziganlia Island was still held by a small force of Serbian infantry who fought with great gallantry, but, in the course of that day, the small remnant of survivors was compelled to evacuate.

The bombardment continued with undi-

BRITISH TROOPS IN SERBIA.

Setting up a quick-firing gun.

THE RETREAT OF SERBIAN SOLDIERS AND CIVILIANS TOWARDS THE MONTENEGRIN FRONTIER,

minished fury throughout the day of October 7. In the morning the British battery at Velike Varchar came into action against batteries across the river, having 24 guns and 4 howitzers over against it. The concentration of fire was such that both the British guns were covered with débris and had to be abandoned until night, when they were cleared and were ready for action again next day. Another British battery was on this day brought from Grotska and got into position on Banovo Hill, which commanded Tziganlia Island. It came into action in the afternoon and was immediately made the object of concentrated fire, but continued in action throughout the remainder of the day. The British guns at Velike Varchar meanwhile had also begun firing again, but one was almost immediately destroyed by a direct hit from a heavy howitzer. The enemy monitors now came out and attempted to take a hand in the fighting. They were at once attacked by the two French guns and the one remaining British gun, and driven off. One of the French guns, however, was also the victim of a direct hit and made useless.

The enemy continued landing men in large numbers during the night of October 7–8, and the morning of the 8th saw him practically in possession of the river front of the city. The city itself was burning fiercely at several points and there remained only one French gun at Topchider, one British gun at Velike Varchar and two British guns at Banovo Hill. Before noon of that day the British gun at Velike Varchar was hit and destroyed. In the afternoon the French destroyed and abandoned their remaining gun. Orders were given to destroy the British battery on Banovo, but, with great gallantry, under cover of the dusk, the men succeeded in bringing up the ox-teams and got the guns away down one side of the hill while the other was already in possession of the enemy infantry. These guns were of valuable assistance later in helping to cover the retreat of the Serbian Army.

The attack having begun on the morning of October 6, Belgrade had fallen by October 8. The little defending force, hopelessly overwhelmed as it was, could not have done more than it did. So far as possible all the war material belonging to the Allies, including surplus ammunition, the picket boat, the *Terror of the Danube*, mines, torpedoes, gun cotton and so forth, were destroyed or put beyond the enemy's reach, some of the operations for the purpose being conducted under heavy infantry as well as artillery fire and at great risk. The Russian, French and British missions all fell back on Torlak, whence they received orders from the Serbian Higher Command at Kraguievatz to proceed by train to Tchupria. Reinforcements from the Serbian Reserve Division, already mentioned, were pushed up to Belgrade on the 8th, but they found the city as well as Banovo Hill and other points already in the enemy's hands and were again withdrawn. Thus the Serbian capital again passed into Austrian hands.

A second crossing of the Danube was made at Semendria, where the attack commenced a day later than that on Belgrade. The bombardment here was equally fierce and overwhelming. It was estimated that the enemy had in action against Semendria throughout the days and nights of October 7 and 8 no less than 200 guns of all calibres, and it was soon discovered that 20 guns had, as had been feared, been got into position on the island under cover of the trees. There was practically nothing to reply to this tremendous fire, and after two days the enemy crossed the river in force and occupied the town, though not until after desperate fighting with the Serbian infantry.

BELGRADE.
Ruined houses in one of the streets.

GENERAL VON GALLWITZ,
Commander of the German Army which captured Semendria.

A small detachment of the British contingent, under command of Lieutenant Bullock, was stationed here with a torpedo battery and a number of mines. There was nothing that they could do of any effectiveness to prevent the landing, which was carried out by a fleet of small boats which had been got ready at Panchevo and behind the island. All that they could do was to remain at their posts, which they did under very heavy fire, as long as there was any chance of their being of service, and then to destroy what material they could not take away, before joining the rest of the British contingent at Torlak.

It should be mentioned that each of the British batteries was under the command of a Serbian officer. All of these officers behaved with great gallantry, and mention should especially be made of No. I. Battery at Veliko Varchar, under Captain Axentia Katitch, which, in the operations already described, lost one officer and 14 men killed or wounded, out of a total strength, British and Serbian, of 2 officers and 22 men.

The general command of the Austro-German army group which was entrusted with the invasion of Serbia was in the hands of Marshal von Mackensen. The army which attacked Belgrade was under the Austrian General Kövess; that which captured Semendria under General von Gallwitz. In the attack on Belgrade both Austrian and German troops were engaged. The artillery was largely German on the whole front. The infantry which made the landing on Tziganlia Island appears to have been Hungarian, while Germans forced the landing on Danube quays. The two forces united in the city and, after some desperate street fighting, the two flags were hoisted side by side on the fortress of Belgrade and over the new Palace.

Some circumstances should be noted here. While the amount of German artillery lent for the invasion of Serbia was large, the actual number of German troops employed seems to have been small. The whole Austro-German army of invasion did not, in the earlier stages, exceed 150,000 men. It is possible that ultimately as many as 250,000 of the combined armies may have been pushed into the country.

The Central Powers had, throughout the preliminary period of preparation and negotiation, declared that this time the invasion was to be in overwhelming force. It is quite certain that even a force of 250,000 would not have been overwhelming if the Serbians could have given it their undivided attention. We have seen that the Serbians were confident of their ability to handle an enemy force of twice that number; and, unaided, it is not to be supposed that the Central Powers would have undertaken the operation with less than half a million men. The point is that they knew that they were not to operate unaided. They knew that they were going to have Bulgaria's assistance, with which the smaller force would be adequate to its task. They must have been confident of this long before the actual attack was delivered—at least for some weeks before—during all of which time the Governments of the Entente Powers were still carrying on negotiations with Bulgaria, still believing that Bulgaria's cooperation might be won.

The story of those negotiations has already been told in Chapter CXIV., but it will be worth while here again to compare some of the dates:

It was on October 3 that Russia addressed her final note of protest to Sofia—the day, that is, on which the preliminary bombardment of Belgrade commenced. It was on October 5 that the Ministers of the Entente Powers at Sofia requested their passports, and not until the 8th did they leave the capital, or the day on which Belgrade fell. Bulgaria had mobilized as long ago as September 28. There i good reason to believe that a secret treaty, by which Bulgaria practically bound herself to the course which she afterwards took, had been signed as far back as August 17.

THE RETREAT OF THE SERBIAN ARMY.
A night bivouac in the Western mountains.

The first actual invasion of Serbia by Bulgarian troops seems to have taken place on October 11 at a point near Kniashevatz, to the north-east of Nish. Later, apparently on the same day, Bulgarian troops also crossed the frontier near Leskovatz, about an equal distance to the south-east of the temporary Serbian capital. The situation in which Serbia now found herself was the worst that her fears could have pictured. She was ringed around with enemies on all sides except the south and extreme south-west. On the north and west the Austro-German forces may not at this period have exceeded, as we have seen, 150,000 men; but they had an overwhelming weight of guns. On the east Bulgaria's army certainly exceeded 300,000. In all, the foes in the field amounted to at least 600,000; against which Serbia had only her 240,000 men, vastly inferior in all details of equipment and hopelessly outclassed in heavy artillery. Of her Allies, Greece had failed her entirely, and the others, moving slowly, were too far away to render any effective help.

The tale of the next two months is a tale of pure tragedy.

GENERAL VON GALLWITZ IN SERBIA.

The first blows in the combined attack had been delivered, as we have seen, with shattering force by the armies of von Kövess and von Gallwitz respectively against Belgrade and Semendria. Both these places were securely in the hands of the Austro-German forces by October 8.

Bulgarian mobilization had been begun on September 23, and the final decrees had been issued on September 28. Bulgarian troops under General Bogatcheff crossed the Serbian frontier and fighting had begun on October 11, but it was not until the 14th that the formal declaration of war against Serbia was made. Before that date Bulgarian troops had invaded Serbian territory at half a dozen points, and active hostilities had begun almost along the whole frontier from the Danube to the Greek border. Besides the first collisions, both on Serbian territory, to the east of Kniashevatz and by Leskovatz, which have already been mentioned, Bulgarian columns had, between the 11th and 13th, pushed into enemy country (1) at Negotin, in the Timok Valley, at the extreme northern corner of Bulgaria; (2) at Zaitchar, halfway between Negotin and Kniashevatz, the terminus of the railway to Paratchin and also of the uncompleted railway to Nish; (3) towards Vrania, on the main railway midway from Nish to the Greek frontier, and (4) on the road from Kustendil to Kumanovo, near to Egri Palanka. A day or two later fierce fighting was also going on between Tsaribrod and Pirot, on the main Nish-Sofia railway, and in the Strumitza region, where the earliest Bulgarian thrust had not been delivered, one may assume, only because, taught by bitter experience, the Serbians held the frontier here in too great force.

The Bulgarian attacks were delivered, therefore, with practical simultaneity at eight different points, showing how well the plans had been prepared. It was, of course, the natural strategy, seeing the enormous numerical advantage which Bulgaria possessed. Even with their smaller forces the Serbians, having the main north-and-south railway line to help them, might have been able to mass troops enough at any one given point to repel an invasion in whatever strength. But they could not be strong everywhere; nor, on the other hand, could they allow any one of the attacks to go unopposed, so permitting the enemy to cut the railway and pierce into the very heart of the country. The position of Serbia, indeed, if it had not been so profoundly pathetic, would have been almost ludicrous.

Belgrade had, we know, been stripped of men, guns, aircraft, searchlights—almost everything needed for its defence. The whole of the northern and north-western fronts had been similarly impoverished, in the hope of being able to offer some adequate resistance to the Bulgarian advance. With her whole army at her disposal, Serbia would have made a brave show either against Bulgaria or against the Austro-German invasion. She had to do her best, sending, perhaps, two-thirds of her strength to the eastern and most vulnerable side, leaving all her northern lines pitiably lightly held, but hoping that by some miracle, as in the preceding winter, even the insufficient screen of troops which she could interpose might be enough to hold the Austro-German advance long enough to enable help to reach her. Without the German heavy artillery, perhaps the miracle would have happened. But against that artillery the Serbians were powerless.

As it was, even the enemy bore testimony to the obstinacy with which the little bands of Serbians contested every mile of the advance. Writers in the German Press, after a fortnight's fighting, complained that it had so far been

THE ENEMY AT NISH.
The Kaiser (1) with the Bulgarian Commander-in-Chief (2); King Ferdinand of Bulgaria (3); Marshal von Mackensen (4).

impossible to bring the Serbian Army as a whole to a general action. The enemy fought, it was explained, "always in small parties," and these small parties "hardly ever surrendered, but fought on bitterly to the end," whence arose "bloody hand-to-hand encounters" and desperate single combats. It is a tragic vision which these pictures, drawn by the enemy, conjure up: the "small parties" of Serbians—all that there were of them—throwing themselves desperately against the enemy masses, not surrendering, but fighting always "to the end" in forlorn defence of their country.

On the east, the Bulgarians tasted the quality of the Serbians in larger doses. Here at several points there was bitter fighting, as notably in the Pirot region, about Kniashevatz and on the road to Kumanovo. At each of these points the invaders suffered very heavy losses, and more than one hard fought day left the numerically inferior Serbians in possession of the field. But everything was useless. The first real calamity on this front came on October 19, when, after some stern fighting, the Bulgarians succeeded in occupying Vrania, thereby cutting the railway between Nish and the south. According to Bulgarian accounts

KING FERDINAND OF BULGARIA
At the Austrian Headquarters.

of the battle, it was a regiment of the Bulgarian Royal Guards which finally broke the Serbian defence and seized the town. With the railway cut, it was as if Serbia's backbone were broken.

Without attempting to follow all the minor operations in detail, it will be well to look at the situation as it stood a fortnight after the attack on Belgrade, and ten days after Bulgaria's first advance into Serbian territory.

On October 21, then, the army of von Kövess, from Belgrade, had forced its way as far as Leskovatz and Stepoyevatz, about 30 miles south and south-west of Belgrade, and was threatening Sopot, slightly to the east of those places. Keeping pace with von Kövess, on his left, von Gallwitz, from Semendria, had occupied Selevatz and, pushing up the valley of the Mlava, was near to Ranovatz. It was on this day, October 21, that the Headquarters Staff thought it best to evacuate Kraguievatz. The Danube and Save had now been crossed at many points, but especially on the extreme west an Austrian column had retaken Shabatz and was thrusting in the direction of Valievo. On the extreme east, after very hard fighting, the enemy had crossed the river at Orsova, close to the Roumanian frontier, thus opening navigation down the river into Bulgaria, an event for which a number of boats laden with ammunition had been gathered at Orsova waiting. Thus the whole Save and Danube frontier was in the enemy's hands, and his forces were already on the average some 30 miles into the country.

On the west the Drina had been crossed at several points, but most important was that a large force operating from Vishegrad, in Bosnia, was slowly pushing back the Serbian resistance and threatening Uzitsha, the terminus of the branch railway on which were Krushevatz and Kralievo.

On the east the fighting was in progress along the whole length of the Bulgarian frontier. Commencing from the north, the Bulgarians had occupied Negotin and Zaitchar, and desperate combats were going on in the immediate vicinity of both Pirot and Kniashevatz. At Vrania, as has been said, the main railway line was already cut, and the enemy had raided down the line as far as Boyanovatz. From Kustendil, after bloody fighting at Egri Palanka, the Bulgarians were close to Kumanovo. Finally, pushing up the valley of the Bregalnitsa, a Bulgarian column had again reached the railway at Veles, and had occupied the half of the town on the eastern bank of the river.

A glance at the map will show how forlorn was Serbia's plight, with the enemy, outnumbering her armies by three to one, and with ten times the weight of guns, thrusting inwards from every side. Not only was the fate of the country sealed, but the whole Serbian Army, as well as the Government, with the King, the Crown Prince and all the foreign missions, were in imminent danger of being surrounded, and compelled to let themselves fall into the enemy's hands.

The sole ray of light in the darkness, and that was but a feeble one, was that the Allies were landing troops at Salonika, and small French and British columns had pushed up along the railway across the frontier at Ghevgeli, the French following the line to Strumitza, and thence heading for Veles, while the British held the railway from the frontier and occupied advance positions about Lake Doiran. At this time the British force, of the 10th Division under Gen. Sir B. Mahon, K.C.B., did not exceed 13,000 men. The French were, perhaps, half as numerous again. On the date at which we have outlined the situation above, October 21, the Allied Fleets, a blockade of the Ægean coasts having been declared four days previously, carried out an effective bombardment of Dedeagatch. On shore, however, the total allied strength in Serbia did not exceed 32,000 or 33,000, which did not go far to redress the balance against Serbia, which was in the neighbourhood of 400,000. There was, however, a hope that even this small force might be of use in preventing the Bulgarians from getting across on this southern part of the theatre, so as to put themselves in rear of the retiring Serbians, until their retirement was made good. This was the best that could now be expected—namely, that the bulk, or some large part, of the Serbian Army would be able to hold itself intact and, having avoided any general engagement, manage to escape from the country, by way of Albania or Montenegro, so as to be able to bear a part when the day of retribution should come. The Allied Powers united in urging Serbia to bend all her energies to this end. Effective resistance now being hopeless, the task was to extricate as much as possible of the Serbian Army from the net which was closing round it. On the enemy's part, the aim now was either to complete the circle of that net till no escape remained, or to overtake and crush the Army in its retreat.

A survey of the situation will show that already the position of Nish was very critical. The task of meeting the Bulgarian attack in this quarter was entrusted to the Serbian 2nd Army, under General Stepanovitch. Every

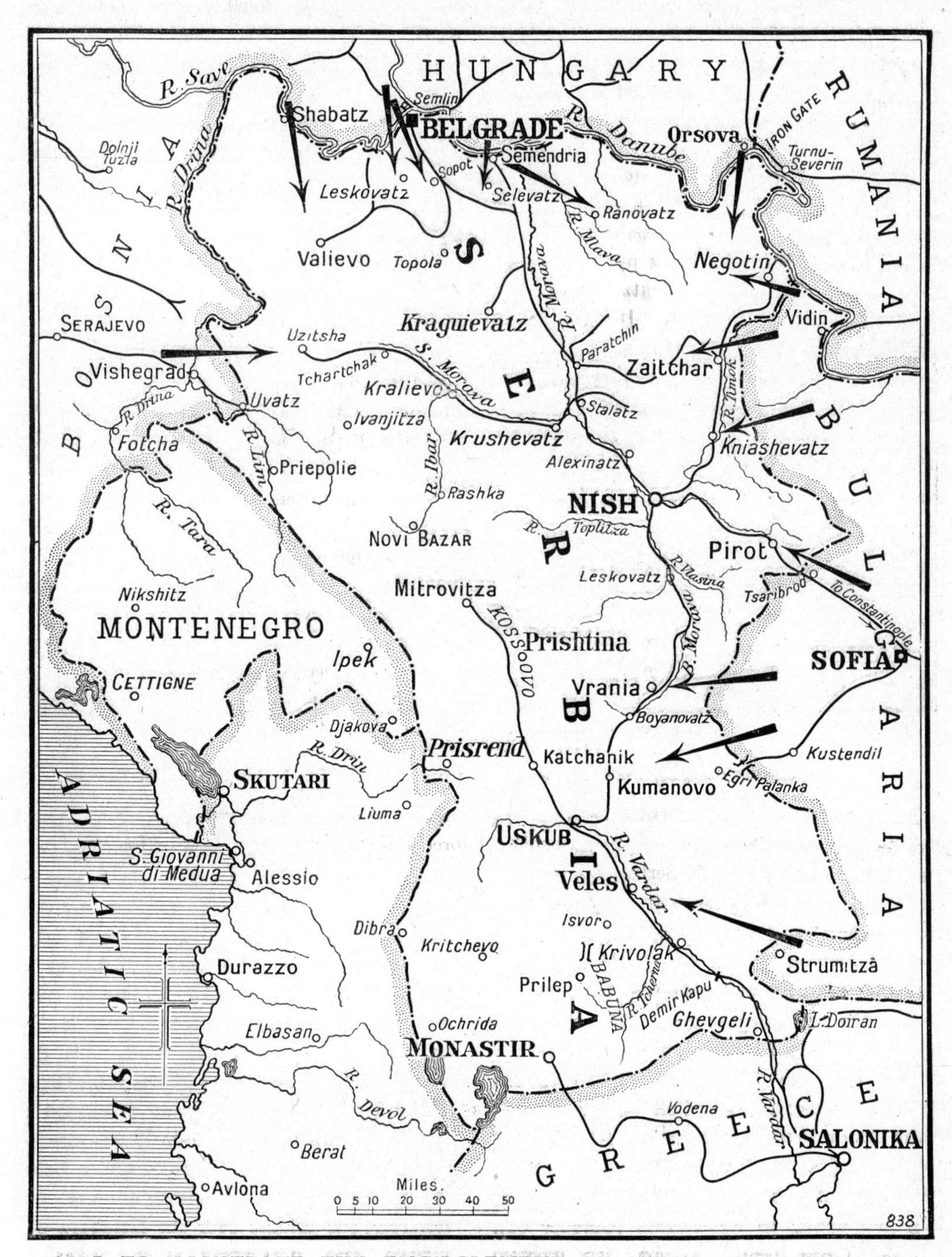

MAP TO ILLUSTRATE THE ENCIRCLEMENT OF SERBIA: SITUATION ON OCTOBER 21, 1915.

mile of Bulgarian advance here cost the invaders heavy losses and days of stubborn fighting. For a week after the Bulgarians claimed to have occupied Zaitchar, fighting of the fiercest description still went on immediately around the town, and Bogatcheff was utterly unable to advance beyond it. Similarly on the Pirot line to the south of Nish the conflict was of the most stubborn and sanguinary character. None the less the danger to the temporary capital itself was evident, and on October 21 the Government decided to remove from Nish, which it did by railway to Stalatz and thence, the main line being cut below that point, over the branch line to Krushevatz. The Allied Legations left Nish on the same date by the same route, but, instead of stopping at Krushevatz, pushed on to Kralievo. There the Government joined them two days later, to remain there until November 3.

THE SERBIAN RETREAT.

Stretcher-bearers carrying wounded men over a damaged wooden bridge across the Morava.

During this period, from October 21 to November 3, while the Serbian 2nd Army continued to offer stubborn resistance to the Bulgarians advancing on Nish, the Northern Serbian Armies—the Army of Belgrade under General Jivkovitch and the 1st Army under General Mishitch—were falling back slowly before the oncoming enemy. The three remaining British batteries, 6 guns, after the fall of Belgrade had been attached to the Army of General Jivkovitch and with that army they retired to Mladnovatz (October 22) to Topola, just north of Kraguievatz (October 25), to a position south of Kraguievatz (October 27), and finally to Krushevatz (October 31), where, as has been said, the Headquarters Staff had been since it left Kraguievatz on October 21. During this retreat the Austro-German forces were continually pressing on the retreating Serbians, the rearguard, with which were the British guns, being almost constantly in touch with the enemy. The last stage of this part of the retreat was done by forced marches in extremely bad weather.

Meanwhile, on General Jivkovitch's left, the 1st Army was also falling back. Between October 6 and 10 the enemy had crossed the Save at several points, but especially at Zabregie near the mouth of the Kolubara. The positions on this north-western section of the Serbian front were probably the strongest in any part of the country, and the Serbian 1st Army under General Mishitch was known for its fighting qualities. But with the fall of Belgrade and the advance of the enemy on the right, there was no choice but for this Army to join in the general retirement. The Staff, therefore, left Valievo for Mionitsa on October 20, and the former place was evacuated two days later, up to which date it was occupied by the famous Sokol Brigade, under Colonel Georgevitch. The evacuation was quite leisurely, the bridges over the Kolubara being wrecked and all material either destroyed or taken away. The town was not entered by the enemy until October 30. The army continued to fall back, not being heavily pressed and mostly without any serious fighting, by way of Mionitsa, Goukosh, Gorni Milanovatz, Rudnik, Blaznava, Bar (to the south-west of Kraguievatz, where the Arsenal had been evacuated since October 22), Knitch and Vitanovitse to Kralievo.

At several of these places, as especially between Mionitsa and Gorni Milanovatz and among the rugged mountain masses of Rudnik, there were positions of great natural strength and this region had been the scene of the chief successes, in which the 1st Army had taken a glorious part, in the campaign of the preceding winter. It was bitterly hard for General Mishitch now to have to fall back from one after another of the lines without serious defence. The enemy was, of course, quite aware of the defensive strength of the country and the German communiqués and other dispatches spoke in grandiose terms of the capturing in succession of the Ub-Kotselievo lines, Valievo, Gorni Milanovatz, etc., at each of which, it was represented, most terrific encounters had taken place and only the heroism of the Austro-German troops had overcome the desperate resistance of the enemy. If the enemy had chosen to resist in earnest, there would have been another story to tell. But the fact was, as has been said, that there was now no question of any longer being able to save Serbia. All that was aimed at was to save as much of the Army as possible, and as much of the stores and materials as could be got away. For this purpose the 1st Army fell back to Kralievo to hold the enemy off while other troops and stores made their way out by the defile of the valley of the Ibar to Mitrovitsa.

We have already seen that a strong Austrian column had pushed in from Vishegrad in Bosnia towards Uzitsha, thus threatening Kralievo from the west. In order to hold both this column and the troops coming down from the north as long as possible, the 1st Army turned at bay at Tchartchak (half-way on the railway between Uzitsha and Kralievo) and here desperate fighting continued for some days, in the course of which Tchartchak itself was taken and retaken many times. The casualties on both sides were large, the fighting being of the most sanguinary description. It was not until

THE GREAT RETREAT.

King Peter being assisted on to a pony from his motor-car, which, owing to the bad state of the roads, could not travel fast enough.

the pressure grew too heavy from all sides, from the north-west as well as from the east, by the arrival of new enemy troops by way of Alexandrovatz and Bruss, that the 1st Army, still fighting, was obliged to continue its retreat southward.

Meanwhile the position of the Second Army under General Stepanovitch had grown critical. We have seen how gallantly it had been holding the enemy above Nish. On November 2, at the request of the Serbian Higher Command, the three remaining British batteries, under Lieut.-Commander Kerr, D.S.O., were sent from Krushevatz to attach themselves to this army. To the south of the Second Army the Third Army, under General Sturm, had also been engaged in hard fighting, but Pirot had finally fallen to the enemy on October 26. On the same date the Bulgarians, now masters of the whole of Veles, had pushed up the railway and taken Skoplie (as the town had been called under the Serbians, though it now resumed its name of Uskub), and three days later they were in the Babuna region. Leskovatz, also the scene of peculiarly heavy fighting, was in the enemy's hands; and with the rapid advance of the main Austro-German forces from the north, which occupied Kraguievatz on October 31, the ring round General Stepanovitch's army was perilously near completion.

If the whole of the Second Army was not to be captured the further defence of Nish had to be abandoned. On November 4, therefore General Stepanovitch's gallant force began its retreat, and the enemy occupied Nish on the following day.

The Second Army then fell back across the Morava, the crossing of the river being covered by the British guns, which remained in their position on the west bank of the river until November 12, when they were ordered to retire in the rear of the army. In getting away, however, two guns became stuck in the mud and had to be stripped and abandoned, thus leaving only four. From the 12th to the 17th the army went by forced marches to Prishtina, the British guns always between the retiring army and the enemy. So severe was the pace that on November 13–14 the men covered 44 miles in 26 hours, and then, after three hours' rest, did 18 miles more. The road to Prishtina was the last possible channel of escape from the enveloping forces of the combined

THE "IRON GATE" OF THE DANUBE.

Formerly one of the most difficult rapids of the Danube below Orsova, improved by difficult and costly engineering work completed in 1898.

enemies, and the extrication of the army was undoubtedly a fine piece of work.

The rapid advance of the enemy from all sides made it no longer safe for the Government to remain at Kralievo or for the Headquarters Staff to remain at Krushevatz. The latter therefore went on to Kralievo on November 2 and on the following day both it and the Government left for Rashka. Both at Kralievo and Krushevatz a great deal of valuable material and, at the former place, 60 guns were left behind and fell into the enemy's hands. Besides the Government and the Headquarters Staff, practically the whole of the Serbian Armies as well as a vast number of civilian refugees were now trying to escape by the same route. The retreat, so far as the armies were concerned, was still orderly; but the road from Kralievo onwards was encumbered along its entire distance by endless trains of slow-moving ox-drawn transport wagons, with troops and refugees. From Rashka the Government no longer travelled as a unit, but all the members had arrived in Mitrovitsa by November 13, the Headquarters Staff getting there on the following day. The Diplomatic corps had been in Mitrovitsa since November 1. After a very short rest, on the news arriving that the enemy had occupied Glisljane on the 15th, the Government, Staff and Diplomatic corps all left for Prisrend, where they arrived on the 16th and 17th. From Prisrend they started again on dates between November 24 and 27, and finally reached Skutari on dates varying from November 30 to December 5.

GENERAL VON KÖVESS.

The Austrian Commander, wearing the Iron Cross presented to him by the Kaiser in recognition of his victory over the Montenegrins.

The British guns, hitherto attached to the Second Army, had arrived at Prishtina, some 30 miles from Prisrend, on November 17. On November 20 the Serbian higher command asked that they be attached to the Third Army under General Sturm. On November 22, therefore, the four surviving guns—the only heavy artillery which was now left to the Serbians—left Prishtina *en route* to Ipek with the Third Army. On the same day two of the guns became hopelessly embedded in the mud of the roads which had been made almost impassable by heavy rains. Every effort was made to extricate them, no less than 250 men and all the available oxen being yoked to them to pull them out of the mud All efforts, however, were useless, and these guns also had to be stripped and left. There were now only two British guns remaining. The enemy occupied Prishtina on November 26, less than 24 hours after the rear guard of the Third Army and the guns had left.

On that same day, the second day out from Prishtina, one of the two last guns fell through a bridge over a small stream, whence it could not be recovered. It was only possible to strip it also and let it lie. For three days more the one remaining British gun continued to accompany the rear of the retiring army On the morning of November 29, however, the British members of the crew—nine in number—found themselves alone and without means to get the gun along. They stripped and buried it; and went on after the army. It had been intended in any case to destroy the guns, if any got so far, at Ipek, where the party arrived on December 1, as beyond that point the transport of artillery over the mountains would have been impossible. It should be added that the Serbians expressed great ad-

THE VETERAN RULER IN THE GREAT RETREAT.

King Peter of Serbia, on an ammunition wagon drawn by oxen, leaving his country in the face of the overwhelming number of his enemies.

miration for the behaviour of the British batteries They continued to be a comfort and a help to the retiring army long after all the Serbian artillery had been captured or abandoned, and it was recognized as an extraordinary feat to have got them as far as they were taken. Of the 103 men, British and Serbian, who had composed the crews of the 8 guns on October 4, 53 had been killed or wounded in action by December 1. The detachment left Ipek for Skutari on December 2. After 11 days it arrived at Podgoritsa, and on the 15th reached Skutari, all the members of the party being very weak and exhausted. In all, the detachment had been fighting or retreating for 67 days, and during most of the time had suffered great privation.

The rest of the British contingent in the International force at Belgrade, the mining and torpedo section, under Major Elliot, since it could no longer serve any useful purpose, had been instructed by Admiral Troubridge to leave Krushevatz for Monastir (provided that route was still open) on October 28. It was fortunate to arrive in time, and reached Monastir on November 26. The French contingent, under Captain Picot, had already gone ahead, and had reached Monastir on November 20, as also had the members of the Russian Mission. Of the other foreigners in Serbia, many of the British hospital units decided to remain and let themselves fall into the enemy's hands, as conspicuously did Lady Paget and her staff at Skoplie. The rest were formed into a party by Sir Ralph Paget at Krushevatz. He himself went ahead to make what arrangements he could for them *en route*, the party itself being under the guidance of Dr. Tchuchin, to whose courage and energy, and to the capacity of Mr. William Smith, of the Scottish Women's Hospital, it was chiefly due that the party finally arrived at Skutari, though having suffered severe privations on the road, without serious catastrophe. The French aviators, with their mechanicians, telegraphists, etc., under Colonel Fournier, the Military Attaché, in all a party of 220 persons, also went by Ipek and Skutari, undergoing great hardships, and losing twenty of their number. They finally reached Skutari on December 3.

In the British party were, of course, a large number of women—doctors, nurses and hospital assistants—who bore the strain of the journey well. That all suffered severely was inevitable in a catastrophe in which the whole Serbian people, from king to peasant, suffered equally. Under the circumstances it was impossible to mitigate the conditions, and all alike testified to the fact that General Jivko Pavlovitch, the Serbian Chief of Staff, did everything in the way of provisioning and transport of the parties that it was in his power to do. That, however, was little.

Such, in barest outline, is the story of the retreat of the Serbians. No mere outline, however, can give any idea of the dreadful nature of that retreat. It must be remembered that it was not the mere retirement of an army. Merely as a retirement of an army, it was probably unique in that it was not one army which retired, but all the armed forces of a nation which withdrew completely from the soil of the country. And with those armies went the King and members of the Royal family, the Government and all the civil *personnel* of the Government, the foreign Legations and the doctors, nurses and staffs of the hospitals of the Allied peoples. Most terrible of all was the great mass of peasant refugees, villagers, peasants and people of the towns who fled in sheer terror Serbians are no strangers to "frightfulness," accustomed as they have been to warring with, and the outrages of, Turks and Bulgarians. But in no former war had more cold-blooded brutality been shown than that of the Austrians in such part of Serbia as they succeeded in overrunning in the preceding winter. All the world, moreover, knew what Germany had done in Belgium. Rather than face the Austro-German occupation, then, and expose their womenfolk to the treatment to which they were almost certain to be subjected if they fell into the invaders' hands, all the Serbian population which was not held by some unbreakable tie gathered together what little household goods it could and took to flight. A great proportion were physically unfit to face the difficulties of the road. Almost none had food enough to last him through the journey. It was not only the armies which retired, it was almost the nation which fled. And swelling the number of those who had to be fed upon the road, almost the most pitiable of all the great concourse of people, were some 20,000 Austrian prisoners who had been captured the year before. The road which the multitude had to travel was always rough. For great part of its way it lay through and over rugged mountains, often by paths dangerous at any time ; and these mountains were peopled by a population of hereditary enemies, largely brigands, who fell upon all small parties and robbed and murdered wherever they dared. The crowning burden was the fact that the weather was most bitter, heavy snow falling for many days, and the temperature in the mountains being for the most part intensely cold. It seems as if no detail which could add to the horror of the march was omitted.

All accounts agree in saying that until after the departure from Kralievo the *moral* of the Serbian Armies was well maintained. Each army had fallen back, however heavy its losses, before the terrible German artillery fire and under pressure of the exigencies of the general movement, in good order and without becoming disorganized. After leaving Kralievo the road was not at first extremely difficult, but the multitude of civilian refugees caused great congestion. Food was still obtainable, if not in any abundance ; and the strain of the march had not yet begun to tell upon the less vigorous. At each stage hereafter, however—at Rashka and at Mitrovitsa—the conditions grew worse. The roads in places were deep in mud. Wagons broke down and cattle died. Some of the weaker persons fell out from fatigue, and hunger began to make itself felt. When the historic plain of Kossovo was reached snow fell, the cold adding to the sufferings of the refugees, and many dropped by the roadside not to rise again. Here it was that the army made its last heroic stand.

The Bulgarians from Uskub had pushed up the railway towards Prishtina, and threatened to cut the route to Prisrend and thence, by Albania, to safety. The road had to be kept open at all costs to allow the slow procession of the fugitives to get away ; and among that slow procession was, the army knew well, the King, travelling in an ox-cart. The army had no heavy guns, but throwing itself in the way of the advancing Bulgars on a line from Lipliane to Ferozevitch, it met them with the rifle and bayonet. For six days the battle continued, the Serbs not only holding the Bulgars, but driving them back some 10 or 12 miles in the direction of Katchanik. Only the failure of the ammunition for their rifles compelled them at last to give way and to follow the King and the people along the road which they had kept open. The Serbian losses from the enemy's artillery fire in this last

THE RETREAT OF THE SERBIAN FIRST ARMY.

SERBIAN SUPPLY COLUMN IN THE GREAT RETREAT.

forlorn stand were very heavy; and the Army, now almost without ammunition, was hardly an army any longer. Terrible scenes were witnessed on the road to Prisrend. Deep snow lay everywhere. There was practically no supply column or commissariat. The men sustained life largely on the carcases of cattle and horses that fell on the road. But the the Bulgarians no longer harassed the army which, almost with its last breath, had taught them so gallant a lesson.

At Prisrend a number of the French contingent, which arrived there on November 24, estimated that there were massed in the neighbourhood of 150,000 refugees, among whom the destitution and the suffering were terrible. From here the only path of escape lay over the forbidding mountains of Albania, to Skutari, over 100 miles away. Here all motor cars, carriages, guns and stores were destroyed or thrown into the waters of the Ibar. To get them over the mountains was impossible. Here Marshal Putnik, very ill, as he had been since mid-summer, arrived in a motor car and left to be carried over the mountains in a chair. Here King Peter left his ox-wagon and, with two officers as companions, went forward on foot. The Crown Prince also went on foot, with an escort of 12 members of the Royal Guard. All arrived finally at their destination, but all suffering and ill, the Crown Prince especially lying for some time seriously ill at Alessio.

Part of the Serbian troops, including the 3rd Army, instead of taking the road by Prisrend, had struck west from Prishtina to Ipek in Montenegro, and so made their way to Skutari. These succeeded in taking with them some batteries of field and mountain guns. Over the Albanian mountains, however, it was not possible to take guns. The road was often of the most precipitous and dangerous character. In the snow, if there was ever likelihood of a detached party missing the route, it was always marked by corpses of those who had fallen out from parties in advance. Immense numbers of people, both soldiers and civilians, died from sheer exhaustion, from weakness and hunger, merely lying down by the road to die. Each more than ordinarily difficult spot, where the road was steep or where a small stream had to be forded, was marked by accumulations of dead. Not a few people and great numbers of the enfeebled and starving transport animals lost their lives by falling from the narrow paths down the mountain sides. No one who made that terrible journey arrived at the end otherwise than worn out, haggard, and in a condition of more or less complete exhaustion. Many died from frostbite and from dysentery, and not a few, both Serbian soldiers and civilians, fell victims

A VIEW OF NISH AFTER THE OCCUPATION OF THE ENEMY.

to the Albanian inhabitants of the mountains. These last seem to have made no attempt to harass the British or French contingents; but Serbian stragglers suffered severely at their hands, even such little baggage as the Headquarters Staff still had with it being pillaged.

This flight of the Serbians from their country—the King, the Government, the Army and the people—will stand as one of the great tragic episodes in history. For many of those who took part in the dreadful exodus, the retreat lasted over two months. For those who started from the centre of the country, as from Kraguievatz or Krushevatz, the time taken was from six to eight weeks. The journey was made in all cases under conditions of great hardship, from lack of food, from the physical difficulties of the latter part of the road and from the bitter weather. The Serbian Army, by the time that it had reached the sea coast, had lost about 120,000 men, or one half of its original strength. The mortality among the civilian population will never be known, but it was very great. No words, no description, can heighten the dreadfulness of the catastrophe which had befallen the Serbian people. Hardly any country in any age has seen so terrible and utter a calamity.

Even at the last, however, the gloom was lightened by a gleam of that fine spirit which the Serbian armies had shown all through their bitter trial. It has been said that some of the troops had made their escape by way of Ipek through Montenegro. Others had endeavoured to take the road by Monastir, but had been cut off by the Bulgarians advancing from the south-east and had been compelled to fall back into southern Albania. Broken, half famished and wasted as the armies were as they arrived at Skutari, General Pavlovitch managed to rally a portion of them, and at once, without any rest for recuperation, columns pushed southwards and got in touch with the scattered bands that had been driven from the road to Monastir, and, putting new spirit into them, concentrated them at Elbasan, Tirana and Kavaia, where they could for the moment rest in comparative security. And when King Peter, old and worn by the hardships of the trail as he was, heard that soldiers of his were in difficulties to the southwards, he insisted on going with the relieving columns to their help.

Skutari, though a temporary haven of refuge, was by no means a place of permanent safety. It was necessary to get everybody, soldier and civilian alike, first, to the coast and, then, to some place beyond the reach of danger. The first thing was to push everybody on as fast as possible to San Giovanni di Medua, an Albanian port which the Montenegrins had seized. By request of the Serbian authorities, Admiral Troubridge, who had accompanied the Headquarters Staff throughout the retreat, took charge of Medua. As a port for embarcation purposes it was extremely dangerous, being too near the enemy's base and, as the torpedoing of several ships arriving with supplies of food or leaving with loads of refugees sufficiently showed, most unsafe as a point from which to attempt to despatch the whole Serbian Army.

On January 11, 1916, the Austrians had captured Mount Lovtchen. On the 18th they occupied Antivari, which gave them command of Skutari Lake, and on the 19th, Dulcigno. Hostile aeroplanes were flying over Medua almost daily, dropping bombs on the camps of refugees surrounding the place and at the shipping in the harbour. Messages from Vienna announced the unconditional surrender of Montenegro. The announcement, however, was soon proved false. On January 18 the Queen and Royal Family of Montenegro embarked at Medua for Brindisi. On January 20 the King of Montenegro followed. By this time all the members of foreign missions, the hospital staffs and so forth, had all been got away. By the advice of Admiral Troubridge no attempt was made to embark the Armies (some of which, as notably the 1st Army, which, having formed the rearguard in the retreat, was farther from the port, were still suffering severely for lack of provisions). The attempt from so inadequate a port so near to the enemy would have been full of danger. The Armies therefore had to march by land yet one more stage southwards to Durazzo. On January 21 San Giovanni di Medua was evacuated by all the Allies. At Durazzo the work of transferring the Serbian Armies to a place of safety, chiefly to Corfu, and of there nursing them back to health and fighting strength, was taken over by the French, under General Mondesir, who had been sent out for the purpose.

There remains only in this sad tale to mention briefly the course of events in connection with the Anglo-French force which, as already narrated, had been landed at Salonika and pushed up into the country in the hope of preventing the Bulgarians from the south from getting round to cut off the Serbian retreat. That it did not succeed in preventing them from getting far enough to block the road to Monastir and in coming perilously near to seizing the road by Prisrend through Albania we have already seen.

One of the most touching aspects of the catastrophe which befell Serbia was the faith which the Serbian Government and people had always had that, if they were loyal to the Entente Powers, those Powers would protect them from ultimate disaster. Perhaps the bitterest blow was dealt by the crisis in Greece, which robbed M. Venizelos of the power to give effect to his belief that Greece was in honour bound to go to Serbia's help.

Serbia still believed that Great Britain and France would save her. On October 26 M. Pashitch addressed a dignified and moving appeal to Great Britain:

> Serbia is making superhuman efforts to defend her existence, in response to the advice and desire of her

KING PETER'S DAUGHTER,
Princess Helena of Serbia, with Prince Alexander.

> great Ally. For this she is condemned to death by the Austro-Germans and Bulgarians.
>
> For twenty days our common enemies have tried to annihilate us. In spite of the heroism of our soldiers our resistance cannot be expected to be maintained indefinitely.
>
> We beg you, the many friends of Serbia in England, to do all that you possibly can to ensure your troops reaching us, that they may help our army, and that we may defend together the common cause that is so gravely menaced.

The reference to Great Britain as Serbia's "great Ally" was, in the mouth of M. Pashitch, no mere figure of speech. It was to Great Britain more than to any other of the Allies that Serbia had always pinned her faith with a complete and almost romantic confidence. This was not by any means the first appeal which Serbia had addressed to Great Britain since the spring of 1915. Sir Edward Grey stated that the Serbian Minister had asked that troops be sent to Serbia as far back as July 7. It is known that the request had been repeated. On September 24 Sir Edward Grey had pledged England's assistance to Serbia "without qualification and without reserve," though he subsequently explained that these words were meant "in a political and not in a military sense." But it was military assistance that Serbia needed and counted upon. When it began to dawn upon the people of Serbia that the Allies were in truth not ready to send her the help that she so sorely needed, feeling against Great Britain and France was bitter, making the position of British representatives with the Serbian Armies sometimes very difficult. The news of the landing of Allied troops at Salonika had been received with enthusiasm; but that again gave way to intense discouragement when it was known how inadequate the strength of those troops was.

That the French and British contingents which pushed up the Valley of the Vardar did all that they could has never been questioned. But a force which could not in any case put as many as 30,000 men all told into the fighting line was not of much use against the enemy forces then in the field. The French, indeed, successfully held the Bulgarians back in the Strumitza neighbourhood and as far up the Vardar as Krivolak, where Bulgarian attacks were more than once repulsed. For a time it appeared as if General Sarrail's force might be able to recapture and hold Veles, and to the west of the river they operated with success in the neighbourhood of Izbor and helped the Serbians for a time to stem the Bulgarian advance by the Babuna defile. Beyond some early cavalry skirmishes it does not appear that the British force was much engaged until close to the end of the operations, when, on December 6 and following days, it was attacked by much superior Bulgarian forces. It behaved well and extricated itself successfully from a difficult position. The French advance on Krivolak was very dashing and the way in which, to distract attention from the Serbians, General Sarrail threw his forces over the Rajec and Tcherna against Bulgarian forces three times his strength, with no line of retreat but by narrow wooden bridges across raging streams, was bold to audacity. In the fighting about Mount Arkangel the French are believed to have inflicted very heavy losses on the enemy. But whatever was done by French or British was done too late. While the struggle about Krivolak was still going on, the Serbian Army was fighting that last desperate fight for existence near Prishtina, and the wretched stream of fugitives was already pouring over the Albanian mountains.

Under these circumstances, prolonged efforts by the little Allied force up the Valley of the Vardar were useless. It was not 30,000 but 300,000 troops at least that were needed. The force which we sent to help Serbia was as much too small as it was too late. Since the errand on which they had come was hopeless and ended, all considerations dictated the Allied withdrawal to Salonika. The exposed position of the force was precarious, but the withdrawal was satisfactorily accomplished, the British troops having to hold the line until the retirement of the French on their left was completed. The fortification of Salonika, the increase in the Allied forces at that point, and the events which followed were the beginning of a new episode in the war. The beginning of the year 1916 saw Serbia's fortunes at their lowest point.

CHAPTER CXIX.

SEA POWER AND NEUTRALITY.

Germany and British Naval Pressure—Position and Policy of the United States—The Meaning of Neutrality—Law of Contraband—Practice of Blockade—The Declaration of London and its Menace to British Sea Power—British Policy during the War—The Orders in Council—The German "War Zone" Policy and British Reprisals—American Arguments and the British Case—Cotton Declared Contraband—German Submarine "Frightfulness"—The Lusitania and other German Crimes—American and German Notes—Statement of British Policy towards Neutrals in January, 1916—Germany and "Armed" Merchant Vessels—Demand in England for a Closer Blockade of Germany—A Minister for Blockade.

THE Great War brought into direct conflict two schools of thought in International Law—the school that gave first place to belligerent rights and the school that gave first place to neutral rights. The war was admirably suited to raise the question in a form that could not be evaded, since, while the main scene of conflict was Europe, the chief neutral was three thousand sea miles away, and her communications with Europe were certain to be cut by British sea power.

That sea power on the first threat of war was swiftly and silently brought into position, and very soon the German flag practically disappeared from the waters of the world. With the German flag driven from the surface of the sea—into home harbours in the case of the High Sea Fleet, and into neutral harbours in the case of that great commercial fleet which had been the pride of the German Empire—there remained, unless or until Germany sent out her fleet, only two hopes for her beyond the Continental chances of war: her over-sea fleet of Zeppelins and other air-craft, her under-sea fleet of submarines. Germany, therefore, considered her only possible policy to lie in an attempt to terrorize the seas by the reckless destruction of all shipping at sight. The policy was from the first calculated to rouse the ire of even the most complaisant of neutrals; it alienated friends with extraordinary speed; it hardened enemies beyond conversion; and at last, after the sinking of the Lusitania, it brought the United States of America not only into closer sympathy than ever with the Allies but into the stage of possible intervention on their side.

The vigour of British sea power in 1915 and again in 1916 saved the American people from war. The Royal Navy devised ways and means for dealing with the submarine menace, and the life of a German submarine became very short. But despite this fact the German short way with neutrals increased, if and where possible, in offensiveness. The submarines that survived in fact ran *amok*. While Great Britain was for ever apologising both to the United States and other neutrals for her strength at sea and was incessantly striving to oblige the most unobliging of neutrals, and in fact was prolonging the war substantially by allowing masses of goods of warlike use through to Germany; while the British Admiralty was thus playing its not unfamiliar part, Germany was engaged by the employment of methods that created repulsion in making the position of neutrals stronger than it had ever been before. It rapidly became clear even to the most pro-German

HOISTING IN A MOTOR-BOAT ON BOARD A BRITISH CRUISER.

neutral that the infamous and shameless conduct of this de-civilized power made the organization of all neutral forces essential to prevent a recurrence of such events. Neutrality throughout the war tended to become more and more an armed neutrality ready to intervene when the moment came. Meanwhile the submarine policy was accompanied by open threats to the United States on the subject of the transport of munitions of war to England, while conspiracies of violence against the manufacturers carrying out contracts for England were organized by Germany and Austria in open defiance of the law of the United States.

From the first the policy of the United States had been absolute neutrality, that is to say, neutrality as a State with freedom for her people to trade at their own risk with any or all the belligerents. Sea power determined the belligerents with whom the nationals of the United States should trade. When Germany lost her sea power she lost the benefit of sea-borne neutral goods other than such as could be supplied by her immediate neighbours. The worlds of the East and the West were practically closed to the Germanic Powers. The realization of this fact led to violent demands to the United States for the suppression of the industry in arms and munitions, demands that were thrice refused. American trade had vastly benefited by the war. Sir Edward Grey made this abundantly plain in his note of February 10, 1915, in reply to ingenuous American complaints. The *ante-bellum* decline in the export trade of the United States had disappeared by the beginning of 1915. It was not only trade with England and her Allies. Immense quantities of food and necessities of war got through to Germany by way of neutral nations, and so dangerous to the Allies was this trade that the British contraband list was tardily enlarged to meet the case. But even this was not enough ; a pure contraband policy was inadequate, and it happened not altogether unfortunately that the reckless German under-sea policy made reprisals legally possible and brought about the famous Order in Council of March 11, 1915.

By this Order what was, in effect, a siege of Germany from the West began. Goods for and from Germany were subjected to restraint, and this action synchronized with a more effective siege on the Russian marshes of Germany and Austria. Sea power came into fuller play from April, 1915. American opinion, which had violently disliked the British contraband policy, was greatly roused by the policy of reprisals, supplementing an ever-increasing contraband list. But two things were forgotten : first, that the American trader was better off under this system of restraint than under a blockade ; and, secondly, that the policy of the Order of March 11, 1915, was based on American as well as British precedents. Moreover, there was a certain incongruity in any complaints against a system of restraint which was full of consideration for neutral trade ; which was aimed at a desperately unscrupulous foe who had proved in a series of reckless attacks on innocent neutral shipping that he was the enemy of mankind ; which was designed to destroy the militancy of a Power that had torn up the Conventions as to warfare to which Germany and the United States were joint parties. Great Britain was compelled by her duty to the whole cause of international life to leave no legal measure untried that would reduce the enemy. Consequently the contraband list was steadily increased. After unpardonable delay and tergiversations on the part of the British Government, cotton came under it, while the siege of Germany from the North Sea proceeded with greater regularity. America was, in fact, doing very well in the matter of trade. It was felt in the British Empire that the complaints of the United States, and indeed of all the neutrals, were in a measure factious and unjustified. But Great Britain did what was possible, as the White Paper of January, 1916, showed. The most meticulous care was taken to safeguard the interests and supply the needs of the populations of European neutral countries, and never in the whole course of the war did England have recourse to an act of violence or injustice to a neutral vessel. Where such vessels were seized and searched and proved innocent the fullest compensation was made or a good price paid.

So gradually the *saeva indignatio* of the United States concentrated, and with reason, on the horrors of German frightfulness at sea. While striving to put the case of the Lusitania on such a footing as would make recurrence impossible, American opinion was continually faced by fresh outbreaks of frightfulness at home and on the sea and on the Continent of Europe. The patience of the American people slowly grew taut, and though the case of the Lusitania at last seemed capable of settlement, a feeling of intense bitterness in March, 1916, swept through the States when it was recognized that in the contemporaneous policy of Germany, by which the right was claimed to sink armed merchantmen, there was a renewed determination to flout and discredit their nation. The States became the angry witness of a new outburst of wickedness on the part of Germany—the deliberate sinking at sight of

DUTCH VESSEL FOUNDERING IN THE NORTH SEA.
After being mined or torpedoed by a German submarine.

BRITISH MOTOR-BOATS IN THE NORTH SEA.
Preparing to board a Norwegian steamer at night.

unarmed neutral liners and passenger ships of an entirely innocent type.

With the broad lines of policy in mind it will be convenient to turn to the great problems of international law that arose for solution.

In order to appreciate the problems of Sea Power and Neutrality raised by the Great War it is essential to bear in mind the modern theory of neutrality. Though, of course, from time immemorial there have been nations and Powers who have stood by while their neighbours have fought, yet the idea of neutrality as the term was understood in 1914—a national status involving both rights and duties in relation to the belligerent operations of other nations—only dates from the period of the Renaissance, when after the fall of Constantinople Europe began to take new shape. For three centuries this idea of a neutral status was indeterminate, varying from war to war. The honour of laying down once for all the current theory of neutrality is due to the United States of America in dealing with the situation created by the French Revolutionary wars. In 1793 Jefferson, on behalf of the Washington administration, declared that a neutral must be, in fact as well as in form, impartial towards all belligerents; must (apart from treaty obligations) give no war service to any party, nor allow troops to be raised in its country, nor vessels armed in its ports. Vattel had already declared that neutrality must not be fraudulent, and Washington adopted this principle with all its implications. On the other hand, this duty of perfect impartiality was not to be regarded as inconsistent with the neutral's right to pursue his commerce as in time of peace, while this right in its turn was not to interfere with the right of one belligerent to deprive the other (if he could do so) of the sinews of war. The neutral Power will not restrain its nationals from trade with any belligerent or any other neutral Power; such restraint, if it is to be exercised at all, must be exercised by the belligerent who is hampered in his lawful warlike operations by such trade. The vital problems of neutrality which took so urgent a shape in the Great War arose out of the indeterminate limitations to which the exercise of such right of restraint is subject. Thus we find that the modern theory of neutrality is intimately bound up with the older doctrines of contraband and blockade. It would be erroneous to suppose that the right of restraint is limited to those doctrines. That right exists in order that the neutral right of commerce shall not be so used as to make the neutrality fraudulent. That right must necessarily exhibit new forms to meet new occasions of fraud.

What is the true adjustment between the neutral right of commerce and the belligerent right of restraint ?—is the question that really underlies all the complex political negotiations between belligerents and neutrals, all the elaborate manifestoes of rights and duties in the realm of international law which from August, 1914, onwards occupied and confused the minds of men. The real principles involved were not complex, but they had to be worked out on such an enormous scale, and affected such a multiplicity of commercial and political interests throughout the world, that the appearance of complexity was inevitable. But if we keep in mind the principles, first, that a neutral nation must always be impartial, must never be fraudulent, but has no duty to place limitations or restraint on the purely commercial activities of its nationals, and, secondly, that a belligerent nation in the course of lawful warlike operations may restrain the nationals of a neutral Power from so exercising their commercial activities as to make their national neutrality elusory, then the course of events is simple enough.

Restraint by sea power of neutral commerce relates primarily to goods. The whole object of the restraint is to prevent goods from reaching the enemy. It is only, in considering first principles, in a secondary fashion that it relates to the means of carriage—namely ships. It is true that until the date of the American Civil War blockade was supposed essentially to refer to ships and not to goods except in relation to the guilt of the ship. But during that war this doctrine was definitely attacked by the American Courts, and the decisions of those courts were acquiesced in by the British Government. No doubt many jurists continued to think up to the date of the Great War that the critical destination in the matter of blockade is that of the ships and not that of the goods, but the war rapidly brought opinion round to the view that in blockade, as in questions of contraband, the critical destination is that of the goods and not that of the ships. The importance of this position became plain when it was seen that Germany could be fully served in every way from neutral ports, and that if those ports could not be closed to goods, then the sea power of one belligerent could not be used to restrain neutral commercial activities that were in fact assisting the other belligerent in every possible way. This difficulty was no new discovery in 1914.

The term contraband (*contra bannum*) is derived from the period when Roman Empe-

THE TRANSPORT "SOUTHLANDS."
Torpedoed by an enemy submarine.

rors and Popes banned the supply of arms and necessaries of war to barbarians and heathens. The great Grotius in 1625 divided goods into three classes : those solely of use in war, those of no warlike utility, and things of use for peace purposes as well as war purposes (*res ancipitis usus*). Here belligerents and neutrals alike are faced with the great difficulty as to the last ambiguous class. If we use Professor Holland's definition of contraband articles as "those which a belligerent is justified in intercepting while in course of carriage to his enemy, although such carriage is being effected by a neutral vessel," it is clear enough that goods solely of use in war so carried are contraband,

COALING A BRITISH CRUISER.

and we may go further and say with Dr. A. T. Walker that all articles "susceptible of direct use in the furtherance of belligerent operations" are contraband if they have what Lord Stowell called "a hostile destination." Now the third or ambiguous class of contraband mentioned above is known as conditional contraband. In the famous Treaty of Whitehall between England and Sweden, signed in 1661, this class was recognized, and from that time onward conditional contraband with a hostile destination has been liable to capture followed by pre-emption of the goods with freight, or in some cases followed by confiscation when the goods were of extreme importance to the military forces of the enemy. This doctrine of conditional contraband was adopted by the United States, but has been largely repudiated on the Continent. The class is determined by the express declaration of the belligerent or by judgment of the Prize Court. England from at least the age of Queen Elizabeth had stood for an elastic contraband list, and her Prize Courts in construing the Treaty of Whitehall introduced the important doctrine of pre-emption with respect to conditional contraband as an alternative to confiscation, a doctrine to some extent accepted by the Declaration of London. This doctrine of pre-emption appeared in its fullest form in the famous Order in Council of March 11, 1915, but it is a doctrine that had had the sanction of English practice during at least three centuries. France and Spain, in the Treaty of the Pyrenees of 1659, endeavoured to establish a different law of contraband, a law that should limit as far as possible contraband to mere munitions of war, and this extraordinarily restricted doctrine eventually was extended to exclude conditional contraband and pre-emption altogether, on the grounds that the existence of such a class made arbitrary conduct on the part of belligerents and their Courts inevitable, and that there is no intermediate state in a neutral between guilt and innocence. However, the nations which adopted this doctrine in theory abandoned it in practice. Thus in the Russo-Japanese War Russia was compelled by the necessities of her position to adopt the doctrine of conditional contraband.

But, whatever view of contraband is held, and the Anglo-American view really dominates the seas, it is clear that that view must be made effective. The geographical intermingling of belligerent and neutral territory long made it difficult for the rights of belligerents in respect of contraband to be enforced. Neutrals have always naturally adopted the position that war should be so conducted as to place the least possible limitations on trade. On the face of things it would seem a mere truism to say that war shall not interfere at all with trade between neutral and neutral. And yet that was the exact problem which faced the world in the late eighteenth-century wars. Goods consigned from a neutral port to the enemy by a ship whose ultimate destination was a neutral port raised a point of supreme importance to Powers which relied for victory on sea power. Were such Powers to allow their admitted rights against contraband to be evaded by the simple device of consigning the goods to the enemy by way of a neutral port? There are still publicists who maintain this position, but the position is not substantially held, since if it is sound the whole doctrine of contraband becomes elusory. It was to meet this position that the really very obvious doctrine of Continuous Voyage was invented. In 1756, at the beginning of the Seven Years' War, France opened the trade between her home and colonial ports to the Dutch, with the result that England claimed the right to capture Dutch vessels so trading, and in 1793, when the same trade was thrown open to all neutrals, England claimed the right to extend the rule and capture all neutral vessels so trading. Neutrals attempted to evade the English claim by interposing a neutral port between the French and the colonial port, but Lord Stowell swept away this evasion of the English claim and so founded the doctrine of Continuous Voyage. Whether the extension of "the Rule of the War of 1756" was sound or not, and it is very generally condemned, the doctrine by which it was enforced was not in any way dependent on the extended Rule. It was a doctrine of common sense invented to prevent the evasion by a neutral of the duty of impartial neutrality. Dr. Walker tells us, in commenting on Lord Stowell's decision in the case of the Maria in 1805, that "the principle underlying this judgment, the principle that in judging of the legitimacy of a certain course of trade reference must be had to the real and ulterior destination of the merchandize existing in the mind of the trader at the place of loading, and that no voyage, illegitimate in its inception on the ground of its ulterior goal, can change its character in consequence of the interposition by design or otherwise of an intermediate port, has become famous as 'the Doctrine of Continuous Voyages.'" In order to prove fraud,

KEEPING UP STEAM ON A BRITISH BATTLESHIP IN THE NORTH SEA.

or the intention under cover of a neutral goal to reach an enemy destination, it has always been possible to go behind the ship's papers and convict the shipper of fraud out of the mouths of his captain or crew, or otherwise. The doctrine of Continuous Voyage was applied both to contraband and blockade by the American Courts in the Civil War, and the attitude was acquiesced in by the British Government, which applied the same doctrine to contraband in the South African War. That is undoubted law. It is always possible to go behind the ship's papers and use any evidence available to prove the hostile destination of the goods. Jurists and Governments throughout the world have felt the overwhelming force of this contention, and the doctrine of Continuous Voyage in the case of contraband was regarded as an established doctrine of International Law on the outbreak of the Great War.

But how far does it go ? Suppose that a neutral shipper without asking any questions at all and with no particular enemy destination in mind ships contraband to a neutral destination, where it becomes part of the stock of a neutral merchant ; can such traffic be stopped on the ground that in fact the goods pour through the funnel into the enemy country ? This was the problem, the apparent extension of the doctrine of Continuous Voyage, by which the Powers exercising sea power were faced in 1914. It was in fact no extension of the ordinary doctrine. In that doctrine the Prize Court has to find what was in the mind of the shipper when he consigned the goods to the neutral port. The Prize Court in the Great War still had to do the same. If a Prize Court finds a shipper who before a war ships to a certain port x tons of goods that have been declared contraband, and during the war, with local neutral conditions of consumption undisturbed, ships $100x$ tons of the same goods to the same port ; and that port is in direct communication with the enemy country ; then the Prize Court is logically bound to find that the shipper had a fraudulent mind and was intent on supplying the enemy by way of the neutral port. That was, in 1914, the view of the English Prize Courts and of the English Privy Council, and it was a view, as we shall see, fully justified by the facts of the case.

The practice of blockade is very different in certain ways to the practice of stopping contraband goods, but they have to-day much the same goal in view. The origin of the idea of blockade is the idea of a siege. If a town is besieged it has always been the practice of the beleaguering forces to cut off the besieged place from all communications with the outside world. No neutral is allowed to cross the lines. This was still true when the beleaguered town was on the sea coast and the lines of investment were on the sea. It is this special case that has been made (to use the words of Dr. Westlake) " the basis of extensions which have resulted in the international doctrine of blockade." In 1584 the Dutch declared a blockade of all the Spanish-Netherlands ports. This was a siege on a huge scale, and in less than half a century the closing of ports (the term used by Grotius in 1625) was distinguished from siege. In 1630 Holland decided to seize neutral ships sailing for those Flemish ports which she had declared closed. The object of this, the first regular blockade, was to shut off from the enemy not only contraband goods but all commerce. The success of this new weapon of war induced the Dutch in 1652 to declare a blockade of the British Isles, and for some years this " paper " blockade tended to limit the operations of blockade to articles useful in war. Before the year 1700 the idea of blockade had become fixed, the lawful exclusion of all commerce from a place definitely invested. The attempt to extend the idea to all trade with the enemy whenever carried on by neutrals failed, and the conception of effective siege of a specific place or area remained, and to some extent still remains, an essential part of the doctrine of blockade. But the idea of siege seems to connote the idea of resistance, and during the Napoleonic Wars and later the blockade of purely commercial ports incapable of defence was stoutly denounced. But after all, if there is any principle in blockade at all it is as manifest in the case of an undefended as in that of a defended port, and there is no real argument against the extension of the doctrine to any specific coast area. Dr. Westlake, not an author who is apt to justify extensions of existing doctrines, declares that " the belligerent right of commercial blockade is well established as a part of the compromise between the exigencies of belligerents and the just claims of neutrals which has been effected by tacit international agreement."

But whatever the nature of the blockade, it must have one characteristic—it must be a reality. In 1856 it was laid down by the

EXAMINING CARGOES FOR CONTRABAND.

Using the X-rays on a bale of cotton to detect any contraband concealed.

Declaration of Paris that "blockades in order to be binding must be real, that is to say, maintained by a force sufficient in fact to prevent access to the coast of the enemy." Both Great Britain and the United States have long contended, and the contention is now almost universally admitted, that such a blockade can be maintained by cruisers forming a distinct blockading squadron in a definite area. Neutral ships entering the area in order to attempt to enter the blockaded ports are liable to capture.

In the Great War a further question as to blockade arose. Could blockade be extended to neutral ports? If blockade is in itself a sound doctrine, it should not be capable of evasion by reason of the existence of neutral ports in the immediate vicinity of the blockaded ports. A complete blockade of a neutral port which is acting as a funnel for the enemy can be justified on the ground that the port in question is only one stage on a journey to the blockaded port; in other words the doctrine of continuous voyage can be applied to blockade. Up to the date of the Great War this extension was

NEUTRALS GUARDING AGAINST GERMAN FRIGHTFULNESS.

The name of a Dutch vessel painted in large letters on the side of the ship.

Smaller picture: Painting on a ship the broad bands of the National colours of Holland.

resisted; it was considered that "if a ship is bound for a neutral port, not as a port of call, no blockade-running has been attempted by her, and her cargo, still innocent, cannot connect her with any such attempt which the ship into which it may be removed may afterwards commit" (Westlake). But in practice the Great War showed that lack of power to stop consignments to neutral ports meant that the whole blockade would become illusory.

The most important questions which arose in the war between neutrals and belligerents arose directly out of the command of the seas exercised by the Royal Navy. Certain series of events must be kept for distinct consideration, in order that a view of the whole development may be possible. The development of British policy from August, 1914, to March, 1915, was in the main an extensive application of the law of contraband

Two main branches of the topic may be distinguished: (i.) The lists of contraband—*i.e.*, what articles may be declared contraband; (ii.) the conditions under which contraband may be captured, and its entrance into enemy territory prevented.

The latest attempt before the Great War to settle the lists of contraband was in the Declaration of London, an ill-advised document drawn up as the result of a naval conference held at London in 1909. The effect of its application would have been to curtail British sea power. Thanks to an agitation conducted by patriotic public men, and to the action of the House of Lords, the document was never ratified, although, long after the beginning of the war, the British Government still endeavoured to retain it as a tentative code of law. Much was said on the German side with regard to the British departures from the Declaration. In so far as that document contained regulations for the lists of contraband, it was substantially observed by the British Government. The Declaration adopted the threefold classification referred to above. Articles exclusively used for war were called absolute contraband: articles of use both in peace and in war were called conditional contraband. Both were contraband, and the only distinction was that absolute contraband could be captured in some cases where conditional contraband could not, a distinction to be dealt with presently.

Three lists were then set out under the heads of absolute and conditional contraband, and goods which could not be declared contraband. The lists were short and contained only well-known articles of commerce, but provision was made for adding to these lists in the proper way —*i.e.*, any other goods of exclusive warlike use might be put under absolute contraband, and so on. The only departures from the Declaration were two: (i.) certain articles which had been declared to be of no use in war, and therefore never to be declared contraband, were made contraband—*e.g.*, rubber, hides, cotton, and metallic ores. It cannot be doubted that in this respect the Declaration must be judged by the departures from it, not the departures by the Declaration. (ii.) Certain articles which were of use in peace as well as in war were made absolute instead of conditional contraband, such as barbed wire, copper, lead, aluminium, sulphuric acid, which became absolute contraband on October 29, 1914. This was a departure justified upon the principles of the Declaration itself. Under the conditions of the Great War these articles had become practically of exclusive use for war, so that they were rightly made absolute contraband. The contraband policy began with a proclamation dated August 4, 1914, which agreed exactly with the lists in the Declaration except that aircraft was made absolute instead of conditional contraband. A different stamp appeared on the lists from December 23, 1914, onwards. It was clear that the expert was at work. Strange metals and chemicals began to appear, but the underlying principles of contraband were not departed from.

In this matter the distinction between absolute and conditional contraband becomes of importance, and it is much more important to appreciate the reasons for the rules than the letter of the rules themselves.

1. The principal difference was in the destination, which had to be proved in the two cases. Absolute contraband consists of those articles which are exclusively used for war, such as munitions. Clearly, therefore, any munitions which are consigned to the enemy territory, whether the consignee be a private merchant or the Government, will be used in the prosecution of the war, and may be properly captured. With regard to conditional contraband the matter is not so simple, since the articles are of use in peace as well as in war. Now, the aim of the law of contraband is to settle what neutral trade a belligerent has a right to intercept, and the line will clearly be drawn at allowing a belligerent to prevent neutral traders from succouring his enemy with supplies for the prosecution of the war. Since these articles of conditional contraband, therefore, may be used for peaceful commercial enterprise, the point was to distinguish between such of them as would be used for such enterprise and those which were destined to be used for war.

ON PATROL DUTY.
A Dutch vessel in the North Sea.

In 1914 the latest formulation of rules for this purpose was in the Declaration of London. Mere consignment to enemy territory was not enough, because the goods might go there for peaceful purposes. If, however, they were consigned to the armed forces of the enemy, or to the enemy governmental authorities, and not to a private merchant, they might be captured as being destined for the furtherance of the war.

2. Another point of difference in the conditions of capture affected trade through neutral ports. The doctrine of continuous voyage which figured largely in the British policy is, as we have shown, perfectly simple. It merely meant for present purposes that contraband could not use neutral ports to evade being intercepted by the fleet of a belligerent, and it was firmly established before August, 1914. The case of the Carthage marked the second point of distinction between absolute and conditional contraband. By way of concession to neutrals it was thought that the doctrine of continuous voyage should only apply to absolute contraband, such as munitions, so that any articles which might have a use in peaceful commerce should gain free entrance into enemy territory through neutral ports. This idea was embodied in the tentative code framed by the London Conference, and the Carthage was decided upon that basis.

Turn now to the circumstances of the war which broke out in 1914. Belligerents were involved upon a scale hitherto unknown; one alliance had undoubted command of the seas, the other had a fringe of neutral countries whose ports could be used as "ports of colourable importation"; while away across the ocean lay a great neutral trading Power, desirous of preserving its economic activity during a world-wide disturbance. Furthermore, the enemy of the Power with naval supremacy was organized through and through for the purposes of war, so that the distinction between peaceful and military activities no longer obtained. The enemy was not a professional army whose fortunes a commercial population followed with patriotic interest, but a nation in arms with peaceful interests suspended for the duration of the war.

The plain result was that articles susceptible of use in peace or in war would undoubtedly be used for warlike purposes. The large German element in the great neutral exporter would be only too ready to send them through. Whether they were consigned to the enemy Government or to private merchants, whether they effected their entrance through enemy or neutral ports, these articles which in other days might support commercial enterprise would certainly become the food of war, the support of a nation at war.

The root principle of contraband is that neutral trade may rightly be intercepted where it provides the food for war, and it was upon this principle that British policy was framed. In statute law the letter must be observed, because judges have no power except to assume that the principle is embodied in the letter; in international law to grasp the principle is vital. To depart from what has hitherto been the letter may be to apply the principle of the law.

No Government in the position of the British Government could well be expected to announce a policy forthwith and adhere to it. The policy was gradually developed as the situation to be met unfolded itself. It became clear that the problem was double-faced—viz., that of the United States as exporter, and that of European neutrals as bases of supply for Germany and her allies. This is apparent from the trade returns in possession of the British Government, and used by them in justification of their policy towards the United States. In his Note of February 10, 1915, Sir Edward Grey made the following observations upon the trade of the United States, based upon the customs returns of that country. In the seven months of 1914, before the outbreak of war, there was a drop of 126 millions of dollars in exports from the United States, as compared with the figures of 1913; if cotton were excluded from consideration, the drop was 161 millions, or 14½ per cent. Turning to the first four months of war, at the end of which the United States presented a Note to the British Government to the effect that our naval policy was ruining their trade, the decline in exports other than cotton was less than 4 per cent. Cotton was excluded from consideration, because—for reasons which are examined below—it remained for the first seven and a half months of war on the free list and was not interfered with by the British policy. Thus it appeared that the effect of the early months of the war was to arrest practically the decline in the export trade from the United States. A circular issued by the Department of Commerce on January 23 showed such a recovery in export trade after the first disturbance caused by the outbreak of war, that in December the exports exceeded those of December, 1913, and were nearly up to the "high record established in December, 1912."

BRITISH PATROL SHIP.

Approaching a suspicious neutral vessel at night.

A detailed examination of the destination of the exports was illuminating as regarded England's attitude towards European neutrals. The point was to discover how exports from the United States to neutral countries had fared since the outbreak of war. This was not discoverable exactly, because the official American figures did not cover a detailed list for each country. The figures for the neutral countries in question had to include Austria. They revealed an increase by over 20,000,000 dollars in exports to neutral countries in the first four months of the war, as compared with the corresponding four months of 1913. Now, it is certain that Austrian imports would show a great decrease, so that the total increase to

GERMAN OFFICERS ARRIVE AT THE LAW COURTS, LONDON.
Naval officers and men, under armed escort, who were witnesses at a Naval Prize Court case.

neutral countries would be correspondingly greater. Even allowing for the fact that certain goods would have to be acquired from America which had before the war been acquired from belligerent countries, the main result undoubtedly showed that there was a double-faced problem for the British Government to meet—the American exporter of supplies and the European neutral distributor to the enemy. This is strikingly confirmed by the figures quoted by Sir Edward Grey in his Note to the United States of January 7, 1915. Taking the period extending from August up to the end of the third week in December, 1914, exports of copper from the United States to Italy, who was then neutral, rose from £15,202,000 in 1913 to £36,285,000; to Europe other than the United Kingdom, Russia, France, Belgium, Austria, Germany, Holland, Italy, the corresponding figures were: £7,271,000 in 1913 and £35,347,000 in 1914. The figures as to food given in the British Note of February 10 were as follows: exports of lard to Denmark in September and October: 1913, nil; 1914, 22,652,598 lbs. Exports of bacon to Denmark in September and October; 1913, nil; 1914, 1,022,195 lbs. Canned beef, pickled beef and pickled pork showed also great increase in exports.

The steps by which the British Government met the situation were simply the working out of the principle that a neutral has no right to furnish the enemy with supplies for the conduct of war. Since peaceful commercial enterprise was at an end in the enemy State, articles of use in peace or war would be used for war. Hence conditional contraband had become to all intents and purposes on the same footing as absolute contraband. Both would be used for war, to support a nation at war, since army and nation were one.

The first thing to do was, therefore, to make conditional contraband capturable on a basis analogous to the principles governing the capture of absolute contraband. This was done by Order in Council of August 20, which provided that (i.) conditional contraband could be captured if it were consigned to an agent of the enemy Government, or to any person under control of the authorities of the enemy State. The distinction between a consignment to the Government and to a private contractor was thus modified. (ii.) It could be captured on its way to a neutral port if its ultimate destination were hostile.

The list of conditional contraband on September 21 included copper, lead, glycerine, iron ore, rubber, and hides. Can it reasonably be said that these should have been allowed entrance into Germany if consigned to private merchants, or if the route chosen was through a neutral port, on the ground that they were adapted for use in peaceful commerce? They were surely supplies of war, as much as ready-made projectiles, or arms.

The next stage in the development of the British contraband policy was the result of a general *modus vivendi* in which the neutral European Governments themselves played a part.

When the Notes which were exchanged between the Governments are examined it is clear that the main complaint is against the general treatment of shipping and cargoes, rather than against any of the rules actually put in force by the British Government. It was natural that irritation should develop. The power to condemn guilty cargoes involves the power to examine the destination of what will turn out to be innocent cargoes. The skill with which modern cargoes are packed, the ruses to which traders in contraband have recourse to evade capture, the heavy presumption against the innocence of cargoes which was raised by the trade returns quoted above, all contributed to make the examination by the British Government particularly searching. Corresponding delays and dislocation occurred.

The British interference with copper had caused particular irritation, and at the end of September, 1914, the United States Senate passed a resolution calling upon the Secretary of State for information as to interference with shipments from the United States to Rotterdam. It was noted, however, in the American Press, that this copper was ultimately destined for Krupps and that a fair price had been paid for intercepted cargoes.

Negotiation led to a modification of British policy by Proclamation of October 29, 1914. The problem to be solved again concerned conditional contraband—*i.e.*, articles of use in peace as well as in war. It had been settled that in the enemy country they were to be used for war, so that they should not be allowed to effect an entrance there even through neutral ports. They would, however, be required for peaceful purposes to a certain extent in the neutral European countries, and it was no wish of the British Government to prevent such supply to neutral countries. The problem was how to sift trade designed to result in supplies for Germany to prosecute the war from supplies for home consumption in the neutral fringe.

The Proclamation of October 29 provided that conditional contraband could be captured on its way to neutral ports only if: (i.) it were

H.M.S. "LARK" ESCORTING A CHANNEL STEAMER.

TORPEDOING OF THE "INDIAN CITY" AND THE "HEADLANDS," MARCH 15, 1915.
Bringing the survivors into St. Mary's.

consigned to an agent of the enemy, (ii.) if it did not appear who the consignee was—*e.g.*, if the consignment was "to order." This meant that consignments to named consignees in neutral countries would be allowed to pass, and some check could be kept upon the real destination of the goods.

The result was equitable. Suppose copper (before it was made absolute contraband) was going to a neutral country, then in face of the fact that it was common knowledge that Germany was drawing supplies through neutral ports, the British Government required that such copper should go to a definite person who was not an agent of the enemy State. Check could then be kept upon the imports, and the order finally provided that if a Secretary of State came to the conclusion that the enemy was drawing supplies from or through a neutral country, conditional contraband could be captured. without further qualification, if on its way to any port of that country

This policy of admitting cargoes of conditional contraband to named consignees was contemporaneous with the development of a *modus vivendi* with the neutral Governments of the countries which had been serving as sources from which Germany drew her supplies. Early in November the British Government announced that the guarantees given by the Governments of Norway, Sweden, and Denmark were satisfactory, that where contraband was consigned to a named consignee it should not be re-exported and so find its way to the enemy. To appreciate this it must again be noticed that conditional contraband embodies articles which are of use in peace as well as war, so that a certain legitimate demand for them would exist in the neutral countries in question. To sift the commodities meeting this demand from the surplus which met the warlike demands of the enemy was the object of the embargo upon re-exportation. If re-exportation were prohibited only, legitimate supplies for home consumption would be imported.

At the beginning of October the State Department of the United States made a statement that food consigned to Holland such as the Dutch Government had made subject to an embargo would not be treated as contraband, and early in January the Dutch Government prohibited the export of live and dead poultry, and of bread: by the end of the first week in January the embargos of Italy and Holland were stringent enough to preclude interference with conditional contraband bound for those countries. In fact, the British Embassy notified the United States that no consignments of copper for Italy had been detained since December 4.

To sum up :—the British policy throughout was directed towards sifting trade which gave Germany the materials for the prosecution of the war from trade which gave neutral countries the materials for commerce. The Note from the United States on December 29, 1914, did not attack this principle in the least, but was confined to the statement that the British policy had caused great suffering to their trade ; that cargoes had been intercepted upon insufficient evidence of hostile destination ; that our methods of visit and search were unjustifiable.

Sir Edward Grey's reply in two notes, January 7 and February 10, 1915, met these points as follows :

1. The trade returns (quoted above) showed that American exports had, in fact, benefited by the war, and that these exports were finding their way into Germany.

2. From August 4 to January 3, of 773 ships which cleared from the United States for Holland, Denmark, Norway, Sweden, Italy, only eight ships had been placed in the Prize Court, of which one was released: only 45 cargoes had been put in Court, in whole or in part.

3. With regard to delay in examining cargoes : the new regulation of the United States that manifests should not be published until 30 days after the vessel had cleared rendered more detailed examination necessary : wherever an innocent owner was aggrieved he had his remedy in the British Courts, and, since no claim had hitherto been made, diplomatic representations upon the matter were deprecated : so desirous of avoiding all possible delay was the British Government that a special committee had been formed to avoid the usual methods of inter-departmental correspondence.

4. Granted that a belligerent had the right to visit and search neutral vessels, it followed that he must be allowed to make such search effective, and often this could only be done in port : such extension of the right had precedent to support it.

THE RESCUED CREWS OF THE "INDIAN CITY" AND "HEADLANDS."

AN OUTPOST.
British submarine rising to the surface.

5. With regard to the evidence upon which vessels had been detained: the universal practice of Prize Courts was to put the burden of proving an innocent destination upon the cargo: the Proclamation of October 29, 1914, was, in fact, a relaxation of previous policy in this respect.

6. The policy with regard to foodstuffs was then defended and instances given of considerate treatment of neutrals by the British Government.

The British claim to stop supplies entering Germany through neutral countries was not challenged. It was natural that this stoppage should cause irritation; delays unavoidable, and sometimes perhaps avoidable, must occur for innocent cargoes under examination: but the main lines of the contraband policy were in harmony with the principles which have always obtained in international law.

The German war-zone policy was announced on February 4; the British declaration of a "counter-blockade" by way of reprisals followed on March 1, 1915. The first part of this declaration was a comment upon the submarine policy of the enemy, and an exposition of the illegalities contained in that policy; in this connexion it will be quoted later. The operative part continued:—"Her opponents are, therefore, driven to frame retaliatory measures in order in their turn to prevent commodities of any kind from reaching or leaving Germany. These measures will, however, be enforced by the British and French Governments without risk to neutral ships, or to neutral or non-combatant life, and in strict observance of the dictates of humanity.

"The British and French Governments will, therefore, hold themselves free to detain and take into port ships carrying goods of presumed enemy destination, ownership, or origin. It is not intended to confiscate such vessels or cargoes unless they would otherwise be liable to condemnation. The treatment of vessels and cargoes which have sailed before this date will not be affected."

Effect was given to this declaration by an Order in Council of March 11, published in the *Gazette* of March 15, 1915. With regard to goods upon neutral ships making for a German destination, it was ordered that no vessel be allowed to proceed on a voyage to a German

IN THE NORTH SEA.
A mine-layer at work.

HELD UP SINCE THE OUTBREAK OF THE WAR.
German goods intended for England at Rotterdam.

port. Unless a pass was given allowing the cargo to make for a neutral market, the goods were to be discharged in a British port, and handed back to the owner upon such terms as the Prize Court should think fit, provided the Crown did not requisition them for its own use. If the cargo had an enemy destination, but was not to be actually discharged at a German, but at a neutral, port, similar treatment was to be applied.

With regard to goods making their exit from Germany, whether they were laden in the vessel at a German or a neutral port, they were to be discharged at a British port. They could then be requisitioned by the Crown if necessary, or they could be detained, or they could be sold by direction of the Court. The proceeds were to remain in Court until the conclusion of peace, unless before the date of the order the goods had become the property of a neutral. If it were neutral property, it might also be released upon application by the proper Officer of the Crown.

Any special claims by persons interested in goods detained could be preferred by proceedings in the Prize Court, but if the goods would have been liable to condemnation as contraband they were to remain liable.

If any country declared that no commerce destined for, or making exit from Germany, or of German ownership, should enjoy the protection of its flag, relaxations might be made in the application of the order to its merchantmen.

In order to mitigate the interference with neutral shipping as far as was possible, instructions were issued giving a wide discretion in the treatment to be accorded to particular vessels as each case arose.

The position which confronted the British Government towards the end of February, 1915, was a difficult one. Germany had been hard hit by the British contraband policy, and had entered upon a course of reprisals, the exact effect of which no one could foresee. At least, it was designed to induce a *modus vivendi* by which the British Government should relax its contraband policy in return for a cessation of the submarine policy; probably it was seriously hoped that England would be definitely cut off from supplies. The illegality and the inhumanity of this policy certainly called for stringent measures, and, with command of the seas at our disposal, it was natural that the aim of British policy should be to cut off Germany in her turn from all commerce whatsoever, whether in contraband goods or not. By virtue of the right to capture private property at sea, this had already been done in so far as German vessels could be used for transport. Such vessels had either been captured or driven to remain in German or neutral ports. It remained to deal with neutral vessels and with commerce proceeding through neutral ports.

The recognized mode of effecting such a commercial isolation of the enemy is by a blockade, and there are certain primary principles which define the legal position in a perfect blockade—(i.) the blockade must be made in fact effective by a sufficient show of force; (ii.) the blockade must not extend to neutral ports; (iii.) the blockade must operate impartially against all neutrals.

It is clear that the obstacle to declaring a perfect blockade was the trade across the Baltic to Germany through Norway and Sweden. Before the British submarine activities in the Baltic began there was no pretence to blockade that portion of the German coast line. Trade from America, as we shall see, could be cut off from approaching Germany through these neutral countries by an application of the doctrine of continuous voyage; but even then the home produce of Norway and Sweden had access to Germany, so that America could complain that she was cut off from trade which was left open to these favoured neutrals. Hence a broad measure of reprisals was declared without notifying a complete blockade, such as was notified on February 23, 1915, against the coast of German East Africa, or on April 24 against the coast of the Cameroons.

American opinion, already irritated by the necessary and legitimate interference with trade in our efforts to stop contraband, received this measure of reprisals with anxiety and disapproval. The feeling was that American trade was being illegally interfered with, and it did not seem to be appreciated that had a perfect blockade been declared the penalties of confiscation would have been much harsher than the policy of buying up the cargoes or handing them back to the neutral owner.

Mr. Balfour, on March 29, 1915, defended the British policy on the basis of the law of reprisals. He argued that international law demands obedience from all parties or its binding effect would be only to load the dice in favour of the disobedient. When rules of international law thus break down, Governments are thrown back upon the laws of morality, and reprisals are justified. Did it follow that such retaliation would be free from all limitation, where the acts which called for it were inhuman? "Assuredly not, I preach no such doctrine. These things were brutal and barbarous before the law of nations took formal shape; they would remain brutal and barbarous if the law of nations fell into desuetude. Germany would indeed have no right to complain of retaliation in kind, but this would not justify us in descending to her level. The policy which I am defending has no resemblance to this. It violates no deep ethical instincts; it is in harmony with the spirit of international law; it is more regardful of neutral interests than the accepted rules of blockade; nor is the injury which it is designed to inflict on the enemy of a different character from that inflicted by an ordinary blockade. And, lastly, it is a reply to an attack which is not only illegal but immoral; and, if some reply be legitimate and necessary, can a better one be devised?"

As a measure of reprisals, therefore, British policy was humane and considerate towards neutrals, and it is difficult to deny that there was just cause for reprisals. The United States adopted the position that reprisals conferred no right upon a belligerent to interfere with neutral rights, and it will be seen that, in answer to the German claim that the war-zone constituted reprisals against our policy in regard to contraband, the United States adopted the same position. This raises a difficult point in theory, and it would seem better to lay down no absolute doctrine as universally applicable. It may surely be said that no policy of reprisals is justified which involves loss of neutral life and absolute destruction of neutral property. Even assuming to the contrary of what we have previously concluded, that Germany was justified in adopting reprisals against the British contraband policy, there can be no doubt that the loss of life, particularly of American life, upon the Lusitania was not legitimately included in those reprisals. The British reprisals were of a radically different nature. They approximated within a very narrow margin to a legal blockade, and by way of set off to the slight illegality there was more favourable treatment of neutrals than that which would have resulted from a blockade. There was no loss of life or destruction of property involved. If, then, it is correct to assume that there was just cause for reprisals in the inhuman methods of Germany, can it not be said that there was a right to

BRITISH SUBMARINE'S VIEW OF A DOOMED GERMAN WARSHIP.

The "field" of a periscope—the marks denote measurements by which the distance of the ship can be gauged.

interfere to some extent with neutrals in adopting those reprisals ?

The British "counter-blockade" vindicated the rights of neutrals as well as the rights of the British; it follows therefore that neutrals should not judge it by the same standards as it would have to be judged by if there were no cause for reprisals. Neutrals could be expected to bear some measure of the burden in this vindication if that burden were proportionate to the violation of their rights.

The violation of neutral right by the war-zone had been gross and inhuman. The measure of reprisals, as Mr. Balfour pointed out, was more favourable to neutrals than the law of blockade, and otherwise it amounted practically to a blockade. Surely there was here no cause for protest.

LIFE-SAVING DRILL ON BOARD A HOSPITAL SHIP.

Such sympathetic treatment of reprisals does not involve a breach of neutrality. A neutral owes certain duties to the belligerents—*e.g.*, to intern armed forces which cross its boundaries; not to allow the equipment of hostile expeditions upon its territory or in its ports; but there is no duty to enforce rights in respect of trade to the enemy country.

Although the counter-blockade was justifiable as a measure of reprisals, the main defence set forth in the British communications to America proceeded upon the fact that the policy was substantially within the law of blockade. The two steps in this defence are simply as follows: (i.) It is recognized that a blockade may cut off all commerce from the enemy: and it is further recognized that neutral ports must not be used for fraudulently evading the blockade. This is the doctrine of continuous voyage which was explained in connexion with contraband. Commerce may be intercepted on its way to a neutral port if it is ultimately destined for the enemy by further transport on sea or land.

It is true that the Declaration of London excluded this in the case of blockade, but it was not law, and the application of the doctrine to blockade in the American Civil War was undoubtedly such as to establish it firmly in the law, especially as it was acquiesced in by the British Government.

The case of the steamship Neches raised the point. She was "of American register, sailing from Rotterdam to a port of the United States, carrying a general cargo," of German origin, so that she was within the terms of the Order in Council of March 11, 1915. She was brought into London and compelled to discharge.

The American Note of April 2 had taken up the curious position that the doctrine of continuous voyage was not applicable to a blockade, but the American precedents in the Civil War were decisive on this. If a cargo destined to break blockade by entrance into the blockaded area may be seized on its way to a neutral port, then equally a cargo making exit from a blockaded area may be seized, even if it be shipped from a neutral port. A blockade is broken outwards, as well as inwards.

To seize commerce entering or making exit from Germany by way of neutral ports was, therefore, well within recognized principles.

(ii.) The second step in the defence of British policy was this: that at no period of the blockade was it attempted to do more than stop commercial intercourse with Germany. It was always the desire of the British Government to sift the trade for home consumption in neutral countries from the trade destined for Germany, just as before March 1 it had been their desire to sift the trade in contraband.

Sir Edward Grey, in his Note of July 23, 1915, emphasized this: "We are taking the utmost possible care not to interfere with commerce genuinely destined for or proceeding from neutral countries. . . . If we are successful in the efforts we are making to distinguish between the commerce of neutral and enemy countries, there will be no substantial interference with the trade of neutral ports, except in so far as they constitute ports of access to and exit from the enemy territory."

In the case of contraband the embargo upon re-exportation rendered possible a less stringent policy of examination upon the part of the British authorities. This policy was developed in order to mitigate inconvenience to neutral innocent cargoes. The Netherlands Overseas Trust may be taken as a type of this development. It was a receiving agency under heavy bonds not to allow export to Germany of the commodities it was allowed to receive. Defective though it proved to be, this cutting off of re-exportation was calculated to ensure that goods entering neutral countries would be such as were genuinely intended for home consumption, and was a legitimate method by which neutrals could secure the least delay to innocent cargoes.

It will be remembered that in the declaration of British policy, and the Order in Council of March 11, the British Government had assumed the right to take goods of German ownership out of neutral vessels. This, of course, would at first sight seem to violate the famous rule —free ships, free goods—which had been formally declared in the Declaration of Paris, 1856. But the words of the Declaration, "The neutral flag covers enemy's goods, with the exception of contraband of war" did not limit rights of blockade, and with a very extended contraband list did not limit large rights of search. The United States, however, made the Order the subject of a protest, and in reply the British Government declared their policy. After hinting that, since the United States had not ratified the Declaration, it was not binding between her and Great Britain, Sir Edward Grey announced that it was not the policy of the Government to take German goods as such out of neutral ships, but that German ownership was only used as strong evidence of enemy origin and destination. The Declaration of Paris was therefore not involved, but the general law of blockade.

The British policy caused a curious agitation upon the subject of cotton. Before the blockade was developed the American cotton trade had been hard hit by the war, although it was not declared contraband. When the

LIFE-BELT DRILL ON A STEAMER.

IN THE NORTH OF ICELAND.

A British Cruiser heading to intercept a neutral vessel suspected of having contraband on board.

blockade was developed, cotton fell within its scope, and, although the treatment accorded to cotton cargoes was much more favourable than the law either of contraband or blockade would have rendered possible, the depression in the cotton trade was put to the account of the British Government, without any consideration of the fact that on plain principle cotton might be declared liable to confiscation as contraband, since it had become of immense importance for warlike purposes.

The Government had a difficult path to follow. The cotton industry was of peculiar strength in America, supporting millions of the population, and providing exports far above any other single industry. The farmers had to pay their way from crop to crop, and the failure to dispose of a crop would at once bring financial distress. As a community giving the tone to opinion in the South, they were open in their distress to the appeals of agitators encouraged by sympathisers with Germany. If they could but find some object upon which to concentrate their anger, a current of American opinion would be created with which that object would have to reckon. That object became the British Government.

Under the policy of the blockade, cotton seized as being ultimately destined for Germany would either be restored to the owner, or, if requisitioned, paid for. On May 18, 1915, the Washington correspondent of *The Times* noted that £2,500,000 worth of cotton was in detention. This was security for 90 days loans to the farmers, so that it would be poor consolation to them to have it returned after delay during which repayment became due. During June and July America was becoming seriously disturbed at the British policy. The meat-packers had only withdrawn a deputation late in May, when assured that negotiations were being conducted on their behalf; in June a deputation of importers to the Secretary of State alleged that £10,000,000 of goods were shut up in Rotterdam, though not contraband; in July the United States registered a caveat that the British Prize Court findings were not accepted.

The general feeling began to develop that cotton should be made contraband. It had not been touched upon the outbreak of war until the blockade was established by Order in Council of March 11, 1915 and, since it was clearly the British policy to interfere with it, it was felt that such interference ought legally to be defined. A blockade was not technically in force, and to make cotton contraband seemed a likely mode of settling the matter. In spite of repeated assurances that the British Government would have no further powers of stopping cotton as contraband than by virtue of the Order in Council, the policy found considerable support at home, and cotton was at length declared contraband towards the end of August. The Foreign Office accompanied the declaration with a memorandum to the effect that the figures for the imports of cotton into Scandinavian countries and Holland led to the inference that since May 1 Germany had not received any considerable supply through those countries, so that it was not expected that the declaration would lead to any appreciable disadvantage in the position of exporters.

Whatever odd precedents may be raked up, there was no doubt that on principle cotton might be made contraband; and the opposition to making it contraband on the part of the legal advisers of the British Government requires much justification. The Declaration of London was against it, but this was on the footing that the framers of that non-prophetic document fatuously considered that cotton could not be of use in war; they thought similarly as to hides, rubber and metallic ores. Under any conditions it was an article of use both in peace and war; under conditions as they were in August, 1915, it was an article which would be used primarily for war, so that it was legitimately made absolute contraband.

To sum up the whole position as to the quasi blockade:

(i.) As a measure of reprisals it was called for; it was not disproportionate to the offence which produced it, and it operated favourably towards neutrals who had suffered gravely by the enemy's offence.

(ii.) As a measure of blockade, in its earlier stages, the only defect was that home produce of Norway and Sweden might find markets where America could not; in its later stages British submarine efforts in the Baltic made it certainly as effective as the vast blockade of the Southern States by the American Government in the Civil War. The doctrine of continuous voyage was correctly applied, since every effort was made to distinguish neutral commerce which was genuine from the surplus which was destined for Germany.

The British policy has now been traced in

[*Swaine*

LORD DEVONPORT.
Chairman of the Port of London Authority.

its relation to neutral States. The main principle underlying that policy was that neutrals had no claim to trade which accrued to them by reason of the war if that trade was of assistance to the enemy. This justified the determination to stop all contraband entering neutral countries in so far as it was not required for home consumption in those countries. Even though contraband was conditional, and consisted of articles which might be used for peaceful industry, the high state of organization in Germany, and the fact that at the opening of the twentieth century war was waged by nations rather than by armies, justified this policy being extended to conditional contraband. The same principles underlay the development of the blockade policy.

If the policy of contraband was justified as against neutrals, it was all the more so as against Germany. Early in February, 1915, however, it was declared that the British policy called for reprisals, and on February 8 notice was given that from February 18 onwards the waters of Britain and the west coast of France would be a zone of war. A memorandum from Berlin in February gave clear indication of what the policy was to be. "Just as England has designated the area between Scotland and Norway as an area of war, so Germany now declares all the waters surrounding Great

EXAMINING SUSPICIOUS CRAFT.
British bluejackets boarding a sailing ship.

Britain and Ireland, including the entire English Channel, as an area of war, thus proceeding against the shipping of the enemy. For this purpose, beginning from February 18, 1915, it will endeavour to destroy every enemy merchant ship that is found in this area of war, without its always being possible to avert the peril that thus threatens persons and cargoes. Neutrals are therefore warned against further entrusting crews and passengers and wares to such ships. Their attention is also called to the fact that it is advisable for their ships to avoid entering this area, for even though the German naval forces have instructions to avoid violence to neutral ships in so far as they are recognizable, in view of the misuse of neutral flags ordered by the British Government, and the contingencies of naval warfare, their becoming victims of an attack directed against enemy ships cannot always be averted. At the same time it is especially noted that shipping north of the Shetland Islands in the eastern area of the North Sea, and in a strip of at least 30 miles in width along the Netherland coasts, is not in peril."

This was a ruthless speculative effort to neutralize legitimately acquired British naval supremacy by illegitimate use of mines and submarines. By way of general comment upon the German policy, the British declaration of March 1 may be quoted:—"Germany has declared that the English Channel, the north and west coasts of France, and the waters round the British Isles are a 'war area,' and has officially notified that 'all enemy ships found in that area will be destroyed, and that neutral vessels may be exposed to danger.' This is in effect a claim to torpedo at sight, without regard to the safety of the crew or passengers, any merchant vessel under any flag. As it is not in the power of the German Admiralty to maintain any surface craft in these waters, this attack can only be delivered by submarine agency. The law and custom of nations in regard to attacks on commerce have always presumed that the first duty of the captor of a merchant vessel is to bring it before a Prize Court, where it may be tried, where the regularity of the capture may be challenged, and where neutrals may recover their cargoes. The sinking of prizes is in itself a questionable act, to be resorted to only in extraordinary circumstances, and after provision has been made for the safety of all the crew or passengers (if there are passengers on board). The responsibility for discriminating between neutral and enemy vessels, and between neutral and enemy cargo, obviously rests with the attacking ship, whose duty it is to verify the status and character of the vessel and cargo, and to preserve all papers before sinking or even capturing it. So also is the humane duty of providing for the safety of the crews of merchant vessels, whether neutral or enemy, an obligation upon every belligerent. It is upon this basis that all previous discussions of the law for regulating warfare at sea have proceeded.

"A German submarine, however, fulfils none of these obligations. She enjoys no local command of the waters in which she operates. She does not take her captures within the jurisdiction of a Prize Court. She carries no prize crew which she can put on board a prize. She uses no effective means of discriminating between a neutral and an enemy vessel. She does not receive on board for safety the crew of the vessel she sinks. Her methods of warfare are, therefore, entirely outside the scope of any of the international instruments regulating operations against commerce in time of war. The

German declaration substitutes indiscriminate destruction for regulated capture." No better statement of the legal position could be desired.

Germany alleged that she could not visit and search because our merchantmen were armed, and sailed under neutral flags, so that a submarine would be destroyed which attempted such action. Further, it is clear that a submarine could not tow captures into port, especially under the nose of the enemy navy. Further, it is clear that she could not provide for the safety of passengers and crew. Two verdicts are possible, either that the inherent disabilities of the submarine released her from existing obligations or that they were such that she should desist from operations for which she was unfitted. "The fundamental error of the German position," said the *New York World*, "is the assumption that submarines have peculiar rights by reason of their disabilities as commerce destroyers."

The conduct of the submarine policy involved the German Government in a controversy with the United States of a different nature from the contemporaneous discussion between that Power and Great Britain. Whereas the basis of one was the interference with trade, the basis of the other was interference with the elementary freedom to live of non-combatants and neutrals. The German Government attempted to harness itself to neutral irritation against British interference with trade, but without success. Although at a certain stage of the proceedings the American Government showed a willingness to help the belligerents to a *modus vivendi* such as that food be allowed to enter Germany in return for the relaxation of the submarine policy, this was not allowed to interfere with the main issue between the two Governments. The announcement of the German policy was immediately followed by a warning Note from the United States that she would hold Germany to a strict accountability for illegal acts which might be committed. At the same time a Note was sent to Great Britain voicing neutral feeling on the advice given by the British Government that the use of the neutral flag should be adopted as a ruse to escape the attentions of the submarine. The ground taken by the British Government

THE BRITISH BLOCKADE.

Boarding party leaving a warship to examine a vessel in the North Sea.

THE NORWEGIAN SHIP "BELRIDGE"

Being towed to Thames Haven after being struck by a torpedo from a German submarine. The smaller picture shows the name painted on the side of the vessel.

was that it was only the neglect of the duty to visit and search by the submarine which would jeopardize neutral safety.

The German reply was somewhat difficult to analyse owing to its disconnected nature. The sore point was clearly that the British naval power had cut off contraband from Germany, while ensuring its entrance into England. Complaint was made that neutrals had not enforced a more lenient British policy. It now became plain that the primary aim of the submarine policy was two-fold: to induce the United States to cease trade with Great Britain in contraband which the condition of German naval power did not allow Germany legitimately to intercept; and, further, to induce Great Britain, at the instance of the United States, to relax her policy with regard to conditional contraband, especially foodstuffs. During these February discussions the Wilhelmina case was pending, and Germany had stated that food imported from America should only be used for the civilian population. The terrorization produced by the submarine policy was calculated to lead to a more favourable state of affairs than German naval power had enabled her to achieve.

Towards the end of February, 1915, the United States suggested a *modus vivendi* on the following lines:—The use of mines to be restricted to the class of anchored mines for defensive purposes; submarines to visit and search in the proper manner; the use of the neutral flag as a ruse to cease; Great Britain to allow foodstuffs to enter Germany consigned to receiving agencies who should distribute to the civil population only. A moment's reflection will show that Great Britain would have gained nothing by such a policy. Germany required that British merchantmen should be unarmed, so that after due visit and search of an unprotected vessel she would have sunk it, if British, and justified her conduct by the inability of a submarine to take a prize into Court. In spite of this, Germany replied that not only foodstuffs but raw materials must be allowed to have free access through neutral countries. Evidently more faith was put in the submarine than results ultimately justified.

Meanwhile, neutral shipping was coming within the scope of submarine activity. Up to the end of the first week in April the Norwegian ships Regin and Nor had been sunk; the Belridge was torpedoed near Folkestone, but managed to reach the Downs, while, on the other hand, the Gazelle had been searched and allowed to go. The Hanna, of Sweden, was sunk without warning, with loss of life. The Dutch ship Zevenbergen was attacked by aircraft, the Mecklenberg was chased by an armed trawler, the Medea was sunk off Beachy Head after removal of the crew. The A.N. Hansen, of Denmark, was searched and allowed to go, and the Portuguese Douro was sunk near the Bristol Channel.

Neutrals were not only affected through their shipping, but by reason of their presence upon British vessels. Four ships, attacked in the war-zone, figured pre-eminently in the Notes between Germany and the United States. The second paragraph of the Note from the United States to Germany, following upon the sinking of the Lusitania, was as follows: "The sinking of the British passenger steamer Falaba by a German submarine on March 28, through which Mr. Leon C. Thrasher, an American citizen, was drowned, the attack on April 28 on the American vessel Cushing by a German aeroplane, the torpedoing on May 1 of the American vessel Gulflight by a German submarine, as the result of which two or more Americans met their death, and finally the torpedoing and sinking of the Lusitania constitute a series of events which the Government of the United States has observed with growing concern, distress and amazement." In the case of the Gulflight no warning was given; in the case of the Lusitania no warning was given; in the case of the Falaba some warning, the extent of which was disputed, was given. Germany considered that the illegal notification of February 8 that neutrals entered the war-zone at their own risk was sufficient. In the case of the Lusitania this was reinforced by an advertisement emanating from the German Embassy in the United States, to the effect that neutral citizens travelled in the war-zone at their own risk. Such was the conduct of an Embassy whose Government had formally asserted the right of its citizens to travel unmolested. The first American Note repudiated the validity of the warning addressed to neutrals on February 8 along with the proclamation of the war-zone, and, in agreement with the comments upon that policy contained in the declaration of the British counter-blockade, represented that the objection to the submarine policy was the "practical impossibility of employing submarines in the destruction of commerce without disregarding those rules of fairness, reason, justice and humanity which all modern opinion regards as imperative." Three things were "confidently expected" of the German Government: disavowal of the acts complained of; reparation; immediate steps to prevent the recurrence of the acts.

The German reply still harped upon the theme that these acts of terrorization would cease if the British contraband policy were relaxed by the mediation of the United States. The Falaba attack was justified on the ground that the vessel sought to escape and was calling for assistance. The Lusitania attack was

THE TORPEDOING OF THE "LUSITANIA," MAY 7, 1915.

A reproduction of a picture postcard which was very popular in Germany. The portrait is ot Admiral von Tirpitz.

THE TORPEDOING OF THE "FALABA."
The German submarine as seen from the "Falaba." Smaller picture: Passengers clinging to an upturned boat.

justified on various grounds: that she had special guns mounted and was, in fact, an auxiliary cruiser; that she carried Canadian troops; that she carried munitions.

The second American Note of June 11, 1915, had no difficulty in disposing of these excuses. The Falaba was entitled to attempt an escape, provided that she did not use armed violence in so doing. The Lusitania was not armed, nor being used as a transport, nor had she an illegal cargo, nor was she a naval vessel, since she cleared as a merchantman.

Apart, however, from these defences, "the sinking of passenger ships involves principles of humanity which throw into the background any special circumstances of detail." Apart from any other consideration, the Note continued, these principles of humanity, and the laws of which they are the source, throw a grave responsibility upon a Government which betrays them. The rights of neutral citizens flowing from these laws are unaffected by any grievance which a belligerent may have against his enemy. Assurances are again demanded that similar occurrences shall not happen again, the representations being made "very earnestly, very solemnly." Mr. Bryan, who had signed the first Note to Germany, resigned, since he could not reconcile the terms of the Note with the policy he had adopted with regard to the peaceful settlement of international differences.

The German rejoinder of July 8, 1915, will always rank as one of the most curious diplomatic documents in history. British treatment of contraband for Germany is again put forward

After being lowered, two of the boats capsized and the people were thrown into the water.

After the torpedo had struck the vessel: Passengers wearing lifebelts waiting to be taken off by the boats.

THE TORPEDOING OF THE "FALABA," MARCH 28, 1915.

ADMIRAL R. D. S. DE CHAIR.

as the justification of Germany's treatment of neutrals, but from reading the document one would gather that a British submarine had torpedoed the liner. The Note declares that Germany has ever been solicitous for proper treatment of non-combatants, and the freedom of the seas, and the rights of neutrals, and continues: "The case of the Lusitania shows with horrible clearness to what jeopardizing of human lives the manner of conducting war employed by our adversaries leads." The curious document ended with an equally curious offer: that neutral passenger steamers, carrying no contraband, should be allowed a free passage through the war-zone if notified sufficiently in advance, and further, that if necessary, free passage would be extended to four enemy passenger steamers, if these were placed under the American flag.

Late in July the third American Note appeared. The possibilities of discussion were apparently exhausted; there was nothing more to be said. The Note emphatically refused Germany's policy of saddling responsibility upon the British Government, and that was the main point so far as British policy was concerned. The Note inexplicably receded from the earlier position that submarines could not operate against commerce while obeying the principles of law and humanity. This surrender of the earlier position was based upon "events of the past two months," but what events precisely these were does not appear. A disavowal was again asked for; and the warning added that a repetition of these occurrences would be treated as deliberately unfriendly.

With this Note it became clear to the German Government that the British maritime policy could not be attacked by the indirect method of violating neutral rights and then directing neutral sentiment against the British Government. Any minor points that Germany chose to assert—*e.g.*, that the Lusitania carried five thousand packages of munitions, do not alter the main judgment of the policy of the war-zone. As an attempt to deprive the British Government of the fruits of its maritime strength it failed, and it failed to embroil the British with the American Government. The subsequent development of the policy, the torpedoing of the Arabic and the sinking of the Hesperian, the attitude of concession developed by Germany as the British began successfully to cope with the submarines, belong to another chapter.

In January, 1916, the British Government issued as a White Paper a statement of the "Measures adopted to intercept the sea-borne commerce of Germany" with the intention of showing "the manner in which the sea power of the British Empire has been used during the present war for the purpose of intercepting Germany's imports and exports." The Memorandum showed that "up to the time of the present war" there had been three methods of dealing with the commerce of the enemy—namely: (1) the capture of contraband of war on neutral ships; (2) the capture of enemy property at sea; and (3) a blockade by which all access to the coast of the enemy is cut off. The capture of enemy property at sea was limited by the Declaration of Paris of 1856, which exempted from capture enemy goods other than contraband on neutral ships. In fact, up to March, 1915, the British Government relied exclusively on the right to capture contraband. The Memorandum goes on to deal with the theory of contraband, to state that the British Government has never challenged the doctrine of continuous voyage, but, in order to secure uniformity of procedure among the Allies, the rules of the Declaration of London were, as we have seen, adopted by France and England, with certain modifications, such as the application of the doctrine of continuous voyage to conditional contraband under circumstances already related. The rules of the Declaration of London so modified enabled the British Government to deal with contraband intended to be discharged in a neutral port in a number of cases, but "there was no power to seize articles of conditional contraband if they could not be shown to be destined for the enemy Government or its armed forces, or non-contraband articles, even if they were on their way to a port in Germany, and there was no power to stop German exports." In March, 1915, Germany having laid herself open to reprisal, "the Allied Governments then decided to stop all goods which could be proved to be going to, or coming from, Germany." The Memorandum goes on to say: "The state of things produced is, in effect, a blockade, adapted to the conditions of modern war and commerce, the only difference in operation being that the goods seized are not necessarily confiscated." It was seen that the stoppage of the enemy's export trade and the consequent power of the enemy to establish neutral credits was all-important, and it was found easy by the system of certificates of origin to identify articles of enemy origin. The method was so effective that, according to the latest returns (those for September, 1915) available when the Memorandum was issued, "over 92 per cent. of the German exports to the United States of America have been

LORD SYDENHAM.

LORD BERESFORD.

stopped." Moreover, much of the remaining 8 per cent. consists of goods allowed through on the ground that they "had been either paid for prior to" March 1, 1915, "or ordered before that date on terms which rendered the neutral purchaser liable to pay whether the goods reached him or not." In such cases it injured the enemy and benefited neutrals to allow the goods to pass. Had the goods been stopped the enemy could have recovered the price and retained goods worth (to the end of 1915) about £3,000,000.

But the problem of German imports was more complicated. The proof of destination necessarily demanded by the British and other Prize Courts had become a matter of great complexity. The goods were universally consigned to neutral ports and the ships' papers conveyed "no suggestion as to their ultimate destination." Times had greatly changed since the days of the American Civil War. "The conditions of modern commerce offer almost infinite opportunities of concealing the real nature of a transaction, and every device which the ingenuity of the persons concerned, or their lawyers, could suggest has been employed to give to shipments intended for Germany the appearance of genuine transactions with a neutral country." In fact, the same difficulty existed in a very acute form during the Napoleonic Wars, and was the subject of close consideration by Lord Stowell. It was not

THE BRITISH LINER "APPAM" CAPTURED BY THE GERMANS, JAN. 15, 1916.
View of the stern of the S.S. "Appam," showing the German Naval Ensign flying.
Bottom picture: One of the crew of the "Moewe."

so new as the author of the Memorandum appeared to think. But it was on an infinitely larger scale, and the Allied Governments had to discover a test of destination to distinguish goods intended for the enemy from goods intended for neutral consumption. A Contraband Committee sitting at the Foreign Office in close touch with the Admiralty, the Board of Trade and War Trade Department dealt with the case, and in all cases where information showed goods to be suspect the goods were stopped. "Nearly every ship on her way to Scandinavian or Dutch ports" was stopped, taken into a British port and her cargo closely scrutinized, and all really suspect articles placed in the Prize Court, while articles of a more doubtful destination were reserved for further scrutiny.

The Memorandum admitted that the method was inadequate to secure "a complete cutting off of the enemy's supplies." The Prize Court could not penetrate in a large number of cases into the mystery of ultimate destination, and, moreover, cargoes with a really neutral destination were nevertheless of vast danger, as the scientific products of those cargoes passed into Germany. Indeed the system in some cases bore hardly on honest neutral trade. There was, however, another method likely to prove both more effective and more equitable—the system of guarantees by importers, not by neutral Governments (which were satisfied to prohibit the exportation of certain imported articles), but by representative associations of merchants. The associations guaranteed that articles consigned to or guaranteed by them, and their products, should not reach the enemy in any form, and in response to this guarantee the British Government undertook not to interfere with shipments to the association except where the shipment was a fraud on the association. Agreements of this type were entered into with the Netherlands Oversea Trust and similar bodies of merchants in Sweden, Norway, Denmark, and Switzerland. These associations would not transmit goods except to receivers who guaranteed under pecuniary penalties that the goods should not leave the country in any form. Agreements with shipping lines were also designed to facilitate honest trade. By those agreements the British Government obtained "the right to require any goods carried by the line, if not discharged in the British port of examination, to be either returned to this country for Prize Court proceedings, or stored in the country of destination until the end of the war, or only handed to the consignees under stringent guarantees that they or their products will not reach the enemy."

Moreover, the public were told that "much use has been made recently of the power which the British Government are in a position to exercise owing to their ability to refuse bunker coal to neutral ships in ports in the British Empire." It was only supplied to owners who could guarantee that their ships were not directly or indirectly trading with the enemy. "The number of owners who accept these conditions increases almost daily." In order to prevent hardships to neutrals the "rationing" system had been introduced, "by which the import of any given article into a neutral country is limited to the amount of its true domestic requirements." This could only effectually be done by agreements with some body representing the trade or sections of the trade of the neutral country and so prevent leakage to Germany on a large scale. Leakage there must be as prices rise, but it will be small under a properly organized rationing system.

This memorandum detailing the position up till January, 1916, revealed a state of affairs that obviously was causing anxiety in Germany. It is possible that the British Government be-

THE BRITISH LINER "APPAM" CAPTURED BY THE GERMANS.
Lieutenant Berg, chief of the prize crew from the "Moewe," with Port Collector Hamilton, who demanded the release from the liner of the British subjects.

lieved the "blockade" to be more effective than it really was, but the German Press at the end of January, 1916, was clearly anxious. The Vienna *Fremdenblatt* declared that "the starvation war is the most serious violation of the rights of nations, which will be indignantly condemned by neutral nations." The reliance of Germany on the laws and rights of nations when German interests were touched was, of course, the obvious complement of the hideous repudiation of those laws and rights when, as in the case of Belgium, such repudiation seemed to be in the interests of the Central Empires. From the date that the blockade began to tighten, German reliance on the laws of nations grew stronger, and perhaps no more significant sign of growing weakness could be detected. Germany in the fulness of her strength knew neither law nor mercy. But if Germany was actually alarmed by the conditions of trade at the end of January, 1916, neutral countries (partly as the result of German agitation) began to express indignation and alarm. In Sweden the alleged leakage into Germany was denied and the attitude of Great Britain denounced as disregarding the legal rights and immunities secured to neutrals by successive international treaties. Considerable discontent was felt in Norway, Sweden, and Denmark, though the trading agreements with the Danish corporations had admittedly brought relief. American opinion was prejudiced against the Orders in Council as not being in accordance with law and as being based on retaliation, the very doctrine used by Germany to justify the sinking of the Lusitania. "Retaliation" and "necessity" were felt to be German, not British, pleas, and Americans were earnestly anxious that Great Britain should have a clean bill of health in this respect. On January 26, 1916, Sir Edward Grey, speaking in the House of Commons while the American Ambassador and the Ministers of Sweden, Norway, Denmark, and Holland were in the Diplomatic Gallery, defended the Government contraband policy and declined to force all ships through a British Prize Court. On the other hand, he informed neutrals that Great Britain would not give up her right to interfere with every trade, and added the significant words, "That we must retain and must press. If the neutrals admitted our right to adapt the doctrine applied in the American Civil War to modern conditions and to prevent enemy trade through neutral countries, let them make it easy for us to distinguish and discriminate. If, on the other hand, they say that we are not entitled to do that, then I would take that as a departure from neutrality."

Meanwhile the German Government, undeterred by their appalling losses of submarines and heedless of the volume of contempt and the hardening of neutral opinion that had followed the infamous and indefensible policy of sinking merchant ships without warning and regardless of the loss of human life, determined on a new exhibition of "frightfulness." On February 11, 1916, the *North German Gazette* issued officially the text of a Memorandum concerning the treatment of armed merchant vessels. The Memorandum, with that singular lack of humour which had characterised so many of these German official papers, protested against merchant ships having any means of defence against submarines, despite the fact that these German instruments of war, contrary to every usage of the law of nations or the practices of humanity, had for months shelled innocent merchant ships without notice or pity. The German Government declared "any warlike activity on the part of enemy merchant vessels to be contrary to international law," but proposed to treat the crews as belligerents and not pirates. The Memorandum alleged that "armed British merchantmen have an official order treacherously to attack German submarines wherever they meet them; that means, mercilessly to wage war against them." Considering that these submarines had proved themselves the enemies of mankind in the sinking of the Lusitania, the Arabic, the Ancona, the Persia, any steps within the sphere of morals to rid the world of such pests would have been allowable; but, in fact, the charge was untrue. Merchant ships had, and have always had, a right of defence against attack. It was this right of defence that the German Government hoped to destroy by the following threat, with which the Memorandum concludes:

> In view of the aforesaid circumstances, enemy merchantmen carrying guns are not entitled to be regarded as peaceful merchantmen. The German naval forces, therefore, after a short interval in the interests of neutrals, will receive an order to treat such vessels as belligerents. The German Government notifies neutral Powers of this state of affairs in order that they may be able to warn their subjects before entrusting their persons or properties to armed merchantmen of Powers at war with the German Empire.

The Memorandum said nothing about summons, detention, visit, search, or even "war zone." The threat was a bold threat to sink

THE MINING OF THE "MALOJA" OFF DOVER, FEBRUARY 27, 1916.
The P. and O. steamer sunk between Folkestone and Dover about half an hour after an explosion caused by a mine.

merchantmen at sight in whatever seas the hunted and terrified German submarines managed to get a momentary glimpse of the sky and respite from the merciless and infinitely ingenious pursuit of the British and French navies. Neutrals were frankly warned of the new policy, but none of them, and certainly not the United States, expected Great Britain and her Allies to surrender that right of arming merchantmen for defence against attack which was an immemorial right and had been specifically affirmed in the Courts of the United States. Possibly the threat was intended to secure some relaxation of the Orders in Council. In

[Elliott & Fry

MR. M. DE C. FINDLAY,
British Minister in Norway.

[Elliott & Fry

SIR HENRY CROFTON LOWTHER,
British Minister in Denmark.

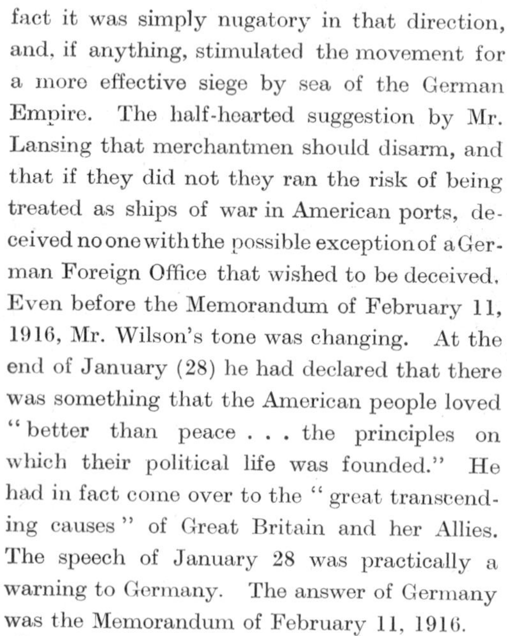

fact it was simply nugatory in that direction, and, if anything, stimulated the movement for a more effective siege by sea of the German Empire. The half-hearted suggestion by Mr. Lansing that merchantmen should disarm, and that if they did not they ran the risk of being treated as ships of war in American ports, deceived no one with the possible exception of a German Foreign Office that wished to be deceived. Even before the Memorandum of February 11, 1916, Mr. Wilson's tone was changing. At the end of January (28) he had declared that there was something that the American people loved "better than peace . . . the principles on which their political life was founded." He had in fact come over to the "great transcending causes" of Great Britain and her Allies. The speech of January 28 was practically a warning to Germany. The answer of Germany was the Memorandum of February 11, 1916.

In the interval occurred the case of the Appam, which brought the German and American Governments into communication once more. A German raider, apparently a converted fruit ship, for some time had been doing a certain amount of mischief in the Atlantic, and toward the end of January she captured the Appam, a British mercantile vessel carrying *inter alios* an ex-Governor of Sierra Leone and some military officers, off the West Coast of Africa. She put a prize crew on the prize and sent her into an American port, relying on certain treaties of the eighteenth century between Prussia and the United States for the securing of the prize. In fact Germany gained nothing by the manœuvre and the passengers were at once released and allowed to return to England. The raider's career was brief, for it gave up operations early in March, and managed to creep through the British blockade in disguise into a Baltic port. This case, like that of the Emden and one or two other cases, shows what an enormous and disastrous effect on England's commerce a bold policy of raiding by the German fleet might have had. The raiders would have been destroyed, of course, but they would have helped the German cause as no other policy could have helped it. But that policy was not adopted at the opening of the war, and after the first few months it was too late. British sea-power had swept the seas and made it practically impossible for German warships other than submarines to find open waters; while the submarine menace was dealt

[Elliott & Fry

SIR ESMÉ W. HOWARD,
British Minister in Sweden.

[Swaine

LORD ROBERT CECIL,
Minister of Blockade.

with in a fashion that undoubtedly made the under-water service less popular in Germany.

But, despite these facts, Germany determined, apparently as an answer to President Wilson's speech, to organize a second submarine campaign. She coupled this determination with a flat defiance of the United States on the subject of the Lusitania atrocity. The German newspapers clearly anticipated a breach of relations on this crime. The crisis was over by February 9, Germany (with the new policy against all commerce in view) pledging herself that "unarmed merchantmen shall not be sunk without warning and unless the safety of the crew can be assured," provided that the vessels did not try to escape or resist. This pledge was regarded as a victory for the United States and for the rights of neutrals, but it was instantly followed by the Memorandum of February 11. The date when the new submarine campaign was to commence was fixed for March 1, 1916. Towards the end of January, 1916, it had become evident that a further development of policy was inevitable. The German submarine policy of 1915 had proved singularly ineffective as a means of blockade. During the whole year, despite desperate attempts at "frightfulness," the German Admiralty had only succeeded in destroying without warning forty unarmed British and fourteen unarmed neutral merchant vessels, while the losses in German submarines had struck terror into the German Navy. But, on the other hand, there had grown up in England a strong feeling that all was not satisfactory in the matter of blockade; that the leakage into Germany of iron ore and other goods essential to the prosecution of the war was of a substantial kind; that the system of "rationing" Scandinavia and Holland—that is to say, the system of allowing through a sufficiency of goods to supply the legitimate demands of those countries—covered an immense amount of smuggling.

At a meeting in the City of London on February 14, 1916, Lord Devonport made these allegations, and there was a demand for a more real blockade of Germany. In a debate in the House of Lords on February 22 Lord Sydenham pressed for a closer blockade and Lord Beresford bluntly declared that the British Navy could "smash" Germany if it were not prevented. These and other speakers showed a large drift of opinion throughout the country, a very general belief that England was not using her Navy as efficiently as she could have done for the purpose of blockading Germany. The task was much wider than the mere blockade of certain belligerent and neutral ports. Trade with persons of neutral nationality but of enemy sympathies had to be checked all over the world. Such traders were dealt with in Egypt as early as February 11, 1916, and on February 29 by the Trading with the Enemy (Neutral Countries) Proclamation, 1916, issued under the Trading with the Enemy (Extension of Powers) Act, 1915, trading with certain persons or bodies of persons of enemy nationality or enemy association in Greece, Morocco, the Netherlands, Norway, Sweden, Portugal, Spain, and Portuguese East Africa was forbidden. All consignments to persons or firms on these statutory black lists were liable to capture. On March 4 firms in Argentina, Uruguay, Brazil, Ecuador, Peru, Central America, the East Indies, the Philippines were blacklisted and supplementary lists were added as occasion served. This was rapidly effective. The case of India, where articles were admitted in certain ports if material of enemy origin did not exceed 25 per cent. of the finished article, showed the difficulty of the position. Continual adjustment and readjustment was necessary in order to strengthen British trade while weakening enemy trade. There was nothing simple about the process at all. The real interests of neutrals had to be safeguarded, while the exigencies of Imperial trade had continually to be kept in mind. Moreover, the problem of freights was becoming acute and Government control over all merchant shipping was gradually asserted. From March 1, 1916, licences were necessary for all voyages to or from the United Kingdom, and a few days later no shipowner could even tender for a contract to carry wheat or flour without official leave. Indeed, the whole problem of foreign trade had to be considered at the same time as the problems of contraband and blockade. In those circumstances it was more than satisfactory to the House of Lords to hear Lord Lansdowne state on February 22 that imports into Germany by way of Holland and Scandinavia were steadily diminishing month by month.

The Government admitted that there was still more leakage than was inevitable into Germany, but the process of quasi-blockade was increasingly successful. Lord Lansdowne further announced that, though the Contraband and War Trading Committees were essential, yet it was realized that the pressure on Germany could be increased by a due coordination of machinery, and he announced that the whole blockade business would be placed in the hands of a single Cabinet Minister who would coordinate the work of all the Committees. It was subsequently stated that Lord Robert Cecil, the Under-Secretary of State for Foreign Affairs, was the new Minister for Blockade. Rear-Admiral Dudley de Chair was appointed as naval adviser to the Foreign Office "on questions connected with foreign trade and blockade." On February 23 Lord Crewe announced, in the continuation of the House of Lords debate, that the list of absolute contraband would inevitably be enlarged as occasion required, and that, though it was not possible to abolish conditional contraband, yet the burden of proof on traders as to the real destination of goods would be increased. Thus the month of March, 1916, which saw certain apparent changes in the German sea policy, as the forerunner of a policy of increased "frightfulness" aimed at all neutral shipping, also saw a very real new development of British sea-power. It was at least possible to hope that this power would now be strenuously applied to the task of shutting out from Germany all and every necessity for the prosecution of the war.

CHAPTER CXX.

THE WORK OF THE MERCANTILE MARINE.

War Traditions of the Merchant Service—Ships "Taken up" by the Navy—Auxiliaries and Transports—The Risk of Capture—Mauretania and Lusitania—The Carmania in Action—Encounters with German Submarines—The Brixham Smack Providence—The Wayfarer—The Lusitania—The Southland—Merchant Ships at the Dardanelles—The Exploits of the German Raider Mowe—Capture of the Appam—The Clan Mactavish—The Greif and the Alcantara—The Patrol Service.

AMONG all the unpredicted developments of the Great War none perhaps was more remarkable than the part taken in it by our Mercantile Marine. There are, of course, as is known to everybody, two branches of the seagoing profession, one military and the other mercantile. A fusion of the two was far from the thoughts of most people. And yet history tells us that Nelson learnt seamanship on board a merchant vessel, and that the merchant seamen of Great Britain in all ages were always ready to take their share in the fighting whenever the cause of their country was involved. Perhaps the best known instance of the sheer audacity of the British Mercantile Marine was when fierce old Commodore Dance, of the Honourable East India Company's Service, ranged his merchant ships in line of battle and beat off the attack of Admiral Linois, who had under his command a line-of-battle ship, three heavy frigates, and a brig, in the Indian Ocean in 1804. From the beginnings of our Island story, deeply interwoven as they are in adventure and enterprise by sea; in all the centuries of battle during which the foundations of our Island Empire have been well and truly laid, the officers and men of our merchant navy have ever been the country's staunch defenders and loyal protectors when danger threatened. And be this also remembered: always they came as volunteers; they invariably flung their weight into the scale "for the fun of the thing." It is true that they were not fighters by profession, but they have always shown an amazing aptitude for mastering the science of sea warfare, and an eagerness to engage in it, which has placed them in line with those to whom they held out a helping and a generous hand.

In all the wars in which England has been engaged there has inevitably occurred much loss of mercantile tonnage. But the Great War was totally unlike any other in which we had ever been engaged before; for although many ships were sunk by the enemy, and we by no means underestimated his capacity for mischief, still the fact remained that the reduction of our commercial carrying capacity was due principally to our naval and military commitments in the war overseas.

The Admiralty Transport Department gradually took up from one-third to one-half of the entire tonnage of our Mercantile Marine; and when we read the category into which the different ships fell we are tolerably certain that this is not an over-statement of the case. Ships were required as mine carriers and layers; troop transports; observation ships; ammunition ships; hospital ships; oilers; store ships; water ships; horse transports; colliers; balloon ships; meat carriers; and for a variety of other services too numerous to recapitulate. To officer these ships recourse was had to the Imperial Merchant Service Guild, and it was stated in one of the reports of that body that it had been instrumental in procuring for

AIRCRAFT v. SEACRAFT.
Auxiliary vessel of the Navy attacked by a bomb-dropping German aeroplane.

the service of the country no less than 2,500 captains and officers. The activities of these gentlemen were widely distributed, as they were employed in Royal Naval Reserve (general service); Royal Naval Reserve (patrol service); Royal Naval Reserve (boom defence); Royal Naval Reserve (mine sweeping); Royal Naval Volunteer Reserve (mine-sweeping service); Royal Naval Reserve (special service); the Government Transport Service; Royal Naval Reserve (salvage service); Special Service Squadron (R.N.R.); Royal Naval Air Service; Trawler Reserve (R.N.R.); Royal Engineers (Inland Water Transport Section); appointments for service under Government on Suez Canal and Nile; Royal Indian Marine (commissions for active service in the East); Royal Indian Marine (transport service); Pilotage Appointments (Trinity House); Royal Fleet Auxiliary (under Government); and Merchant Fleet Auxiliary (under Government).

The officers employed in the various services enumerated were, of course, all directly under the Government, no matter in which branch they were serving. But there remained still the great bulk of the Mercantile Marine, carrying on its ordinary business, fetching and carrying from the uttermost ends of the earth to the wharves and the warehouses of London, Glasgow, Liverpool, and all the minor ports with which the United Kingdom is ringed. The result is that we have to regard the Mercantile Marine in war from a dual standpoint: first as auxiliary to the Royal Navy in all those services enumerated above; secondly in its ordinary capacity for the transport of commodities to and from our shores. Nevertheless it stood one and indivisible; whether it was employed in actual warlike operations, or in the ordinary avocations of commerce, it deserved the recognition of all inhabitants of our Empire for the coolness and dogged courage that it displayed. Nothing could bring home better to the mind of the land folk how imperturbable was the quality of our merchant sailors than the study of the advertisements that figured in the front pages of our great shipping newspapers. Did you desire to cross the Western Ocean, to proceed "up the Straits," to visit the Far East, South America, the Pacific, Australia, or the Scandinavian ports, you could take your choice among the regular steamship lines that plied for your convenience:

> Swift shuttles of an Empire's loom
> That bind us main to main

have never ceased to connect Great Britain with the uttermost ends of the earth. The sea is a jealous mistress, and year in year out never ceases to take toll of the ships that use the sea; wreck, collision, fire, grounding, hazards innumerable, encircle the calling of the mariner in the piping times of peace ; the war risks that were added would have tried the temper and the nerves of any men less constitutionally fearless.

The King, ever sympathetic where his seamen were concerned, early in the war placed his appreciation in words in a letter through his secretary to Lord Muskerry :

"The King realises what magnificent work has been done by the brave officers and crews of his Merchant Service during the past months of war."

Admiral Sir Henry Jackson, First Sea Lord of the Admiralty, in a letter to the Secretary of the Imperial Merchant Service Guild, said :

The promptitude with which the country's call on their merchant officers and seamen has been met is invaluable. The wonderful facility with which they have learnt to carry out their duties as part of a trained fighting force is extraordinary. The Allied nations owe them a deep debt of gratitude for these responses, as well as for their indomitable pluck and endurance.

Admiral Sir John Jellicoe wrote as follows :

I beg to assure you that no one could possibly appreciate more than myself the services of the officers and men of the Mercantile Marine, as I know so well their work during the war, and how splendidly it has been carried out.

Admiral Lord Beresford wrote :

The country never really appreciates what it owes to the officers and men of the Mercantile Marine. During peace, their loyalty to duty and hardihood in encountering the endless difficulties connected with the sea ensures the punctual and certain delivery of food and raw material. Now in war their readiness of resource and gallantry has been exhibited on many occasions. The German pirates have discovered that an unarmed British merchant ship can tackle a submarine by skill of seamanship and the art of handling a vessel. I believe we have now some 2,500 vessels, not men-of-war—namely merchant ships, trawlers, drifters, yachts, etc., employed doing men-of-war work, half of them undertaking patrols. The British Mercantile Marine have well maintained their splendid traditions during the war.

It would be possible to quote many similar opinions of other distinguished and representative men.

As far as the Mercantile Marine is concerned the war divided itself into two periods : first, from the declaration of war on August 4, 1914 ; and second, from the declaration by Germany that from February 18, 1915, she would torpedo at sight all vessels found in what she was pleased to denominate "the war area."

Naturally the question in the minds of all persons interested in shipping when the war began was : Supposing German men-of-war capture British merchant vessels, what procedure will they adopt, there being no ports into which prizes can be taken ? This query was answered by that ingenious officer, the Captain of the Emden, in no uncertain fashion. Between September 10 and 14, 1914, he captured no less than seven vessels ; of these six were sunk, and the captured crews transferred to the seventh. Again, on September 30, he captured six ships, when the same procedure was adopted, five being sunk, and one released. The ancient

MOTOR-BOAT RESERVE IN ATTENDANCE ON TRANSPORTS.

THE BRITISH MAIL BOATS' ESCORT: KEEPING THE ROAD OPEN TO FRIENDLY AND NEUTRAL SHIPPING.

rules of warfare were set at naught, and our foes showed that by sea, as by land, they would be bound by no restrictions of law or of humanity.

In the first phase of the war our merchant seamen were confronted with the fact that a number of enemy warships were distributed about the ocean, and the risk of capture from them was considerable. They knew that a certain class of neutral would be only too ready to serve as ocean spies, and that they would have to use their wits to avoid the dangers with which they were threatened. Those who knew our merchant captains knew also that in any emergency they might be relied upon to display that courage, resourcefulness, and aptitude which is the heritage of their profession. Some cases may be cited which show how this confidence was not misplaced.

The Mauretania, the splendid 32,000-ton ocean flyer belonging to the Cunard Company, sailed from Liverpool on August 1, 1914, with a large complement of saloon, second cabin and third-class passengers, and war was declared when she was in mid-Atlantic. During the night of August 5 she received information by wireless that a German cruiser was on her track. Captain Charles, C.B., R.N.R., hesitated not an instant; he screened all lights on board, altered course to the northward, and made the British port of Halifax, Nova Scotia, in record time. We can well imagine the excitement that reigned on board, but this excitement was translated into action by the toiling firemen at the furnaces below. The safety of all on board, the escape of a ship, the value of which was nearer two millions than one and a half, rested principally with the men who handled the shovel and the slice. When Halifax Harbour was won a deputation of passengers waited on Captain Charles to compliment him upon the manner in which he had manœuvred his ship and saved all hands from a watery grave or a German prison.

The sister ship of the Mauretania, the Lusitania, the ship whose name afterwards branded the German name with eternal infamy, left New York for Liverpool on August 4, the day that war was declared. Shortly after leaving the Ambrose Channel she encountered an unknown cruiser, which signalled to her to consider herself captured, and at the same time steered so as to cut her off. But Captain Dow, of the Lusitania, was of a different opinion to the German commander; he altered course to the northward of the usual

FULL SPEED AHEAD.
Craft of the Motor-boat Reserve on active service.

track, telling his engine-room staff that there was hurry toward. Fortune favoured the brave on this occasion, and the Lusitania ran into a fog which sheltered her from her pursuer, whom she never saw again, and she arrived in Liverpool without encountering any other enemy craft.

On another occasion, on February 10, 1915, Captain Dow, when off the Irish coast, deceived enemy vessels by hoisting the American flag: this action caused a good deal of comment in the United States of America, but no complaint was made by the Government of the United States. The stratagem is of course perfectly legitimate and as old as the time when first ships went to sea flying the banner of the countries to which they belonged.

It is, of course, well known that a large number of merchant vessels were taken up by the Admiralty at the beginning of the war to act as auxiliary cruisers to protect our trade routes; the work that they did was of incalculable value. In this provision of commissioned merchant cruisers we were copied by the enemy, and it so happened that a British mercantile cruiser, H.M.S. Carmania, met with a German vessel of similar type on the coast of South America, on September 14, 1914. The Carmania was just a month from home, having left Liverpool on August 15. Shortly after land was sighted a ship was made out ahead, a liner somewhat similar to the Carmania. This vessel was the German armed merchantman Cap Trafalgar, mounting eight 4-inch guns and pom-poms. When first made out by the Carmania she had two colliers alongside from which she was taking in coal. On sighting the Carmania the colliers were cast off from the Cap Trafalgar, and the two departed in different directions. The Cap Trafalgar after apparently trying to make her escape, thought better of it and headed for the English ship. The weather was fine and sunny with a moderate breeze from north-east. At 8,500 yards Captain Noel

THE BRITISH MOTOR-BOAT RESERVE.
Arrival at the depôt ship for orders.

THE SINKING OF THE " CAP TRAFALGAR," SEPTEMBER 14th, 1914.
The German armed merchantman taking a list to starboard after a twenty-five minute fight with H.M.S. " Carmania."
Specially drawn for " The Times History of the War."

Grant, R.N., of the Carmania, fired a shot across the bows of the German ship. She replied by firing at the Carmania from her starboard-after gun. The battle thus begun soon became animated, but Captain Grant reported that most of the German shots were aimed too high: in consequence rigging, masts, funnels, ventilators, and derricks, suffered the most damage at first. Whether the German gunners were flurried or not it is difficult to say, but one who was present at the action said that at first the Cap Trafalgar was firing five shots to the Carmania's one. One German shell passed through the cabin under the fore bridge of the Carmania and started a fire which was rather a serious matter, as the chemical fire extinguishers proved of very little use, and the Carmania's fire main (used for the extinguishing of fire on board ship) had been shot through. So firm a hold did the fire obtain that the fore bridge had to be abandoned and the ship conned from aft. At the beginning of the action the range was closing, and at one period the ships were as close as 3,200 yards. Captain Grant, however, finding himself annoyed by pompom fire at the shorter ranges, opened out the distance, and always handled his ship with the greatest ability and discretion. She was a huge target; in consequence he manœuvred to keep her bows on, in which position he could use four guns, or again, stern on, he could use four guns.

In this duel the ships were very evenly matched, as both were magnificent vessels, the Cap Trafalgar being an almost brand new liner of 18,170 tons. Such being the case, it was a question of handling; and here we will let one speak who was aboard the Carmania.

After about twenty-five minutes there was only one ship in it, and that was not her (*sic*). She broke out in flames forward, and the fire seemed to spread like lightning. Smoke was coming from her from end to end. She, however, continued firing, although we noticed she was not firing so many guns. About this time she decided to run away, but this was useless, as she had taken a slight list to starboard in the first quarter of an hour, and this had continued to increase. Consequently, when she decided to run she could hardly budge. The list continued, and we still kept on showing her no mercy. It was then noticeable that only one gun was firing, the starboard after; the list had increased to such an extent by this time that she seemed as if she was going to turn turtle. We had practically ceased firing at her by now, watching her, when the gunlayer at the after gun must have elevated his gun and fired at us in his last effort, for we saw the gun flash and the projectiles dropped about what appeared to us 20 yards from his own ship, but I expect it was three or four hundred yards. She then began to settle—you could see her propellers.

The captain seeing that she had not hauled down her flag ordered three rounds to be fired into her, which was done on the port side. She then gradually heaved over until you could see right in her funnels, which were level with the water. There was then a sort of explosion and her bows disappeared, bringing her stern out of the water. Then there seemed a second explosion and she disappeared altogether, leaving five boats full, which were picked up by one of the colliers.

CAPTAIN NOEL GRANT,

Of H.M.S. "Carmania," leaving the Admiralty Court after the award of the prize bounty to the officers and crew of the "Carmania," for the destruction of the "Cap Trafalgar."

The official report gives the time of the action as one hour and forty minutes. The Carmania was unable to pick up the survivors as the ship had to be put in front of the wind at once in order to deal with the fire beneath the fore bridge: she was hit by seventy-nine projectiles which made 304 holes; the ship had been rendered unseaworthy and practically all communications and navigational instruments were destroyed. She was escorted into harbour by H.M.S. Cornwall, and there effected temporary repairs. Nine men were killed and twenty-six wounded on board the ship. How many lost their lives on board the Cap Trafalgar is not known, but the collier landed 279 officers and men of the German ship at Buenos Aires.

Under the Naval Prize Act the Carmania was awarded prize bounty of £2,115 for the destruction of the Cap Trafalgar.

In November, 1914, the Admiralty decided that the whole of the North Sea must henceforward be considered as a military area. They were led to this decision by the fact that the Germans had been scattering mines indiscriminately in the open sea on the main trade routes from America to Liverpool via the North of Ireland. Already merchant ships had been blown up and sunk by these engines of destruction, and the toll would have been far greater had it not been for the warnings of British cruisers. It was pointed out that these mines had been laid by merchant vessels flying a neutral flag, the watch on the trade routes having been far too close for the laying of mines by German warships. Further, that mine laying under a neutral flag and reconnaissance conducted by trawlers, hospital ships, and neutral vessels, were the ordinary features of German naval warfare. Accordingly, as guardians of the seas, the Admiralty felt it incumbent upon them to take exceptional measures, and gave the notice spoken of above. Within the area of the North Sea merchant shipping of all kinds, traders of all countries, and fishing craft, were exposed to the gravest dangers from the mines that we on our side had been obliged to lay, and from warships searching diligently by night and day for suspicious craft.

All merchant ships and fishing vessels were accordingly warned of the dangers they encountered by entering this area save in strict accordance with Admiralty directions. Every effort was made to convey the warning to neutral countries and vessels at sea, but from November 5 onwards the Admiralty announced that all ships passing a line drawn from the northern point of the Hebrides through the Faroe Islands to Iceland did so at their own peril. Routes were given for ships to follow in order that they might reach their destinations in safety.

This scattering of mines broadcast, in the manner indicated, was the first indication of the German policy of frightfulness upon the high seas. By it they intended so to frighten the mariner of the British Mercantile Marine that he would refuse to put to sea in so dangerous an area. In this the Teuton showed his constitutional incapacity to understand the dauntless courage of the men against whom this danger was directed. While one section of the sailors of England swept diligently for mines, the other section pursued their ordinary business upon the seas as unconcernedly as if no such persons as Germans existed, and as if

ON BOARD A BRITISH TORPEDO BOAT.
Gun practice in the North Sea.

ON BOARD THE KITE BALLOON SHIP H.M.S. "CANNING."

The balloon about to make an ascent. Smaller picture: Balloon observers above the hold.

no such contrivances as mines had ever been invented. It is true that ships were sunk, and that the mine sweepers were exposed to the most dreadful peril. One of the men engaged in mine sweeping expressed the opinion "that this 'ere *is* a bit thick," on the third occasion on which he was blown up, and when the trawler's winch weighing three-quarters of a ton whizzed past his head as he stood at the tiller. This, however, did not prevent him from shipping in a fourth mine sweeper after he had been picked up and taken back to an East Coast port.

On April 12, 1915, there limped into Hampton Roads, U.S.A., the Kronprinz Wilhelm. She was a deplorable spectacle, with her sides streaming red rust and carrying a very perceptible list: yet she had done an extraordinary amount of damage to her enemy, which is best told in the words of her own commander:—

Our work is not yet finished. We are going back to sea. This ship is unkempt inside and out, I admit, but that is because we had to coal at sea, and the only way that could be done was by taking coal on deck and carrying it down through the saloons to the bunkers. We had no guns when we left New York, but we knew what we were about. Our original intention was to get armament from the Karlsruhe, but we ran into the British steamer La Correntina, which was armed, but without ammunition. We took her guns. We had no ammunition to waste, and most of the ships that we took we sank by opening the seacocks. We rammed the Nova Scotian, a schooner, and took off her crew. We took more than 1,000 prisoners from various craft, and kept most of them for two months. We found this expensive, and got into communication with the collier Holgar, which landed the prisoners at Buenos Aires. . . . The biggest prize of our entire trip was the British steamer La Correntina. We came upon her in the South Atlantic. She showed no fight. We boarded her, took two 3-inch guns and five million pounds of beef, and then opened her seacocks. The Indian Prince, which was captured on September 7, did not prove a rich prize. On November 11 we secured 3,100 tons of coal from the French barque Union. We stored the coal in the saloon and first-class cabins. After that our ship never looked clean. On December 23 we captured the Hemisphere and took 500 tons of coal. On January 10 we ran into the British steamer Potaro in ballast. We opened her seacocks. On January 14 we secured the Royal Mail steamship Highland Brae; she carried 51 passengers and a crew of 94. We took these aboard and large quantities of provisions. Later on the same day we got the British steamer Wilfred loaded with fish and potatoes. The only neutral ship we sank was the Norwegian sailing vessel Sonantha, with a cargo of wheat bound for Liverpool. On February 22 we overtook the British freighter Chase Hill . . . instead of sinking him I transferred 400 men and women to his vessel, and told him to take them ashore.

This raider also sank the French steamer Guadaloupe and the British s.s. Tamar with 68,000 sacks of coffee on March 24. Four days later the Coleby, laden with wheat, met the same fate. Although the career of the Kronprinz Wilhelm was neither so meteoric nor so destructive as was that of the Emden, it is perhaps even more remarkable ; there must also be much left to tell.

One by one, however, the raiders were captured or driven off the seas to be interned in the ports of neutrals. The oversea commerce of Germany, strangled from the outset of the war, had not been redeemed by any specially dashing exploits by the High Sea Fleet. But the German naval authorities felt that something must be done. Accordingly on February 18, 1915, was published the infamous decree that Germany had declared all the coasts of the United Kingdom "a war area," and within that area all ships were to be torpedoed at sight and without warning. At first, civilized humanity would not believe that even Germany would go to such lengths as this ; but they found that they were entirely mistaken. The system of sea murder began. Passenger liners, refugee ships, hospital ships, coasters, freighters, trawlers and drifters, all were to (and all did) fall a prey to these cowardly assassins. Thereafter, to risk of floating mine and of prowling German cruiser was added the terror that stalked beneath the sea for our ships and our men. Once more they rose to the occasion. Deep sea long-voyage sailors and firemen, the men who man our coasters, the fishermen, or rather such of them as were left who were not fishing for mines, continued "to go down to the sea in ships and occupy their business in great waters," and, not only did they do this, but they applied for and got guns with which to defend themselves. This latter proceeding caused genuine annoyance to the Germans. To paraphrase a famous saying, they described the average British merchant vessel as "a treacherous animal that defends itself when attacked."

Examples of the manner in which the merchant ships resisted their assailants were given by the Germans themselves. On February 10, 1916, the representatives of the neutral Powers at Berlin were handed a memorandum in which the German Government announced its decision to treat all armed merchantmen as warships on and from March 1, thus rendering them liable to be sunk at sight. In annexe No. 4 of this memorandum, which was transmitted by wireless to the German Embassy at Washington on February 26, a list of eighteen cases was given in which merchant vessels opened fire when attacked by German or Austrian submarines. In fifteen instances the defence of the merchant ships was successful, and they escaped destruction, illustrating the great advantage of a gun armament in such circumstances. The following were typical cases in the German compilation:

September 10, 1915.—In the Western Mediterranean an unknown steamer was asked to show her flag, and thereupon she opened fire with about 10-centimetre guns from her stern. The submarine escaped by submerging quickly.

November 23, 1915.—In the Western Mediterranean the British steamer, City of Marseilles, was fired at by a submarine as a warning. A large freight steamer without flag turned round, and by artillery fire from ten cannon of about 10 centimetre calibre opened fire. The submarine had to abandon the pursuit and the steamer escaped. A newspaper telegram from Bombay of January 14, 1916, corroborated details of the event, and the steamer stated that it had sunk the submarine.

This German list of encounters between merchantmen and submarines was naturally confined to episodes from which the submarines returned unharmed. From other sources it was known that on certain occasions the submarines never returned at all, but were sunk by their mercantile opponents. The facts revealed the determination of the British merchant seamen to defend their ships to the utmost when attacked, and showed that the men in those vessels which had been provided with guns of small calibre for their protection knew how to use them. Owing to the action of the submarines there had come about a return to the practice of olden days, when every ship had to carry guns for defence or else sail under the protection of a convoying squadron. In those days it was the privateers and pirates who constituted the menace to the sea trader ; in this war, means of defence were needed against the submarine pirates. The psychological processes of the Teuton are hard to fathom. He gloried in the most cowardly system of sea murder that had ever been invented. By processes of logic, which seemed to him irrefutable, he set the seal of his approval on this new form of frightfulness ; but that submarines should, if possible, be sunk on sight by a merchantman that had had the effrontery to arm herself with a gun, called forth from him the strongest reprobation.

On January 1, at 3 a.m., H.M.S. Formidable was torpedoed by a German submarine in the Channel, some 15 miles from Berry Head. The tale of this tragedy has been told elsewhere; it is referred to here to bring into prominence once again the part taken in the rescue of 68 men of the ill-fated battleship by the Brixham fishing smack Providence, owned and skippered by William Pillar. This little craft was running for shelter before the gale then blowing for Brixham, but when off the Start had to heave to owing to the violence of the wind and the tremendous run of the sea. Those who know the fisherman are aware that it is no trifle that causes him to heave to, especially when he has his home port close under his lee. Presently the third hand of the smack noticed, to his amazement, a small boat to leeward driving through the sea with one oar upended, to which was attached a sailor's scarf. There was no hesitation on board the smack. In some miraculous fashion they managed to put another reef in the mainsail and to bend and hoist the storm jib. The Providence had then to manœuvre to get the boat alongside, and to do this she had to gybe—which means passing her stern to the wind. Nothing but most desperate and urgent necessity would have caused that fine seaman in command of the smack to have done this, as he risked dismasting his craft. Having accomplished the manœuvre he had to run down to the boat and get her alongside; to do this he had to round to and bring the head of the smack up to the wind again. Further, there was imminent risk when the boat was approached that she might be run down and sunk. How in the darkness, the shouting gale, and the monstrous sea that was running, this was accomplished is nothing short of miraculous. But the iron nerve of William Pillar at the helm, the alertness of his little handful of a crew, never failed for an instant: it was one of those tense and wonderful moments in which the British seaman rises to heights of achievement seemingly impossible, when nerve and brain and hand and muscle, subordinated to the will of one master mind, work together for the accomplishment of the incredible. Four times did the smack approach close enough to heave a rope to the boat—and four times she failed; each failure meant a fresh manœuvre for position, a renewed chance of the sinking of the boat by collision in seas that ran thirty feet from trough to crest, topped with breaking foam that showed a wan yellow in the fitful moonlight. At last a light warp was passed on board the man-of-war boat, brought to the capstan of the smack, and, with infinite precaution, the one craft was warped up close enough astern of the other for a transference to begin and for the sailors in the small boat to jump on board the smack. True to the traditions of the great service to which he belonged, Torpedo Gunner Hurrigan, the senior officer in the cutter, was the last man to leave; then the warp was cut, the cutter drifted astern, and the smack headed for Brixham. They arrived safely and the shipwrecked mariners were tenderly cared for, while, during the passage, all the available food in the smack had been served out to the rescued men. This is the story of that well-named Brixham fishing vessel Providence; and no man or woman who reads it can fail in passionate admiration for the rescuers of that sorely tried remnant of the crew of the Formidable, who were adrift in a small, overcrowded boat in that terrible January gale; a boat, moreover, that had been stove and was kept

THE GERMAN RAIDER "KRONPRINZ WILHELM."
At anchor at Hampton Roads, U.S.A.

WAR-PAINT IN A LONDON DOCK.
Armed British Liners being painted "Man-o'-war grey."

afloat by a pair of trousers stuffed into the hole.

From the very beginning of the submarine campaign by the Germans there appears to have been only one pronounced determination among our merchant seamen, and that was to assume the offensive on every possible occasion. One and all seem to have been animated by the same spirit. Thus Captain H. Gibson, of the steam tug Homer, belonging to South Shields, was awarded a gold watch and a letter on vellum from the Admiralty expressing their admiration of his conduct.

The Homer was towing the French barque General de Sonis when she was hailed by a German submarine and told to surrender. Captain Gibson's method of surrender was to slip the tow rope and steer straight for the submarine, in spite of a shower of bullets from a machine gun. Unfortunately, the Homer missed the stern of the submarine by a few feet, whereupon the U boat turned and chased the tug She even went so far as to fire a torpedo at her contemptuous opponent, which was, when one considers it, a high compliment. However, the torpedo missed its mark, and Captain Gibson brought the Homer triumphantly into Bembridge, Isle of Wight, with his vessel peppered and scarred with bullet marks.

Captain J. W. Bell was the fortunate officer to win the sum of £500 offered by the paper *Syren and Shipping* for the first merchant service captain to sink an enemy submarine; other awards totalled up the sum he received to £1,160. This is the entry from the ship's official log:

About 9.30 this morning, while proceeding from Blyth towards Plymouth, Beachy Head, distant 8 to 10 miles, observed the periscope of a submarine on the starboard bow. Ordered all hands on deck in case of emergency. Then observed the submarine to pass across our bow on to the port beam, where it took up a position 30 to 40 yards off. Shortly after noticed the wake of a torpedo on the starboard beam; put the helm hard over to starboard and ran over the periscope, when I and the crew heard and felt the crash under our bottom. Did not see the submarine after, but saw oil floating on the water.

(Signed) J. W. BELL, *Master.*
JOHN PEGG, *Mate.*

The ship was docked for examination and the statement of Captain Bell was fully borne out by the marks on the bottom; and not only did this fortunate mariner reap the reward that has been mentioned, but he was decorated with the Distinguished Service Cross and granted a temporary Lieutenant's commission in the Royal Naval Reserve.

When Captain T. Atkinson of the s.s. Oceola was proceeding down Channel he sighted the ss. Western Coast and Rio Parana, both of which had been torpedoed, and also another ship making in towards the land as fast as she could steam. Prudence would have dictated a course in the opposite direction to the torpedoed vessels, but Captain Atkinson was not one of the prudent breed. He accordingly approached the torpedoed ships on a zig-zag course, picked up the boats of the Western Coast and brought them safely into port; while the people of the Parana were being attended to by a British destroyer that had arrived upon the scene. On a later occasion Captain Atkinson was followed by a submarine, from which he escaped by running into thick weather; and he also had the experience of having bombs dropped at him by two enemy Taube aeroplanes; from which attentions he escaped by the skilful handling of his ship.

When the transport Wayfarer was torpedoed in the Atlantic on April 11, 1915, she had on board 700 horses and a yeomanry detachment. After the explosion the ship was abandoned by the crew and the troops in boats, and they proceeded to the s.s. Framfield, which fortunately happened to be in the vicinity. Finding that the Wayfarer did not sink, the captain, Captain D. G. Cownie, called for volunteers to return. Accompanied by all his officers, some of the crew, and a proportion of the yeomanry, headed by the Major in command and the two subalterns, Captain Cownie returned to the damaged vessel. Captain Bain of the Framfield, with 35 of the crew and 169 of the yeomanry on board, then made fast a wire hawser and towed the Wayfarer to within 16 miles of Queenstown, from which port she was 108

BOARDING AND EXAMINING A SUSPICIOUS VESSEL.
British sailors leaving the ship after examination.

miles distant when torpedoed, and there handed her over to two Government tugs. Lord Derby, at the Liverpool Town Hall, at the request of the Admiralty, presented inscribed gold watches to Captain Cownie; Mr. H. L. Pritchard, Chief Officer; Mr. E. R. Bury, Second Officer; Mr. E. Davies, Third Officer; and also to the engineers. Seeing that she had a hole in her side thirty-five feet by twenty-five, and one interior bulkhead entirely destroyed, we can appreciate the courage and determination of Captain Cownie, his officers and crew, and those gallant yeomen who stood by the ship and her lading of dumb animals in that perilous voyage back to Queenstown.

NORWEGIAN STEAMER "TRONDHJEMAJORD."
Torpedoed by a German submarine.

But Germany's crowning deed of shame was the torpedoing of the Cunard Liner Lusitania on May 6, 1915. In this wholesale massacre twelve hundred and twenty-five persons, men, women and children, lost their lives. This outrage was received with shouts of joy in Germany; but even so an attempt was made to palliate the deed. Instantly the German Press began to explain. It was stated that the Lusitania was an armed cruiser that was laden with munitions of war, and in consequence of this the submarines were quite justified in sinking the ship. That this was a deliberate and calculated lie is known to all the world. To reinforce the lies told in print, pictures were produced in the illustrated newspapers depicting the sinking of the Lusitania, and showing guns mounted both forward and aft. At the time of the disaster there was a good deal of discussion as to why the Lusitania was allowed to enter the danger zone in the Irish Sea unaccompanied by an escort; but nothing transpired at the inquest on the bodies of the victims of the outrage, or subsequently, to account for this apparent neglect. According to the evidence of Captain Turner, the master of the Lusitania, the ship remained afloat only some eighteen minutes after being struck; and it was only owing to the fact that the sea was dead smooth at the time of the explosion that even the minority who were saved escaped with their lives.

The contention that the Lusitania was carrying munitions of war, and was torpedoed on this account, was not borne out even by the actions of the German submarines. The next ship to leave New York after the Lusitania was the passenger liner Transylvania, and the Germans were boasting that she also would be sunk. The captain of that vessel declared that an attempt was made to sink his command, but that he escaped by skilful manœuvring. Not even the German Press pretended that the Transylvania was armed; yet it was thanks to the mercy of Providence and the skill of her captain that she did not share the fate of the Lusitania. The only consolation for the tragedy of the Lusitania was the splendid behaviour of those on board. Doomed to certain death, as they with good cause believed themselves to be, no man or woman flinched; all, according to the evidence of the captain, behaved with that coolness which is the hallmark of the race to which they belonged.

As time went on the activities of the submarines were not confined to the sea that washes our coasts, and what happened to the Southland occurred in the Mediterranean. She was a British transport conveying Australian troops to the scene of hostilities, and some forty miles from Mudros she was torpedoed abaft the foremast and two of her forward compartments were blown into one. The ship was crowded with men, and with a gaping rent in her 30 feet in length might be expected to founder at any moment. "Fall in," was the order, and, even as the men of the Birkenhead fell in sixty-six years before, so did the Australians line up—to die if so ordained—but to die as became men of British birth and blood. Fortunately it was fine weather and not much sea was running. The boats were

A BRITISH CAPTURE ON THE HIGH SEAS.

The "Presidente Mitre," of the Hamburg-South American Line, was captured by H.M.S. "Orama" in November, 1915. The picture shows the mails being slung from the captured vessel on board the "Orama."

A BRITISH PATROL-VESSEL ESCORTING A TROOPSHIP AND SIGNALLING TO A PASSING OUTWARD-BOUND STEAMER—"ENEMY SUBMARINE IN THE VICINITY."

swung out in orderly methodical fashion, they were lowered, and the men embarked. But no man moved until he got the order to do so from his officer. Across the sea the S.O.S. signal was picked up by the British India s.s. Neuralia employed as a hospital ship. Quickly she was on the scene, and some 470 men were transferred to her in her own boats, that were got into the water as soon as she arrived on the scene. The Neuralia carried a Lascar crew; seamen and firemen of these Eastern fellow-subjects of ours almost came to blows in their desperate anxiety to man the boats and assist in the saving of life from what appeared to be a sinking ship. To the last the men of the damaged Southland maintained their coolness, their instinct to do the right thing. As the boats of the Neuralia approached the boats of the transport these parted right and left to give them passage, to enable them the more quickly to arrive at the scene of the disaster. Unfortunately 22 deaths resulted. Three men were killed outright by the explosion, the remainder being lost by the capsizing of one of the life rafts. The Southland got into Mudros, whence, after temporary repairs, she was able to proceed to England.

In any account of the work of the Mercantile Marine notice should be taken of the part played by our merchant seamen in the Mediterranean, and particularly in the wonderful and agonizing drama of Gallipoli. Few people have any idea of the size of the fleet of transports necessary for the conveyance of troops and stores to this distant scene of action; and if it were only to record the seamanlike competence of our brethren of the merchant service notice should be taken of the feat that they performed. From ocean-going leviathans, like the Aquitania, of 46,000 tons, and the Mauretania, of 33,000 tons, down to tugs and small coasters, the operations confided to their extremely competent hands were carried out without a hitch. Gallipoli was not only a supreme test for the men officially registered as combatants, it also called for qualities of the highest description among those not so catalogued. The functions of the merchant ship in wartime are, and always have been, necessarily hazardous; that is to say, when these vessels are carrying out their ordinary commercial avocations. The danger to which they are exposed is, of course, vastly increased when they are "taken up" to be used for warlike purposes by the Government. Ships that are

PRISONERS OF WAR FROM A GERMAN MERCHANT SHIP.
After being searched on board a British cruiser, the prisoners were put under guard.

transporting an army overseas are liable to be sunk at sight by enemy warships, and yet in the case of the Gallipoli Expedition this was only the beginning of the troubles that had to be incurred.

Even from the first the transports had to run in so close to land their cargoes that they came under the direct fire of the Turkish batteries. There was no possible means of avoiding this obligation: thousands upon thousands of tons of stores had to be landed, and this not merely upon one day, but on every day of the week for months on end. A big merchant ship returned from this scene of action with her upper works riddled. The mate explained that this had been all one day's work landing stores on "the beaches." "Oh yes," he said, "they had got it pretty hot on that occasion, but then that was the usual thing when old Johnny Turko got the range of you. It was true that the cook made a bitter complaint about his oven being perforated, but then he was always a chap a bit inclined to grouse." This attitude of taking shrapnel fire as all in the day's work seems to be characteristic of the Mercantile Marine in this war.

Subsequently came the danger to the transports of the attack by submarine. That fine ship the Royal Edward was lost with some hundreds of lives; nor was she the only victim, and we may instance the Middleton, sunk between Alexandria and Mudros, when several of her crew were killed by shell fire. So it will be seen that these "non-combatants" entered the danger zone as soon as they left Alexandria for Mudros, and, after their arrival at this latter port, sailed for Suvla, Anzac, and Cape Helles, where they became the unresisting targets of the Turkish batteries. Considering the exceptional circumstances of this act of war, it may be said with justice that for this there was no help; yet too much recognition cannot be paid to the services rendered by the Mercantile Marine and the complete disregard of danger shown by them on all occasions when duty called ships and men into the firing line.

In January, 1916, there occurred what had long been expected, a fresh attempt to interfere with the commercial activities of the Allies by the attacks of armed merchant cruisers on the ocean trade routes. At the end of the month the Elder Dempster liner Appam, from West Africa, was much overdue, and grave anxiety was felt for this and some half dozen other

SINKING OF A GERMAN RAIDER.

[*Specially drawn for "The Times History of the War."*

The fight between the armed German raider "Greif," disguised as a Norwegian merchant vessel, and H.M. armed merchant cruiser "Alcantara" in the North Sea, February 29, 1916. The engagement resulted in the loss of both vessels, the German raider being sunk by gunfire, and the "Alcantara" by a torpedo.

important vessels. The Appam should have arrived at Plymouth on January 20, but the only sign or sound of her was a broken boat which was picked up between Madeira and Gibraltar on the 16th. When her loss was considered certain, and had been attributed either to bad weather or to a submarine attack, the ship made a dramatic appearance at Norfolk, U.S.A., on February 1. She had been taken there by a prize crew from a German raider which had stopped her on January 16, and had on board a number of prisoners from other merchant ships which were sunk about the same time. By this it became known that an attempt to break through the British North Sea guard had at length succeeded. The vessel making it was called the Möwe, but in reality was understood to be a fruit trader named the Ponga, converted into an auxiliary cruiser. She was stated to have left a German base in December, and, taking advantage of a snowstorm, had managed to elude the cordon of watching British cruisers. Her first captures were made in the neighbourhood of the Canary Islands. During January and February she held up fifteen Allied vessels, including one French and one Belgian. Their aggregate value exceeded that of the loss inflicted by any other German raider, even the Emden. On March 4 the German Admiralty announced her safe return to a German port, and gave the name of her commander as Captain Count von und zu Dohna-Schlodien. The principal interest in her raid was the encounter between the German ship and the British steamer Clan Mactavish. When summoned to stop, this vessel refused, being suspicious of the appearance of her questioner, and when the Möwe's canvas screens fell away and disclosed her battery of guns, which opened fire, the Clan Mactavish still held on her course, and replied from a two-pounder gun mounted in her stern as a protection against submarines. This unequal combat illustrated the pluck and daring of the personnel of the Mercantile Marine in a striking manner. The Clan Mactavish kept up her fire until it became evident that further resistance was useless. Her action was commended by the British people, and aroused great enthusiasm. In a telegram to the owners of the vessel, Admiral Sir John Jellicoe said that the fight put up by the Clan Mactavish filled the seamen in the Grand Fleet with admiration.

The measure of success which attended the Möwe's adventure led to an early attempt at repetition. On February 29, 1916, the Alcantara was carrying out her ordinary patrolling duties in the North Sea when she sighted a large steamer flying Norwegian colours and with Norwegian colours painted on her side. The Alcantara ran down to the stranger, and, as is usual in such cases, the crew went to their quarters. Exactly what distance separated the vessels when the Alcantara stopped is not known, but the range must have been extremely short, as she asked the name and destination of the supposed Norwegian. The answers being apparently satisfactory, the British cruiser lowered a boat to board the ship and verify the information supplied. As soon as the boat shoved off and was pulling towards the stranger her true character was revealed. She dropped her false bulwarks, displayed a formidable array of guns, and opened fire on the boat and the ship to which she belonged. But the Alcantara was ready for her—which perhaps she did not expect—and action was joined at once. Both were very large ships, the Alcantara being well over 15,000 tons, and presented such targets that to miss was almost impossible at the short range. It appears that the Germans fired one, if not two, torpedoes at once and missed, showing very poor marksmanship. They then had a remarkable stroke of luck as one of their shells struck the rudder of the Alcantara, rendering her unmanageable. The German ship was then able so to manœuvre as to get in a torpedo on the side of her foe, thus

ON THE LOOK-OUT.
A British destroyer out on patrol duty.

reducing that vessel to a sinking condition. Had it not been for the proximity of the Andes, another of our large armed merchantmen, the raider might have got away with the honours of war, although she had been badly mauled by the Alcantara, and was on fire in several places. As soon as the Andes was sighted the Greif, for such was the name of the raider, made off at full speed, the Andes in hot pursuit. A stern chase is a long one, and the Greif, doubling like a hare, fired several torpedoes at her pursuer, but without effect.

The practice from the Andes seems to have been very pretty; she wrecked the tophamper of the Greif, driving the men away from the guns. Her shooting must have been remarkably good, as not only was the range altering rapidly, but to avoid torpedoes the ship must have been swinging on her helm from side to side. Just as the end was inevitable a light cruiser appeared, apparently from nowhere, and joined in the fray. At some very extreme distance her gunlayers picked up the range. But there was no occasion for the participation of the cruiser. Already the German was on fire fore and aft, and presently she blew up with a terrific explosion. It is related, though for the truth of the story no guarantee can be given, that as the cruiser ramped up to the Andes, travelling at the rate of an express train, she made the signal, "Sorry, your bird." It is thought that the Greif was laden with mines, and this it was that caused the violence of the explosion.

When we think of our merchant seamen it is well to think of the patrol service. From Archangel to the Line, from the Line to the Horn, in bitter biting cold, in roasting torrid heat, in shouting gales that whirl the snow wreaths mast high; in latitudes where the pampero, the cyclone and the mistral reign, the merchant service was at work. Stark men of their hands are they, rough in speech, instant in action. Auxiliary to the fighting sea service they proved that the breed has not deteriorated. The seed of Drake, of Frobisher, of John Hawkins, and of stout Sir Richard Grenville, he who lay "at Flores in the Azores" and fought the fight of "the one and the fifty-three," still survived. It may have been that in the days, the drowsy days, of peace, there were misgivings as to our reserves of seamen; but such apprehensions passed when all the sailors of Britain and the Empire proved themselves a company one and indivisible.

CHAPTER CXXI.

FISHERMEN AND THE WAR.

Use of Fishermen by the Royal Navy—The Trawler Section—Size of the British Fishing Fleet—Trawling in Peace and Mine-sweeping in War—Heroism of the Mine-sweepers—Fishermen at the Dardanelles—Some Famous Adventures—Attacks by German Aircraft—Fishermen off the Belgian Coast—Patrols and Motor-boat Work—Some Brave Deeds.

So vast soon became the number of fishermen, mostly of the deep sea, who were mine-sweeping and patrolling in connexion with the Royal Navy, and so great was the number of steam trawlers and steam drifters which were requisitioned by the Admiralty, that it is hard to realize that before the war this invaluable auxiliary was practically non-existent. There was a nucleus, a skeleton, and that was all; but it was enough to allow of the building of a superstructure in the shape of the Trawler Section, which did so much to secure the safety of the Grand Fleet and the lesser fleets of the British Navy. At the outbreak of war there were very few naval officers, either at the Admiralty or elsewhere, who knew anything of the deep sea fisherman and his possibilities of service in connexion with the Navy, and for a long period no adequate use had been made of these unrivalled men. The war caused a complete change in the official attitude towards fishermen and they were gladly absorbed, to become one of the most remarkable of the many remarkable auxiliaries of the Navy. It is to the work of the fishermen in combating the deadly menace of the mine that the failure of many of the German plans for our defeat was due. It was a North Sea skipper, in an old beam-trawler, who gave one of the very first alarms of German mine-layers; and after that opening period of the war trawlermen were the means of destroying enormous numbers of German mines which had the power of causing incredible loss in ships and lives.

At the outbreak of war the fishing industry was in full swing. Four fleets of steam trawlers were at work on the North Sea—the Red Cross, the Great Northern, the Gamecock, and Messrs. Hellyers; single-boaters were everywhere, from Iceland downward; steam drifters, which had begun the season at the Shetlands, were following the herring southward, and many beam-trawlers and liners were making profitable trips. The fleets were the direct successors of the old fleets of sailing smacks, which worked the Dogger and other banks, sending their catches to Billingsgate by steam carrier, and remaining at sea for eight or more weeks at a time, returning to port only for a few days, to refit and get fresh water and stores. Small paddle tugs at north country ports had been equipped with beam trawls and had proved a great success; these picturesque pioneers had been succeeded by screw trawlers, which used an improved and more efficient trawl known as the Otter, and were formed into fleets as the smacks had been formed. These steam trawlers, 40 or 50 to the fleet, remained on the fishing banks in an unbroken succession, a vessel leaving for port, to recoal and get fresh water and stores, when she had been at sea for four or five weeks and her supplies had come to an end. The old system of boarding the fish and sending it to market by carrier was maintained, and a very high degree of efficiency in trawling was reached, each fleet being under the control of an experienced and specially selected fisherman, who was known as the admiral. This important leader, whose duty was to select

A NORTH SEA MINE-SWEEPER AT WORK.

the best fishing-grounds and so secure the most satisfactory results, had under him a vice-admiral who, in his chief's absence or at other times of need, could take over the direction of the fleet

Grimsby, the world's greatest fishing port, was the headquarters of an enormous fleet of steam trawlers, mostly engaged in single boating; that is to say, the vessels worked individually, going to sea and fishing until enough fish had been caught to make it worth while to return to port. Many of these trawlers, exceptionally fine craft, made the Iceland trip, lasting about three weeks, and there were voyages to the White Sea and elsewhere. The fleeters belonged mostly to Hull. Extensive operations were conducted from other bases, such as Aberdeen, and great numbers of vessels worked from the lesser ports like Scarborough. Yarmouth and Lowestoft maintained their position as the chief ports for the steam drifters. Before the war, therefore, there was a vast aggregation of first-rate steam fishing vessels, manned by crews of whom many members practically spent their lives on the North Sea, for out of a whole 12 months a fleeter would enjoy only about three weeks ashore. The rest of his life was lived in his little steamboat, far from land, and in this environment he had to contend with the bitterest and heaviest of the winter gales. This compulsion made him what he was—an unrivalled sailor and an expert in knowledge of the North Sea grounds.

Fortunate indeed was it that there were available these wonderful *personnel* and *matériel*: doubly fortunate that prompt and comprehensive steps were taken to secure them for the Royal Navy. At the very outbreak of war the Germans realized what a precious asset our deep sea fishermen were to us, and they tried hard to destroy or seize the vessels. In one swoop in August, 1914, they captured a number of steam trawlers which were fishing in the North Sea and made prisoners of the crews, but beyond minor successes of that description their efforts failed. Subsequently many steam trawlers were lost, some by submarine attacks, most by striking mines; a large number of brave fellows perished, and a lesser number were made prisoners of war. After a year and a half of war there were nearly 300 fishermen prisoners of war in Germany. Many of them suffered cruelly through neglect and ill-treatment, and it is comforting to know that special help was provided for them by means of the Fishermen Prisoners of War Fund, which was organized and administered by the Royal National Mission to Deep Sea Fishermen. Further reference will be made to losses amongst fishermen and their vessels; but it may be stated here, as an indication of the extent of both, that Grimsby alone during the year 1915 lost 57 steam trawlers, with a death-roll of 287 men. In some cases the crew escaped; but in most instances they perished. Twenty of the vessels carried a crew of nine each; in one case, the Horatio, the number was 14.

When the war broke out the number of first-class British steam fishing vessels was more than 3,000, mostly trawlers and drifters. In 1913 more than 1,600 steam drifters were at work, in addition to motor and sailing craft;

and of these about 1,000 had their headquarters at Yarmouth. The total number of whole-time fishermen was upwards of 125,000, and it was calculated that the entire industry supported one-twentieth of the population, with an invested capital of about £200,000,000. It was remarkable that while the British steam drifter industry developed with extreme rapidity there was no such progress in the German drifter fleets. The Germans, however, had made full use of English and Scottish markets for their catches of fish, and their Iceland boats especially did a large business at Aberdeen. The Germans were also quick to see the advantages of wireless telegraphy on North Sea fishing vessels, and they established installations well in advance of the experiments which were carried out by British enterprise.

Heavy demands were made by the Admiralty on the ships and men, and these demands grew rapidly as the necessities of the war increased. It was publicly known that nine months after war broke out there were 14,000 fishermen engaged in mine-sweeping, and a thousand of their vessels.

The Otter gear had reached a high state of development, and the fishermen had become very proficient in its use. It is important to bear this fact in mind in considering what the mine-sweepers accomplished; because without experience they could not have achieved their astonishing success in dealing with the mines. The net of the Otter gear was of the usual bag-shaped variety, the size varying according to the power and dimensions of the vessel using it; but an average size was about 100 ft. in length, with a spread of from 80 to 90 ft. The principal features of the gear were fore and after gallows, with fairleaders, a towing-block, a powerful steam-winch, the Otter boards, and the towing-warps. A steam trawler used hundreds of fathoms of heavy wire warp and the handling of these warps called for the greatest skill and care. It was not difficult to adapt the method of trawling for fish to sweeping for mines, the great difference being that, while a trawler in fishing worked alone to get her catch, in sweeping they worked in pairs. What had been done by the towing-warp was accomplished by the sweeping-wire.

In the system of sweeping employed there was a "kite" and a "shoot," and great skill and care had to be exercised in using them. Many accidents happened which were unavoidable—for example, a man engaged on board a sweeper was working between the "kite" and the "shoot" when the vessel rolled and the "kite" swung over and killed him.

In sweeping, the pair of trawlers, steaming abreast at a certain distance, dragged a weighted steel hawser which, striking the mooring of a mine, brought the mine to the surface, where

A NORTH SEA TRAWLER IN A GALE.

MINE-SWEEPERS AT WORK.

it was promptly exploded by gun-fire from an accompanying destroyer or armed trawler or by rifle-fire. At the very outset the sweepers encountered perils and hardships which continuously attended their calling. Mines exploded and destroyed vessels and crews, and the danger was always present with trawlers which were carrying out fishing in the ordinary manner in the areas indicated by the Admiralty and made known to fishermen. The Grimsby trawler Uxbridge had a mine in the net when the gear was hauled. As the net reached the side of the vessel the mine exploded and the Uxbridge was so severely damaged that she sank in ten minutes. Her crew of nine men, of whom three were wounded, were just able to escape in their small boat, and they were lucky enough to be picked up by another trawler.

Sometimes sweeping was done under actual fire, and a fisherman in a letter described what happened to him and his comrades when they were sweeping in a winter gale. The perilous and excessively uncomfortable work was in progress, warships being in attendance, when German cruisers appeared, and the little sweepers had to leave the scene under shell-fire. "They must have taken us for Dreadnoughts," wrote the fisherman sarcastically. Two days later the sweepers were recompensed, for they ran into some German mines and immediately set to work to sink them. This sweeper alone, within a very short period, blew up no fewer than 18 German mines, "any one of which," the writer said with truth and pride, "might have destroyed a battleship." On this point it may be recalled that during the first winter of the war Admiral Jellicoe's secretary, writing from the Iron Duke, the flagship of the Grand Fleet, to a little blind girl who had sent the admiral a knitted scarf, said :—"We often pass German mines floating about in the water, and we know that if we did not see them, but ran into them, the Iron Duke would be blown up. . . . It is very cold on the North Sea, and very stormy, too, and sometimes the snow falls so heavily that we cannot see at all where we are going, and very often the great seas sweep right over the ship." That truly lovable letter, reminiscent of Collingwood and his little Sarah, gives at once a picture of the appalling menace of the mine and the saving work of sweepers. The peril to the super-Dreadnought, with her vast bulk and tonnage, was precisely the same as that which confronted the little sweeper, with her tonnage in the neighbourhood of a hundred register.

In addition to the floating mines there were the anchored mines, which were frequently encountered by vessels fishing in the ordinary way—a Grimsby trawler caught two of them in her trawl, and as they could not be disentangled, part of the fishing-gear had to be cast away; but the position of the mines was carefully noted, so that they could be subsequently found and destroyed.

Mine-sweepers very soon established a roll of honour and the announcements of rewards for their deeds contained the only details that were made public concerning the work of officers and men in trawlers and drifters December 19, 1914, was a day of uncommon activity amongst them. The Orianda was

BRITISH FISHERMEN PRISONERS OF WAR IN GERMANY.

blown up by a mine, but the gallantry of Lieutenant H. Boothby, R.N.R., her commander, resulted in all the crew being saved except one man, who was killed. Lieutenant Boothby was given another vessel, and in this he was again blown up, but he again escaped and received a companionship of the Distinguished Service Order. Another officer, Lieutenant C. V. Crossley, R.N.R., on December 19, was in command of a sweeper near which no fewer than three mines exploded. The little ship was badly damaged, and she was saved only by the perfect discipline of the crew and the courage of the officer, who crawled into the cramped space near the screw shaft, found out where the leak was, plugged it sufficiently to enable the pumps to keep the water down, and so kept the ship from sinking. For this splendid performance Lieutenant Crossley received the Distinguished Service Cross. Then, on the

ON A BRITISH PATROL SHIP.
Washing down the decks after coaling.

night of Christmas Day, 1914, in total darkness, Skipper T. W. Trendall, in the sweeper Solon, of 121 tons, went to the assistance of a vessel which had been mined. The steamer was not showing any lights; it was low water, and she had to be searched for in the mine-field. Utterly disregarding the danger to himself and crew, and bent only on giving help to brother seamen in distress, Skipper Trendall and his crew succeeded in reaching and helping the mined steamer, and for this gallant conduct he also was decorated by the King. Splendid also was the conduct of Lieutenant Godfrey Parsons, R.N., who, on December 19, despite the fact that he had been mined in his trawler, continued to command his group of sweepers. On that great day his group exploded eight mines and brought up half-a-dozen more. While these operations were being carried out the lieutenant's ship and another trawler were damaged by explosions, and a third trawler was blown up. And all this happened in ten minutes.

The achievements of the sweepers at that period were the preliminary of the gallant exploits of British fishermen in the Dardanelles operations. Concerning those doings there was not for the public so much of the fog of war as enveloped other undertakings. Time after time the sweepers carried out their work under heavy fire, and in the mine-infested waters there were serious losses. On a March night, when the Okino and Beatrice were sweeping in partnership, the Beatrice at the end of the sweep slipped her sweeping wire, leaving her partner to heave it in. Having got the wire aboard, the Okino steamed away full speed for the fleet; but in a few minutes she foundered, having been in contact with a mine or struck by a stray shell. She carried a large crew—15—and of these 10 were killed or drowned. Another pair of trawlers were sweeping when one of them, the Manx Hero, was blown up; but her crew of 11 men were saved through the skill and heroism of Skipper Woodgate and his crew in the Koorah. On returning from the Dardanelles Skipper Woodgate gave an account of his experiences in which he said: "When we were up in the Dardanelles there were what we call three groups—One, Two and Three—and each group had to go up, one at a time. The vessel I was in belonged to the second group. The night we were going to make the final dash in the Dardanelles, up in the Narrows, we went, no lights up, everything covered in. They let us get right up to the Narrows, and as we turned round to take our sweeps up one of our number was blown up. Then they peppered us from each side, from $1\frac{1}{2}$ to 2 miles. We heard cries for help. I said, 'We shall have to do the best we can, and go back and pick up.' There was no waiting, no saying 'Who shall go?' As soon as I called for volunteers three jumped in. I kept the vessel as close as I could to shelter them. I did not think any would come back alive, but they did come back. No one was hit, and I said 'Now we'll get the boat in.' Just as we got the boat nicely clear of the water, along came a shot and knocked it in splinters. I shouted, 'All hands keep under cover as much as you can,' and I got on the bridge, and we went full steam ahead. I could not tell you what it was like, with floating and sunken mines and shots everywhere. We got knocked about, the mast almost gone, rigging gone, and she was riddled right along the starboard side. One of the hands we picked up had his left arm smashed with shrapnel; that was all the injury we got. When we got out the commander came alongside and said, 'Have you seen any more trawlers?' I said 'Yes, we've got the crew of one on board, the Manx Hero.' We were the last out, and I can tell you I never want to see such a sight again. . . . I thought of the three men in the fiery furnace, how they were preserved, and of Daniel in the lions' den, and I think of the 24 of us coming out under that terrible fire and the water covered with floating and sunken mines."

In what appeared to be the final list of naval awards to officers for services in the Dardanelles operations the names were given of eight skippers in command of trawlers who were commended, and these were "specially selected from over a hundred names." The awards were for service between the time of landing on the Gallipoli Peninsula in April, 1915, and the evacuation in December, 1915–January, 1916. Of the eight skippers four received the Distinguished Service Cross. The only details officially given were in the case of Skipper F. W. Barnes, R.N.R., and they were comprised in the sentence, "While off Anzac gallantly took in tow a tug under heavy fire." In the other cases the skippers "performed long, arduous, and dangerous duties." How dangerous those duties were was indicated by the official lists of naval casualties announced by the Secretary of the Admiralty. Between February 26 and March 18, 1916, five skippers were reported killed, no reference being made as to locality; while during about the same period, under the headings "H.M. Ships" and "Mediterranean" there were announced as killed a large number of fishermen who had died at the post of duty.

Apart from the direct work of the fishermen in protecting the Navy and the Mercantile Marine by their wonderful mine-sweeping operations a most important work was done in making the seas safe for the fishermen who went to sea and continued to help largely in keeping up the food supply of the country. The arrangements of the Admiralty made it possible for a small composite fleet of steam trawlers to work in a safe area, and other dispositions enabled sailing and steam fishing vessels to carry out their work in comparative security, and very often, indeed, in most cases,

WAR "PASS LIGHTS" AT SEA.

A neutral vessel proceeding to port after obtaining leave from an examination ship.

at great profit. Record after record was made by steam trawlers, drifters, beam-trawlers and smaller craft, and skippers and mates in particular, because of the share system on which they are employed, made abnormal incomes. In April, 1916, a few days before Good Friday, when fish was scarce and prices high, the Hull trawler Elf King landed a catch of fish which realized the record sum of £3,670. The same vessel held the previous record of £3,480. The Elf King had made the Iceland trip, lasting nearly four weeks, and the skipper's share of the profit came to about £300, being at the rate of nearly £5,000 a year. In other directions there were inevitable hardships, and a correspondent of *The Times* pointed out that the skilled and industrious females who, irrespective of age, are known as fisher-girls, had found their occupation of "gipping" and packing gone, and had taken to munitions, postal work and other uncongenial tasks, though many of them found it hard to make the living to which they had been accustomed.

A remarkable feature of the absorption by the Admiralty of such great numbers of fishermen was the steady effort made by prominent naval officers at naval bases to provide means of satisfying the moral needs of men who were far from home for long periods. Every encouragement, therefore, was given to organizations apart from the Naval Chaplains' Department, such as the Young Men's Christian Association and the Royal National Mission to Deep Sea Fishermen In this direction Rear-Admiral Ballard showed great interest and resource, and other naval officers did the same. Two of the Mission's fine hospital steamers were taken over by the Admiralty for patrol work, the third became a hospital steamer, at the cost of Sir Charles Chadwyck-Healey; one Mission sailing smack was permitted to work amongst the sweepers and patrollers attached to the Grand Fleet, and another was allocated to a great naval base on the North Sea shore. The value of these societies was warmly admitted by officers, who of necessity had had little or no experience in dealing with a class of men who were unaccustomed to the rigid discipline of the Royal Navy, of which they had become a part, and asserted their independence in a manner not in keeping with the strict traditions of the Senior Service.

So ubiquitous were the fishermen in sweepers, patrollers and other craft that there was no great mishap at sea in connection with which they did not take a part in helping and saving· while fishermen were associated with many strange happenings, such as the loss of the German naval airships L 19 and L 15. Reference has been made in the previous chapter to the gallant conduct of the crew of the little Brixham beam-trawler Providence when the Formidable was torpedoed in the Channel; and the same resource and heroism were shown in all the home and foreign waters when warships, liners and other vessels were lost or damaged through torpedoes wantonly discharged, striking mines, or in action. On the night of January 31, 1916, a squadron of German airships raided some of the Eastern and Midland counties of England, killed a large number of inoffensive civilians, including women and children, and caused serious damage to property. The airships escaped from England, but one of them, which is believed to have shared in the raid, was found, a helpless wreck, floating on the North Sea. The discovery was made by the skipper and crew of a Grimsby steam trawler, the King Stephen. The fishermen counted twenty-two Germans on the wrecked airship, and as the trawler carried only nine hands and had no weapons the skipper adopted the only course which was open to him—he declined to rely on the worthless word of such an enemy, and left the airship and reported the matter as soon as he possibly could to a British naval vessel. It was inevitable that there should be in Germany fierce outbursts in referring to the trawler and the airship, and that our North Sea fishermen should be accused of cowardice, brutality and inhumanity. In making these charges the Germans forgot, or did not wish to remember, the courage which was consistently shown by North Sea fishermen in rescuing perishing German sailors and passengers. An outstanding illustration is that of the North German Lloyd Company's express mailboat, Elbe, on January 30, 1895, in an exceptionally bitter winter. The loss of this vessel through collision, in itself one of the most terrible disasters to Atlantic liners, had its horror lessened through the skill and courage of North Sea smacksmen, who saved the few survivors. The Elbe foundered within twenty minutes. There were 352 people on board, and of these only 20 were saved—rescued by Skipper Wright and his little crew in the smack Wildflower. It needed half an hour's excessive effort to haul the trawl, and instantly the skipper fought his way to the boat which

WITH A DESTROYER PATROL.
"Periscope astern to starboard, Sir!"

held the survivors and plucked them from the very grasp of death. The rescued Germans were crowded into the smack's tiny cabin, and were fed and warmed and clothed to the last generous limit, for when the smack reached port there was not even a biscuit left. The last had been given to Miss Anna Böcker, who was afterwards commanded to Osborne to tell the story of the wreck and rescue to Queen Victoria and the Empress Frederick. That is merely one of unnumbered instances of the courage and skill of our deep sea fishermen.

SHIPPING HELD UP IN THE SCHELDT, ANTWERP.

It was an auxiliary patrol trawler which on April 1, 1916, discovered the wrecked L 15 off the mouth of the Thames. Being everywhere, as they were, fishing vessels were particularly liable to attacks from German airships and such German craft as dared to venture from the refuge of the Kiel Canal and other hiding places. The Germans declared their intention of using all means within their power to destroy British fishing vessels, and on more than one occasion they tried to destroy these vessels by dropping bombs on them from the air. From this peril, against which the fishermen were utterly unable to defend themselves, a number of the men and their craft had amazingly narrow escapes.

In the course of his speech in the House of Commons on March 7, 1916, on the motion for going into Committee on the Navy Estimates, Mr. Balfour, the First Lord of the Admiralty, paid a warm tribute to the mine-sweepers, the armed trawlers, and other fishermen engaged on war work in various areas. "I am afraid," he said, "I cannot do justice to all that I feel about the work of these men. Necessarily, it is little known to the public. They do not work in the presence of great bodies of men, to admire and applaud them for their gallantry. Small crews in stormy seas suddenly face to face with unexpected peril, they never seem to me to fail. No danger, no difficulty, is too great for them. The debt of this country to them is almost incalculable." A short time previously Lord Selborne, speaking in public, declared that our fishermen had been a priceless asset to the nation in connexion with the war. "It was known," he said, "that the Germans would make the mine one of their principal instruments, but we did not realize that the German fleet would not dare to fight, and would resort to mines as almost its sole instruments." He did not know how many mines the Germans had sown round our coasts during the last eighteen months, but he was prepared to risk the statement that it was many, many thousands, of a most extraordinary ingenuity of construction, charged with an explosive calculated to destroy a most powerful ship, and to blow a small fishing craft to matchwood. Many vessels were destroyed in this manner, including some belonging to neutral countries; but, on the other hand, there were some remarkable instances of sweepers and patrollers and larger ships being salved, in spite of serious damage sustained through striking mines, owing to the skill and courage of their crews. Fishermen, accustomed to their little steamboats in time of peace being badly damaged in gales and collision, had acquired the knack of salving seemingly hopeless wrecks, so that they were peculiarly well able to bring lame ducks to port and safety.

For the purposes of the mine-sweeping the trawlers, by reason of their build and equipment, were with ease and quickness adapted, and under the direction of their skippers, in most cases men who had been given warrant rank and were officially described as "Mr.", they carried out their dangerous work with unflinching fortitude, though many a brave man willingly admitted that at first he found the new and unfamiliar task "a bit nervy." In the other and equally important and perilous work of dealing with enemy submarines, the steam drifters were available in large numbers, ready for immediate service. Just before the outbreak of the war, when the herring season had opened and was in full operation in the north, there were assembled at Lerwick, in the Shetland Islands, between 500 and 600 of these fine and seaworthy little vessels, manned by fishermen who, though they did not keep the deep sea in the same manner as the fleeters and single-boaters, were yet hardy and reliable in every way.

We have seen that the steam trawler worked with a huge net, dragging on the bed of the sea; the drifter adopted a different method, for while the trawler secured the demersal fish the drifter netted the pelagic fish, mostly herrings, which swim close to the surface of the water. Accordingly the drifter when at sea got overboard about a mile of fine netting which hung vertically in the water, and while the vessel drifted with the tide, the fish, dashing in shoals against the net, were caught.

Gathered in from their respective stations on the East Coast, the stout little ships were set to work to take their share in combating the menace of the submarine, not only in the North Sea, but elsewhere, and we know, from official statements, that at least one of them achieved renown in the Dardanelles. Let it be borne in mind that these craft were very small, with cramped deck space and extremely limited cabin accommodation, and that they had practically no freeboard, and the task of getting across the Bay of Biscay and up the Mediterranean will be recognised as no light one. Many steam drifters in use were built of wood, and a representative vessel—oak, built in 1909, was 75 feet long, $17\frac{1}{2}$ feet broad, and $8\frac{1}{4}$ feet deep; bunkers, eight tons; and compound engines developing a speed of nine knots. Such a vessel, and there were many like her,

HELD UP OWING TO THE MINES IN THE NORTH SEA.
A fleet of fishing boats at Flushing.

A BRITISH DESTROYER STOPS A NEUTRAL SAILING SHIP IN NORTHERN WATERS.

was for sale in March, 1916, and by way of comparison it may be said that at the same time there was on offer a steel-built trawler, constructed in 1908, 126 feet long, 20½ feet wide, and 12¼ feet deep; flush-decked; bunkers, 130 tons; boiler with a working pressure of 180 lbs., engines developing 11 knots; winch, 1,200 fathoms; electric light. These vessels were representative. There were larger craft in both classes, but there were very many smaller, and in these the fishermen had to keep the stormy seas in winter and not only fight the gales, but also run the constant risk of destruction from mines or attack by enemy war vessels.

"We arrived in port after being at sea 19 days, and we sail again in the morning. . . . I should love to spend an hour amongst the flowers, instead of looking for submarines on the briny . . ." wrote one fisherman from sea. "We have had a very stormy week," another reported; while a man over military age said in a letter: "They have taken a lot of trawlers for mine-sweeping and other purposes. When I am better I may go mine-sweeping. I should be doing a little, and it is better for me to let the younger men go in the Naval Reserve. I have just had letters from my two sons—one says he has had terrible weather: four vessels disabled. The other says he is waiting for the Germans to come out. He likes it very well." Later, this man over military age, with the gallant son who was waiting for the Germans, and liked it very well, wrote and said, "I have joined the mine-sweepers." Such was the spirit in which the British fishermen undertook the dangerous duties of their calling in connexion with the war.

In a humorous but very true description of the sweepers and their work the writer of "A Grand Fleet Chaplain's Note-Book," published in the *Westminster Gazette*, said of mines: "There are some kinds that have horns, like a dilemma. . . . Some are arranged to come up to the surface long after they were hidden in the depths, and at unexpected times, like regrettable incidents from a hectic past. Others are constructed with fiendish ingenuity to wait after touching a ship until they have felt out its most vulnerable spot before exploding. Some are made to float about at random; and others, more dangerous still, drift when they were meant to remain anchored. The task of sweeping for all these different brands of tinned doom is almost as great as that of the old lady in the nursery rhyme whose job it was to sweep the cobwebs out of the sky. The labour of Sisyphus was child's play compared to it. For this labour must go on incessantly, over a vast area, and often with a doubt whether the desired results have been fully or only partly accomplished."

In the dispatch issued by the Admiralty on January 12, 1916, from Vice-Admiral Bacon, commanding the Dover Patrol, reference was made to the part played by fishermen in the operations off the Belgian coast between August 22 and November 19, 1915. Three vessels were lost—the armed yacht Sanda, sunk by gunfire; the drifter Great Heart, sunk by mine, and the mine-sweeper Brighton Queen, sunk by mine. The Admiral said that their lordships would appreciate the difficulties attendant on the cruising in company by day and night under war conditions of a fleet of 80 vessels comprising several widely different classes, manned partly by trained naval ratings, but more largely by officers of the Naval Reserve, whose fleet training had necessarily been scant, and by men whose work in life had hitherto been that of deep sea fishermen. The protection of such a moving fleet by the destroyers in waters which were the natural home of the enemy's submarines had been admirable, and justified the training and organization of the personnel of the flotilla.

A VESSEL BEING STRUCK BY A TORPEDO.

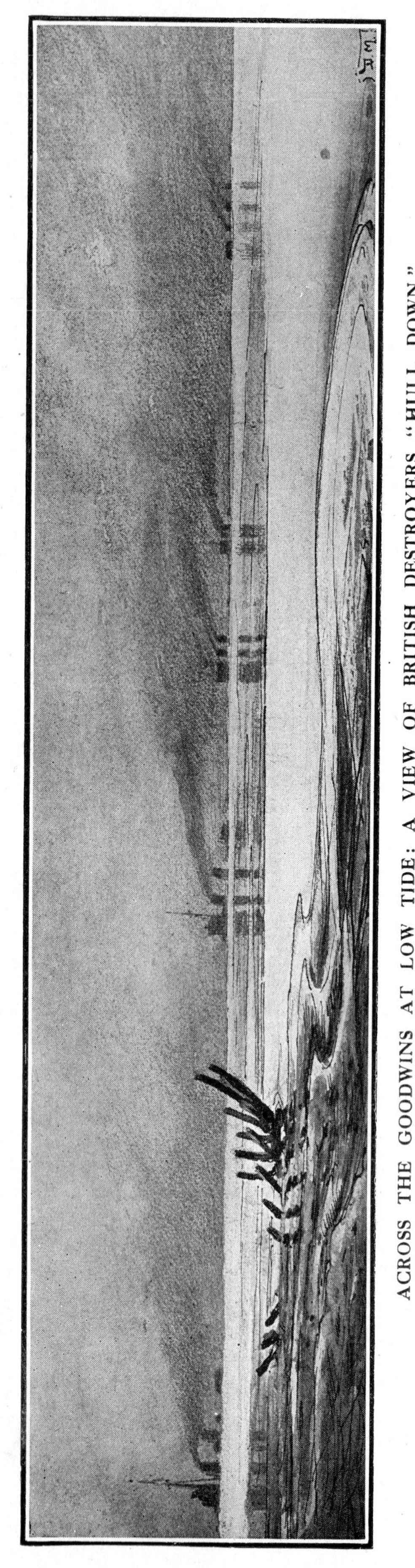

ACROSS THE GOODWINS AT LOW TIDE: A VIEW OF BRITISH DESTROYERS "HULL DOWN."

The Admiral added: "But more remarkable still, in my opinion, is the aptitude shown by the officers and crews of the drifters and trawlers, who in difficult waters, under conditions totally strange to them, have maintained their allotted stations without a single accident. Moreover, these men under fire have exhibited a coolness well worthy of the personnel of a service inured by discipline. The results show how deeply sea adaptability is ingrained in the seafaring race of these islands."

Skipper L. Scarlett, of the drifter Hyacinth, was specially recommended for his great coolness in action off Zeebrugge on September 25, when, although he was exposed to heavy gunfire, he remained and completed his task. Mr. Scarlett received the Distinguished Service Cross, and the Distinguished Service Medal was awarded to Second Hand Thomas John Prior; while other skippers and men were commended for service in action. At this period in many directions skippers, second hands, deck hands, enginemen and trimmers in every sphere of sweeping and patrolling were daily showing courage which was acknowledged by the bestowal of the Distinguished Service Medal, and in other ways. These recognitions were naturally a source of the greatest pride to a body of men who previously had been but little in the public eye, and of whom practically nothing was ever heard unless some great calamity happened to a fishing fleet—and then they were soon forgotten. The war in its earliest stages firmly established the deep sea fishermen in an honourable place in the naval defences of the Empire.

In the less exciting work of patrolling and in connexion with motor-boat work fishermen were also of invaluable service, and in these capacities they served all around our coasts and in much more distant regions. Keeping the seas, as they did, in all weathers, they had to endure much discomfort and danger, apart from the perils of war. A skipper of one little vessel never left the bridge for three days and nights owing to the fearful weather, and that sleepless vigil was the experience of many more like him.

The method employed by the Germans in laying mines was made known at the time of the bombardment of Scarborough and the Hartlepools. In reference to that affair a memorandum was furnished by the Admiral commanding the East Coast mine-sweepers, detailing the mine-sweeping operations off Scarborough. It was stated that from

AN AWKWARD MOMENT.
A Mine-sweeper drawing a mine up under the stern.

December 19 to December 31, 1914, sweeping operations were conducted with the object of clearing the minefield which had been laid off Scarborough. At the beginning there was no indication of the position of the mines, although, owing to losses of passing merchant ships, it was known that mines had been laid. In order to ascertain how the mines lay it was necessary to work at all times of the tide, with a consequent large increase in the element of danger. Commander Richard H. Walters, R.N., A.M.S. Staff, was in charge of the whole of the mine-sweeping operations from December 19 to December 31. During that period a large number of mines had been swept up and destroyed, and by Christmas Day a channel had been cleared, and traffic was able to pass through by daylight. It was in association with these operations that Lieutenant Parsons and other officers, already referred to, distinguished themselves. Other officers were specially noticed for their services during the operations. Commander Lionel G. Preston, R.N., H.M.S. Skipjack, on the 19th proceeded at once into the middle of the area where the mines had exploded to give assistance to damaged trawlers. He anchored between the trawlers and the mines which he had brought

THE BRITISH STEAMER "NORDMAN."
Torpedoed by a German submarine near Kara Burnu.

to the surface, and proceeded to sink them. Skipper Ernest V. Snowline, drifter Hilda and Ernest, was commodore of the flotilla of Lowestoft drifters under Chief Gunner Franklin. He kept to his station in heavy weather, and stood by the steamship Gallier after she had been damaged by a mine. Very fine was the performance of Skipper T. B. Belton, of the drifter Retriever, who, when all the other drifters had been driven in by the weather, kept to his station, marking the safe channel for shipping. A skilful and courageous rescue was effected by Sub-Lieutenant W. L. Scott, R.N.R., of the drifter Principal. He went alongside the trawler Garmo in a dinghy to rescue a man, running great risk to himself and his boat, for at the time the vessel was floating nearly vertical, with only the forecastle above water. A few minutes after the boat left her she turned completely over and sank.

The lead of the officers in these dangerous operations, all the more dangerous because in those early stages of the war there was not the wide experience in dealing with mines which became available later, was nobly followed by the men, and a number of second hands, enginemen, deck hands and a cook were commended for good service. To those who visited Scarborough and the Hartlepools soon after the German raid, and looking seaward from amongst the ruins could observe the sweepers at their work, there was brought home with impressive force the vastness of the debt which the country owed to the crews—the skilled, courageous fighters who had been our toilers of the deep.

CHAPTER CXXII.

ARTILLERY: CONSTRUCTION AND USE.

FIELD GUNS—QUICK-FIRERS—HOWITZERS—SIEGE ARTILLERY—IMMOBILE ARTILLERY—NAVAL GUNS—"ALL-BIG-GUN" ARMAMENT—BARBETTES—ANTI-TORPEDO CRAFT ARMAMENT—CONSTRUCTION OF GUNS—THE GUN AN EXPLOSION ENGINE—BUILT-UP GUNS—SHRINKING ON A TUBE—WIRE-WINDING—EROSION—METHODS OF REPAIR—BREECH MECHANISMS—OBTURATION—FUNCTIONS OF ARTILLERY—EQUIPMENT OF CONTENDING ARMIES—USE OF HEAVIER WEAPONS—ACCURACY AND DIRECTION OF FIRE—CURTAIN FIRE—FRENCH SYSTEM—TRENCH MORTARS.

FORMERLY the term artillery was used generally of all implements of war, but it has come to be applied specifically to the larger firearms which are discharged from carriages, as well as to the troops which serve them, and to the science of organizing and directing their employment. Small arms such as rifles, which are hand weapons, are therefore excluded, nor are machine guns usually reckoned among artillery. The guns may be classified as heavy or light according to their size, which may be defined by the diameter of their bore, or their weight, or the weight of the projectile they throw; those of 7·5-inch bore and upwards are classed as heavy, those of 4 to 6-inch bore as medium, and the smaller ones as light. Another division is into mobile and immobile. The former category includes pieces, such as field guns, which are adapted to be moved more or less readily from place to place, and the latter those that are mounted in fixed positions, such as a fortress; the distinction, however, is not very definite, and, thanks partly to mechanical traction, unexpected feats were performed in the Great War in the way of moving heavy guns. So far as naval guns are concerned, the distinction between mobile and immobile becomes meaningless; the guns themselves, from the smallest to the largest, are immobile, but a warship may be regarded as nothing else but a mobile gun-carriage, designed for the express purpose of bringing guns into action at any desired point.

Field guns may be taken as typical of mobile artillery, almost all countries possessing such weapons, which have a bore in the neighbourhood of 3 inches, and throw shells weighing from 13 to 18 lbs. The gun is mounted on a two-wheeled carriage, which is attached to another two-wheeled carriage—the limber. The weight of the whole does not exceed 2 tons, and in most countries is less; and drawn by a team of six horses, the equipment is expected to operate with infantry, its normal pace being something like four miles an hour. Horse artillery is intended to work with cavalry, and therefore moves more rapidly; in the British Army the guns are somewhat lighter, and the gunners are mounted on horses, instead of, as with field artillery, riding on the limber of the gun and the waggon which accompanies it. The design of mountain guns, another form of light artillery, is limited by the consideration that they have to be carried by pack animals. Therefore the weights of the pieces into which the gun and its carriage are divided have to be kept within the capacity of the load which the animals can carry, and the dimensions of the pieces are also limited

ON THE WESTERN FRONT.

A British 18-pounder quick-firing gun in action.

No. 1 (the sergeant), with his hand on the spade, gives instructions to the rest of the detachment. At the actual moment when this picture was taken No. 2 was lying down. If the gun were actually firing his position would be to the right of the breech. No. 3 is ready to fire the gun; No. 4 has the shell in the correct position for placing in the bore; No. 5 adjusts the fuse and hands the shell to No. 4; No. 6, the farthest away, also prepares the ammunition and hands it to No. 5. The upper portion of the gun has been partially covered in order to conceal it from observers.

for the same reason. The calibre of mountain guns is the same as of field guns, or a little less. British mountain batteries have been supplied with a weapon of 2·75-inch bore, throwing a 10 lb. projectile, and the French have one of 65 mm. (2·5 inch).

The modern field gun is always a quick-firer, capable of delivering some 20 or 25 rounds a minute. A variety of factors contribute to make this result possible. In the first place, rapid loading is ensured by means of a breech action which can be quickly manipulated, and by the use of "fixed" ammunition, in which the projectile and the propelling charge are combined in a metallic cartridge, so that they can be placed in the breech by a single operation, instead of having to be inserted one after the other, as in the case of large guns. In the second place, rapidity of aiming is facilitated by mechanical arrangements, by virtue of which one gunner lays the gun on the target while another gives it the elevation required to enable the shot to reach its mark. In this connexion it must be remembered that no shot travels in a straight line after it leaves the muzzle of the gun; if it did the task of the gunner would be very much simpler than it is in fact. Gravity is always at work pulling it towards the earth, and its path is therefore a curve. It follows that if a gun were pointed straight at the target the shot would hit the ground before it reached its mark, except perhaps at very short ranges, and therefore the muzzle has to be elevated to such a degree that the curve described by the shot may pass through the object aimed at

Another improvement relates to the method of dealing with the recoil. When the old guns were fired the gun and its carriage ran back a considerable distance, owing to the reaction from the shot as it left the muzzle, and had to be brought back into position by the gunners. At the end of last century Sir George Clarke (Lord Sydenham) introduced a spring spade arrangement, whereby on discharge the spade was forced into the earth and the spring was compressed, its subsequent extension running the gun back into position. In modern practice the gun proper slides back in a cradle on the carriage, which does not move, the recoil being taken up by a hydraulic buffer consisting of a cylinder filled with oil or glycerine, in which moves a piston attached to the gun. Grooves or ports cut in the walls of the cylinder permit the liquid to escape past the piston, their depth, and therefore the resistance offered to the movement of the piston, being so arranged that the gun is brought gently to rest. The gun is returned to the firing position by springs or, as in French practice, by compressed air. To prevent the carriage from running backwards the trail is provided with a spade, which digs into the ground when a shot is fired, and generally also there are brakes on the wheels. On the discharge taking place there is a tendency for the wheels to be lifted from the ground, the whole gun pivoting round the trail, but this is overcome by careful attention to the design, so that the forces involved may be counteracted, and in fact the carriage remains in position—a contrast to the behaviour of British guns in the Boer War, according to the picturesque description of Laughton O. Zigler, as reported by Mr. Kipling: "They'd jolt into action and wiggle around and skid and spit and prize 'emselves back again during our hours of bloody warfare till I could have wept, sir, at the spectacle of modern white men chained up to those old hand-power, back-number, flint-and-steel mowing machines."

Another advantage of taking up the recoil in the modern manner is that the gunners do not, as formerly, have to stand clear to avoid the gun as it runs back, but can remain within the shelter of a steel shield, which protects them from shrapnel and rifle bullets.

The famous 75 mm. (2·95 inch) gun of which the French are so justly proud for its power, rapidity of fire, and precision, may be taken as an example of field artillery. Of unusual length in relation to its bore, it is credited with an extreme range exceeding four miles, and it throws a shrapnel shell weighing nearly 16 lbs. with a muzzle velocity of about 1,740 feet a second, or a high-explosive shell weighing 11¾ lbs. at about 1,915 feet a second. It weighs with its limber about 37 cwt. A somewhat lighter type with the same bore but a lower muzzle velocity has also been introduced. The German field gun of 77 mm. (3·05 inch) bore, is generally regarded as an inferior weapon to that of the French. The shrapnel shell it fires is a little lighter, its range shorter, and its muzzle velocity lower, and though its weight is rather less it requires more men to serve it. The British field gun is of rather larger bore (3·3 inch) than that used by other countries, and the shrapnel shell it fires is heavier—18½ lbs. Still larger guns are found in heavy field artillery, which in Great Britain is defined as artillery equipped with mobile guns of 4-inch calibre and upwards; an example is the 5-inch gun, which fires a 60-lb. projectile with a muzzle velocity exceeding 2,000 feet a second.

Light howitzers are also classed among field guns. It has already been explained that every shot travels in a curve after it leaves the muzzle, not in a straight line In the case of a gun proper the designer tries to make the path of the shot as little curved as possible, to get a "flat trajectory," and for this purpose he employs a long barrel and a large charge of

BRITISH 60-POUNDER IN THE ACT OF FIRING.

FRENCH GUNNERS TAKING A "SEVENTY-FIVE" INTO ACTION.

powder, giving a high muzzle velocity. In the howitzer, on the contrary, the shot is intentionally made to travel in a curved path, and instead of being fired directly at the target it is projected up into the air in such a way that it may fall more or less vertically upon the target, the muzzle being given a considerable elevation for this purpose. Thus, while a gun might fire directly at the parapet of a trench without damaging the men protected by it, the howitzer would reach them effectively by dropping its shell among them behind it. The howitzer has a shorter barrel and a lower muzzle velocity than a gun, and requires a smaller charge of powder. This smaller charge means that the stress of discharge is smaller, and thus for a given weight of shell a howitzer is lighter and therefore more mobile than a gun; or alternatively it can fire a heavier projectile than a gun of the same weight. Its range can be varied by employing reduced charges, as has been explained in the chapter on Ammunition (Vol. V., p. 417); by resorting to the same device a gun can be used as a howitzer provided that, as is the case for instance with the Italian 75 mm. field gun, it can be given sufficient elevation. In passing, it may be mentioned that a distinguishing characteristic of anti-aircraft guns is that they are so mounted as to be capable of extreme elevation.

Field howitzers have a calibre of about 4½ inches, and throw a shell weighing from 35 to 45 lbs. They use fixed ammunition, and their breech action resembles that of a quick-firing gun, though special arrangements have to be made in mounting them to prevent the breech from striking the ground on recoil when they are being fired at high elevations.

Guns and howitzers heavier than those already mentioned are classed as heavy artillery, and when they become heavier still they are known as siege artillery. But it is impossible to draw a definite line between these categories, and the Germans, fully alive to the value of heavy guns, contrived to bring into the field pieces which before the war would have been regarded as light or even heavy siege units. Their heavy field howitzer, with a bore of 15 cm. (5·9 inch), was able to fire two or three rounds a minute of shells weighing 87 lbs., and they also employed in field actions still heavier weapons, such as the 21 cm. (8·27 inch) and 28 cm. (11 inch) mortars, the latter firing a shell weighing 750 lbs. for a distance of six miles. Drawn by a motor tractor these heavy units were fired from a special carriage, having its wheels provided with a "wheel belt" consisting of a series of feet so arranged as to distribute the pressure. It should be explained that a mortar was originally a very short smoothbore muzzle-loading piece, but in Germany it became the custom to apply the name to a shortened form of howitzer.

The weapons already referred to do not represent the extreme limit of size, even apart from naval guns. The Germans, for example, had a Krupp siege howitzer of 42 cm. (16·6 in.), and the Austrians were credited, by their own papers, with using in the fighting round Tarnow in May, 1915, 52 cm. (20·5 in.) mortars, a shot from one of which was said to have entirely destroyed a large tower at a distance of eleven miles. Such pieces can scarcely be regarded as mobile, and their transport is no easy task. The 42 cm., and also some smaller but still very heavy weapons, were described as being moved by rail, mounted on a steel truck supported on two six-wheeled bogies. When they were fired the reaction was taken, not by the wheels, but by hydraulic rams interposed between them and the ballast. In this connexion it may be noted that the combatants on both sides took advantage in another way of railways for increasing the mobility of their artillery, by mounting guns of various sizes on completely armoured trains, which thus became miniature travelling fortresses. Somewhat similarly, too, guns were mounted on armoured motor cars.

No doubt Germany paid special attention to the development of very heavy ordnance in the knowledge that she would have to batter down the powerful forts erected by her neighbours along their frontiers. But even if it be true that the French were disposed to put their trust too exclusively in their 75's, their heavier equipment included pieces that could be matched with those of the Central Powers. They had in 1906 heavy siege units in the shape of a 6·1-inch gun and a 10·7-inch howitzer, and in the great assault on Verdun in the spring of 1916 they were described as defending themselves with pieces up to 305 mm. (12 in.), while about the same time reports appeared of the production of a 16 inch howitzer, the equivalent of the German 42 cm. Their lighter siege artillery comprised an interesting piece in the 155 mm. (6·1 in.) Rimailho

THE FRENCH 250 MM. HOWITZER.

One of the battery that took part in the Battle of Champagne, September-October, 1915.

howitzer, firing a shell weighing about 95 lbs. with an effective range of nearly four miles. One of its features was that the breech opened automatically after each shot, and it was claimed that it could fire four or five rounds a minute. It was transported in two parts, the barrel being conveyed on a special travelling carriage, but it was said that the two portions could be put together ready for action in a couple of minutes. The larger 10·7 inch howitzer of the French was transported in four parts—piece, carriage, slide, and platform.

The characteristic application of immobile artillery is to coast defence and permanent fortification, and the armament employed for such purposes includes all sorts and sizes of pieces, from small quickfirers up to large guns for direct fire, and heavy howitzers for high-angle fire. In the United States a 16 inch coast defence gun has been produced, dis-

LOADING A BIG GUN.

The French artillerymen wearing masks for protection against asphyxiating gasses.

charging a projectile of a weight of 2,400 lb. by means of 640 lb. of smokeless powder. Much ingenuity has been devoted to the design of mountings for such guns; they are now only placed behind earthen parapets as the experience of the War indicates that permanent fortifications cannot withstand the assaults of the heavy artillery which modern methods can bring to bear upon them. At one time disappearing mountings were favoured in England. The gun was carried on the upper end of an arm the lower end of which was pivoted below in a pit, and the energy of the recoil was utilized to swing it down into the pit, where it could be loaded under protection, and then to raise it again to the firing position Another form of mounting is the cupola, in which the gun is protected by a flat dome of armour, rising but little above the ground. The gun fires through an aperture in the dome, which with the gun can be revolved on a central pivot or a roller ring so that during loading the opening is turned away from the enemy. Sometimes also the cupola is made to sink flush with the ground. In any case it offers a poor mark, though here a new factor, by no means of advantage to it, has been introduced through spotting and direction of fire by aeroplanes. In barbette mountings the guns are placed on a platform of such a height that they can fire over the parapet below which their mechanism is protected.

Naval ordnance represents the extreme development of the art of the gunmaker, and thanks to the cooperation of the engineer and the metallurgist it is continually being improved in power and effectiveness. The guns used in the various types of war vessels are of all sizes and calibres, from quick-firing 3-pounders and upwards, but the most characteristic of the service are those that form the main armament of capital ships. Of large bore (12 inches or more) and great length (often 50 times their bore) they fire an enormous shell, which, propelled by a heavy charge of smokeless powder, leaves the muzzle with a velocity of 3,000 feet a second, and as the result of all these factors they have a very long range. It was probably by the use of naval guns, specially mounted, that the Germans were able to drop shells into Dunkirk from a distance exceeding 20 miles; but they were far from being the first to employ such guns on land, and it may be recalled that 4·7-inch and 6-inch guns, taken off a cruiser and fitted on improvised mountings by Sir Percy Scott, did good service at Ladysmith during the Boer War. For such long ranges considerable elevation must be given to the gun. On one occasion Sir Percy Scott told his fellow guests at a City dinner that if the Dreadnought were planted on the Derby racecourse at Epsom, 26,400 yards away from the hall in which they were sitting, they would not be out of reach of her 12-inch guns, and that they would be wrong if they thought they would be saved by the intervening hills, since even if Mont Blanc were interposed the projectiles would pass 700 feet above its summit.

The Dreadnought was the first of a new type of battleship, distinguished by the possession of an "all-one-calibre" big gun armament. What this means may be discovered by taking a list of the armoured ships in the British Navy, and comparing her armament with that of some battleships that immediately preceded her.

The Duncan, completed three years before her, in 1903, is described as mounting (apart from anti-torpedo-boat armament) four 12-inch and twelve 6-inch guns; the King Edward VII., completed in 1905, four 12-inch, four 9·2-inch, and ten 6-inch; while the Lord Nelson, which was designed in 1903 though not completed till 1908, had four 12-inch, and ten 9·2-inch. But the Dreadnought stood forth in the sweet sim-

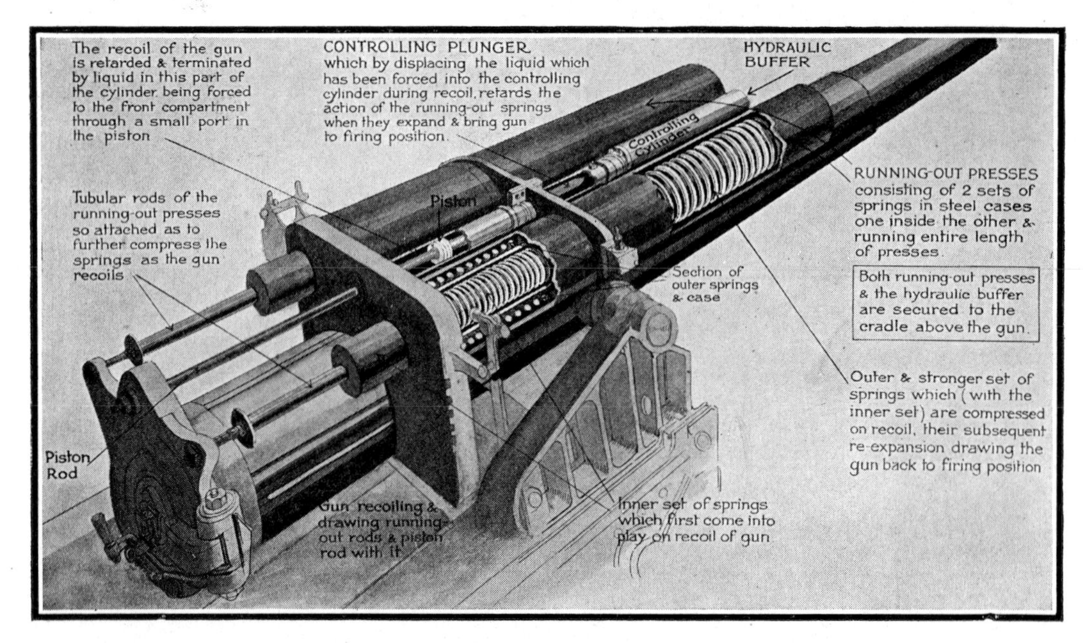

SECTIONAL VIEW OF THE HYDRAULIC BUFFER AND RUNNING-OUT PRESSES OF A 60-POUNDER.

BARBETTES OF A BATTLESHIP.
The "Queen Elizabeth's" 15-inch Guns.

plicity of ten 12-inch guns only. The same tendency towards uniformity in the heavy guns is observable also in the armoured cruisers. Thus the Achilles, completed in 1907, was fitted with six 9·2-inch and four 7·5-inch guns, and the Minotaur (1908) with four 9·2-inch and ten 7·5 inch, but the battle cruiser Inflexible, completed in the same year as the Minotaur, but of later design, had simply eight 12-inch.

Various considerations combined to bring about the adoption of the all-big-gun armament, which, however, by no means secured universal approbation. One was that the "danger space" (the limit within which the range must be known in order that a target of a given height may be hit) is smaller for small guns than for big ones, and therefore the latter can come into effective action before it is possible for the former to do so. Another was that once the range has been found for a gun it is also known fairly accurately (with calibration) for companion guns of the same size, but has to be separately ascertained for others of a different size; while a third was that the concentration of the gun power in a small number of heavy pieces enables them to be mounted on the middle line of the ship, so that they can fire all round. In the Dreadnought eight of the ten 12-inch guns could be fired on either broadside, and six directly ahead and six directly astern. In later ships—the Neptune, Hercules, and Colossus—one pair of guns was placed in a turret forwards, two pairs in turrets *en échelon* on the beam, and two pairs in turrets aft, one of these last turrets being superimposed on the other; the result was that all of the guns could fire on either broadside, eight of them astern, and six of them ahead. In subsequent Dreadnoughts all the guns were placed on the centre line of the ship, two in a turret amidships, four in superimposed turrets at the bow, and four in superimposed turrets at the stern.

Coincidentally with these improvements in the arrangement of the guns their power was gradually increased. The 12-inch guns in the Dreadnought weighed 58 tons, were 45 calibres long, and with a charge of cordite weighing 260 lbs. fired a shell of 850 lbs. with an initial velocity of 2,700 feet a second. In the St. Vincent (1910) and her sister ships the guns were made longer (50 calibres) and weighed 66 tons, and with a larger charge of cordite gave the projectile a muzzle velocity of about 3,000 feet a second. In the Orions, according to *The Times Book of the Navy*, the calibre of the guns was increased to 13·5 inches, and the weight of the shell to 1,250 lbs., while in the four ships of the King George V. class the shell thrown by guns of the same calibre weighed 1,400 lbs. In the Queen Elizabeth, which made her debut at the Dardanelles, the calibre was increased to 15 inches (though the number was reduced to eight), and the shells weighed nearly a ton. It is interesting to note that in the past the British Navy possessed still larger guns, for in the 'eighties six weighing 110 tons, with a bore of 16·25 inches, and throwing a projectile of 1,800 lbs., were made at Elswick and mounted in the Victoria, Sans Pareil, and Benbow. As fighting machines, however, they were far inferior to modern guns, not only because their power was less but because they could fire only one round in three minutes, whereas the later 12-inch guns could fire two rounds in one

IN A PRESS ROOM AT KRUPP'S.

minute. In America guns of still larger calibre were made in the shape of Rodman cast-iron pieces, having a bore of 20 inches, but even these were surpassed by the 36-inch mortar, which Robert Mushet designed for use in the Crimea, but which never reached the seat of war.

The turrets, or more properly barbettes, in which the large guns of a battleship are mounted may be described as great armoured shafts, 40 feet in diameter, extending from the upper deck downwards into the interior of the ship. Near the top of the shaft there is a platform or turntable, which is supported on a ring of live rollers and can be rotated by means of motors, and on this turntable are mounted two guns with their recoil and elevating gear. Below the platform is the working chamber, to which the ammunition is brought up from the magazines below by hoists in the central trunk, which also rotates. Carried by overhead travellers from the shell stores deep down in the ship, the shells are deposited in receiving trays at the bottom of the trunk and raised by a hoist to the working chamber, where they are transferred into the loading cage. The same thing happens with the charge of powder, which has also been hoisted up the trunk, and the two are then lifted by another hoist to the breech of the gun. In the most recent practice they are presented in line with the axis of the gun, whatever may happen to be the angle of elevation of the latter, so that they can be loaded into it by a mechanical rammer without loss of time; formerly loading could be effected only at certain elevations, and even only with the gun trained in certain positions, an arrangement which evidently did not conduce to rapidity of firing. Practically all the operations required for training, elevating, and loading big guns on board ship are performed mechanically; usually the power is hydraulic, but electricity is often employed, and in some Krupp barbettes water, electricity, and compressed air are all utilized. Hand-worked mountings are used only for the smaller guns, 6-inch or less; the 7·5-inch guns carried in the Triumph and Swiftsure were the largest in which hand-working was adopted.

As has already been explained, what used to be known as the secondary armament, composed often of 6-inch guns, was abandoned on our battleships at the beginning of the twentieth century in favour of a homogeneous primary armament composed solely of guns of the largest calibre. But another important part of a battleship's armament—that intended for her defence against torpedo craft—was retained, and indeed increased in power in order to cope with the increasing range of the torpedo. To take the classes of battleship which have already been referred to, in the Duncan and the King Edward VII. twelve 12 pounders and in the Lord Nelson twenty-four 12 pounders were relied upon for anti-torpedo craft armament, and a few 3 pounders and machine guns were also provided. In the Dreadnought, in view particularly of the chances of torpedo attack towards the end of an action, it was considered advisable to separate the anti-torpedo-boat guns as widely as possible from each other, so that they might not all be disabled by one or two heavy shells; and twenty-four 12 pounder quick-firing guns were fitted, of a longer and heavier type than those previously employed, and possessing a higher muzzle velocity. These guns were replaced by sixteen 4-inch guns (25 pounders) in the battleships built after the original Dreadnought, until in the Iron Duke (1914) and her sister ships twelve 6-inch guns were mounted instead. Thus the old " secondary " armament reappeared, though in a new guise—that of defence against torpedo craft. Many of the light cruisers mount 6-inch guns as their main armament, and 4-inch guns are found in the later destroyers, the earlier types of which had 12 pounders and 6 pounders.

The gun is an internal combustion or explosion engine exactly analogous to the engine of a motor-car. The barrel represents the cylinder, and the projectile the piston, but the latter, instead of being constrained to a limited length of travel as in the motor-car, is free in the gun to continue its course as far as its momentum will carry it. The driving force behind the piston, as behind the shot, is produced by the explosion or combustion of a mixture that gives rise to a large volume of gas —in the one case petrol vapour and air, and in the other a nitro-explosive that contains within itself the oxygen required for its combustion. But the pressure produced in the cylinder of a motor-car engine is trifling compared with that set up in the barrel of a gun, where it may be 18 tons to the square inch or more; and while a simple iron casting is sufficient for the former, one of the great problems that have to be solved by the designer of a gun is that of making it strong enough to withstand the disruptive forces that are put upon it at the

ITALIAN OCCUPATION OF FORT HERMANN.
One of the Italian pieces that was in action against the Austrian stronghold.

moment when it is fired. These forces come into play in two directions ; on the one hand there is a circumferential stress that tends to burst the barrel outwards, and on the other a longitudinal stress that tends to rend it lengthwise.

It might be supposed that strength to resist the circumferential stress might be obtained by increasing the thickness of the metal of the barrel ; but in fact this expedient is effective only to a limited extent, and in a solid gun, made of a single homogeneous mass of metal, there soon comes a time when additional thickness gives little additional strength, the reason being that the internal layers of metal may be strained beyond their bursting point before the outer ones have reached the limit of resistance. A stronger gun can be made by arranging that the inner layers are initially in a state of compression, gradually increasing past the neutral point till the outer layers are in a state of tension This can be accomplished by building up the gun of successive layers of metal, and this principle, which was employed in the first guns made by Armstrong about 1856, is now adopted in one form or another for all large ordnance. Armstrong, in the first place, used a jacket formed by winding a wrought-iron bar round a mandrel and welding the turns together into a continuous cylinder, the internal diameter of which was slightly smaller than the tube or barrel of the gun. This cylinder was expanded by heat and slipped over the barrel, the contraction produced by its cooling then producing the desired states of compression and tension in the interior and exterior metal. Later the system was introduced of producing the required compression by winding on the barrel successive layers of steel wire, or rather tape, which were in turn enclosed in an outer steel tube.

Formerly guns were made of bronze, cast-iron, wrought-iron, steel, or combinations of those metals, but now it is almost the universal practice to employ special steels, the strength and reliability of which have been enormously increased by improvements in composition and by close attention to their heat-treatment. Gun-steel is made by the open hearth process, and cast into ingots which may weigh as much as 80 tons. All the unsound portions having been removed, the first operation, when a large gun is being made, is "trepanning," by which the ingot is formed into a rough tube by having a hole bored in it. It is next reheated and placed in a huge hydraulic press which forges it to shape and elongates it, a tubular mandrel, kept cool by flowing water, being inserted in the hole during the operation. The forging process, if not carried to excess, greatly improves the quality of the metal; the mass of steel retains its heat sufficiently long to enable it to be worked in the press for from two to four hours. The forging is next annealed by heating it and allowing it to cool slowly, and then, after being rough-turned and bored, it is hardened. For this purpose it is heated in a gas furnace, and as soon as the required temperature of about 1,600 deg. F. has been attained it is plunged vertically into a tank of rape oil, which is kept cool by a water jacket. Another annealing process follows, in which it is heated to about 1,200 deg. F., and allowed to cool slowly, the object being to remove the internal strains which may have been set up by the hardening and other treatments to which it has alrea ly been subjected. At various stages pieces of the metal are tested, and if the results are satisfactory the forging is rough-turned in a lathe, and bored out to nearly the final size.

After this point the procedure varies according as the gun is to be wire-wound, the method especially favoured in British practice, or is to be built up with a series of plain tubes. In the latter case the interior of the tube or hoop that is to be slipped over the barrel is bored out and finished, and the final adjustment in size, needed so that the shrinkage may produce the required degree of compression in the metal, is made not on it but on the outside of the barrel, where it can be more easily effected. The hoop is then heated by gas jets internally and externally so that by expansion its diameter becomes greater than that of the barrel, and is dropped by means of a crane over the barrel, which is placed in a vertical position. As it

THE AUSTRIAN 28-CM. HOWITZER.

Mounted on a steel and concrete base. This view shows the various parts of the gun, including the cradle and the recoil chamber.

cools it contracts upon the barrel, which must be sufficiently strong to resist the action, and the metal composing it is thus put in the desired state of compression. The contraction is both circumferential and longitudinal, and must be carefully controlled. If, for instance, the two ends of the hoop were cooled simultaneously and thus caused to grip the barrel, it is evident that the middle portion, being held fast at its extremities, would be stretched longitudinally, or would compress the barrel longitudinally, when it in its turn came to cool and contract. Cooling is therefore determined at one end by the application of water jets, while rings of gas flames, which are gradually extinguished as required, prevent other parts from cooling prematurely. The interior of the barrel is also kept cool by water, so that the hoop may cool from the inside outwards. After the various courses of hoops have been put in place by a repetition of this process, the interior of the barrel is fine-bored and rifled, and the gun fitted with its breech mechanism.

In wire-wound guns the wire, which consists of steel ribbon, ¼ inch wide and 0·06 inch thick, of enormous strength, is wound on the barrel, layer after layer, by the aid of a machine which enables the tension to be exactly regulated. The tension starts at about 50 tons per square inch for the first layers, and is reduced to 40 or 35 tons for the outer ones. A 12-inch gun requires 117 miles of wire, weighing about 13½ tons. When all the wire is in place, a protective outer steel tube, which also gives longitudinal strength (a quality in which the wire winding is deficient) is placed over it. For this purpose the tube is expanded by heat in the same way as described for guns without wire-winding, but its size is so calculated as to give little if any shrinkage upon the wire covering.

The number and size of the tubes or hoops shrunk upon the barrel in built-up guns vary in different countries, some of which prefer a larger number of short thin tubes while others adopt a few longer thick tubes. In any case care must be taken not to heat them excessively during the shrinking-on process, else there is a risk of undoing the good effects of the heat treatments to which the steel has been previously subjected. Different arrangements are also adopted to secure longitudinal strength by hooking or screwing the hoops together, and special precautions are necessary as regards the breech portion and its attachment to enable it to resist the pressure of the explosion, which tends to blow it off. In large British wire-wound guns the barrel really consists of two parts—the inner A tube, which is the barrel proper in which the projectile travels, and the A tube by which it is enclosed. The wire is wound upon the A tube, and is surrounded by the protective or B tube, over which is shrunk the jacket at the breech end. The breech bush is screwed into the A tube.

The object of fitting the inner A tube is to enable the gun to be repaired when it has become worn by use. The gases produced by the explosion of the charge, rushing out from

HEAVY FRENCH GUN MOUNTED ON TRAIN FOR TRANSPORT.

GERMAN SOLDIERS MOVING A HEAVY HOWITZER.

the powder chamber at great speed and at a high temperature, wash away the metal of the bore and gradually destroy the rifling, until finally accurate shooting becomes impossible. The larger the calibre of the gun and the heavier the charges the more rapidly does this erosion take place. With full charges a large gun may fire only about 150 rounds or fewer before its barrel becomes too seriously eroded for further use, and its active life is literally to be measured in seconds, supposing it to be fired continuously, and remembering the extremely short interval of time required for the projectile to travel along the bore to the muzzle after the charge has been fired. Large guns are not only very expensive, but also require a long time for manufacture, and therefore it is obviously of great importance to have some means of repairing the damaged barrel of a piece which is otherwise good. The inner A tube enables this need to be met. It is made of a slightly tapered form externally, and when it is worn out it is removed by hanging the gun in a vertical position, breech downwards, heating it and then suddenly cooling the interior of the inner A tube with cold water, thus causing it to contract. It can then be knocked out, and a new one substituted for it. Another method of repairing an eroded bore, applicable when a single A tube is employed, is to make the walls of the barrel so thick that the worn portion can be bored out. A liner is then inserted and rifled, and thus the gun is again rendered serviceable.

Breech-loading guns possess numerous advantages over the now obsolete muzzle loaders, but before they could be adopted many difficulties had to be overcome in regard to closing

A BIG GUN IN THE MAKING.

Heated in a metal tower: hardened in an oil bath. Lowering an "A" tube for a 50-calibre 12-inch gun into the oil.

the breech, after the projectile and charge had been inserted, in such a way that while it could be manipulated with reasonable ease, it was strong enough to resist the pressure of the explosion and that the escape of gas was prevented. An enormous number of mechanisms have been devised for the purpose, but they may be reduced to two main classes. In one, of which Krupps are the great exponents, the breech is closed by a sliding block or wedge which is solid at one end but at the other has a hole that is brought opposite the bore when the gun is being loaded. The other class depends on the use of a screwed plug, which is inserted in the breech when the gun is being fired, and is carried on a hinge, so that it can be swung out of the way when the charge is being put in position.

Obviously, if a long screw be employed—and a short one with a small number of threads would not give sufficient strength—a considerable time will be required to screw it home or withdraw it, and thus the operation of loading will be slow. To get over this difficulty the screw is "interrupted" or cut away over certain portions of its circumference. For instance, if the circumference be supposed to be divided into six equal parts, three of them will have screw threads cut upon them and three will be smooth. Similarly the breech opening into which the plug screws will be divided into six sections—three smooth and three threaded. Then if the plug be inserted into the opening in such a way that its three threaded sections are opposite the three smooth sections of the latter, it will no longer be necessary to turn it a number of complete revolutions corresponding to the number of threads screwed upon it, but a single turn through one-sixth of a circle will suffice to engage all the threads. The circumference of the plug may be divided into a larger number of screwed and plain sections, and the larger the number the smaller will be the amount of circumferential twist needed to close the breech; but whatever the number of sections, only half of

POURING AN INGOT.

[Courtesy of Messrs. Vickers.

MACHINING THE INTERIOR AND EXTERIOR SIMULTANEOUSLY.

Small picture: Boring a gun tube.

ON BOARD H.M.S. "HIGHFLYER."—A 6-INCH GUN IN ACTION.

the surface will be screwed and available for resisting the pressure of the explosion.

In the Welin screw the plug is again provided with screwed and plain portions, but the former, instead of being of the same diameter throughout, are stepped. The circumference, for example, may be divided into three sections, each comprising a plain portion which is of least diameter, a screwed portion which is of greater diameter, and another screwed portion which is of the full diameter of the plug. Then, the breech opening having corresponding plain and screwed surfaces, a turn through only one-ninth of a circle will suffice to screw the plug fully home, and two-thirds of its total circumference will be available for resisting the pressure when the gun is fired. In the Elswick coned screw, used for the smaller guns of from 3 to 6-inch calibre, the portion of the plug that enters the gun first is tapered, while the back portion is cylindrical. Both have interrupted screws, but the interruptions of the former are in line with the screwed portions of the latter, The surface of the breech opening being similarly formed, the result is that not only is the entry of the plug facilitated, but when it is screwed home the pressure of the explosion is distributed round the whole of its circumference, and not taken merely by a portion, as in the arrangements previously mentioned.

The French 75 mm. field gun has a breech mechanism which at first sight appears to belong to the screw class, but is really of the sliding type. The plug is of larger diameter than the bore of the gun and mounted eccentrically to it. In it is pierced a hole, also eccentric, which is brought opposite the bore when the cartridge is being inserted, but is turned away from it when the gun is being fired, half a turn screwing the solid portion up against the breech opening.

In opening the breech a single pull on a lever in the smaller guns, or the turning of a hand-wheel in the larger ones, suffices to rotate the plug till its threads are free in the breech opening, to withdraw it, and to swing it back. By reversing the lever or wheel the same operations are performed in the reverse order and the breech is closed. In large naval guns hydraulic or electric power is employed, though hand gear is fitted in addition for use should the power fail.

Breech mechanisms also embody devices for preventing the possibility of the charge being fired before the breech is properly closed and for extracting the cartridge cases, when such are used, or the firing tubes which are employed when the shell and the charge are loaded separately. As has already been explained in the chapter on Ammunition (Vol. V., p. 416) in quick-firing guns "fixed" ammunition is used, the shell being attached to a brass cartridge case which contains the charge and the primer by which it is ignited. Here the brass case acts as an efficient means of "obturation," that is to say, under the pressure produced by the explosion the metal expands closely against the walls of the powder chamber, thus preventing the escape of gas backwards through the breech opening. But in large guns for which "separate loading" ammunition is adopted, other arrangements must be made to secure obturation. A favourite method, introduced by Colonel de Bange, is to place a ring-shaped canvas bag, containing a highly compressed mixture of asbestos and mutton suet, over the front of the breech screw, holding it in position by means of a steel mushroom-head with a spindle which projects through the ring down the middle of the breech screw. The force of the explosion acting on the mushroom-head squeezes the plastic material in the bag closely against the sides of the chamber, and an effective gas seal is formed. The spindle may be drilled to receive the firing tube, when the part is known as a "vent axial."

[*Courtesy of Messrs. Vickers.*

EXPANDING A GUN TUBE IN A HYDRAULIC PRESS.

The part played by the artillery in the war was relatively far more important, compared with the other arms, than in any former campaign. Generally regarded as an auxiliary of the infantry in the conduct of battles, the artillery showed itself during the greater part

GERMAN HEAVY GUNS IN THE SERBIAN CAMPAIGN.

The enemy got over the difficulty of travelling over soft ground by laying a plank and hurdle gangway over which the guns were hauled.

of the struggle to be the predominant partner in the alliance between the two. The reasons for this were, broadly speaking, two: the one was the siege-like character which was the prominent feature of the operations after the Germans were driven back to the Aisne, the other the greatly enhanced power of the gunner's weapons, which made their fire so much more efficacious and destructive. In the retreat from Mons towards Paris the fighting was of a fairly open nature. The infantry, of course, entrenched itself whenever it made a stand, as it always will do if given even half-an-hour to prepare—as it is a routine precaution to obtain any cover possible from the assailant's fire—but there was no time to construct the elaborate trenches and to cover the approaches to them with the impassable wire entanglements which formed part of the later battle-field organizations. The other reason was an example of action and reaction. The increased value of fire brought about increased precautions to escape from its effects, and this in turn made all nations lose no efforts to produce still more powerful weapons to destroy the improved defences.

The Germans had indeed before the war broke out made considerable progress in this direction. All armies, in addition to the guns with which the horse and ordinary field batteries were equipped, had introduced field howitzers firing a shell of about 30 to 40 lbs This weapon was intended to be used for demolition purposes or against troops behind cover where the flat trajectory gun could not reach them. The German guns used in the Great War, the majority of which doubtless were in being before it broke out, were as follows:—The field gun fired a 15 lb. shrapnel, also a high-explosive common shell and a universal shell, *i.e.*, one of which the front part was a high-explosive common shell, the rear part a shrapnel. When used as a shrapnel the head was blown off and the bullets freed, while the head itself went on and acted as a common shell. When used for demolition purposes the whole shell burst on impact and could be arranged to act immediately or with delayed action.

Two other field guns were used, viz., the 9-cm., which has a shrapnel of about 17 lbs., and a steel high-explosive shell of about 16½ lbs. The heavy field gun was of later date. Its calibre was 4·68 inches (10 cm.), and it fired both shrapnel and high-explosive shell weighing 40 lbs. It was a formidable weapon, having

An aeroplane in sight.
Smaller picture: "Spotting" enemy aircraft.

A gun in action.

BRITISH ANTI-AIRCRAFT GUNS ON THE WESTERN FRONT.

an extreme range of 11,500 yards. A still larger field gun was the 13 cm., firing a shell of 88 lbs., whether shrapnel or high explosive. Its range was 13,000 yards—*i.e.*, over six miles. The largest size field gun was the 15 cm.—*i.e.*, 6 inch; the projectiles weighed approximately 112 lbs., and were of two natures, shrapnel and high explosive. The field howitzers employed by the Germans were of two kinds, the light, which fired shrapnel, high explosive and universal shell and common shell. The latter were those most commonly in use; they weighed approximately 39 lbs. The common shell was of cast iron and was probably introduced because there was a shortage of forged steel. A similar shell for the same reason was used with the 77 mm. field gun The next form of field howitzer was the far heavier 15 cm. (6-inch) pattern, firing two types of projectile —a high explosive of 90 lbs. and an incendiary of considerably less weight. Other larger weapons were the 21 cm. (8·27 inches) mortar, firing a high explosive shell of 262 lbs., and the 28 cm. (11 inches) with a high-explosive shell of 770 lbs. In addition, a number of far heavier pieces were employed of varying but large size, both guns and howitzers, up to the notorious 32 and 42 cm. howitzers which proved so fatal to the Belgian and French permanent fortifications.

The equipment of the French artillery was somewhat similar, although at first our Allies had not such a full measure of heavier natures available as the enemy. The British Army began the struggle with only six divisions, but they were well equipped with a large proportion of artillery. The British division had 76 pieces. Of these 54 were 18-pounders—*i.e.*, the ordinary field guns, firing a shrapnel of that weight. It had been thought better not to employ high-explosive shell with this gun because of the very small charge of high explosive the common shell would hold. Indeed, it was not so necessary, considering that every division had 18 howitzers which used a high-explosive shell of 35 lbs. and four 60-pounder guns which had a similar projectile of the weight given. This was the most powerful field gun forming part of the regular equipment of any modern army. However, after the war

THE FRENCH 75 MM. GUN.
Cleaning the gun behind the lines.

A GERMAN 77 MM. FIELD GUN,
After being hit by a French gun.

had begun it was thought desirable to give high-explosive shells even to the 18-pounders as soon as it was seen how continuous the struggle between the fortified positions held by us and those of the Germans was likely to be. Shrapnel of the 18-lb. size, while still necessary for the destruction of wire entanglements, give very little effect against parapets or the troops behind them. They are, of course, much more useful than any high-explosive shell of this calibre against unprotected troops and continued to be largely used for this purpose.

Summing up, therefore, it may be said that there was very little difference in the weapons used by the contending Powers, though the initial advantage gained by the French by the superiority of the field-gun persisted, and the same may be said of our 18-pounder, which was far better than the field gun of the German army.

So long as the warfare was of the ordinary open character similar in nature to that of former campaigns, very little was heard of the heavier calibres which were afterwards so much in evidence. So long as fighting and marching were fairly evenly divided the artillery employed was necessarily of the most mobile character. There was no time to make the special platforms necessary for the larger pieces, and even the lighter natures were so difficult to move, requiring either traction engines or very powerful horse teams, that they could not be brought into action before the tide of battle had flowed away from the part of the country where they had been deployed. But once the ordinary field encounters had given place to the siege-like operations which later became the feature of the war, the practical absence of all change in the general line held by the contending armies permitted both sides to bring into use the heavier weapons, which could be brought up and placed in positions carefully prepared for them.

Nor was this kind of warfare any great novelty. In the days of the Crimea, the fortress of Sevastopol was constructed under the eyes of the English and French, who failed to rush the position before the Russian works had become formidable. The guns on both sides, it is true, were feeble in comparison with those of 60 years later, but they sufficed to keep at bay both the French and English infantries. The Allies, therefore, had to make their forward movement by the siege methods of sap and trench-work.

By sapping is meant the process by which trenches are executed under cover either of the ground or of shields which serve to protect the squad working at the trench. Formerly sap-rollers were used to cover the head of the sap, the side of which, if exposed to fire only on one side, was protected by gabions; where both sides were so exposed a double sap—*i.e.*, two side by side—had to be used. The sap-roller was a long, bottomless basket of cylindrical shape in which was another similar cylinder, the space between the two being packed with fascines—*e.g.*, long faggots. This was superseded by steel shields, and finally it was found necessary to rely only on the solid earth, and the trench was, therefore, excavated to sufficient depth to cover the men working in it. Gabions were bottomless baskets about 2 ft. 9 in. high and 2 ft. in diameter. Placed on end, they were filled with earth by the excavators and served to protect them more rapidly than if the earth were

A THREE-INCH DYNAMITE GUN,
Used in East Africa.

simply thrown up into a parapet, which would have required far more material and therefore a longer time for construction. When modern rifles were introduced these contrivances became inefficient, and, whether saps or trenches were made, the solid earth alone was relied on. It is quite true, in the latter case, that where troops have to work with the portable entrenching tool which the men carry on their backs the process of excavating to any depth is a lengthy one; but, even after an hour's work, fair cover can be obtained against rifle fire, and when the warfare is of a stationary character, ordinary picks and shovels are served out, which facilitate the construction of the deeper and more perfect trenches required.

Sevastopol marked the commencement of the era of improvised fortresses, constructed where necessary during hostilities. Experience shows that they are much better capable of resisting attacks, because much less exposed to destruction than the so-called permanent fortifications, which are permanent only until heavy weapons are brought against them. The French after the 1870 war expended not far short of £100,000,000, practically the whole of which was absolutely thrown away. The Germans, too, fell into the same error, but not to the same extent. The great Belgian engineer, the late General Brialmont, who deserved the well-known epitaph placed over an architect's grave,

> Lie heavy on him, Earth, for he
> Laid many heavy loads on thee,

thought he had discovered the impregnable method when he built the forts of concrete with steel cupolas round Liège and Namur. Yet none of these proved capable of any serious defence against the formidable shells the Germans used for their destruction. The French did not even attempt to defend the fort of Douaumont, near Verdun, constructed to a great extent on this system, as experience had shown that earthen works with deep-down dug-outs were much more capable of resistance.

Plevna, again, in 1878 showed the value of such improvized defences. The Russians at first possessed no weapons which could produce any effect on them; their field guns were quite useless because not sufficiently powerful. For months the Turks held out, bringing the Russian advance to a standstill, as it was impossible for them to move forward over the Balkans leaving the army which held the Turkish position on their flank. It was not till more powerful guns were brought up and regular approaches constructed that Todleben was able to capture this fortress which had grown up under the eyes of the attacking force. It is noteworthy that Todleben, who first came into fame by constructing Sevastopol, should have made his last campaign against a similar hastily constructed stronghold.

In the South African War we found the deep, narrow trenches of the Boers formidable obstacles. Our heavy howitzers produced but little effect, finding it very difficult to hit so small a target, and the artillery assistance to the infantry was practically limited to keeping down the hostile rifle fire by pouring shrapnel on the trenches, the bullets from which served to force the firing line in them to keep under cover, till the near approach of our infantry compelled our guns to cease firing

The outcome of the Russo-Japanese War established similar results. But here the Japanese used some heavy howitzers (11-in. calibre) which are said to have produced con-

THIS MORTAR BEARS THE ARMS OF LOUIS PHILIPPE AND THE DATE 1846, AND HAS BEEN USED DURING THE WAR FOR THROWING BOMBS INTO THE GERMAN TRENCHES.

siderable effect. Both sides made use of machine guns and the Japanese of small pieces of artillery in the front trenches. A study of the fighting shows the germs of the more fully-grown plans employed in the present struggle.

Let us now examine the various methods in which the artillery was used by the contending armies. In the fighting from Mons back towards Paris, and in the offensive return made by the Allies which drove the Germans over the Marne, there was little change to be seen in the manner of handling the guns from that which had prevailed in previous wars. The artillery prepared the way by a preliminary bombardment, and then supported the infantry in its attack on the enemy's position. Its action was, however, greater because the weapons were more powerful than any which had been previously employed, but it differed only in degree, not in kind. The results were greater because the shooting was much better, owing to greatly improved sights, and because shells, both high explosive and shrapnel, were much more efficacious. Statistics as to the percentage of loss inflicted by the various arms are always of a somewhat doubtful character, being largely based on the wounded. It is impossible to examine the slain to ascertain what they died of, and therefore there is always a tendency to an indeterminate amount of error. It is said that in the Franco-German War only 5 per cent. of the German losses were due to

ONE OF THE BRITISH 4·7 GUNS USED IN THE SOUTH-WEST AFRICAN CAMPAIGN.

MOBILE BATTERY CONSTRUCTED AT THE CREUSOT WORKS IN FRANCE.
Showing the observation tower, the howitzers on their turn-tables, and the ammunition waggon.

artillery fire. The French guns were signally inefficient. On the other hand, 20 per cent. of the French losses were attributed to the German artillery. In the Great War German authorities said 85 per cent. of the casualties were due to the guns. No doubt this chiefly applied to the siege-works period; but in any case, allowing for a considerable margin of error, it showed an enormous increase in the amount to be attributed to the artillery.

It is worth while to examine a little more closely the way in which this greatly enhanced proportion was attained. The telescopic dial sight of the modern field gun was twenty times more accurate than the old form of sight with its V notch, which took up a varying amount of the foresight, depending on the idiosyncrasy of the individual using it. The special advantage of the dial sight is that it enables the gun to be laid for direction on any aiming point to the front, flank, or rear.

Guns are now often fired from a concealed position—*i.e.*, from behind a fold of the ground, which serves to screen them from the enemy. At first glance it might seem that this would be very detrimental to accurate practice. This is not the case: the battery commander, by various contrivances, can so order the fire of each gun as to ensure its proper direction, although the guns may not be able to see the target. When the gun is behind cover, provided it is about twelve or thirteen feet below it, the flash of the gun is no longer visible to the enemy. It is this flash which betrays the modern gun's place, not so well perhaps as the smoke of the old black powder, but still well enough to enable the enemy to range on. It will, therefore, be easily understood that the concealed position is the one most sought for when bringing guns into play. It may be necessary to bring some of them more forward to support the infantry when closing, but as long as possible the safety of the hidden position will be preferred. If the gunlayer cannot see the object to be fired at, he can, if he can see a point in between the gun and the object, lay his piece on that. This is what is done. Aiming posts are placed in alignment with the target in front of the battery (see Plates I and II), and then the Battery Commander takes the Director (see Plate III), and aligns on them. He then measures the angle back to some one gun (D in the plates), which he selects as the gun of direction, as it may be called. The gunlayer of this now brings his

FIRING A FRENCH HOWITZER.

Smaller picture: Shells for the howitzer.

gun parallel to the line from the aiming post to the target by means of the dial sight. Suppose the measured angle to be 135 deg., then, as shown in Fig. 7, Plate II, by means of the arc on the dial sight, he puts the gun parallel to the line from the aiming posts to the target. A similar process will align all the six guns in positions parallel to the same line. The six guns in the battery occupy a front of roughly 100 yards, and the fire from the individual guns would be disseminated in six groups in front of the target, and not all on it. To avoid this, each gun is dealt with by each using a "corrector angle" obtained from the table of correcting angles. This is clearly shown on Fig. 8, Plate II. The result is that each gun is now pointing straight on the target. This is roughly the system used, but there are many details too complicated to be dealt with here.

Acting with the battery there will be an observing officer placed in some convenient spot whence he can see the target at which the guns are aiming. By means of the telephone he can send back information to the battery after each shot, so that the gunlayers may know exactly what has happened to each shell. It may not always be possible to find such a place. Foreign artilleries use a ladder, up which the observing officer can climb to note where the shells fall. This, however, has the disadvantage very often of betraying the situation of the guns, as it forms rather a conspicuous object with a man on the top of it.

The long ranges of modern guns also allow much more choice of positions for them, and permit the concentration of fire from a wide arc against any particular point which it is sought to batter. Moreover, the modern gunner never hesitates to fire over guns or infantry of

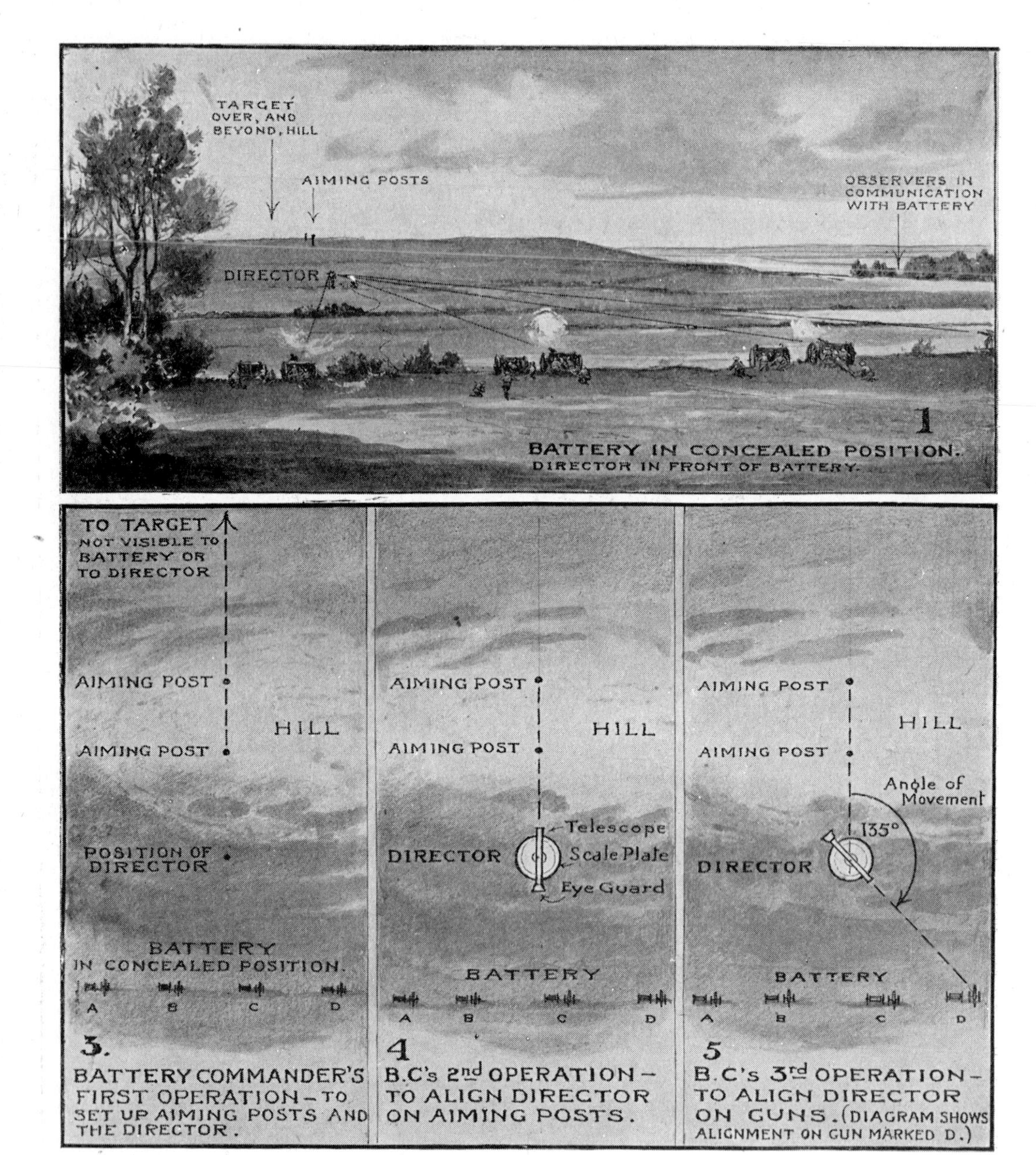

PLATE I. BRITISH
Methods of the Artillery in

his own side; his sighting is so accurate, the fuses are so absolutely to be relied on, and the velocities obtained by the nitro powders so constant, that he knows exactly how the shells will behave, and there is no danger from this action.

But the progress of aeronautics provided the aeroplane which is able to fly over the enemy's lines, observe the positions of his various gun emplacements and other works, and signal them back by various simple signals previously agreed on. Moreover, it is now the custom to make as quickly as possible a map or to use an existing map which is divided up into squares so that it suffices to indicate the particular square and the position of the target in it to enable the exact position of the point in question to be indicated. The aeroplane has greatly increased the power of the gun because it not only reconnoitres for it but also directs its fire by pointing out how it fails in accuracy whether in direction or length of range. It is especially useful when no observation post can be established.

One great advantage of the long range of modern guns is that it is no longer necessary to shift their position with anything like the frequency which was necessary when the effective range was much less. The effective

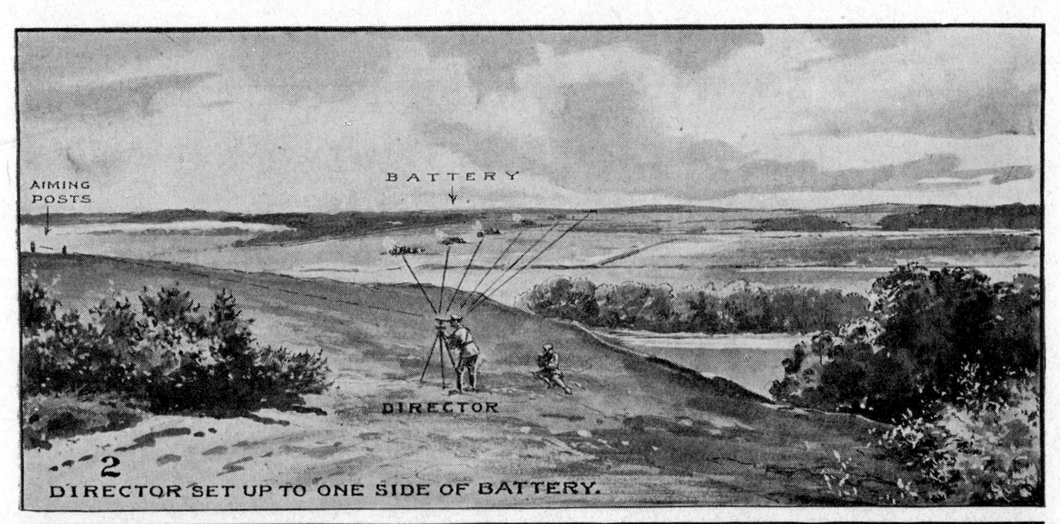

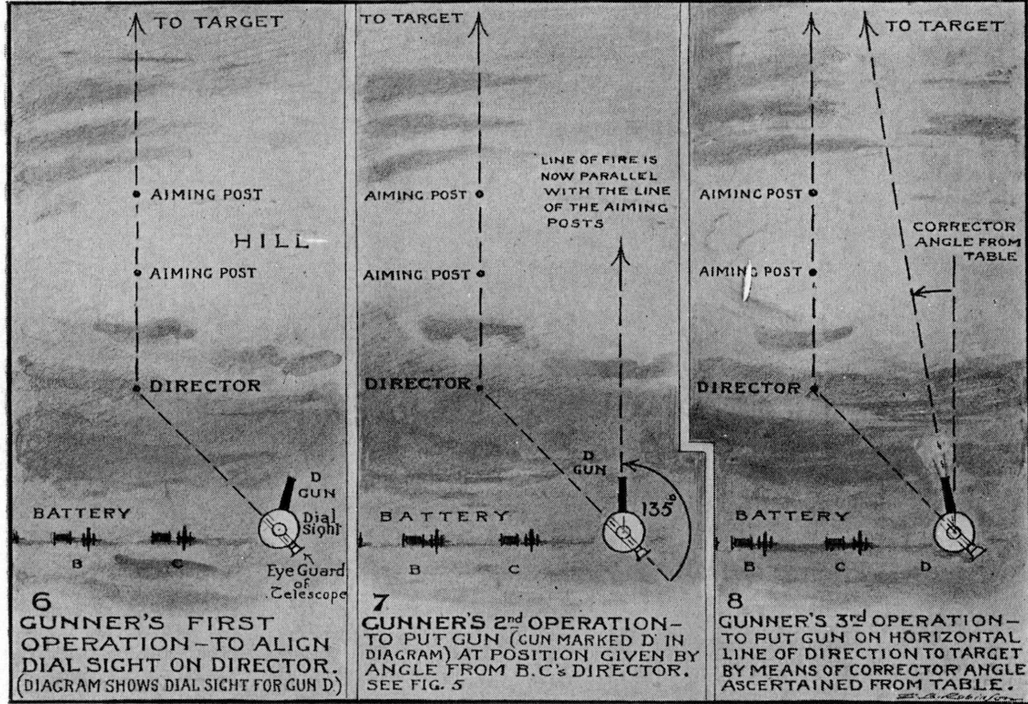

GUN-LAYING. **PLATE II.**

aiming at Invisible Targets.

distance now lies anywhere between 2,500 and 4,000 yards for field guns. Over 4,000, and up to 5,000, is considered long, and over 5,000 to 6,500 distant. But the fire from heavy batteries has a much longer range, and, indeed, in the case of guns, the heavier they are the longer the range at which they can engage. Thus with them the effective range extends up to 5,000 yards; up to 6,500 yards is considered only "long," while "distant" fire may go as far as 10,000 yards.

The way in which the various calibres are combined together for action now becomes clear. The heavier one will fire from comparatively secluded positions. The smaller guns will do so from closer ranges from positions nearer the point to be battered. The mission of each class will vary. Those firing larger shells will direct their fire against the entrenched position to break it down; the smaller will be directed against objects requiring less force to destroy them. Thus shrapnel will be used to destroy wire entanglements, and to keep down the enemy's infantry, so as to prevent them from firing on the assailants when they came forward to the assault. All guns, when the infantry do come out to attack, will "lift" their fire—*i.e.*, direct it farther on so as to form

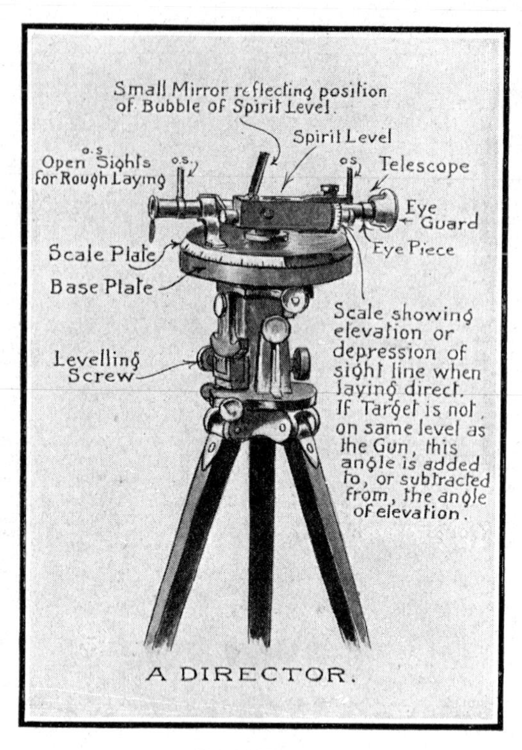

PLATE III.
THE DIRECTOR,
An Instrument used in Indirect Gun-laying.

a barrier through which the enemy's reserves cannot penetrate to come up to aid their front line of trench holders.

This proceeding is called forming a "curtain," or, as the French say, "barrier." It is quite commonly employed, and has been very successful. It is an entirely new method of procedure which only came forward in the Great War. Twenty years earlier the suggestion of any such action would have been received with ridicule and characterized as a wicked waste of ammunition. At one time the great object appears to have been to have plenty of ammunition, but not to use it. We have progressed since then, and it is acknowledged that it is desirable to cover the target with an absolute deluge of projectiles. When this proposition was made by an English officer a good many years ago it was received with derision and not thought worthy of a moment's serious consideration. It seems an elementary proposition that the more you fire the more you are likely to hit, provided your fire is delivered in the right direction. But it took a good many years for this idea, so subversive of what was then called "fire discipline," to penetrate. Fire discipline then meant as little fire as possible; now it means as much as possible, provided it is properly applied—a terrible subversion of old notions horrifying to those who had been imbued with the tradition of the older school.

But prodigality of ammunition is of no value unless it is well directed. It is to the French that we owe the scientific arrangement of rapid fire, which they introduced with their field gun, the renowned "75," in 1900. A brief description of their methods is therefore desirable.

The French battery consists of four guns and twelve ammunition wagons. The gun has a shield against musketry, and the construction of the wagon when it is up-ended also affords the same protection. When in action each gun has a wagon beside it, and two others are brought up to the battery so that half the ammunition supply is at once available. The battery commander takes shelter behind one of the two wagons alluded to, which is placed on the flank. The gun works smoothly backwards and forwards over its recoil cylinder and is securely anchored, so that it remains in the same position while firing in which it was originally fixed. This obviates all delay due to relaying the gun on its target.

The main principle of the French system of fire is to open effective fire as quickly as possible after coming into action. This gives the enemy no time for elaborate arrangements before returning fire, and if he indulged in them, the destructive methods used by the French artillery would snuff him out before he had begun a serious reply. The range, besides being found from maps on which the enemy's position may have been located by the observation of airmen, or by range-finders, is confirmed by the actual fire of the guns. The method is similar to that in use in all artilleries, but is simpler and more rapid. All alike endeavour to get one shot short and one over the target. The right range is obviously in between the two, which are called a bracket. The French having obtained even a long one, do not endeavour to gain further accuracy by seeking for a smaller one. As soon as the bracket is obtained by a salvo fired at each of two different elevations of 400 metres difference, or less if the range be close, the battery commander orders "Tir progressif"—*i.e.*, progressive fire, which is executed as follows: Starting with an elevation of 100 m. less than the shorter range of the bracket (which is, if time allow, reduced to 200 m.), each gun fires two rounds, followed by two others at an increased range of another

100 m. (50 m. if the battery commander thinks it better), and so on, till each gun has fired eight rounds. This takes about a minute. After this the ranges are corrected and fire proceeds at any ordinary rate, broken where necessary by "rafales" (squalls)—*i.e.*, several rounds of rapid fire from each gun. This is really a reversion to the old method of noting a road, brook, or some similar well defined object, ascertaining its range, and then firing as rapidly as possible when the enemy arrives at it. But in the French plan it is the target itself which, when it is observed, has the rapid fire poured on it.

When it is thought desirable to distribute the fire in breadth, advantage is taken of the traversing arrangement by which the gun can be turned, right or left, on its carriage without moving the latter. On the command "Fauchez" (literally "Mow," the action of mowing resembling the swinging movement given to the gun), each gun, after the first round, is traversed three turns of the traversing-wheel to the left, then three more, and then moved back so that the gun is in its original position. The same process is then gone through to the right. By this method at a range of 2,500 m. each gun distributes its fire over a front of 50 m. Mowing and progressive fire can be combined if necessary.

The normal manner of aiming the French gun is indirect—*i.e.*, on an aiming post. But as that would not suit all the guns of a battery, each is given a special deflection determined by the battery commander, which is called "echeloning," because the increments of deflection increase by successive and equal increments. If the left gun is aimed on the post with a deflection of 50, No. 3 would, for example, with an "echelon" of 5, use 55, No. 2 60, No. 1 65. This is similar to our plan which has been previously explained.

Advantage is taken of any intervals in the firing to ascertain the range by trial shots of any ground over which an enemy is likely to pass. The results are recorded for use if required.

Such in brief outline is the French method. It is chiefly intended for use with shrapnel, and the object is to cover the ground with a rain of bullets. It will be seen that "curtain" fire, previously alluded to, is but an example of this procedure.

But efficient as modern guns were in the kind of fighting seen in the Great War, there was need for another weapon. The object fired at, a trench, had so little depth that although the artillery might knock away anything in the shape of a parapet, and although a certain amount of damage might be done by large howitzer shells, it is plain that considering how close the hostile lines of entrenchments were to one another, sometimes not more than fifty yards apart, there was need for a weapon which could, as it were, "lob" a projectile into them. For this purpose the trench

A FRENCH "155 SHORT" GUN.

A BRITISH 60-POUNDER GUN.

mortar was employed. This assumed many forms, from an empty cartridge case to special constructions throwing anything from a small hand grenade to the huge 190 lb. shell of the German mine thrower, or the so-called aerial torpedo. These supplemented the regular artillery; their projectiles fell into the narrow trench, destroyed the "dug-out" cover there, and killed and wounded the occupiers. Hand grenades thrown by the attacking infantry formed another auxiliary means of destruction. It is difficult not to picture to oneself the terrible nature of the combination of all these various means of destruction concentrated against some sector of the enemy's defences selected for destruction. From time to time accounts appeared in the newspapers describing what the observers had seen: parapets blown out of existence, wire entanglements swept away, and when the assaulting infantry arrived on the scene, the remnants of the original garrison—*i.e.*, those not blown to fragments—dazed and half-unconscious. Verily, modern artillery means of destruction are as efficacious as they are dreadful. Nor does night lead to any serious interruption in the struggle. Searchlights, star-shells, and flares give a bright illumination which betrays any hostile advance.

We have seen that the artillery depend largely on aircraft for reconnoitring and informing them of likely targets, and even of the effect of their shells. This produced in turn the anti-aircraft gun, specially designed for firing at very high angles against the Zeppelin or aeroplane. At night the shells leave a brilliant light behind them from the "tracer" fitted to them, which, as its name implies, enables the gunner to watch their flight by the trace left behind. By day this tracer leaves a smoke track for the same purpose.

Artillery has become far more complicated and scientific and infinitely more deadly and destructive, and the part it plays far more important and decisive. But still the gunner cannot do without the infantryman. He occupies and holds the ground the former has prepared, and he suffers more heavily in the successive captures he has to undertake of the trenches bombarded by the guns. Neither can do without the other; the two combined make the deciding factor of war.

There are also other minor factors to be taken into consideration. The increased use of machine guns gives greater power to the infantry and represents the fire power of many men concentrated in a small space. Numerous examples might be quoted showing how attacks have been brought to a standstill by them.

Lastly, it may be remarked that subterranean warfare was employed to an extent never before seen. Mines not only blew up defences, but the craters formed convenient places for starting new works, and marked steps in the continuous advance against the enemy.

END OF VOLUME SEVEN.

INDEX TO VOLUME VII.

A

B

C

D

I

J

K

L

M

N

O

P

R

S

T

N

O

P

R

S

T

MAPS AND PLANS.

ILLUSTRATIONS IN VOLUME VII.

PORTRAITS.

PLACES.